LABOR & EMPLOYMENT ARBITRATION
LEADING CASES & DECISIONS

LABOR & EMPLOYMENT ARBITRATION
LEADING CASES & DECISIONS
A Practical Approach to the Study of Arbitration

Floyd D. Weatherspoon

Published by:

Vandeplas Publishing, LLC – July 2016

801 International Parkway, 5th Floor
Lake Mary, FL. 32746
USA

www.vandeplaspublishing.com

ISBN 978-1-60042-284-3

LABOR & EMPLOYMENT ARBITRATION
LEADING CASES & DECISIONS

A Practical Approach to the Study of Arbitration

FLOYD D. WEATHERSPOON
ASSOCIATE DEAN FOR DISPUTE RESOLUTION
PROFESSOR OF LAW
CAPITAL UNIVERSITY LAW SCHOOL
COLUMBUS, OHIO

PREFACE

The primary objective of this casebook is to present material which both students and practitioners will find useful in analyzing, writing, and interpreting arbitration awards and cases. Unlike the traditional casebook, there are less theoretical concepts and historical developments. Instead, the book includes a broad collection of arbitration court cases and arbitration awards to analyze, followed by discussion questions, case problems, and summaries.

Court cases and arbitration awards were selected which set forth clear and practical substantive and procedural arbitration principles. In addition, leading Supreme Court cases, which outline and identify federal common law rules and policies on arbitration, are included to illustrate the judicial process for establishing precedent and federal common arbitration laws. Similarly, a selected number of secondary readings, which should enhance the reader's understanding and application of specific arbitration concepts, are inserted to give the reader an immediate opportunity to synthesize a wealth of arbitration concepts and principles.

During the past twenty years, there has been an increase of judicial review of arbitration awards by courts at the state and federal levels. The reoccurring issues have been whether awards violate public policy, and therefore should be vacated. There has also been a stream of cases challenging awards based on allegations that the arbitrator engaged in misconduct and exceeded their authority. The book incorporates a line of court cases where these issues are explored and anaylzed.

The book is divided between labor and employment arbitration with a major emphasis on labor arbitration. The labor arbitration section provides a wide range of reoccurring labor issues such as, management rights, seniority, subcontracting, benefits, wages and hours, off duty conduct, and safety policies. Because disciplinary actions remain the dominant issue arbitrated, a significant amount of material is included on the "just cause" principles. Through arbitration awards, each element of the "just cause" principal is explained and analyzed. Even though there is some controversy over whether labor arbitrators consider all the seven elements of "just cause" in their awards, the analysis still remains a basic concept of labor arbitration. This section also includes the "just cause" analysis in Federal sector arbitration, known as the *Douglas Factors*.

Aside from disciplinary issues, the book also covers issue grievances, which primarily involve contract interpretation. Topics in this section include the plain meaning rule, ambiguous contract language, pattern and practices issues, and the parol evidence rule.

Arbitrators are also called to assist parties in reaching agreements on the content and terms within the collective bargaining agreement. This process is called interest arbitration. A select few of interest arbitration cases are included to provide the reader with a basic understanding of the criteria used by arbitrators to make recommendations to the parties on terms, which are fair and reasonable.

The last section of the book discusses the development of employment arbitration. This area of arbitration has rapidly expanded in the private sector. The catalyst for this expansion was caused in part by The Supreme Court's liberal interpretation of the Federal Arbitration Act and most recently, the validation of mandatory arbitration provisions in employment contracts. This section of the book includes the leading Supreme Court decisions on compulsory arbitration and the application of these cases on discrimination claims, employment statutes, and contract disputes.

Floyd D. Weatherspoon

ACKNOWLEDEMENTS

I would like to thank the following research assistants who assisted in researching and editing this textbook: Alysha Clark, Jessica Doogan, Joshua Farnsworth, Kadawni Scott, Michelle Lanham and Jennifer Rohrbaugh. I would like to thank Marcus Lashley, Labor Arbitrator Apprentice, for his assistance in proof reading and editing. I am also grateful to Soni Shoemaker, Faculty Assistant for her administrative support on this project. I am especially thankful to my Lead Research Assistant, Helen Robinson for the detailed research and editing of this book.

COPYRIGHT PERMISSIONS

The author gratefully acknowledges the copyright permissions granted by the following individuals and organizations:

1. The American Arbitration Association to reprint Lexis Arbitration decisions and Lexis Employment Arbitration decisions. Copyright 2015 by the American Arbitration Association. (800-778-7879). https://adr.org.

2. The American Arbitration Association to reprint Robert L. Arrington, Aaron Duffy, and Elizabeth Rita's article *When Worlds Collide: An Arbitrator's Guide to Social Networking Issues in Labor and Employment Cases*, 66 Disp. Resol. J. 4 (2011).

3. The American Arbitration Association to reprint *Kathleen Birkhofer, Last Chance Agreements: How Many Chances Is an Employee Entitled To, 2005 J. Disp. Resol. 467 (2005).*

4. The Bureau of National Affairs, Inc., to reprint *Labor Relations Reporter-Labor Arbitration Reports'* decisions. Copyright 2015 by the Bureau of National Affairs, Inc. (800-372-1033). http://www.bna.com.

5. *Past Practice and the Administration of Collective Bargaining Agreements* by Richard Mittenthal, Reproduced with permission from Labor Relations Reporter-Labor Arbitration Reports, 134 BNA LA 276 (Sept. 22, 2014). Copyright 2014 by The Bureau of National Affairs, Inc. (800-372-1033) <http://www.bna.com.

6. Jay E. Grenig to reprint his article, *Principles of Contract Interpretation: Interpreting Collective Bargaining Agreements*, 16 Cap. U. L. Rev. 31 (1986).

7. Juris Publishing, Inc., and the ACResolution Magazine to reprint my article entitled, *Eliminating Barriers for Minority ADR Neutrals,* Originally published in ACResolution Magazine (Spring, 2006).

8. The Yale University Law Journal Association for permission to reprint Julius G. Getman's *Labor Arbitration and Dispute Resolution,* 88 Yale L. J. 916 (April, 1979).

TABLE OF CONTENTS

TABLE OF CASES

The leading cases are in bold type.

Local 1099 134 LA 1066 (J. Fullmer, 2015)

City of Des Plaines v. Metro. Alliance of Police, Chapter No. 240, 2015 IL App (1st) 140957; 2015 Ill.App. LEXIS 223

City of Hartford v. Hartford Mun. Employees Ass'n, 134 Conn.App. 559, 39 A.3d 1146 (2012).

City of Mason and Mason Professional Firefighters, IAFF Local 4039 BNA LA 1165 (Tolley, 2015)

City of Philadelphia, 127 BNA LA 1384 (K. Lang, 2010)

Circuit City Stores, Inc. V. Adams, 532 U. S. (2001)

City of Richmond v. Service Employees Intern. Union, Local 1021, 189 Cal. App.4th 663, 118 Cal. Rptr. 3d 315 (2010)

City of Seldovia, 2013-01 and 2013-02, 133 BNA LA 1593 (Landau, 2014)

City of Sidney, Ohio v. Fraternal Order of Police, Common Pleas Court of Shelby County, Ohio, Case No. 10VC000497 (2011)

City of Wadsworth and The Ohio Patrolmen's Benevolent Association, 134 BNA LA 641 (Bell, 2015)

City of Willowick, OH, 110 LA 1150 (Ruben 1998)

Colfax Envelope Corp. v. Local No. 458-3M, Chicago Graphic Communications Internat'l Union, AFL-CIO, 20 F.3d, 750 (7th Cir. 1994)

Collyer Insulated Wire, A Gulf And Western Systems Co. and Local Union 1098, International Brotherhood of Electrical

Workers, AFL CIO 192, N.L.R.B. 837 (J. Fitzpatrick, 1971)

Commonwealth of Pennsylvania, 65 LA 280 (1975)

Communications Workers v. New York Telephone Co., 327 F.2d 94 (2d Cir. 1964)

Connick v. Meyers, 461 U.S. 138 (1983)

Council of Prison Locals, AFL-CIO, American Federation of Government Employees, Local 607 and U.S. Department of Justice, Federal Bureau of Prisons, FCI Elkton, Ohio: Federal Arbitration (2007)

County of Allegheny and Allegheny Court Association of Professional Employees, Acape Unit 1603, 134 BNA LA 977 (Kobell, 2015)

County of Riverside v. Phillip Tamoush, 2012 Cal. App. Unpub. LEXI S 2677

Craft v. Campbell Soup Co., 177 F.3d 1083 (C.A. 1999)

Crane Plumbing, 96/15354-6, 107 BNA LA 1084 (J. Fullmer, 1996)

Cummins Sales, 54 LA 1071 (Seinsheimer, 1970)

Curtis Douglas V. Veterans Administration, 981 MSPB LEXIS 886 (1981)

CVS Pharmacy, 2012 BNA LA Supp. 147419 (E. Goldstein, 2012)

Decatur Police Benevolent and Protective Ass'n Labor Committee v. City of Decatur, 2012 IL App (4th) 110764, 360 Ill. Dec. 256 (2012).

Delaware Transit Corp. v. Amalgamated Transit Union Local 42 34 A.3d 1064 (2011)

Department of Veterans Affair v. VA Medical Center, 2010 LA Supp. 119534 (F. Weatherspoon, 2010)

District 2A v. Gov't of the Virgin Islands,

AMERICAN ARBITRATION ASSOCIATION CASES

I. DEVELOPMENT OF LABOR ARBITRATION

A. BRIEF HISTORICAL REVIEW OF LABOR ARBITRATION

The U.S. State's engagement in World War II had a direct impact on the increased use of arbitration to resolve labor disputes. It was crucial that labor organizations and employers provided resources to support the War. To facilitate the resolution of labor disputes, President Roosevelt in 1942 created the National War Labor Board. The Labor Board's primary objective was to resolve labor disputes and avoid labor strikes. Labor arbitrators were used to assist parties in resolving labor disputes. The process of selecting labor arbitrators to resolve labor grievances has expanded and evolved as the final step in grievance procedures of most collective bargaining agreements.

To further the growth and development of collective bargaining and particularly arbitration, Congress passed the Labor Management Relations Act of 1947. Section 301 of the Act provided for the enforcement of arbitration awards in federal district courts. Section 203 of the Act encouraged the parties to a collective bargaining agreement to develop a process to settle labor disputes that may arise when interpreting the agreement.

B. LEGAL STATUS OF LABOR ARBITRATION: THE CREATION OF FEDERAL COMMON LAW

U.S. SUPREME COURT DECISIONS

In 1957, the Supreme Court held in Lincoln *Mills* that federal courts had jurisdiction to hear cases brought under 301 of the Labor Management Relations Act of 1947. The

Court made it clear that parties to a collective bargaining agreement were required to comply with the arbitration provision as agreed by the parties. The Court also held that federal courts had authority to grant relief under either state or federal laws. This was the first time the Supreme Court gave judicial recogntion of collective bargaining agreements.

In 1960, the Supreme Court issued three decsions all on the same day which began the development of basic federal common law on labor arbitration and collective bargaining. These cases were brought by the United Steelworkers Union. These cases are known as the *Steelworkers Trilogy* Cases. The *Lincoln Mills* and the *Steelworkers Trilogy* Cases provided the foundation for expansions of the use of labor arbitration to resolve labor disputes.

Arbitrators rely on *Lincoln Mills to* support the application of federal substantive law in rendering arbitration awards. Moreover, the *Steelworkers Trilogy* cases provided arbitrator with guidance on how to resolve arbitrability issues, how to determine the appropriate sources of law to apply, and explained the use and importance of the collective bargaining agreement in reaching decisions. More importantly, the Supreme Court set forth the limits of judicial review of arbitration decision, as well as the limits of arbitrators' authority in rendering decisions. However, the Supreme Court made it very clear that arbitrators have the ultimate authority to resolve grievances based on their knowledge and experience, but within the limits of the collective bargain8ng agreement.

TEXTILE WORKERS UNION V. LINCOLN MILLS
353 U.S. 448 (1957)

Mr. Justice DOUGLAS delivered the opinion of the Court.

Petitioner-union entered into a collective bargaining agreement in 1953 with respondent-employer, the agreement to run one year and from year to year thereafter, unless terminated on specified notices. The agreement provided that there would be no strikes or work stoppages and that grievances would be handled pursuant to a specified procedure. The last step in the grievance procedure-a step that could be taken by either party-was arbitration.

This controversy involves several grievances that concern work loads and work assignments. The grievances were processed through the various steps in the grievance procedure and were finally denied by the employer. The union requested arbitration, and the employer refused. Thereupon the union brought this suit in the District Court to compel arbitration. *issue* *PH*

The District Court concluded that it had jurisdiction and ordered the employer to comply with the grievance arbitration provisions of the Collective Bargaining Agreement. The Court of Appeals reversed by a divided vote. 230 F.2d 81. It held that, although the District Court had jurisdiction to entertain the suit, the court had no authority founded either in federal or state law to grant the relief. The case is here on a petition for a writ of certiorari which we granted because of the importance of the problem and the contrariety of views in the courts. 352 U.S. 821, 77 S.Ct. 54, 1 L.Ed.2d 46.

The starting point of our inquiry is s 301 of the Labor Management Relations Act of 1947, 61 Stat. 156, 29 U.S.C. s 185, 29 U.S.C.A. s 185, which provides: *301*

'(a) Suits for violation of contracts between an employer and a labor organization representing employees in an industry affecting commerce as defined in this chapter, or between any such labor organizations, may be brought in any district court of the United States having jurisdiction of the parties, without respect to the amount in controversy or without regard to the citizenship of the parties.

'(b) Any labor organization which represents employees in an industry affecting commerce as defined in this chapter and any employer whose activities affect commerce as defined in this chapter shall be bound by the acts of its agents. Any such labor organization may sue or be sued as an entity and in behalf of the employees whom it represents in the courts of the United States. Any money judgment against a labor organization in a district court of the United States shall be enforceable only against the organization as an entity and against its assets, and shall not be enforceable against any individual member or his assets.'

There has been considerable litigation involving s 301 and courts have construed it differently. There is one view that s 301(a) merely gives federal district courts jurisdiction in controversies that involve labor organizations in industries affecting commerce, without regard to diversity of citizenship or the amount in controversy. Under that view s 301(a) would not be the source of substantive law; it would neither supply federal law to resolve these controversies nor turn the federal judges to state law for answers to the questions. Other courts-the overwhelming number of them-hold that 301(a) is more than jurisdictional-that it authorizes federal courts to fashion a body of federal law for the enforcement of these collective bargaining agreements and includes within that federal law specific performance of promises to arbitrate grievances under collective bargaining agreements. Perhaps the leading decision representing that point of view is the one rendered by Judge Wyzanski in Textile Workers Union of America (C.I.O.) v. American Thread Co., D.C., 113 F.Supp. 137. That is our construction of s 301(a), which means that the agreement to arbitrate grievance disputes, contained in this collective bargaining agreement, should be specifically enforced.

From the face of the Act it is apparent that s 301(a) and s 301(b) supplement one another. Section 301(b) makes it possible for a labor organization, representing employees in an industry affecting commerce, to sue and be sued as an entity in the federal courts. Section 301(b) in other words provides the procedural remedy lacking at common law. Section 301(a) certainly does something more than that. Plainly, it supplies the basis upon which the federal district courts may take jurisdiction and apply the procedural rule of s 301(b). The question is whether s 301(a) is more than jurisdictional.

The legislative history of s 301 is somewhat cloudy and confusing. But there are a few shafts of light that illuminate our problem.

* * * *

It seems, therefore, clear to us that Congress adopted a policy which placed sanctions behind agreements to arbitrate grievance disputes, by implication rejecting the common-law rule, discussed in Red Cross Line v. Atlantic Fruit Co., 264 U.S. 109, 44 S.Ct. 274, 68 L.Ed. 582, against enforcement of executory agreements to arbitrate. We would undercut the Act and defeat its policy if we read s 301 narrowly as only conferring jurisdiction over labor organizations.

The question then is, what is the substantive law to be applied in suits under s 301(a)? We conclude that the substantive law to apply in suits under s 301(a) is federal law, which the courts must fashion from the policy of our national labor laws. See Mendelsohn, Enforceability of Arbitration Agreements Under Taft-Hartley Section 301, 66 Yale L.J. 167. The Labor Management Relations Act expressly furnishes some substantive law. It points out what the parties may or may not do in certain situations. Other problems will lie in the penumbra of express statutory mandates. Some will lack express statutory sanction but will be solved by looking at the policy of the legislation and fashioning a remedy that will effectuate that policy. The range of judicial inventiveness will be determined by the nature of the problem. See *Board of Commissioners of Jackson County v. United States*, 308 U.S. 343, 351, 60 S.Ct. 285, 288, 84 L.Ed. 313. Federal interpretation of the federal law will govern, not state law. Cf. *Jerome v. United States*, 318 U.S. 101, 104, 63 S.Ct. 483, 485, 87 L.Ed. 640. But state law, if compatible with the purpose of s 301, may be resorted to in order to find the rule that will best effectuate the federal policy. See *Board of Commissioners of Jackson County v. United States*, supra, 308 U.S. at pages 351-352, 60 S.Ct. at pages 288-289. Any state law applied, however, will be absorbed as federal law and will not be an independent source of private rights.

It is not uncommon for federal courts to fashion federal law where federal rights are concerned. See *Clearfield Trust Co. v. United States*, 318 U.S. 363, 366-367, 63 S.Ct. 573, 574-575, 87 L.Ed. 838; *National Metropolitan Bank v. United States*, 323 U.S. 454, 65 S.Ct. 354, 89 L.Ed. 383. Congress has indicated by s 301(a) the purpose to follow that course here. There is no constitutional difficulty. Article III, s 2, extends the judicial power to cases 'arising under * * * *the Laws of the United States * * *.' The power of Congress to regulate these labor-management controversies under the Commerce Clause is plain. *Houston East & West Texas R. Co. v. United States*, 234 U.S. 342, 34 S.Ct. 833, 58 L.Ed. 1341; *National Labor Relations Board v. Jones & Laughlin Corp.*, 301 U.S. 1, 57 S.Ct. 615, 81 L.Ed. 893. A case or controversy arising under 301(a) is, therefore, one within the purview of judicial power as defined in Article III.

* * * *

The judgment of the Court of Appeals is reversed and the cause is remanded to that court for proceedings in conformity with this opinion.

Reversed.

APPLICATION AND DISCUSSION QUESTIONS

The *Lincoln Mill* decision resolved the conflict among district courts over the issue of whether 301 (a) was purely a jurisdictional provision and not a source of power to allow the courts to develop federal common law for enforcing collective bargaining provisions. The Court held that the Federal courts had the authority to develop and apply federal common law. The decision ensured that collective bargaining agreements would be enforced. In other words, employers and unions could not escape the enforcement of an agreement that they agreed to comply with. Thus, collective bargaining agreements are binding on all parties and a breach of the agreement could be enforced in Federal court.

1. How does *Lincoln Mills* ensure industrial peace between the parties?

2. If federal courts have jurisdiction to enforce collective bargaining agreements, what substantive law will the court apply? How will the court determine what is substantive law? Can substantive law be developed from other federal labor statutes, legislative history, and/or state labor laws?

3. How can arbitrators use *Lincoln Mills* to support their arbitration awards?

THE STEELWORKERS TRILOGY CASES

UNITED STEELWORKERS V. WARRIOR & GULF NAVIGATION COMPANY
363 U.S. 574 (1960)

Opinion of the Court by Mr. Justice DOUGLAS, announced by Mr. Justice BRENNAN.

Respondent transports steel and steel products by barge and maintains a terminal at Chickasaw, Alabama, where it performs maintenance and repair work on its barges. The employees at that terminal constitute a bargaining unit covered by a collective bargaining agreement negotiated by petitioner union. Respondent between 1956 and 1958 laid off some employees, reducing the bargaining unit from 42 to 23 men. This reduction was due in part to respondent contracting maintenance work, previously done by its employees, to other companies. The latter used respondent's supervisors to lay out the work and hired some of the laid-off employees of respondent (at reduced wages). Some were in fact assigned to work on respondent's barges. A number of employees signed a grievance which petitioner presented to respondent, the grievance reading:

'We are hereby protesting the Company's actions, of arbitrarily and unreasonably contracting out work to other concerns, that could and previously has been performed by Company employees.

'This practice becomes unreasonable, unjust and discriminatory in lieu (sic) of the fact that at present there are a number of employees that have been laid off for about 1 and 1/2 years or more for allegedly lack of work.

'Confronted with these facts we charge that the Company is in violation of the contract by inducing a partial lock-out, of a number of the employees who would otherwise be working were it not for this unfair practice.'

The collective agreement had both a 'no strike' and a 'no lockout' provision. It also had a grievance procedure which provided in relevant part as follows:

'Issues which conflict with any Federal statute in its application as established by Court procedure or matters which are strictly a function of management shall not be subject to arbitration under this section.

'Should differences arise between the Company and the Union or its members employed by the Company as to the meaning and application of the provisions of this Agreement, or should any local trouble of any kind arise, there shall be no suspension of work on account of such differences but an earnest effort shall be made to settle such differences immediately in the following manner:

'A. For Maintenance Employees:

'First, between the aggrieved employees, and the Foreman involved;

'Second, between a member or members of the Grievance Committee designated by the Union, and the Foreman and Master Mechanic.

'Fifth, if agreement has not been reached the matter shall be referred to an impartial umpire for decision. The parties shall meet to decide on an umpire acceptable to both. If no agreement on selection of an umpire is reached, the parties shall jointly petition the United States Conciliation Service for suggestion of a list of umpires from which selection shall be made. The decision of the umpire will be final.'

Settlement of this grievance was not had and respondent refused arbitration. This suit was then commenced by the union to compel it.

The District Court granted respondent's motion to dismiss the complaint. 168 F.Supp. 702. It held after hearing evidence, much of which went to the merits of the grievance that the agreement did not 'confide in an arbitrator the right to review the defendant's business judgment in contracting out work.' Id., at page 705. It further held that 'the contracting out of repair and maintenance work, as well as construction work, is strictly a function of management not limited in any respect by the labor agreement involved here.' Ibid. The Court of Appeals affirmed by a divided vote, 269 F.2d 633, 635, the majority holding that the collective agreement had withdrawn from the grievance procedure 'matters which are strictly a function of management' and that contracting out fell in that exception. The case is here on a writ of certiorari. 361 U.S. 912, 80 S.Ct. 255, 4 L.Ed.2d 183.

* * * *

The collective bargaining agreement states the rights and duties of the parties. It is more than a contract; it is a generalized code to govern a myriad of cases which the draftsmen cannot wholly anticipate. Shulman, Reason, Contract, and Law in Labor Relations, 68 Harv.L.Rev. 999, 1004-1005. The collective agreement covers the whole employment relationship. It calls into being a new common law-the common law of a particular industry or of a particular plant. As one observer has put it:

> * * * *(I)t is not unqualifiedly true that a collective-bargaining agreement is simply a document by which the union and employees have imposed upon management limited, express restrictions of its otherwise absolute right to manage the enterprise, so that an employee's claim must fail unless he can point to a specific contract provision upon which the claim is founded,. There are too many people, too many problems, too many unforeseeable contingencies to make the words of the contract the exclusive source of rights and duties. One cannot reduce all the rules governing a community like an industrial plant to fifteen or even fifty pages. Within the sphere of collective bargaining, the institutional characteristics and the governmental nature of the collective-bargaining process demand a common law of the shop which implements and furnishes the context of the agreement. We must assume that intelligent negotiators acknowledged so plain a need unless they stated a contrary rule in plain words.

A collective bargaining agreement is an effort to erect a system of industrial self-government. When most parties enter into contractual relationship they do so voluntarily, in the sense that there is no real compulsion to deal with one another, as opposed to dealing with other parties. This is not true of the labor agreement. The choice is generally not between entering or refusing to enter into a relationship, for that in all probability pre-exists the negotiations. Rather it is between having that relationship governed by an agreed-upon rule of law or leaving each and every matter subject to a temporary resolution dependent solely upon the relative strength, at any given moment, of the contending forces. The mature labor agreement may attempt to regulate all aspects of the complicated relationship, from the most crucial to the most minute over an extended period of time. Because of the compulsion to reach agreement and the breadth of the matters covered, as well as the need for a fairly concise and readable instrument, the product of negotiations (the written document) is, in the words of the late Dean Shulman, 'a compilation of diverse provisions: some provide objective criteria almost automatically applicable; some provide more or less specific standards which require reason and judgment in their application; and some do little more than leave problems to future consideration with an expression of hope and good faith.' Shulman, supra, at 1005.

Gaps may be left to be filled in by reference to the practices of the particular industry and of the various shops covered by the agreement. Many of the specific practices which underlie the agreement may be unknown, except in hazy form, even to the negotiators. Courts and arbitration in the context of most commercial contracts are resorted to because there has been a breakdown in the working relationship of the parties; such resort is the unwanted exception. But the grievance machinery under a collective bargaining agreement is at the very heart of the system of industrial self-government. Arbitration is the means of solving the unforeseeable by molding a system of private law for all the problems which may arise and to provide for their solution in a way which will generally accord with the variant needs and desires of the parties. The processing of disputes through the grievance machinery is actually a vehicle by which meaning and content are given to the collective bargaining agreement.

Apart from matters that the parties specifically exclude, all of the questions on which the parties disagree must therefore come within the scope of the grievance and arbitration provisions of the collective agreement. The grievance procedure is, in other words, a part of the continuous collective bargaining process. It, rather than a strike, is the terminal point of a disagreement.

The labor arbitrator performs functions which are not normal to the courts; the considerations which help him fashion judgments may indeed by foreign to the competence of courts.

> 'A proper conception of the arbitrator's function is basic. He is not a public tribunal imposed upon the parties by superior authority which the parties are obliged to accept. He has no general charter to administer justice for a community which transcends the parties. He is rather part of a system of self-government created by and confined to the parties. * * *' Shulman, supra, at 1016.

The labor arbitrator's source of law is not confined to the express provisions of the contract, as the industrial common law-the practices of the industry and the shop-is equally a part of the collective bargaining agreement although not expressed in it. The labor arbitrator is usually chosen because of the parties' confidence in his knowledge of the common law of the shop and their trust in his personal judgment to bring to bear considerations which are not expressed in the contract as criteria for judgment. The parties expect that his judgment of a particular grievance will reflect not only what the contract says but, insofar as the collective bargaining agreement permits, such factors as the effect upon productivity of a particular result, its consequence to the morale of the shop, his judgment whether tensions will be heightened or diminished. For the parties' objective in using the arbitration process is primarily to further their common goal of uninterrupted production under the agreement, to make the agreement serve their specialized needs. The ablest judge cannot be expected to bring the same experience and competence to bear upon the determination of a grievance, because he cannot be similarly informed.

The Congress, however, has by s 301 of the Labor Management Relations Act, assigned the courts the duty of determining whether the reluctant party has breached his promise to arbitrate. For arbitration is a matter of contract and a party cannot be required to submit to arbitration any dispute which he has not agreed so to submit. Yet, to be consistent with congressional policy in favor of settlement of disputes by the parties through the machinery of arbitration, the judicial inquiry under s 301 must be strictly confined to the question whether the reluctant party did agree to arbitrate the grievance or did agree to give the arbitrator power to make the award he made. An order to arbitrate the particular grievance should not be denied unless it may be said with positive assurance that the arbitration clause is not susceptible of an interpretation that covers the asserted dispute. Doubts should be resolved in favor of coverage.

We do not agree with the lower courts that contracting-out grievances were necessarily excepted from the grievance procedure of this agreement. To be sure, the agreement provides that 'matters which are strictly a function of management shall not be subject to arbitration.' But it goes on to say that if 'differences' arise or if 'any local trouble of any kind' arises, the grievance procedure shall be applicable.

Collective bargaining agreements regulate or restrict the exercise of management functions; they do not oust management from the performance of them. Management hires and fires, pays and promotes, supervises and plans. All these are part of its function, and absent a collective bargaining agreement, it may be exercised freely except as limited by public law and by the willingness of employees to work under the particular, unilaterally imposed conditions. A collective bargaining agreement may treat only with certain specific practices, leaving the rest to management but subject to the possibility of work stoppages. When, however, an absolute no-strike clause is included in the agreement, then in a very real sense everything that management does is subject to the agreement, for either management is prohibited or limited in the action it takes, or if not, it is protected from interference by strikes. This comprehensive reach of the collective bargaining agreement does not mean, however, that the language, 'strictly a function of management,' has no meaning.

'Strictly a function of management' might be thought to refer to any practice of management in which, under particular circumstances prescribed by the agreement, it is permitted to indulge. But if courts, in order to determine arbitrability, were allowed to determine what is permitted and what is not, the arbitration clause would be swallowed up by the exception. Every grievance in a sense involves a claim that management has violated some provision of the agreement.

Accordingly, 'strictly a function of management' must be interpreted as referring only to that over which the contract gives management complete control and unfettered discretion. Respondent claims that the contracting out of work falls within this category. Contracting out work is the basis of many grievances; and that type of claim is grist in the mills of the arbitrators. A specific collective bargaining agreement may exclude contracting out from the grievance procedure. Or a written collateral agreement may make clear that contracting out was not a matter for arbitration. In such a case a grievance based solely on contracting out would not be arbitrable. Here, however, there is no such provision. Nor is there any showing that the parties designed the phrase 'strictly a function of management' to encompass any and all forms of contracting out. In the absence of any express provision excluding a particular grievance from arbitration, we think only the most forceful evidence of a purpose to exclude the claim from arbitration can prevail, particularly where, as here, the exclusion clause is vague and the arbitration clause quite broad. Since any attempt by a court to infer such a purpose necessarily comprehends the merits, the court should view with suspicion an attempt to persuade it to become entangled in the construction of the substantive provisions of a labor agreement, even through the back door of interpreting the arbitration clause, when the alternative is to utilize the services of an arbitrator.

The grievance alleged that the contracting out was a violation of the collective bargaining agreement. There was, therefore, a dispute 'as to the meaning and application of the provisions of this Agreement' which the parties had agreed would be determined by arbitration.

The judiciary sits in these cases to bring into operation an arbitral process which substitutes a regime of peaceful settlement for the older regime of industrial conflict. Whether contracting out in the present case violated the agreement is the question. It is a question for the arbiter, not for the courts.

Reversed.

APPLICATION AND DISCUSSION QUESTIONS

In *Warrior & Gulf,* the Supreme Court explained how the collective bargaining agreement is "more than a contract; it is a generalized code to govern a myriad of cases which the draftsman cannot wholly anticipate." The Court answered a number of unsolved questions on the use of arbitration to resolve labor grievances. The Court also defined the role of the arbitrator and the Court. Specifically, the Court explained that the parties agreed to give the arbitrator power to issue awards. The arbitrator's source of law is not limited by the express language in the collective bargaining agreement, but also includes common law and practices of the industry and the shop.

The Court also pointed out that federal judges do not have the same experience as arbitrators. Thus, arbitrators' awards should be set aside only on a limited basis.

Discuss how the court addressed each of the following questions:

1. How can arbitrators use the Court's language to resolve substantive arbitrability issues?

2. How should arbitrators "fill in gaps" in the collective bargaining agreement to determine the parties' intentions?

3. How did the arbitrator determine "the common law' of a particular plant or industry?

4. How does the Court define the functions and roles of arbitrators and the courts?

5. How did the Court determine that arbitrators have "broad general powers"?

6. How should an arbitrator resolve the issue of whether an arbitration clause covers a dispute?

Opinion of the Court by Mr. Justice DOUGLAS, announced by Mr. Justice
BRENNAN.

This suit was brought by petitioner union in the District Court to compel arbitration of a 'grievance' that petitioner, acting for one Sparks, a union member, had filed with the respondent, Sparks' employer. The employer defended on the ground (1) that Sparks is estopped from making his claim because he had a few days previously settled a workmen's compensation claim against the company on the basis that he was permanently partially disabled, (2) that Sparks is not physically able to do the work, and (3) that this type of dispute is not arbitrable under the collective bargaining agreement in question.

The agreement provided that during its term there would be 'no strike,' unless the employer refused to abide by a decision of the arbitrator. The agreement sets out a detailed grievance procedure with a provision for arbitration (regarded as the standard form) of all disputes between the parties 'as to the meaning, interpretation and application of the provisions of this agreement.'

The agreement reserves to the management power to suspend or discharge any employee 'for cause.' It also contains a provision that the employer will employ and promote employees on the principle of seniority 'where ability and efficiency are equal.' Sparks left his work due to an injury and while off work brought an action for compensation benefits. The case was settled, Sparks' physician expressing the opinion that the injury had made him 25% 'permanently partially disabled.' That was on September 9. Two weeks later the union filed a grievance which charged that Sparks was entitled to return to his job by virtue of the seniority provision of the collective bargaining agreement. Respondent refused to arbitrate and this action was brought. The District Court held that Sparks, having accepted the settlement on the basis of permanent partial disability, was estopped to claim any seniority or employment rights and granted the motion for summary judgment. The Court of Appeals affirmed, 264 F.2d 624, for different reasons. After reviewing the evidence it held that the grievance is 'a frivolous, patently baseless one, not subject to arbitration under the collective bargaining agreement.' Id., at page 628. The case is here on a writ of certiorari, 361 U.S. 881, 80 S.Ct. 152, 4 L.Ed.2d 118.

Section 203(d) of the Labor Management Relations Act, 1947, 61 Stat. 154, 29 U.S.C. s 173(d), 29 U.S.C.A. s 173(d), states, 'Final adjustment by a method agreed upon by the parties is hereby declared to be the desirable method for settlement of grievance disputes arising over the application or interpretation of an existing collective-bargaining agreement.* * * *' That policy can be effectuated only if the means chosen by the parties for settlement of their differences under a collective bargaining agreement is given full play.

A state decision that held to the contrary announced a principle that could only have a crippling effect on grievance arbitration. The case was *International Ass'n of Machinists v. Cutler-Hammer, Inc.*, 271 App.Div. 917, 67 N.Y.S.2d 317, affirmed 297 N.Y., 519, 74 N.E.2d 464. It held that 'If the meaning of the provision of the contract sought to be arbitrated is beyond dispute, there cannot be anything to arbitrate and the contract cannot be said to provide for arbitration.' 271 App. Div. at page 918, 67 N.Y.S.2d at page 318. The lower courts in the instant case had a like preoccupation with ordinary contract law. The collective agreement requires arbitration of claims that courts might be unwilling to entertain. In the context of the plant or industry the grievance may assume proportions of which judges are ignorant. Yet, the agreement is to submit all grievances to arbitration, not merely those that a court may deem to be meritorious. There is no exception in the 'no strike' clause and none therefore should be read into the grievance clause, since one is the quid pro quo for the other. The question is not whether in the mind of the court there is equity in the claim. Arbitration is a stabilizing influence only as it serves as a vehicle for handling any and all disputes that arise under the agreement.

The collective agreement calls for the submission of grievances in the categories which it describes, irrespective of whether a court may deem them to be meritorious. In our role of developing a meaningful body of law to govern the interpretation and enforcement of collective bargaining agreements, we think special heed should be given to the context in which collective bargaining agreements are negotiated and the purpose which they are intended to serve. See *Lewis v. Benedict Coal Corp.*, 361 U.S. 459, 468, 80 S.Ct. 489, 495, 4 L.Ed.2d 442. The function of the court is very limited when the parties have agreed to submit all questions of contract interpretation to the arbitrator. It is confined to ascertaining whether the party seeking arbitration is making a claim which on its face is governed by the contract. Whether the moving party is right or wrong is a question of contract interpretation for the arbitrator. In these circumstances the moving party should not be deprived of the arbitrator's judgment, when it was his judgment and all that it connotes that was bargained for.

The courts, therefore, have no business weighing the merits of the grievance, considering whether there is equity in a particular claim, or determining whether there is particular language in the written instrument which will support the claim. The agreement is to submit all grievances to arbitration, not merely those which the court will deem meritorious. The processing of even frivolous claims may have therapeutic values of which those who are not a part of the plant environment may be quite unaware.

The union claimed in this case that the company had violated a specific provision of the contract. The company took the position that it had not violated that clause. There was, therefore, a dispute between the parties as to 'the meaning, interpretation and application' of the collective bargaining agreement. Arbitration should have been ordered. When the judiciary undertakes to determine the merits of a grievance under the guise of interpreting the grievance procedure of collective bargaining agreements, it usurps a function which under that regime is entrusted to the arbitration tribunal.

here

Reversed.

APPLICATION AND DISCUSSION QUESTIONS

In *American Manufacturing Company*, the Supreme Court further discussed the role of the Court in reviewing arbitration awards. The Court explained it was not the role of the Court to determine the merits of a grievance. The role of the Court was very limited, especially where the parties have agreed for the arbitrator to interpret the collective bargaining agreement. The Supreme Court cautioned lower courts not to usurp the role of the arbitrator to interpret the agreement.

Discuss how the Court addressed each of the following questions:

1. What role does the Court have in 'weighing the merits of grievances'?

2. Are there any benefits to arbitrating a grievance that may be frivolous if the collective bargaining agreement permits all grievances to be arbitrated, if requested?

3. Can and should the Court place limitations on arbitrating such claims that appear on its face to be frivolous?

4. Cite some examples of when the arbitrator should cite the *American Manufacturing* decision.

UNITED STEELWORKERS' V. ENTERPRISE WHEEL & CAR CORPORATION

363 U.S. 593 (1960)

Opinion of the Court by Mr. Justice DOUGLAS, announced by Mr. Justice BRENNAN

Petitioner union and respondent during the period relevant here had a collective bargaining agreement which provided that any differences 'as to the meaning and application' of the agreement should be submitted to arbitration and that the arbitrator's decision 'shall be final and binding on the parties.' Special provisions were included concerning the suspension and discharge of employees.

The agreement stated:

'Should it be determined by the Company or by an arbitrator in accordance with the grievance procedure that the employee has been suspended unjustly or discharged in violation of the provisions of this Agreement, the Company shall reinstate the employee and pay full compensation at the employee's regular rate of pay for the time lost.'

The agreement also provided:

'* * * *It is understood and agreed that neither party will institute civil suits or legal proceedings against the other for alleged violation of any of the provisions of this labor contract; instead all disputes will be settled in the manner outlined in this Article III-Adjustment of Grievances.'

A group of employees left their jobs in protest against the discharge of one employee. A union official advised them at once to return to work. An official of respondent at their request gave them permission and then rescinded it. The next day they were told they did not have a job any more 'until this thing was settled one way or the other.'

A grievance was filed; and when respondent finally refused to arbitrate, this suit was brought for specific enforcement of the arbitration provisions of the agreement. The District Court ordered arbitration. The arbitrator found that the discharge of the men was not justified, though their conduct, he said, was improper. In his view the facts warranted at most a suspension of the men for 10 days each. After their discharge and before the arbitration award the collective bargaining agreement had expired. The union, however, continued to represent the workers at the plant. The arbitrator rejected the contention that expiration of the agreement barred reinstatement of the employees. He held that the provision of the agreement above quoted imposed an unconditional obligation on the employer. He awarded reinstatement with back pay, minus pay for a 10-day suspension and such sums as these employees received from other employment.

Respondent refused to comply with the award. Petitioner moved the District Court for enforcement. The District Court directed respondent to comply. 168 F.Supp. 308. The Court of Appeals, while agreeing that the District Court had jurisdiction to enforce an arbitration award under a collective bargaining agreement, held that the failure of the award to specify the amounts to be deducted from the back pay rendered the award unenforceable. That defect, it agreed, could be remedied by requiring the parties to complete the arbitration. It went on to hold, however, that an award for back pay subsequent to the date of termination of the collective bargaining agreement could not be enforced. It also held that the requirement for reinstatement of the discharged employees was likewise unenforceable because the collective bargaining agreement had expired. 269 F.2d 327. We granted certiorari. 361 U.S. 929, 80 S.Ct. 371.

The refusal of courts to review the merits of an arbitration award is the proper approach to arbitration under collective bargaining agreements. The federal policy of settling labor disputes by arbitration would be undermined if courts had the final say on the merits of the awards. As we stated in *United Steelworkers of America v. Warrior & Gulf Navigation Co.*, 363 U.S. 574, 80 S.Ct. 1347, the arbitrators under these collective agreements are indispensable agencies in a continuous collective bargaining process. They sit to settle disputes at the plant level-disputes that require for their solution knowledge of the custom and practices of a particular factory or of a particular industry as reflected in particular agreements.

When an arbitrator is commissioned to interpret and apply the collective bargaining agreement, he is to bring his informed judgment to bear in order to reach a fair solution of a problem. This is especially true when it comes to formulating remedies. There the need is for flexibility in meeting a wide variety of situations. The draftsmen may never have thought of what specific remedy should be awarded to meet a particular contingency. Nevertheless, an arbitrator is confined to interpretation and application of the collective bargaining agreement; he does not sit to dispense his own brand of industrial justice. He may of course look for guidance from many sources, yet his award is legitimate only so long as it draws its essence from the collective bargaining agreement. When the arbitrator's words manifest an infidelity to this obligation, courts have no choice but to refuse enforcement of the award.

The opinion of the arbitrator in this case, as it bears upon the award of back pay beyond the date of the agreement's expiration and reinstatement, is ambiguous. It may be read as based solely upon the arbitrator's view of the requirements of enacted legislation, which would mean that he exceeded the scope of the submission. Or it may be read as embodying a construction of the agreement itself, perhaps with the arbitrator looking to 'the law' for help in determining the sense of the agreement. A mere ambiguity in the opinion accompanying an award, which permits the inference that the arbitrator may have exceeded his authority, is not a reason for refusing to enforce the award. Arbitrators have no obligation to the court to give their reasons for an award. To require opinions free of ambiguity may lead arbitrators to play it safe by writing no supporting opinions. This would be undesirable for a well-reasoned opinion tends to engender confidence in the integrity of the process and aids in clarifying the underlying agreement. Moreover, we see no reason to assume that this arbitrator has abused the trust the parties confided in him and has not stayed within the areas marked out for his consideration. It is not apparent that he went beyond the submission. The Court of Appeals' opinion refusing to enforce the reinstatement and partial back pay portions of the award was not based upon any finding that the arbitrator did not premise his award on his construction of the contract. It merely disagreed with the arbitrator's construction of it.

The collective bargaining agreement could have provided that if any of the employees were wrongfully discharged, the remedy would be reinstatement and back pay up to the date they were returned to work. Respondent's major argument seems to be that by applying correct principles of law to the interpretation of the collective bargaining agreement it can be determined that the agreement did not so provide, and that therefore the arbitrator's decision was not based upon the contract. The acceptance of this view would require courts, even under the standard arbitration clause, to review the merits of every construction of the contract. This plenary review by a court of the merits would make meaningless the provisions that the arbitrator's decision is final, for in reality it would almost never be final. This underlines the fundamental error which we have alluded to in *United Steelworkers of America v. American Manufacturing Co.*, 363 U.S. 564, 80 S.Ct. 1343. As we there emphasized, the question of interpretation of the collective bargaining agreement is a question for the arbitrator. It is the arbitrator's construction which was bargained for; and so far as the arbitrator's decision concerns construction of the contract, the courts have no business overruling him because their interpretation of the contract is different from his.

We agree with the Court of Appeals that the judgment of the District Court should be modified so that the amounts due the employees may be definitely determined by arbitration. In all other respects we think the judgment of the District Court should be affirmed. Accordingly, we reverse the judgment of the Court of Appeals, except for that modification, and remand the case to the District Court for proceedings in conformity with this opinion. It is so ordered.

Judgment of Court of Appeals, except for its modification of District Court's judgment, reversed and case remanded to District Court with directions.

Mr. Justice WHITTAKER, dissenting. (Omitted)

APPLICATION AND DISCUSSION QUESTIONS

In *Enterprise Wheel*, the Supreme Court continued with a discussion of the limited role that courts play in reviewing arbitration decisions. The Court stated that, "federal labor policy of settling labor disputes by arbitration would be undermined if courts had the final say on the merits of the awards." The court explained that arbitrators bring to the process, "knowledge and experience in formulating remedies."

Discuss how the Court addressed each of the following questions:

1. Explain the Court's reasoning that the arbitrator had authority to issue an award when the collective bargaining agreement had expired.

2. How did the arbitrator have authority to reduce the penalty from a termination to a 10-day suspension?

3. The Court cautioned aribtrators not to "dispense [their] own brand of industrial justice." Explain what the Court meant by this phrase. How can arbitrators ensure they don't cross the line of dispensing such justice?

4. Isn't reducing a termination to a 10-day suspension a violation of this priniciple?

5. What is the Court's reasoning for not reviewing the merits of a grievance?

6. What federal common law principle does the court develop regarding an ambiguity in an arbitrator's award?

7. For a historical review of the trilogy, see, Martin H. Malin, Forward: *Labor Arbitration Thirty Years After the Steelworkers Trilogy,* 66 Chi-Kent L. Rev. 551 (1990); William B. Gould IV, The Trilogy at 50-Foundations For the 21st Century; A Half Century of the *Steelworkers Trilogy:* Fifty Years of Ironies

Squared, in Proceedings of the Sixty-Third Annual Meeting National
Academy of Arbitrators, May 26-27, 2010, pp.35-100.

C. ARBITRABILITY ISSUES

PROCEDURAL ARBITRABILITY

Case
merged corp
must arb

JOHN WILEY & SONS, INC. V. LIVINGSTON
376 U.S. 543 (1964)

Mr. Justice HARLAN delivered the opinion of the Court.

Q

This is an action by a union, pursuant to s 301 of the Labor Management Relations Act, 61 Stat. 136, 156, 29 U.S.C. s 185, to compel arbitration under a collective bargaining agreement. The major questions presented are (1) whether a corporate employer must arbitrate with a union under a bargaining agreement between the union and another corporation which has merged with the employer, and, if so, (2) whether the courts or the arbitrator is the appropriate body to decide whether procedural prerequisites which, under the bargaining agreement, condition the duty to arbitrate have been met. Because of the importance of both questions to the realization of national labor policy, we granted certiorari (373 U.S. 908, 83 S.Ct. 1300, 10 L.Ed.2d

A

411) to review a judgment of the Court of Appeals directing arbitration (313 F.2d 52), in reversal of the District Court which had refused such relief (203 F.Supp. 171). We affirm the judgment below, but, with respect to the first question above, on grounds which may differ from those of the Court of Appeals, whose answer to that question is unclear.

I.

District 65, Retail, Wholesale and Department Store Union, AFL-CIO, entered into a collective Pubishers, Inc., a with Interscience Pubishers, Inc., a publishing firm, for a term expiring on January 31, 1962. The agreement did not contain an express provision making it binding on successors of Interscience. On October 2, 1961, Interscience merged with the petitioner, John Wiley & Sons, Inc., another publishing firm, and ceased to do business as a separate entity. There is no suggestion that the merger was not for genuine business reasons.

In discussions before and after the merger, the Union and Interscience (later Wiley) were unable to agree on the effect of the merger on the collective bargaining agreement and on the rights under it of those covered employees hired by Wiley. The Union's position was that despite the merger it continued to represent the covered Interscience employees taken over by Wiley, and that Wiley was obligated to recognize certain rights of such employees which had 'vested' under the Interscience bargaining agreement. Such rights, more fully described below, concerned matters typically covered by collective bargaining agreements, such as seniority status, severance pay, etc. The Union contended also that Wiley was required to make certain pension fund payments called for under the Interscience bargaining agreement.

Wiley, though recognizing for purposes of its own pension plan the Interscience service of the former Interscience employees, asserted that the merger terminated the bargaining agreement for all purposes. It refused to recognize the Union as bargaining agent or to accede to the Union's claims on behalf of Interscience employees. All such employees, except a few who ended their Wiley employment with severance pay and for whom no rights are asserted here, continued in Wiley's employ.

No satisfactory solution having been reached, the Union, one week before the expiration date of the Interscience bargaining agreement, commenced this action to compel arbitration.

II.

The threshold question in this controversy is who shall decide whether the arbitration provisions of the collective bargaining agreement survived the Wiley-Interscience merger, so as to be operative against Wiley. Both parties urge that this question is for the courts. Past cases leave no doubt that this is correct.1 'Under our decisions, whether or not he company was bound to arbitrate, as well as what issues it must arbitrate, is a matter to be determined by the Court on the basis of the contract entered into by the parties.' *Atkinson v. Sinclair Refining Co.*, 370 U.S. 238, 241, 82 S.Ct. 1318, 1320, 8 L.Ed.2d 462. Accord, e.g., *United Steelworkers of America v. Warrior & Gulf Navigation Co.*, 363 U.S. 574, 582, 80 S.Ct. 1347, 4 L.Ed. 2d 1409. The problem in those cases was whether an employer, concededly party to and bound by a contract which contained an arbitration provision, had agreed to arbitrate disputes of a particular kind. Here, the question is whether Wiley, which did not itself sign the collective

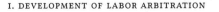

bargaining agreement on which the Union's claim to arbitration depends, is bound at all by the agreement's arbitration provision. The reason requiring the courts to determine the issue is the same in both situations. The duty to arbitrate being of contractual origin, a compulsory submission to arbitration cannot precede judicial determination that the collective bargaining agreement does in fact create such a duty. Thus, just as an employer has no obligation to arbitrate issues which it has not agreed to arbitrate, so a fortiori, it cannot be compelled to arbitrate if an arbitration clause does not bind it at all.

The unanimity of views about who should decide the question of arbitrability does not, however, presage the parties' accord about what is the correct decision. Wiley, objecting to arbitration, argues that it never was a party to the collective bargaining agreement, and that, in any event, the Union lost its status as representative of the former Interscience employees when they were mingled in a larger Wiley unit of employees. The Union argues that Wiley, as successor to Interscience, is bound by the latter's agreement, at least sufficiently to require it to arbitrate. The Union relies on s 90 of the N.Y. Stock Corporation Law, McKinney's Consol. Laws, c. 59, which provides, among other things, that no 'claim or demand for any cause' against a constituent corporation shall be extinguished by a consolidation. Alternatively, the Union argues that, apart from s 90, federal law requires that arbitration go forward, lest the policy favoring arbitration frequently be undermined by changes in corporate organization.

Federal law, fashioned 'from the policy of our national labor laws,' controls. *Textile Workers Union of America v. Lincoln Mills*, 353 U.S. 448, 456, 77 S.Ct. 912, 918, 1 L.Ed.2d 972. State law may be utilized so far as it is of aid in the development of correct principles or their application in a particular case, id., 353 U.S. at 457, 77 S.Ct. 912, 1 L.Ed.2d 972, but the law which ultimately results is federal. We hold that the disappearance by merger of a corporate employer which has entered into a collective bargaining agreement with a union does not automatically terminate all rights of the employees covered by the agreement, and that, in appropriate circumstances, present here, the successor employer may be required to arbitrate with the union under the agreement.

* * * *

IV.

Wiley's final objection to arbitration raises the question of so-called 'procedural arbitrability.' The Interscience agreement provides for arbitration as the third stage of the grievance procedure. 'Step 1' provides for 'a conference between the affected employee, a Union Steward and the Employer, officer or exempt supervisory person in charge of his department.' In 'Step 2,' the grievance is submitted to 'a conference between an officer of the Employer, or the Employer's representative designated for that purpose, the Union Shop Committee and/or a representative of the Union.' Arbitration is reached under 'Step 3' 'in the event that the grievance shall not have been resolved or settled in 'Step 2.'" Wiley argues that since Steps 1 and 2 have not been followed, and since the duty to arbitrate arises only in Step 3, it has no duty to arbitrate this dispute. Specifically, Wiley urges that the question whether 'procedural' conditions to arbitration have been met must be decided by the court and not the arbitrator.

We think that labor disputes of the kind involved here cannot be broken down so easily into their 'substantive' and 'procedural' aspects. Questions concerning the procedural prerequisites to arbitration do not arise in a vacuum; they develop in the context of an actual dispute about the rights of the parties to the contract or those covered by it. In this case, for example, the Union argues that Wiley's consistent refusal to recognize the Union's representative status after the merger made it 'utterly futile—and a little bit ridiculous to follow the grievance steps as set forth in the contract.' Brief, p. 41. In addition, the Union argues that time limitations in the grievance procedure are not controlling because Wiley's violations of the bargaining agreement were 'continuing.' These arguments in response to Wiley's 'procedural' claim are meaningless unless set in the background of the merger and the negotiations surrounding it.

Doubt whether grievance procedures or some part of them apply to a particular dispute, whether such procedures have been followed or excused, or whether the unexcused failure to follow them avoids the duty to arbitrate cannot ordinarily be answered without consideration of the merits of the dispute which is presented for arbitration. In this case, one's view of the Union's responses to Wiley's 'procedural' arguments depends to a large extent on how one answers questions bearing on the basic issue, the effect of the merger; e.g., whether or not the merger was a possibility considered by Wiley and the Union during the negotiation of the contract. It would be a curious rule which required that intertwined issues of 'substance' and 'procedure' growing out of a single dispute and raising the same questions on the same facts had to be carved up between two different forums, one deciding after the other. Neither logic nor considerations of policy compel such a result.

Once it is determined, as we have, that the parties are obligated to submit the subject matter of a dispute to arbitration, 'procedural' questions which grow out of the dispute and bear on its final disposition should be left to the arbitrator. Even under a contrary rule, a court could deny arbitration only if it could confidently be said not only that a claim was strictly 'procedural,' and therefore within the purview of the court, but also that it should operate to bar arbitration altogether, and not merely limit or qualify an arbitral award. In view of the policies favoring arbitration and the parties' adoption of arbitration as the preferred means of settling disputes, such cases are likely to be rare indeed. In all other cases, those in which arbitration goes forward, the arbitrator would ordinarily remain free to reconsider the ground covered by the court insofar as it bore on the merits of the dispute, using the flexible approaches familiar to arbitration. Reservation of 'procedural' issues for the courts would thus not only create the difficult task of separating related issues, but would also produce frequent duplication of effort.

In addition, the opportunities for deliberate delay and the possibility of well-intentioned but no less serious delay created by separation of the 'procedural' and 'substantive' elements of a dispute are clear. While the courts have the task of determining 'substantive arbitrability,' there will be cases in which arbitrability of the subject matter is unquestioned but a dispute arises over the procedures to be followed. In all of such cases, acceptance of Wiley's position would produce the delay attendant upon judicial proceedings preliminary to arbitration. As this case, commenced in January 1962 and not yet committed to arbitration, well illustrates, such delay may entirely eliminate the prospect of a speedy arbitrated settlement of the dispute, to the disadvantage of the parties (who, in addition, will have to bear increased costs) and contrary to the aims of national labor policy.

No justification for such a generally undesirable result is to be found in a presumed intention of the parties. Refusal to order arbitration of subjects which the parties have not agreed to arbitrate does not entail the fractionating of disputes about subjects which the parties do wish to have submitted. Although a party may resist arbitration once a grievance has arisen, as does Wiley here, we think it best accords with the usual purposes of an arbitration clause and with the policy behind federal labor law to regard procedural disagreements not as separate disputes but as aspects of the dispute which called the grievance procedures into play. With the reservation indicated at the outset, the judgment of the Court of Appeals is affirmed.

APPLICATION AND DISCUSSION QUESTIONS

Shortly after the Supreme Court trilogy decisions, the court issued a decision in *John Wiley & Sons* to determine whether the Court or the arbitrator is the appropriate body to decide procedural and substantive arbitrability issues. The Court first points out that issues such as whether a decision is arbitrable is for the Court to decide. It is the role of the arbitrator to decide procedural issues.

Discuss how the court addressed each of the following questions:

1. Is it the role of the arbitrator to determine substantive issues? What about procedural arbitrability issues? What is the difference between the two? Identify the substantive and procedural issues in *Wiley*.

2. Why does Wiley object to arbitration?

3. What are some examples of procedural arbitrability issues?

NOLDE BROTHERS, INC. V. LOCAL NO. 348, BAKERY & CONFECTIONARY WORKERS UNION, AFL-CIO

430 U.S. 243 (1977)

care

post–CBA dispute

Mr. Chief Justice BURGER delivered the opinion of the Court.

This case raises the question of whether a party to a collective-bargaining contract may be required to arbitrate a contractual dispute over severance pay pursuant to the arbitration clause of that agreement even though the dispute, although governed by the contract, arises after its termination. Only the issue of arbitrability is before us.

Q

In 1970, petitioner Nolde Brothers, Inc., entered into a collective-bargaining agreement with respondent Local No. 358, of the AFL-CIO, covering petitioner's Norfolk, Va., bakery employees. Under the contract, 'any grievance' arising between the parties was subject to binding arbitration. In addition, the contract contained a provision which provided for severance pay on termination of employment for all employees having three of more years of active service. Vacation rights were also granted employees by the agreement; like severance pay, these rights were geared to an employee's length of service and the amount of his earnings. By its terms, the contract was to remain in effect until July 21, 1973, and thereafter, until such time as either a new agreement was executed between the parties, or the existing agreement was terminated upon seven days' written notice by either party.

term

In May 1973, the parties resumed bargaining after the Union advised Nolde, pursuant to s 8(d) of the National Labor Relations Act, 29 U.S.C. s 158(d), of its desire to negotiate certain changes in the existing agreement. These negotiations continued without resolution up to, and beyond, the July 21 contract expiration date. On August 20, the Union served the requisite seven days written notice of its decision to cancel the existing contract. The Union's termination of the contract became effective August 27, 1973.

Despite the contract's cancellation, negotiations continued. They ended, however, on August 31, when Nolde, faced by a threatened strike after the Union had rejected its latest proposal, informed the Union of its decision to close permanently its Norfolk bakery, effective that day. Operations at the plant ceased shortly after midnight on August 31. Nolde then paid employees their accrued wages and accrued vacation pay under the canceled contract; in addition, wages were paid for work performed during the interim between the contract's termination on August 27 and the bakery's closing four days later. However, the company rejected the Union's demand for the severance pay called for in the collective-bargaining agreement. It also declined to arbitrate the severance-pay claim on the ground that its contractual obligation to arbitrate disputes terminated with the collective-bargaining agreement.

The Union then instituted this action in the District Court under s 301 of the Labor Management Relations Act, 29 U.S.C. s 185, seeking to compel Nolde to arbitrate the severance-pay issue, or in the alternative, judgment for the severance pay due. The District Court granted Nolde's motion for summary judgment on both issues. It held that the employees' right to severance pay expired with the Union's voluntary termination of the collective-bargaining contract and that, as a result, there was no longer any severance-pay issue to arbitrate. It went on to note that even if the dispute had been otherwise arbitrable, the duty to arbitrate terminated with the contract that had created it. 382 F.Supp. 1354 (ED Va.1974).

On appeal, the United States Court of Appeals for the Fourth Circuit reversed. 530 F.2d 548 (1975). It took the position that the District Court had approached the case from the wrong direction by determining that Nolde's severance-pay obligations had expired with the collective-bargaining agreement before determining whether Nolde's duty to arbitrate the claim survived the contract's termination. Turning to that latter question first, the Court of Appeals concluded that the parties' arbitration duties under the contract survived its termination with respect to claims arising by reason of the collective-bargaining agreement. Having thus determined that the severance-pay issue was one for the arbitrator, the Court of Appeals expressed no views on the merits of the dispute. We granted certiorari to review its determination that the severance-pay claim was arbitrable.

In arguing that Nolde's displaced employees were entitled to severance pay upon the closing of the Norfolk bakery, the Union maintained that the severance wages provided for in the collective-bargaining agreement were in the nature of 'accrued' or 'vested' rights, earned by employees during the term of the contract on essentially the same basis as vacation pay, but payable only upon termination of employment. In support of this claim, the Union noted that the severance-pay clause is found in the contract under an article entitled 'Wages.' The inclusion within that provision, it urged, was evidence that the parties considered severance pay as part of the employees' compensation for services performed during the life of the agreement. In addition, the Union pointed out that the severance-pay clause itself contained nothing to suggest that the employees' right to severance pay expired if the events triggering payment failed to occur during the life of the contract. Nolde, on the other hand, argued that since severance pay was a creation of the collective-bargaining agreement, its substantive obligation to provide such benefits terminated with the Union's unilateral cancellation of the contract.

As the parties' arguments demonstrate, both the Union's claim for severance pay and Nolde's refusal to pay the same are based on their differing perceptions of a provision of the expired collective-bargaining agreement. The parties may have intended, as Nolde maintained, that any substantive claim to severance pay must surface, if at all, during the contract's term. However, there is also 'no reason why parties could not if they so chose agree to the accrual of rights during the term of an agreement and their realization after the agreement had expired.' *John Wiley & Sons v. Livingston*, 376 U.S. 543, 555, 84 S.Ct. 909, 917, 11 L.Ed.2d 898 (1964). Of course, in determining the arbitrability of the dispute, the merits of the underlying claim for severance pay are not before us. However, it is clear that, whatever the outcome, the resolution of that claim hinges on the interpretation ultimately given the contract clause providing for severance pay. The dispute therefore, although arising after the expiration of the collective-bargaining contract, clearly arises under that contract.

* * * *

Nolde contends that the duty to arbitrate, being strictly a creature of contract, must necessarily expire with the collective-bargaining contract that brought it into existence. Hence, it maintains that a court may not compel a party to submit any post-contract grievance to arbitration for the simple reason that no contractual duty to arbitrate survives the agreement's termination. Any other conclusion, Nolde argues, runs contrary to federal labor policy which prohibits the imposition of compulsory arbitration upon parties except when they are bound by an arbitration agreement. In so arguing, Nolde relies on numerous decisions of this Court which it claims establish that 'arbitration is a matter of contract and (that) a party cannot be required to submit to arbitration any dispute which he has not agreed so to submit.' *Steelworkers v. Warrior & Gulf Nav. Co.*, 363 U.S. 574, 582, 80 S.Ct. 1347, 1352, 4 L.Ed.2d 1409 (1960).

Our prior decisions have indeed held that the arbitration duty is a creature of the collective-bargaining agreement and that a party cannot be compelled to arbitrate any matter in the absence of a contractual obligation to do so. Adherence to these principles, however, does not require us to hold that termination of a collective-bargaining agreement automatically extinguishes a party's duty to arbitrate grievances arising under the contract. Carried to its logical conclusion that argument would preclude the entry of a post-contract arbitration order even when the dispute arose during the life of the contract but arbitration proceedings had not begun before termination. The same would be true if arbitration processes began but were not completed, during the contract's term. Yet it could not seriously be contended in either instance that the expiration of the contract would terminate the parties' contractual obligation to resolve such a dispute in an arbitral, rather than a judicial forum. Nolde concedes as much by limiting its claim of nonarbitrability to those disputes which clearly arise after the contract's expiration.

The parties agreed to resolve all disputes by resort to the mandatory grievance-arbitration machinery established by their collective-bargaining agreement. The severance-pay dispute, as we have noted, would have been subject to resolution under those procedures had it arisen during the contract's term. However, even though the parties could have so provided, there is nothing in the arbitration clause that expressly excludes from its operation a dispute which arises under the contract, but which is based on events that occur after its termination. The contract's silence, of course, does not establish the parties' intent to resolve post-termination grievances by arbitration. But in the absence of some contrary indication, there are strong reasons to conclude that the parties did not intend their arbitration duties to terminate automatically with the contract. Any other holding would permit the employer to cut off all arbitration of severance-pay claims by terminating an existing contract simultaneously with closing business operations.

By their contract the parties clearly expressed their preference for an arbitral, rather than a judicial-interpretation of their obligations under the collective-bargaining agreement. Their reasons for doing so, as well as the special role of arbitration in the employer-employee relationship, have long been recognized by this Court:

> 'The labor arbitrator is usually chosen because of the parties' confidence in his knowledge of the common law of the shop and their trust in his personal judgment to bring to bear considerations which are not expressed in the contract as criteria for judgment. ... The ablest judge cannot be expected to bring the same experience and competence

to bear upon the determination of a grievance, because he cannot be similarly informed.' *Warrior & Gulf Nav. Co.,* 363 U.S., at 582, 80 S.Ct., at 1353.

Indeed, it is because of his special experience, expertise, and selection by the parties that courts generally defer to an arbitrator's interpretation of the collective-bargaining agreement:

'(T)he question of interpretation of the collective bargaining agreement is a question for the arbitrator. It is the arbitrator's construction which was bargained for; and so far as the arbitrator's decision concerns construction of the contract, the courts have no business overruling him because their interpretation of the contract is different from his.' *Enterprise Wheel & Car Corp.,* 363 U.S., at 599, 80 S.Ct., at 1362.

While the termination of the collective-bargaining agreement works an obvious change in the relationship between employer and union, it would have little impact on many of the considerations behind their decision to resolve their contractual differences through arbitration. The contracting parties' confidence in the arbitration process and an arbitrator's presumed special competence in matters concerning bargaining agreements does not terminate with the contract. Nor would their interest in obtaining a prompt and inexpensive resolution of their disputes by an expert tribunal. Hence, there is little reason to construe this contract to mean that the parties intended their contractual duty to submit grievances and claims arising under the contract to terminate immediately on the termination of the contract; the alternative remedy of a lawsuit is the very remedy the arbitration clause was designed to avoid.

It is also noteworthy that the parties drafted their broad arbitration clause against a backdrop of well-established federal labor policy favoring arbitration as the means of resolving disputes over the meaning and effect of collective-bargaining agreements. Congress has expressly stated:

'Final adjustment by a method agreed upon by the parties is hereby declared to be the desirable method for settlement of grievance disputes arising over the application or interpretation of an existing collective-bargaining agreement.' 29 U.S.C. s 173(d).

In order to effectuate this policy, this Court has established a strong presumption favoring arbitrability:

(T)o be consistent with congressional policy in favor of settlement of disputes by the parties through the machinery of arbitration, . . . (a)n order to arbitrate the particular grievance should not be denied unless it may be said with positive assurance that the arbitration clause is not susceptible of an interpretation that covers the asserted dispute. Doubts should be resolved in favor of coverage. *Warrior & Gulf Nav. Co.*, supra, 363 U.S., at 582-583, 80 S.Ct., at 1353.

The parties must be deemed to have been conscious of this policy when they agree to resolve their contractual differences through arbitration. Consequently, the parties' failure to exclude from arbitrability contract disputes arising after termination, far from manifesting an intent to have arbitration obligations cease with the agreement, affords a basis for concluding that they intended to arbitrate all grievances arising out of the contractual relationship. In short, where the dispute is over a provision of the expired agreement, the presumptions favoring arbitrability must be negated expressly or by clear implication.

We therefore agree with the conclusion of the Court of Appeals that, on this record, the Union's claim for severance pay under the expired collective-bargaining agreement is subject to resolution under the arbitration provisions of that contract.

Affirmed.

Mr. Justice STEWART, with whom Mr. Justice REHNQUIST joins, dissenting. (Omitted)

APPLICATION AND DISCUSSION QUESTIONS

1. The dissent states that the "court today says that a union-employer dispute must be settled by arbitration even though the dispute did not even arise until after the contract containing an agreement to arbitrate had been terminated by action of the Union, and the employer had closed its business." Is this the conclusion that the majority reached? If so, does it make sense?

2. What reasons did the court state as to why parties prefer an arbitrator to hear their dispute than the court?

3. Why is there a strong presumption favoring arbitration?

Timeliness of Grievances

In disputes regarding timeliness, the threshold issue for the Arbitrator to decide is whether the grievance is arbitrable based on a claim that the grievance was untimely filed. The issue of procedural arbitrability arises when a party fails to meet a required timeframe or step in the grievance process. Typically, the CBA outlines the procedural requirement for each party to meet at each stage of the grievance process. The failure to meet the procedural requirement of processing a grievance may deny the arbitrator authority to rule on the substantive issue. Unless there are mitigating factors, the arbitrator is bound by the strict procedural language in the CBA. The Arbitrator will consider arguments presented by the parties on how to interpret and apply the contract provision on filing grievances. The primary arbitrable principle on analyzing procedural defects has been described in the following manner:

> An Arbitrator is bound by the agreement of the parties relating to timeliness and other requirements contained in the grievance procedure and appeal to arbitration, unless the parties themselves, by their actions or omissions, have in some way excused compliance with the procedure. (*Stone Container*, 105 LA 385 (Berquist, 1995).

THE GREEN BAKERY COMPANY, INC.[*]

I. STATEMENT OF FACTS

* * * *The facts indicate that this arbitration involves four grievances. These grievances were consolidated in accordance with a previous arbitration between the parties. All four grievances involve the same issue. The facts indicate that a production line shutdown occurred on four different occasions in 2007. On each shutdown, after the employees cleaned the production line, the employees were sent home.

Grievance 81 was filed on August 13, 2007, Grievance 85 was filed August 31, 2007 (Joint Exh 5), Grievance 84 was filed September 14, 2007, and Grievance 80 was filed November 21, 2007. The grievances all contend that the Employer violated the contract when the employees were sent home and not given the option to work for the remainder of their shift. The grievances went through the various stages of the grievance procedure. The grievances were denied. Arbitration was requested pursuant to Article 15 of the CBA.

---

[*]   Unpublished Decision, (Floyd D. Weatherspoon, 2008)

II. ISSUES

At the arbitration hearing, the Company raised two procedural issues:

1. Were the four grievances timely appealed to arbitration?

2. Do Grievances 80, 81, and 84 meet the requirements of the CBA which specifies that the grievances identify the employees affected?

The parties stipulated to the following substantive issue: Did the Company violate Article 6, Section 8, involving the four grievances, if so, what is the appropriate remedy?

III. RELEVANT CONTRACT PROVISIONS

Article 15: Grievance Procedure and Arbitration

Step 1. The grievant shall individually or with the Union Steward within five (5) work days after the grievant knew, or with reasonable diligence should have known, of the event giving rise to the grievance, first attempt to settle the controversy by discussion with the Foreman or Superintendent who shall give the aggrieved employee a verbal answer within two (2) work days from the time of the discussion.

Step 2. If the grievance is not satisfactorily settled in the manner provided for in Step 1, the grievance shall be reduced to writing and signed by the grievant on a form to be supplied by the Union. In reducing the grievance to writing, the following information shall be stated with reasonable clearness: The exact nature of the grievance, the act or acts complained of, by whom and when they occurred, the identity of the employee or employees who claim to be aggrieved, the provisions of this Agreement that the employee or employees claim that the Company has violated and the remedy sought.

5. In the event that the dispute cannot be satisfactorily settled by the above steps of the grievance procedure, the Union may request arbitration by giving the Company written notice of its desire to arbitrate signed by an authorized Union Representative within one (1) calendar week of the Company's final answer or failure to answer after the passage of the prescribed time limit at Step 2.

IV. POSITION OF THE PARTIES

A. Union's Position

The Union contends that the Company violated the contract when it sent employees home instead of giving the employees the option to work, when the production line shut down. The Union further contends that the parties bargaining history and the past practice establishes that the contract language was changed in 2001 to permit the Company to keep the employees at work when the production line shut down. The Union maintains that the intent was not to give the Company the discretionary power to send employees home in the event of a line shutdown. The Union further contends that the parties established a binding past practice that when a line shutdown occurred, the employees would either be given work or ask the supervisor to release them to go home. The Union maintains that the Company violated the contract when it didn't follow that practice in these four grievances.

U arg

B. Management's Position

Initially, the Company raises two procedural issues: the Company contends that the four grievances were not timely appealed to arbitration and that grievances 81, 84, and 80 did not comply with the requirements of Article 15 because the grievance do not name the grievants. The Company further contends that the contract does not require it to create work for an employee when the production line shuts down. The Company maintains that when a production line shuts down, it must assign work if there is a need, but it does not have to create work.

ER arg

V. DISCUSSION AND ANALYSIS

A. Procedural Issues

The Employer raises two procedural issues, the first procedural issue is whether all four grievances were timely appealed to arbitration. The second procedural issue involves grievances 80, 81, and 84 and whether they meet the requirements of the CBA which specifies that the grievance identify the employees affected.

The Arbitrator determined at the hearing that the failure to specifically list the grievants' names on the grievances forms did not violate the CBA in this instance. The Arbitrator rationalized that the Employer could reasonably determine what employees were affected from the language on the grievance form. Therefore, the absence of employee names did not disadvantage the Employer, since the Employer had sufficient notice of the employees affected. Despite the fact that the Arbitrator ruled on this procedural issue at the arbitration hearing, the Employer still challenges the issue in its post-hearing brief. However, the arguments raised by the Employer do not change the Arbitrator's previous ruling. Nevertheless, the Arbitrator will address the Employer's arguments.

The Employer argues that Article 15, Section 3 specifies what information must be provided in a written grievance. The Employer further emphasizes that the Arbitrator has no power to add, subtract, or modify the terms of the agreement. The Employer contends that since employee identification is a requirement in accordance with Article 15 to disregard this requirement would be a clear modification of the terms of the agreement.

> Article 15, Section 3, provides in relevant part;
>
> If the grievance is not satisfactorily settled in the manner provided for in Step 1, the grievance shall be reduced to writing and signed by the grievant on a form to be supplied by the Union. In reducing a grievance to writing, the following information shall be stated with reasonable clearness: The exact nature of the grievance, the act or acts complained of, by whom, and when they occurred, the identity of the employee or employees who claim to be aggrieved.

Initially, the Arbitrator notes that "[a] general presumption exists that favors arbitration over dismissal of grievances on technical grounds." (Elkouri & Elkouri, How Arbitration Works, 6th Ed. pg. 206). However, the Arbitrator finds, again, that the grievances substantially comply with the requirements of Article 15, Section 3. Article 15 provides that the grievance shall state the identity of the employees with reasonable clearness. The Arbitrator acknowledges that the most clear way to identify an employee is by name. However, the Arbitrator further notes that Article 15 does not explicitly state that the Grievant's name has to be the identifier; the requirement is that the identity of the employee be stated with reasonable clearness. Grievance 80 states that the grievance affects the 1000 and 800 line employees at Green Road. Therefore, this grievance identifies the affected employees with reasonable clearness. Grievance 81 states that the grievance affects "all 800 employees". Therefore, this grievance identifies the affected employees with reasonable clearness. Finally, Grievance 84 states that the grievance affects 1000 line employees at Green Road. Therefore, this grievance identifies the employees with reasonable clearness. The objection is denied.

The Arbitrator will now address the remaining procedural issue raised by the Employer, which is whether the grievances were timely appealed to arbitration. The Employer argues that the Union untimely appealed the four grievances to arbitration under Article 15, Section 5 of the parties' contract. Step 2 of Article 15, provides, in relevant part, "[t]he grievant and/or a Union Representative may meet with the Bakery Manager or his representative to discuss the grievance at a time and place mutually agreeable to the parties. The Bakery Manager or his representative shall make a written reply to the grievance within three (3) work days following the meeting. "

Paragraph 5 of Article 15, provides in relevant part, "[i]n the event that the dispute cannot be satisfactorily settled by the above steps of the grievance procedure, the Union may request arbitration by giving the Company written notice of its desire to arbitrate signed by an authorized Union Representative within one (1) calendar week of the Company's final answer or failure to answer after passage of the prescribed time limit at Step 2."

The resolution of this issue is predicated upon a determination of when the Company gave its "final answer". It is the Company's contention that the time for the Union to request arbitration began to run when the Company gave its Step 2 written reply. At the arbitration hearing, the Union vehemently argued that the Company's final answer was not the same as the step 2 written reply. Thus, the issue requires a determination of whether the "final answer" language in Article 15 means the same thing as the Step 2 "written reply". While both parties put thought and development into its contentions at the hearing of whether the "final answer" and Step 2 "written reply" were merely interchangeable terms or had different meanings, the Employer makes no attempt to develop the argument any further in its post-hearing brief. Rather, the Employer cites the provision, states the date on which it denied the grievance, and concludes that the appeal to arbitration is untimely, without regard to interpretation of terms. However, the Employer's contention that the grievances are not timely requires the determination that the "final answer" means the same thing as the Step 2 "written reply"

The Union maintains that appeal period does not start to run until the Company gives its "final answer" which is not the same as its Step 2 "written reply". The Union emphasizes that Paragraph 5, specifically says the Company's final answer as opposed to the Step 2 written reply. The Union contends that the parties continue to discuss the grievances following the written reply, therefore, the final answer is not the written reply. According to the Union the Company's final answer typically occurs at a monthly meeting, after the Company's Step 2 reply. The Union further states that the Company's final answer is when the Company informs the Union that there will be no more discussion of the grievance. The Union states that it is this event that triggers the time to appeal to arbitration.

The evidence demonstrates that the parties continue to discuss grievances even after the Company has issued a Step 2 written denial. Thus, the Union argues that the parties have never operated such that the Union has to file its notice to arbitrate within seven days of the Step 2 written reply. The Human Resources Manager testified that the parties continue to discuss grievances after the grievances have been denied. Thus, the Company acknowledges that the parties continue to discuss the grievances and sometimes even resolve them. The Company argues, however, that if the parties later on negotiate a possible resolution of the grievance or attempt to do so, doesn't extend the time period for the Union to appeal the grievance to arbitration.

* * * *

The Union provided sufficient evidence that the Company's final answer occurs at a monthly meeting between the Company and the Union, when the Human Resources Manager informs the Union that the Company is no longer willing to discuss the grievance, thereby indicating that the Company's position on the matter is final. Once this event occurs, the Union files for arbitration. The Union maintains that each of these grievances were appealed within one week of the Company's final answer. The Arbitrator will look at each of the four grievances individually.

Grievance 81

The evidence indicates that the Union appealed this grievance to arbitration on September 26, 2007. The evidence further indicates that a meeting was held where this grievance was discussed on September 12, 2007. The letter states that the Company requested an opportunity to review the grievance, thus, the Company did not give its "final answer" at this meeting. In his letter, dated September 26, 2007, the Financial Secretary Treasurer of the Union, states that the HR Manager requested an opportunity to review the grievance in the September 12, 2007 meeting and to respond to the Union. The letter goes on to state that since the Union has not heard anything from the Company, the letter serves as its notice of arbitration. This letter confirms the parties' practice to discuss grievances subsequent to the Step 2 written reply. Moreover, this letter demonstrates that the Company did not yet give its final answer, so the appeal period had not yet run. Thus, the appeal was timely.

Grievances 84 and 85

The evidence demonstrates that these grievances were appealed to arbitration on October 3, 2007. The evidence demonstrates that a meeting was held about November 6 or 7, where the Company gave its final answer. Therefore, the evidence demonstrates that the appeal for these grievances came prior to the final answer. Therefore, the appeal was timely.

Grievance 80

The evidence demonstrates that this grievance was appealed on December 7, 2007. The evidence further reveals that a meeting occurred on December 7, 2007, wherein, the Company gave its final answer. Therefore, the appeal was timely.

B. Substantive Issues (omitted)

APPLICATION AND DISCUSSION QUESTIONS

1. The arbitration clause in collective bargaining agreements will outline the process the parties are to follow prior to the arbitration hearing. Often, the parties will be required to share documents related to the grievance. In addition, the parties may be required to exchange their witness lists within a certain time period. The exchange of documents and witness lists prior to the hearing, may avoid lengthy delays during the hearing. Where one party fails to comply with the request of documentation, the other party may request that the arbitrator issue a subpoena or disallow the admission of such evidence. The opposing party may also file a motion to compel a party to comply with the request. What documents are normally presented in disciplinary and issues grievances?

2. Why is there a presumption in favor of arbitration over dismissal of a grievance? Was the failure to provide the witness list prior to the hearing more than a harmless non-prejudicial technical violation? Can you think of a situation where the failure to provide requested documentation prior to the hearing could be prejudicial?

3. When the parties continued to have conversations and e-mails related to the issue, were they engaged in collective bargaining? If yes, what impact would it have on the timeliness issue? What options did the parties have to resolve this issue?

4. Did the previous arbitration award leave a number of issues unresolved? How should the arbitrator approach these issues, if raised in the second arbitration case?

5. Technically, the Union did not comply with Article 15, section 3 of the agreement which required "the identity of the employee or employees who claim to be aggrieved." Why does the arbitrator still permit the grievances to go forward?

6. The arbitrator determined that the grievances were timely. Now the parties will schedule another arbitration, which will normally be months away. Would it make more sense to schedule the procedural issue and the substantive issue in one hearing? What are the advantages and disadvantages of having two separate hearings?

COUNTY OF ALLEGHENY AND ALLEGHENY COURT ASSOCIATION OF PROFESSIONAL EMPLOYEES, ACAPE UNIT 1603
134 BNA LA 977 (KOBELL, 2015)[*]

ARTICLE III

Grievance Procedure

3. Procedural Steps for Grievance Processing:
   A. Level One - Department of Human Resources

Any alleged grievance shall be reduced to writing within seven (7) work days from the alleged occurrence of the grievance, or within seven (7) work days from the time the grievant reasonably should have known or have been aware of the existence of

---

[*] Reprinted with permission from *Labor Relations Reporter- Labor Arbitration Reports.* 134 BNA LA 977. Copyright 2015 by the Bureau of National Affairs, Inc. (800-372-1033).http://www.bna.com.

the situation giving rise to the alleged grievance. The written grievance, which must be submitted on the approved form and signed by the grievant and an authorized representative, will be filed with the Manager of Labor Relations of the County's Department of Human Resources. The Manager or his representative and the Union shall meet, either with or without the grievant, and attempt to settle the grievance. Failing settlement, the Manager or his representative shall provide the Union with a written response, unless not reasonably possible within ten (10) workdays.

* * * *

ARTICLE VIII (omitted)

Statement of Facts

The facts of this case are not in dispute. What is in dispute are the timeliness of the instant grievance, and the significance of the facts in the context of the bargaining history, the Award of Arbitrator Lewis R. Amis, and the collective bargaining agreement. This case involves a collective bargaining unit of approximately 330-340 probation officers who are appointed by the Allegheny County Court System and covered by the Agreement, which is administered by the Allegheny County Department of Human Resources. The contractual issues relating to the bargaining unit are controlled by Act 195, which provides for interest arbitration in the event of a collective bargaining impasse.

According to the testimony of Association President, Probation Officer Stephen J. Bechtold, the sole witness at the hearing, and whose testimony was undisputed, the parties reached an impasse with respect to wages and benefits on July 18, 2013. By letters dated December 5, 2013, and April 8, 2014, 6 the County advised the Association that it, in accordance with another interest arbitration award not involved herein, the County desired to implement a new health insurance plan when 75 percent of the eligible employees had transferred to a new plan, and that this had already occurred.

In accordance with Act 195, which prohibits strikes by employees in this bargaining unit, impasses are to be resolved by an impartial arbitrator. Arbitrator Lewis R. Amis was appointed as the neutral arbitrator to resolve all of the issues upon which an impasse had been reached, which included the 2 or 2.25 percent employee contribution for healthcare, among several other issues. The other two arbitrators were the counsel for the respective parties in this proceeding, Daniel R. Delaney, Esq. for the Association, and Diego Correa, Esq., Assistant Solicitor for Allegheny County.

Arbitrator Amis conducted a hearing on February 7, 2014 and an executive session on April 9, 2014, and he issued his Award on May 6, 2014.

* * * *

This brings this narrative to the core of the dispute, i.e., that portion of Arbitrator Amis' Award with respect to the "Cost Containment" paragraph. After modifying Article VIII, Sections 1.A, 2B 3, and 3E, all of which appear to have been before him in the impasse arbitration, he stated the following with respect to Section 3 H Cost Containment, "Continue 2 percent contribution of base salary towards premium for hospitalization insurance for the life of this Agreement. Retain existing relevant conditions, rights, and restrictions contained in this section."

Apparently, the parties did not agree that the Amis Award definitively resolved all of the issues in dispute. The Association submitted its version of those provisions of the Agreement to succeed the agreement, which expired on December 31, 2013, including a two percent participation in Article VIII, Section H. In May 2014, the Association also submitted a summary of its version of the Arbitration Award, covering the salary schedule and other benefits. The submitted document also provides for the two percent contribution towards the health care premium under the heading of "PREMIUM CONTRIBUTION." The Association, despite the extant disputes, ratified the Agreement, based upon its understanding of it, on May 29, 2014.

The County's objectives with respect to a new plan with increased employee contributions in excess of 2 percent of base salary were common knowledge at the time of the arbitration proceeding, even though that goal was reached before Arbitrator Amis issued his Award. The County's letters dated December 5, 2013 and April 8, 2014 make that abundantly clear. On or about May 1, 2014, the County announced that it had reached the threshold of 75 percent of the represented employees in the County who had agreed to accept a new health insurance plan. The County believed that this phenomenon also included acceptance of the 2.25 percent employee contribution for the balance of 2014 and 2015, which in the following two years, would be raised to 2.5 percent.

* * * *

According to ACAPE President Bechtold's testimony, there was much left to be resolved, including shift differentials and health care language.

* * * *

ACAPE President Bechtold testified that in the Union and Union counsel's view, all of the foregoing conversations and e-mails were part of the past practice oral discussions and the oral discussions referred to in the County's grievance form, and were for the purpose of resolving all of the remaining outstanding issues, including but not limited to the 2-2.25 percent controversy, that prevented the execution and distribution of the contract, and which was already almost one year old. Until September 25, 2014, ACAPE believed that the issue of 2 percent employee participation was "still in play" along with the other remaining issues.

On the same day, September 25, 2014, Attorney Correa replied that the position previously taken by the County remained unchanged that the 2 percent payroll deduction was subject to modification with the "me too" clause, which allows the County to implement a new healthcare program. Attorney Correa added that this position is consistent with the County's position all along. Attorney Correa further added that the County would not agree to submit the issue to Arbitrator Amis for resolution, and the Union could choose to contest the interpretation, in any manner it desired. If the Union elected to file a grievance, the County would agree to "fast tracking" the grievance to the arbitration level so as to address the matter in the timeliest manner possible. Last, Attorney Correa added that as discussed, in agreeing to the accelerated schedule, the County reserved the right to raise any and all procedural defenses, including but not limited to timeliness.

The grievance herein was filed on October 6, 2014, which was within seven days (work days) of September 25, the prescribed time period for the filing of a grievance.

Positions of the Parties

A. *The Association*

1. Timeliness

The Association argues that ACAPE has often experienced delay with respect to efforts to resolve matters with the County, and the instant dispute with respect to the employee participation rate is part of the pattern of past practice. In this connection, ACAPE points out that over one year has passed since the expiration of the prior Agreement, and even the scheduling of the arbitration to interpret Arbitrator Amis' award was overly delayed.

* * * *

B. The County

1. Timeliness

The County argues that as a matter of law, the parties to a collective bargaining agreement are bound by its time limits, * * * * "the collective bargaining agreement herein provides, in Article III, Section 3, that "Any alleged grievance shall be reduced to writing within seven (7) work days from the time the grievant reasonably should have known or been aware of the existence of the situation giving rise to the alleged grievance." Moreover, the Agreement in Article III, Section 4 also provides that "any grievance must be presented under the procedures of this Article promptly, and within the prescribed time limitations."

* * * *

The County disagrees with the Association that it did not make its position clear in the August e-mails. It was clearly stated in those e-mails. Moreover, the Union's approach to this case (i.e. that the County's position remained unclear) has been considered in a similar situation by the Pennsylvania Labor Relations Board. In Pennsylvania State Corrections Officers Association v. Commonwealth of Pennsylvania Department of Corrections, the Association claimed that it received "mixed signals" from the Commonwealth regarding compliance with a grievance settlement, and that it was not aware of management's official position until the parties conducted their monthly labor management meeting. However, the Association's Local President was aware of the Commonwealth's position, and the Association knew or should have known that the Commonwealth was not complying with the grievance settlement previously negotiated. Therefore, the Association's grievance, which was filed more than four months after the deadline, must be dismissed as untimely. The County, in reliance upon the above case, therefore argues that the Association, well aware of the County's position, may not plead ignorance to toll the negotiated contractual time limitations.

* * * *

The County also rejects the Association's argument that the deduction of 2.25 percent instead of 2 percent is a continuing violation, i.e. each paycheck constitutes a new actionable violation of the Agreement. This interpretation would effectively nullify the concept of timeliness as it applies to any pay-related claim, with each paycheck resurrecting the cause of action for review. The Pennsylvania Labor Relations Board and the Pennsylvania Courts have concluded that such interpretations must be denied.

* * * *

2. The Merits (Omitted)

The Issue

There was general agreement at the Arbitration hearing that this case presents two issues, as follows:

1. Was the Association's grievance filed on October 6, 2014 timely, with respect to the provisions of the Agreement providing for the filing of a grievance within seven (7) workdays of the occurrence or when the grievant should have been reasonably aware of the occurrence?

2. Did Arbitrator Amis' Arbitration Award, pursuant to Act 195, in Section 3H, Cost Containment on page 6, continue the 2 percent of base salary payroll deduction towards the premium contribution to the new Health Plan, for the life of the new Agreement, notwithstanding the other retained language in the Cost Containment section providing for the imposition of a new healthcare plan?

Discussion

The threshold question for me is the timeliness of the grievance that was filed on October 6, 2014. Clearly, if the contract precludes the filing of the grievance involved herein because it was filed more than seven (7) work days after the Association knew, or should have known, in June 2014, or certainly on August 21, 2014, that the County had increased the payroll deduction from 2 to 2.25 percent, I cannot grant the grievance. Even though some arbitrators, after finding a grievance to be untimely, still consider and decide the merits, I would not be required to do so.

In order to decide the timeliness question, at the outset, I must determine how the parties came to be apart on this issue. There is no dispute towards the end of calendar year 2013 and into 2014, the parties were engaged in bargaining for a new collective bargaining agreement to replace the one that was scheduled to expire on December 31, 2013. They did so pursuant to Act 195, which has special provisions for employees such as Probation Officers. The Act clearly spells out that after mediation efforts have been unsuccessful, and an impasse still remains, the dispute should be submitted to a panel of arbitrators, whose decision shall be final and binding.

The uncontradicted testimony and argument in this case, which is clearly reflected in the Award, is that the Arbitrator considered the bargaining proposals of the parties, and engaged in "give and take," agreeing on some occasions with the County, and on others with the Association.

* * * *

On the basis of the foregoing, I conclude that the grievance was timely filed in accordance with the seven (7) day contractual time limits. In so finding, I am not unmindful of the cases cited by the County with respect to the inelasticity of contractual time limits with respect to the filing of grievances. I agree with those cases which state, in substance, that the time limits for the filing of a grievance begin to run when the grievant ether knew or should have known that conduct occurred which was allegedly in violation of the collective bargaining agreement and for which a grievance could be filed. Here, I have found that the terms of a new contract had not been completely agreed upon either pursuant to negotiation or the subsequent arbitration under Act 195, and the parties were negotiating with respect to a means to resolve the remaining disputes. This is an entirely different situation and no cases cited are apposite to it.

Moreover, there is an estoppel issue here as well. The County, based upon this record, either knew or should have known at the executive session on January 29, 2014 that it either had already reached or, in a matter of days, would reach the threshold percentage to change the existing healthcare plan. That was the time to clearly state to the Association's Arbitrator (Attorney Daniel Delaney) that the Arbitration Award which was about to issue providing for a 2 percent employee participation would increase as soon as possible to 2.25 percent and in later years, to 2.50 percent. There is no testimony and certainly no documentation in the record that such a communication occurred. The County should not have been surprised, therefore, when ACAPE objected for the first time in August about the increased deduction, and about ACAPE's efforts to quickly resolve the issue by communicating with Arbitrator Amis. The County, at the hearing before me, through cross-examination of ACAPE President Bechtold, expressed concern about the difficulty or delay in contacting Arbitrator Amis, getting his schedule, refreshing his recollection about the issue, and providing a methodology to resolve it. It may well be that the final conclusion on September 25, 2014 to present the issue to a new arbitrator on an expedited basis was the best alternative, but the negotiations to reach that result cannot be construed as delay in order to deny the grievance as untimely, and I decline to do so.

* * * *

AWARD

Allegheny County is ordered to reimburse all of the employees in Bargaining Unit 1603, Allegheny Court Association of Professional Employees, ACAPE for health care participation payments in excess of 2 percent, within thirty (30) days of this Award, and to continue the 2 percent deduction for the life of the Agreement ending December 31, 2017. Jurisdiction is retained until compliance with the Award has been obtained. Interest shall only begin to accrue after 30 days of the issuance of this Award if restitution is not made by that time in accordance with the rate used by the Court of Common Pleas of Allegheny County.

APPLICATION AND DISCUSSION QUESTIONS

Grievance procedures will require grievants or the Union to file a grievance within a set time period. A failure to follow strict time frames at the initial filing and each step of the grievance process may cause the grievance to be dismissed. In the *County of Alleghany*, the Court acknowledged the "inelasticity of contractual time frames." The Court cited the arbitration principle that the "time limits for filing of grievances begin to run when the grievant either knows or should have known that conduct occurred, which was allegedly in violation of the [CBA] and for which a grievance could be filed."

Discuss how the Court addressed each of the following questions:

1. Why didn't the parties agree to ask the previous arbitrator to clarify the agreement in place of having another arbitration on the same issues previously decided? What is the dufference between interest arbitration and grievance arbitration ? {See Interest arbitration Chapter}

2. What is a continuing violation and how can it impact the time frame to file a greivane. How could this principle be applied in this grievance?

3. What does the phrase "inelasticity of contractual time limits" suggest and how did the arbitrator apply this principle in this grievance?

4. What is the estoppel issue identified by the arbitrator and how was this principle applied in this grievance?

5. Why did the arbitrator order interest if the employer had not implemented the award within 30 days? {See Remedy Chapter}

DEPARTMENT OF VETERANS AFFAIR V. VA MEDICAL CENTER
2010 LA SUPP. 119534 (FLOYD WEATHERSPOON, 2010)[*]

I. STATEMENT OF FACTS

The facts indicate that American Federation of Government Employees, hereinafter (Union) and Department of Veterans Affairs, hereinafter (Agency) are parties to a collective bargaining agreement, hereinafter (CBA or Agreement).

The facts indicate that the Grievant was a Licensed Practical Nurse (LPN) at the Community Living Center in Fort Thomas Kentucky. About May 1, 2009, Linda Smith, Medical Center Director, convened an Administrative Investigative Board to conduct an investigation into whether the Grievant was following nursing procedures for administering medications at the Community Living Center. Approximately, June 5, 2009, the Board submitted the findings of the investigation. The conclusion of the Board was that the Grievant did not follow policy and procedure when she administered medication. On July 20, 2009, Nurse Manager, Sylvia Samuelson conducted a fact-finding with the Grievant with regard to the Grievant's patient care issues. About September 3, 2009, the Grievant received a "notice of proposed removal' informing her that the Agency proposed to remove her from her position as a LPN for the reasons listed in the letter. The Grievant provided an oral response to the charges set forth in the "notice of proposed removal'. A removal decision was issued which notified the Grievant that her employment was terminated effective October 21, 2009.

About October 21, 2009, a grievance was filed challenging the Grievant's termination. (Joint Exh. 2) The grievance went through the various stages of the grievance

---

[*] Reprinted with permission from *Labor Relations Reporter- Labor Arbitration Reports*. 210 LA Supp. 119534. Copyright 2015 by the Bureau of National Affairs, Inc. (800-372-1033). http://www.bna.com.

procedure. The grievance was denied. Arbitration was requested pursuant to Article 40 of the CBA. (Joint Exh 1).

II. ISSUES

Whether this grievance is properly before the Arbitrator?

The parties stipulated that the issue is whether the Grievant was terminated for just cause, and if not, what is the appropriate remedy?

III. RELEVANT CONTRACT PROVISIONS

Article 13 - Discipline and Adverse Action (Omitted)

IV. POSITION OF THE PARTIES (Just cause issue omitted)

V. DISCUSSION AND ANALYSIS

Procedural Issue

It is noted at the outset, that the Agency has raised a procedural issue. The Agency maintains that the current grievance is not properly before the Arbitrator. The Agency contends that the grievance concerns a matter for which a full remedy has already been granted.

The facts indicate that the Grievant received a "Notice of Proposed Removal" dated September 3, 2009. The Grievant received a Removal Decision letter dated, October 13, 2009, which notified the Grievant that she was terminated effective October 21, 2009. About October 21, 2009, the Grievant filed a grievance challenging her removal. The Grievant received a letter dated, October 27, 2009, notifying her that the letter dated October 13, 2009 which originally terminated her employment October 21, 2009, was rescinded and replaced by the the letter dated October 27, 2009, which terminated her employment effective November 5, 2009. About November 27, 2009, the Union submitted a "notice to invoke arbitration" About December 10, 2009, the Union filed a second grievance challenging the Grievant's November 5, 2009 termination. The grievance was dismissed as untimely. That issue is not before this Arbitrator.

Basically, the Agency argues that the current grievance before the Arbitrator is moot because the Grievant received the full remedy and was made whole, as requested in the grievance filed October 21, 2009. This contention is not persuasive. This Arbitrator follows the principle that "(a) general presumption exists that favors arbitration over dismissal of grievances on technical grounds.' See, generally, Elkouri & Elkouri, <u>How Arbitration Works</u>, 6th Ed. pg. 206. The Agency maintains that the Grievant didn't grieve the "Notice of Proposed Removal', but rather only grieved the Removal Decision. The Agency contends that the two are separate and distinct and the Grievant only grieved the removal decision. The Arbitrator agrees that the Grievant challenges her removal. However, it is undisputed that the Grievant was ultimately terminated or removed based on the facts as stated in the "Notice of Proposed Removal'. The Arbitrator acknowledges that the procedure followed in this process is not as clean as it could be. However, the fault does not rest solely with the Union or the Grievant. It was the Agency that issued a second letter to correct an error that the Agency made. It is clear that the Agency never intended to rescind its decision to terminate the Grievant. Moreover, it is clear that the Union grieved the Grievant's termination, despite the fact that the Grievant's original termination was rescinded and she was given a new termination date. The point is that the the Grievant was ultimately terminated and it was the termination that was grieved. Therefore, the Arbitrator finds that the issue is properly before the Arbitrator. The Arbitrator will now address the substantive issues.

APPLICATION AND DISCUSSION QUESTIONS

1. Often governmental employers will issue "Notice of Proposed Removal" and 14-days later issue a "Removal Decision". As in this grievance, the effective date of the termination occurs at a later date. If the agreement is silent, which date triggers the running of the time frame to file a grievance? What arguments should the employer and the union raise as to which event starts the time to file a grievance?

2. In this grivance the employer rescinded and replaced the "Removal Decsion" letter, after the Grievant had filed a grievance. Should the Grievant be required to file a new grievance?

3. The Arbitrator points out that "the procedure followed in this process is not as clean as it could be" and suggest that both parties are at fault.When

parties to an agreement fail to consistently follow time frames as outlined in the grivance procedure, or is very laxed, arbitrators normally will not allow a grievance to be dismissed when a party attempts to strictly follow the timeframes without notice that the timeframes will be followed in future grievances.

OHIO EDUCATION ASSOCIATION, STATE COUNCIL OF PROFESSIONAL EDUCATORS
1995 LA SUPP. 119206 (WEATHERSPOON, 1995)[*]

In OEA, the arbitrator outlines a number of basic arbitration principles related to the obligation of employers to object to processing an untimely filed grievance. First, the employer is obligated to notify the Union prior to the arbitration hearing that the grievance was not filed in a timely manner. In other words, the employer must challenge the procedural arbitrability of the grievance. A failure to do so will result in the challenge being waived. If the employer "clearly and timely" raises the arbitrability issue, the waiver is reserved.

THE ISSUES

The Employer raised the issue of procedural arbitrability. After hearing the parties' arguments on this issue the Arbitrator accepted the issue of arbitrability over the Union's objection.

The parties stipulated to issue 2.

1. Whether the grievance and the request for arbitration of the grievance were timely filed in accordance with the Collective Bargaining Agreement (CBA); thus is arbitrable?

2. Was the three day suspension of teacher Raj Ahuja from the Apple Creek Development Center Institution for just cause?

---

[*] Reprinted with permission from *Labor Relations Reporter- Labor Arbitration Reports.* 1995 LA Supp. 119206. Copyright 2015 by the Bureau of National Affairs, Inc. (800-372-1033). http://www.bna.com.

II. APPLICABLE CONTRACT PROVISIONS

5.08 - DISCIPLINARY GRIEVANCE PROCEDURE.

B. Procedure

An employee with a disciplinary grievance or an authorized Association representative shall file a grievance under the procedures listed below unless mutually agreed otherwise.

1. Step 3

An employee or an authorized Association representative may file a grievance directly to the Agency Head/Director or designee of the employing agency at Step 3 either within ten (10) days of the effective date of the action or within ten (10) days after receipt of the notice as to the action, whichever is later. When different work locations are involved, transmittal of grievance appeals and subsequent responses shall be made by U.S. mail. The grievance may be submitted by serving written notice (including a copy of the grievance) presented to the Agency Head/Director or designee. The mailing of the grievance appeal shall constitute a timely appeal, if it is postmarked within the appeal period. Envelopes lacking a legible postmark shall be assumed to have been mailed three (3) days prior to their receipt.

Upon receipt of the grievance, the Agency Head/Director or designee shall schedule a meeting to be held within ten (10) days. An Association representative may attend the hearing and shall represent the employee if requested. The Agency Head/ Director or designee shall render a decision in writing and return a copy to the grievant and the Association representative within forty-five (45) days after the meeting.

A representative of the Office of Collective Bargaining may be present at such meeting and the Director of the Office of Collective Bargaining or designee shall review the written decision of the Agency Head/Director or designee, prior to its being mailed to the grievant and/or Association. The Association shall designate an individual within the organization to whom copies of Step 3 responses shall be mailed. The notification shall be sent to the Office of Collective Bargaining by the President of the Association.

By mutual agreement, the Association and agency may waive any preceding step of the grievance procedure.

2. Step 4 - Request for Arbitration

If the Association is not satisfied with the answer at Step 3, it may submit the grievance to arbitration, by serving written notice of its desire to do so (including a copy of the grievance) by U.S. Mail. The notice shall be presented to the Director of the Office of Collective Bargaining, with a copy sent to the Agency Head/Director or designee. This notice shall be mailed within fifteen (15) days after the receipt of the decision at Step 3 or the date such answer was due, whichever is earlier. The mailing of a letter requesting a grievance appeal shall constitute a timely appeal, if it is postmarked within the appeal period. Envelopes lacking a legible postmark shall be assumed to have been mailed three (3) days prior to their receipt.

ARTICLE 13 - PROGRESSIVE DISCIPLINE (Omitted)

III. STATEMENT OF FACTS

A. Arbitrability Issue

The Grievant, Raj Ahuja is employed as a teacher at The Apple Creek Development Center. Grievant has been employed by the State since April 12, 1976. Grievant received a ten day suspension for violating the Employer's work rule, (inconsiderate treatment) which occurred on January 31, 1994. Grievant's suspension was later reduced to a three-day suspension which he served on March 28 through March 30, 1994.

The Apple Creek Development Center, is a residential facility of the Ohio Department of Mental Retardation and Disabilities. The facility provides housing and services to retarded patients. The Grievant has been employed with the Employer for 19 years and has no prior disciplinary record.

A pre-disciplinary conference was held on February 25, 1994 which upheld the Employer's decision to suspend the Grievant. Subsequently, the Grievant filed a grievance regarding his suspension.

Aside from the above facts the parties agreed to very little else as to the filing and processing of the grievance, and the January 31, 1994 incident. However, the parties did agree to submit joint exhibits which provided information on the dates the grievance was filed, the Step 3 hearing, and the request for arbitration.

1. Union's Position

The Union argues that the Grievant first filed a grievance on March 31, 1994 regarding the three day suspension. The Union again filed the grievance on June 1, 1994 The Union further argues that the grievance filed on March 31, 1994, was timely and that the Employer never raised the issue that the grievances filed on either March 31, 1994 or June 1, 1994 were untimely. Moreover, the Union claims that the Employer never objected to their September 2, 1994 letter requesting arbitration.

The Union's position is that the Employer never raised the issue of arbitrability at any time during the processing of the grievance. According to the Union, the Employer raised for the first time the timeliness issue at the arbitration hearing. The Union stated during the hearing that the Employer "has not given a single document that can show that they raised this issue".

The Union further states in their Brief that "while substantive arbitrability claims may be legitimately raised as late as the hearing, arbitrators have long held that questions of procedural arbitrability must be raised during the grievance process; that failure to do so constitutes a waiver of such claim. The Union cited, Sterling Engineering Products, 92 LA 340 (1989) to support this principle.

2. Employer's Position

The Employer's position is that the grievance is not arbitrable because the grievance was never filed at Step three (3) in a timely manner and the Union never requested arbitration in a timely manner

Specifically, the Employer states in its Brief: "[T]he employee received notice of a suspension for three days to be served on March 28 through 30, 1994, however, a grievance was not filed until June 3, 1994 by Register U.S. mail, a total of 66 days after knowledge of the event". The Employer also argues that the grievance dated March 31, 1994, was never filed in accordance to the CBA.

"If this is not sufficient to show a procedural flaw, the grievance trail shows that a Step 3 meeting took place on June 27, 1994, however the request for arbitration was not made until September 3, 1994, a total of 68 days after the meeting".

B. THREE DAY SUSPENSION ISSUE (Omitted)

A. ARBITRABILITY ISSUE

The Arbitrator finds that the grievance and the request for arbitration were untimely filed; therefore not in compliance with Section 5.08 of The Collective Bargaining Agreement. However, it is clear that the Employer waived its right to challenge the timeliness of the grievance and the request for arbitration by processing the grievance without giving notice to the Union their challenge to the timeliness of the grievance.

With regard to the filing of the grievance on March 31, 1994, the Union failed to submit any documentation or testimony which support their contentions that the grievance was actually filed late. The Grievant's testimony only revealed that he gave the grievance form to a union representative name "Hilda Herra" (sp.). There was no evidence that the grievance was hand delivered, mailed, or any way given to the Employer for processing from the Union or the Grievant. The burden is initially on the Union to establish that a grievance was filed in accordance with the CBA. This typically is a lenient burden to meet.

Mr. Jim Kovack, Labor Relations Officer at the ACDC testified that the Grievant "never personally gave him a grievance--never put it in his hand or his office." Mr. Kovack also denied that he discussed the issue of timeliness of the grievance with Henry Stevens, Union representative. Carolyn Collins, Labor Relations Officer, for the Department of Mental Retardation, located in the Central Office testified that she is designated to hear Step 3 hearings. She testified she never received any other grievance filed by the Grievant other than the grievance dated June 1, 1994.

In reviewing the grievance dated March 31, 1994, Collins testified her office could not have received the form because it did not have a grievance number, a post office mark written on it, or a date stamp.

The Union failed to present what would have been their best witness, Hilda Herra. She could have testified that she gave the grievance form to the Employer. The Union provided no explanation why she was absent from these proceedings or her statement.

* * * *

The record indicates that the Grievant served his suspension on March 26, 27, and 28, 1994. More than two months elapsed before the Union filed a viable grievance, much too late to be in compliance with Step 3 requirements.

Even if the Arbitrator had accepted the Union's contention that a grievance was filed on March 31, 1994, or that the June 1, 1994 grievance was timely, the Union would have "won the battle but lost the war" because the request for arbitration was untimely filed. Section 5.08(B)(2) states:

If the Association is not satisfied with the answer at Step 3, it may submit the grievance to arbitration, by serving written notice of its desire to do so (including a copy of the grievance) by U.S. Mail. The notice shall be presented to the Director of the Office of Collective Bargaining, with a copy sent to the Agency Head/Director or designee. This notice shall be mailed within fifteen (15) days after the receipt of the decision at Step 3 or the date such answer was due, whichever is earlier.

As stipulated by the parties, the Step 3 meeting was held on June 27, 1994, and the request for arbitration was made on September 3, 1994. The Union had 15 days after receipt of a decision from the Employer at Step 3 or the date such answer was due. The Employer did not give an answer within forty-five days as permitted by the grievance procedure, thus the Union was required to request arbitration in late August. The request of September 3, 1994 was untimely. The Union attempts to make a major issue of the fact that a Step 3 response was not given. Collins testified she did not write a response at Step 3. She stated her "office receives more than 300-400 grievances a year and probably 4 or 5 percent may not get an answer." She also testified that the contract permits the Union to appeal when a Step 3 step hearing response has not been given.

With regard to the waiver of time limits, the Employer correctly cited a number of arbitration decisions and the leading treatise on arbitration, How Arbitration Works, which set forth the basic principles on "clear and unambiguous language" in contracts, the burden on the Union to persuade an Arbitrator to ignore such language, and the prohibition against arbitrators exceeding their authority.

The Employer also relies on ORC 4117.03(A)(5) which according to the Employer prohibits them from refusing to accept a grievance, even a grievance filed late for processing. Lastly, the Employer cites the Steelworker Trilogy for the principle that the "Employer may not unilaterally dismiss a grievance that suffers from either procedural or substantive defects; thus the Employer "had no choice but to accept and process the grievance."

The Employer's arguments, in theory, may be correct. The Employer, however fails to incorporate one basic arbitration principle which would modify their analysis and conclusion. That basic arbitration principle is that the Employer must at some time prior to the arbitration hearing give notice directly or indirectly by their action, that they challenge the procedural arbitrability of the grievance. In other words, the

Employer must give notice that the grievance is untimely filed or other procedural time limits have not been met.

Numerous arbitration decisions in Elkouri and Elkouri, How Arbitration Works, 4th ed. (1985) supports this rule. Arbitrators have held that the time limit objection is waived by the employer if the grievance is processed through the preliminary steps of the grievance procedure without timeliness being asserted as a defense. See, for example, In re Unit Parts Company, 86 Lab. Arb. 1241 1986, citing Owen Fairweather, Practice and Procedure in Labor Arbitration, 2nd ed., p.104.

Where an employer clearly and timely objects to an untimely filed grievance or request for arbitration, the employer has not waived the time requirement by processing the grievance on the merits through the grievance process. Elkouri, id., 195; Also see, *In re Phillips, 66 Company, Houston Chemical Complex*, 92 LA 1037 (1992). Indeed, employers are encouraged to process all grievances through the grievance process to attempt resolution of the dispute. However, the parties are expected to put all issues and defenses on the table which will facilitate efforts to resolve the dispute. *Denver Post*, 41 LA 200 (1963). Susan May's testimony confirms that the Employer never raised the issue of arbitrability during the time she was scheduling the grievance for mediation or arbitration.

Based upon the above evidence and the arguments, the Arbitrator finds the Employer waived their rights to raise the issue of timeliness at the arbitration hearing and therefore, this grievance is arbitrable. The case now will be decided on its merits.

B. SUSPENSION ISSUE (Omitted)

APPLICATION AND DISCUSSION QUESTIONS

Employers must raise any arbitrability challenges in a timely manner or their right to challenge is waived. Based on this principle, how would you respond to the following questions?

1. What arguments did the employer raise and why did the arbitrator reject the employer's argument?

2. What steps should the employer have taken to preserve their right to raise the procedural arbitrability challenge at the hearing?

3. What is the policy reason for allowing a procedurally defective grievance to be processed through arbitration?

4. Does the evidence suggest that both parties failed to strictly follow the steps of the grievance process, thus the arbitrator should not strictly apply the rules?

SUBSTANTIVE ARBITRABILITY

More than fifty years after the Supreme Court issued the trilogy cases favoring labor arbitration, courts have continued to support labor arbitration as the preferred method of resolving disputes under the CBA. For example in *Mitsubishi Motors Corp. Solar Chrysler –Plymouth, Inc.*, 473 U.S. 614 (1985), the Supreme Court held that an anti-trust dispute was subject to arbitration under the FAA, finding that the federal body of substantive arbitrability law counsels, "...questions of arbitrability must be addressed with a healthy regard for the federal policy favoring arbitration.... The Arbitration Act establishes that, as a matter of federal law, any doubts concerning the scope of arbitrable issues should be resolved in favor of arbitration." (quoting *Moses H. Cone Memorial Hospital*, 460 U.S. at 24-25, 103 S.Ct. at 941-942).

Again in *Granite Rock Co. v. Int'l Bd. of Teamsters*, 130 S.Ct. 2847 (2010), the Court reconfirmed that federal labor policy favors the use of labor arbitration to resolve disputes. Justice Thomas, writing for the Majority, discussed the presumption of arbitrability stating, "...the presumption...reflects its foundation in the federal policy favoring arbitration. As we have explained, this policy is merely an acknowledgment of the FAA's commitment to overrule the judiciary's longstanding refusal to enforce agreements to arbitrate and to place such agreements upon the same footing as other contracts". (quoting *Volt*, 489 U.S. at 478, 109 S.Ct. 1248) .

AT&T TECHNOLOGIES, INC. V. COMMUNICATIONS WORKERS OF AMERICAN

475 U.S. 643 (1986)

Justice WHITE delivered the opinion of the Court.

The issue presented in this case is whether a court asked to order arbitration of a grievance filed under a collective-bargaining agreement must first determine that the parties intended to arbitrate the dispute, or whether that determination is properly left to the arbitrator.

AT & T Technologies, Inc. (AT & T or the Company), and the Communications Workers of America (the Union) are parties to a collective-bargaining agreement which covers telephone equipment installation workers. Article 8 of this agreement establishes that "differences arising with respect to the interpretation of this contract or the performance of any obligation hereunder" must be referred to a mutually agreeable arbitrator upon the written demand of either party. This Article expressly does not cover disputes "excluded from arbitration by other provisions of this contract." Article 9 provides that, "subject to the limitations contained in the provisions of this contract, but otherwise not subject to the provisions of the arbitration clause," AT & T is free to exercise certain management functions, including the hiring and placement of employees and the termination of employment. "When lack of work necessitates Layoff," Article 20 prescribes the order in which employees are to be laid off.

On September 17, 1981, the Union filed a grievance challenging AT & T's decision to lay off 79 installers from its Chicago base location. The Union claimed that, because there was no lack of work at the Chicago location, the planned layoffs would violate Article 20 of the agreement. Eight days later, however, AT & T laid off all 79 workers, and soon thereafter, the Company transferred approximately the same number of installers from base locations in Indiana and Wisconsin to the Chicago base. AT & T refused to submit the grievance to arbitration on the ground that under Article 9 the Company's decision to lay off workers when it determines that a lack of work exists in a facility is not arbitrable.

The Union then sought to compel arbitration by filing suit in federal court pursuant to § 301(a) of the Labor Management Relations Act, 29 U.S.C. § 185(a).4 *Communications Workers of America v. Western Electric Co.*, No. 82 C 772 (ND Ill., Nov. 18, 1983). Ruling on cross-motions for summary judgment, the District Court reviewed the provisions of Articles 8, 9, and 20, and set forth the parties' arguments as follows:

"Plaintiffs interpret Article 20 to require that there be an actual lack of work prior to employee layoffs and argue that there was no such lack of work in this case. Under plaintiffs' interpretation, Article 20 would allow the union to take to arbitration the threshold issue of whether the layoffs were justified by a lack of work. Defendant interprets Article 20 as merely providing a sequence for any layoffs which management, in its exclusive judgment, determines are necessary. Under defendant's interpretation, Article 20 would not allow for an arbitrator to decide whether the layoffs were warranted by a lack of work but only whether the company followed the proper order in laying off the employees."

Finding that "the union's interpretation of Article 20 was at least 'arguable,' " the court held that it was "for the arbitrator, not the court to decide whether the union's interpretation has merit," and accordingly, ordered the Company to arbitrate. *Id.*, at 11A.

The Court of Appeals for the Seventh Circuit affirmed. *Communications Workers of America v. Western Electric Co.*, 751 F.2d 203 (1984). The Court of Appeals understood the District Court to have ordered arbitration of the threshold issue of arbitrability. *Id.*, at 205, n. 4. The court acknowledged the "general rule" that the issue of arbitrability is for the courts to decide unless the parties stipulate otherwise, but noted that this Court's decisions in *Steelworkers v. Warrior & Gulf Navigation Co.*, 363 U.S. 574, 80 S.Ct. 1347, 4 L.Ed.2d 1409 (1960), and *Steelworkers v. American Mfg. Co.*, 363 U.S. 564, 80 S.Ct. 1343, 4 L.Ed.2d 1403 (1960), caution courts to avoid becoming entangled in the merits of a labor dispute under the guise of deciding arbitrability. From this observation, the court announced an "exception" to the general rule, under which "a court should compel arbitration of the arbitrability issue where the collective bargaining agreement contains a standard arbitration clause, the parties have not clearly excluded the arbitrability issue from arbitration, and deciding the issue would entangle the court in interpretation of substantive provisions of the collective bargaining agreement and thereby involve consideration of the merits of the dispute." 751 F.2d, at 206.

All of these factors were present in this case. Article 8 was a "standard arbitration clause," and there was "no clear, unambiguous exclusion from arbitration of terminations predicated by a lack of work determination." *Id.*, at 206-207. Moreover, although there were "colorable arguments" on both sides of the exclusion issue, if the court were to decide this question it would have to interpret not only Article 8, but Articles 9 and 20 as well, both of which are "substantive provisions of the Agreement." The court thus "decline[d] the invitation to decide arbitrability," and ordered AT & T "to arbitrate the arbitrability issue." *Id.,* at 207.

The court admitted that its exception was "difficult to reconcile with the Supreme Court's discussion of a court's duty to decide arbitrability in [*John Wiley & Sons, Inc. v. Livingston,* 376 U.S. 543, 84 S.Ct. 909, 11 L.Ed.2d 898 (1964)]." The court asserted, however, that the discussion was "dicta," and that this Court had reopened the issue in *Nolde Brothers, Inc. v. Bakery Workers,* 430 U.S. 243, 255, n. 8, 97 S.Ct. 1067, 1074, n. 8, 51 L.Ed.2d 300 (1977). 751 F.2d, at 206.

We granted certiorari, 474 U.S. 814, 106 S.Ct. 56, 88 L.Ed.2d 46 (1985), and now vacate the Seventh Circuit's decision and remand for a determination of whether the Company is required to arbitrate the Union's grievance.

The principles necessary to decide this case are not new. They were set out by this Court over 25 years ago in a series of cases known as the *Steelworkers Trilogy: Steelworkers v. American Mfg. Co., supra; Steelworkers v. Warrior & Gulf Navigation Co., supra;* and *Steelworkers v. Enterprise Wheel & Car Corp.,* 363 U.S. 593, 80 S.Ct. 1358, 4 L.Ed.2d 1424 (1960). These precepts have served the industrial relations community well, and have led to continued reliance on arbitration, rather than strikes or lockouts, as the preferred method of resolving disputes arising during the term of a collective-bargaining agreement. We see no reason either to question their continuing validity, or to eviscerate their meaning by creating an exception to their general applicability.

The first principle gleaned from the *Trilogy* is that "arbitration is a matter of contract and a party cannot be required to submit to arbitration any dispute which he has not agreed so to submit." *Warrior & Gulf, supra,* 363 U.S., at 582, 80 S.Ct., at 1353; *American Mfg. Co., supra,* 363 U.S., at 570-571, 80 S.Ct., at 1364-1365 (BRENNAN, J., concurring). This axiom recognizes the fact that arbitrators derive their authority to resolve disputes only because the parties have agreed in advance to submit such grievances to arbitration.

The second rule, which follows inexorably from the first, is that the question of arbitrability-whether a collective-bargaining agreement creates a duty for the parties to arbitrate the particular grievance-is undeniably an issue for judicial determination. Unless the parties clearly and unmistakably provide otherwise, the question of whether the parties agreed to arbitrate is to be decided by the court, not the arbitrator.

* * * *

The third principle derived from our prior cases is that, in deciding whether the parties have agreed to submit a particular grievance to arbitration, a court is not to rule on the potential merits of the underlying claims. Whether "arguable" or not, indeed even if it appears to the court to be frivolous, the union's claim that the employer has violated the collective-bargaining agreement is to be decided, not by the court asked to order arbitration, but as the parties have agreed, by the arbitrator. "The courts, therefore, have no business weighing the merits of the grievance, considering whether there is equity in a particular claim, or determining whether there is particular language in the written instrument which will support the claim. The agreement is to submit all grievances to arbitration, not merely those which the court will deem meritorious." *American Mfg. Co.,* 363 U.S., at 568, 80 S.Ct., at 1346 (footnote omitted).

Finally, it has been established that where the contract contains an arbitration clause, there is a presumption of arbitrability in the sense that "[a]n order to arbitrate the particular grievance should not be denied unless it may be said with positive assurance that the arbitration clause is not susceptible of an interpretation that covers the asserted dispute. Doubts should be resolved in favor of coverage." *Warrior & Gulf,* 363 U.S., at 582-583, 80 S.Ct., at 1352-1353. See also *Gateway Coal Co. v. Mine Workers, supra,* 414 U.S., at 377-378, 94 S.Ct., at 636-637. Such a presumption is particularly applicable where the clause is as broad as the one employed in this case, which provides for arbitration of "any differences arising with respect to the interpretation of this contract or the performance of any obligation hereunder...." In such cases, "[i]n the absence of any express provision excluding a particular grievance from arbitration, we think only the most forceful evidence of a purpose to exclude the claim from arbitration can prevail." *Warrior & Gulf, supra,* 363 U.S., at 584-585, 80 S.Ct., at 1353-1354.

* * * *

With these principles in mind, it is evident that the Seventh Circuit erred in ordering the parties to arbitrate the arbitrability question. It is the court's duty to interpret the agreement and to determine whether the parties intended to arbitrate grievances concerning layoffs predicated on a "lack of work" determination by the Company. If the court determines that the agreement so provides, then it is for the arbitrator to determine the relative merits of the parties' substantive interpretations of the agreement. It was for the court, not the arbitrator, to decide in the first instance whether the dispute was to be resolved through arbitration.

The Union does not contest the application of these principles to the present case. Instead, it urges the Court to examine the specific provisions of the agreement for itself and to affirm the Court of Appeals on the ground that the parties had agreed to arbitrate the dispute over the layoffs at issue here. But it is usually not our function in the first instance to construe collective-bargaining contracts and arbitration clauses, or to consider any other evidence that might unmistakably demonstrate that a particular grievance was not to be subject to arbitration. The issue in the case is whether, because of express exclusion or other forceful evidence, the dispute over the interpretation of Article 20 of the contract, the layoff provision, is not subject to the arbitration clause. That issue should have been decided by the District Court and reviewed by the Court of Appeals; it should not have been referred to the arbitrator.

The judgment of the Court of Appeals is vacated, and the case is remanded for proceedings in conformity with this opinion.

It is so ordered.

Justice BRENNAN, with whom THE CHIEF JUSTICE and Justice MARSHALL join, concurring. (Omitted)

APPLICATION AND DISCUSSION QUESTIONS

Based on the AT & T decision, how would you respond to the following questions?

1. What is the Court's reasoning for the presumption of arbitrability for labor disputes?

2. Does the Court place too much power in the hands of arbitrators for interpreting collective-bargaining agreements?

3. Should arbitrators be limited to resolving only those issues specified by the parties?

4. When can the arbitrator determine substantive arbitrability issues?

5. Should arbitrators be empowered to determine their own jurisdiction? What would be the advantages and disadvantages? See, Cox, *Reflection Upon Labor Arbitration*, 72 Harv. L.Rev. 1482 (1959).

6. May a court determine the merits of a grievance when determining the arbitrability issues, when it is clear the grievance has no merit?

7. Does an employer waive their right to challenge the authority of the arbitrator to hear the merits of a case if the parties proceed to arbitration, even if the employer repeatedly objects and argues that the arbitrator lacked authority to hear the case? See *Square Plus Operating Corp. v. Local Union No. 917*, 140 LRRM 2389 (S.D. N.Y. 1992).

COMMUNICATIONS WORKERS V. NEW YORK TELEPHONE CO.

327 F.2D 94 (2D CIR. 1964)

WATERMAN, Circuit Judge:

Plaintiff, Communications Workers of America, AFL-CIO, brought suit below to compel defendant, New York Telephone Company, to arbitrate grievances caused by the temporary promotion of certain employees without regard to a seniority roster. Both parties agreed that no genuine issues of fact were involved in the case and both moved for summary judgment. The United States District Court for the Southern District of New York, Tyler, J., in a written opinion reported at 209 F.Supp. 389, granted defendant company's motion. He dismissed plaintiff's action on the ground that the dispute was one expressly excluded from arbitration by the parties' collective bargaining agreement. Plaintiff union has appealed. We affirm.

The dispute sought to be arbitrated involves the proper criteria to be used by defendant company in deciding which employees to promote. It is the union's position that all promotions, whether temporary or permanent, must be based on seniority if all other relevant qualities of employee candidates are substantially equal. The company disagrees, maintaining that the parties' collective bargaining agreement requires that consideration of the seniority of employees is applicable to permanent promotions only, and, though requested by the union to do so, refused to arbitrate the dispute.

Resolution of the differences between petitioner and the company depends upon the proper construction of two sections of the parties' collective bargaining agreement.

The section of the contract which provoked the disagreement over the proper method of handling promotions is Section 9.08 of Article 9, which states:

'9.08. In selecting employees for promotion to occupational classifications within the bargaining unit, seniority shall govern if other necessary qualifications are substantially equal. In no event shall any grievance or dispute arising out of this Section 9.08 be subject to the arbitration provisions of this Agreement.'

The bargaining agreement's basic arbitration provision, which the plaintiff union maintains requires arbitration of the dispute, is Section 12.01 of Article 12. That section provides as follows:

> '12.01. Either the Union or the Company may arbitrate a grievance regarding the true intent and meaning of a provision of this Agreement, or a grievance involving a claim referable to arbitration as provided in Articles 7, 8, 10 and 15, provided in all cases that the grievance has been processed in accordance with the provisions of Article 11 and has not been adjusted, and that written notice of intention to arbitrate is given to the other party within thirty (30) calendar days after the review in Step 4 of Article 11 has been completed. It is understood that the right to require arbitration does not extend to any matters other than those expressly set forth in this Article.'

* * * *

According to the Steelworkers cases, though a party may be held to arbitrate only those disputes contracted to be arbitrated, a very strong presumption exists in favor of the arbitrability of a disagreement over the meaning of a labor contract. A grievance or dispute must be regarded as arbitrable 'unless it may be said with positive assurance that the arbitration clause is not susceptible of an interpretation that covers the asserted dispute. Doubts should be resolved in favor of coverage.' *United Steelworkers of America v. Warrior & Gulf Nav. Co.*, supra, 363 U.S. at 582-583, 80 S.Ct. at 13538 4 L.Ed.2d 1409. Parties to a labor agreement containing an arbitration clause may, of course, exclude certain types of disputes from arbitration. But an exclusionary clause, to be effective, must be clear and unambiguous.

It is difficult to imagine a clearer or more direct exclusionary clause than the one in Section 9.08 above set forth. It expressly provides that *'in no event'* shall *'any grievance or dispute'* arising out of the section be subject to the contract's arbitration provisions. (Emphasis supplied.) We believe these words convey a clear and unambiguous directive that no Section 9.08 disputes of any kind are arbitrable.

The union, nevertheless, seeks to saddle the exclusionary clause of Section 9.08 with ambiguity, by arguing that it only definitely forecloses review by an arbitrator of the company's estimate of the comparative abilities of employees eligible for promotion. According to the union, the clause does not clearly prohibit arbitral inquiry into the true meaning of the terms used in the section. Thus, the union's argument amounts to pointing out two types of disputes which might arise under Section 9.08, and then contending that the section's exclusionary clause clearly covers but one of them.

One obvious difficulty with this argument is that Section 9.08 states that arbitration proceedings shall not be invoked with regard to 'any grievance or dispute' arising under the section. (Emphasis supplied.) But there is another reason, relating to the only way in which the contract's arbitration clause could cover Section 9.08 disputes absent an exclusionary clause, for rejecting the argument. Section 12.01, above quoted, the basic arbitration provision, is so drawn as to compel arbitration in two categories of cases: (1) those involving claims referable to arbitration as provided in Articles 7, 8, 10 and 15 of the contract; and (2) those involving disputes as to the true intent and meaning of any provision in the contract.

For the exclusionary clause of Section 9.08 to have any meaning at all, it must be regarded as referring to that part of Section 12.01 which, except for that clause, would extend to disputes under Section 9.08. Since Section 9.08 is in Article 9 (and not Article 7, 8, 10 or 15), the only way disputes under it could be arbitrable would be through application of Section 12.01's 'true intent and meaning' clause. Therefore, the exclusionary clause of Section 9.08, unless we hold it to be devoid of any meaning whatever, must be viewed as referring to and foreclosing disputes as to the meaning of the terms used in that section. And as this is precisely the sort of dispute the union argues is not covered by Section 9.08's exclusionary clause we find no merit in its argument.

We are not unmindful of the 'federal policy of promoting industrial peace and stability, especially with reference to arbitration procedures set up in collective bargaining agreements.' *Livingston v. John Wiley & Sons, Inc.*, supra, 313 F.2d at 56. The advantages of arbitration are obvious and compelling indeed, and absent a legitimate contractual restriction prohibiting it, the most desirable method of resolving this dispute would no doubt be through its submission to arbitration. But, if the strong presumption in favor of arbitrability established in the Steelworkers cases is not to be made irrebuttable, we cannot close our eyes to the plain meaning of the words used in this contract. The union also argues that if the company is not compelled to arbitrate this grievance it will be able to exercise almost unlimited discretion over the operation of matters arising under an entire section of the agreement. This argument does not impress. We cannot bring ourselves to accept this invitation to ignore the plain meaning of the Section 9.08 exclusionary clause, and to find ambiguity where none exists, by indulging ourselves in speculation as to what types of disputes a union might be likely to require an employer to settle by arbitration. The union concedes it intended to give the company unlimited discretion with respect to certain facets of Section 9.08's operation. If, at the bargaining table, the union's true intent was to reserve a different sort of Section 9.08 question for an arbitrator, it should not have consented to the incorporation into that section of an exclusionary clause so broad and sweeping.

Affirmed.

APPLICATION AND DISCUSSION QUESTIONS

1. How did the court delineate the roles of the arbitrator and the court?

2. What is an exclusionary clause in a collective bargaining agreement?

3. What conclusion did the court reach in analyzing the exclusionary clause in the above case?

4. What were the union's arguments regarding the exclusionary clause?

5. Is the court's decision in conflict with federal common law which encourages the use of arbitration?

LITTON FINANCIAL PRINTING DIVISION V. NATIONAL LABOR RELATIONS BOARD
111 s. ct., 2215 (1991)

Justice KENNEDY delivered the opinion of the Court.

This case requires us to determine whether a dispute over layoffs which occurred well after expiration of a collective-bargaining agreement must be said to arise under the agreement despite its expiration. The question arises in the context of charges brought by the National Labor Relations Board (Board) alleging an unfair labor practice in violation of §§ 8(a)(1) and (5) of the National Labor Relations Act (NLRA), 49 Stat. 449, as amended, 29 U.S.C. §§ 158(a)(1) and (5). We interpret our earlier decision in *Nolde Bros., Inc. v. Bakery Workers.* 430 U.S. 243, 97 S.Ct. 1067, 51 L.Ed.2d 300 (1977).

Petitioner Litton operated a check printing plant in Santa Clara, California. The plant utilized both coldtype and hottype printing processes. Printing Specialties & Paper Products Union No. 777, Affiliated with District Council No. 1 (Union), represented the production employees at the plant. The Union and Litton entered into a collective-bargaining agreement (Agreement) which, with extensions, remained in effect until October 3, 1979. Section 19 of the Agreement is a broad arbitration provision:

"Differences that may arise between the parties hereto regarding this Agreement and any alleged violations of the Agreement, the construction to be placed on any clause or clauses of the Agreement shall be determined by arbitration in the manner hereinafter set forth."

Section 21 of the Agreement sets forth a two-step grievance procedure, at the conclusion of which, if a grievance cannot be resolved, the matter may be submitted for binding arbitration. *Id.*, at 35.

Soon before the Agreement was to expire, an employee sought decertification of the Union. The Board conducted an election on August 17, 1979, in which the Union prevailed by a vote of 28 to 27. On July 2, 1980, after much postelection legal maneuvering, the Board issued a decision to certify the Union. No contract negotiations occurred during this period of uncertainty over the Union's status.

Litton decided to test the Board's certification decision by refusing to bargain with the Union. The Board rejected Litton's position and found its refusal to bargain an unfair labor practice. *Litton Financial Printing Division*, 256 N.L.R.B. 516 (1981). Meanwhile, Litton had decided to eliminate its coldtype operation at the plant, and in late August and early September 1980, laid off 10 of the 42 persons working in the plant at that time. The laid off employees worked either primarily or exclusively with the coldtype operation, and included 6 of the 11 most senior employees in the plant. The layoffs occurred without any notice to the Union.

The Union filed identical grievances on behalf of each laid off employee, claiming a violation of the Agreement, which had provided that "in case of layoffs, lengths of continuous service will be the determining factor if other things such as aptitude and ability are equal." App. 30. Litton refused to submit to the grievance and arbitration procedure or to negotiate over the decision to lay off the employees, and took a position later interpreted by the Board as a refusal to arbitrate under any and all circumstances. It offered instead to negotiate concerning the effects of the layoffs.

On November 24, 1980, the General Counsel for the Board issued a complaint alleging that Litton's refusal to process the grievances amounted to an unfair labor practice within the meaning of §§ 8(a)(1) and (5) of the NLRA, 29 U.S.C. §§ 158(a) (1) and (5). App. 15. On September 4, 1981, an Administrative Law Judge found that Litton had violated the NLRA by failing to process the grievances. *Id.*, at 114–115. Relying upon the Board's decision in *American Sink Top & Cabinet Co.*, 242 N.L.R.B. 408 (1979), the Administrative Law Judge went on to state that if the grievances remained unresolved at the conclusion of the grievance process, Litton could not refuse to submit them to arbitration. App. 115–118. The Administrative Law Judge held also that Litton violated §§ 8(a)(1) and (5) when it bypassed the Union and paid severance wages directly to the 10 laid off employees, and Litton did not contest that determination in further proceedings.

Over six years later, the Board affirmed in part and reversed in part the decision of the Administrative Law Judge. 286 N.L.R.B. 817 (1987). The Board found that Litton had a duty to bargain over the layoffs, and violated § 8(a) by failing to do so. Based upon well-recognized Board precedent that the unilateral abandonment of a contractual grievance procedure upon expiration of the contract violates §§ 8(a)(1) and (5), the Board held that Litton had improperly refused to process the layoff grievances. See *Bethlehem Steel Co.,* 136 N.L.R.B. 1500, 1503 (1962), enforced in pertinent part, 320 F.2d 615 (CA3 1963). The Board proceeded to apply its recent decision in *Indiana & Michigan Electric Co.,* 284 N.L.R.B. 53 (1987), which contains the Board's current understanding of the principles of postexpiration arbitrability and of our opinion in *Nolde Brothers, Inc. v. Bakery Workers, supra.* The Board held that Litton's "wholesale repudiation" of its obligation to arbitrate any contractual grievance after the expiration of the Agreement also violated §§ 8(a)(1) and (5), as the Agreement's broad arbitration clause lacked "language sufficient to overcome the presumption that the obligation to arbitrate imposed by the contract extended to disputes arising under the contract and occurring after the contract had expired. Thus, [Litton] remained 'subject to a potentially viable contractual commitment to arbitrate even after the [Agreement] expired.' " 286 N.L.R.B., at 818 (citation omitted).

Litton did not seek review of, and we do not address here, the Board's determination that Litton committed an unfair labor practice by its unilateral abandonment of the grievance process and wholesale repudiation of any post-expiration obligation to arbitrate disputes.

In fashioning a remedy, the Board went on to consider the arbitrability of these particular layoff grievances. Following *Indiana & Michigan,* the Board declared its determination to order arbitration "only when the grievances at issue 'arise under' the expired contract." 286 N.L.R.B., at 821 (citing *Nolde Brothers, Inc. v. Bakery Workers,* 430 U.S. 243, 97 S.Ct. 1067, 51 L.Ed.2d 300 (1977)). In finding that the dispute about layoffs was outside this category, the Board reasoned as follows:

> "The conduct that triggered the grievances ... occurred after the contract had expired.
> The right to layoff by seniority if other factors such as ability and experience are equal
> is not 'a right worked for or accumulated over time.' *Indiana & Michigan,* supra at 61.
> And, as in *Indiana & Michigan Electric,* there is no indication here that 'the parties

contemplated that such rights could ripen or remain enforceable even after the contract expired.' *Id.* (citation omitted). Therefore, [Litton] had no contractual obligation to arbitrate the grievances." 286 N.L.R.B., at 821–822.

Although the Board refused to order arbitration, it did order Litton to process the grievances through the two-step grievance procedure, to bargain with the Union over the layoffs, and to provide a limited backpay remedy.

The Board sought enforcement of its order, and both the Union and Litton petitioned for review. The Court of Appeals enforced the Board's order, with the exception of that portion holding the layoff grievances not arbitrable. 893 F.2d 1128 (CA9 1990). On that question, the Court of Appeals was willing to "assume without deciding that the Board's *Indiana & Michigan* decision is a reasonably defensible construction of the section 8(a)(5) duty to bargain." *Id.*, at 1137. The court decided, nevertheless, that the Board had erred, because the right in question, the right to layoff in order of seniority if other things such as aptitude and ability are equal, did arise under the Agreement. The Court of Appeals thought the Board's contrary conclusion was in conflict with two later Board decisions, where the Board had recognized that seniority rights may arise under an expired contract, *United Chrome Products, Inc.,* 288 N.L.R.B. 1176 (1988), and *Uppco, Inc.,* 288 N.L.R.B. 937 (1988).

* * * *

In the absence of a binding method for resolution of postexpiration disputes, a party may be relegated to filing unfair labor practice charges with the Board if it believes that its counterpart has implemented a unilateral change in violation of the NLRA. If, as the Union urges, parties who favor labor arbitration during the term of a contract also desire it to resolve postexpiration disputes, the parties can consent to that arrangement by explicit agreement. Further, a collective-bargaining agreement might be drafted so as to eliminate any hiatus between expiration of the old and execution of the new agreement, or to remain in effect until the parties bargain to impasse. Unlike the Union's suggestion that we impose arbitration of postexpiration disputes upon parties once they agree to arbitrate disputes arising under a contract, these alternatives would reinforce the statutory policy that arbitration is not compulsory.

* * * *

. . . we come to the crux of our inquiry. We agree with the approach of the Board and those courts which have interpreted *Nolde Brothers* to apply only where a dispute has its real source in the contract. The object of an arbitration clause is to implement a contract, not to transcend it. *Nolde Brothers* does not announce a rule that postexpiration grievances concerning terms and conditions of employment remain arbitrable. A rule of that sweep in fact would contradict the rationale of *Nolde Brothers.* The *Nolde Brothers* presumption is limited to disputes arising under the contract. A postexpiration grievance can be said to arise under the contract only where it involves facts and occurrences that arose before expiration, where an action taken after expiration infringes a right that accrued or vested under the agreement, or where, under normal principles of contract interpretation, the disputed contractual right survives expiration of the remainder of the agreement.

Any other reading of *Nolde Brothers* seems to assume that postexpiration terms and conditions of employment which coincide with the contractual terms can be said to arise under an expired contract, merely because the contract would have applied to those matters had it not expired. But that interpretation fails to recognize that an expired contract has by its own terms released all its parties from their respective contractual obligations, except obligations already fixed under the contract but as yet unsatisfied. Although after expiration most terms and conditions of employment are not subject to unilateral change, in order to protect the statutory right to bargain, those terms and conditions no longer have force by virtue of the contract. See *Office and Professional Employees Ins. Trust Fund v. Laborers Funds Administrative Office of Northern California, Inc.,* 783 F.2d 919, 922 (CA9 1986) ("An expired [collective-bargaining agreement] ... is no longer a 'legally enforceable document' " (citation omitted)); cf. *Derrico v. Sheehan Emergency Hosp.,* 844 F.2d 22, 25–27 (CA2 1988) (Section 301 of the LMRA, 29 U.S.C. § 185, does not provide for federal court jurisdiction where a bargaining agreement has expired, although rights and duties under the expired agreement "retain legal significance because they define the *status quo"* for purposes of the prohibition on unilateral changes).

* * * *

We apply these principles to the layoff grievances in the present case. The layoffs took place almost one year after the Agreement had expired. It follows that the grievances are arbitrable only if they involve rights which accrued or vested under the Agreement, or rights which carried over after expiration of the Agreement, not as legally imposed terms and conditions of employment but as continuing obligations under the contract.

The contractual right at issue, that "in case of layoffs, lengths of continuous service will be the determining factor if other things such as aptitude and ability are equal," App. 30, involves a residual element of seniority. Seniority provisions, the Union argues, "create a form of earned advantage, accumulated over time that can be understood as a special form of deferred compensation for time already worked." Brief for Respondent Union 23–25, n. 14. Leaving aside the question whether a provision requiring all layoffs to proceed in inverse order of seniority would support an analogy to the severance pay at issue in *Nolde Brothers,* which was viewed as a form of deferred compensation, the layoff provision here cannot be so construed, and cannot be said to create a right that vested or accrued during the term of the Agreement or a contractual obligation that carries over after expiration.

* * * *

For the reasons stated, we reverse the judgment of the Court of Appeals to the extent that the Court of Appeals refused to enforce the Board's order in its entirety and remanded the cause for further proceedings.

It is so ordered.

Justice MARSHALL, with whom Justice BLACKMUN and Justice SCALIA join, dissenting. (Omitted in part)

A.

The majority grossly distorts *Nolde's* test for arbitrability by transforming the first requirement that posttermination disputes "arise under" the expired contract. The *Nolde* Court defined "arises under" by reference to the *allegations* in the grievance. In other words, a dispute "arises under" the agreement where "the resolution of [the Union's] claim hinges on the interpretation ultimately given the contract." *Id.,* at 249, 97 S.Ct. at 1071.

By contrast, the majority today holds that a postexpiration grievance can be said to "arise under" the agreement only where the court satisfies itself (1) that the challenged action "infringes a right that accrued or vested under the agreement," or (2) that "under normal principles of contract interpretation, the disputed contractual right survives expiration of the remainder of the agreement." *Ante,* at 2225. Because they involve inquiry into the substantive effect of the terms of the agreement, these determinations require passing upon the merits of the underlying dispute. Yet the *Nolde* Court expressly stated that "in determining the arbitrability of the dispute, the merits of the underlying claim ... are not before us."

Justice STEVENS, with whom Justice BLACKMUN and Justice SCALIA join, dissenting. (Omitted)

APPLICATION AND DISCUSSION QUESTIONS

The Court in *Litton* clarified their earlier decision in *Nolde Bros., Inc.* The Court held that, "...grievances are arbitrable only if they involve rights which accrued or vested under the Agreement, or rights carried over after expiration of the Agreement, not as a legally imposed terms and conditions of employment but as a continuing obligation under the contract."

The Court was unwilling to permit all grievances filed under an expired contract to proceed to arbitration. The Court will permit only those grievances that "arise under" the expired contract. Based on Nolde and Litton, answer the following questions:

1. Why was the Court willing to permit grievances in *Nolde* to be processed when the contract had expired, but not in *Litton*?

2. What reasons did the dissent offer to permit the post expiration grievance to be processed?

3. What was the Court's explanation as to why the employer may still be obligated to process the layoff grievances, even though the agreement had expired?

4. Why was the Court relunctant to order the layoff grievamces to be processed through arbitration?

MEDCO HEALTH SOLUTIONS OF COLUMBUS WEST, LTD. V. ASSOCIATION OF MANAGED CARE PHARMACISTS

2011 WL 4572002 (S.D. OHIO 2011)

OPINION AND ORDER

MICHAEL H. WATSON, District Judge.

Plaintiff employer in this labor dispute seeks a declaratory judgment that a grievance is not arbitrable under the Labor Management Relations Act, 29 U.S.C. § 185. Defendant labor union counterclaims to compel arbitration. Both sides move for summary judgment on the issue of arbitrability. ECF Nos. 19 & 20. For the reasons that follow, the Court holds that the grievance is not arbitrable because the only remedies sought in the grievance are either outside the scope of the arbitrator's authority or moot. Accordingly, the Court grants Plaintiff's summary judgment motion and denies Defendant's summary judgment motion.

I. BACKGROUND

The facts are undisputed. Plaintiff Medco Health Solutions of Columbus West, Ltd. ("Medco") provides pharmacy services at a facility in Columbus, Ohio. Defendant Association of Managed Care Pharmacists ("AMCP") is the exclusive bargaining representative for approximately 244 pharmacists who work at Medco's Columbus facility. The parties' relations are governed by a collective bargaining agreement ("CBA").

In February 2006 and again in February 2007, Medco granted stock options to twenty-three newly hired pharmacists. In March 2008, AMCP filed a grievance, Grievance No. 08–001, asserting the aforementioned stock options violated the CBA. As remedies for the grievance, AMCP demanded (1) that Medco grant all staff pharmacists the same options it granted the twenty three newly-hired pharmacists and (2) that Medco cease and desist any further violation of the CBA.

The grievance was not resolved between the parties, and AMCP filed a demand for arbitration in February 2009. In August 2009, Medco agreed in writing to cease and desist from issuing stock options other than those explicitly set forth in the CBA. Hence, the only remedy remaining for the arbitrator to consider was to order Medco to issue the same stock options it issued to the new hires in February 2007 and February 2008 to all of the pharmacists in the bargaining unit. Medco asserted the grievance was not arbitrable because the CBA precludes the arbitrator from imposing such a remedy. Medco initiated the instant lawsuit in September 2009. By agreement of the parties, the arbitration is stayed pending the Court's decision on arbitrability.

II. SUMMARY JUDGMENT

The standard governing summary judgment is set forth in Federal Rule of Civil Procedure 56(a), which provides: "The court shall grant summary judgment if the movant shows there is no genuine dispute as to any material fact and the movant is entitled to judgment as a matter of law." Fed.R.Civ.P. 56(a).

* * * *

III. DISCUSSION

Medco argues that the grievance is not arbitrable because the CBA precludes the arbitrator from ordering Medco to issue the disputed stock options to all of the pharmacists in the collective bargaining unit, and the request that Medco cease and desist is moot. AMCP contends that the grievance is arbitrable because it entails the " 'application, interpretation and enforcement of the terms and provisions' " of the CBA. Def.'s Mem. Supp. Mot. Summ. J. 2, ECF No. 21 (quoting CBA 28, ECF No. 21–1).

It is well-settled that federal policy favors arbitration of labor disputes. (citation omitted). It is equally well-established, however, that arbitration is strictly a matter of consent. The Sixth Circuit "has consistently adhered to the principle that an arbitrator may construe ambiguous contract language, but lacks authority to disregard or modify plain or unambiguous contract provisions." *Sears, Roebuck & Co. v. Teamsters Local Union No. 243*, 683 F.2d 154, 155 (6th Cir.1982).

Here, the CBA provides: "In no event shall the arbitrator have any authority to modify, add to, disregard or abolish, in any way, any of the terms and provisions of" the CBA. CBA 28, ECF No. 21–1. Medco argues that it would be beyond the authority of the arbitrator to impose a remedy requiring Medco to issue the disputed stock options to all of the pharmacists in the bargaining unit because to do so would "modify, add to, disregard or abolish" provisions in the CBA because the CBA does not obligate or authorize Medco to issue stock options in that manner. Notably, AMCP's designee under Federal Rule of Civil Procedure 36(b)(6), Randy DePoy, directiy conceded that very point during his deposition. DePoy Dep. 67, ECF No. 20–3. Where an arbitrator lacks authority to grant the relief sought, the matter is not arbitrable. *Printing Indus. Ass'n of N. Ohio v. Inter. Printing and Graphic Comrnc'n Union, Local 56*, 578 F.Supp. 555, 557 (N.D.Ohio 1983) (declining to compel arbitration where arbitrator had no authority to reform collective bargaining agreement); *see also In re Continental Airlines, Inc.,* 484 F.3d 173, 181 (3d Cir.2007) ("[W]e will not compel the airline to participate in an arbitration whose award cannot be enforced against it."). For the above reasons, the Court concludes that the grievance is not arbitrable to the extent it seeks to require Medco to issue the disputed stock options to all of the pharmacists in the bargaining unit because the arbitrator lacks authority to grant such relief.

AMCP attempts to avoid the conclusion that the grievance is not arbitrable by noting the grievance also seeks a cease and desist order, which would be within the arbitrator's authority to grant. Medco responds by pointing out that it has already agreed in writing to cease and desist, thus rendering that aspect of the grievance moot. See *Int'l Bhd., Local Union No. S–251 v. Thyssenkrupp Elevator Mfg.,* 365 F.3d 523, 527–28 (6th Cir.2004) (declining to enforce arbitrator's award reinstating union employee where second basis for employee's termination rendered moot the basis challenged in the grievance). The Court agrees that the moot remedy is likewise not arbitrable.

Because the only remedies sought in the grievance are either outside the scope of the arbitrator's authority or moot, the Court holds as a matter of law that the grievance is not arbitrable.

IV. DISPOSITION

Based on the above, the Court GRANTS Medco's summary judgment motion, ECF No. 20, and DENIES AMCP's summary judgment motion, ECF No. 19.

The Clerk shall enter final judgment in favor of Medco, and against AMCP, declaring that Grievance No. 08–001 presented by AMCP is not arbitrable, and dismissing this action with prejudice.

The Clerk shall remove ECF Nos. 19 and 20 from the Civil Justice Reform Act motions report.

IT IS SO ORDERED.

APPLICATION AND DISCUSSION QUESTIONS

1. Why did the Court determine that the "remedies sought in the grievances [were] either outside the scope of the arbitrator's authority or moot?"

2. Was the language in the CBA clearly unambiguous as the Court suggests?

3. The Court cites the rule that "whether an arbitrator lacks authority to grant the relief sought, the matter is not arbitrable". But in this case, couldn't the arbitrator issue a cease and desist order?

ROGER WILLIAMS UNIV. FACULTY ASS'N V. ROGER WILLIAMS UNIV. UNITED STATES DISTRICT COURT FOR THE DISTRICT OF RHODE ISLAND

14 F. SUPP. 3D 27 C.A. NO. 13-16L (2014 U.S. DIST.)

Opinion by: Ronald R. Lagueux

MEMORANDUM AND DECISION

This matter is before the Court on cross motions for summary judgment brought to resolve the appeal of Plaintiff Roger Williams University Faculty Association ("the Union") from an arbitration award. The arbitration award ("the Award") held that the Union's complaint was not arbitrable under the collective bargaining agreement with Defendant Roger Williams University ("the University"). For reasons explained herein, the Court upholds the Award. The Court also rules that the Union's retaliation claim, which the Union argues had been reserved, was waived by the Union.

* * * *

Discipline and resulting grievance

On August 16, 2011, DeLucca was suspended for two weeks without pay. Shortly thereafter, she filed a grievance, claiming that the suspension was in retaliation for her 2010 grievance. Two weeks later, the Union amended DeLucca's grievance, adding an additional claim that her suspension was not based on just cause, in violation of Articles V and IX of the Contract.

DeLucca's grievance went through established procedures. It was denied at Step 1 by the provost in November 2011; and denied at Step 2 by the University president in March 2012 following a grievance meeting attended by DeLucca and several representatives of both the University and the Union. President Farish's denial letter explains that he has "carefully considered yours and the Union's grievance submissions, as well as the positions and statements of all parties in attendance at the Step 2 meeting."

* * * *

Similarly, DeLucca's other claims, that her discipline was without just cause and that it was imposed without due process, were rejected by Farish as without merit, with several pages of explanation. Among the arguments set forth by Farish on the issue of whether or not there was just cause for DeLucca's suspension was the University's contention that the Contract contained no provision that set a standard for discipline, or that limited the University's ability to impose discipline in any way.

The arbitration

The Union then sought arbitration on its claims. Prior to the arbitration, the parties framed the issues for the arbitrator, and agreed on the documents to be presented. The threshold issue was the one articulated by President Farish in the Step Two grievance denial letter: was the discipline imposed upon DeLucca subject to the Contract's grievance and arbitration procedures? The University's position was that DeLucca's suspension was not arbitrable, because the Contract had no provision limiting the University's ability to discipline its employees, and because the parties could only seek arbitration for violations of the Contract. In an email submitted by the Union to the arbitrator, the issues to be arbitrated were posed:

> On the arbitrability question the issue is framed as follows: Is the Union's challenge to the University's August 2011 decision to suspend Professor DeLucca for two weeks arbitrable under the 2008-2012 CBA between Roger Williams University and the RWUFA/NEARI? The University would bear the burden of proof on this issue.

> If you determine the matter not to be arbitrable the grievance would be denied on that basis and his [sic] analysis would stop there.

> If the you [sic] determine the matter to be arbitrable you would next address the "procedural fairness" question in your preliminary award. On the "procedural fairness" question the issue is framed as follows: "Was the investigation leading to the University's decision to suspend Grievant so procedurally flawed so as to warrant reversal of the discipline on its face?" The Union would bear the burden of proof on this issue.

If you determine the process was so procedurally flawed as to warrant a reversal, the discipline would be removed and the analysis would stop there.

If you determine the matter to be arbitrable, but not procedurally unfair so as to warrant a reversal, we'd move to the merits and schedule a hearing for that purpose.

With those issues settled by agreement, the University next petitioned the arbitrator to bifurcate the proceedings, so that the arbitrability issue could be decided first and separately. The Union objected. The arbitrator denied the University's request, and the arbitration proceeded with both issues before the arbitrator.

In its brief, the Union conceded that the Contract did not address disciplinary measures directly, but urged the arbitrator to interpret the Contract broadly in order to find an implied requirement of just cause for the University's actions. On its side, the University argued that disciplining its employees was the right of management, and that, moreover, the arbitrator could not exceed his authority by adding provisions to the Contract, or finding implied provisions, that had not been negotiated by the parties. The arbitrator ruled in favor of the University, writing, inter alia:

> [T]he Supreme Court stated that to be substantively arbitrable the parties must have
> clearly stated in the contract that they agreed to arbitrate the matter. Such a statement
> does not appear in this contract and for that reason the dispute is not arbitrable. In
> light of the decision on the arbitrability issue, it is not necessary to address the second
> issue.

The arbitrator, and the University, considered the matter at an end, but the Union chose to pursue it further before this Court.

The Complaint

In its federal court complaint, the Union seeks to vacate the arbitrator's Award. Its central claim is that the arbitrator exceeded his authority because he relied on the parties' bargaining history in formulating the Award, in violation of the Contract. Beyond that, the Complaint's allegations are conclusory: the Award does not draw its essence from the Contract; the Award is not based on a plausible interpretation of the Contract; the Award is completely irrational; and the arbitrator disregarded the law.

Analysis

The Court will address three issues that are in contention between the parties. First, the Court will review the arbitration Award and its determination of non-arbitrability. This analysis will include the sub-issue raised in the Union's complaint: that the arbitrator improperly relied upon bargaining history in rendering the Award. Second, the Court will determine whether or not the retaliation claim was effectively reserved by the Union for further review. And, third, the Court will address the Union's concerns over the process that was due and provided to DeLucca during the course of the University's investigation.

Arbitrability

Both sides agree that the Contract contains no express provision governing disciplinary measures. However, the Union argues that the University's obligation to impose discipline only when there is just cause is implied by the totality of the Contract's language. Without an implied just cause requirement, the Union argues, the notion of progressive discipline is meaningless. The University could, hypothetically, suspend a professor repeatedly for no good reason, then terminate that professor because of the accumulated suspensions. The Union argues further that there is extensive precedential support for the principle that matters that are excluded from the reach of arbitration must be expressly excluded by the Contract.

On the other side, the University argues that, while the Contract requires just cause for the termination of a tenured professor, the omission of a standard for discipline was intentional. According to the University, discipline, though not expressly listed, falls into the provision of retained management rights found in Article III:

> It is recognized that the RWU, through its Chief Executive Officer, has the authority
> and responsibility to effectively formulate the University's curriculum, budget, grading
> systems, admissions and matriculation standards, academic calendars, size of the stu-
> dent body, tuition and fees, hiring and termination and other traditional management
> functions.

Moreover, the express inclusion of a just cause requirement for discipline in two other contemporaneous contracts between these same parties demonstrates that the parties will purposefully include such a provision when there is an agreement to do so. The other contracts cover facilities workers and professional support staff at the University. The University also points to two faculty contracts for the years 1984-89 which included a provision imposing an "arbitrary and capricious" standard for discipline - a provision that was omitted from subsequent agreements.

The University cites additional provisions in the Contract in support of its position. First, the language of Article X of the Contract limits the proper subject of a grievance to "a violation, misinterpretation, or misapplication" of the Contract, and, consequently, does not cover every potential dispute between the parties. If a dispute is not grievable, it cannot be subject to arbitration, pursuant to Step 3 the grievance procedure as provided by Article X, section B. Secondly, Article X also contains a limitation on the power of the arbitrator: "The arbitrator shall not alter, add to or subtract from the terms of this Agreement..."

* * * *

The implied 'just cause' provision

The Court believes the arbitrator's reasoning is unassailable. To the points made by the arbitrator, the Court would add a few observations. Article IX of the Contract requires the University to have just cause in order to dismiss a tenured faculty member. However, non-tenured faculty members may be dismissed as long as such dismissal is not arbitrary or capricious - a less rigorous standard. This discrepancy weakens the Union's argument that the Contract in its entirety should be read as including an implied just cause provision.

Moreover, when courts have found an implied just cause provision, the cases have frequently involved the more compelling circumstance of dismissal, rather than discipline. In a case cited by the Union, *Smith v. Kerrville Bus Co., Inc.*, 709 F.2d 914, 917 (5th Cir. 1983), the court recognized that arbitrators often infer a just cause provision for dismissals from parts of the contract governing seniority or the grievance procedure.

To hold as a matter of law that management could, at its sole discretion, terminate an employee without cause would in effect allow it the unqualified power to avoid contractually mandated rights and benefits.

The other contracts and "bargaining history" (Omitted)

The retaliation claim (Omitted)

Due process (Omitted)

Conclusion

For these reasons, the Court grants the University's Motion for Summary Judgment, and denies the Union's motion for summary judgment. The Award of the arbitrator is affirmed. The Clerk shall enter judgment accordingly. So ordered.

APPLICATION AND DISCUSSION QUESTIONS

1. Why did the University request that the arbitrator bifurcate the procedural and substantive arbitrability issues? Wouldn't this require more time and cost?

2. What are the reasons the Union asked for the award to be vacated?

3. What is the standard of review to be applied when the court reviews the arbitrator's finding of facts?

4. How can the arbitrator apply a just cause standard in disciplinary actions if just cause is not listed in the agreement? The Court recognized that a standard often implies a just cause provision, if it is not in the CBA. Why didn't the Court imply just cause in this case?

II. JUDICIAL REVIEW OF ARBITRATION AWARDS

A. PUBLIC POLICY ISSUES

W.R. GRACE & CO. V. RUBBER WORKERS
461 U.S. 757 (1983)

case

conciliation agreement
+ firing

Justice BLACKMUN delivered the opinion of the Court.

Faced with the prospect of liability for violations of Title VII of the Civil Rights Act of 1964, as amended, petitioner signed with the Equal Employment Opportunity Commission (Commission or EEOC) a conciliation agreement that was in conflict with its collective bargaining agreement with respondent. Petitioner then obtained a court order, later reversed on appeal that the conciliation agreement should prevail. The issue presented is whether the Court of Appeals was correct in enforcing an arbitral award of backpay damages against petitioner under the collective bargaining agreement for layoffs pursuant to the conciliation agreement.

Q

* * * *

The sole issue before the Court is whether the Barrett award should be enforced. Under well established standards for the review of labor arbitration awards, a federal court may not overrule an arbitrator's decision simply because the court believes its own interpretation of the contract would be the better one. *Steelworkers v. Enterprise Wheel & Car Corp.*, 363 U.S. 593, 596, 80 S.Ct. 1358, 1360, 4 L.Ed.2d 1424 (1960). When the parties include an arbitration clause in their collective bargaining agreement,

rule

they choose to have disputes concerning constructions of the contract resolved by an arbitrator. Unless the arbitral decision does not "dra[w] its essence from the collective bargaining agreement," a court is bound to enforce the award and is not entitled to review the merits of the contract dispute. This remains so even when the basis for the arbitrator's decision may be ambiguous.

Under this standard, the Court of Appeals was correct in enforcing the Barrett award, although it seems to us to have taken a somewhat circuitous route to this result. Barrett's initial conclusion that he was not bound by the Sabella decision was based on his interpretation of the bargaining agreement's provisions defining the arbitrator's jurisdiction and his perceived obligation to give a prior award a preclusive effect. Because the authority of arbitrators is a subject of collective bargaining, just as is any other contractual provision, the scope of the arbitrator's authority is itself a question of contract interpretation that the parties have delegated to the arbitrator. Barrett's conclusions that Sabella acted outside his jurisdiction and that this deprived the Sabella award of precedential force under the contract draw their "essence" from the provisions of the collective bargaining agreement. Regardless of what our view might be of the correctness of Barrett's contractual interpretation, the Company and the Union bargained for that interpretation. A federal court may not second-guess it. *Steelworkers v. Enterprise Wheel & Car Corp.*, 363 U.S., at 599, 80 S.Ct., at 1362.

Barrett's analysis of the merits of the grievances is entitled to the same deference. He found that the collective bargaining agreement provided no good faith defense to claims of violations of the seniority provisions, and gave him no authority to weigh in some other fashion the Company's good faith. Again, although conceivably we could reach a different result were we to interpret the contract ourselve, we cannot say that the award does not draw its essence from the collective bargaining agreement.

As with any contract, however, a court may not enforce a collective bargaining agreement that is contrary to public policy. See *Hurd v. Hodge,* 334 U.S. 24, 34–35, 68 S.Ct. 847, 852–53, 92 L.Ed. 1187 (1948). Barrett's view of his own jurisdiction precluded his consideration of this question, and, in any event, the question of public policy is ultimately one for resolution by the courts. See *International Brotherhood of Teamsters v. Washington Employers, Inc.,* 557 F.2d 1345, 1350 (CA9 1977); *Local 453 v. Otis Elevator Co.,* 314 F.2d 25, 29 (CA2 1963), cert. denied, 373 U.S. 949, 83 S.Ct. 1680, 10 L.Ed.2d 705 (1963); Kaden, Judges and Arbitrators: Observations on the Scope of Judicial Review, 80 Colum.L.Rev. 267, 287 (1980). If the contract as interpreted by Barrett violates some explicit public policy, we are obliged to refrain from enforcing it. *Hurd v. Hodge,* 334 U.S., at 35, 68 S.Ct., at 853. Such a public policy, however, must be well defined and dominant, and is to be ascertained "by reference to the laws and legal precedents and not from general considerations of supposed public interests." *Muschany v. United States,* 324 U.S. 49, 66, 65 S.Ct. 442, 451, 89 L.Ed. 744 (1945).

* * * *

Enforcement of the Barrett award will not inappropriately affect this public policy. *here* In this case, although the Company and the Commission agreed to nullify the collective bargaining agreement's seniority provisions, the conciliation process did not include the Union. Absent a judicial determination, the Commission, not to mention the Company, cannot alter the collective bargaining agreement without the Union's consent. See *Alexander v. Gardner-Denver Co.,* 415 U.S., at 44, 94 S.Ct., at 1017 (Commission's power to investigate and conciliate does not have coercive legal effect). Permitting such a result would undermine the federal labor policy that parties to a collective bargaining agreement must have reasonable assurance that their contract will be honored. *Charles Dowd Box Co. v. Courtney,* 368 U.S. 502, 509, 82 S.Ct. 519, 523, 7 L.Ed.2d 483 (1962). Although the ability to abrogate unilaterally the provisions of a collective bargaining agreement might encourage an employer to conciliate with the Commission, the employer's added incentive to conciliate would be paid for with the union's contractual rights.

Aside from the legality of conferring such power on the Commission and an employer, it would be unlikely to further true conciliation between all interested parties. Although an innocent union might decide to join in Title VII conciliation efforts in order to protect its contractual position, neither the employer nor the Commission would have any incentive to make concessions to the union. The Commission and the employer would know that they could agree without the union's consent and that their agreement would be enforced.

In fact, enforcing the award here should encourage conciliation and true voluntary compliance with federal employment discrimination law. If, as in this case, only the employer faces Title VII liability, the union may enter the conciliation process with the hope of obtaining concessions in exchange for helping the employer avoid a Title VII suit. If, however, both the union and the employer are potentially liable, it would be in their joint interests to work out a means to share the burdens imposed by the Commission's demands. On this view, the conciliation process of Title VII and the collective bargaining process complement each other, rather than conflict.

For the foregoing reasons, the Barrett award is properly to be enforced. The judgment of the Court of Appeals is therefore affirmed.

It is so ordered.

APPLICATION AND DISCUSSION QUESTIONS

1. The arbitrator concluded that there is "no good faith defense to claims of violations of the seniority provisions..." Is this correct? Could the arbitrator have considered that an implied good faith defense exist? Does the court suggest that it could have conceivably reached a different conclusion on this issue, if so, why did the court refuse to interpret the argument?

2. The court acknowledges that it has authority to refuse to "enforce a collective bargaining agreement that is contrary to public policy." Does a seniority system which perpetuates racial and/or sex discrimination violates public policy. How does the court view public policy? Title VII of the Civil Rights Act prohibits discrimination in employment. Could the court have cited Title VII as a "well defined and dominate law which prohibited discrimination in seniority systems?" If the company had refused to comply with a conciliatory agreement which was approved by the court, would they have violated public policy?

3. For an early discussion of the court's authority to overturn an arbitration award based on public policy, the court cited *Hurd v. Hodge*, 334 U.S. 24 (1948); Kaden, Judges and Arbitrators Observations on the Scope of Judicial Review, 80 COLUM. L. REV. 287 (1980).

Case

paper Converting + drugs

UNITED PAPERWORKERS INTERNATIONAL UNION, AFL-CIO V. MISCO, INC
484 U.S. 29 (1987)

Justice WHITE delivered the opinion of the Court.

Q The issue for decision involves several aspects of when a federal court may refuse to enforce an arbitration award rendered under a collective-bargaining agreement.

I.

Misco, Inc. (Misco, or the Company), operates a paper converting plant in Monroe, Louisiana. The Company is a party to a collective-bargaining agreement with the United Paperworkers International Union, AFL-CIO, and its union local (the Union); the agreement covers the production and maintenance employees at the plant. Under the agreement, the Company or the Union may submit to arbitration any grievance that arises from the interpretation or application of its terms, and the arbitrator's decision is final and binding upon the parties. The arbitrator's authority is limited to interpretation and application of the terms contained in the agreement itself. The agreement reserves to management the right to establish, amend, and enforce "rules and regulations regulating the discipline or discharge of employees" and the procedures for imposing discipline. Such rules were to be posted and were to be in effect "until ruled on by grievance and arbitration procedures as to fairness and necessity." For about a decade, the Company's rules had listed as causes for discharge the bringing of intoxicants, narcotics, or controlled substances on to plant property or consuming any of them there, as well as reporting for work under the influence of such substances. At the time of the events involved in this case, the Company was very concerned about the use of drugs at the plant, especially among employees on the night shift.

Isiah Cooper, who worked on the night shift for Misco, was one of the employees covered by the collective-bargaining agreement. He operated a slitter-rewinder machine, which uses sharp blades to cut rolling coils of paper. The arbitrator found that this machine is hazardous and had caused numerous injuries in recent years. Cooper had been reprimanded twice in a few months for deficient performance. On January 21, 1983, one day after the second reprimand, the police searched Cooper's house pursuant to a warrant, and a substantial amount of marijuana was found. Contemporaneously, a police officer was detailed to keep Cooper's car under observation at the Company's parking lot. At about 6:30 p.m., Cooper was seen walking in the parking lot during work hours with two other men. The three men entered Cooper's car momentarily, then walked to another car, a white Cutlass, and entered it. After the other two men later returned to the plant, Cooper was apprehended by police in the backseat of this car with marijuana smoke in the air and a lighted marijuana cigarette in the frontseat ashtray. The police also searched Cooper's car and found a plastic scales case and marijuana gleanings. Cooper was arrested and charged with marijuana possession.

On January 24, Cooper told the Company that he had been arrested for possession of marijuana at his home; the Company did not learn of the marijuana cigarette in the white Cutlass until January 27. It then investigated and on February 7 discharged Cooper, asserting that in the circumstances, his presence in the Cutlass violated the rule against having drugs on the plant premises. Cooper filed a grievance protesting his discharge the same day, and the matter proceeded to arbitration. The Company was not aware until September 21, five days before the arbitration hearing was scheduled, that marijuana had been found in Cooper's car. That fact did not become known to the Union until the hearing began. At the hearing it was stipulated that the issue was whether the Company had "just cause to discharge the Grievant under Rule II.1" and, "[i]f not, what if any should be the remedy." App. to Pet. for Cert. 26a.

The arbitrator upheld the grievance and ordered the Company to reinstate Cooper with backpay and full seniority. The arbitrator based his finding that there was not just cause for the discharge on his consideration of seven criteria. In particular, the arbitrator found that the Company failed to prove that the employee had possessed or used marijuana on company property: finding Cooper in the backseat of a car and a burning cigarette in the front-seat ashtray was insufficient proof that Cooper was using or possessed marijuana on company property. Id., at 49a-50a. The arbitrator refused to accept into evidence the fact that marijuana had been found in Cooper's car on company premises because the Company did not know of this fact when Cooper was discharged and therefore did not rely on it as a basis for the discharge.

The Company filed suit in District Court, seeking to vacate the arbitration award on several grounds, one of which was that ordering reinstatement of Cooper, who had allegedly possessed marijuana on the plant premises, was contrary to public policy. The District Court agreed that the award must be set aside as contrary to public policy because it ran counter to general safety concerns that arise from the operation of dangerous machinery while under the influence of drugs, as well as to state criminal laws against drug possession. The Court of Appeals affirmed, with one judge dissenting. The court ruled that reinstatement would violate the public policy "against the operation of dangerous machinery by persons under the influence of drugs or alcohol." 768 F.2d 739, 743 (CA5 1985). The arbitrator had found that Cooper was apprehended on company premises in an atmosphere of marijuana smoke in another's car and that marijuana was found in his own car on the company lot. These facts established that Cooper had violated the Company's rules and gave the Company just cause to discharge him. The arbitrator did not reach this conclusion because of a "narrow focus on Cooper's procedural rights" that led him to ignore what he "knew was in fact true: that Cooper *did* bring marijuana onto his employer's premises." Even if the arbitrator had not known of this fact at the time he entered his award, "it is doubtful that the award should be enforced today in light of what is now known."

* * * *

Because the Courts of Appeals are divided on the question of when courts may set
aside arbitration awards as contravening public policy,7 we granted the Union's petition for a writ of certiorari, 479 U.S. 1029, 107 S.Ct. 871, 93 L.Ed.2d 826 (1987), and now
reverse the judgment of the Court of Appeals.

[margin handwriting: SC]

II.

The Union asserts that an arbitral award may not be set aside on public policy grounds
unless the award orders conduct that violates the positive law, which is not the case
here. But in the alternative, it submits that even if it is wrong in this regard, the Court
of Appeals otherwise exceeded the limited authority that it had to review an arbitrator's award entered pursuant to a collective-bargaining agreement. Respondent,
on the other hand, defends the public policy decision of the Court of Appeals but
alternatively argues that the judgment below should be affirmed because of erroneous findings by the arbitrator. We deal first with the opposing alternative arguments.

A.

Collective-bargaining agreements commonly provide grievance procedures to settle
disputes between union and employer with respect to the interpretation and application of the agreement and require binding arbitration for unsettled grievances. In
such cases, and this is such a case, the Court made clear almost 30 years ago that the
courts play only a limited role when asked to review the decision of an arbitrator.
The courts are not authorized to reconsider the merits of an award even though the
parties may allege that the award rests on errors of fact or on misinterpretation of
the contract. "The refusal of courts to review the merits of an arbitration award is the
proper approach to arbitration under collective bargaining agreements. The federal
policy of settling labor disputes by arbitration would be undermined if courts had the
final say on the merits of the awards." *Steelworkers v. Enterprise Wheel & Car Corp.,*
363 U.S. 593, 596, 80 S.Ct. 1358, 1360, 4 L.Ed.2d 1424 (1960). As long as the arbitrator's award "draws its essence from the collective bargaining agreement," and is not
merely "his own brand of industrial justice," the award is legitimate. *Id.,* at 597, 80
S.Ct., at 1361.

[margin handwriting: rule]

    "The function of the court is very limited when the parties have agreed to submit
all questions of contract interpretation to the arbitrator. It is confined to ascertaining
whether the party seeking arbitration is making a claim which on its face is governed

by the contract. Whether the moving party is right or wrong is a question of contract interpretation for the arbitrator. In these circumstances the moving party should not be deprived of the arbitrator's judgment, when it was his judgment and all that it connotes that was bargained for.

"The courts, therefore, have no business weighing the merits of the grievance, considering whether there is equity in a particular claim, or determining whether there is particular language in the written instrument which will support the claim."

* * * *

B.

The Company's position, simply put, is that the arbitrator committed grievous error in finding that the evidence was insufficient to prove that Cooper had possessed or used marijuana on company property. But the Court of Appeals, although it took a distinctly jaundiced view of the arbitrator's decision in this regard, was not free to refuse enforcement because it considered Cooper's presence in the white Cutlass, in the circumstances, to be ample proof that Rule II.1 was violated. No dishonesty is alleged; only improvident, even silly, factfinding is claimed. This is hardly a sufficient basis for disregarding what the agent appointed by the parties determined to be the historical facts.

Nor was it open to the Court of Appeals to refuse to enforce the award because the arbitrator, in deciding whether there was just cause to discharge, refused to consider evidence unknown to the Company at the time Cooper was fired. The parties bargained for arbitration to settle disputes and were free to set the procedural rules for arbitrators to follow if they chose. Article VI of the agreement, entitled "Arbitration Procedure," did set some ground rules for the arbitration process. It forbade the arbitrator to consider hearsay evidence, for example, but evidentiary matters were otherwise left to the arbitrator. Here the arbitrator ruled that in determining whether Cooper had violated Rule II.1, he should not consider evidence not relied on by the employer in ordering the discharge, particularly in a case like this where there was no notice to the employee or the Union prior to the hearing that the Company would attempt to rely on after-discovered evidence. This, in effect, was a construction of what the contract required when deciding discharge cases: an arbitrator was to look only at the evidence before the employer at the time of discharge. As the arbitrator noted, this approach was consistent with the practice followed by other arbitrators. And it was consistent with our observation in *John Wiley & Sons, Inc. v. Livingston*, 376 U.S. 543, 557, 84 S.Ct. 909, 918, 11 L.Ed.2d 898 (1964), that when the subject matter of a dispute is arbitrable, "procedural" questions which grow out of the dispute and bear on its final disposition are to be left to the arbitrator.

Under the Arbitration Act, the federal courts are empowered to set aside arbitration awards on such grounds only when "the arbitrators were guilty of misconduct ... in refusing to hear evidence pertinent and material to the controversy." 9 U.S.C. § 10(c). See *Commonwealth Coatings Corp. v. Continental Casualty Co.*, 393 U.S. 145, 89 S.Ct. 337, 21 L.Ed.2d 301 (1968). If we apply that same standard here and assume that the arbitrator erred in refusing to consider the disputed evidence, his error was not in bad faith or so gross as to amount to affirmative misconduct. Finally, it is worth noting that putting aside the evidence about the marijuana found in Cooper's car during this arbitration did not forever foreclose the Company from using that evidence as the basis for a discharge.

*   *   *   *

C.

The Court of Appeals did not purport to take this course in any event. Rather, it held that the evidence of marijuana in Cooper's car required that the award be set aside because to reinstate a person who had brought drugs onto the property was contrary to the public policy "against the operation of dangerous machinery by persons under the influence of drugs or alcohol." 768 F.2d, at 743. We cannot affirm that judgment.

A court's refusal to enforce an arbitrator's award under a collective-bargaining agreement because it is contrary to public policy is a specific application of the more general doctrine, rooted in the common law, that a court may refuse to enforce contracts that violate law or public policy. *W.R. Grace & Co. v. Rubber Workers*, 461 U.S. 757, 766, 103 S.Ct. 2177, 2183, 76 L.Ed.2d 298 (1983); *Hurd v. Hodge*, 334 U.S. 24, 34-35, 68 S.Ct. 847, 852-853, 92 L.Ed. 1187 (1948). That doctrine derives from the basic notion that no court will lend its aid to one who founds a cause of action upon an immoral or illegal act, and is further justified by the observation that the public's interests in confining the scope of private agreements to which it is not a party will go unrepresented unless the judiciary takes account of those interests when it considers whether to enforce such agreements. *E.g., McMullen v. Hoffman*, 174 U.S. 639, 654-655, 19 S.Ct. 839, 845, 43 L.Ed. 1117 (1899); *Twin City Pipe Line Co. v. Harding Glass Co.*, 283 U.S. 353, 356-358, 51 S.Ct. 476, 477-478, 75 L.Ed. 1112 (1931). In the common law of contracts, this doctrine has served as the foundation for occasional exercises of judicial power to abrogate private agreements.

* * * *

As we see it, the formulation of public policy set out by the Court of Appeals did not comply with the statement that such a policy must be "ascertained 'by reference to the laws and legal precedents and not from general considerations of supposed public interests.' " *Ibid.* (quoting *Muschany v. United States, supra,* 324 U.S., at 66, 65 S.Ct., at 451). The Court of Appeals made no attempt to review existing laws and legal precedents in order to demonstrate that they establish a "well-defined and dominant" policy against the operation of dangerous machinery while under the influence of drugs. Although certainly such a judgment is firmly rooted in common sense, we explicitly held in *W.R. Grace* that a formulation of public policy based only on "general considerations of supposed public interests" is not the sort that permits a court to set aside an arbitration award that was entered in accordance with a valid collective-bargaining agreement.

Even if the Court of Appeals' formulation of public policy is to be accepted, no violation of that policy was clearly shown in this case. In pursuing its public policy inquiry, the Court of Appeals quite properly considered the established fact that traces of marijuana had been found in Cooper's car. Yet the assumed connection between the marijuana gleanings found in Cooper's car and Cooper's actual use of drugs in the workplace is tenuous at best and provides an insufficient basis for holding that his reinstatement would actually violate the public policy identified by the Court of Appeals "against the operation of dangerous machinery by persons under the influence of drugs or alcohol." 768 F.2d, at 743. A refusal to enforce an award must rest on more than speculation or assumption.

In any event, it was inappropriate for the Court of Appeals itself to draw the necessary inference. To conclude from the fact that marijuana had been found in Cooper's car that Cooper had ever been or would be under the influence of marijuana while he was on the job and operating dangerous machinery is an exercise in factfinding about Cooper's use of drugs and his amenability to discipline, a task that exceeds the authority of a court asked to overturn an arbitration award. The parties did not bargain for the facts to be found by a court, but by an arbitrator chosen by them who had more opportunity to observe Cooper and to be familiar with the plant and its problems. Nor does the fact that it is inquiring into a possible violation of public policy excuse a court for doing the arbitrator's task. If additional facts were to be found, the arbitrator should find them in the course of any further effort the Company might have made to discharge Cooper for having had marijuana in his car on company premises. Had the arbitrator found that Cooper had possessed drugs on the property, yet imposed discipline short of discharge because he found as a factual matter that Cooper could be trusted not to use them on the job, the Court of Appeals could not upset the award because of its own view that public policy about plant safety was threatened.11 In this connection it should also be noted that the award ordered Cooper to be reinstated in his old job or in an equivalent one for which he was qualified. It is by no means clear from the record that Cooper would pose a serious threat to the asserted public policy in every job for which he was qualified.

The judgment of the Court of Appeals is reversed.

So ordered.

Justice BLACKMUN, with whom Justice BRENNAN joins, concurring. (Omitted)

APPLICATION AND DISCUSSION QUESTIONS

1. What are the parties' arguments regarding why the Court of Appeals' decision should be affirmed or reversed?

2. Where does the Court derive its authority to limit or modify an arbitrator's awards? What were the reasons outlined by the Court of Appeals for affirming the lower court decisions to set aside the award?

3. How does the Court define the public policy doctrine? Where is this doctrine derived from? How does the Court formulate public policy?

CITY OF SIDNEY, OHIO V. FRATERNAL ORDER OF POLICE
COMMON PLEAS COURT OF SHELBY COUNTY, OHIO,
CASE NO. 10vc000497
MARCH 11, 2011

On November 2, 2010, Plaintiff City of Sidney, Ohio (City), filed its Complaint and Motion to Vacate Arbitration Award. On November 29, 2010, Defendant, Fraternal Order of Police, Ohio Labor Council, Inc. (FOP), filed its Answer with an Application to Confirm Arbitration Award. Subsequently, the parties filed additional motions and memoranda in support of their respective positions and this Court heard oral arguments on February 9, 2011. The facts in this case are not in dispute, only the decision of the Arbitrator.

A   For the reasons that follow, this Court confirms the Arbitrator's award of September 13, 2010.

Issues:

Q   The issue before this Court is whether the Arbitrator in his award exceeded the authority provided to him by statute and contract.

Standards of Review:

Rule   Revised Code Section 2711.10 provides four circumstances in which a Court of Common Pleas shall vacate an arbitration award. Those circumstances include: A) Award procured by corruption, fraud, or undue means; B) Evident partiality or corruption on the part of the arbitrators; C) The arbitrators were guilty of misconduct... or D) The arbitrators exceeded their powers...

The City contends that the Arbitrator exceeded his power such that this Court should vacate the award pursuant to Revised Code Section 2711.10(D).

Facts:

In February, 2010, City sent the Tactical Response Team to New Mexico for six days of training. Both third shift supervisors were members of the Tactical Response Team. During the six days, instead of assigning a supervisor from another shift to the third shift, the City assigned a patrol officer as "officer-in-charge."

The FOP complained that appointing an officer-in-charge instead of using supervisors from another shift violated the Collective Bargaining Agreement. The FOP contended that the City could only designate an officer-in-charge if the absence was for an extended period of time. The FOP contended that six days was not an extended period of time as contemplated by the Collective Bargaining Agreement.

All parties agree that the phrase "extended period of time" is not defined in the Collective Bargaining Agreement. The City, however, contends that the proper definition of extended period of time should be interpreted as any period of time more than three days. In support of that position, the City points to a paragraph which references, "Vacation of short duration, one to three days." The City argued that if a vacation of short duration was defined as one to three days, any period in excess of three days would be considered an extended period of time. The FOP contends that since "extended period of time" is not defined the Arbitrator must determine the intent of the parties in the use of that language. In doing so, the Arbitrator was free to use any information, including how that phrase was used in the past to decide the intent of the parties.

The Arbitrator conducted a hearing. At the conclusion of the hearing, the Arbitrator, after considering the evidence presented, including evidence of the past practices, determined that the proper interpretation of the phrase "extended period of time" would be a period of time commencing at thirty days.

The City, disputing the Arbitrator's interpretation, filed this action.

Discussion:

The City argues that the Arbitrator exceeded his powers because the Arbitrators award "fails to draw its essence from the labor agreement." The City contends that the Arbitrator, in effect, modified the terms and conditions of the Collective Bargaining Agreement by the Arbitrator's interpretation of the contract.

Further, the City contends that the arbitration award violated the terms and conditions of the Collective Bargaining Agreement by the use of past practices to interpret the agreement. The City points to language in Article 8, which specifies that the City is not obligated to continue any "...past practice which is not covered or contained in this Agreement."

If there was a clear definition or understanding of what the phrase "extended period of time" meant, there would have been no need for the Arbitrator to determine a definition or meaning. The very fact that the parties dispute the meaning of the phrase "extended period of time" demonstrates a need for an interpretation. The person to make that interpretation is the Arbitrator.

If either party wanted a specific definition of "extended period of time," they could have bargained for it. In the absence of a definition, "...the function of the arbitrator is to determine and carry out the mutual intent of the parties by interpreting the agreement and applying its provisions to the issues before him or her.

This Court disagrees with the City that the Arbitrator cannot use past practices to interpret the contract. It is true that the contract does not require the City to continue past practices not covered in the contract. For example, if the City had a past practice of providing free coffee and donuts to each shift but there was no provision in the contract for the providing of free coffee and donuts, then the City could change that practice. However, this Court does not believe that language of Article 8 prevents the Arbitrator from considering past practices as a means of determining the intent of the parties to interpret a phrase in the contract. In interpreting the contract, the

Arbitrator had to determine the intent of the parties. In interpreting the intent of the parties, the Arbitrator could look to not only the contract but also the practices outside the contract that might help the Arbitrator in determining the parties' intent.

Similarly, this Court is not of the opinion that the decision of the Arbitrator violates the anti waiver provisions of the contract. The issue here is not whether the City had a right that was waived or not waived, but, rather, how a particular undefined phrase of the collective bargaining agreement should be interpreted.

The role of the Court in reviewing an arbitration award is strictly limited. The Arbitrator's award is presumed valid and must be upheld whenever it is possible to do so. A trial court may not reverse an Arbitrator's award simply because it disagrees with the Arbitrator's findings of facts or interpretation of the contract.

The Arbitrator's role is to interpret the contract if the contract is vague or ambiguous. It is not the function of the Court to second-guess the interpretation of the Arbitrator. "When a provision in a collective bargaining agreement is subject to more than one reasonable interpretation and the parties to the contract have agreed to submit their contract interpretation disputes to final and binding arbitration, the arbitrator's interpretation of the contract, and not the interpretation of a reviewing court, governs the rights of the parties thereto. This is so because the arbitrator's interpretation of the contract is what the parties bargained for in agreeing to submit their disputes to final and binding arbitration. The arbitrator's interpretation must prevail regardless of whether his or her interpretation is the most reasonable under the circumstances."

It is true that if there is no rational basis for the Arbitrator's decision it can be found that the Arbitrator exceeded his authority. The City argues that that happened in this case. The City point to the case of *Trumbull County Sheriff v Ohio Patrolmen's Benevolent Association*[6] as analogous to the case sub judice. However, in that case the Arbitrator apparently imposed a new condition i.e. an expiration date, to the collective bargaining agreement not contemplated by the parties. In the case of *International Assoc. of Fireman v Columbus* also cited by the City, the arbitrator went beyond the plain meaning of the language i.e. the term "disability" and imposed an additional condition not contemplated by the terms of the collective bargaining agreement.

This Court cannot say that in this case the Arbitrator added a new condition to the contract or went beyond the plain meaning of the language in the contract. An "extended period of time" was a condition contemplated by the parties, just not clearly defined. In this case, the meaning of the phrase "extended period of time" is not plain. It cannot be defined by merely looking up a dictionary definition. The issue here is what were the parties contemplating when placing that phrase in the collective bargaining agreement.

It is certainly reasonable, as the City argues, that if a "vacation of short duration" is three days as is used in other parts of the collective bargaining agreement then an "extended period of lime' is more than three days. The Arbitrator considered that argument, but found it not persuasive. It is not for the court to decide which of the two arguments is best. That is the responsibility of the Arbitrator.

The FOP has also requested interest from the date of the arbitration award until paid. The City has not provided any authority opposing that request. As noted in *Board of Trustees of Miami Township v Fraternal Order of Police, Ohio Labor Council* "...to make the aggrieved party whole, the party should be compensated for the lapse of time between accrual of the claim and judgment."

Conclusion:

Accordingly, this Court finds that the Arbitrator did not exceed his powers in interpreting the contract and determining the award. This Court confirms the arbitration award and enters judgment in favor of the FOP and against the City.

Further, interest is awarded pursuant to law from the date of the award, September 13, 2010, until paid.

Costs charged to Plaintiff:

The Clerk of this Court is directed to deliver copies of the within Entry to the attorneys of record and to any parties not represented by an attorney.

IT IS SO ORDERED.

APPLICATION AND DISCUSSION QUESTIONS

1. Under Ohio law, the four circumstances in which the court "shall" vacate an arbitration award include:
   a. Award procured by corruption, fraud, or undue means
   b. Evidence of partiality or corruption on the part of the arbitrators
   c. The arbitrators were guilty of misconduct
   d. The arbitrators exceeded their power

   Which of these reasons did the arbitrator present to the Court?

2. The employer argues that the award should be vacated because the award "fails to draw its essence from the labor agreement" and the "award violated the terms and conditions of the CBA by the use of past practices

to interpret the argument". Explain the terms "draw its essence" and the concept of "past practices."

3. What is the role of the arbitrator if a term is not defined in the CBA? What factors do arbitrators consider in defining the term? How does the arbitrator determine intent of the parties?

4. The Court makes it clear that it is the role of the arbitrator to interpret the contract if the contract is vague or ambiguous. It is not the role of the Court to second-guess the interpretation of the arbitrator. What terms were ambiguous? If the terms could have more than one meaning, should the Court have the final interpretation? What is the role of the Court if there is no rational basis for the arbitrator's decision?

5. Why did the court award interest and cost to the plaintiff? How should the arbitrator rule if there are two arguments, which are credible?

MEDCO HEALTH SOLUTIONS OF COLUMBUS WEST V. THE ASSOCIATION OF MANAGED CARE PHARMACISTS
2009 U.S. DIST. LEXIS 106256 (2009)

JUDGES: GREGORY L. FROST, UNITED STATES DISTRICT JUDGE. Magistrate Judge Mark R. Abel.

OPINION BY: GREGORY L. FROST

For the reasons that follow, the Court DENIES Plaintiff's Motion for Summary Judgment and GRANTS Defendant's Motion for Summary Judgment.

I. Background

Plaintiff is a large mail order pharmacy that processes approximately 380,000 prescriptions per week. On March 19, 2007, a calling technician, Tiffany Harper, received a file that contained patient information, but did not contain a prescription. Because the prescription was missing, Harper placed a call to the patient. The patient began to discuss clinical information, so Harper telephoned the pharmacist, Brian Scott, who then spoke to the patient. After speaking to the patient, Scott wrote "per MD Seidt" on the order, falsely indicating in the records that Dr. Seidt had issued an oral prescription for the drug Lipitor. Harper twice asked Scott if he wanted her to call the doctor, and twice Scott told her to put the order through. When questioned about the incident by his superiors, Scott was untruthful and said that he had spoken to the doctor's office. On March 27, 2007, Plaintiff terminated Scott as a result of this incident.

issue

fired

Scott was a member of a collective bargaining unit represented by Defendant. Plaintiff and Defendant are parties to a collective bargaining agreement ("CBA") that covers a collective bargaining unit of pharmacists employed by Plaintiff. The CBA states in its pertinent parts:

CBA

VI. DISCIPLINE/DISCHARGE

A. The Employer will not discipline or discharge any employee, except for just cause. The Employer will follow the principles of progressive discipline to the extent just cause requires.

CBA

XVI. GRIEVANCE AND ARBITRATION . . .

In no event shall the arbitrator have any authority to modify, add to, disregard or abolish, in any way, any of the terms and provisions of this Agreement. The decision of the arbitrator shall be final and binding. However, the foregoing shall not waive the rights of either party to move in a court of competent jurisdiction to vacate an arbitrator's award in accordance with applicable law.

A grievance protesting Plaintiff's action as a violation of the CBA was filed and processed to arbitration before Arbitrator Floyd D. Weatherspoon, Professor of Law, Capital University Law School. An arbitration hearing was held on April 3, 2008, at which both Plaintiff and Defendant were represented by counsel, and given full opportunity to present testimony, examine and cross-examine witnesses, and to present other evidence. At the hearing Plaintiff and Defendant stipulated the issue as follows:

[W]hether the grievant was terminated for just cause and, if not, what the appropriate remedy should be. The parties also stipulated that: [T]he grievance is properly before the arbitrator and there are no procedural issues.

Following the filing of post-hearing briefs by Plaintiff and Defendant, Arbitrator Weatherspoon issued his award on September 19, 2008, wherein he determined that Scott was terminated without just cause. The award ordered that Scott's termination be reduced to a one year and five and one half month suspension without pay. The arbitrator stated the following, in part, regarding his decision to reduce the penalty imposed by Plaintiff:

> Article VI, Section A, of the parties CBA, provides that the Employer will follow the principles of progressive discipline to the extent just cause requires. In determining whether there are mitigating factors which may impact the level of discipline that an employee may receive for violating a work rule or policy, arbitrators often consider the employee's work record, service time, gravity of the offense, and any other special circumstances. *Paperworkers v. Misco, Inc.*, 484 U.S. 29, 41, 108 S. Ct. 364, 98 L. Ed. 2d 286 (1987).

The Union put forth undisputed evidence that the Grievant had an excellent work record. Indeed, the evidence establishes that in a seven year period, the Grievant had only one dispensing error. However, the Company states that even the Grievant acknowledges that falsely recording information on a prescription is in violation of the law and would jeopardize his job. Thus, the Company argues that just cause didn't require progressive discipline in this case.

The Arbitrator acknowledges that strict rules must be followed when processing patient prescriptions. If stringent rules and proper procedures are not followed, both patients and the pharmacy are put at risk. It poses a health and safety risk for patients and risk of liability for the pharmacy. The evidence supports the conclusion that the Company had sufficient evidence to conclude that the Grievant knowingly attempted to process a prescription without first confirming that prescription with the doctor. The Grievant's actions clearly constituted intentional misconduct. However, it was not the kind of malicious and reckless disregard that posed a serious threat to the health and safety of the patient. The evidence indicates that the prescription was already in the system, it just needed to be verified and confirmed. Moreover, as stated earlier, the Grievant did not falsify a prescription. Therefore, while the evidence supports that the Grievant engaged in misconduct, it was not the kind of intentional disregard for human health that should end in discharge.

The CBA calls for progressive discipline. The evidence demonstrates that the Grievant had an excellent work record, seven years of seniority, and only a minor dispensing error. Clearly, the Grievant's conduct 'was very serious,' however; his past record and the facts surrounding the misconduct are mitigating factors to support a reduction in the penalty. Thus, the Arbitrator finds that the discharge was too severe. Therefore, the Grievant shall be reinstated with full seniority. However, because the evidence supports that the Grievant actions constituted intentional misconduct, he is awarded no back pay.

Plaintiff has refused to comply with the award of the arbitrator.

On December 17, 2008, Plaintiff filed this action seeking to vacate the arbitration award as contrary to public policy, and Defendant counterclaimed for confirmation of the award and to have Scott compensated for all earnings and benefits lost from the date of the arbitration award to the date of his requested reinstatement. The parties have filed cross motions for summary judgment.

Standard (omitted)

III. Analysis

"[C]ourts play only a limited role when asked to review the decision of an arbitrator." *United Paperworkers Int'l Union v. Misco, Inc.*, 484 U.S. 29, 36, 108 S. Ct. 364, 98 L. Ed. 2d 286 (1987). *See also DBM Techs., Inc. v. Local 227, United Food & Commercial Workers Int'l Union*, 257 F.3d 651, 656 (6th Cir. 2001) (noting that a federal court's review of an arbitration award is " 'one of the narrowest standards of judicial review in all of American jurisprudence' ") The United States Supreme Court has cautioned that "the federal policy of settling labor disputes by arbitration would be undermined if courts had the final say on the merits of the awards." *Steelworkers v. Enter. Wheel & Car Corp.*, 363 U.S. 593, 596, 80 S. Ct. 1358, 4 L. Ed. 2d 1424 (1960). When, as here, there is no claim that the arbitrator acted outside his authority, the arbitrator's award must be treated as if it represents a contractual agreement between the employer and union as to the meaning of the CBA.

Despite this deferential review, a court must "refrain from enforcing" an arbitration award "if the contract as interpreted by [the arbitrator] violates some explicit public policy." *W.R. Grace & Co. v. Local Union 759*, 461 U.S. 757, 766, 103 S. Ct. 2177, 76 L. Ed. 2d 298 (1983). This is "a specific application of the more general doctrine, rooted in the common law that a court may refuse to enforce contracts that violate law or public policy." "[A] court's refusal to enforce an arbitrator's *interpretation* of such contracts is limited to situations where the contract as interpreted would violate some explicit public policy that is well defined and dominant," which, in turn, must be "ascertained by reference to the laws and legal precedents and not from general considerations of supposed public interests." ("A court may refuse to enforce an award when specific terms in the contract would violate public policy, but there is no broad power to set aside an arbitration award as against public policy."). Whether the contract, as interpreted by the arbitrator, is contrary to public policy is a question to be resolved by the courts. *See Misco*, 484 U.S. at 43.

In the instant action, Plaintiff argues that reinstatement of Scott would force it to risk compromising public safety and would expose Plaintiff to possible liability for Scott's potential future misconduct. In support of the public policies at issue, Plaintiff relies upon Ohio Revised Code, Sections 2925.23(A) and 4729.01, and the regulations of the Ohio Pharmacy Board. It is a criminal violation of Ohio's drug laws to knowingly make a false statement in any prescription, order, report, or record. Ohio Rev. Code § 2925.23(A). The Board of Pharmacy regulations address the situation when a pharmacist takes an oral order from a doctor:

> The pharmacist shall make a record of the full name of the prescriber and, if transmitted by the prescriber's agent, the full name of the agent, on the original prescription and, if used, on the alternate system of record keeping. The pharmacist is responsible for assuring the validity of the source of the oral prescription.

Defendant argues that the question for the Court to decide is whether the arbitrator's decision, not Scott's conduct, violated public policy and that the answer to that question is that it did not. This Court agrees.

The United States Court of Appeals for the Sixth Circuit has been clear that in cases like the one *sub judice* " 'the issue is not whether grievant's conduct for which he was disciplined violated some public policy or law, but rather whether the award requiring the reinstatement of a grievance, *i.e.*, the contract as interpreted, *W.R. Grace*, 461 U.S. at 766, violated some explicit public policy.' " Thus, the issue before this Court is whether the CBA as interpreted by Arbitrator Weatherspoon, *i.e.*, to suspend without pay rather than to discharge Scott, falls within the legal exception that makes unenforceable a collective-bargaining agreement that is contrary to public policy.

* * * *

More appropriate is Defendant's reliance upon *Way Bakery v. Truck Drivers Local No. 164*, 363 F.3d 590 (6th Cir. 2004). In *Way Bakery*, a white union member was terminated for making a racially offensive remark to a black coworker. The employee grieved the termination through arbitration and the arbitrator ordered reinstatement. The *Way Bakery* court explained:

In *Eastern [Associated Coal Corp.*, 531 U.S. at 62)], the Supreme Court held that public policy considerations did not require courts to refuse to enforce an arbitrator's award reinstating a truck driver who twice tested positive for marijuana use. Id. at 59. The Court reasoned that the arbitrator's award was not contrary to the relevant public policies, including policies "against drug use by employees in safety-sensitive transportation positions" and policies in favor of drug testing, id. at 65, holding as follows:

The award before us is not contrary to these several policies, taken together. The award does not condone Smith's conduct or ignore the risk to public safety that drug use by truck drivers may pose. Rather, the award punishes Smith by suspending him for nearly three months, thereby depriving him of nearly $ 9,000 in lost wages; it requires him to pay the arbitration costs of both sides; it insists upon further substance-abuse treatment and testing; and it makes clear (by requiring Smith to provide a signed letter of resignation) that one more failed test means discharge.

Way Bakery, 363 F.3d at 596. The appellate court concluded:

Similarly, the arbitration award in the present case did not condone Zentgraf's behavior, but rather punished him by depriving him of his salary for six months and placing him on probation for five years. Way Bakery cites no case, nor have we found any, that establishes a public policy of flatly prohibiting the reinstatement of a worker who makes a racially offensive remark. We therefore hold that the arbitrator's award in this case did not violate public policy.

Like the Court in *Eastern* and the *Way Bakery* court, this Court concludes that the arbitration award here was not contrary to the relevant public policies nor did it condone Scott's behavior, but rather punished him by depriving him of his salary for one year and five and one-half months. Also like the *Way Bakery* employer, Plaintiff here "cites no case, nor [has this Court] found any, that establishes a public policy of flatly prohibiting the reinstatement of a worker who" falsifies a prescription.

[margin note: *Issue*]

IV. Conclusion

For the reasons set forth above, the Court DENIES Plaintiff's Motion for Summary Judgment (Doc. # 15) and GRANTS Defendant's Motion for Summary Judgment (Doc. # 16). Plaintiff is ORDERED to comply with the arbitration award that requires reinstatement of Brian Scott. Plaintiff is also ORDERED to compensate Scott for all earnings and benefits lost from the date of the arbitration decision to the date of his reinstatement.

[margin note: *held*]

IT IS SO ORDERED.

APPLICATION AND DISCUSSION QUESTIONS

1. What must the plaintiff prove for the arbitrator's decision to be against public policy?

2. What public policy did the employer argue the award violated?

3. Why did the parties negotiate a provision in the "Grievance and Arbitration" clause of the CBA that either party may sue to vacate the arbitrator's award, especially when the clause also states the arbitrator's award was final and binding?

4. How do courts determine the existence of a public policy?

5. What factors did the arbitrator consider to mitigate the penalty? The arbitrator concluded that the employee had "knowingly" attempted to violate policies and procedures and intentionally engaged in misconduct. How could the arbitrator still require the employee to be reinstated?

case abusive cop (handwritten annotation)

CITY OF DES PLAINES V. METRO. ALLIANCE OF POLICE, CHAPTER NO. 240
2015 IL APP (1ST) 140957; 2015 ILL. APP. LEXIS 223

Disposition: Reversed and remanded.

Judges: JUSTICE LIU delivered the judgment of the court, with opinion. Presiding Justice Simon concurred in the judgment and opinion. Justice Pierce dissented, with opinion.
Opinion by: LIU

Issue (handwritten annotation)   Plaintiff, City of Des Plaines (City), sought to terminate City police officer John Bueno (Bueno) after conducting an investigation into allegations that Bueno had used unnecessary or excessive force against arrestees and had failed to report that use of force in violation of the General Orders of the Des Plaines Police Department (Department). Defendant, Metropolitan Alliance of Police, Chapter No. 240 (the Union), represented Bueno, and the parties submitted the grievance over his termination to arbitration. Although the arbitrator concluded that Bueno had violated certain General Orders, he nevertheless determined that termination was not an appropriate remedy because of "due process" considerations—specifically, the City's delay in investigating the complained-of incidents and the Department's condonation of Bueno's conduct.

The City filed a motion to vacate the arbitration award in the circuit court, arguing that the award violated public policy. The circuit court agreed and vacated the arbitration award; it also denied the Union's motion to remand to the arbitrator for additional findings concerning Bueno's likelihood of engaging in the same misconduct following reinstatement. The Union appeals. We find that a remand to the arbitrator is necessary to clarify the award; in the absence of a clarification, we cannot fully assess its public policy implications. We therefore reverse the circuit court's judgment and remand for further proceedings consistent with this opinion.

BACKGROUND

Bueno had been a City police officer since 2002. In 2011, the city manager, Jason Slowinski (Slowinski), received a letter alleging that Bueno had physically beaten four arrestees, with the alleged instances occurring in 2009 and 2010. After receiving the letter, Slowinski initiated an investigation into the allegations.

Based on the investigation, the City identified three incidents where Bueno allegedly misapplied force against arrestees: (1) in August 2010, he punched in the face a handcuffed arrestee who was seated in the back of his squad car; (2) in January 2010, he punched an arrestee in the nose inside the police station; and (3) in June 2009, he pushed an arrestee in a holding cell. Bueno had not reported any of these incidents as required by Department General Order 10.01.

After the investigation was complete, the City filed a complaint with the City's Board of Fire and Police Commissioners, requesting that Bueno be terminated. Bueno challenged his termination through grievance arbitration as allowed by the City-Union Collective Bargaining Agreement. The City terminated Bueno, and the parties proceeded to arbitration. After a three-day hearing, the arbitrator issued an award (1) reinstating Bueno without back pay, benefits or accumulated seniority for "time away from work"; (2) deeming Bueno's time away as "a disciplinary suspension"; (3) conditioning Bueno's reinstatement on a "last chance" basis for a period of three years from the date of reinstatement, such that any violation of the City's use-of force and reporting policy and/or truthfulness requirements will result in immediate discharge; and (4) allowing the City, at its discretion, to provide Bueno with "a reasonable amount and type of training in the appropriate use of force."

In the award, the arbitrator addressed each of the three identified use-of-force incidents. First, with respect to the August 2010 occurrence, the parties did not dispute that Bueno had been driving his squad car with another officer in the passenger seat and a handcuffed arrestee, who had been charged with aggravated battery, in the backseat. Bueno drove the car into a parking garage within close proximity to the police station. He then exited the vehicle, opened the backseat door, and punched the arrestee in the face. During an investigation interrogation in November 2011, Bueno explained that he punched the arrestee because he thought the prisoner was trying to defeat the handcuffs. According to Bueno, he wanted to distract the prisoner so that he could confirm that the handcuffs were still secure.

The arbitrator found that this explanation was "not remotely credible" and would "not be credited." In reaching this conclusion, the arbitrator emphasized that Bueno's explanation was undermined by both his failure to ask the other officer in his squad for assistance and the proximity of the police department to the parking garage, where officers could have assisted Bueno...

* * * *

Finally, with respect to the June 2009 incident, Bueno admitted that he pushed an arrestee after hearing that the latter had made vulgar comments about Bueno's daughter. The Union admitted that Bueno should not have pushed the arrestee, and the arbitrator found that Bueno's actions were "not necessary, not justified, and not intended to accomplish any police task." The arbitrator therefore determined that Bueno's conduct during this incident violated the general orders because he used unnecessary force and also failed report the incident.

Concluding that Bueno had engaged in misconduct, the arbitrator next assessed the Union's position that the City lacked just cause to discharge Bueno because either (1) he was subject to disparate treatment; (2) the City delayed action to discipline him: or (3) the Department condoned his conduct. The arbitrator ultimately agreed that Bueno's discharge was unjustified as a result of certain "due process considerations," namely, the City's delay in investigating the incidents and the Department's condonation of Bueno's conduct.

As to the City's delay in investigating the incidents, the arbitrator explained that it "may have resulted in the loss of pertinent video evidence of these incidents" that "might have been helpful to the Union's defense." Additionally, "witness memories may have faded during" the delay. As a result, the "delay may have prejudiced" the Union's defense, and the "City's discharge of the Grievant was procedurally flawed."

Regarding the Department's condonation of Bueno's conduct, the arbitrator found that members of the Department's command staff were aware of the use-of-force incidents yet did not initiate an investigation into his conduct. The command staff, he determined, "sen[t] a signal" that the conduct was acceptable. Because the Department essentially condoned Bueno's behavior, the arbitrator concluded that the City could not discharge him for just cause. Despite finding that the City could not discharge Bueno for his misconduct, the arbitrator nevertheless acknowledged that some discipline was warranted with respect to Bueno's unnecessary use of force, his failure to report the use of force, and his untruthfulness during the November 2011 investigation.

Based on these findings, the arbitrator determined that the appropriate remedy was to reinstate Bueno by June 3, 2013, as a full-time, paid police officer without back pay, benefits, or accumulated seniority for his time away from work; record his time away from work as a disciplinary suspension; and reinstate him on a "last chance" basis for a three-year period during which any "similar misconduct" by Bueno would entitle the City to immediately discharge him. Instead of reinstating Bueno, the City filed its motion to vacate the arbitration award in the circuit court on June 12, 2013. The circuit court granted the City's motion to vacate on December 13, 2013, agreeing with the City that the award violated public policy:

> "In the instant case, the statutes and cases presented by the City clearly state a public policy against police officers assaulting prisoners and lying about matters related to the specific duties of the officer. The arbitrator * * * * found that the grievant engaged in this egregious conduct but made no finding * * * that the grievant was likely not to do so again in the future. Thus, the Court finds that the [public policy] exception applies, and the arbitrator's order reinstating the grievant violated public policy."

In addition, the circuit court denied the Union's subsequent motion to remand the case to the arbitrator to make a factual finding concerning Bueno's likelihood to reoffend upon reinstatement. The Union timely appealed, and we have jurisdiction pursuant to Supreme Court Rule 303. Ill. S. Ct. R. 303 (eff. Jan. 1, 2015).

ANALYSIS

On appeal, the Union contends that the circuit court erred in vacating the arbitration award. The Union argues that the award of reinstatement did not violate public policy because there is no well-defined public policy that mandates termination of a police officer who engaged in misconduct involving unnecessary use of force, failure to report, or untruthfulness. Additionally, the Union maintains that public policy supports the award because the Department condoned the conduct, the City delayed its investigation of the incidents, and the City destroyed relevant video evidence that resulted in prejudice to Bueno's defense. In the alternative, the Union argues that the court erred in denying its motion to remand the cause to the arbitrator for additional findings concerning Bueno's likelihood to re-engage in the misconduct upon his reinstatement as a police officer under the terms of the award.

A. Public Policy Exception

*　*　*　*

The public policy analysis involves two steps: We must first determine "whether a well-defined and dominant public policy can be identified"; and if so, we then assess "whether the arbitrator's award, as reflected in his interpretation of the agreement, violated the public policy." This inquiry "is necessarily fact dependent"; however, the question of whether an award violates public policy is one of law, which we review de novo.

*　*　*　*

When the issue is properly framed, we find that the arbitration award here implicates a well-defined and dominant public policy, namely, the public policy against police officers unnecessarily using force against prisoners and being dishonest about that use of force during a subsequent investigation.

*　*　*　*

Turning to the second prong, we next must consider whether the arbitrator's award, i.e., reinstatement of Bueno as a police officer under the terms and conditions attached to his reinstatement, resulted in a violation of the established public policy of ensuring that law enforcement officers refrain from using unnecessary or unreasonable force, failing to report such incidents if they occur, and being untruthful during investigations of the incidents. The arbitrator found that Bueno unnecessarily used force against prisoners, failed to report the misconduct, and subsequently lied about his actions—conduct which contravenes public policies, poses physical danger to innocent third parties and exposes the City to liability. In AFSCME, our supreme court reiterated our obligation to ensure that an arbitration award does not threaten such dominant and well-defined public policies. AFSCME, 173 Ill. 2d at 333 ("[W]hen public policy is at issue, it is the court's responsibility to protect the public interest at stake."). What is not addressed in the award, however, is any finding by the arbitrator concerning the likelihood of recidivism, namely, whether Bueno is likely to engage in similar misconduct involving the use of force, reporting requirements or truthfulness following reinstatement as a police officer. Without such a finding, we do not have the necessary information to conclude that the arbitration award contravenes public policy. If the arbitrator had entered his award based on a "rational finding" that Bueno is unlikely to engage in the offending conduct upon reinstatement, the court "would be obliged to affirm the award." But here, as the Union concedes, the arbitrator never made an express finding on this point. Although authority supports the position that an implicit finding may suffice, we find the award ambiguous on this point.

* * * *

C. Destruction of Video Evidence and D. Completeness of the Arbitration
   Award (omitted)

* * * *

Here, we find that the award is incomplete, or at least ambiguous, as it does not include any findings from which we can reasonably infer that the arbitrator found Bueno was unlikely to reengage in the offending conduct upon his reinstatement. Without such findings, we are unable to fully assess the public policy implications of Bueno's reemployment as a City police officer. Accordingly, we find that a remand to the circuit court to further remand the cause to the arbitrator with instructions to clarify the award is appropriate.

The City's arguments to the contrary are not persuasive. According to the City, the award is not incomplete—and, therefore, a remand is not necessary—because the arbitrator lacked the authority to address Bueno's amenability to rehabilitation. That issue, the City maintains, went "beyond the scope of the stipulated questions that were submitted to the Arbitrator." We disagree.* * *

CONCLUSION

For the above reasons, we reverse and remand to the circuit court with directions to remand the cause to the arbitrator, consistent with this opinion, for the limited purpose of issuing a finding, based on the record, as to whether Bueno is likely to engage in similar misconduct upon reinstatement.

Reversed and remanded.

JUSTICE PIERCE, dissenting.

* * * *

I respectfully disagree with the majority decision to remand this matter to the arbitrator for findings regarding whether Officer Bueno is likely to reoffend. There is no requirement that an arbitrator use specific words or phrase in an order of reinstatement where there is a finding the employee has violated public policy. I would find that a commonsense reading of the detailed award clearly demonstrates the arbitrator implicitly found that Officer Bueno was amenable to rehabilitation and is unlikely to reoffend. The arbitrator noted Officer Bueno's otherwise favorable work history and the mitigating circumstances justifying reinstatement after imposition of substantial penalties. The award penalized the officer by treating his time off as an unpaid 14-month disciplinary suspension without benefits and without seniority accruals, the reinstatement was subject to a three-year "last chance agreement" under the collective bargaining agreement where any future misconduct would be a dischargeable offense and the arbitrator himself retained jurisdiction over the officer during the three-year period. Lastly, the arbitrator gave the City the option of providing additional use of force training to Officer Bueno which, in my view, is further support for the conclusion that there was an implicit finding of an unlikelihood of repeat conduct.

Simply stated, the arbitrator would not have conditioned reinstatement and given the City the option to provide additional training if he found, explicitly or implicitly, a likely risk of further misconduct. We have previously found that "[i]f it is clear from the award that the arbitrator made a rational finding that an employee could capably return to and perform his duties without impinging or undermining the public policy and without posing a risk to public safety and welfare and that the employee will refrain from the misconduct, the court is obligated to affirm the award." *AFSCME II*, 321 Ill. App. 3d at 1043. In my view, the remedy in this award demonstrates an implicit finding by the arbitrator that Officer Bueno can capably return to and perform his duties without undermining public policy or posing a risk to public safety or welfare.

I have little doubt that, on remand, the arbitrator will find that officer Bueno is unlikely to re-offend, the City will again seek vacation of the award by requesting the court to substitute its judgment for that of the arbitrator which, again, a court cannot do. I would affirm this arbitral award, not because we agree with the decision, but because we are bound to follow established law regarding the deference given to arbitration awards based on a collective bargaining agreement. I respectfully dissent.

APPLICATION AND DISCUSSION QUESTIONS

Based on the Court's rules on vacating an award, how would you respond to the following questions?

1. When will the court vacate an arbitration award based on common law principles?

2. What reasoning did the Court of Appeals provide to support its conclusion?

3. What is the two-prong test to determine whether the award violated public policy?

4. What were the major arguments that the award did not violate public policy?

5. What is the well-defined public policy that the court states violates public policy?

6. Do you agree with the dissent, it was not necessary to remand the case back to the arbitrator?

There has been an increase in the number of cases where the parties have asked the courts to set side an arbitrator's award based on public policy. The following is a sample of cases where the courts have reviewed the impact of public policy on an arbitrator's award. As you review these cases identify the public policy at issue and determine whether there was sufficient evidence to support a claim that the award violated such a policy.

SUMMARY OF CASES ON JUDICIAL REVIEW

BOEHRINGER INGELHEIM VETMEDICA, INC. V. UNITED FOOD & COMMERCIAL WORKERS,
739 F.3D 1136 (8TH CIR. 2014) (FALSIFYING WORK RECORDS).

The dispute arose when BIVI discharged a Lab Technician for falsifying work records. The Union grieved the discharge, and BIVI and the Union then submitted the dispute to arbitration. The arbitrator concluded, BIVI "in assessing the discipline did not give sufficient consideration to the circumstances of the case." The arbitrator partially sustained the grievance, reinstating the technician with unbroken seniority but denying back pay. The Employer brought an action to vacate the award. The court stated that "it will give substantial deference to labor arbitration awards; however, the arbitrator may not ignore the plain language of the contract, but as long as the arbitrator is even arguably construing or applying the contract and acting within the scope of his authority, that a court is convinced he committed serious error does not suffice to overturn his decision." The court also held that 'an employer's failure to raise a public policy issue at the arbitration hearing will likely be fatal." Additionally, the court held that "BIVI did not make a factual and legal showing required for the court to invoke the narrow public policy exemption and vacate an arbitration award that fully acknowledge the technician's misconduct. The judgment of the district court was affirmed.

LOCAL 342 V. TOWN OF HUNTINGTON, 2012 N.Y. MISC. LEXIS 2298,

2012 NY SLIP OP. 31268U. (PHYSICAL ALTERCATION)

Former employee engaged in a physical altercation while on the job. During the investigation, employee filed a grievance on the basis that the Town did not provide him with an attorney. The CBA states that the employer should provide legal counsel to defend employee as a result of assault while in the scope of employment. The court found the Town's arguments unconvincing, and confirmed the arbitrator's decision and award, holding that it did not violate any strong public policy, nor was the award totally irrational.

DECATUR POLICE BENEVOLENT AND PROTECTIVE ASS'N LABOR COMMITTEE V. CITY OF DECATUR,

2012 IL APP (4TH) 110764, 360 ILL. DEC. 256 (2012).
(DOMESTIC BATTERY)[VACATED].

Police officer was discharged after allegations of domestic battery and subsequent untruthfulness about the alleged incident. The trial court vacated the arbitrator's award of employee reinstatement. The Fourth District Appellate Court of Illinois affirmed the trial court, and held the arbitration award violated the strong public policies against domestic violence, and truthfulness of police officers during investigations.

CITY OF HARTF ORD V. HARTFORD MUN. EMPLOYEES ASS'N,

134 CONN.APP. 559, 39 A.3D 1146 (2012). [EMPLOYEE MISCONDUCT].

Employee was terminated from her supervisory position in a tax collector's office. The Appellate Court of Connecticut reversed and remanded the Superior Court's decision to vacate the arbitrator's award, which reduced disciplinary sanctions and ordered reinstatement. The appellate court reasoned that the arbitrator's award did not violate public policy. The arbitrators found employee to be grossly negligent, but also found mitigating circumstances such as employer's lack of written policies and procedures. The appellate court concluded that the employee's conduct "did not rise to the level of apparent and egregious misconduct" to support vacating the award.

CHICAGO TRANSIT AUTHORITY V. AMALGAMATED TRANSIT UNION, LOCAL 241,

399 III.APP.3D 689, 339 ILL.DEC. 444 (2010). SEXUAL ABUSE][VACATED]

Bus driver was terminated from his position after it was discovered he had been convicted of aggravated criminal sexual abuse of his 12-year old daughter. The arbitrator's award reinstated the bus driver, and the Transit Authority sought to vacate award. The trial court granted summary judgment to the Union, and the transit authority appealed. The First District Appellate Court of Illinois reversed the trial court, and held that "public policies existed in favor of the safe and secure transportation of the public, including children, and the protection of the public, especially juveniles, from convicted sex offenders; and the labor arbitrator's reinstatement of the bus driver violated public policy."

STATE V. CONNECTICUT STATE EMPLOYEES ASS'N,

287 CONN. 258, 947 A.2D 928 (2008). WORKPLACE DISPUTE].

Corrections officer sought a transfer to a different corrections facility, and engaged in a romantic relationship (which turned violent) with an employee of the new facility. The State unilaterally removed the corrections officer from the transfer list. The arbitrator awarded the corrections officer's transfer to his desired facility. The trial court held that the award did not "violate public policy" nor was "in manifest disregard of the law." The Supreme Court of Connecticut affirmed all of the above, also holding that the State failed to demonstrate the award violated public policy against workplace violence and sexual harassment, therefore, vacation of award was not required.

LAKE COUNTY FOREST PRESERVE DISTRICT V. LLLINOIS FRATERNAL ORDER OF POLICE,

2012 ILL.APP. 2D. 110280U (2012) DISOBEDIENT EMPLOYEE).

Police officer was terminated after leaving his post without permission, and was later inconsistent in his statements about his conduct. The trial court erroneously vacated an arbitration award that reinstated the officer, because the district did not demonstrate the existence of a clear and dominant public policy. The district tried to identify the public policy in terms of employing a mendacious and disobedient officer. However, the court rejects this argument.

SEXUAL HARASSMENT ISSUES

BETHEL PARK SCHOOL DIST. V. BETHEL PARK FEDERATION OF TEACHERS, LOCAL 1607

55 A.3D 154, 193 L.R.R.M. (BNA) 3597(2012)

OPINION BY Judge COVEY.

Bethel Park Federation of Teachers, Local 1607, American Federation of Teachers, and AFL–CIO (collectively, Federation) appeal the Allegheny County Court of Common Pleas' (trial court) August 4, 2011 order vacating the Arbitrator's award and affirming the Bethel Park School District's (District) decision to terminate Michael W. Lehotsky's (Grievant) employment. There are two issues before the Court: (1) whether the Arbitrator's award was rationally derived from the collective bargaining agreement, i.e., whether it met the essence test; and (2) whether the Arbitrator's award should have been vacated under the public policy exception to the essence test. We affirm.

Grievant has been employed by the District as a seventh grade mathematics teacher since 1991. The District alleges that although Grievant performed satisfactorily early in his career, more recently, his conduct has become unacceptable. Since approximately 2003, Grievant has engaged in various forms of misconduct which have resulted in disciplinary proceedings or formal improvement plans. During the 2008–2009 school year, parents and students reported to the District that Grievant was engaging in unwelcome contact with seventh grade female students which included holding their hands, and/or rubbing their backs or legs when he would assist them.

Before the 2009–2010 school year began, the District required Grievant to be evaluated by psychiatrists to determine whether and under what conditions he could safely return to the classroom. Among the psychiatric experts' recommendations was that Grievant should not have any contact with students outside of a structured classroom setting. In addition to his five teaching periods per day, Grievant had historically conducted a math lab, also known as "Lunch and Learn." During math lab, students with questions could bring their lunches to the classroom and obtain additional assistance, complete assignments that they had missed, or retake tests. The improvement plan prohibited Grievant from conducting a math lab and from contacting students outside of the structured classroom setting. Grievant defied those directives. He met with students during lunch in other teachers' classrooms, continued to have physical contact with them, and engaged in other unacceptable conduct, including making death threats against members of the administration. Because Grievant did not meet the improvement plan conditions, the District concluded that he could not remain employed as a teacher in the District.

By letter dated November 24, 2009, the District's Board of Directors informed Grievant of its intention to discharge him from his employment for violating provisions of Pennsylvania's Public School Code of 1949, as well as the District's own policies prohibiting sexual harassment. The November 24, 2009 correspondence also charged Grievant with unprofessionalism because of his conduct toward colleagues and administrators. The correspondence informed Grievant of his right to a hearing before the Board of Directors to determine whether the charges were substantiated or, in the alternative, to challenge his proposed dismissal through the contractual grievance and arbitration procedure.

On December 2, 2009, the Federation informed the District that Grievant preferred to challenge any proposed action through the contractual grievance and arbitration procedure and, on that same date, the Federation submitted a formal grievance on Grievant's behalf, asserting that he was suspended and dismissed from his employment without just cause, in violation of Article 7 of the collective bargaining agreement (CBA). Because the parties were unable to resolve their dispute through the preliminary stages of the grievance procedure set forth in the CBA, the matter was referred to an Arbitrator for full, final and binding resolution.

Hearings were held on June 30, July 1, August 10, August 12, August 25, August 31, September 14, September 28, and October 18, 2010. On February 10, 2011, the Arbitrator sustained the grievance in part. The Arbitrator directed that Grievant's employment discharge be set aside and that he be restored to compensated status, without loss of seniority, effective on the date of the award. The award specified that the time between Grievant's November 2009 suspension and his reinstatement to payroll status is to be regarded as an unpaid, disciplinary suspension. The Arbitrator's award further directed the District to begin compensating Grievant at the rate contemplated by the CBA, effective as of the date of the award. The award allowed the District to delay returning Grievant to classroom teaching until the next academic year, if reinstatement at that time would disrupt the educational process. Between the date of the Arbitration award and Grievant's reinstatement to teaching duties, he could be assigned alternative duties, subject to any limitations in the CBA. According to the award, any time between Grievant's return to compensated status and his return to active duty shall be regarded as paid administrative leave without disciplinary consequences. Upon reinstatement to active teaching duties, Grievant was to be subject to the September 14, 2009 teacher improvement plan, unless the parties mutually agree on alternative conditions for his reinstatement. The Federation's remaining claims for relief, including back pay and benefits were denied because, as stated by the Arbitrator, "persuasive evidence establishes that the Grievant is guilty of grievous misconduct which would ordinarily warrant discharge .... [and] so long as he persisted in his behavior, the Grievant was unfit to teach." Reproduced Record (R.R.) at 35a–36a. The District appealed to the trial court. On August 4, 2011, the trial court vacated the Arbitrator's award and affirmed the District's decision to terminate Grievant's employment. The Federation appealed to this Court.

The Federation first argues that the Arbitrator's award should be upheld because it draws its essence from the CBA. Specifically, the Federation contends that the award is within the terms of, and rationally derived from, the CBA. We disagree.

* * * *

The issue before the Arbitrator in the instant matter was whether Grievant was discharged for just cause. Article 7 of the CBA specifically states: "No professional employee shall be disciplined, reprimanded, reduced in rank or compensation without just cause." R.R. at 48a. The issue, therefore, is within the CBA's terms. Accordingly, both parties agree that the Arbitrator's award meets the first prong of the essence test.

Concerning the second prong of the essence test, the Federation argues that because just cause is not defined in the CBA, pursuant to *Office of Attorney General v. Council 13, American Federation of State, County Municipal Employees, AFL–CIO,* 577 Pa. 257, 844 A.2d 1217 (2004), the Arbitrator was within his authority to define it. Thus, the Federation contends the award is rationally derived from the CBA. The District, on the other hand, argues that the Arbitrator based his award on a due process procedure outlined in the District's Unlawful Harassment Policy which is not part of the CBA; hence, the award does not meet the second prong of the essence test. We agree with the District.

We recognize that the *Attorney General* Court held:

By failing to agree upon and incorporate a definition of just cause into the collective bargaining agreement, and by casting the arbitrator into the role of resolving disputes arising under the collective bargaining agreement, we believe that it is clear that the parties intended for the arbitrator to have the authority to interpret the terms of the agreement, including the undefined term 'just cause' and to determine whether there was just cause for discharge in this particular case.

However, in this case, the Arbitrator did not reinstate Grievant based on a finding that the District did not prove just cause to discharge him. Instead, the Arbitrator specifically stated: "Grievant has not been spared discharge because he is not guilty, but because the District violated significant due process rights in conducting its investigation." R.R. at 36a. The only due process clause in the CBA is Article 12, which essentially provides that, before a teacher can be summoned to a meeting that may result in discipline, he must receive notice in writing and have the opportunity to have a representative of the Federation accompany him. *See* R.R. at 80a–81a. It is undisputed that the CBA does not contain a due process procedure for responding to sexual harassment complaints. As such, the Arbitrator clearly went outside the CBA in making his determination.

The essential requirements of due process ... are notice and an opportunity to respond. The opportunity to present reasons, either in person or in writing, why proposed action should not be taken is a fundamental due process requirement. The tenured public employee is entitled to oral or written notice of the charges against him, an explanation of the employer's evidence, and an opportunity to present his side of the story. To require more than this prior to termination would intrude to an unwarranted extent on the government's interest in quickly removing an unsatisfactory employee.

* * * *

Finally, even if the Arbitrator's award satisfied the essence test, the trial court properly vacated the award on the basis that it violates the well-defined and established public policy of protecting students from sexual harassment during school hours, on school property. The district has a specific policy against Unlawful Harassment, which provides that "it shall be the policy of the [D]istrict to maintain an educational environment in which harassment in any form is not tolerated. R.R. at 66a. Harassment for purposes of the policy includes "sexual harassment" and includes "physical conduct" and "touching" 6 R.R. at 66a.-67a.

The District's Unlawful Harassment Policy cites as its authority: Title IX of the Civil Rights Act of 1964, 20 U.S.C. § 1681, and the Pennsylvania Human Relations Act.7 Notwithstanding that the Arbitrator did not make an express ruling finding Grievant guilty of sexual harassment, his findings leave no doubt that Grievant, an adult male in power over the seventh grade female students, persisted in unwelcome inappropriate touching during the performance of academic work which made the seventh grade female students uncomfortable.

The Arbitrator specifically stated "there appears to be sufficient evidence that some inappropriate touching occurred.... A number of female students reported to the principal and the assistant principal that the Grievant had made them uncomfortable when he assisted them with classroom assignments. They testified that the Grievant would either hold their hands for protracted periods of time or would caress their backs, necks and shoulders." R.R. at 26a–27a (emphasis added). The Arbitrator in finding the female students credible concluded that "persuasive evidence establishes that grievant is guilty of grievous misconduct which would ordinarily warrant discharge." R.R. at 35a (emphasis added). The Arbitrator continued: "Grievant has not been spared discharge because he is not guilty...." R.R. at 36a (emphasis added).

* * * *

The instant case, however, is exactly that case. The Arbitrator's award reinstating Grievant to the classroom after finding that he was guilty of inappropriately touching seventh grade female students during academic lessons unequivocally violates public policy as pronounced in Title IX of the Civil Rights Act, the Federal Civil Rights Act,9 the Pennsylvania Human Relations Act, as well as the District's zero-tolerance sexual harassment policy. In addition, the likelihood of Grievant's "grievous misconduct" continuing, and thus placing the safety and well-being of the seventh grade female students in jeopardy, was well founded by the Arbitrator, wherein he stated:

Because the Grievant had been repeatedly and unequivocally cautioned that he must refrain from physical contact with students.... The Grievant's insubordinate contact was compounded by his refusal to respect supervisory directive that he not meet with students during lunchtime.... The Grievant was not to meet with students during extracurricular activities or school events and he knew or should have known that lunchtime contact with students in any context was a violation of his improvement plan. The Grievant was not attempting to conscientiously comply with the plan, but attempting to evade its restrictions.

Thus, *Westmoreland* applies, and the trial court properly vacated the Arbitrator's award.

For all of the above reasons, the trial court's order is affirmed.

* * * *

CONCURRING OPINION BY Senior Judge FRIEDMAN. (Omitted)

[Also see, Philadelphia Housing Authority v. American Federation of State, County, and Municipal Employees, District Council 33, local 934, 956 A. 2d 477 (2008) (Vacated on same principles).

APPLICATION AND DISCUSSION QUESTIONS

1. Should the arbitrator discuss the public policy exception if the employer never raises the argument or only mentions it without supporting evidence?

2. The following cases involve claims of sexual harassment and the public policy principle. Should the arbitrator's decision be vacated? Explain your position in each case:

SUMMARY OF CASES ON SEXUAL HARASSMENT AND PUBLIC POLICY

STATE V. AFSCME, COUNCIL 4, LOCAL, 69 A. 3D 927 (2013) [VACATED].

The grievant was fired for engaging in an open pattern of sexual harassment in knowing violation of the administrative directive of his employer, the Department of Correction (DOC)An arbitrator found that the grievant's dismissal was not for just cause and reduced the dismissal to a one-year suspension without pay or benefits. The intermediate appellate court held that the trial court correctly vacated the arbitration award on the ground that it violated the public policy against workplace sexual harassment. The high court agreed. The state statute explicitly indicated that the maintenance of a hostile work environment constituted sexual harassment and was prohibited by the laws of Connecticut. Therefore, the arbitrator's interpretation of the ²just cause² provision of the collective bargaining agreement as barring the grievant's dismissal for sexual harassment violated a clearly established public policy against sexual harassment in the workplace.

CITY OF SAN JOSE V. INTERNATIONAL ASSOCIATION OF FIREFIGHTERS,

2010 CAL. APP. UNPUB. LEXIS 8812; 110 FAIR EMPL. PRAC. CAS. (BNA) 1477.

(SEXUAL HARASSMENT)

Fire inspector was discharged by the City for sexually harassing his co-workers. Even though the accusations were substantiated, arbitrator found the City failed to implement progressive discipline, and thus awarded reinstatement. The appellate court upheld the trial court's affirmation of the arbitration award, holding there were no public policy grounds for vacating. The court stated, "Although there is a well-defined public policy against sexual harassment in the workplace, that policy does not mandate automatic discharge of an offending employee, particularly where, as here, the discharge violates progressive discipline principles reflected in the governing labor agreement and the employer's own policies."

CITY OF RICHMOND V. SERVICE EMPLOYEES INTERN.UNION, LOCAL 1021,

189 CAL. APP. 4TH 663, 118 CAL. RPTR. 3D 315 (2010)

(SEXUAL HARASSMENT).

City employee was terminated based on alleged sexual harassment claims by a subordinate. The labor arbitrator awarded reinstatement, holding the claims were time-barred. The superior court vacated the award on the grounds of public policy against sexual harassment. The court of appeal reversed and remanded, holding that the arbitrator did not violate public policy, as the City failed to implement disciplinary action on the sexual harassment claims during the CBA's imposed time limit of 6 months.

SUMMARY OF RULES ON JUDICIAL REVIEW

· Courts will give "considerable deference" to arbitrator's awards, but willing to vacate awards, if the decision clearly and specifically violates an identifiable public policy.

- Public policy can be based on a statute or common law, but the court insists on evidence of a specific violation of public policy. Broad allegations of a violation are insufficient.

- Courts continue to follow a two-step test in public policy challenges: (1) is there a "well-defined and dominant policy?" and (2) did the award violate the policy?

- The public policy exception to enforcing an arbitration award is very narrow. In cases of sexual harassment, it appears that court will find that the prevention and correction of sexual harassment is a well defined and a dominant policy; thus reinstating an individual who has violated such policies may be cause to vacate the award. (There are similar rules on domestic violence).

- If the employer fail to raise the public policy exception during the arbitration hearing, the court may not permit the argument to be raised in court. [One court of appeals says it can be raised-[see above].

B. Challenges Based On Claims That The Arbitrator Exceeded Their Powers

OAKWOOD HEALTHCARE, INC. V. OAKWOOD HOSPITAL EMPLOYEES, LOCAL 2568

2014 U. S. DIST. LEXIS 107089 (2014)

JUDITH E. LEVY, District Judge.

This is a labor union arbitration case that is before the Court on plaintiff Oakwood Healthcare, Inc.'s motion to vacate an arbitration award.

I. Background

Plaintiff employed Shannon "Ken" Curry, and at the time of his termination he was employed as a Dietary Assistant II. Curry's duties included cleaning the hospital kitchen, in which food was prepared for patients, visitors, and employees. The employment relationship was governed by a Collective Bargaining Agreement ("Oakwood CBA") (and Employee Work Rules issued pursuant to the Oakwood CBA.

A. July 16, 2012 Incident, Termination, and Arbitration

On July 16, 2012, one of plaintiff's cooks, Robert Ebbing, spilled potatoes on the hospital kitchen floor and then left the area to bring food to an event. Curry swept the potatoes up along with some other debris from the kitchen floor and placed the waste on a sanitary food preparation table. He did this two successive times. The incident was captured on a video, which was later shown to Curry after he denied putting any debris on the table. Plaintiff suspended Curry pending investigation on July 30, 2012. Curry was found to have violated Major Work Rule 17 of the Employee Work Rules by failing "to fulfill the responsibilities of the job to an extent that might reasonably or does cause injury to a patient, visitor or another employee." The penalty for a Major Work Rule violation is either a three-or five-day suspension, or termination. Plaintiff conducted an investigation of the incident and based on the outcome of the investigation, Curry was discharged on August 6, 2012.

Curry was a member of a union, AFSCME Local 2568, and the union filed a grievance on Curry's behalf. On July 26, 2013, an arbitration hearing was held pursuant to the Oakwood CBA. On October 25, 2013, the arbitrator issued his opinion and award, in which he agreed with plaintiff that Curry had violated a Major Work Rule. The arbitrator set forth his reasons, stating that "what Mr. Curry did on July 16, 2012 is just unacceptable to say the least. And then, in the view of this Arbitrator, he aggravated the situation by accusing Mr. Ebbing of using the N word, which did not happen, and further aggravated [sic] by claiming that the words that were used caused him to react when in fact his actions took place for the most part before any statements were made to Curry."

Despite finding that Curry had violated Major Work Rule 17, the arbitrator ordered Curry reinstated with full seniority and a 15–month suspension due to "mitigating factors" which he took into consideration based upon the Oakwood CBA's just cause standard. Those factors included Curry's ten years of seniority, a positive performance evaluation, and two certificates of appreciation. The arbitrator also determined that plaintiff, at its discretion, may require Curry to attend an anger management program sponsored by the Hospital's Employee Assistance Program.

Instead of implementing the arbitrator's award, plaintiff filed suit in this Court on November 18, 2013, and filed this motion to vacate the arbitrator's award on April 25, 2014. Oral argument was held on July 14, 2014, and the case is now ready for decision.

B. Relevant Language From the Oakwood CBA and Work Rules Section 3.2, Step 4(c) of the Oakwood CBA:

The arbitrator shall not have jurisdiction to add to, subtract from, or modify any of the terms of this Agreement ... or to substitute discretion for that of any of the parties hereto or to exercise any of their functions or responsibilities.

Section 4.1(a) of the Oakwood CBA:

The Employer has the right to employ any person who is satisfactory to the Employer, and also to discharge or discipline a seniority employee for just and proper cause. The principle of progressive discipline is recognized except in cases of serious offenses justifying immediate discharge.

Section 8.1 of the Oakwood CBA:

The Employer retains the sole right and shall have a free hand to manage and operate its Hospital, subject only to the condition that it shall not do so in any manner which is inconsistent with this Agreement.... The Employer also shall have the right to make at any time and to enforce any rules and regulations which it considers necessary or advisable for the safe, effective, and efficient operation of the Employer so long as such rules and regulations are not inconsistent herewith, and any employee who violates or fails to comply therewith may be subject to discipline, and may have recourse to the Grievance Procedure of this Agreement in the event the employee feels aggrieved by such discipline.

Employee Work Rules, Procedures for Major Infractions:

Infractions of a major nature will result in corrective action that may begin with Step 4, a 3 or 5 Day Suspension or may result in immediate Termination, Step 5.

II. Analysis

Plaintiff argues that under the plain language of the Oakwood CBA, it had the sole discretion to discipline or discharge employees who commit a major infraction, and that the Oakwood CBA did not give the arbitrator jurisdiction to determine whether the employer's exercise of discretion in deciding between a suspension or termination meets the standard for just cause.

The standard for vacating an arbitrator's award is a very high one. So long as "an arbitrator is even arguably construing or applying the contract and acting within the scope of his authority, the fact that a court is convinced he committed serious error does not suffice to overturn his decision." *Totes Isotoner Corp. v. Int'l Chem. Workers Union Council/UCFW Local 664C*, 532 F.3d 405, 411 (6th Cir.2008) (quoting *Major League Baseball Players Assoc. v. Garvey*, 532 U.S. 504, 509, 121 S.Ct. 1724, 149 L.Ed.2d 740 (2001)). The arbitrator's award, however, "must draw its essence from the contract and cannot simply reflect the arbitrator's own notions of industrial justice." *United Paperworkers Int'l Union, AFL–CIO v. Misco, Inc.*, 484 U.S. 29, 38, 108 S.Ct. 364, 98 L.Ed.2d 286 (1987).

The Sixth Circuit uses a "procedural aberration" standard on a motion to vacate an arbitration award to determine whether an arbitrator acted outside the scope of his or her authority. An award may only be overturned when the Court answers one of the following questions in the affirmative:

1) Did the arbitrator act "outside his authority" by resolving a dispute not committed to arbitration?

2) Did the arbitrator commit fraud, have a conflict of interest or otherwise act dishonestly in issuing the award?

3) In resolving any legal or factual disputes in the case, was the arbitrator not "arguably construing or applying the contract"? *Mich. Family Res., Inc. v. Serv. Emp. Int'l Union Local 517M*, 475 F.3d 746, 753 (6th Cir.2007). "So long as the arbitrator does not offend any of these requirements, the request for judicial intervention should be resisted even though the arbitrator made serious, improvident or silly errors in resolving the merits of the dispute." Id. (internal quotation marks omitted).

The dispute in this case is ultimately over how to read Sections 4.1(a) and 8.1 of the Oakwood CBA in harmony with Section 3.2, Step 4(c) and the Procedures for

Major Infractions. Section 4.1(a) grants the employer the right to "discharge or discipline a seniority employee for just and proper cause." Section 8.1 also grants the employer "the right to make at any time and to enforce any rules and regulations which it considers necessary or advisable for the safe, effective, and efficient operation of the Employer so long as such rules and regulations are not inconsistent herewith." Section 3.2, Step 4(c) creates a jurisdictional bar preventing the arbitrator from "substitut[ing] discretion for that of any of the parties hereto or … exercise[ing] any of their functions or responsibilities."

It is undisputed that the arbitrator had authority to determine whether Curry committed a major infraction of the rules worthy of discipline or discharge. Plaintiff, however, argues that the arbitrator's authority ended there, and that plaintiff had the sole discretion to determine Curry's punishment, supported by Sections 3.2, Step 4(c) and 8.1, the Employee Work Rules, and the Procedures for Major Infractions. By determining whether just and proper cause existed for the employer to enforce its chosen discipline for an "infraction of a major nature", the plaintiff argues that the arbitrator acted outside of his authority by resolving a dispute not committed to arbitration, and was not arguably construing or applying the contract.

Defendant argues that the phrase "just and proper cause" is ambiguous, and that by evaluating the chosen discipline, the arbitrator was, at the very least, arguably construing and applying the contract. Further, the defendant argues that whenever a range of punishments is available, the determination over which punishment is appropriate is properly committed to the arbitrator to determine.

The Sixth Circuit has determined that where collective bargaining agreements commit the right to discipline and discharge solely to employers, arbitrators overstep their authority when they substitute their discretion for that of the employer. (Citation omitted); *Accord Int'l B'hood of Elec. Workers, Local 429 v. Toshiba Am., Inc.,* 879 F.2d 208 (6th Cir.1989) (holding that once union stipulated that an employee committed a dischargeable offense, arbitrator lacked authority under the contract to overturn the employer's decision to discharge employee for just cause); see also *SEIU Healthcare Michigan v. St. Mary's Acquisition Co., Inc.,* 09–13215, 2010 WL 2232218 (E.D.Mich. May 27, 2010).

126

The overarching rule of these cases is that where the collective bargaining agreement is unclear or ambiguous as to whether the arbitrator has the authority to determine the appropriate discipline, as in *Eberhard* or *Dixie*, the arbitrator has unquestioned authority to act in the ambiguous space. However, if the collective bargaining agreement clearly prohibits the arbitrator from considering a matter, as in *Amanda Bolt, Morgan,* and *International Brotherhood,* the arbitrator oversteps his or her authority if he or she alters the employer's chosen remedy.

This case is similar to International Brotherhood. There, the arbitrator had unquestioned jurisdiction to determine whether employees were terminated for just cause and found that the employer had just cause to terminate the employees, but he ordered the employees reinstated. The collective bargaining agreement stated that "[a]ny disciplinary action, including discharge taken as a result of the violation of [the no-strike clause] ... shall not be altered or amended in the grievance and arbitration procedures[.]"The collective bargaining agreement clearly stated that all disciplinary actions were removed from the arbitrator's jurisdiction, and the arbitrator was found to have overstepped his authority by reconsidering the employer's decision on discipline.

Here, Section 4.1(a) of the Oakwood CBA grants the employer the discretion to discharge or discipline a seniority employee (which Curry was) for just and proper cause. Section 8.1 of the Oakwood CBA grants the employer the right to make and enforce rules and regulations giving rise to discipline, so long as those rules are not inconsistent with the Oakwood CBA. The Employee Work Rules were issued pursuant to Section 8.1. Critically, Section 3.2, Step 4(c) expressly prohibits the arbitrator from substituting his or her discretion for that of any of the parties to the Oakwood CBA, or from exercising any of the parties' functions or responsibilities. Finally, the applicable work rule regarding the "Procedures for Major Infractions" gives the employer the discretion to suspend or terminate an employee who is found to have engaged in an "infraction of a major nature".

This case is distinguishable from both Eberhard and Dixie Warehouse. In both of those cases, the collective bargaining agreements committed to the arbitrator the issue of whether employees were discharged for just cause, and afforded sole discretion to the employer to discharge employees. However, unlike the Oakwood CBA and the collective bargaining agreement in International Brotherhood, those agreements did not restrict the arbitrator's jurisdiction over the employer's discharge decisions.

The language of the Oakwood CBA is "sufficiently clear so as to deny the arbitrator the authority to interpret the agreement as he did." The defendant is correct that the phrase "just and proper cause" is itself ambiguous, and that the arbitrator may determine the meaning of that phrase under the Oakwood CBA. That, however, is not the issue in this case. The issue in this case is whether the arbitrator had jurisdiction over the employer's exercise of discretion in disciplining Curry once he determined that Curry had engaged in an infraction of a major nature such that he could apply the "just and proper cause" standard to the employer's discretionary disciplinary decisions. The Court holds that this exercise of jurisdiction was outside of the arbitrator's authority.

The arbitrator's jurisdiction under the Oakwood CBA ends at the point he determines there is just cause for the employer to exercise its discretion, and he is barred by the plain language of the Oakwood CBA from substituting his discretion for the employer's to reflect his own notion of "industrial justice." The arbitrator did so here, and as a result, the Court is required to vacate the arbitrator's award of reinstatement.

Plaintiff also argues that the arbitrator's reinstatement of Curry violated an explicit public policy providing for sanitary food preparation areas, and so should also be vacated on that ground. See *W.R. Grace & Co. v. Local Union 759*, 461 U.S. 757, 766, 103 S.Ct. 2177, 76 L.Ed.2d 298 (1983); *Shelby Cnty. Health Care Corp. v. Am. Fed. of State, Cnty. & Mun. Emps. Local 1733*, 967 F.2d 1091, 1095 (6th Cir.1992). In support of this argument, plaintiff cites a series of state and federal statutes and regulations whose collective purpose is to prevent contamination of the food preparation process in various facilities. Because the Court is vacating the arbitration award on jurisdictional grounds, it does not reach the issue of whether Curry's reinstatement violated public policy.

III. Conclusion

For the reasons stated above, the Court determines that the Oakwood CBA did not grant the arbitrator jurisdiction over disciplinary and discharge decisions reserved solely for the employer once he determined that Curry had violated Major Work Rule 17 and had therefore engaged in an "infraction of a major nature."

Accordingly, Plaintiff's motion to vacate the arbitration award is GRANTED; and the arbitration award is HEREBY VACATED.

IT IS SO ORDERED.

APPLICATION AND DISCUSSION QUESTIONS

1. What factors did the arbitrator consider in mitigating the penalty from termination to a 15-month suspension?

2. *In Mich. Family Res., Inc. v. Service Employer Int'l Union Local*, 517M, 475 F.3d 746 (6th Cir. 2000), the Sixth Circuit uses a "procedural aberration"

standard in determining whether to vacate an arbitration award. What are those factors?

3. This is a case where the arbitrator has authority to determine whether the employee has committed a major infraction of the work rules which could lead to discipline. However, another section of the CBA gives the employer "sole discretion in determining the appropriate discipline". The Court made it clear that if the CBA is ambiguous as to the arbitrator's authority in determining discipline, the arbitrator has authority to determine whether discipline is appropriate.

SCHLAGE LOCK COMPANY LLC V. UNITED STEELWORKERS AFL-CIO, LOCAL NO. 7697,

202 L.R.R.M. 3058 (S.D. OHIO, 2014)

Sandra S. Beckwith, Senior United States District Judge.

ORDER

Plaintiff, Schlage Lock Company filed this lawsuit seeking to vacate an arbitration award in favor of Defendant, United Steelworkers AFL-CIO, Local 7697. The arbitration grew out of the termination of two Schlage employees, Saal and Smith, who were involved in a physical altercation at work. Both employees were terminated for violating Schlage's work rules. The Union sought arbitration over Saal's discharge; Saal is Caucasian. It did not seek arbitration on behalf of Smith, an African-American employee. After a hearing, the arbitrator ordered that Saal be returned to work but without back pay or restoration of seniority.

Schlage's complaint alleges that the award should be vacated because the arbitrator exceeded his authority in ordering Saal's reinstatement without back pay, and because the award violates public policy. The parties have submitted cross-motions seeking entry of judgment on the arbitration record. For the following reasons, the Court will grant the Union's motion and will deny Schlage's motion.

Background

The relevant facts established by the record are that Saal worked for Schlage (and its predecessor, Steelcraft Manufacturing) for approximately 16 years. Smith worked at the plant for about 7 years. Saal and Smith were apparently on friendly terms, and had spoken to each other earlier the day of the incident (May 31, 2012). Saal had agreed to take Smith after work to pick up some furniture using Saal's truck.

Just before noon that day, Saal was walking by Smith's work area; their stories about what happened next were quite different. Saal claimed that Smith suddenly turned and punched him in the mouth for no reason whatsoever. Saal denied touching or saying anything to Smith, and could not explain why Smith would punch him with no reason. Smith claimed that Saal "grabbed his ass," and Smith turned around and hit Saal. Smith said that two or three months earlier, he had complained to his team leader about Saal's harassment. Schlage's investigator (Carl Parson) interviewed Smith's team leader after the incident; he denied receiving any previous complaint from Smith. Parson interviewed eleven other employees who were in the vicinity at the time of the incident. Many of them said that horseplay and behavior they called "ass-grabbing," "dry humping," making suggestive comments about "cute mouths" and about employees' mothers, were relatively common in the plant. None of the employees had seen Saal touch Smith that day. And most of them, including Saal, told Parsons that it was out of character for Smith to punch someone for no reason.

Saal was suspended the same day for violation of "Serious Conduct [Rules] #2/6." On June 6, 2012, Schlage terminated Saal's employment, sending him a letter that cited his violation of Serious Conduct Rule #6: "Engaging in harassment (Sexual, Racial or any other reason) of other employees or the general public while on Company premises or Company business."

Article 12 of the collective bargaining agreement between Schlage and the Union describes the progressive grievance system, which culminates in submission of an unresolved grievance to binding arbitration by a mutually agreeable arbitrator. Section 5 of that Article states: "The arbitrator shall have no power to add to, subtract from or modify any of the terms of this Agreement."

The parties agreed on an arbitrator, and on a written statement of the issue being submitted for arbitration: "Did the Company have just cause when they discharged Jeremiah Saal under 'Serious Rules of Conduct' #2 and #6. Horseplay and Harassment; and if not, what is the remedy?" The arbitrator conducted a hearing on July 11, 2013, at which Smith, Saal, Parson, and Terry Mullins (the Union's President) testified. Exhibits and post-hearing briefs were submitted by both parties. The arbitrator's written decision reviewed the evidence and the testimony, and summarized the parties' contentions. He ultimately concluded that the grievance ... must be sustained to a very limited extent. The basis for this finding is that the Company proved that the Grievant did something wrong that day, but it could not prove that he provoked Smith sufficiently that being punched in the face was a reasonable response. However, because of the Grievant's lack of cooperation and veracity, nothing other than a return to work order is merited.

Specifically, the arbitrator found that Schlage's Work Rules were not mutually negotiated and should not be treated as binding to the same extent as the terms of the CBA. While the Union conceded that the rules had been posted for some time and they had not filed a grievance about them, the rules were not bilateral. The arbitrator stated that he had the power to enforce the CBA, which controlled the Rules and their enforcement in appropriate circumstances.

* * * *

The Parties' Contentions

Schlage contends that the arbitrator did not construe the CBA when he awarded what Schlage calls "the unprecedented remedy of an unpaid suspension with reinstatement following Serious Conduct Work Rules violations." Schlage argues that in doing so, the arbitrator exceeded his authority. According to Schlage, the parties agreed that the only question for the arbitrator was whether Schlage had "just cause" to discharge Saal, an issue limited to whether or not Saal's behavior actually occurred. The Union argued at arbitration that Saal did not violate the Work Rules, and just cause therefore did not exist. But the arbitrator went beyond determining what Saal did: he considered whether or not Saal violated the work rules, and then fashioned what he believed was an appropriate penalty.

Schlage also contends that the arbitration award violates public policy against sexual harassment, as it could leave the company exposed to charges from other potential future victims that it "tolerated" a known harasser. It also suggests that the order violates public policy banning racial discrimination. Two employees, one African-American and one Caucasian, both violated Serious Conduct Work Rules and both were discharged, yet only the Caucasian employee was reinstated.

In seeking to affirm the arbitration award, the Union cites the narrow standards that apply to judicial review of an arbitration award. As long as the arbitrator even arguably applies the contract, serious errors or disagreement with the merits of the decision do not permit the court to set aside an arbitrator's decision. The Union contends that the arbitrator did not exceed his authority. The issue submitted by agreement was not merely whether just cause existed for Saal's discharge; the issue was whether there was just cause and if not, "what is the remedy?" Schlage's Serious Conduct Work Rules do not mandate immediate discharge for any first violation. Rather, the rules state: "Serious conduct, which ordinarily justifies discharge for the first offense, includes but [is] not limited to the following examples ..." (emphasis added). The examples include fighting or acts of physical violence; unsafe "horseplay and/or practical jokes ... which might endanger the safety or lives of others;" possession of firearms; using or possessing drugs or alcohol at work; harassment; insubordination; falsification of documents; stealing company property; and leaving work without clocking out. Schlage does not contend that any employee who engages in any of this conduct is automatically fired, without any consideration of the facts of the incident.

The Union further contends that the arbitration award does not violate public policy against sexual harassment or racial discrimination. In order to fall within this narrow exception, the award itself must violate some clearly articulated public policy, and not the conduct that gives rise to an arbitration proceeding. An order reinstating an employee who engaged in the type of "horseplay" that was common at the plant does not violate any clearly established policy. And Smith's discharge was not before the arbitrator. His decision to reinstate Saal cannot be reasonably understood to condone racial discrimination.

Standard of Review

The Federal Arbitration Act restricts a district court's review of an arbitration award. The Court's task is to determine whether the arbitrator's decision "draws its essence from the contract." If the arbitrator was "even arguably construing or applying the contract," the award must be confirmed. Id. "Only when the arbitrator strays from interpretation and application . . . does he enter the forbidden world of effectively dispensing his own brand of industrial justice, making the arbitrator's decision unenforceable."

Discussion

The Court concludes that the arbitrator did not exceed his authority in ordering Saal's reinstatement without back pay or restoration of seniority. In arguing for the opposite conclusion, Schlage repeatedly asserts that the "only issue" submitted to the arbitrator was whether there was "just cause" for Saal's discharge. But the written stipulation between Schlage and the Union of the issue being submitted to the arbitrator was not limited to whether just cause existed. The parties plainly authorized the arbitrator to address the "remedy" if he concluded that just cause was lacking. The arbitrator framed the question presented to him as having two components: the question of fact [what happened], and the question of just cause [did what happened amount to just cause for discharge]. This framework does not exceed the authority granted by both parties in their stipulated statement of the issue they presented for arbitration.

* * * *

The Supreme Court has cautioned that the public policy exception is a narrow one, and cannot be based upon "general considerations of supposed public interests." Applying that narrow exception here, the Court concludes that the arbitrator's decision does not violate a clearly established public policy.

CONCLUSION

For all of the foregoing reasons, the Court finds that the November 4, 2013 Opinion and Award by Arbitrator Michael Paolucci should be affirmed.

The Union's motion for summary judgment affirming that order is granted. Schlage's motion to vacate that award is denied. Schlage's complaint is dismissed with prejudice.
SO ORDERED.
THIS CASE IS CLOSED.

APPLICATION AND DISCUSSION QUESTIONS

1. The employer argues that the arbitrator exceeded his authority when the arbitrator modified the termination to "the unprecedented remedy of an unpaid suspension with reinstatement." The employer insists that the arbitrator was to determine only whether there was just cause. The arbitrator had no authority to reinstate the grievant. The Court points out that the stipulated issue included the authority of the arbitrator to determine the remedy if there was no just clause for the termination prior to the start of a hearing. The parties routinely agree that the arbitrator is to determine the appropriate remedy, if there is no just cause. In this

case, the Court relied on the stipulation between the parties to find the arbitrator did not exceed his.

2. What narrow standard did the court cite that would apply to judicial review of an arbitration award? What is the standard of review for a court's review of an arbitration award?

3. Can you make an argument that the arbitrator's award violates public policy against sexual harassment and racial discrimination?

4. Did the arbitrator exceed his authority? Did the parties limit the authority of the arbitrator by restricting the issue?

MASS. BD. OF HIGHER EDUCATION V. MASS. TEACHERS ASS'N,
79 MASS. APP. CT. 27 (2011)

Judges: Present: McHugh, Meade, & Milkey, JJ.

MILKEY, J. In 2006, Holyoke Community College posted a position for an assistant professor of nutrition. Elizabeth Hebert, who many years earlier had been a tenured faculty member at the college, received an initial interview for the position. However, she did not advance to the final round, and the college eventually hired one of the three candidates who did. Based on a grievance that Hebert's union, Massachusetts Teachers Association/Massachusetts Community College Council/ National Education Association, pressed on her behalf, an arbitrator ruled that the college violated its collective bargaining agreement by choosing its preferred candidate over Hebert. He ordered the college to appoint Hebert to the posted position with full back pay, or to pay broadscale damages on an ongoing basis. A Superior Court judge vacated the arbitrator's award, and the union seeks to have it reinstated on appeal. We agree with the judge that the arbitrator exceeded his authority in some respects, but we conclude that the case must be remanded for additional proceedings.

Background.

Hebert has a "master's degree in food and nutrition." In 1981, she began working as a "program coordinator" in the dietetic technology program at the college. She was promoted to assistant professor in 1986, and she obtained tenure in 1988. In May of 1989, the college eliminated the entire dietetic technology program because of severe budgetary issues, and Hebert therefore lost her position. The college offered her a "retraining sabbatical" designed to qualify her for a position in the biology department. She initially accepted that offer, but eventually decided that she did not want to leave the nutrition field. Therefore, she resigned her position at the college. However, at many points over the ensuing years she taught courses at the college as an adjunct professor.

On January 6, 2006, the college posted the assistant professor position in nutrition. The posting listed various "required" and "preferred" qualifications. Among the required qualifications was that the candidate have a "[m]aster's degree in Nutrition or closely related field."

Hebert applied for the posted position, and she was among the five candidates asked to make presentations to the search committee. The committee recommended three finalists, including Hebert. In the committee's report, the chair had particularly positive things to say about Hebert's candidacy, referring to her as "exceed[ing] all candidates [in the pool] in required and preferred job qualifications." However, the college decided not to hire from the existing pool. Instead, it reposted the position on December 21, 2006. Although the new posting was slightly modified, it continued to list having a master's degree as a "required" qualification. The membership of the search committee had changed in the intervening months; for example, the chair, who had been a booster of Hebert's in the earlier process, no longer was on the search committee.

Hebert reapplied, and, as before, made the search committee's initial cut and was brought in for an interview. The reconstituted search committee asked each candidate a set series of questions, which was a different format than had been used in the earlier search. Hebert found the process "very strange," and she acknowledged to the arbitrator that it "threw her a bit." She did not advance further in the process.

The search committee chose three finalists, including Clement Ameho, who held a Ph.D in nutrition from Tufts University; Laura Hutchinson, a Ph.D candidate at the University of Massachusetts who had completed her course work and comprehensive examinations, but had not yet finished her doctoral dissertation; and Kim Teupker, who held a master's degree in nutrition and who -- in the arbitrator's words -- had "professional and teaching experience similar to Hebert's." The college eventually hired Hutchinson for the position.

On May 18, 2007, the day that Hebert learned that she was not a finalist, she filed a grievance claiming that the college had violated the collective bargaining agreement then in effect by having "acted in an arbitrary, capricious, and unreasonable manner in failing to offer her a second interview." After the college denied the grievance on multiple grounds and mediation proved unsuccessful, the union requested that the dispute be arbitrated.

The assigned arbitrator held a hearing on November 20, 2008, and he ruled in Hebert's favor by a decision dated March 2, 2009. With the college having completed its hiring process after Hebert had filed her grievance, the arbitrator framed the issues before him as follows:

"Is the grievance of Elizabeth Hebert arbitrable?

"If so, did the College violate the parties' collective bargaining agreement by failing to appoint the grievant to a full-time faculty position in the Nutrition Department?

"If so, what shall be the remedy?"

The arbitrator determined that the grievance was arbitrable, because, having lost her teaching position two decades earlier, Hebert was a "retrenched" union member who enjoyed certain preferences under the collective bargaining agreement. He concluded that Hebert no longer was entitled to some of these preferences, either because of the sheer passage of time or because she had not followed required notification procedures in the interim.

However, the arbitrator found that Hebert still was entitled to a preference with regard to article XVI of the collective bargaining agreement, the general provision governing the "filling of vacancies." Section 16.02 of the collective bargaining agreement requires the college president or designee to fill any vacancies with unit members within the college "when in the professional judgment of the President of the College or designee such unit members are the best-qualified applicants." It further states that retrenched unit members must be given first preference "[i]f the President of the College or designee determines that two (2) or more applicants are equally best qualified."

After reviewing their respective qualifications, the arbitrator found Hebert better qualified than Hutchinson, and "[a]t the very least, Hebert should have been found [by the college] to be equally qualified as Hutchinson." Indeed, he determined that

Hutchinson was per se unqualified given that, although she had completed her doctoral course work and examinations, she did not possess a master's degree. Based on this, the arbitrator concluded that, in choosing Hutchinson over Hebert, the college failed to give Hebert preference as a "retrenched faculty member" and thereby violated the collective bargaining agreement.

As to remedy, the arbitrator ordered the college to hire Hebert for the posted position (plus back pay). Recognizing doubt as to whether he could order the college to hire Hebert, the arbitrator further ordered that, in the event that his preferred remedy was struck, the college must pay Hebert the full salary of the position for as long as that job continued to exist. A Superior Court judge summarily vacated this award, stating: "Hebert is not entitled to reinstatement and not entitled to retrenchment. Where it is clear that the arbitrator exceeded his authority, and [his award] is against public policy, his decision must be VACATED."

Discussion.

* * * *

An arbitrator exceeds his authority when he intrudes upon decisions that cannot be delegated, but that are instead left by statute to the exclusive managerial control of designated public officials. *Higher Educ. Coordinating Council/Roxbury Community College v. Massachusetts Teacher's Ass'n/Mass. Community College Council,* (hereinafter Roxbury Community College). "This gloss on public sector collective bargaining statutes is deemed necessary in order that the collective actions of public employees do not distort the normal political process for controlling public policy." *Boston Teachers Union, Local 66 v. School Comm. of Boston.* However, the principle of nondelegability is to be applied only so far as is necessary to preserve the college's discretion to carry out its statutory mandates. Thus, although the principle applies to the administration of community colleges, "unless the arbitrator's decision infringed on an area of educational policy reserved for the exclusive judgment of the administrators of the college, it cannot be disturbed." *Roxbury Community College.*

Section 22 of G. L. c. 15A, inserted by St. 1991, c. 142, § 7, specifically delegates to the community college administrators the responsibility to "appoint, transfer, dismiss, promote and award tenure to all personnel of said institution." Few issues are as central to setting educational policy as choosing which faculty members to hire or promote. ("It has been observed that '[t]he success of a school system depends largely on the character and the ability of the teachers. Unless a school committee has authority to employ and discharge teachers it would be difficult to perform properly its duty of managing a school system"), quoting from Davis v. School Comm. of Somerville. Not surprisingly, the Supreme Judicial Court long has recognized that "specific appointment determinations" cannot be delegated to an arbitrator.

While a college cannot delegate specific appointment decisions, it can bind itself to the process that is to be used in making such decisions, including the criteria by which the candidates will be judged. See, e.g., *School Comm. of Holbrook* ("bargained-for procedures governing the appointment and reappointment of teachers, such as posting and evaluation requirements, are specifically enforceable"); *School Comm. of New Bedford v. New Bedford Educators Ass'n,* (same principle). Sorting out when arbitrators tread into the forbidden realm of nondelegable decision-making, or are instead properly enforcing agreed-to procedures, requires nuanced analysis on a case-by-case basis. See, e.g., *School Comm. of Boston v. Boston Teachers Union, Local 66, Am. Fedn. of Teachers (AFL-CIO).*

Liability.

Following these principles, we conclude that it is beyond the authority of an arbitrator to question the judgment that a college administration exercises in evaluating candidates for a faculty appointment, regardless of whether the applicable collective bargaining agreement can be interpreted as subjecting such issues to arbitration. Put differently, whether a college administration erred in exercising its judgment as to which candidate was best qualified is not an arbitrable issue. See *Department of State Police v. Massachusetts Org. of State Engrs. & Scientists* (absent alleged procedural violation or discrimination based on membership in constitutionally protected class, State police colonel's decision to terminate chemist was not arbitrable). If an arbitrator were allowed to overturn a college administration's discretionary judgments on how to rank job candidates, then, absent proof of fraud, we would be compelled to let the arbitrator's decision stand regardless of the reason, if any reason at all, the arbitrator gave for finding an abuse of discretion. This would render the arbitrator the ultimate decision maker on faculty hiring decisions, a result that is plainly inconsistent with G. L. c. 15A, § 22.

Accordingly, to the extent that the arbitrator here substituted his judgment for that of the college administration in making his own evaluation of the job candidates, that decision cannot stand. We are not done, however, because the union argues that the arbitrator's decision can be sustained without intruding upon matters of judgment. Specifically, it contends that the college was not free to choose Hutchinson over Hebert because Hutchinson was per se unqualified for the posted position given that she lacked a master's degree (a "required" qualification, as propounded by the college). See *School Comm. of New Bedford*, (arbitrator's review of whether school committee hired candidate who did not meet posted minimum job requirements, including that candidate possess master's degree, does "not impermissibly limit the committee's discretion").

The college counters that the arbitrator's reasoning lacks an appreciation for how the academic world weighs such credentials. It suggests that being a doctoral candidate with "all but dissertation" (ABD) status is generally considered to provide higher rank than having a mere master's degree, and that its judgment in this regard cannot be second guessed. This argument is not without some force. However, we ultimately conclude that, having drafted its posting expressly to require that candidates have a master's degree, the college was not free to determine that a candidate who had obtained neither a master's degree nor a higher degree nevertheless possessed "better" credentials than one with a master's degree. We note that the college easily could have written its job posting so as to require a "master's degree or equivalent," a phrase that the college used in the collective bargaining agreement. Having established the minimum job requirements as it did, the college had a good faith obligation to employ them, and it lay within the arbitrator's purview to determine whether the college had done so. *School Comm. of Newton v. Newton Sch. Custodians Ass'n, Local 454, SEIU*, (although principal retains "actual, first-line determination of whom to hire," he is bound to make "good-faith effort" to apply criteria to which he has agreed). See *School Comm. of New Bedford*, supra (school committee bound itself to follow its own appointment criteria). In sum, although the arbitrator was without authority to substitute his judgment for that of the college administration, insofar as he ruled that the college violated the collective bargaining agreement by selecting someone who did not meet the minimum requirements set forth in the posting, his ruling cannot be disturbed.

Remedy.

It does not follow, however, that the arbitrator then could appoint Hebert an assistant professor against the wishes of the college administration. The cases consistently recognize that arbitrators do not have authority to grant such relief, because it would directly intrude upon the appointment authority left to the exclusive purview of the college administration.

* * * *

What relief then is appropriate to remedy the procedural violation that occurred? As the college acknowledged at oral argument, if it erred by hiring someone who did not meet the posted job requirements, then the obvious way to address the problem directly would be to start the process again.

* * * *

Although full-scale damages plainly exceed the arbitrator's authority, this does not rule out the possibility of Hebert obtaining more limited damages. School Comm. of Holbrook, (award of one-year's back pay upheld). What, if any, damages might be appropriate is, at this point, far from obvious given that the collective bargaining agreement expressly limits the compensation that an arbitrator can award for a breach of the agreement to "actual damages directly attributable to such breach." Nevertheless, under the cases, the question of damages is one for the arbitrator to resolve so long as he does not exceed his authority.

Conclusion.

In light of the foregoing, we reverse the judgment vacating the arbitrator's award. A new judgment shall enter reversing so much of the arbitrator's award as ordered that Hebert be appointed with full back pay and benefits, or that she receive full pay for each year the position exists. The new judgment also should remand the case to the arbitrator for further proceedings consistent with this opinion. So ordered.

APPLICATION AND DISCUSSION QUESTIONS

1. How does the court determine whether an arbitrator has exceeded their authority? The Court indicated that the arbitrator still had to order other remedies. What remedies could the arbitrator order and not exceed their authority?

2. The following cases illustrate when courts will vacate an arbitrator's award. The evidence must be clear that the arbitrator exceeded their authority. Review each of the following cases and explain the court's reasoning for its decision:

SUMMARY OF RULES ON THE ARBITRATOR'S AUTHORITY

WASH. HOSP. V. SEIU HEALTHCARE INC. PA.,
2014 U. S. DIST. LEXIS 115679.

The employer requested the court to vacate the award which reinstated an employee. The court rejected the Employer's argument that the Arbitrator's award failed to "draw its essence from the CBA". Citing the U.S. Supreme Court decision in *Oxford Health Plans, LLC v. Sutter, 133 S. Ct. 2064 (2013)* held that the Federal Arbitration Act permits vacating an award when "the arbitrator strayed from his [her] delegated task of interpreting a contract, not when he [her] performed the task pooly." Here the Arbitrator reviewed the facts in the record and pointed to specific contract provisions that were violated.

CHARDON LOCAL SCH. DIST. BD. OF EDUC. V. CHARDON EDUC. ASSOC.,
3 N. E. 3D 1224, COURT OF APPEALS OF OHIO. ELEVENTH APPELLATE DISTRICT (2013).

Whether a trial court had the authority to interpret a CBA between the parties in a way that differed from that of an arbitrator .The trial court had the authority to interpret the CBA differently and to vacate an arbitration award of back pay to a teacher because the arbitrator misinterpreted the CBA when the interpretation was not justified or necessary. The direct, clear and unambiguous language of the CBA required, pursuant to R.C. 3319.16, a ²just cause² analysis of a school district's termination of the teacher. Therefore, the arbitrator exceeded his authority and improperly executed his powers when he utilized a standard not provided for in the CBA and ignored the application of the good and just cause standard to the termination. Pursuant to R.C. 2711.12, the trial court properly charged a teacher's association with the costs of the arbitration. Judgment affirmed. [Vacated]

COUNTY OF RIVERSIDE V. PHILLIP TAMOUSH

2012 CAL. APP. UNPUB. LEXI S 2677.

Supervising network administrator was terminated from her position based on her accessing email accounts without authorization, and the arbitrator awarded reinstatement to her position at the County. On appeal, the county argued that the arbitrator substituted his own judgment for the district attorney, and therefore exceeded his authority granted to him under the Memorandum of Understanding (M OU) between the union and the county. The appellate court affirmed the trial court's upholding of the arbitration award, finding that the arbitrator did not exceed his power. The court stated, "Here, an issue explicitly submitted by the parties and squarely addressed by the arbitrator was whether the employer had just cause to terminate [employee]."

HUMILITY OF MARY HEALTH PARTNERS, ET AL., V. LOCAL 377 TEAMSTERS,

U.S. DIST. LEXIS 83794; 193 L.R.R.M. 2890 (N.D. OHIO 2012).

Neurosurgeon technician diagnosed with Crohn's Colitis and Rheumatoid Arthritis (and deemed FMLA ineligible) was terminated due to excessive absences. Arbitrator concluded employer did not have just cause for termination, and awarded reinstatement and lost wages. Employer argued that the arbitrator exceeded his authority. The court disagreed and upheld the arbitration award, finding that the arbitrator properly interpreted the CBA - "The judgment of the arbitrator should be left alone with respect to the facts and merits of the case."

FORREST V. WAFFLE HOUSE,

2012 U.S. DIST. LEXIS 70725, (M.D. AL. MAY 22, 2012).

Former employee brought action against former employer for alleged sexual harassment and inappropriate touching. Arbitrator found Title VI I claims were time barred, but state tort claims of assault and invasion of privacy were substantiated. The employer sought to vacate based on arbitrator's exceeded authority and manifest disregard of the law. The employer claimed that the arbitrator applied the wrong state law to the claim. This court upheld the arbitration award and found both arguments unsubstantiated: (1) the arbitrator's award "constitutes more than a simple result and easily meets the standard for a reasoned opinion," and (2) "errors of law are not sufficient to set aside an arbitration award." Thus, so long as the arbitrator makes a reasonable effort to apply the correct law, the award is valid.

SUMMARY OF RULES ON MISCONDUCT OF ARBITRATORS

- Courts will follow the rigorous standard for enforcement of awards as outlined in the FAA.

- A party challenging an award "must clear a high hurdle" to obtain relief from an award.

- If it is clear that the parties agreed to submit an issue for arbitration, the court will uphold the decision.

- "The Court must uphold an arbitrator's decision if an arbitrator is even arguably construing or applying the contract and acting within the scope of his authority." (Misco)

- The arbitrator's award can be vacated if the decision does not flow from the CBA, but is based on the arbitrator's "own brand of industrial justice."

C. Allegations that the Arbitrator Was Guilty of Misconduct or Partiality

DELAWARE TRANSIT CORP. V. AMALGAMATED TRANSIT UNION LOCAL 42
34 A.3D 1064 (2011)

Before HOLLAND, JACOBS and RIDGELY, Justices.

Delaware Transit Corporation ("DTC") filed a complaint with the Court of Chancery of the State of Delaware against the Amalgamated Transit Union, Local 842 ("Union") and Harry Bruckner ("Bruckner") in the nature of a declaratory judgment action ("Complaint"), pursuant to Title 10, Chapter 65. The Complaint sought an order vacating or modifying a labor arbitration award ("Award") issued by Arbitrator Alan A. Symonette ("Arbitrator"), pursuant to a collective bargaining agreement ("CBA") between DTC and the Union. The Award reinstated Bruckner, who was terminated by DTC, with back pay less interim earnings.

The Court of Chancery granted the Union's motion for summary judgment. DTC's sole argument in this appeal is that the Arbitrator's decision should be vacated due to the appearance of bias or partiality on the part of the Arbitrator. We have concluded that argument is without merit. Therefore, the judgment of the Court of Chancery must be affirmed.

* * * *

Arbitrator's Award

On November 9, 2009, a hearing was held before the Arbitrator. At the arbitration hearing, the Union and DTC, who were both represented by counsel, stipulated to the issue to be decided by the Arbitrator: "Was the grievant, Mr. Harry Bruckner, terminated for just cause? If not, what shall the remedy be?" On January 5, 2010, the Arbitrator issued an opinion and Award in which he sustained the grievance and ordered Bruckner to be reinstated with back pay less any interim earnings.

In rendering his decision, the Arbitrator relied upon several sections of the CBA. First, he cited Section 13 of the Miss Rules, which outlines progressive discipline for up to eight misses within a floating twelve-month period. Second, he quoted from Section 20, Leaves of Absence, which gives the DTC discretion to provide unpaid leaves of absence to employees who make a written request. Third, he quoted, in part, Section 35, Bid Shifts, which describes the process by which employees may bid on particular runs at DTC ("Bidding Rules"). Although the Arbitrator did not specifically mention Section 10, Discipline, he did rely upon it in finding that DTC did not have "just cause" in terminating Bruckner. Section 10 states, in pertinent part, that "[n]o employee who has successfully completed the probationary period shall be discharged or disciplined without just cause."

The Arbitrator found that DTC's failure to consider the option of allowing Bruckner to switch runs was either arbitrary or constituted disparate treatment:

In this case, management's failure to consider that option at least to the extent of consulting with the Union to reach an accommodation was at least arbitrary or at most an instance of disparate treatment. It was clear that the grievant was attempting to correct his situation and had come to management for help. Even though the solution may have been a deviation from the language of the contract, given the history between the parties in which waivers have been granted and that this accommodation would not have affected any other employees, management could have at least spoken to the Union to determine whether this is a possibility. It is for this reason that I sustain this grievance.

As a remedy, the Arbitrator directed DTC to return Bruckner to his former position with back pay less any interim earnings. The Arbitrator also directed that Bruckner be placed on the disciplinary step of the Miss Rules that he was on at the time of his termination.

Court of Chancery Ruling

On March 17, 2010, DTC filed the Complaint in the Court of Chancery seeking to vacate the Award to Bruckner. The Union filed a motion for summary judgment, arguing that none of the three grounds for vacating a labor arbitration award applied in this case. Therefore, the Union argued that the Arbitrator's Award should be affirmed summarily.

The standards for judicial intervention in arbitration proceedings are always narrowly drawn. The role of the Court of Chancery in conducting post-arbitration judicial review is limited in a labor dispute to three issues:

Delaware has long had a policy favoring arbitration, and its courts have applied a deferential standard when reviewing labor arbitration awards. [The Court of Chancery] will not disturb a labor arbitration award unless (a) the integrity of the arbitration has been compromised by, for example, fraud, procedural irregularity, or a specific command of law; (b) the award does not claim its essence from the CBA; or (c) the award violates a clearly defined public policy.

Where a grievance is arbitrated under a collective bargaining agreement, courts will not review the merits of the arbitration award other than on the grounds listed above. To do otherwise would give courts the final say on the merits of arbitration awards and undercut benefits of labor arbitration-namely, speed, flexibility, informality and finality.In opposing the Union's motion for summary judgment, DTC argued that the Award should be vacated on the grounds that the integrity of the arbitration was compromised because the Arbitrator failed to disclose to the parties that his wife had died of cancer a few months before the arbitration hearing. According to DTC, this created the appearance of bias or partiality because Bruckner argued that he failed to arrive at work in a timely fashion after his mother-in-law, who had provided daycare for his children, died of cancer. DTC raised no other issue in opposition to the Union's motion for summary judgment.

In this appeal, DTC does not argue that the Award violates public policy. It also does not argue that the Award "does not claim its essence from the CBA." The only grounds for vacating the Award that DTC raises in its opening brief to this Court is that the integrity of the arbitration was compromised because the Arbitrator's shared life experience gave the appearance of bias or partiality.

Labor Arbitration Rule 17

In support of its sole argument on appeal, DTC relies upon Rule 17 (Disclosure and Challenge Procedure) of the American Arbitration Association Labor Arbitration Rules ("Rule 17"). Rule 17 states, in pertinent part:

> No person shall serve as a neutral arbitrator in any arbitration under these rules in which that person has any financial or personal interest in the result of the arbitration. Any prospective or designated neutral arbitrator shall immediately disclose any circumstance likely to affect impartiality, including any bias or financial or personal interest in the result of the arbitration.

The rule requires that "any circumstance likely to affect impartiality" be disclosed. DTC submits that if an arbitrator has a shared personal life experience that might possibly cause the arbitrator to be sympathetic or empathetic to the position of one of the parties, it must be disclosed and is a basis for disqualification. Thus, DTC contends that the Arbitrator's failure to disclose his wife's death from cancer to the parties constituted a violation of Rule 17, and, therefore, requires vacating the Award.

The Court of Chancery concluded that Rule 17 concerns actual financial or personal relationships between the arbitrator and a party, an agent of a party, or an attorney for a party. The ethics rules for arbitrators, written and approved by the American Arbitration Association ("AAA"), the National Academy of Arbitrators, and the Federal Mediation and Conciliation Service, support that conclusion. The AAA requires its arbitrators to abide by the Code of Professional Responsibility for Arbitrators of Labor Management Disputes. Under section 2(B)(1), arbitrators presiding over labor-management disputes are required to disclose (1) "any current or past managerial, representational, or consultative relationship with any company or union involved in a proceeding in which the arbitrator is being considered for appointment or has been tentatively designated to serve" and (2) "any pertinent pecuniary interest. "Additionally, section 2(B)(3) states that "[a]n arbitrator must not permit personal relationships to affect decision-making."

* * * *

Evident Partiality Standard

Commonwealth Coatings Corp. v. Cont'l Cas. Co. is the leading case addressing arbitrator disclosure and is relied upon by DTC in this appeal. Commonwealth Coatings involved a dispute between a prime contractor and a subcontractor. The member of the three-person arbitration panel selected as a "neutral" was an engineering consultant. The prime contractor was one of the engineering consultant's regular customers. As the Supreme Court explained, "[a]n arbitration was held, but the facts concerning the close business connections between the third arbitrator and the prime contractor were unknown to [the other party] and were never revealed to it by this arbitrator, by the prime contractor, or by anyone else until after an award had been made." In a plurality decision by Justice Black, the Supreme Court stated:

> [A]ny tribunal permitted by law to try cases and controversies not only must be unbiased but also must avoid even the appearance of bias. We cannot believe that it was the purpose of Congress to authorize litigants to submit their cases and controversies to arbitration boards that might reasonably be though biased against one litigant and favorable to another.

* * * *

Ever since *Commonwealth Coatings* was decided, it has been generally accepted that an arbitrator's failure to disclose a substantial relationship with a party or a party's attorney justifies vacatur under an "evident partiality" standard. Nevertheless, courts are divided on what constitutes "evident partiality." Some courts follow Justice Black's plurality opinion in Commonwealth Coatings, by adopting a standard whereby a failure to disclose may be grounds for vacatur of an arbitration award if the undisclosed relationship creates an appearance or impression of bias. In other courts, however, this standard is limited in favor of a more narrow reasonableness standard, requiring "more than a mere appearance of bias," such that an award will be vacated where the undisclosed relationship would lead a reasonable person to conclude that the arbitrator actually lacked impartiality. Most courts have concluded that evident partiality requires more than an appearance of bias but less than actual bias. The evolving standard of judicial review is that a reasonable person would have to conclude that a neutral arbitrator was partial or biased In *Kaplan v. First Options of Chicago, Inc.*, the Third Circuit Court of Appeals recognized that after *Commonwealth Coatings* the proper standard for considering a claim of arbitrator bias is "evident partiality" and joined the courts that have adopted the reasonable person test. The Third Circuit stated:

In order to show "evident partiality," "the challenging party must show 'a reasonable person would have to conclude that the arbitrator was partial' to the other party to the arbitration." "Evident partiality" is strong language and requires proof of circumstances "powerfully suggestive of bias."

* * * *

We agree that arbitrators should disclose all of their past and present personal or financial relationships with the parties, their agents, and their attorneys. We hold that to demonstrate evident partiality sufficient to require vacatur, however, the record must reflect that an arbitrator failed to disclose a substantial personal or financial relationship with a party, a party's agent, or a party's attorney that a reasonable person would conclude was powerfully suggestive of bias. The question presented in this appeal is whether an undisclosed shared life experience is sufficient to constitute evident partiality and to require vacatur. DTC acknowledges that under Rule 17 and the applicable ethics rules, the Arbitrator in this case had no duty to disclose before the arbitration hearing commenced because he had no past or present personal or financial relationship with any party, their agent, or their attorney. Arbitrators are under an ongoing obligation, however, to disclose information they acquire that might make them partial. In addition to the rules for mandatory disclosure, the AAA's ethics rules also provide that "[i]f the circumstances requiring disclosure are not known to the arbitrator prior to acceptance of appointment, disclosure must be made when such circumstances become known to the arbitrator." DTC contends that, when Bruckner's mother-in-law's death from cancer became known during the hearing, the Arbitrator was required to disclose his shared life experience with his wife's death from cancer.

In deciding whether an arbitrator's personal life experiences should be disclosed either before acceptance of an appointment or during the course of arbitration proceedings, the rules for judicial officers' recusal and disqualification are not binding on arbitrators. However, they are didactic. The general rule is that a judge "is not disqualifiable because of his [or her] own life experiences." "[L]ifetime experiences, good or bad, are something all judges bring with them to the bench, and only in unusual circumstances would a judge be required to recuse" because of a shared life experience. "Obviously a judge is not disqualified from presiding at an automobile accident trial merely because he was once himself in an automobile accident. Nor is a judge disqualified from trying a divorce case either because he is himself married or divorced, or from trying a contested adoption case because he has either natural children or adopted children."

The party seeking the disqualification of an arbitrator bears the burden of establishing the basis for a recusal. Other courts have concluded that to set aside an award for evident partiality, the moving party must identify an undisclosed relationship between the arbitrator and a party or the party's agent that is "so intimate—personally, socially, professionally or financially—as to cast serious doubt on [the arbitrator's] impartiality." We agree. In addition, the alleged past or present conflicting personal or financial relationship with the arbitrator "must be direct, definite, and capable of demonstration rather than remote, uncertain or speculative."

The alleged bias or partiality which DTC attributes to the Arbitrator in this matter fails to meet the "evident partiality" standard. The mere fact that an arbitrator may share a personal life experience with a party or a party's agent is legally insufficient to constitute a substantial relationship that a reasonable person would conclude is powerfully suggestive of bias. We hold that arbitrators are not disqualified because of their shared life experience with a party or a party's agent and that the disclosure of a shared life experience is not mandatory. In this case, the Arbitrator had no obligation to disclose that his wife had recently died from cancer.

Conclusion

The judgment of the Court of Chancery is affirmed.

APPLICATION AND DISCUSSION QUESTIONS

In *Beebe Med. Ctr., Inc. v. InSight Health Servs. Corp.*, the Court of Chancery also recognized and applied the "evident partiality" standard arising from Commonwealth Coatings and adopted the reasonable person test. The Court of Chancery stated:

> "In the wake of Commonwealth Coatings, it is almost universally accepted that an arbitrator's failure to disclose a substantial relationship with a party or a party's attorney justifies vacatur under the evident partiality standard. Judges have spilled many words on the pages of the federal reporters trying to put this standard into simple terms, but most agree that an arbitrator's nondisclosure of a relationship [with a party or the party's attorney] substantial enough to create a reasonable impression of bias will ordinarily dictate vacatur".

The Court of Chancery deermined that the reasonable person test was satisfied where the arbitrator, a lawyer, failed to disclose that one of the corporate parties to an arbitration he heard was represented by a law firm that was simultaneously representing the arbitrator in litigation in a Delaware Court.

1. Which party has the burden of establishing the basis for recusal of the arbitrator? What must the party show to have an award set aside because of evident partiality?

2. Courts have considered whether an advocate is too "intimate--personally, socially, professionally or financial as to cast serious doubt on [the arbitrator] impartiality." *Id.* Can you give an example of each of the above possible conflicts?

3. The Court outlined three factors it would consider in vacating an arbitration award. What are these three factors? Are any of those factors present in this case?

ORDER ACCEPTING FINDINGS AND RECOMMENDATION OF THE UNITED STATES MAGISTRATE JUDGE

REED O'CONNOR, District Judge.

After reviewing all relevant matters of record in this case, including the Findings, Conclusions, and Recommendation of the United States Magistrate Judge and any objections thereto, in accordance with 28 U.S.C. § 636(b)(1), the undersigned District Judge is of the opinion that the Findings and Conclusions of the Magistrate Judge are correct and they are accepted as the Findings and Conclusions of the Court.

FINDINGS, CONCLUSIONS, AND RECOMMENDATION OF THE UNITED STATES MAGISTRATE JUDGE

IRMA CARRILLO RAMIREZ, United States Magistrate Judge.

Pursuant to Special Order No. 3–251, this case was referred for pretrial management, including the determination of non-dispositive motions, and issuance of findings of fact and recommendation on dispositive motions. Before the Court are Motion of Chester Shane McVay to Vacate Final Arbitration Award and Brief in Support filed June 20, 2007, and HES' Opposition to McVay's Motion to Vacate Arbitration Award and Cross–Motion to Confirm the Award and Brief filed July 10, 2007. Based on the relevant filings, evidence, and applicable law, the Court recommends that Plaintiff's motion to vacate the final arbitration award be DENIED, Defendant's cross-motion to confirm the award and its request for prejudgment and post-judgment interest be GRANTED, and Defendant's request for attorney's fees be DENIED.

I. BACKGROUND

This case arises from an intellectual property ("IP") agreement between Plaintiff, Chester Shane Mcvay, and his one-time employer, Halliburton Energy Services,

Inc. ("HES"). In early 2001, Plaintiff executed an IP agreement with HES and began working there as an employee. A few years later, Plaintiff accepted a job offer from another employer and announced his resignation to HES. During his exit interview, HES asked Plaintiff to return all documents, electronic or otherwise, belonging to HES. Plaintiff responded by claiming intellectual property ownership of a software program that he had worked on while an HES employee. HES subsequently filed a lawsuit and obtained a temporary restraining order against Plaintiff to compel production of the disputed documents. As a result of the restraining order, Plaintiff produced some documents and electronic files but retained possession of others. After substantial legal wrangling, HES initiated arbitration against Plaintiff for breach of their IP agreement. On March 21, 2007, the arbitrator found that Plaintiff had breached the agreement and awarded HES injunctive relief, breach of contract damages, reasonable and necessary attorney's fees, and expert witness costs. Plaintiff now moves the Court to vacate the arbitration award, and HES cross-moves to confirm the award.

II. PLAINTIFF'S MOTION TO VACATE ARBITRATION AWARD

Plaintiff moves for vacatur of the arbitration award on three grounds. He first moves to vacate the final award arguing that the arbitrator was partial in making the award. Alternatively, he moves to vacate portions of the award, claiming that the arbitrator exceeded her powers and acted in manifest disregard of the law.

A. Legal Standard

Pursuant to the Federal Arbitration Act ("FAA"), if the parties have agreed that a judgment of the court shall be entered upon the entry of an arbitration award, then upon application by a party, the court must grant such an order unless the award is vacated, modified, or corrected.

9 U.S.C. § 9. The FAA authorizes a district court to vacate an arbitration award where: (1) the award was procured by corruption, fraud, or undue means; (2) there is evidence of partiality or corruption among the arbitrators; (3) the arbitrators were guilty of misconduct which prejudiced the rights of one of the parties; or (4) the arbitrators exceeded their powers. 9 U.S.C. § 10(a). The Court may vacate an arbitration award under the FAA only for these statutory reasons.

B. Partiality

Plaintiff first moves the Court to vacate the final award claiming that the arbitrator was partial in making the award.

Section 10(a)(2) of the FAA authorizes a district court to vacate an arbitration award if there is "evident partiality2 or corruption in the arbitrators." 9 U.S.C. § 10(a) (2). The party asserting evident partiality has the burden of proof. *Mantle v. Upper Deck Co.*, 956 F.Supp. 719, 729 (N.D.Tex.1997) (Fitzwater, J.). The party carrying this "onerous burden" must produce specific facts. Additionally, "the alleged partiality must be direct, definite and capable of demonstration rather than remote, uncertain, or speculative." (citations and internal quotations omitted). A party "can establish evident partiality by demonstrating that the arbitrator failed to disclose relevant facts or that he displayed actual bias at the arbitration proceeding." *Weber v. Merrill Lynch Pierce Fenner & Smith*, 455 F.Supp.2d 545, 549 (N.D.Tex.2006) (Fitzwater, J.) (citations omitted). Plaintiff seeks to establish evident partiality by showing non-disclosure and actual bias.

1. Non–Disclosure

To evaluate evident partiality in non-disclosure cases, the Fifth Circuit has adopted a "reasonable impression of bias" standard. *Positive Software Solutions Inc. v. New Century Mortg. Corp.*, 476 F.3d 278, 283 (5th Cir.2007). Under this standard, a party seeking to vacate an arbitration award must demonstrate something more than a mere appearance of bias emanating from the arbitrator's failure to disclose a contact or relationship; it must show a reasonable impression of bias created by the arbitrator's non-disclosure. See id. at 282–84, see also *Bernstein Seawell & Kove v. Bosarge*, 813 F.2d 726, 732 (5th Cir.1987). To rise to the level of evident partiality, "[a]n arbitrator's failure to disclose must involve a significant compromising connection to the parties," not something "trivial and insubstantial." *Positive*, 476 F.3d at 282–83.

Plaintiff argues that the arbitrator demonstrated evident partiality by waiting until after the arbitration hearing to disclose a social relationship. Plaintiff alleges that the arbitrator and her husband were neighbors with, and had a social relationship with, the son of a named party to the proceeding. He claims that the arbitrator's husband corresponded with the neighbor and even picked up his mail. He further claims that the arbitrator revealed this social relationship after the arbitration hearing even though the relationship was discoverable a month before the hearing. This suspiciously-timed revelation, he alleges, created a reasonable impression of bias.

Even though the arbitrator disclosed the social relationship two months before she issued the final arbitration award, Plaintiff waited until after the arbitration award to claim partiality based on non-disclosure. Plaintiff waived any objection based on non-disclosure when he failed to object to the continued service of the arbitrator after she disclosed the relationship. See *Ergobilt, Inc. v. Neutral Posture Ergonomics, Inc.*, 2002 WL 1489521, at *5 (N.D.Tex.2002) (Lindsay, J.). A party cannot stand by during arbitration, withhold certain arguments, and upon losing, raise those arguments in federal court. *Gateway Techs. Inc. v. MCI Telecomms. Corp.*, 64 F.3d 993, 998 (5th Cir.1995). Since Plaintiff has waived any objections based on non-disclosure, the Court should not vacate the award on these grounds.

2. Actual Bias

Here, Plaintiff claims that the arbitrator displayed actual bias by improperly reviewing HES' proposed award while not giving him an opportunity to present his own for consideration. He concedes that the arbitrator refused to consider the proposed award when HES submitted it for consideration, but relies on similarities in language in the proposed and final awards to conclude that the arbitrator improperly reviewed the proposed award. Plaintiff does not account for the fact that the final award's language is much more similar to language in a reply brief that HES properly submitted to the arbitrator for consideration. Given these facts, a reasonable person would not have to conclude that the arbitrator improperly reviewed and relied on HES' proposed award thus displaying actual bias towards Plaintiff.

Plaintiff also claims actual bias by alleging that the arbitration was "marred with irregularities from files used as evidence having been resaved and modified, personal files going missing from computers after searches, and disregard for the clear terms of a questionably-obtained temporary restraining order." However, he does not provide specific facts to show that the irregularities, if any, were linked to the arbitrator. Plaintiff's allegations of actual bias are at most remote, uncertain, and speculative rather than direct, definite, and capable of demonstration. See Mantle, 956 F.Supp. at 729. Since Plaintiff has failed to meet his burden to show actual bias, the Court should deny vacatur of the arbitration award on these grounds.

C. Exceeding Powers (Omitted)

D. Manifest Disregard of the Law

Plaintiff moves the court to set aside the award of injunctive relief and attorney's fees on the grounds that the arbitrator made the awards in manifest disregard of the law. The Fifth Circuit previously recognized manifest disregard of the law as a non-statutory or common law ground for vacating an arbitration award. See e.g. *Sarofim v. Trust Co. of the West*, 440 F.3d 213, 216 (5th Cir.2006). Recently, however, it overruled its own precedent in Citigroup Global and held that manifest disregard of the law is no longer an independent, non-statutory basis for vacating an arbitration award under the FAA. 562 F.3d at 355, 358. Under *Citigroup Global*, a court may vacate an arbitration award only for reasons provided in § 10 of the FAA. Id. at 358 (citing *Hall Street*, 128 S.Ct. at 1405).

In this case, Plaintiff raises manifest disregard of the law as a non-statutory basis for vacating the arbitrator's award of injunctive relief and attorney's fees. Under the specific holding of *Citigroup Global*, the Court is foreclosed from reviewing this non-statutory ground. See *Saipem Am. v. Wellington Underwriting Agencies, Ltd.*, 335 Fed. Appx. 377, 379–80 (5th Cir.2009).

III. DEFENDANT'S CROSS–MOTION TO CONFIRM THE AWARD

HES moves the Court to confirm the award, and to grant prejudgment interest, post-judgment interest, and attorneys fees and costs for the current litigation.

Pursuant to the FAA, a court may enter judgment on the arbitration award if the parties have agreed that the court may do so, and the award has not been vacated, modified, or corrected. See 9 U.S.C. § 9; *McKee v. Home Buyers Warranty Corp.* II, 45 F.3d 981, 985 (5th Cir.1995) (citing 9 U.S.C. § 9). In this case, Plaintiff and HES agree that the Court may enter judgment on the arbitration award. DRR 31.D specifically provides for this agreement when it states that the "Parties to these rules shall be deemed to have consented that judgment upon the award of the arbitrator may be entered and enforced in any federal or state court having jurisdiction of the Parties." Given the parties' consent that the Court may enter judgment on the award and the Court's ruling that the award should not be vacated, the Court should confirm the arbitrator's final award.

(Prejudgment Interest, Post–Judgment Interest, Attorney Fees and Costs (Omitted)

IV. CONCLUSION

Plaintiff's motion to vacate the arbitration award should be DENIED. Defendant's motion to confirm the award and its request for prejudgment and post-judgment interest should be GRANTED, and its request for attorney's fees should be DENIED. SO RECOMMENDED, on this 13th day of November, 2009.

APPLICATION AND DISCUSSION QUESTIONS

1. The Supreme Court held in *Hall Street Assocs., L.L.C. v. Mattel, Inc.,* 552 U.S. 576, 128 S.Ct. 1396, 1403, 170 L.Ed.2d 254 (2008) that § 10 of the FAA provides the exclusive grounds for expedited vacatur.

2. The court in *McVay* states that the party challenging an award has the "onerous burden" of submitting sufficient evidence that the award should be set aside. What are some examples of conflicts of interest that would meet this high standard? Why have courts set such a high standard?

3. How does the court determine whether the arbitrator has exceeded his authority?

The following cases illustrate how arbitrators have engaged in misconduct or engaged in conduct that might appear to be impartial. What conduct did the arbitrator engaged in that could be perceived as being impartial or engaged in misconduct? What impact could such conduct have on the arbitration process?

SUMMARY OF COURT CASES INVOLVING THE MISCONDUCT OF ARBITRATORS

QUESADA V. CITY OF TAMPA,
2012 FLA. APP. LEXIS 10892 (VACATED)

Employee was terminated following drug tests that indicated usage of anabolic steroids. The arbitration award was in favor of the City, and the arbitrator admitted to conducting an independent investigation on the supplement. The Second District Court of Appeals held that the arbitrator's independent research constituted misconduct, and the employee was prejudiced by the misconduct. The court stated, "Arbitration panels, should not, in the course of their deliberations, have gone outside the evidence presented to them." The arbitrator's misconduct also prejudiced the employee, as the independent research yielded information both different from the record, but also damaging to the employee's case. In addition, the CBA did not provide for the arbitrator's independent research.

MORAN V. NEW YORK CITY TRANSIT AUTHORITY
45 AD. 3D 484, 846 N.Y.S.2D 162 (2007).

Petitioner claimed that arbitrator engaged in misconduct (e.g., falling asleep during critical portions of the proceeding, engaging in ex *parte* communication) and partiality (e.g., refusal to allow petitioner's lawyer of question complainant) were not upheld by the court during the proceedings. The Supreme Court (Appellate Division) of New York held that petitioner failed to establish arbitrator misconduct or partiality, as there were no indications in the record and there was a lack of supporting evidence.

SUMMARY OF RULES ON MISCONDUCT OF ARBITRATORS

- An arbitrator's independent research or investigation of a grievance constitutes misconduct, unless the parties agree or permitted by the CBA.

- To support vacating an arbitration award because of errors during the hearing, the plaintiff must present the court an adequate record to review.

- Arbitrator's legal error or mistake of fact is not sufficient to establish arbitrator misconduct that would justify vacating the award. The standard for arbitrator misconduct is higher and more egregious, and may involve establishing corruption or fraud.

- Arbitrator must disclose any and all past and present contacts with the parties and their representatives, e.g. prior hearings, bar Committees, social gathering, etc. The arbitrator should provide the details of any contacts and place on the record that the parties accept the appointment of the arbitrator.

III. THE ARBITRATION PROCESS

A. THE GRIEVANCE PROCESS

LABOR ARBITRATION AND DISPUTE RESOLUTION
88 YALE L.J. 916 (APRIL, 1979)[*]
JULIUS G. GETMAN

There is a widespread perception that our judicial system needs changing. It is expensive, unnecessarily technical, intrusive on private relations, and it gives unfair advantage to the wealthy and powerful. Labor arbitration, by contrast, is frequently pointed to as the paradigm of private justice.

It is understandable that labor arbitration is widely admired. When it functions properly it achieves in an impressive fashion the goals by which any system of dispute resolution should be measured. These are:

(1) *Finality.* Once decided, are cases likely to be retried or appealed?

(2) *Obedience.* Are the decisions put into effect or are they rendered meaningless by subsequent refusals to carry them out?

(3) *Guidance.* Do the decisions provide necessary guidance to the parties involved in the dispute? Can they subsequently structure behavior in a reasonable fashion and avoid future litigation?

---

[*] Reprinted with permission of The Yale University Law Journal Association, 88 Yale L. J. 916 (April, 1979).

(4) *Efficiency.* Are the majority of disputes settled without a formal hearing? When cases are tried, are the procedures adequate, flexible, and suited to the particular issue? Are the benefits achieved from the system economical compared to the costs?

(5) *Availability.* Is the dispute-resolution machinery routinely available without undue expense to people whose behavior is governed by the system, and are they provided with adequate representation?

(6) *Neutrality.* Do the decisionmakers avoid favoritism and bias for one side or another?

(7) *Conflict Redaction.* Does the entire process, including the adjudication, lead to more amicable relations and contribute to mutual respect among the potential disputants?

(8) *Fairness.* Will the disputes be resolved in a way that appropriately recognizes the interests of the various parties likely to come before the system?

The perception that labor arbitration successfully achieves these various purposes has led some commentators to the erroneous conclusion that it offers a technique for dispute resolution that can be routinely applied, with only minor adjustments, in other situations. This conclusion, which has been fostered by prominent labor arbitrators and by prestigious groups such as the American Arbitration Association and the National Academy of Arbitrators, overlooks the idiosyncratic nature of labor arbitration and its crucial interrelationship with unionization and collective bargaining.

Collective bargaining shapes labor arbitration and gives it power. The collective-bargaining relationship itself reflects the strength and purpose of unions. It is only when unions are powerful, well established, and responsive to the needs of their members that labor arbitration works successfully. Without unions and collective bargaining, key aspects of labor arbitration would become meaningless Or counterproductive. Therefore, proposals to utilize arbitration in various contexts cannot be justified by reference to the labor experience, although the effort to do so is common.

* * * *

Conclusion

To understand labor arbitration one must understand its complex relationship with other aspects of collective bargaining. Through labor arbitration the parties continue and refine their bargaining. Their agreement takes on a more precise meaning, and issues not dealt with during formal negotiations are resolved in a way likely to recognize their interests and priorities. This process is enhanced by the system of private selection of arbitrators. The private aspects of the process make arbitrators less able than judges to facilitate prelitigation settlement, but this is relatively unimportant because settlement is achieved through the lower steps of the grievance system.

The constant focus on the informality of arbitration is misleading. The procedures used vary, but they frequently involve presentation of cases through lawyers, oaths, subpoenas, transcripts, briefs, and carefully written awards following a common form and citing precedent. The entire process serves to legalize the administration of a unionized enterprise to a remarkable extent.

Labor arbitration also serves as a mechanism by which unions that have given up the right to strike can apply pressure on employers during the term of an agreement. This feature, which increases the value of arbitration to unions, occasionally makes it a source rather than a substitute for conflict.

The collective-bargaining relationship and the collective agreement give considerable power to arbitration awards. Primarily they provide the substantive standards to be applied and make the results acceptable to the parties. Because both sides develop a strong interest in the smooth functioning of the process, arbitration awards are routinely obeyed and infrequently challenged. The other provisions of the agreement serve to protect the integrity of the process. Because they limit managerial discretion they make it difficult to undercut the impact of an unfavorable award through retaliation.

The interconnection between labor arbitration and collective bargaining means that grievance systems in other situations without this feature will be vastly different. The private aspects of labor arbitration that have served to make it attractive to commentators are likely to be a hindrance in nonunionized contexts in which collective bargaining does not take place. Protection for nonunionized workers, for example, probably requires more direct government involvement, and even then it is unlikely to achieve the same results as are achieved by the combination of collective bargaining and labor arbitration in the unionized sector.

APPLICATION AND DISCUSSION QUESTIONS

1. What goals are achieved when parties use labor arbitration to resolve labor grievance? What is the "idiosyncratic" nature of labor arbitration that Professor Getman describes?

2. How has arbitration become more formal and less informal? How has the formality of arbitration improved the process of resolving grievances, as well as made it less efficient?

3. Professor Getman describes how arbitrators are less engaged in the pre-litigation and settlement of disputes than judges. What are some advantages and disadvantages to arbitrators of being more engaged in pre-litigation and settlement of grievances?

B. SELECTION OF THE ARBITRATOR

Organization that select arbitrators to hear labor and employment disputes have a number of readily available resources to use to select arbitrators from. Arbitrators may be selected from a roster of arbitrators that is maintained by various state and federal agencies. Rosters of arbitrators are also maintained by private ADR organizations and companies. In addition to availability of external rosters of arbitrators, organizations which regularly arbitrate cases may maintain a permanent roster of internal arbitrator.

The FMCS and AAA are the primary organizations that maintain rosters ADR panels of arbitrators. However, there are a number of other private and public organizations at the local. State and national level that also maintains rosters and panels of neutrals to serve as arbitrators.

1. FEDERAL MEDIATION AND CONCILIATION SERVICES (FMCS)

The FMCS maintains a roster of labor arbitrators. The FMCS does not allow advocates to serve on its roster as an arbitrator. Roster members are required to have extensive experience in labor relations and knowledge of collective nargaining, with experience conducting administrative hearings. For a description of the criteria to serve on the Roster, see FMCS at:

https://www. fmcs.gov.

2. NATIONAL MEDIATION BOARD (NMB)

The NMB maintains a roster of arbitrators to hear railroad and airline collective bargaining disputes. The primary qualification for placement on the NMB's roster is to have extensive "substantive experience in connection with collective bargaining or labor agreement administration in the railroad and airline industries. An arbitrator is also eligible for placement on the roster if they are a current member of the National Academy of Arbitrators. See NMB at: https://www. nmb.gov.

3. AMERICAN ARBITRATION ASSOCIATION (AAA)

The AAA is a not-for-profit organization which maintains a number of national rosters of arbitrators, including labor and employment arbitrators. The AAA also provides administrative support to parties in processing a dispute through arbitration. See, https//www.adr.org

4. PERMANENT ARBITRATORS

In lieu of selecting an arbitrator from a roster of arbitrators, the union and the employer may agree on maintaining a permanent panel of arbitrators to use on a rotating basis. These arbitrators have extensive knowledge of and experience with the practices of the industry.

5. AD HOC ARBITRATORS

Organizations may select arbitrators on an as needed basis. This normally occurs when disputes have not been successfully resolved through the labor grievance process or under terms of an employment contract. The organization will then contact either a private or public ADR organization to provide a list of qualified arbitrators.

D. Diversity In Arbitration

ELIMINATING BARRIERS FOR MINORITY ADR NEUTRALS

35 ACRESOLUTION SPRING 2006[*]

FLOYD D. WEATHERSPOON

The use of alternative dispute resolution (ADR) has grown by leaps and bounds during the past 25 years. Indeed, ADR has expanded from its traditional use in labor arbitration into the judicial systems, educational systems, community disputes, state and federal agencies, and complex commercial disputes. Corporations have found ADR to be so cost effective that many have made ADR mandatory in resolving employment disputes. Similarly, the banking industry has incorporated the use of ADR as a mandatory method for resolving credit card and contract disputes. The use of ADR is also expanding in the health care field, in special education, natural disasters and on-line disputes.

Exclusionary Practices

As the use of ADR has grown, so has the need for competent ADR professionals, e.g., mediators, arbitrators, facilitators, etc. In addition, ADR organizations, including state and federal governments and corporations have created and expanded ADR rosters and panels to provide arbitration, mediation and facilitation services. Unfortunately, minority ADR neutrals have been intentionally and unintentionally excluded from receiving such opportunities.

Not only have minorities been disproportionately excluded from ADR rosters and panels, they are often not selected as trainers in a myriad of training programs provided by colleges and universities, private training organizations and governmental agencies. Ironically, minorities are aggressively recruited to attend such programs but rarely chosen to serve as a facilitator or trainer. Often, those opportunities are only made available to the same select non-minority trainers and facilitators. With few exceptions, minorities are also often excluded from the high-paying lucrative rosters.

* * * *

---

[*] Originally published in ACResolution Magazine (Spring, 2006).

Minorities seem to have no trouble serving on community mediation rosters or doing pro bono work. However, with few exceptions, minority ADR neutrals report a difficulty in making the transition from serving as a voluntary neutral to being compensated as a professional ADR neutral. Even in the judicial system with court appointed neutrals, minorities are often under-represented on rosters. Minority neutrals identified exclusionary selection criteria as a major obstacle to placement on rosters and panels. ADR providers were described as the "gate keepers" who "sit at the door" to disperse ADR opportunities to those who have met their subjective requirements.

The selection of individuals to the various rosters and panels reminds me of when I pledged a fraternity. I was required to engage in a selection process that felt somewhat meaningless and arbitrary until it was determined by those in power that I was acceptable for admission into the exclusive club. At the end, I felt I had endured too much to turn back, even though the process did not make me a loyal frat brother. Similarly, the criteria for entrance into the exclusive ADR club are often not relevant and at times, the process can even be arbitrary and discriminatory. Those who make it through the process buy into and propagate a selection system that has a disparate impact on women and minority neutrals. They too take the position, "I met the criteria and every one interested in becoming a part of this exclusive club must also meet the same criteria." This appears to be the sentiment of those who become a part of a system that may unintentionally exclude minority and women neutrals.

In Search of a Mentor

Finding a compatible and committed mentor is a challenge for any new ADR practitioner, but can be especially daunting for minority neutrals. It is crucial to locate a mentor who is well-respected in the field and who can introduce new minority neutrals to advocates and ADR providers.

* * * *

Racial and Ethnic Discrimination

In my experience, many minority neutrals believe discrimination exists in selecting minority neutrals to serve on various rosters and panels. ADR organizations and administrators readily deny any such practice exists and are angered when such allegations are suggested. However, many minority ADR neutrals perceive that the selection processes are exclusionary and that these processes discriminate against minority neutrals. This theory of discrimination was articulated by the Supreme

Court's decision in *Griggs v. Duke Power.* The Supreme Court determined that discrimination is not only overt "but also practices that are fair in form but discriminatory in operation" is still discrimination. (401 U.S. 424, 431 (1971)).

* * * *

As *Griggs* illustrates, discrimination is not always blatant; indeed it is often delivered with a smile. Minority neutrals often share their experiences of communicating with administrators of ADR programs and providers around the country who advise them of the process and selection criteria for placement on their roster. The code words for exclusion are terms such as "qualification," "criteria," "quality of service" and "standards." Depending on the manner in which these terms are presented, minority ADR neutrals may interpret these terms to mean "minorities need not apply." Clearly, all of these factors can and should be a consideration for placement on the various ADR rosters. However, the question is whether these factors are related to what neutrals do. Do these criteria predict performance as a neutral? Often there is no real correlation.

Elimination of Discriminatory Practices

* * * *

ADR providers should evaluate whether their selection devices are having a disproportionate impact on minority ADR neutrals. If their selection devices can be justified based on a business necessity, they should also explore whether other selection devices could be used which would have fewer discriminatory effects on minority neutrals but still achieve their overall goals. This principle was also mandated in *Griggs.*

* * * *

Often minority ADR neutrals are unaware or the last to know about new developments and expansion of opportunities in the field of ADR. By the time the information accidentally filters down to the minority ADR network, the new ADR initiative is already in place, the qualifications have been established, the roster is closed and the same select group of non-minority neutrals has been selected by their associates. For example, a permanent panel of neutrals was being selected at a federal agency and three months after the panel of non-minorities was selected, I received a call inquiring whether I was aware of any minority neutrals who could be considered when they select members for their roster in a few years. Why the absence of minority neutrals was not considered when the list was first established?

The lack of information sharing with minority ADR neutrals is not limited to any one field. Minority ADR neutrals are often ignored and excluded from opportunities involving disputes related to banking, special education, construction, federal labor issues, and even sports. Recently, I tried to organize a training program on sports arbitration as a part of our Minority ADR Initiative. I learned very quickly that information on opportunities in this field is closely held and reserved for only a few non-minorities. The failure on the part of ADR providers, including governmental agencies, to make a conscious effort to circulate information within the minority ADR network is not necessarily intentional discrimination but just indifference. Nevertheless, the end result is still the same—the exclusion of minority neutrals.

The solution to this barrier is quite simple. If there is a good faith intention to share information regarding paid opportunities and to diversify rosters, then ADR providers should make a concerted effort to circulate information in a timely manner to various minority professional organizations. Diversity means more than selecting one superstar minority neutral. In addition, ADR organizations can establish a network of minority neutrals in the various fields. ADR providers can circulate their announcements to organizations such as the Association for Conflict Resolution and the National Bar Association, as well as to minority networks such as the Mediators of Color Alliance (MOCA).

Helping minority ADR neutrals to gain opportunities and acceptance in the field of ADR requires ADR providers to continue evaluating their selection procedures for placement on rosters and panels. In addition, lawyers who now play a major role in selecting neutrals to serve in private disputes must also look outside their network for diversity. Finally, minority ADR neutrals must be vigilant in their efforts to seek opportunities and acceptance in the field.

The role of minorities in ADR is more vital today than it has ever been. Changes to the current processes must be made to ensure equal and effective ADR. The future of ADR depends upon the increased inclusion of minority neutrals. It is my belief that increasing the number of minority neutrals will lead to an increase in the use of ADR and will enhance users' satisfaction with ADR outcomes.

APPLICATION AND DISCUSSION QUESTIONS

1. What additional obstacles can you identify that Minority and Women ADR professionals may face when entering the field of ADR?

2. Why is the role of minority ADR more vital today than it has ever been? What is the benefit of having minority ADR professionals on panels and rosters?

3. Why are minority ADR professionals often overlooked when parties are selecting neutrals?

THE IMPACT OF THE GROWTH AND USE OF ADR PROCESSES ON MINORITY COMMUNITIES, INDIVIDUAL RIGHTS, AND NEUTRALS
39 CAP. U. L. REV. 789 (2011)
FLOYD D. WEATHERSPOON

VI. Selection of Minority Neutrals

As the ADR field has grown, opportunities for neutrals have also grown. However, such opportunities for minority neutrals have been limited, and in some cases, minority neutrals have been totally excluded. The lack of diversity in the pool of potential neutrals raises suspicion among minorities who must use the ADR process to resolve their dispute. Unfortunately, minorities who participate voluntarily or involuntarily in an ADR process may find that the ADR participants are similar to those in court where all the participants are white. Often the mediator or arbitrator will be white as well as the attorneys and other participants. The absence of minority neutrals on ADR rosters, panels, and court appointments stems from a system of exclusion and invisibility. When plaintiffs have challenged the lack of diversity on ADR rosters, they fail to garner support from the courts.

The pool of neutrals has been primarily white males, especially in labor, construction, and commercial disputes. Minority mediators are often placed on family and domestic rosters, juvenile programs, and community and volunteer rosters. Rarely are they placed on highly paid lucrative rosters. Those are typically reserved for white males.

The major ADR providers and organizations have offered and developed many initiatives to increase the presence of minorities on their rosters, but the number remains relatively small after years of promoting diversity in the ADR field. With the explosion of the use of ADR processes and the commitment on the part of ADR providers to increase the numbers of minorities on their rosters of neutrals-why are the numbers still relatively small? There are few scientific studies which address this issue. However, the Barriers Research Study, conducted at John Jay College of Criminal Justice of the City University of New York, did reveal a number of "informational and professional barriers," "social and institutional barriers," and "economic barriers."Also, although not a scientific study, surveys completed and collected during Capital University Law School's ADR conferences and institutes reveal that minority neutrals face such barriers as lack of mentors, stealth selection procedures, lack of information regarding ADR opportunities, and superficial qualification requirements.

In addition to the barriers mentioned above, other factors explain why minority neutrals are rarely listed on rosters, and even if listed, are rarely selected. Judge Timothy K. Lewis spoke of an incident he witnessed while attending a conference of corporate general counsels where he was hosting a seminar on diversity. The following question was raised by an attendee: "You know, this sounds very nice and is all well and good, but what are we supposed to do as a result of the drop off in quality we're going to have to deal with from hiring a minority arbitrator or mediator?"According to Judge Lewis, this sentiment of a corporate general counsel, who has the authority to select mediators or arbitrators, was unfortunately the sentiment of a majority of the attendees.

Blatant race and national origin discrimination may also explain why minority neutrals are excluded. These factors are often ignored or deemed too sensitive to address.[86] Based on racial and ethnic stereotypical biases, minority neutrals may be ignored intentionally or assumed not qualified. Even when highly experienced minority neutrals gain placement on ADR rosters, they rarely are scheduled to serve. Some scholars suggest that minority neutrals may need to develop better strategies for marketing their services to gain recognition and acceptance. It appears then that there are a number of factors explaining why minority neutrals are excluded, isolated, and ignored. Courts, corporations, and advocates must reach beyond the traditional methods of selecting neutrals and provide minority neutrals opportunities for growth and development.

VII. Conclusion

This article has raised more questions than it has answered. The hope is that this symposium will lay the foundation for continued study, evaluation, and dialogue on the impact of ADR on the minority community, individual rights, and the selection of minority neutrals.

APPLICATION AND DISCUSSION QUESTIONS

1. The above article raises a number of questions related to the lack of diversity in the field of arbitration. For example: Do minorities benefit more by resolving disputes through ADR processes versus the courts, where they rarely prevail? Will the rule of law established by courts diminish, thus, forcing minorities to rely on private instead of public justice? What is your response to these conerns?

2. There is substantial evidence that ADR processes lessen the cost and time of litigating disputes and reduce the court's docket. But do these benefits overshadow the rights of minorities who are often involuntarily thrust into these processes?

3. Why is it important to have a diverse roster of arbitrators for the parties to select from?

4. The article gave a number of suggestions for diversifying rosters and panels of neutrals. Which suggestions would you have concern with if implemented by ADR providers? What additional suggestions would you make to further diversify roster?

5. There is also evidence that women face similar barriers in entering the profession as arbitrators. See, Cynthia Alkon, *Women Labor Arbitrators: Women Members Of The National Academy Of Arbitrators Speak About The Barriers Of Entry Into The Field,* 6 Appalachian J.L. 195 (Spring 2007). Also see, Andrea Kupfer Schneider, Gina Viola Brown, *Gender Differences In Dispute Resolution Practice,* 20 No. 3 Disp. Resol. Mag. 36 (Spring, 2014). What solutions would you propose to increase the number of women arbitrators?

6. The National Labor Relations Board may deter the unfair labor practice charge, if the issue is resolved through arbitration. The NLRB first established this policy in *Collyer Insulational Wire*, 192 NLRB 837 (1971) and in *United Technologies* 208 NLRB 557 (1984).

E. NLRB DEFERRAL OF ARBITRATION

In resolving a contractual dispute under a collective bargaining agreement (CBA), an arbitrator's decision may at the same time resolve an unfair labor practice claim (ULP) filed with the National Labor Relations Board (NLRB). This occurs when the underlying facts are applicable to the grievance, filed under the CBA, and the complaint, filed under the Nation Labor Relations Act. When this occurs the NLRB may defer to the arbitrator's decision and decline to hear the unfair labor practices complaint. Prior to arbitration, the NLRB may delay the processing of an ULP claim for similar reasons. Thus, the deferral may be a pre-arbitration deferral or a post-arbitration deferral.

This has been the policy of the NLRB since its ruling in *Spielberg Mfg. Co.*, 112 NLRB 1080 (1955), and *Olin Corp.*, 268 NLRB 573 (1084). In *Olin,* the NLRB set forth the standard it would apply in post arbitral deferrals. Similarly, the NLRB set forth standards to apply in pret-arbitration deferrals in *Collyer Insulated Wire*, 192 NLRB 837 (1971) and in *United Technologies Corp.*, 208 NLRB 557 (1984). However, on December 15, 2014 in *Babcock & Wilcox Construction Co.*, 361 NLRB 132 (2014), the NLRB modified its deferral standard and set forth a stricter standard to apply in deferral of arbitration cases. On February 15, 2015, the NLRB General Counsel issued Memorandum GC 15-02 to explain the modified deferral standard.

COLLYER INSULATED WIRE, A GULF AND WESTERN SYSTEMS CO. AND LOCAL UNION 1098, INTERNATIONAL BROTHERHOOD OF ELECTRICAL WORKERS AFL-CIO

N.L.R.B. 837 (J. FITZPATRICK, 1971)

* * * *

IV. DISCUSSION

We find merit in Respondent's exceptions that because this dispute in its entirety arises from the contract between the parties, and from the parties' relationship under the contract, it ought to be resolved in the manner which that contract prescribes. We conclude that the Board is vested with authority to withhold its processes in this case, and that the contract here made available a quick and fair means for the resolution of this dispute including, if appropriate, a fully effective remedy for any breach of contract which occurred. We conclude, in sum, that our obligation to advance the purposes of the Act is best discharged by the dismissal of this complaint.

In our view, disputes such as these can better be resolved by arbitrators with special skill and experience in deciding matters arising under established bargaining relationships than by the application by this Board of a particular provision of our statute. The necessity for such special skill and expertise is apparent upon examination of the issues arising from Respondent's actions with respect to the operators' rates, the skill factor increase, and the reassignment of duties relating to the worm gear removal. Those issues include, specifically: (a) the extent to which these actions were intended to be reserved to the management, subject to later adjustment by grievance and arbitration; (b) the extent to which the skill factor increase should properly be construed, under article IX of the agreement, as a "change in the general scale of pay" or, conversely, as "adjustments in individual rates . . . to remove inequalities or for other proper reason"; (c) the extent, if any, to which the procedures of article XIII governing new or changed jobs and job rates should have been made applicable to the skill factor increase here; and (d) the extent to which any of these issues may be affected by the long course of dealing between the parties. The determination of these issues, we think, is best left to discussions in the grievance procedure by the parties who negotiated the applicable provisions or, if such discussions do not resolve them, then to an arbitrator chosen under the agreement and authorized by it to resolve such issues.

The Board's authority, in its discretion, to defer to the arbitration process has never been questioned by the courts of appeals, or by the Supreme Court. Although Section 10(a) of the Act clearly vests the Board with jurisdiction over conduct which constitutes a violation of the provisions of Section 8, notwithstanding the existence of methods of "adjustment or prevention that might be established by agreement," nothing in the Act intimates that the Board must exercise jurisdiction where such methods exist. On the contrary in Carey v. Westinghouse Electric Corporation, 375 U.S. 261, 271 (1964), the Court indicated that it favors our deference to such agreed methods by quoting at length with obvious approval the following language from the Board's decision in *International Harvester Co.:*

> "There is no question that the Board is not precluded from adjudicating unfair labor practice charges even though they might have been the subject of an arbitration proceeding and award. Section 10(a) of the Act expressly makes this plain, and the courts have uniformly so held. However, it is equally well established that *the Board has considerable discretion to respect an arbitration award and decline to exercise its authority over alleged unfair labor practices if to do so will serve the fundamental aims of the Act.*
>
> The Act, as has repeatedly been stated, is primarily designed to promote industrial peace and stability by encouraging the practice and procedure of collective bargaining. Experience has demonstrated that collective-bargaining agreements that provide for final and binding arbitration of grievance and disputes arising thereunder, 'as a substitute for industrial strife,' contribute significantly to the attainment of this statutory objective". [Emphasis supplied.]

* * * *

As already noted, the contract between Respondent and the Union unquestionably obligates each party to submit to arbitration any dispute arising under the contract and binds both parties to the result thereof. It is true, manifestly, that we cannot judge the regularity or statutory acceptability of the result in an arbitration proceeding which has not occurred. However, we are unwilling to adopt the presumption that such a proceeding will be invalid under Spielberg and to exercise our decisional authority at this juncture on the basis of a mere possibility that such a proceeding might be unacceptable under *Spielberg* standards. That risk is far better accommodated, we believe, by the result reached here of retaining jurisdiction against an event which years of experience with labor arbitration have now made clear is a remote hazard.

Member Fanning's dissenting opinion incorrectly characterizes this decision as instituting "compulsory arbitration" and as creating an opportunity for employers and unions to "strip parties of statutory rights."

We are not compelling any party to agree to arbitrate disputes arising during a contract term, but are merely giving full effect to their own voluntary agreements to submit all such disputes to arbitration, rather than permitting such agreements to be sidestepped and permitting the substitution of our processes, a forum not contemplated by their own agreement.

Nor are we "stripping" any party of "statutory rights." The courts have long recognized that an industrial relations dispute may involve conduct which, at least arguably, may contravene both the collective agreement and our statute. When the parties have contractually committed themselves to mutually agreeable procedures for resolving their disputes during the period of the contract, we are of the view that those procedures should be afforded full opportunity to function. The long and successful functioning of grievance and arbitration procedures suggests to us that in the overwhelming majority of cases, the utilization of such means will resolve the underlying dispute and make it unnecessary for either party to follow the more formal, and sometimes lengthy, combination of administrative and judicial litigation provided for under our statute. At the same time, by our reservation of jurisdiction, we guarantee that there will be no sacrifice of statutory rights if the parties' own processes fail to function in a manner consistent with the dictates of our law. This approach, we believe, effectuates the salutary policy announced in *Spielberg*, which the dissenting opinion correctly summarizes as one of not requiring the "serious machinery of the Board where the record indicates that the parties are in the process of resolving their dispute in a manner sufficient to effectuate the policies of the Act."

We are especially mindful, finally, that the policy of this Nation to avoid industrial strife through voluntary resolution of industrial disputes is not static, but is dynamic. The years since enactment of Section 203(d) have been vital ones, and the policy then expressed has helped to shape an industrial system in which the institution of contract arbitration has grown not only pervasive but, literally, indispensable. The Board has both witnessed and participated in the growth, a complex interaction where the growth of arbitration in response to Congress' will has called forth and nurtured gradually broader conceptions of the basic policy. The Supreme Court which in Lincoln Mills, first upheld the enforceability of agreements to arbitrate disputes has recently, in *Boys Markets, Inc. v. Retails Clerks*, suggested that arbitration has become "the central institution in the administration of collective bargaining contracts." After *Boys Market* it may truly be said that where a contract provides for arbitration, either party has at hand legal and effective means to ensure that the arbitration will occur.

We believe it to be consistent with the fundamental objectives of Federal law to require the parties here to honor their contractual obligations rather than, by casting this dispute in statutory terms, to ignore their agreed-upon procedures.

V. REMEDY

Without prejudice to any party and without deciding the merits of the controversy, we shall order that the complaint herein be dismissed, but we shall retain jurisdiction for a limited purpose. Our decision represents a developmental step in the Board's treatment of these problems and the controversy here arose at a time when the Board decisions may have led the parties to conclude that the Board approved dual litigation of this controversy before the Board and before an arbitrator. We are also aware that the parties herein have not resolved their dispute by the contractual grievance and arbitration procedure and that, therefore, we cannot now inquire whether resolution of the dispute will comport with the standards set forth in *Spielberg*. In order to eliminate the risk of prejudice to any party we shall retain jurisdiction over this dispute solely for the purpose of entertaining an appropriate and timely motion for further consideration upon a proper showing that either (a) the dispute has not, with reasonable promptness after the issuance of this decision, either been resolved by amicable settlement in the grievance procedure or submitted promptly to arbitration, or (b) the grievance or arbitration procedures have not been fair and regular or have reached a result which is repugnant to the Act.

ORDER

Pursuant to Section 10(c) of the National Labor Relations Act, as amended, the National Labor Relations Board orders that the complaint herein be, and it hereby is, dismissed; provided, however, that: Jurisdiction of this proceeding is hereby retained for the limited purposes indicated in that portion of our Decision and Order herein entitled "Remedy."

APPLICATION AND DISCUSSION QUESTIONS

1. Why does the Board feel that arbitrators are better skilled to resolve the contract dispute than the Board?

2. Under what authority does the Board have in deferring disputes to arbitration? How does the Board rely on Supreme Court decisions in *Lincoln Mills* and *Boys Markets* to support the use of arbitration to resolve collective bargaining disputes?

3. The dissenting opinion characterizes the Board's decision as a form of "mandatory arbitration." Do you feel there are some merits to this statement?

4. As you read *Babcock & Wilcock,* supra, outline the new standard the NLRB will apply in pre-arbitration deferral?

BABCOCK & WILCOX CONSTRUCTION CO., INC. AND COLETTA KIM BENELI

2014 NLRB LEXIS 964; 201 L.R.R.M. 2057; 2014-15 NLRB DEC. (CCH) P15, 892; 361 NLRB NO. 132 (2014)

Panel: By Mark Gaston Pearce, Chairman, Kent Y. Hirozawa, Member, Nancy Schiffer, Member.

Administrative Law Judge: JAY R. POLLACK

DECISION AND ORDER

On April 9, 2012, Administrative Law Judge Jay R. Pollack issued the attached decision. The General Counsel filed exceptions and a supporting brief; the Respondent filed an answering brief; and the General Counsel filed a reply brief.

The National Labor Relations Board has considered the decision and the record in light of the exceptions and briefs, and has decided to affirm the judge's rulings, findings, and conclusions and to adopt the recommended Order.

The National Labor Relations Act. The Board's standard for deferral is solely a matter for the Board's discretion. Section 10(a) of the Act expressly provides that the Board is not precluded from adjudicating unfair labor practice charges even though they might have been the subject of an arbitration proceeding and award, and the courts have uniformly so held.

In its seminal decision in *Spielberg Mfg. Co., 112 NLRB 1080 (1955)*, the Board held that it would defer, as a matter of discretion, to arbitral decisions in cases in which the proceedings appear to have been fair and regular, all parties agreed to be bound, and the decision of the arbitrator is not clearly repugnant to the purposes and policies of the Act. Id. at 1082. The deferral doctrine announced in Spielberg was intended to reconcile the Board's obligation under Section 10(a) of the Act to prevent unfair labor practices with the Federal policy of encouraging the voluntary settlement of labor disputes. Thirty years later, in *Olin Corp., 268 NLRB 573 (1984)*, the Board adopted the current deferral standard, holding that deferral is appropriate where the contractual issue is "factually parallel" to the unfair labor practice issue, the arbitrator was presented generally with the facts relevant to resolving that issue and the award is not "clearly repugnant" to the Act.

The General Counsel contends that the current deferral standards, as explicated in Olin, are inadequate to ensure that employees' statutory rights are protected in the arbitral process. He urges the Board to adopt a more demanding standard in 8(a)(3) and (1) cases, specifically those alleging that employers have retaliated against employees for exercising their rights under Section 7 of the Act. Under the General Counsel's proposed standard, the Board would defer only if the statutory right was either incorporated in the collective-bargaining agreement or presented to the arbitrator by the parties, and if the arbitrator "correctly enunciated the applicable statutory principles and applied them in deciding the issue." Under the General Counsel's proposed standard, the party favoring deferral would have the burden of showing that those criteria were met. On such a showing, if the proceedings appeared to have been fair and regular, and all parties agreed to be bound, the Board would defer unless the award was "clearly repugnant" to the Act, as under the current standard. See GC Memorandum 11-05 at 6-7 (January 20, 2011).

On February 7, 2014, the Board invited the parties and interested amici to file briefs addressing the following questions. (Question 3 and 4 omitted)

1. Should the Board adhere to, modify, or abandon its existing standard for postarbitral deferral under *Spielberg Mfg. Co., 112 NLRB 1080 (1955)*, and *Olin Corp., 268 NLRB 573 (1984)*?

2. If the Board modifies the existing standard, should the Board adopt the standard outlined by the General Counsel in GC Memorandum 11-05 (January 20, 2011) or would some other modification of the existing standard be more appropriate: e.g., shifting the burden of proof, redefining "repugnant to the Act," or reformulating the test for determining whether the arbitrator "adequately considered" the unfair labor practice issue?

The Board also invited the parties and amici to submit empirical and other evidence bearing on those questions.

After careful consideration, we agree with the General Counsel that the existing deferral standard does not adequately balance the protection of employees' rights under the Act and the national policy of encouraging arbitration of disputes arising over the application or interpretation of a collective-bargaining agreement. The current standard creates excessive risk that the Board will defer when an arbitrator has not adequately considered the statutory issue, or when it is impossible to tell whether he or she has done so. The result is that employees are effectively deprived of their Section 7 rights if disciplinary actions that are, in fact, unlawful employer reprisals for union or protected concerted activity are upheld in arbitration. Accordingly, we have decided to modify our standard for postarbitral deferral in 8(a)(3) and (1) cases, but not precisely along the lines suggested by the General Counsel.

We agree that the burden of proving that deferral is appropriate is properly placed on the party urging deferral. We also agree that deferral is appropriate only when the arbitrator has been explicitly authorized to decide the statutory issue, either in the collective-bargaining agreement or by agreement of the parties in the particular case. We believe, however, that the General Counsel's proposal that deferral is warranted only if the arbitrator "correctly enunciated the applicable statutory principles and applied them in deciding the issue" would set an unrealistically high standard for deferral. Our modified standard, by contrast, will require that the proponent of deferral demonstrate that the parties presented the statutory issue to the arbitrator, the arbitrator considered the statutory issue or was prevented from doing so by the party opposing deferral, and Board law reasonably permits the award. On such a showing, the Board will defer. Our reasons follow.

I. DISCUSSION

A. Statutory Background [omitted]

B. A Brief History of Postarbitral Deferral

The Board's postarbitral deferral policy has traveled a long and winding road. The Board began almost 60 years ago, as an exercise of discretion, to defer in what it deemed appropriate circumstances to arbitral decisions involving alleged unfair labor practices. In its 1955 Spielberg decision, the Board announced that it would defer if the proceedings appeared to have been fair and regular, all parties had agreed to be bound, and the arbitrator's decision was "not clearly repugnant to the purposes and policies of the Act." 112 NLRB at 1082. After some years of experience applying Spielberg, the Board held it improper to defer when the arbitrator had not considered the unfair labor practice issue, explaining that "[w]e cannot, in giving effect to arbitration agreements, neglect our function of protecting the rights of employees granted by our Act." Raytheon Co., 140 NLRB 883, 886 (1963), enf. denied 326 F.2d 471 (1st Cir. 1964). The Raytheon rule was extended in *Airco Industrial Gases*, 195 NLRB 676, 677 (1972), to cases where the arbitration award gave no indication whether the arbitrator ruled on the unfair labor practice issue. *Id.* at 677. Then, in Yourga Trucking, the Board held that the party urging deferral bore the burden of showing that the deferral standards were met.

Two years later, however, the Board abruptly reversed course, citing concern that under the existing standard, parties would withhold evidence relevant to the unfair labor practice issue in arbitral proceedings in an attempt to have the Board decide the issue. *Electronic Reproduction Service Corp.*, 213 NLRB 758, 761 (1974). To avoid such piecemeal litigation, the Board held that it would defer to arbitral awards unless the party opposing deferral could show that special circumstances prevented that party from having a full and fair opportunity to present evidence relevant to the statutory issue.

Six years later, the Board overruled Electronic Reproduction Service, and returned to the principles laid down in *Raytheon, Airco,* and *Yourga Trucking. Suburban Motor Freight, Inc.,* 247 NLRB 146, 146-147 (1980). In *Suburban Motor Freight*, the Board ruled that it would "give no deference to an arbitration award which bears no indication that the arbitrator ruled on the statutory issue of discrimination in determining the propriety of an employer's disciplinary actions." *Id.* The Board also returned to the previous burden of proof allocations, under which the party seeking deferral was required to show that the standards for deferral had been met. *Id.*

Four years later, however, the Board in Olin overruled *Suburban Motor Freight* and held that it would find that an arbitrator has adequately considered the unfair labor practice if: (1) the contractual and unfair labor practice issues were factually parallel, and (2) the arbitrator was generally presented with the facts relevant to resolving the unfair labor practice. The Board also placed the burden on the party opposing deferral to demonstrate that the standards for deferral had not been met. *Id.*

C. The New Standard for Postarbitral Deferral

Having carefully considered the arguments of the parties and amici, we are persuaded that the existing deferral standard does not adequately protect employees' exercise of their rights under Section 7. In practice, the standard adopted in Olin amounts to a conclusive presumption that the arbitrator "adequately considered" the statutory issue if the arbitrator was merely presented with facts relevant to both an alleged contract violation and an alleged unfair labor practice. The presumption is theoretically rebuttable, but, as indicated above, the burden is on the party opposing deferral to show that the conditions for deferral are not met. In many, if not most arbitral proceedings, the parties do not file written briefs; there is no transcript of proceedings; and decisions often are summarily stated. In such situations, it is virtually impossible to prove that the statutory issue was not considered. For example, in *Airborne Freight Corp.,* 343 NLRB 580, 581 (2004), the Board deferred the 8(a)(3) discharge allegation even though the record did not show what arguments and evidence were presented in the grievance proceeding, because the General Counsel was unable to show that the statutory issues were not presented to the grievance panel. In our view, deferral in such circumstances amounts to abdication of the Board's duty to ensure that employees' Section 7 rights are protected.

Accordingly, we have decided to modify our deferral standard as follows. If the arbitration procedures appear to have been fair and regular, and if the parties agreed to be bound, the Board will defer to an arbitral decision if the party urging deferral shows that: (1) the arbitrator was explicitly authorized to decide the unfair labor practice issue; (2) the arbitrator was presented with and considered the statutory issue, or was prevented from doing so by the party opposing deferral; and (3) Board law reasonably permits the award. This modified framework is intended to rectify the deficiencies in the current deferral standard in a way that provides greater protection of employees' statutory rights while, at the same time, furthering the policy of peaceful resolution of labor disputes through collective bargaining. Thus, as discussed below, this approach will enable us to determine whether the arbitrator has actually resolved the unfair labor practice issue in a manner consistent with the Act, without placing an undue burden on unions, employers, arbitrators, or the arbitration system itself.

1. The arbitrator must be explicitly authorized to decide the statutory issue

> Arbitration is a consensual matter. The Supreme Court has expressly held that "arbitration is a matter of contract and a party cannot be required to submit to arbitration any dispute which he has not agreed so to submit."

2. The arbitrator must have been presented with and considered the statutory issue, or have been prevented from doing so by the party opposing deferral

Under the current deferral standard, an arbitrator will be found to have adequately considered the unfair labor practice issue if it and the contractual issue are "factually parallel" and if the arbitrator was "presented generally" with the facts relevant to resolving the statutory issue. *Olin, 268 NLRB at 574.* As discussed above, this amounts to a presumption that if an arbitrator is presented in some fashion with facts relevant to both an alleged contract violation and an alleged unfair labor practice, the arbitrator necessarily was presented with, and decided, the latter allegation in the course of deciding the former.

*   *   *   *

Accordingly, we shall defer to arbitral decisions only where the party urging deferral demonstrates that the arbitrator has actually considered the unfair labor practice issue, or that although the statutory issue is incorporated in the collective-bargaining agreement, the party opposing deferral has acted affirmatively to prevent the proponent of deferral from placing the statutory issue before the arbitrator. We emphasize, however, that we are not returning to the rule of Electronic Reproduction Services, wherein the Board held that in the absence of "unusual circumstances" it would defer to arbitral awards dealing with discharge or discipline so long as there was an opportunity to present the statutory issue to the arbitrator, even where the record did not disclose whether the arbitrator had considered, or been presented with, the unfair labor practice issue involved.

*   *   *   *

3. Board law must reasonably permit the award

If the previous requirements are met, deferral normally will be appropriate if the party urging deferral shows that Board law reasonably permits the arbitral award. By this, we mean that the arbitrator's decision must constitute a reasonable application of the statutory principles that would govern the Board's decision, if the case were presented to it, to the facts of the case. The arbitrator, of course, need not reach the same result the Board would reach, only a result that a decision maker reasonably applying the Act could reach. In deciding whether to defer, the Board will not engage in the equivalent of de novo review of the arbitrator's decision.

4. The proponent of deferral has the burden to show that the standards for deferral have been met

Finally, we return to the rule enunciated in *Yourga Trucking, Inc., 197 NLRB at 928*, and reaffirmed in *Suburban Motor Freight, 247 NLRB at 147*, that the party urging deferral has the burden to prove that the substantive requirements for deferral have been met. It is well settled that deferral is an affirmative defense.

APPLICATION AND DISCUSSION QUESTIONS

1. What new standard did the Board set forth for post-arbitral deferral in 8(a)(3) and (1) cases? How is the Board's modified standard different from what the Board announced almost sixty years ago in *Spielburg Mfg. Co.,* 112 NLRB 1080 (1955) and *Olin Corp.,* 268 NLRB (1984)?

2. What should the arbitrator include in their award when 8(a)(3) and (1) issues are included in the contract dispute? Should arbitrators specifically spell out in their award whether the unfair practices claim was addressed, and if so, explain in details the basis of the decision?

3. What impact does *Babcock & Wilcox* have on collective bargaining agreements? Should the parties negotiate language in the CBA on deferral arbitration? What language would you recommend to the parties to be included?

FROM: Richard F. Griffin, Jr., General Counsel /s/

SUBJECT: Guideline Memorandum Concerning Deferral to Arbitral Awards, the Arbitral Process, and Grievance Settlements in Section 8(a)(1) and (3) cases

I. Introduction

In its seminal decision in *Spielberg Manufacturing Co.*, the Board decided that it would defer, as a matter of discretion, to an arbitrator's decision in cases where the arbitral proceedings appear to have been fair and regular, all parties agreed to be bound, and the arbitrator's decision was not clearly repugnant to the purposes and policies of the Act. After some years of experience applying *Spielberg*, the Board expanded on that test by requiring an arbitrator to have considered the unfair labor practice issue (i.e., the "statutory issue"). In *Olin Corp.*, the Board relaxed the consideration requirement, holding that it was satisfied if the contractual and statutory issues were factually parallel and the arbitrator was presented generally with the facts relevant to resolving the unfair labor practice. In addition, *Olin* placed the burden on the party opposing deferral to demonstrate that the deferral criteria were not met.

In *Babcock & Wilcox Construction Co.*, the Board revisited *Olin* and held that the existing postarbitral deferral standard did not adequately balance the protection of employee rights under the Act and the national policy of encouraging arbitration of disputes over the application or interpretation of collective-bargaining agreements. The Board reasoned that the existing standard created excessive risk that the Board would defer when an arbitrator had not adequately considered the unfair labor practice issue, or when it was impossible to tell whether that issue had been considered.

In order to adequately ensure that employees' Section 7 rights are protected in the course of the arbitral process, *Babcock* announced a new standard for deferring to arbitral decisions in Section 8(a)(1) and (3) cases. In so doing, the Board also modified the standards for prearbitral deferral and deferral to grievance settlements in these types of cases. This memorandum explains these new standards, describes the circumstances in which they apply to pending and future cases, and provides guidance on handling cases that implicate these issues.

II. Postarbitral Deferral

A. Overview of the Babcock Standard and Burden Allocation

Under *Babcock*, deferral to an arbitral decision is appropriate in Section 8(a)(1) and (3) cases where the arbitration procedures appear to have been fair and regular, the parties agreed to be bound, and the party urging deferral demonstrates that: (1) the arbitrator was explicitly authorized to decide the unfair labor practice issue; (2) the arbitrator was presented with and considered the statutory issue, or was prevented from doing so by the party opposing deferral; and (3) Board law "reasonably permits" the arbitral award. The meaning of each of these three new prongs in the postarbitral deferral test is discussed in more detail below. It is important to underscore that *Babcock* places the burden of proving that the deferral standard is satisfied on the party urging deferral, typically the employer, which is another significant change from the *Olin* standard.

B. Explanation of the *Babcock* Requirements

1. Explicit Authorization

Under *Babcock*, an arbitrator must be explicitly authorized to decide the statutory issue in order to defer to the arbitral award. This requirement can be met by showing either that: (1) the specific statutory right at issue was incorporated in the collective-bargaining agreement, or (2) the parties agreed to authorize arbitration of the statutory issue in the particular case.

Significantly, the *Babcock* standard treats explicit authorization as a threshold requirement, that is, deferral is never warranted if this requirement is not met. The Board reasoned that arbitration is a consensual matter and it will not assume that the parties have agreed to submit statutory claims to the grievance process. Consequently, each party to a collective-bargaining agreement has the prerogative to decide not to arbitrate statutory claims by refusing to agree to a contract incorporating the statutory right or to otherwise agree to arbitrate the statutory issue. That is, a party will retain the option of adjudicating a statutory claim before the Board in the event the arbitrator denies the grievance where the collective-bargaining agreement is silent as to the statutory right and the party refused to authorize arbitration of the claim in the particular case.

2. Statutory Issue was Presented and Considered

The *Babcock* standard requires that the arbitrator was "actually presented" with and "actually considered" the statutory issue in order to defer to an arbitral award. It therefore abandons *Olin*'s *de facto* presumption that "if an arbitrator is presented in some fashion with facts relevant to both an alleged contract violation

The *Babcock* Board observed that either party can raise the statutory issue before the arbitrator. Merely informing the arbitrator of the unfair labor practice allegation in a pending charge will usually be sufficient to show that the issue had been presented.

In order to show that the arbitrator actually considered the statutory issue, the Board will require that the arbitrator "identified that issue and at least generally explained why . . . the facts presented either do or do not support the unfair labor practice allegation." The Board will not require that an arbitrator conduct a "detailed exegesis" of Board law, since many arbitrators, as well as union and employer representatives in arbitral proceedings, are not trained in labor law. But the Board will not assume that an arbitrator implicitly ruled on the statutory issue if the award merely upholds disciplinary action under a "just cause" analysis; rather, the arbitrator must make explicit that the action was not in retaliation for an employee's protected activities.

APPLICATION AND DISCUSSION QUESTIONS

1. What explicit language should the arbitrator include in their decisions to comply with the General Counsel's instructions? How should the arbitrator address the statutory issues?

2. What impact does *Babcock & Wilcox* have on settlement of grievances which may also settle an unfair labor practices claim? What standard would the NLRB apply?

3. After the NLRB issued the new deferral standard, the Board declined to apply to pending cases. See, *Verizon New Eng., Inc.,* 2015 NLRB LEXIS 151.

"In *Babcock & Wilcox Construction Co.,* 361 NLRB No. 132 (2014), the Board modified its postarbitral deferral standard, but decided that it would not apply the modified standard in pending cases. Id., slip op. at 14. Accordingly, we decide this case under the standard adopted in *Olin Corp.*, 268 NLRB 573 (1984 ')"; *Heartland-Plymouth Court MI, LLC,* 2015 NLRB LEXIS 49, "We agree with the judge that deferral to the arbitral award is not appropriate in this case under the standard articulated in *Spielberg Mfg. Co.,* 112 NLRB 1080 (1955), *and Olin Corp.,* 268 NLRB 573 (1984). We do not apply our current deferral standard here because this case was pending as of the date we prospectively adopted that standard. See *Babcock & Wilcox Construction Co.";* *Graymont PA, Inc.,* 2014 NLRB LEXIS 1007, "...by its terms, the standards articulated in *Babcock & Wilcox* do not apply to cases, such as this one, pending at the time of the issuance of the decision in *Babcock & Wilcox".*

IV. DISCIPLINARY ACTIONS, SUSPENSIONS, DEMOTIONS, AND TERMINATION DISPUTES

A. DEVELOPMENT OF THE TRADITIONAL JUST CAUSE ANALYSIS

In discharge grievances, typically, the employer has the burden of demonstrating that the employee was terminated for just cause. See, generally, Elkouri & Elkouri, <u>How Arbitration Works</u>, 6th ed. pg. 949. Under this just cause standard the School District cannot act arbitrarily, capriciously, discriminatorily, or make a decision not based on fact. Therefore in this grievance, the School District, has to prove the Grievant was terminated for just cause pursuant to Article L (3) of the CBA. In determining whether an employee was terminated for just cause, the School District must first prove the Grievant engaged in wrongdoing, once this is established, the arbitrator must review the reasonableness of the penalty imposed by the School District. (Elkouri, <u>How Arbitration Works</u>, 6th ed. pg. 948).

[handwritten margin note: A just cause]

The elements of the just cause analysis are further developed by Arbitrator Carroll Daugherty in the seminal cases, *Grief Bros. Cooperage Corp*; 42 LA 555, 557-59, (Daugherty, 1964*); Enterprise Wire Co.*, 46 LA 359, 363-365 (Daugherty,1966). The seven elements of just cause include: the employee must be forewarned, the rule or order the employee violated must be reasonably related to the efficient and safe operation of the business or agency, the employer conducted an investigation before discharge, the investigation was fair, there is substantial evidence that supports the charge against the employee, there was no discrimination, and the degree of discipline was reasonably related to the nature of the offense and the employee's past record. See, Norman Brand, ed. <u>Discipline and Discharge in </u>Arbitration, pp.31-33 (BNA Books, 1998; Also see, Koven, Smith and Farwell, "Just Cause: The Seven Tests", eds., pp.21-23 (BNA Books, 1992); Dunsford, "Arbitral Discretion: The Tests of Just Cause," <u>Proceeding of the 42nd Annual Meeting of NAA</u>, 23, 35-37 (BNA Books, 1990).

[handwritten margin note: A elements]

GRIEF BROS. COOPERAGE CORP.

42 LA 555 (DAUGHERTY, 1964)[*]

FINDINGS OF MATERIAL FACT

On December 13, 1963 the young aggrieved employee, classified as a machine operator and representing the Union in his department as a steward, was capping Ro-Con
fiber drums with metal tops. He capped several hundred that day. The operation
involved tapping the top on to the fiber body with a wooden mallet and fastening the
top with attached metal clips.

facts
kicked
caps,
fired w/o
investigation
+ fight

That afternoon his foreman, one Little, observed that two of said tops had been
damaged by unduly hard blows from the mallet and that grievant X— had kicked or
shoved with his foot, with some force, one of the drums, producing a mark and some
damage thereto. The foreman made no further investigation on the spot, told X— that
he was fired, ordered him to the foreman's office, and after an interval went to get
the local Union president. In Little's office X— asked for grievance forms to take with
him and was told they were Company property. After some discussion, not harmonious, an altercation developed during which Little manhandled X— until the president
intervened. X— finally clocked out.

unclear
if accident
or intent

It appears also from the record that the foreman had not warned X— on December
13 not to hit the caps so hard, but X— knew how to do the job properly. There is no
evidence on which to base a firm conclusion either that X— inadvertently damaged
the two tops with too hard a mallet-blow or that he did same with willful and deliberate intent. But he did damage them.

It appears further that, after one of X—'s more recent earlier offenses, higher management wished to discharge X—, but the foreman intervened in X—'s behalf and
induced management to give him another chance to develop his potential.

bad
record

The Arbitrator finds from the uncontroverted facts of record that X—'s record had
been unfavorable, although he was a fast and competent employee with considerable
potential. Out of a number of incidents he had received several oral warnings and
had twice been suspended, once for a portion of a day and once for three days.

---

[*] Reprinted with permission from *Labor Relations Reporter- Labor Arbitration Reports*. 42 LA 555, 557-559. Copyright 2015
by the Bureau of National Affairs, Inc. (800-372-1033). http://www.bna.com.

Arbitrator's Opinion

The above-stated issue in this case of protested disciplinary action requires a definition of "just and proper cause." Since the Parties' Agreement contains no such definition, the Arbitrator will here apply to the above-summarized facts the guide lines or questions that are to be found in the document appended to this decision.

From said application the Arbitrator now finds as follows: (1) Young X— knew that in effect he was on probation. He had been warned and penalized or previous offenses, but none was like the one involved here. It may not be said that he was specifically aware that to damage two or three drums out of several hundred, in the manner he did, would result in his discharge. Nevertheless, he knew that he would have to "watch his step."

The answer to Question 1 must be "yes." (2) The Company's requirement of careful work was reasonable. The answer to Question 2 is "yes." (3) Foreman Little thought he had the evidence of his eyes in respect to X—'s damaging actions when Little told X— he was fired. Little, however, made no effort, through conversation with X—, to discover whether Little's eyes had conveyed a correct impression. Little's announced disciplinary decision must be held to have been hasty. The visual evidence may well have been correct and a proper reason for discipline; but Little should have checked said evidence out for verification and for the purpose of learning whether X—'s behavior had justification. On balance, the answer to Question 3 must be "no." (4) Similarly the answer to Question 4 must be "no," and for the same reasons. (5) The same answer must be given to Question 5, for the same reasons. There was no proper pre-discharge investigation. (6) The answer to Question (6) must be "yes," because the record contains no probative evidence that the Company discriminated against X—. (7) If the aggrieved's guilt had been properly established by a fair predischarge investigation, so that Questions 3, 4, and 5 could have been answered "yes," then X—'s discharge would have to be upheld. The reason: Although his proven offense, as such might not have been serious enough to warrant dismissal if the offense had been a first one, X—'s record was poor; even a proven minor offense would have been enough to justify his discharge.

Given all the above answers to the seven tests or questions, the Arbitrator finds further as follows: (1) Little's behavior, including his post-discharge manhandling of X—, makes it impossible for the Arbitrator to rule that the discharge must "stick." That is, even though the "no" answers to Questions 3, 4, and 5 might appear to have been made on technical grounds, said answers have great weight in any discipline case. Every accused employee in an industrial democracy has the right of "due process of law" and the right to be heard before discipline is administered. These rights are precious to all free men and are not lightly or hastily to be disregarded or denied. The Arbitrator is fully mindful of the Company's need for, equity in, and right to require careful, safe, efficient performance by its employees. But before the Company can discipline an employee for failure to meet said requirement, the Company must take the pains to establish such failure. Maybe X— was guilty as hell; maybe also there are many gangsters who go free because of legal technicalities. And this is doubtless unfortunate. But company and government prosecutors must understand that the legal technicalities exist also to protect the innocent from unjust, unwarranted punishment. Society is willing to let the presumably guilty go free on technical grounds in order that free, innocent men can be secure from arbitrary, capricious action. (2) The Arbitrator then has only two alternatives: (a) reinstate X— with pay for all time lost; and (b) reinstate him without such pay. (3) In the light of all the instant facts, the Arbitrator is of the opinion that the proper decision here is to reinstate X— as of the date of his discharge but without back pay. The Company is now so directed.

AWARD

Grievant X— is to be reinstated as of discharge date, all rights unimpaired, but with no pay for time lost.

Tests Applicable For Learning Whether Employer Had Just And Proper Cause For Disciplining An Employee

Few if any union-management agreements contain a definition of "just cause." Nevertheless, over the years the opinions of arbitrators in innumerable discipline cases have developed a sort of "common law" definition thereof. This definition consists of a set of guide lines or criteria that are to be applied to the facts of any one case, and said criteria are set forth below in the form of questions.

A "no" answer to any one or more of the following questions normally signifies that just and proper cause did not exist. In other words, such "no" means that the employer's disciplinary decision contained one or more elements of arbitrary, capricious, unreasonable, and/or discriminatory action to such an extent that said decision constituted an abuse of managerial discretion warranting the arbitrator to substitute his judgment for that of the employer.

The answers to the questions in any particular case are to be found in the evidence presented to the arbitrator at the hearing thereon. Frequently, of course, the facts are such that the guide lines cannot be applied with slide-rule precision.

test Qs

The Questions

1. Did the Company give to the employee forewarning or foreknowledge of the possible or probable disciplinary consequences of the employee's conduct?

   Note 1: Said forewarning or foreknowledge may properly have been given orally by management or in writing through the medium of typed or printed sheets or books of shop rules and of penalties for violation thereof.

   Note 2: There must have been actual oral or written communication of the rules and penalties to the employee.

   Note 3: A finding of lack of such communication does not in all cases require a "no" answer to Question No. 1. This is because certain offenses such as insubordination, coming to work intoxicated, drinking intoxicating beverages on the job, or theft of the property of the company or of fellow employees are so serious that any employee in the industrial society may properly be expected to know already that such conduct is offensive and heavily punishable.

   Note 4: Absent any contractual prohibition or restriction, the company has the right unilaterally to promulgate reasonable rules and give reasonable orders; and same need not have been negotiated with the union.

2. Was the company's rule or managerial order reasonably related to the orderly, efficient, and safe operation of the Company's business?

   Note: If an employee believes that said rule or order is unreasonable, he must nevertheless obey same (in which case he may file a grievance thereover) unless he sincerely feels that to obey the rule or order would seriously and immediately jeopardize his personal safety and/or integrity. Given a firm finding to the latter effect, the employee may properly be said to have had justification for his disobedience.

3. Did the company, before administering discipline to an employee, make an effort to discover whether the employee did in fact violate or disobey a rule or order of management?

Note 1: This is the employee's "day in court" principle. An employee has the right to know with reasonable precision the offense with which he is being charged and to defend his behavior.

Note 2: the Company's investigation must normally be made *before* its disciplinary decision is made. If the company fails to do so, its failure may not normally be excused on the ground that the employee will get his day in court through the grievance procedure after the exaction of discipline. By that time there has usually been too much hardening of positions.

Note 3: There may of course be circumstances under which management must react immediately to the employee's behavior. In such cases the normally proper action is to suspend the employee pending investigation, with the understanding that (a) the final disciplinary decision will be made after the investigation and (b) if the employee is found innocent after the investigation, he will be restored to his job with full pay for time lost.

4. Was the Company's investigation conducted fairly and objectively?

   Note: At said investigation the management official may be both "prosecutor" and "judge," but he may not also be a witness against the employee.

5. At the investigation did the "judge" obtain substantial evidence or proof that the employee was guilty as charged?

   Note: It is not required that the evidence be preponderant, conclusive or "beyond reasonable doubt." But the evidence must be truly substantial and not flimsy.

6. Has the company applied its rules, orders, and penalties evenhandedly and without discrimination to all employees?

   Note 1: A "no" answer to this question requires a finding of discrimination and warrants negation or modification of the discipline imposed.

   Note 2: If the company has been lax in enforcing its rules and orders and decides henceforth to apply them rigorously, the company may avoid a finding of discrimination by telling all employees beforehand of its intent to enforce hereafter all rules as written.

7. Was the degree of discipline administered by the company in a particular case reasonably related to (a) the seriousness of the employee's proven offense and (b) the record of the employee in his service with the company?

Note 1: A trivial proven offense does not merit harsh discipline unless the employee has properly been found guilty of the same or other offenses a number of times in the past. (There is no rule as to what number of previous offenses constitutes a "good," a "fair," or a "bad" record. Reasonable judgment thereon must be used.)

Note 2: An employee's record of previous offenses may never be used to discover whether he was guilty of the immediate or latest one. The only proper use of his record is to help determine the severity of discipline once he has properly been found guilty of the immediate offense.

Note 3: Given the same proven offense for two or more employees, their respective records provide the only proper basis for "discriminating" among them in the administration of discipline for said offense. Thus, if employee A's record is significantly better than those of employees B, C, and D, the company may properly give A a lighter punishment than it gives the others for the same offense: and this does not constitute true discrimination.

APPLICATION AND DISCUSSION QUESTIONS

1. Arbitrator Daugherty outlined in detail the seven elements of just cause. He explained the application of each element. Why does a negative response to just one of the elements result in a no just cause finding? Is the test for just cause too structural and does it favor the Union?

   b/c 1 no = element of arbitrary, capricious, unreasonable discr.;

2. Which of the seven elements did the arbitrator weigh most heavily in his finding of no just cause? Were there other circumstances that influenced the arbitrator's conclusion? *no investigation; yes, the fight*   *yes*

3. Why did the arbitrator find there was no just cause to discharge the grievant, even though the grievant had been warned and penalized on prior occasions and he knew that "in effect he was on probation?"

   b/c no investigation

(handwritten margin note: Case)
(handwritten margin note: wire rod cleaner fired)

ENTERPRISE WIRE CO.

46 LA 359 (DAUGHERTY, 1966)[*]

Factual Background

(handwritten margin note: fired reason)
On October 8, 1965, the Company communicated to grievant X— an employment termination notice, signed by the plant manager and by the assistant plant superintendent and giving as the reasons for X—'s dismissal unsatisfactory work, including absenteeism, plus insubordination or refusal to work as directed.

The aggrieved employee had been hired on April 13, 1965, and had been trained as a wire rod cleaner in the Cleaning Department, second shift. The Company receives coils of wire rod from its suppliers, and said coils vary in diameter and metallurgical composition. Before the coils reach the cleaner employee, they are welded together at the ends in sets of three to form a "pin" and are tagged for identification as to diameter and composition. The cleaner's job is to clean the pins in an acid tank, preserve their identities, and respectively to re-tag them after they have been so pickled and as they are left suspended from a sort of beam called a "yoke." The tag is a rectangular piece of carboard with spaces to be filled in as to size and other characteristics of the wire rod in the pin and as to the identity of the wire-drawing machine to which the pin is to go. At the top of the tag is a reinforced hole through which a fine, flexible wire is placed by the cleaner, fastened to a strand of rod in the pin, and wound or twisted to prevent detachment.

(handwritten margin note: fired b/c)
Failure properly to tag each pin results in production delays, cost increases, and customer dissatisfaction (when orders for wire are not filled according to specifications). Alleged continued failure to tag some of his pins properly—either through allegedly not tagging some pins at all or through allegedly not marking the machine number on some of them—was the immediate cause of X—'s discharge.

Other material facts are set forth below under *Findings and Opinion* in respect to the issue of "just cause."

Contract Provisions (Selected Provisions Omitted)

The provisions of the Parties' controlling Agreement cited by the Company read as follows:

[*]   Reprinted with permission from *Labor Relations Reporter- Labor Arbitration Reports*. 46 LA 359, 363-365. Copyright 2015 by the Bureau of National Affairs, Inc. (800-372-1033). http://www.bna.com.

ARTICLE VIII

Discipline

Section 1. Proper Cause. No employee shall be discharged or otherwise disciplined except for proper cause.

The Arbitrator has found that all seven Questions merit affirmative answers. Accordingly, he must now rule that there is no proper basis for sustaining X—'s grievance.

* * * *

AWARD

The grievance is denied.

TESTS APPLICABLE FOR LEARNING WHETHER EMPLOYER HAD JUST AND PROPER CAUSE FOR DISCIPLINING AN EMPLOYEE

Few if any union-management agreements contain a definition of "just cause." Nevertheless, over the years the opinions of arbitrators in unnumerable discipline cases have developed a sort of "common law" definition thereof. This definition consists of a set of guide lines or criteria that are to be applied to the facts of any one case, and said criteria are set forth below in the form of questions.

A "no" answer to any one or more of the following questions normally signifies that just and proper cause did not exist. In other words, such "no" means that the employer's disciplinary decision contained one or more elements of arbitrary, capricious, unreasonable, or discriminatory action to such an extent that said decision constituted an abuse of managerial discretion warranting the arbitrator to substitute his judgment for that of the employer.

The answers to the questions in any particular case are to be found in the evidence presented to the arbitrator at the hearing thereon. Frequently, of course, the facts are such that the guide lines cannot be applied with precision. Moreover, occasionally, in some particular case an arbitrator may find one or more "no" answers so weak and the other, "yes" answers so strong that he may properly, without any "political" or spineless intent to "split the difference" between the opposing positions of the parties, find that the correct decision is to "chastize" both the company and the disciplined employee by decreasing but not nullifying the degree of discipline imposed, by the company—e.g., by reinstating a discharged employee without back pay.

It should be clearly understood also that the criteria set forth below are to be applied to the employer's conduct in making his disciplinary decision *before* same has been processed through the grievance procedure to arbitration. Any question as to whether the employer has properly fulfilled the contractual requirements of said procedure is entirely separate from the question of whether he fulfilled the "common law" requirements of just cause before the discipline was "grieved."

Sometimes, although very rarely, a union-management agreement contains a provision limiting the scope of the arbitrator's inquiry into the question of just cause. For example, one such provision seen by this arbitrator says that "the only question the arbitrator is to determine shall be whether the employee is or is not guilty of the act or acts resulting in his discharge." Under the latter contractual statement an arbitrator might well have to confine his attention to Question No. 5 below—or at most to Questions Nos. 3, 4, and 5. But absent any such restriction in an agreement, a consideration of the evidence on all seven Questions (and their accompanying Notes) is not only proper but necessary.

can limit arb via k

The Questions (Omitted, See *Grief*)

APPLICATION AND DISCUSSION QUESTIONS

reasonable analysis ?

For more than fifty years arbitrators have applied the seven elements of just cause as outlined by Arbitrator Daugherty. More recently, there are indications that labor arbitrators are using the test less and are applying a reasonableness analysis. In 2008, a study published by the National Academy of Arbitrators determined that only about 8.5 percent of arbitrators strictly follow the seven elements of just cause.

1. Should an employer be required to satisfy all elements of the Daugherty Test to meet the "Just Cause" standard"? What is your definition of just cause? *no - reasonable cause*

2. Which of the just cause elements were the most crucial in the arbitrator's decision here and why? *Q2?*

3. Should a grievant's cumulative work record and history of offenses and warnings be considered to determine if an employer had just cause for discharge? *yes*

B. The Elements of Just Cause

ADVANCE WARNING OF POSSIBLE DISCIPLINARY ACTION TO EMPLOYEE

GREATER CLEVELAND REGIONAL TRANSIT AUTHORITY AND AMALGAMATED TRANSIT UNION, LOCAL 268
134 BNA LA 859 (SKULINA, 2015)[*]

Issue

Whether there was just case to discharge the grievant? If not, what should be the remedy?

Facts

On April 25, 2014, the appellant was operating a passenger train eastbound. At the time of this incident, there were no passengers on her train.

She was employed on the rail system since June 14, 1995. On April 22, 2014, a general notice was posted indicating a red stop sign is positioned at the crossover known as West Green. All must stop at this sign, and if the westbound station is occupied, the control center should be called for instructions while the train is stopped.

The appellant overran the red stop sign, fouled the westbound rail and made contact with a westbound train and damaged a mirror on that train.

If she had done this one or two seconds earlier, there would have been a head on collision with all the effects of same such as repairs, possible loss of life, equipment damage and major service interruptions.

---

[*]   Reprinted with permission from *Labor Relations Reporter- Labor Arbitration Reports.* 134 BNA LA 859. Copyright 2015 by the Bureau of National Affairs, Inc. (800-372-1033). http://www.bna.com.

Because of this incident, according to the Rail Operations Rule Book, she was to make a "Three Emergency Broadcast" and immediately report the accident. She did not do so and when she returned, she was disciplined and ultimately discharged.

Conclusion

Under Section 4, "The Arbitrator's decision shall be binding on the parties except that the arbitrator shall have no power to add to, subtract from, or modify any terms of the Agreement.

In Article 12, "Discipline", the parties agreed that Section 1 "Violation of rules and regulations necessary to effect adequate and efficient operation in the public interest will constitute just cause for discipline or discharge."

The Employee Performance Code, which is promulgated to exercise its management rights, list offenses that may result in immediate discharge. It lists protection of safety rules which impose a risk of harm to persons or property (No. 9) as one violation.

At 12, it also states "Failure to notify the Authority immediately of an accident" as a dischargeable event.

Going through a stop sign after being warned days before of its presence is certainly a serious offense. In effect, the appellant was operating the wrong way on the rail and seriously endangered any train proceeding towards her. Along with the failure to promptly report, and the contact with the other train, is an egregious error.

The employer had the option to discharge the grievant. In the absence of some abuse of this authority, the arbitrator does not have the power to set some other form of discipline short of that decided by the Greater Cleveland Regional Transit Authority.

AWARD

The decision to discharge the Appellant was in accordance with the Company's rules and, therefore, is sustained.

APPLICATION AND DISCUSSION QUESTIONS

1. What are the public policy implications of the arbitrator's decision?

2. Do grievants employed in positions that affect public safety have fewer due process rights than others?

3. Why did the arbitrator conclude he did not have the power to impose a lesser form of discipline than discharge?

SAN DIEGO TROLLEY, INC. AND INTERNATIONAL BROTHERHOOD OF ELECTRICAL WORKERS, LOCAL 465
112 BNA LA 323 (PRAYZICH, 1999)*

Issue

At the outset of the hearing, the Parties stipulated that the following mutually agreed upon Issue is properly before the Arbitrator for a final and binding decision:

Was the Grievant, C_, discharged for just cause?

If not, what is the appropriate remedy?

Contract Language

The relevant provisions of the Collective Bargaining Agreement, are set forth below:
(Article 2--Union Recognition, Article 4—Seniority (Omitted)

ARTICLE 5--GRIEVANCE AND ARBITRATION PROCEDURE

* * * *

F. Arbitration Procedure.

(1) The issue(s) to be submitted to arbitration shall be limited to those set forth and defined in the original grievance, and the arbitrator's

---

*   Reprinted with permission from *Labor Relations Reporter- Labor Arbitration Reports.* 112 BNA LA 323. Copyright 2015 by the Bureau of National Affairs, Inc. (800-372-1033). http://www.bna.com.

authority shall be limited to the determination of the issue(s) thus set forth.

(2) The arbitration shall be held before an impartial arbitrator jointly selected by the Employer and Union. If the parties are unable to agree on an arbitrator, a list of seven (7) arbitrators shall be obtained from an appropriate agency and the parties shall alternatively strike names from the list until only one arbitrator remains who shall hear the grievance.

(3) As soon as possible after the arbitrator is selected, a hearing shall be held before the arbitrator. The arbitrator shall issue an award in writing pertaining only to the issues submitted to arbitration. The award of the arbitrator shall be final and binding on all parties.

* * * *

ARTICLE 6--GENERAL PROVISIONS

A. Rule and Regulations. The Union recognizes that the Employer may, from time to time, promulgate rules and regulations for the management of the business and direction of its working force.

B. Just Cause. No employee may be disciplined or discharged without just cause.

* * * *

D. Employees to Advance Welfare of Employer. The Union agrees for its members (who are employees of the Employer) that they will individually and collectively perform loyal and efficient work and service, that they will use their best efforts to protect the property of the Employer, and that they will cooperate in promoting and advancing the welfare of the Company and the protection of its service to the public at all times. The Employer will cooperate with Union in its efforts to promote harmony and efficiency among the employees.

Background

The Grievant, C_, was employed as a Train Operator for San Diego Trolley, Inc., ("Company" or "Employer"). C_ was hired on or about June 26, 1995 and terminated on or about June 4, 1998. The Grievant's classification is set forth in a Collective Bargaining Agreement between the Company and International Brotherhood of Electrical Workers, Local 465, ("Union").

In late May 1998, the Employer received reports that the Grievant had made threats of physical harm against supervision and/or other employees of the Company. An investigatory meeting to discuss those alleged threats with the Grievant took place on May 22, 1998. Those present at the meeting were both Management and Union Representatives, including Assistant Business Manager, Mr. Hal Engstrom, and Mr. Fecher, Counsel for the Union. During the course of that meeting, the Grievant consented to a search of his locker on Company premises, and a loaded revolver was found among his personal belongings in the locker. The meeting was over at that point, and the Grievant proceeded to go on a pre-planned vacation. Upon his return, he was advised by letter of an intent to terminate. The basis for discharge is what the Company determined to be a most serious violation of its work rule prohibiting weapons of any kind on Company property.

According to the Employer, the violation was such, that immediate termination was warranted. Further, any discussion of a "fitness for duty evaluation," as a penalty, took place before the Company was made aware that there was in fact a loaded gun in the Grievant's locker.

The Union asserts, that there was in fact a promise by the Employer that the "fitness for duty evaluation" was the only penalty that would be imposed. Additionally, the Grievant had valid reasons, including personal safety, for carrying the gun. The Union argues, that the Company's action of discharge violated an understanding between the Company and the Union. Moreover, progressive discipline is generally imposed for Rule violations. The Union requests that the Arbitrator reinstate the Grievant with full back pay and benefits.

Positions of the Parties (Omitted)

It is well established that a company has a "duty to protect the health and safety of its employees. The Grievant's reasons, (though valid in his mind), for carrying the gun onto the Company premises on May 22, 1998 and other dates, cannot be deemed controlling. In keeping with the requirement that companies have a duty to "make safe" the premises for its employees, a reasonable Rule had been promulgated and distributed, (Work Rule No. 1.4.12). The Company's Rule prohibiting the bringing of a weapon onto the premises is not only reasonable but consistent with its right to do so as set forth in Article 6, A., of the Collective Bargaining Agreement. At the hearing, the Grievant stated that he did not have knowledge of Rule 1.4.12 prohibiting the bringing of a weapon onto Company property. However, not only was the Rule issued to him in writing, which he acknowledged receipt of in writing, but the Arbitrator must note that common sense dictates, (particularly in today's society), that the Rule in question is so basic and essential that it is implied.

The Union argues, inter alia, that not only had there been an agreement to submit the Grievant to a fitness for duty evaluation, but that the discipline imposed was improper, because the Company was required to follow the steps of progressive corrective discipline. Generally, discipline falls into two basic categories. First, those relatively minor infractions which deserve the benefit of attempts to correct the behavior by progressive discipline, starting with a verbal warning, a written warning, and finally, one or more suspensions, (as the Union correctly stated in its brief). Those infractions however generally involve matters such as attendance problems, minor work deficiencies, tardiness, minor rule violations, and other misconduct, which deserve progressive attempts at correction. The second category of infractions are the serious violations. They include acts of insubordination, dishonesty, drug and alcohol violations on the premises, and other such most serious misconduct. The violation involved in the instant matter must reasonably be placed within the second category of offenses, which generally warrant summary discharge. The Grievant's misconduct was most serious and inexcusable, and any discipline short of termination would establish and condone a standard of conduct which is clearly unacceptable. Accordingly, while it is unfortunate that the Grievant placed his employment in jeopardy, the evidentiary record mandates a conclusion that the Employer has carried its burden of proving just cause for discharge, and the grievance must be denied.

AWARD

After careful consideration of all evidence and argument, and for the reasons offered above, it is the decision of the Arbitrator that with regard to the submitted Issue:

The Grievant, C_, was discharged for just cause. Accordingly, the grievance is denied in its entirety.

APPLICATION AND DISCUSSION QUESTIONS

1. Is carrying a gun on company premises, against the company's policy, sufficient for termination without a "fitness for duty evaluation?"

2. How did the employer carry its burden of proving just cause for the Grievent's termination?

3. What are your views on using common sense to determine whether or not an employee is knowledgeable of company policies? Was it properly used in this case?

DONALDSON MINING COMPANY AND UNITED MINE WORKERS OF AMERICA, DISTRICT 17, LOCAL 340
91 BNA LA 471 (M. ZOBRAK, 1988)[*]

* * * *

The question to be resolved is whether or not the Company's drug testing policy violates the Agreement.

Cited Portions of the Agreement (Omitted)

The following portions of the Agreement were cited:

ARTICLE IA -- SCOPE AND COVERAGE
Section (d) Management of the Mines
  The management of the mine, the direction of the working force and the right to hire and discharge are vested exclusively in the Employer.

Factual Background

Donaldson Mining Company (hereafter the "Company") requires employees who have been off from work for over one year to undergo a physical examination before they are permitted to return to work. On May 19, 1987, L.C. Howe, Company President

---

[*] Reprinted with permission from *Labor Relations Reporter- Labor Arbitration Reports.* 91 BNA LA 471. Copyright 2015 by the Bureau of National Affairs, Inc. (800-372-1033). http://www.bna.com.

and Chief Executive Officer, expanded the scope of the physical examination when he issued the following correspondence to management employees only:

> In the future all new employees or employees returning from an extended period of disability (over one year) will be required to take a medically supervised test to detect drug abuse. This will apply to both hourly and salaried employees.

Howe testified that he was aware that some employees had entered drug and alcohol rehabilitation programs, and he suspected that other employees were having similar problems on the job. Howe cited an occasion in the late 1970's when employees were caught using drugs in the mine parking lot. Officers of the United Mine Workers of America, District 17, Local Union 340 (hereafter the "Union") were not notified of the Company's new drug testing policy. Howe's May 19, 1987 correspondence is the only written statement concerning the Company's drug testing policy.

The Grievant had been off from work for a period of 16 months due to an injury. Near the end of October, 1987, he contacted Kent Smith, Manager of Office Services, and indicated that he was ready to return to work. Smith scheduled the Grievant to take his physical examination at a local hospital on October 30, 1987. He did not inform the Grievant that a drug test would be administered during the physical. The Grievant reported for the physical as scheduled and signed a consent form for the drug test. Company witnesses said that an employee would be talked to if he refused to sign the consent form. They stated that they would investigate the reasons given for not submitting to the drug test, and the employee's return to work would be dependent upon the results of the investigation. The Company presented documents signed by the Grievant indicating a chain of custody for the urinalysis. The sample was then sent to Internal Clinical Laboratories (ICL) for testing.

The Grievant was permitted to return to work after passing the portions of the physical administered by the hospital. He received annual retraining on November 2, 1987. The Grievant worked his assigned shift at the Mine on November 3 and 4, 1987. There is no evidence on the record that the Grievant was impaired in any way from performing his duties. On November 5, 1987, the Company received the results of the drug test. The Grievant had tested positive for cannabinoids at the 100 nanograms/milliliter (ng/ml) threshold...

* * * *

Contentions of the Parties (Omitted)

Company Contentions (Omitted)

Discussion and Findings

Howe communicated the drug testing policy to only a few members of his management staff. His correspondence of May 19, 1987 was not shared with the Union or any classified employees of the Company. It is observed that the correspondence only applies to employees returning to employment from an extended period of disability (over one year). No mention is made in the May 19, 1987 correspondence of what actions the Company would take if the employee refused to take the drug test or what would occur if the drug test was positive. The Parties stipulated that the drug policy has been verbal and that it was not posted for the employees' notification.

It is generally accepted that the Company has the right to promulgate reasonable rules and regulations governing its operations. The question of the Company's right to institute a drug testing policy for its employees has been addressed by the General Counsel of the National Labor Relations Board. In Memorandum GC-87-5 issued September, 1987, the General Counsel took the position that drug testing for current employees and job applicants is a mandatory subject for bargaining under Section 8(d) of the Act. The General Counsel also took the position that implementation of a drug testing program is a substantial change in working conditions, even where physical examinations previously have been given. It is recognized that the opinion of the General Counsel is subject to appeal. The Parties did not present evidence of this question being resolved by a court of final appeal. Clearly in this matter, the Company did not negotiate with the Union concerning the implementation of the drug testing policy. While the Union has taken the position that the Company's actions constitute a violation of the National Labor Relations Act, the findings in this matter flow from an application of the terms and conditions of the Agreement.

The Agreement preserves the Company's right to manage its operations including its right to implement reasonable rules and regulations. In order for the rule or regulation to be deemed reasonable, certain conditions must be met. In this matter neither the Grievant, other classified employees, nor the Union were notified of the newly instituted drug testing policy. Those employees affected by the policy, and those employees returning from an extended period of absence of over one year, were not notified of the new conditions set upon their return to work. Howe testified that he was aware of drug problems at the Mine in the late 1970's. He also stated that he was aware that present employees had sought rehabilitation for drug and alcohol related problems. Clearly, Howe's reason for implementing the drug policy was to make it clear the Company would not condone drug use by its employees. He failed, however, to communicate that message to the employees.

The lack of a written policy communicated to the Union and employees makes it impossible to rule on the reasonableness of said policy. The policy does not appear in writing. When questioned on cross-examination, members of management were hesitant or could not clearly explain what would take place if an employee refused to undergo the testing procedure. When he took his return-to-work physical, the Grievant had no idea of the consequences of taking and failing the drug test. As of November 5, 1987, the Grievant was not given notice that even if he produced a report of a negative drug test finding, he would still be subject to random drug testing for the text fifteen (15) months. The drug testing policy appears to have been evolving in response to the circumstances encountered by the Grievant. It can only be concluded that the Company, as of the period encompassed by this grievance, had not devised a drug testing policy that clearly spelled out what it expected from the employees and what disciplinary actions it would take if the employee failed to abide by the policy.

In the absence of a clearly stated, published, and communicated drug policy, this arbitrator is foreclosed on making any judgment on the reasonableness of the drug testing policy employed by the Company in matters related to the Grievant. This verbal policy, unwritten and unpublished, simply does not rise to the level of a policy that can bind employees. The Company cannot demand compliance with a policy that has not been communicated to the affected employees, nor can the employees be disciplined for violating a policy they do not know exists. As concluded by Arbitrator William Hannan in City of Pittsburgh and Pittsburgh Fire Fighters, Local 1, LAIG 3834 (1987), the purpose of drug testing is not to catch employees, but to warn them that they will be disciplined if found to be drug users. In the instant matter, such a warning was not provided to the employees prior to returning to work and their submitting to the enhanced physical examination.

Based on all the foregoing, it is found that the Company has not implemented and communicated a clearly defined drug policy. Reviewing the facts contained on the record, it is not possible to make any finding on the question of the policy's reasonableness. Employees, such as the Grievant, cannot be disciplined for violating a policy that they have not been aware of through publication or posting. For all these reasons, the Grievant is to be made whole for all wages and benefits lost as the result of his suspension, effective November 18, 1987. Contract benefit days used by the Grievant between November 5, 1987 and November 18, 1987 shall not be restored. Furthermore, he shall not be required to undergo random drug testing for the next fifteen (15) months as stated in the correspondence dated November 24, 1987. Any documents related to the drug testing and subsequent discipline issued the Grievant are to be removed from the Grievant's personnel file and destroyed. The Company is directed to cease and desist from implementing the drug testing policy that had its origins in Howe's memorandum of May 19, 1987. The arbitrator will retain jurisdiction over this matter for a period of forty-five (45) calendar days to resolve any disputes arising from the implementation of this Award.

AWARD

The grievance is timely filed. The grievance is sustained and the remedy is set forth herein.

APPLICATION AND DISCUSSION QUESTIONS

1. The change to the company's policy on physical examinations was only shared with management employees. Do you think it is okay to hold managers responsible for communicating policy updates to their staff?

2. Was the employer able to establish that the Grievent's brain was impacted by drug use, causing him to be impaired on the job? Why or why not?

3. Do you agree with the employer's decision to let the Grievent work until the results of his drug test were in?

JUDGES: RICHARD M. BERMAN, UNITED STATES DISTRICT JUDGE
OPINION BY: RICHARD M. BERMAN

I. Introduction

This Decision and Order resolves the parties' respective cross-motions to confirm and to vacate NFL Commissioner Roger Goodell's July 28, 2015 Arbitration Award imposing a four-game suspension on New England Patriots quarterback Tom Brady, pursuant to Section 301 of the Labor Management Relations Act, 29 U.S.C. § 185, and Section 10 of the Federal Arbitration Act, 9 U.S.C. § 10.

Based upon the foregoing and applicable legal authorities, the Court hereby denies the Management Council's motion to confirm the Award and grants the Players Association's motion to vacate the Award, thereby vacating the four-game suspension of Tom Brady, effective immediately.

II. Background

Pash/Wells Investigation & Wells Report

Shortly after the conclusion of the AFC Championship Game on January 18, 2015, senior NFL officials undertook an extensive (reportedly $3+ million) investigation into the circumstances surrounding the use by the Patriots of seemingly under-inflated footballs during that game's first half. On January 23, 2015, the NFL publicly announced that it had retained Theodore V. Wells, Jr. and his law firm to conduct an "independent" investigation, together with NFL Executive Vice President and General Counsel Jeff Pash.

The Investigation specifically was conducted pursuant to the NFL Policy on Integrity of the Game & Enforcement of Competitive Rules, dated February 11, 2014 ("Competitive Integrity Policy"), which provides, in part:

> Policy on Integrity of the Game & Enforcement of Competitive Rules...The follow-
> ing updated memorandum was sent on February 11, 2014 to Chief Executives, Club

Presidents, General Managers, and Head Coaches from Commissioner Goodell
Regarding the Policy on Integrity of the Game & Enforcement of Competitive Rules . .
.Actual or suspected violations will be thoroughly and promptly investigated. Any club
identifying a violation is required promptly to report the violation, and give its full
support and cooperation in any investigation. Failure to cooperate in an investigation
shall be considered conduct detrimental to the League and will subject the offending
club and responsible individual(s) to appropriate discipline.

The Wells Report includes the following narrative: During the course of the January 18, 2015 AFC Championship Game, Colts linebacker D'Qwell Jackson intercepted a pass thrown by Patriots quarterback Tom Brady. The intercepted ball was apparently handed to the Colts equipment staff, who used a pressure gauge and determined that the football was inflated to approximately 11 psi, i.e., below the range of 12.5 to 13.5 psi specified in Rule 2, Section 1 of the 2014 NFL Official Playing Rules ("Playing Rules"). NFL officials collected and tested eleven Patriots game balls and four Colts game balls at halftime and concluded that all eleven of the Patriots' game balls measured below 12.5 psi. The balls were re-inflated to approximately 13 psi and placed back in play. Wells Report at 63-70.

On May 6, 2015, the findings of the Pash/Wells "independent" Investigation were made public. The Investigation included reviews of player equipment, security footage, text messages, call logs, emails, press conferences, League rules and policies, and interviews with no less than sixty-six Patriots and NFL personnel. The Wells Report was accompanied by a separately commissioned analysis prepared by the consulting firm "Exponent."

The Wells Report concluded, among other things, that "in connection with the AFC Championship Game, it is more probable than not that New England Patriots personnel participated in violations of the Playing Rules and were involved in a deliberate effort to circumvent the rules." Wells Report at 2. It determined that Patriots employees Jim McNally ("McNally"), who was the Officials Locker Room attendant, and John Jastremski ("Jastremski"), who was a Patriots equipment assistant in charge of footballs, "participated in a deliberate effort to release air from Patriots game balls after the balls were examined by the referee [on January 18, 2015]."

As to Brady, the Wells Report concluded that "it is more probable than not that Brady was at least generally aware of the inappropriate activities of McNally and Jastremski involving the release of air from Patriots game balls." The Wells Report also concluded that "it is unlikely that an equipment assistant and a locker room attendant would deflate game balls without Brady's knowledge and approval."

The Wells Report acknowledged that "there is less direct evidence linking Brady to tampering activities than either McNally or Jastremski.". It also stated that "[t]he evidence does not allow us to reach conclusions as to when McNally and Jastremski began their efforts to release air from Patriots game balls on game day . . . exactly how long those efforts have been ongoing, how frequently they occurred, how the idea originated or the full scope of communication related to those efforts.

Brady has denied "any knowledge of or involvement in any efforts to deflate game balls after the pre-game inspection by the game officials."

The Wells Report exonerated all (other) members of the Patriots staff. "[W]e do not believe there was any wrongdoing or knowledge of wrongdoing by Patriots ownership, Head Coach Belichick or any other Patriots coach in the matters investigated. We also do not believe there was any wrongdoing or knowledge of wrongdoing by Patriots Head Equipment Manager David Schoenfeld."

Following the issuance of the Wells Report on May 6, 2015, both McNally and Jastremski were indefinitely suspended without pay by the Patriots.

The Arbitral Process

On May 14, 2015, Brady, through the Players Association, appealed the four-game suspension. Thereupon, Commissioner Goodell designated himself as arbitrator to hear Brady's appeal pursuant to CBA Art. 46 § 2(a), which provides that "the Commissioner may serve as hearing officer in any appeal under Section 1(a) of this Article at his discretion."

On May 19, 2015, Patriots owner Robert Kraft is reported to have stated that "I don't want to continue the rhetoric that's gone on for the last four months. I'm going to accept, reluctantly, what he [Commissioner Goodell] has given to us [the Patriots' organization], and not continue this dialogue and rhetoric, and we won't appeal."

Brady's Motion for Recusal

On May 19, 2015, the Players Association filed a motion seeking Goodell's recusal from arbitrating Brady's appeal, arguing (1) "You cannot lawfully arbitrate whether you committed a CBA violation by delegating exclusive conduct detrimental disciplinary powers to Troy Vincent," (2) "You cannot lawfully arbitrate a hearing in which you are a central witness," (3) "You cannot lawfully arbitrate issues which you have publicly prejudged" [apparently referring to Commissioner Goodell's public comments on May 6, 2015 about the Wells Report: "I want to express my appreciation to Ted Wells and his colleagues for performing a thorough and independent investigation, the findings and conclusions of which are set forth in today's comprehensive report"], and (4) "You cannot lawfully arbitrate a matter implicating the competence and credibility of NFL staff."

On June 2, 2015, Commissioner Goodell issued his "Decision on NFLPA's Motion to Recuse," concluding that "[o]ur Collective Bargaining Agreement provides that 'at his discretion,' the Commissioner may serve as hearing officer in 'any appeal' involving conduct detrimental to the integrity of, or public confidence in, the game of professional football. I will exercise that discretion to hear Mr. Brady's appeal."

Brady's Discovery Motion(s) [Omitted]

Arbitral Hearing [Omitted]

Goodell's Award or Final Decision

On July 28, 2015, Commissioner Goodell published a 20-page Award or Final Decision on Article 46 Appeal of Tom Brady, which, as noted, upheld Brady's four-game suspension. In the Award, Goodell states, among other things, (1) "[i]n appeals of Commissioner discipline under Article 46, the hearing officer gives appropriate deference to the findings of the disciplinary decision under review; that is so even when the Commissioner serves as hearing officer [i.e., as in this case]," (2) "I am bound, of course, by standards of fairness and consistency of treatment among players similarly situated," (3) "[i]t bears emphasis [] that my finding of tampering with the game balls is not based solely on the Exponent study and the testimony of the scientific experts, but instead on consideration of all of the evidence in the record, including the conduct, text messages, and other communications discussed in both the Wells Report and at the hearing," (4) "it is unlikely that an equipment assistant and a locker room attendant would deflate game balls without Brady's knowledge and approval and that Mr. McNally and Mr. Jastremski would not personally and unilaterally have engaged in such conduct in the absence of Brady's awareness and consent," (5) "[t]he most significant new information that emerged in connection with the appeal was evidence that on or about March 6, 2015 — the very day that that he was interviewed by Mr. Wells and his investigative team — Mr. Brady instructed his assistant to destroy the cellphone that he had been using since early November 2014, a period that included the AFC Championship Game and the initial weeks of the subsequent investigation," and (6) "the conduct at issue here — specifically the willful destruction of potentially relevant evidence — goes well beyond Mr. Brady's failure to respond to or fully cooperate with the investigation."

Goodell determined that "the available electronic evidence, coupled with information compiled in the investigators' interviews, leads me to conclude that Mr. Brady knew about, approved of, consented to, and provided inducements and rewards in support of a scheme by which, with Mr. Jastremski's support, Mr. McNally tampered with the game balls." Id. at 10 (emphasis added). This finding by Goodell goes far beyond the "general awareness" finding in the Wells Report or in Vincent's May 11, 2015 Disciplinary Decision Letter to Brady. Compare Award at 10 with Report at 2 and Vincent Letter to Brady at 1.

* * * *

As for discipline, Goodell stated "I am very aware of, and believe in, the need for consistency in discipline for similarly situated players." Id. at 14. "In terms of the appropriate level of discipline, the closest parallel of which I am aware is the collectively bargained discipline [31] imposed for a first violation of the policy governing performance enhancing drugs [four-game suspension] . . . ." Id. at 16.

Commissioner Goodell concluded as follows: "(1) Mr. Brady participated in a scheme to tamper with the game balls after they had been approved by the game officials for use in the AFC Championship Game, and (2) Mr. Brady willfully obstructed the investigation by, among other things, affirmatively arranging for destruction of his cellphone knowing that it contained potentially relevant information that had been requested by the investigators." Id. at 13. "All of this indisputably constitutes conduct detrimental to the integrity of, and public confidence in, the game of professional football," stated Goodell. Id. (emphasis added).

III. Legal Standard [Citation Omitted]

"Although judicial scrutiny of arbitration awards necessarily is limited, such review is sufficient to ensure that arbitrators comply with the requirements of the statute at issue." "The deference due an arbitrator does not extend so far as to require a district court to countenance, much less confirm, an award obtained without the requisites of fairness or due process." (Citation Omitted).

Under the Federal Arbitration Act ("FAA"), "the validity of an award is subject to attack only on those grounds listed in [9 U.S.C.] § 10, and the policy of the FAA requires that an award be enforced unless one of those grounds is affirmatively shown to exist." For example, FAA § 10 provides that the Court may vacate an arbitral award "where the arbitrators were guilty of . . . refusing to hear evidence pertinent and material to the controversy." 9 U.S.C. § 10(a)(3). The Court may also vacate an arbitral award "where there was evident partiality . . ." 9 U.S.C. § 10(a)(2).

* * * *

It is the "law of the shop" to provide professional football players with advance notice of prohibited conduct and potential discipline. In In the Matter of Reggie Langhorne ("Langhorne"). Arbitrator Richard R. Kasher vacated the discipline of a player who had refused to take part in practice, holding that the player "was entitled at some time to be placed on notice as to what consequences would flow from his refusal to participate in . . . practice. Any disciplinary program requires that individuals subject to that program understand, with reasonable certainty, what results will occur if they breach established rules." Slip op. at 25 (Apr. 9, 1994. Arbitrator Michael H. Beck vacated a fine imposed upon a player for missing a mandatory weigh-in, and observed that "adequate notice is the fundamental concept in discipline cases." Slip op. at 10 (July 16, 2010)

* * * *

IV. Analysis

An arbitrator's factual findings are generally not open to judicial challenge, and we accept the facts as the arbitrator found them.

The Court is fully aware of the deference afforded to arbitral decisions, but, nevertheless, concludes that the Award should be vacated. The Award is premised upon several significant legal deficiencies, including (A) inadequate notice to Brady of both his potential discipline (four-game suspension) and his alleged misconduct; (B) denial of the opportunity for Brady to examine one of two lead investigators, namely NFL Executive Vice President and General Counsel Jeff Pash; and (C) denial of equal access to investigative files, including witness interview notes.

(A) Inadequate Notice of Discipline and Misconduct
(i) No Notice of Four-Game Suspension: [35] Steroid Use Comparison
The Court finds that Brady had no notice that he could receive a four-game suspension for general awareness of ball deflation by others or participation in any scheme to deflate footballs, and non-cooperation with the ensuing Investigation. Brady also had no notice that his discipline would be the equivalent of the discipline imposed upon a player who used performance enhancing drugs.

* * * *

The Court finds that no player alleged or found to have had a general awareness of the inappropriate ball deflation activities of others or who allegedly schemed with others to let air out of footballs in a championship game and also had not cooperated in an ensuing investigation, reasonably could be on notice that their discipline would (or should) be the same as applied to a player who violated the NFL Policy on Anabolic Steroids and Related Substances. Brady had no such notice. "When it is clear that the arbitrator 'must have based his award on some body of thought, or feeling, or policy, or law that is outside the contract [] and not incorporated in it by reference . . . the arbitrator has failed to draw the award from the essence of the collective bargaining agreement." *In re Marine Pollution Serv., Inc.*, 857 F.2d 91, 94 (2d Cir. 1988) (quoting *Ethyl Corp. v. United Steelworkers*, 768 F.2d 180, 184-85 (7th Cir. 1985), cert. denied 475 U.S. 1010, 106 S. Ct. 1184, 89 L. Ed. 2d 300); see also Bounty-Gate, slip op. at 6 ("In other words, rightly or wrongly, a sharp change in sanctions or discipline can often be seen as arbitrary and as an impediment rather than an instrument of change.").

(ii) No Notice of Any Discernible Infraction [Omitted]
(iii) No Notice of Suspension as Opposed to Fine: Competitive Integrity Policy vs. Player Policies

The Players Association argues that "[u]nder the Player Policies, Brady had notice only of fines — not suspensions — for player equipment violations designed to gain a competitive advantage." Def.'s Countercl. With respect to "Other Uniform/Equipment Violations," and as noted supra p. 15 n.14, the Player Policies state in relevant part, the following:

League discipline may also be imposed on players whose equipment, uniform, or On

Field violations are detected during postgame review of video, who repeat violations on the same game day after having been corrected earlier, or who participate in the game despite not having corrected a violation when instructed to do so. First offenses will result in fines.

* * * *

Brady was on notice that equipment violations under the Player Policies could result in fines. He had no legal notice of discipline under the Competitive Integrity Policy, which is incorporated into the Game Operations Manual and distributed solely to

— and, therefore, provides notice to — "Chief Executives, Club Presidents, General Managers, and Head Coaches," and not to players. Game Operations Manual at A2.

* * * *

Conduct Detrimental [Omitted]

(B) Commissioner Goodell Improperly Denied Brady the Opportunity to Examine Designated Co-Lead Investigator Jeff Pash

The Players Association contends that Commissioner Goodell's denial of the testimony of Jeff Pash at the arbitral hearing was fundamentally unfair because (1) "the NFL publically declared that NFL Executive Vice President and General Counsel Jeff Pash was the co-lead investigator on the Wells-Pash Investigation," and (2) Pash was allowed to review a draft of the Wells Report and to provide Paul, Weiss with written comments or edits prior to the Report's release to the public. Def.'s Countercl.

The Management Council responds that Mr. Wells "testified that Pash had played 'no substantive role in the investigation,' and any comments he may have provided on a draft of the report 'did not impact' the Paul, Weiss findings," and that "[i]n light of the fact that 'arbitrators have substantial discretion to admit or exclude evidence,' the decision not to have cumulative testimony from Pash is not subject to challenge." Pl.'s Mem. of Law in Supp. at 11 (quoting *Kolel Beth Yechiel Mechil of Tartikov, Inc. v. YLL Irrevocable Trust*, 729 F.3d 99, 107 (2d Cir. 2013)) (emphasis added).

In determining what evidence to admit, "[a]n arbitrator need not follow all the niceties observed by the federal courts." *Tempo Shain Corp. v. Bertek, Inc.*, 120 F.3d 16, 20 (2d Cir. 1997) (quoting *Bell Aerospace Co. Div, of Textron v. Local 516*, 500 F.2d 921, 923 (2d Cir. 1974)). "However, although not required to hear all the evidence proffered by a party, an arbitrator 'must give each of the parties to the dispute an adequate opportunity to present its evidence and argument.'" Id. (quoting *Hoteles Condado Beach v. Union De Tronquistas Local 901*, 763 F.2d 34, 39 (1st Cir. 1985). "A fundamentally fair hearing requires that the parties be permitted to present evidence and cross-examine adverse witnesses." *Kaplan*, 1996 U.S. Dist. LEXIS 16455, 1996 WL 640901, at *5: see also *Tempo Shain*, 120 F.3d at 20 ("[T]here was no reasonable basis for the arbitration panel to determine that . . . omitted testimony would be cumulative . . . . [T]he arbitration panel must "indicate in what respects [] testimony would be cumulative.")

* * * *

The Court finds that Commissioner Goodell's denial of Brady's motion to compel the testimony of Mr. Pash was fundamentally unfair and in violation of 9 U.S.C. § 10(a)(3). Given Mr. Pash's very senior position in the NFL, his role as Executive Vice President and General Counsel, and his designation as co-lead investigator with Ted Wells, it is logical that he would have valuable insight into the course and outcome of the Investigation and into the drafting and content of the Wells Report. It is also problematic to the Court that there was no specification by Goodell as to the ways Pash's testimony would have been "cumulative."

* * * *

VI. Conclusion & Order

For the reasons stated herein, the Management Council's motion to confirm the arbitration award [ECF No. 4] is denied and the Players Association's motion to vacate the arbitration award [ECF No. 28] is granted. Brady's four-game suspension is vacated, effective immediately. The Clerk is respectfully requested to close cases 15 Civ. 5916 and 15 Civ. 5982.

APPLICATION AND DISCUSSION QUESTIONS

1. What statutes were used to vacate the arbitration award?

2. Should Goodell have been recused as the arbitrator? Explain your response.

3. Why did the District Court vacate the arbitrator's award? Did the court fail to give deference to the arbitrator's findings?

4. When can an award be vacated under the FAA? Which provision of the FAA was violated?

5. Do you agree with the court that Brady had no notice of possible discipline? Did Brady raise a valid argument regarding the failure of the Comission to provide requested documents?

6. What is the "law of the shop?" Should it include rules of "common sense?" Should players understand they could receive a disciplinary action for misconduct even if there is no written rule?

7. In April of 2016, the Court of Appeals for the Second District reversed the District Court's ruling. The Court of Appeals held that " the Commissioner properly excercised his broad discretion under the [CBA] and his procedural rulings were properly grounded in that agreement and did not deprive Brady of fundamental fairness." *See, National Football League v. Brady, No. 15-2801(L0, No.15-2805(Con) (2016)*

THE VIOLATED POLICY/RULE IS REASONABLE

ATMOS ENERGY CORP. AND INT'L CHEM. WORKERS UNION AND COMMERCIAL WORKERS UNION LOCAL 1047c
121 BNA LA 908 (HOWELL, 2005)*

Issue

The parties stipulated that the issue is as follows:

Was the Company's decision to discharge the Grievant done in a reasonable manner? If not, what is the appropriate remedy?

Relevant Agreement Provisions (Selected Provisions)

* Reprinted with permission from *Labor Relations Reporter- Labor Arbitration Reports.* 121 BNA LA 908. Copyright 2015 by the Bureau of National Affairs, Inc. (800-372-1033). http://www.bna.com.

ARTICLE IV

NO DISCRIMINATION

Section 1. Neither the Company nor the Union will discriminate against any employee because of his race, color, sex, religious belief, age, disability or national origin.

Section 2. No employee nor any member of the Union shall be either discriminated against or intimidated in any manner by the Company or the Union because of the employee's membership in the Union or lack thereof.

ARTICLE VIII

RIGHTS OF MANAGEMENT

Section 2. The management of the Company also has the right to discipline, demote, suspend or discharge any employee, but will do so in a reasonable manner.

Background

* * * *

There is little, if any, dispute as to the basic facts in this case. In the summer of 2004, the Company's construction crews were working on a project in an area principally populated by African-Americans. No one is certain of the exact date the incident occurred, although Union witnesses indicated they believed it occurred in July of 2004. Two construction crews were working on the project site, although in slightly separate areas. One crew was led by Crew leader F, an African-American. The other crew was led by the Grievant. All of the crew members, with one exception, were African-Americans. The Grievant is Caucasian.

According to the testimony at the arbitration hearing, the Grievant and an African-American member of F's crew, P's, had a long-running, allegedly friendly,

banter during which they would call each other by various names which had arguably racial connotations, e.g. Jefferson Davis, Trent Lott, etc. On the day in question,
P's allegedly called the Grievant "Trent Lott", although Mr. Johnston's notes indicate
P's denied that. In the wake of this alleged comment, Grievant decided to walk over to
the excavation site in which P's and F were working and turned his hard hat around
backward, causing a white cotton wipe to be draped over his face, reminiscent of a
Ku Klux Klan hood. Apparently, the white cotton wipes were reinforced paper towels
sometimes used by employees to shield the backs of their necks from the sun. The
testimony conflicted as to whether the eye and mouth holes were fashioned purposefully, or by happenstance, or that they existed. Mr. Sharp testified on both direct, as
well as on cross-examination, that he did not see any eye or mouth holes cut in the
cotton wipe. In any event, the record reflects that the Grievant intended his actions to
be interpreted as simulating a KKK hood. The Grievant's actions all took place in an
area adjacent to a public street. Houses were also located in the area of the work site,
at least some occupied by African-Americans. All employees were wearing Company
uniforms and trucks and equipment bearing the Company logo and name were present at the site.

Two days after the incident, the President of Local 1047C, Ricky Lawrence, was
made aware of the Grievant's conduct at the job site when he was contacted by
Mike McCrory, a member of the local and the shop steward for the Construction
Department, the same department the Grievant worked in. Lawrence was contacted
by McCory on or about July 30, 2004. After learning of the incident from McCrory,
Lawrence contacted the Grievant and confirmed the incident had occurred. He then
directed the Grievant to approach each individual at the job site where the incident
occurred and offer a personal apology. Subsequently, Lawrence was contacted by the
Grievant and advised by him that he had met with each individual and offered his
apologies which had been accepted.

Company management learned about the incident involving the Grievant on
September 9, 2004, when Eddie Johnston, Jackson District Operations Manager, was
confronted by Company employee Gelston McCornell who told him about the incident and to also let him know that a group of individuals intended to go to the
Company President, Kevin Akers, to complain about the situation. The record reflects
that McCornell was not present and did not see the events about which he was complaining. This is the first time Johnston had heard of the incident.

After learning about the incident, Johnston immediately began an investiga-
tion. Johnston first contacted Ross Aven (at the time Mississippi Valley Gas's Vice-
President of Human Resources) and John McDill, the Vice-President of Operations.
Johnston then contacted Local Union President Lawrence to inform him of the

investigation. Lawrence told Johnston that Pat Pope would serve as the Union's representative during the investigation. Johnston then began conducting interviews of everyone present at the work site. Some interviews were conducted on the afternoon of September 9 and the remainder were conducted on September 10. Johnston interviewed everyone present, including the Grievant. Johnston then went back to the Company Management Team on September 16, 2004, and reported his findings and conclusions. After discussion, the Management Team decided to terminate the Grievant's employment. Johnston and McDill informed the Grievant of his discharge on September 17, 2004, which was his last day of employment. Also present at the Grievant's discharge were Union officers Jimmy Jones and Dan Lindsey.

On October 11, 2004, the Union filed a grievance regarding the Grievant's discharge. The matter was not settled at previous steps in the grievance procedure. The parties stipulated that the grievance is properly before the arbitrator and there are no procedural issues which preclude the arbitrator from addressing the substantive merits of the grievance.

Arguments of the Parties

COMPANY'S ARGUMENTS

The Company points out that there are no serious factual disputes in this matter. The Grievant admittedly and deliberately fashioned a cotton wipe to resemble a Ku Klux Klan mask and did so in a public place, in a Company uniform around trucks and equipment emblazoned with Company logos. In addition to the Company's Harassment Policy, the Grievant also admitted he had attended meetings in which Johnston told the attendees that racial "nitpicking and name-calling" was going to stop or "someone was going to the house." One would think that anyone who lived in the Deep South in the 60's, 70's, 80's, 90's and into the current decade would understand the extreme sensitivity of pretending to wear a KKK hood in front of their African-American co-workers.

* * * *

The Company will not concede the issue that the Grievant did not receive a prior warning. Johnston testified he expressly told his employees in meetings that he had zero tolerance for racial joking and horseplay. The Company contends that the Union will likely argue that the Grievant was treated differently than other employees who engaged in similar conduct. At the hearing, the Union brought up an argument that one Company employee called another employee an "Uncle Tom." The witness reciting this event admitted that both employees were African-American. The Union also alluded to the fact that P's the employee who allegedly called the Grievant "Trent Lott", was not disciplined as part of this process. The Company claims that one employee calling another employee "Trent Lott", does not in any sense equate to simulating a KKK hood.

* * * *

UNION'S ARGUMENTS

The Union argues that the discharge of the Grievant cannot be sustained because the discipline, when evaluated with all events and circumstances, was not done in a reasonable manner. Several prior cases were cited in support of this position. The Union points out that the Grievant had been employed by the Company for over 11 years prior to his termination on September 17, 2004. During his time of employment with the Company, the only prior discipline imposed on him was a warning letter issued after he revved the engine of the Company's vehicle too much. The Grievant's work ethic and job reviews reflect that he was viewed as an employee requiring little direct supervision.

The Union states that notwithstanding his employment history, the Grievant did engage in racial horseplay which precipitated his discharge. The Union also states that it cannot be emphasized in strong enough terms that the Union neither condones nor tolerates such conduct. Local Union President Lawrence contacted the Grievant, determined that the incident had occurred, and directed the Grievant to apologize to each employee at the job site.

The Union claims that beyond the incident in this case, racial joking and jesting goes on between members of the Company's work force. The fact that racial jesting occurs was supported by testimony from three different Union witnesses, as well as the Company's Operations Manager as reflected in his interview notes dated September 15, 2004. Moreover, one of the utility workers has admitted to Johnston that he has called this Grievant "Jeff Davis" in the past. The Union contends that the fact that an employee is a member of an ethnic minority does not give a license or greater immunity to engage in acts of ethnic harassment. As such, even though the Grievant's actions were wrong, he was not the only one engaged in severe race-related teasing and taunting in the work place. Prior cases are also cited in support of this position. The Union argues that given the testimony and evidence at the arbitration hearing in this matter, consistency in the enforcement of the Company's

Harassment Policy has been totally lacking. As such, the decision of the Company to discharge the Grievant fell far short of the contractual standard of reasonableness and cannot be sustained. No other employee of the Company has ever been terminated for participating in racial humor, racial teasing or racial joking.

The Union claims that another factor to be considered is the Grievant's knowledge of the Company's rules. The Union contends it is a commonly recognized principle in arbitration of discipline cases that there be reasonable rules which are consistently applied and enforced and widely disseminated. In this case, the Company's Harassment Policy as contained in the Employee Handbook was disseminated to all employees. However, the discipline to be imposed for a violation of that policy was not widely disseminated. Johnston only indicated that a future racial incident could result in "someone going to the house." Other than that potential discipline could be imposed, there was no other testimony or evidence presented that a violation of the Company's Harassment Policy would result in discharge for a first-time offense.

Discussion

* * * *

It is well established in arbitration that management has the fundamental right to unilaterally establish reasonable rules not inconsistent with the law or the collective agreement. The Harassment Policy is a reasonable rule and/or policy in its content. However, rules/policies must be reasonable not only in their content but also in their application.

* * * *

The Arbitrator is convinced that the Grievant was aware, or should have been aware, that racial taunting and teasing was not appropriate conduct in the workplace, but his knowledge of the consequences of such actions is questionable. He had received a copy of the Company's Harassment Policy, and signed an acknowledgement of receiving it. However, the Union's argument that the discipline to be imposed for a violation of that policy was not widely understood by the employees has some merit. Why does the Arbitrator reach this conclusion?

The question of "notice" in this case is related to and/or intermingled with the "equal treatment" (consistency) question. Part of the "notice" requirement is that the employee must not only know the rule/policy but also "foreknowledge of the possible or probable consequences of the employee's disciplinary conduct." The Harassment Policy does state: "Discipline, up to and including termination, shall take precedent over job performance regardless of how outstanding it may be." The record also reflects that Operations Manager Johnston held a "tailgate" meeting in which he indicated a future racial incident could result in "someone going to the house." The Harassment Policy and tailgate meeting standing alone could constitute notice under some circumstances. However, these types of notices can be weakened and even negated by failure to consistently enforce the Policy. The employee may be lulled into thinking no disciplinary action will be taken for violating the rule/policy, and certainly not discharge.

The Arbitrator realizes that management cannot know everything that takes place in the workplace, and certainly not all the words said by employees to each other. However, this does not negate the fact that if such teasing and taunting does routinely take place without any discipline, another employee may not be discharged for engaging in the same activity. Management at the minimum knew some racial teasing and taunting was taking place. Two African-Americans had engaged in "Uncle Tom" calling. The Company may be correct in that the Grievant's actions were more serious, but no discipline was given these two minority workers. The Company learned in the investigation that some minority employees had called the Grievant "names like Jefferson Davis and Trent Lott." Even if the Grievant was not called "Trent Lott" on the day of the incident, as the Grievant claims, the record clearly indicates that he had been called such names intended as racial related in the past. The Company at least learned this in the interviews during the investigation.

* * * *

It has already been ruled by this Arbitrator that the Harassment Policy is reasonably related to the orderly, efficient, and safe operation of the Company's business, and required by law. The Harassment Policy is reasonable in content, but it is the application of the Policy in question in this case of the Grievant. Proof is not an issue in this case. The Grievant has admitted engaging in the activity as charged, and even apologized for his actions.

In summary, the Arbitrator finds the Grievant was guilty of turning his hard hat around backward, causing a white cotton wipe to be draped over his face, reminiscent of a Ku Klux Klan hood, before other employees who were African-American—racial harassment. On the other hand, the Grievant had approximately 11 years of service with the Company without any prior discipline for racial harassment. The Grievant admitted his actions, and apologized to the employees who saw the incident. Minority employees had made comments to the Grievant in the past that had a racial intended meaning. The Company was aware of these racially intended comments made to the Grievant before he was discharged. No other employee was disciplined for racial harassment. Therefore, as explained above, the Company had some problems in the "notice" and "consistency" requirements. Thus, the discharge of the Grievant was not done in a "reasonable manner" as required by Article VIII, Section 2, of the Agreement. This decision is not based on "leniency" but the principles of just cause and industrial jurisprudence.

* * * *

AWARD

For all of the above reasons, explained in some detail, it is ruled that the Company's decision to discharge the Grievant was not done in a reasonable manner. The Grievant is to be reinstated immediately to the Crew leader "A" position, without loss of seniority, but without any back pay.

APPLICATION AND DISCUSSION QUESTIONS

1. The arbitrator outlines a number of arbitration principles on notice, reasonable work rules, and disparate treatment. Can you cite each rule as set forth in this award? Was there sufficient notice to the grievant regarding the harassment policy and that he could be terminated for violating the policy?

2. Once the arbitrator determined that the grievant was aware of the work rule and that the work rule was reasonable, why didn't the arbitrator uphold the termination? Was the discipline "fair and just"? Why did the arbitrator state the decision was not based on "leniency"?

3. Does the award "negate" the company's policy on zero tolerance of harassment? How does the arbitrator address this concern? Should the company be held responsible if management was unaware that other employees may have violated the harassment policy?

QUAKER STATE CORP. AND OIL, CHEMICAL AND ATOMIC WORKERS INT'L UNION, LOCAL 8-481

92 BNA LA 898 (R. TALARICO, 1989)[*]

* * * *

Background

The Employer, Quaker State Corporation, is engaged in the refining and marketing of petroleum products. One of several Quaker State Facilities engaged in the refining of crude oil was located at Emlenton, Pennsylvania. This facility was the oldest refinery in the Corporation with the smallest refining capacity. In early 1980, it became apparent to management that the plant could no longer be operated profitably due to its small refining capacity and outdated equipment. Management elected to discontinue refining operations and to convert the Emlenton plant to a specialty wax operation with a sizeable reduction in the work force.

The grievants, A, J and W, were all previously employed by Quaker State at its Titusville facility. As a result of a cutback in crude gathering operations in central Pennsylvania, a number of Titusville employees were scheduled for layoff in May 1986. A job vacancy referral request form was distributed to Titusville production employees who were facing layoff. The purpose of the form was for these workers to express an interest in employment at other Quaker State facilities should job openings arise.

Representatives of the Employer contacted grievant A in early 1987 regarding a job opening at the Emlenton facility. During the job interview, A was told that he would have to move to the Emlenton area within 150 days of his employment as a condition of obtaining employment. There are some questions as to the specific terms and conditions of this "residency requirement" as they were related to the grievant which will be discussed later in this opinion. However, nothing exists in writing as to the alleged "understanding" reached with A.

Grievants W and J were also offered employment at the Emlenton facility on November 23, 1987, and December 1, 1987, respectively. They were also advised in general terms that they would have to move to the Emlenton area within 150 days of employment as a condition of accepting employment. Again, the specific terms and

---

conditions of the "residency requirement" as related to these grievants are also in dispute and will be discussed later.

Approximately ten to fifteen days before his 150 day probationary period expired, A was reminded by a Company representative of his obligation to move within the Emlenton area. A few days later, A was told that he would have several days to relocate or be permanently suspended. That weekend, A found residence in the Emlenton area in the home of his wife's aunt. He moved to that residence and stayed there approximately two to three months, but his wife and family did not relocate to that address. Thereafter, he vacated that address and returned to his Titusville home. On March 18, 1988, after more than one year of employment, A was requested to and did sign the following letter:

> "It has been explained to me and I fully understand that as a condition of my employment at Quaker State Corporation's Emlenton Plant, I am required to establish legitimate residency within the local Emlenton area.
>
> Note: For the purpose of this requirement, 'local Emlenton area' will be defined as within a 10 mile radius of the Emlenton Plant as determined by Quaker State.
>
> I also understand that failure to establish and maintain such residency will be cause for immediate termination, and that this requirement will be in effect for the full Term of my employment at Emlenton Plant.
>
> Signature_____ Date_____ "

Shortly after signing this document, A and his wife started looking for houses in the Emlenton area but did so reluctantly because of their fear that employment at the Emlenton facility may not be permanent.

On June 8, 1988, it came to the attention of the plant management that A failed to maintain a residence within the Emlenton area and was permanently suspended until further notice. Shortly thereafter, the Union President was able to work out a temporary solution of having the grievant again rent from his wife's aunt until the issue could be settled by Arbitration.

Grievants J and W also were requested to execute the same document as A and did so on March 18, 1988. On June 8, 1988, management also became aware that J and W had not moved into the Emlenton area and they were similarly suspended. These grievants also became the beneficiary of the temporary settlement worked out with the Local Union until the within issues could be presented to Arbitration.

Issues

1. Whether the Employer violated the Collective Bargaining Agreement when it unilaterally promulgated a residency requirement for new hires at its Emlenton facility?

2. Whether the Employer had just cause for suspending the grievants for failure to comply with the residency requirement?

Position of the Employer

While the Collective Bargaining Agreement does not contain a Management Rights Clause, Arbitrators still recognize the Employer's reserved rights to manage. It is the Company's position that it retains the right to establish a residency rule at the Emlenton plant as an incident of its implied right to manage and direct the working forces. Furthermore, local officers did not protest when told in November 1986, March and November 1987, that new hires had to relocate to Emlenton as a condition of employment.

Each of the grievants testified that they were advised in pre-employment interviews that any offer of employment would be contingent on their relocating to the Emlenton area. Each grievant fully understood the move requirement and agreed to move in order to be offered employment.

It must be noted that the Union's grievance attacks the penalty imposed for violating the residency rule but not the rule itself. The written grievance clearly sets forth the nature of the grievance:

"We protest the indefinite suspension of A, W and J as being too harsh a disciplinary action."

* * * *

Position of the Union

It is well established that there is a duty to bargain about mandatory subjects of bargaining. The residency requirement at issue is a condition of employment and thus a mandatory subject to that duty to bargain, notwithstanding the Company's attempt to suggest that this residency requirement is nothing more than a work rule, which the Company has the free unfettered right to implement. An Employer only has the right to unilaterally establish a reasonable plant rule which is not inconsistent with either the law or the Collective Bargaining Agreement. The Employer has failed to meet these requirements.

* * * *

The Company produced no evidence showing that its alleged residency requirement is necessary. The fact that the residency rule is grandfathered for the existing employers hired before the grievance, underscores the fact that the residency requirement is, in fact, not necessary. Moreover, the Company rule is overly broad and vague and unenforceable. The residency requirement varied according to who was being interviewed. More importantly, the stated purposes behind the residency requirement were met by all the grievants, i.e., overtime, call-out and emergency response. Thus, the Union has demonstrated that the Employer does not have the right to unilaterally impose a residency requirement on some of the employees but not all, without negotiations with the Union, particularly where there is, in fact, no general uniform established policy throughout the bargaining unit impacting upon the administration of the discipline and just cause obligations of the Company. The within policy fails to properly account for the necessary distinction between an employee's work-related concerns and other aspects of life which must necessarily remain private.

Under these circumstances, there can be no other conclusion warranted than that the Union's grievance must be sustained, the employees reinstated and all benefits lost restored, a determination that the residency requirement is unenforceable and that the Union's grievance must be sustained.

Findings and Discussion

* * * *

Let us turn now to a close examination of the circumstances and rationale under which the Emlenton residency rule was promulgated. The Employer argues that its residency rule is reasonably related to the efficient operation of its Emlenton facility. More specifically, the residency requirement for new employees is designed to ensure that they are available for overtime work assignments which occur, as well as work beyond regular quitting time, Saturdays or emergency call-outs without having to travel several miles to accommodate the needs of the facility. In further support thereof, the Employer notes that the matter of job security for present refinery employees was discussed during contract negotiations and the Union agreed to make every effort to provide maximum employment by eliminating inefficient work practices.

The within agreement does not contain a Management Rights Clause nor any specific authority to promulgate work rules unilaterally. Despite that, Arbitrators still recognize an Employer's reserved rights to manage and operate its business which includes the right to unilaterally establish reasonable Plant rules not inconsistent with law or the Collective Bargaining Agreement. Since there is no express provision in the agreement prohibiting a residency rule, any challenge to the residency requirement must be premised on the basis that it is unfair, arbitrary or discriminatory. The most common ground for challenging a work rule is an asserted lack of reasonableness. The basic standard of reasonableness of a unilaterally promulgated work rule is whether it is reasonably related to a legitimate interest of management, without imposing undue hardships on employees. After evaluating all of the circumstances and rationale surrounding the development and implementation of the residency rule; and balancing its impact on the grievants in relation to the interests of the Employer, I conclude that the residency requirement is not reasonably related to the efficient operation of the Emlenton facility. I reach this conclusion for several reasons:

1. The express reason for the residency requirement is to ensure that new hires, who comprise a very small portion of the total working force, will be readily available for overtime, extra work, call-outs, etc., since they will not have to travel more than ten miles to reach the Plant. However, such a residency requirement in and of itself does not guarantee nor even offer reasonable assurances that employees will be available to work overtime. Traffic and road conditions on one side of the ten mile radius may vary significantly from traffic and road conditions on the other side of the ten mile radius. So distance itself is not necessarily the determinative factor in evaluating response time or availability; just as the Employer cannot account for cars that won't start, unplowed rural driveways, etc.

2. Rapid response is not a critical factor in most of the overtime situations which are of concern to the Employer. For example, it makes no difference where an employee lives if he is asked to extend an existing shift. The same can generally be said for working extra days.

3. The Employer already has at its disposal a broad and clear Mandatory Overtime provision set forth in Article II of the Collective Bargaining Agreement which provides that employees must accept overtime work when it is assigned to them. This provision would be applicable to all employees (new hires or others) when needed to stay after their shift has ended, to be called out early for their shift, or to work extra days. Refusals can be met with disciplinary action. With such a powerful tool in hand, I fail to see what more can be gained by the Employer by imposing a residency requirement upon new hires only.

4. Even if implemented, the residency requirement cannot impinge upon an employee's free time or private life. There is absolutely no requirement thereunder that the grievants remain on stand-by status. Consequently, what does the residency requirement accomplish if an employee decides to go hunting or fishing or to visit friends (who live more than ten miles from the plant) and decides to stay over until he has to report for his next scheduled shift. A residency requirement under these circumstances does not guarantee the availability or rapid response of that employee. In fact, the same scenario applies to exempt/grandfathered employees and their ability to rapidly respond to call-outs, etc.

5. While circumstances can always change, one extremely significant element is the fact that since being hired by Quaker State at its Emlenton facility, all of the grievants have had an exemplary work record, but even more importantly, have met all overtime work assignments requested of them. The Employer attempts to make much of a situation where one of the grievants was canvassed about the possibility of working overtime one day and he stated that he would like to be passed over if possible inasmuch as he needed a ride home. Apparently, his personal request was granted without any inconvenience to the Employer. However, even under a residency requirement, employees will always have occasions where personal reasons may force them to seek an exemption from an overtime requirement. Even the agreement's Mandatory Overtime provision recognizes such exceptions.

6. The grievants, by choosing where they want to live in relationship to the Plant, are fully cognizant of the mandatory overtime requirements and their normal duty to arrive at work on time. Should their choice of residence hinder their performance, they are well aware of the fact that disciplinary action (including discharge) may be imposed.

7. The residency requirement is not being applied evenhandedly. While the Employer offered testimony that it believes the majority of its present employees (who are not subject to the residency requirement) live within a ten to twelve mile radius of the Plant, it did not conduct a survey to determine what percentage of its work force actually does live within that radius. More importantly, however, there is no restriction on such employees from ever moving outside that radius.

8. The residency requirement poses an unnecessary and undue hardship on these employees. The Employer's requirement is to establish a permanent domicile within ten miles of the Plant. This means uprooting their families; selling their homes and double mortgages if it doesn't sell quickly; transferring their children to another school district; a spouse having to quit her job; being unable to care for ill parents who may live nearby, etc. When balancing these hardships in relation to the benefits derived by the Employer, it is readily apparent to this Arbitrator that the imposition of a residency rule serves no appreciable purpose.

* * * *

AWARD

The grievance is sustained. The grievants are to be reimbursed for any lost wages and benefits as a result of their temporary suspensions. Moreover, the residency rule promulgated by the Employer is not enforceable against the grievants.

APPLICATION AND DISCUSSION QUESTIONS

1. The primary question presented in the grievance is whether the new work rule (residency requirements) was reasonable. In determining whether a

work rule is reasonable, management must establish that the work rule "is reasonably related to a legitimate interest of management." What evidence did the employer present to prove that the residency rule was "reasonably related to the efficient operation of its Emlenton facility?

2. The arbitrator cited several reasons why the residency work rule was not reasonable. Do you agree with each of the reasons outlined by the arbitrator? Explain the hardships the employees would face and the benefits the employer would receive.

PAN AMERICAN AIRWAYS CORP. AND AIR LINE PILOTS ASSOCIATION

116 BNA LA 757 (NOLAN, 2001)[*]

A. Background

The Grievant is an experienced pilot with about 20,000 hours of flight time. He has flown as a pilot for 33 years, 28 of which were for commercial airlines. He has worked for Pan Am and its predecessor, Carnival, for 11 years. During that entire period, he has never been disciplined by an employer or the FAA. The termination prompting this grievance occurred after a single incident involving a dispute over the interpretation of a Federal Air Regulation (FAR).

One of the most debated issues affecting air crews is the permissible length of service without a break. Everyone agrees that it would be unsafe for pilots to fly too long without a substantial rest period, but people differ about how long is "too long." The applicable FAR is 14 CFR §121.471, which prohibits a carrier from scheduling, and a pilot from accepting, any assignment that would require duty for more than 16 hours in any 24-hour period. Until recently, the consensus in the industry about the meaning of that section was that while a pilot could not be scheduled for more than 16 hours, he or she could complete a properly scheduled flight that would take the pilot beyond 16 hours, provided the delay was due to weather, mechanical, or air traffic delays. Section 12.A.2 of the collective bargaining agreement reflects that consensus

---

[*]   Reprinted with permission from *Labor Relations Reporter- Labor Arbitration Reports.* 116 BNA LA 757. Copyright 2015 by the Bureau of National Affairs, Inc. (800-372-1033). http://www.bna.com.

by allowing extension of a pilot's duty period to 18 hours when properly scheduled flights are delayed for those reasons.

The FAA recently upset that consensus by interpreting the FAR as prohibiting a pilot from even initiating a delayed flight if the anticipated arrival time would cause the pilot to exceed the 16-hour limit. Further, the FAA now asserts that a pilot who has pushed off the gate and subsequently encounters a delay before takeoff must return to the gate if he or she could not complete the flight within the 16 hour limit. These changes were announced in a November 20, 2000 letter from the FAA's Deputy Chief Counsel, James W. Whitlow; the interpretation is thus commonly known as the Whitlow Letter. (The Union prefers the term "clarification" to the word "change," but there is no doubt that the Whitlow Letter represented a new and different position. "Change" is an appropriate description even if the FAA merely gave a new interpretation to an existing regulation.)

The Union communicated the Whitlow Letter to its Master Executive Committee chairmen on December 1, 2000. The chairman of the Pan Am MEC, Captain Lanny Schott, circulated the letter to his pilots early in December. Interestingly, Captain Schott himself faced a similar scheduling problem in early December of 2000. He discussed the problem with Crew Scheduling and was released from duty without incurring any discipline.

B. The January 3 Incident and Subsequent FAA Action

On January 3, 2001, the Grievant was scheduled to fly Pan Am Flight 2 from Portsmouth-Bangor-Pittsburgh-Sanford-Portsmouth. That trip should have taken 0745 of flight time and 1320 of duty time. He reported for duty at 0545 and should have been released at 1905, well before his 16-hour mark at 2145. Although this schedule complied with the FAR, a mechanical problem delayed the flight at Sanford. The Grievant calculated that he would have to push back by 1855 in order to reach Portsmouth within his 16-hour period. He reported his concern to Crew Scheduling (as did Captain Schott, with whom the Grievant had spoken.) He then learned for the first time that the Company did not agree with the Grievant's interpretation of the FAR.

Around 1900, when he believed that he could no longer complete the flight within the 16-hour period, the Grievant asked Crew Scheduling if he and his crew could get a room at a hotel. The request was granted, but Pan Am's Director of Operations, Captain Jim Baker, contacted the Grievant shortly after he arrived at the hotel. Baker explained that the FAA interpretation of the FAR was in dispute and warned the crew of serious trouble if they did not fly as scheduled. When the Grievant still refused to fly, citing his "take on the law" for his conclusion that to take the flight would "break an FAR," Baker terminated him for insubordination. The other two crewmembers reluctantly agreed to fly, with Captain Schott serving as the replacement pilot. It should be noted that the Grievant has never claimed that he was too fatigued to fly. His sole reason for refusing the flight was his interpretation of the FAR.

When the FAA learned of the incident and of the Company's general position on the interpretive dispute, it initiated enforcement action against the Company and the other two crewmembers. The action against the Company is still pending but the FAA withdrew the actions against the crewmembers because they flew only under the threat of losing their jobs. That explanation of the FAA's decision not to discipline the other crewmembers (or Captain Schott for flying with crewmembers who were exceeding the 16-hour limit) refutes the Company's assertion that the FAA found there was no violation in its orders to the crew.

The FAA's current position is that Pan Am is bound by the Whitlow Letter's interpretation of the FAA and that it will take enforcement action if the Company again directs a crewmember to fly in similar circumstances. In fact, the Company may already have had employees complete flights that ended beyond the 16-hour period, but there is no evidence that the FAA knew of those incidents.

C. The Motion to Postpone (Omitted)

III. The Issues

Did the Company have just cause to terminate the Grievant? If not, what shall the remedy be?

V. The Employer's Position

The Company views this as a simple case of insubordination. The Grievant willfully refused a direct order from his supervisor, even after being told that the Company disputed the Whitlow Letter and that the legitimacy of the new interpretation was unsettled. The Company has a contractual right to manage and direct its pilots, which is what it did on January 3. Several arbitration awards have held that a refusal to fly for any reason other than a belief that the aircraft was unsafe is "blatant insubordination." Insubordination, in turn, presents just cause for discipline.

The Company rejects the Union's claim that a pilot may refuse an order if he or she believes it to be illegal. The only recognized exception to the "obey now, grieve later" rule, it argues, is when the pilot believes a flight would be unsafe.

VI. The Union's Position

The Union initially argues that the Company's order to the Grievant was illegal because it conflicted with the FAA's interpretation of the controlling FAR. Second, discharge would be inappropriate even if the Grievant was wrong in his interpretation, because he acted in good faith. Third, the Company treated the Grievant disparately because it excused Captain Schott from a flight when he raised the identical issue in December of 2000. Finally, discharge would be too severe for a long-term employee with an exemplary record.

The Union therefore asks that the Grievant be reinstated with full back pay and other benefits, and that he receive interest on his back pay. The Union also asks that he be reimbursed for his out-of-pocket expenses incurred in seeking other employment.

VII. Discussion

A. The Appropriateness of a Decision

The Company's brief reiterated its earlier argument against deciding the case at this time. So did the dissenting arbitrator, who charged that deciding this case before a final court decision on the merits of the Whitlow Letter's interpretation of the FAR would amount to a "rush to judgment."

That argument mistakes the ultimate issue in this case. If the question before the System Board was whether the Grievant was right or wrong in his interpretation of the FAR, we would, of course, have to wait until the final court decision on the pending cases. That is not the issue posed by the parties. Rather, we are to determine whether the Company had just cause to terminate the Grievant-quite a different matter. The Board can resolve that issue without deciding the proper meaning of the FAR. Because we can do so, there is no reason to delay the case any further.

B. Controlling Principles

Ultimately, this case turns not on the proper interpretation of the FAR-something that will not be determined for months, if not years-but on the applicability of an exception to a fundamental principle of labor arbitration. The normal rule is that an employee who believes an order to be improper should "obey now and grieve later." The rationale for the rule is obvious and universally accepted: it would be impossible to operate a business if every employee could refuse any he or she deemed improper. That rule usually works well. The employer gets uninterrupted production during the pendency of the resulting grievance, and an employee who prevails is made whole for any losses.

There are a few cases, however, where application of the rule would produce unacceptable consequences. These have caused arbitrators to create a few very narrow exceptions. A standard reference work in the field provides a concise statement of the rule, its exceptions, and the qualifications to the exceptions:

(1) An employee who disagrees with a work order or work rule normally must obey the order or rule and challenge its legitimacy through the grievance and arbitration procedure or other channels. Failure to do so may constitute insubordination.

(2) An employee need not immediately obey an order or rule if he or she

　(a) reasonably believes it to be illegal, unethical, or immoral;

　(b) reasonably believes that obedience would place the employee or others in imminent danger of harm; or

　(c) would suffer immediate and substantial harm, and would lack any satisfactory remedy after the fact.

Even in these cases, however, disobedience will be excused only if the employee has no other feasible way to resolve the dispute.

The rationales for the exceptions are as obvious and universally accepted as for the rule itself. First, no employee should be punished for disobeying an order that is illegal, unethical, or immoral, or that would endanger the employee or others. If there were no such exceptions, employees would be forced to choose between a job and following an order that conflicts with important societal rules. Clearly, a discharge for such a reason would not be "just." Second, a "good faith belief" must satisfy the exception because it is often impossible to know, immediately and with absolute certainty, whether a given order is lawful or safe. Employees have to act on the basis of what they know at the time, or else the mere risk of an error would deter them from doing what they should, or force them to do what they should not. Third, the risk of loss to the employer is reduced to a reasonable level by the qualifications that the employee's disobedience must be reasonable and in circumstances that eliminate other feasible ways of resolving the dispute.

The Company argues that, at least in the context of an order to fly an airplane, there is no recognized defense other than a good faith belief that the plane was unsafe. The Company submitted and relied upon five arbitration awards. Because its assertion departs from the general understanding of the "obey now, grieve later" rule, it is essential to examine the authorities on which it relies. Doing so leads us to the conclusion that the cited cases do not support the Company's position.

* * * *

In sum, the Company failed to provide any evidence or authority that the illegality exception to the general rule does not or should not apply in this industry. We therefore conclude that a pilot's good faith and reasonable belief that a flight would violate an FAR provides a valid exception to the usual "obey now, grieve later" rule. Furthermore, the illegality exception does not require that the employee's interpretation be the one the courts eventually approve. That would require pilots to carry a crystal ball with them in the cockpit, and would force them to gamble their jobs on decisions to be made by others long afterward. For the same reason, it is proper to resolve this grievance without waiting for the decision in the ATA's challenge to the FAA interpretation. Whether the ATA or the FAA prevails in that case will not affect the propriety of the Grievant's decision on January 3.

A pilot asserting the illegality defense to an order must of course act reasonably, which means that he or she must have good reason to believe that his interpretation is correct. The pilot must also act in good faith, which means that he or she cannot use an assertion of illegality as a cover for a different but unacceptable reason. Finally, the pilot must try to exhaust all other reasonable means of determining the law's requirements before refusing an order to fly.

C. Application of the Principles

The Grievant relies solely on the exception covering his good faith belief that flying the last leg of his scheduled trip would have violated the FAR. Because the Company does not challenge his good faith, that exception would protect him from discipline so long as his belief was reasonable and he had no other way of escaping his dilemma.

Was the Grievant's interpretation reasonable? He saw and relied on the Whitlow Letter. That letter's meaning is not disputed. Nor did the Company challenge Whitlow's authority to issue that interpretation on behalf of the FAA. Whether Whitlow was right or wrong, he clearly stated the FAA's considered interpretation that the FAR barred a captain from beginning a flight if he knew the trip would carry him past his 16-hour limit. The Grievant's reliance on that apparently authoritative interpretation was therefore not unreasonable.

Did the Grievant have any other way to escape his dilemma? The Company suggested none and we can think of none. He read the latest controlling authority and discussed it with the MEC chairman and with the Company's Director of Operations. He had to make a decision within a matter of minutes, so there was no time to obtain any further advice from the FAA. As he reasonably saw the situation, he had to grasp one horn or the other-risk losing his certificate or risk losing his job. In those circumstances, making a reasonable decision to protect his certificate was the best that he could do.

We conclude that the Grievant met the qualifications for the illegality exception to the "obey now, grieve later" rule. It follows that the Company did not have just cause to fire him. The grievance must be sustained.

D. The Appropriate Remedy

Part of the appropriate remedy is standard and obvious: a wrongfully terminated employee should be reinstated with full back pay and other benefits, less alternative earnings. A second portion is almost as obvious: the Grievant should received interest on his back pay. The Neutral Chairman's decision eight years ago in another airline case explains that conclusion:

> In virtually all other forums-courts and administrative agencies-a prevailing party
> routinely receives interest on delayed payments. That is a matter of simple justice:
> getting a sum a year late does not make the recipient whole. Interest is the normal
> way to compensate the injured party for delayed payment. Interest awards are rela-
> tively unusual in labor arbitration, apparently only because parties seldom seek them.
> Marvin F. Hill, Jr. and Anthony V. Sinicropi, Remedies in Arbitration 450 (BNA 2nd
> ed. 1991). There is no logical reason why labor arbitration remedies should differ from
> those applied, for example, by the National Labor Relations Board.
>
> Some arbitrators have used interest awards as a form of punitive damages, award-
> ing interest only when the employer's conduct is reprehensible. That misinterprets the
> concept of interest. Since its purpose is to compensate the injured employee for the

delay in payment, it is appropriate regardless of the nature of the employer's breach. A wrongly discharged employee's right should not depend on whether the employer was a sinner as well as a contract breacher.

Atlantic Southeast Airlines, Inc., 101 LA 515, 525-26 (1993).

APPLICATION AND DISCUSSION QUESTIONS

1. What is the ultimate issue in this case?

2. Do you agree with the pilot's interpretation of the Federal Air Regulation? If not, what are some alternatives to terminating his employment? How does the arbitrator apply the "good faith and reasonable belief" principle? Was the pilot's belief reasonable?

3. What is the "obey now, grieve later" rule? What are the exceptions to this rule and what role did it play in this case?

AN INVESTIGATION WAS COMPLETED BEFORE DISCIPLINE ISSUED

TRINITY EAST AND OHIO COUNCIL 8, AFSCME LOCAL 2934
131 LA 1242 (FULLMER, 2013)[*]

This case concerns a three day suspension given to the Grievant, D, on April 10, 2012 for "threatening, intimidating or interfering with an employee or supervisor, a failure to cooperate with others, and dishonesty for denying that you acted in such a manner."

---

[*] Reprinted with permission from *Labor Relations Reporter- Labor Arbitration Reports.* 131 LA 1242. Copyright 2015 by the Bureau of National Affairs, Inc. (800-372-1033). http://www.bna.com.

I. Facts

A. Background Facts

The Employer operates a hospital in Steubenville, Ohio. The Union represents a unit of staff employees which includes Nursing Assistants. One of these is the Grievant, D. She has been employed by the Employer for some four years. There is a separate bargaining unit of registered nurses. One of these is M, R.N. The remaining personages in the case include, in "descending" order: Fred B. Brower, President and CEO; Leslie C. Musso, Vice President-Human Resources; Leslie Heavilin, Clinical Manager; Jamie D'Angelo, Director; Valery Ann Smith, Nursing Supervisor and a flotilla of Nursing Assistants. Three of these were going "off-shift" at 3:00 p.m. [the Grievant, Marjorie Campbell and Ann McAffe] and three were coming "on-shift" at that point [Lynn Lane, Brenda Cook and another]. There were two patients involved, designated here as "Patient 805" and "Patient 808 (B)".

The Employer maintains a set of rules and takes disciplinary actions thereunder when it deems it necessary. The Grievant's record in this respect was indicated in the eventual Notice of Suspension: (Disciplinary Record Omitted)

B. Facts Leading to the Grievance

On April 7, 2012 there was an incident which was described in the eventual Notice of Suspension in the following terms:

> "On April 7, 2012, at approximately 3:00 p.m., you became involved in a heated discussion with M, RN, your supervisor on that shift, regarding a patient assignment. As the discussion continued, you swiftly rose from your chair, approached M, pointed your finger in her face and stated, 'I am forty years old and you better get out of my face while you still can.' You repeated this statement three times in a very threatening manner. Your actions were observed by Valery Smith, Nursing Supervisor, as well as several other staff members...."

The matter was investigated and it was decided to impose a three day suspension. The letter imposing the suspension in question was dated April 10, 2012. The remaining portion of that letter stated in relevant portion that:

> "Your insubordinate actions, as outline above, are a serious violation of the Medical Center's rules of Conduct which prohibit threatening, intimidating or interfering

with an employee or supervisor, a failure to operate with others, and dishonesty for denying that you acted in such a manner. In addition, your actions violate the following Standards of Behavior, Attitude, Respect, Accountability, Sense of Ownership, Commitment to Co-workers, and Communications.

The appropriate disciplinary action for such conduct is disciplinary suspension.

A review of your disciplinary record over the past twenty-four (24) month period reveals the following: ...."

In addition, the following disciplinary actions were taken for attendance:

"...Therefore, as a result of your actions on April 7, as outlined above, and your previous disciplinary record, I am giving you this three (3) day suspension from work without pay as disciplinary action. This suspension commenced on April 9 and included April 9 and April 11. You will be expected to return to work on Friday, April 13 at 7:00 a.m., your previously scheduled shift and time.

I am hopeful that you will take this opportunity to correct your improper conduct and perform all duties and responsibilities required of your in your job. If you fail to do so, I will be compelled to take further appropriate action including discharge and termination of your employment with Trinity East."

Two days later, on April 12, 2012 the Union filed the grievance in this case. It provided in relevant portion that:

"STATEMENT OF GRIEVANCE, List Applicable violation: Article XIII, Section 1 Unjust Discipline.

Adjustment required: Grievant be cleared of 3 day suspension from record & Grievant be made whole."

The grievance was thence processed through the steps of the grievance procedure to arbitration.

II. Potentially Applicable Contract Provisions

ARTICLE VI

Section 2. The Hospital retains the right to discipline and/or discharge employees for just cause and also the right to adopt and enforce reasonable work rules, and once adopted, to revise any and all such; provided that, in the exercise of those rights, the Hospital will not act in an violation of the express terms set forth in this Agreement. Complaints that the Hospital has violated this Section 2 may be appealed through the grievance procedure.

III. Stipulated Issue

Was the three day suspension given to the Grievant, D, on April 10, 2012 for just cause? If not, what shall be the remedy?

IV. Positions of the Parties

The Union Position

The Union emphasizes that the Employer failed to conduct a proper pre-disciplinary investigation. It failed to interview the Grievant prior making the decision to suspend her. The Employer did not deny this failure and apparently thinks hearing only one side of the story is sufficient. The Employer also failed to interview two Nursing Assistants who observed the incident, i.e. Marjorie Campbell and Ann McAfee. Ms. Campbell even asked to be interviewed. The Employer basically wanted to avoid interviewing anyone whose account differed from RN M.

* * * *

The Employer Position

* * * *

Here the Grievant was not discharged, only suspended for three days, a lesser penalty. She, like the other employees of the Employer is subject to the Rules of Conduct. These prohibit threatening, intimidating or interfering with an employee or supervisor. The Standards of Behavior include standards regarding attitude, respect, accountability, sense of ownership, commitment to co-workers, and communications. Employees are advised of these provisions and there is no contention that the Grievant did not know of them.

* * * *

V. Discussion

A. Introduction

The present case is a discipline case in which the Grievant was given a three day suspension without pay on April 10, 2012 for what were described as "insubordinate actions". The parties have stipulated to an issue on the basis of just cause. Within that overall issue the following sub-issues potentially merit discussion. One is the nature of the offense involved. The second is as to the nature of the rules involved. The third is whether there has been a failure by the Employer to adequately investigate the matter. The fourth is as to the precise nature of the Grievant's alleged offense. The fifth is as to whether there was disparate enforcement of the of the rules involved vis a vis registered nurse M.

We turn to these issues in the order stated, as necessary.

(B. The Nature of the Offense, C. The Rules Involved Omitted)

D. The Claimed Failure to Properly Investigate

The Union claims that the Employer failed to fulfill its duty to properly investigate the matter before imposing the suspension on the Grievant, principally by its failure to interview the Grievant prior to imposing the discipline.

There is arbitration authority that an employer has the duty to make an adequate investigation of the facts before imposing discipline. Grief Bros. Cooperage Corp., 42 LA 555, 557-59 (Daugherty, Arb., 1964). Brand, Discipline and Discharge in Arbitration, p. 32, 184 (BNA, 1998). One of the prime elements of this duty is to ascertain the potential grievant's view of the facts, again prior to imposing the discipline. It is often said that an employee must be given an adequate opportunity to present his or her side of the case. Elkouri & Elkouri, How Arbitration Works, p. 15-44 (BNA, 2012). See Crane Pluming, 107 LA 1084 (Fullmer, Arb., 1996). In many work establishments there is a more or less formalized procedure for such a pre-disciplinary interview. Here the "opportunity to present her side of the case" aspect was especially important because the Grievant maintains that she never made the "I am forty years old and you better get out of my face while you still can" statement.

Here the incident occurred on April 7, 2012 at the time of the change in shifts, i.e. 3:00 p.m. The Clinical Manager of the Employer at the time was Leslie Heavilin. Ms. Heavilin was not a witness to the actual incident.

The Grievant's testimony is that she went home after the incident and that evening [April 7] received a telephone call from Manager Heavilin indicating that she [the Grievant] should not come into work the next day, i.e. April 8. She [the Grievant] was instead told to come to work a half hour early on April 9 so that they could discuss the incident. The Grievant prepared to do so on April 9, but received still another telephone call from Manager Heavilin telling her [the Grievant] that she should not return to work until April 12 because they had decided to suspend her. The written Notice of Suspension was dated April 10, 2012. The suspension was described as follows:

"This suspension commenced on April 8 and included April 9 and April 11."

Manager Heavilin's version of whether she interviewed the Grievant prior to the suspension was not available because she did not attend the arbitration hearing or, obviously, testify. Two documents were submitted for the limited purpose of proving that Manager Heavilin did interview the Grievant prior to imposing discipline. One is described by the Employer as "Summary of Statement given by Lynn Lane" allegedly authored by Manager Heavilin. The other is described by the Employer as "Statement from Brenda Cook"). Mss. Lane and Cook were "coming on shift" Nursing Assistants.

There are some difficulties with the documents. The Union argues that they are hearsay because not supported by the live testimony of the purported authors. But, putting those questions aside, the more important issue is whether the two documents contribute anything with respect to the substance of the issue with which we are here dealing. They appear to be merely the recollections of Mss. Lane and Cook as to the substance of the incident, i.e. who said what to who and the utterance or non-utterance of the "I am forty years old and you better get out of my face while you still can." statement. There is no text in the statements as to whether the Grievant admitted making the statements attributed to her or still less any text as to whether Manager Heavilin was on the scene and interviewed the Grievant as to her actions.

Based on this record, the Grievant's testimony that she was not interviewed prior to the imposition of the disciplinary suspension is credited.

We turn to an overall conclusion.

VI. Conclusion

As indicated at the outset, a three day suspension given to the Grievant, D, on April 10, 2012 for "threatening, intimidating or interfering with an employee or supervisor, a failure to cooperate with others, and dishonesty for denying that you acted in such a manner." The issue has been stipulated to in terms of just cause.

The Employer has every right to enforce the cited provisions of its rules against threatening, intimidating and interfering conduct. It is especially important in a hospital setting where the health of the patients is at stake. Alleged comments along the lines of "... get out of my face while you still can...", deserve investigation and, if established, enforcement. But, as indicated in the authorities cited above, one of the important elements of just cause is the conducting of a fair investigation prior to the imposition of discipline. In almost all cases this includes interviewing the potential grievant or otherwise ascertaining his/her side of the story. Here the evidentiary record leads to the conclusion that this was not done and therefore just cause precepts were violated. This conclusion makes it unnecessary to consider the other issues raised by the parties.

To the extent that it may not be otherwise clear, the stipulated issue i.e. that concerning the merits, is answered in the negative, i.e. the three day suspension given to the Grievant, D, on April 10, 2012 was not for just cause. The award draws its essence from the arbitrator's interpretation of Article VI, Section 2 of the parties' agreement and from the terms of the stipulated issue itself.

VII. AWARD

Grievance sustained. The three day suspension given to the Grievant, D, on April 10, 2012 is rescinded. The Grievant is awarded back pay for the days of April 8, 9, and 11, 2012. Should the parties not be able to agree on the amounts of back pay owing, jurisdiction is retained until February 4, 2014 to resolve only such disputes.

APPLICATION AND DISCUSSION QUESTIONS

1. What is an example of a "just cause" termination? Do you believe the termination was justified in this case?

2. What do the standards of behavior include?

3. Were the nurse's actions considered "threatening, intimidating, and interfering?" Why or why not?

INVESTIGATION

This case concerns the discharge of the Grievant, G, on March 18, 1996 for violation of Company Rules 6, 15, and 17.

I. Facts

A. Background Facts

The Company manufactures plumbing fixtures at its Mansfield, Ohio facility. The Union represents a contractually defined unit. Up until March 18, 1996 the Grievant was employed within the unit, in the Kiln operations.

The Company maintains a set of Plant Rules, last revised on October 22, 1993. The first paragraph of these rules indicates that:

"... To enforce plant rules, it is often necessary to invoke disciplinary action that may range from verbal warning to immediate discharge."

Among the substantive rules are those against:
"6. The use of profane, threatening or abusive language towards a supervisor or co-worker.

15. Entering the plant or Company property at any time other than those specified as regular working hours. . . .

17. Interfering in any way with the work of another employee."

The Grievant worked under the direct supervision of a foreman named Joe Lauinger. Among his fellow workers was one S. The Grievant and S made a $25.00 bet on the 1996 Super Bowl. The Grievant won. S did not pay up.

---

[*] Reprinted with permission from *Labor Relations Reporter- Labor Arbitration Reports.*107 BNA LA 1084. Copyright 2015 by the Bureau of National Affairs, Inc. (800-372-1033). http://www.bna.com.

B. Facts Leading to the Grievance

On Friday, March 15, at about 5:30 p.m., S was working at the plant. It was pay day. The Grievant was not scheduled for work. Nevertheless he came to the plant to see if he could collect his money. He looked for S in the cafeteria, but he was not there. The Grievant then headed for the Kiln Department and encountered S along the way. The Grievant asked for his $25.00, but S said that he couldn't make it that week.

According to S, the Grievant then pulled a knife on him and told him that he, the Grievant, would "get" him. The Grievant claimed, he just sort of shrugged, said "forget it" and then left the plant.

S relayed his version of the event to Supervisor Lauinger who in turn called the Company's Manager of Human Resources, Charles Cain at his home. Mr. Cain told Mr. Lauinger that he should suspend the Grievant pending an investigation. That investigation commenced the following Monday morning.

The investigation indicated to the Company that S's version of the event was essentially correct and it decided to discharge the Grievant. A Notice of Disciplinary Action dated March 19 was prepared and sent to the Grievant:

"OFFENSE VIOLATION OF PLANT RULES #15, #6 and #17
On Friday, March 15, 1996 you entered the plant without permission, interrupted the work place and threatened another employee. This is a serious violation of the rules that cannot be tolerated. As a result of this action you are discharged effective immediately."

On March 20, 1996 the grievance at issue was filed:
Protest Company for discharging me. Request my job back, all lost earnings, and to be made whole in every way.

The grievance proceeded through the steps of the grievance procedure to arbitration.

II. Potentially Applicable Contract Provisions

ARTICLE II RESPONSIBILITIES OF THE PARTIES

SECTION A--FUNCTIONS AND PREROGATIVES OF MANAGEMENT
The right to exercise the functions of management are vested exclusively in the Company; including the right to select and hire, and to make such rules not inconsistent with the terms of the Agreement, relating to its operation as it shall deem

advisable, and the right to suspend, discharge or discipline an employee for violation of such rules or for other proper cause. . . .

ARTICLE VIII

Section A.
The right to discharge or discipline employees for just cause shall remain with the Company.

III. Stipulated Issue

Was the discharge of the Grievant, G, on March 18, 1996 for just cause? If not, what shall be the remedy?

IV. Positions of the Parties

The Company Position

The Company's right to discharge for just cause is unquestioned. "Just Cause" is defined in the management rights clause as the violation of Company rules "or for other proper cause." In this case, the company properly discharged the Grievant because of his threatening conduct, which violated at least three separate Plant rules.

In addition to the just cause standard, the Company is prohibited from discriminating against an employee because of his age, national origin or ancestry. Accordingly the arbitrator's opinion should find that the Union did not show any violation of the discrimination clause despite an opportunity to raise and argue the issue.

The Grievant's conduct violated three separate plant rules, i.e. Rules 15, 17, and 6, pertaining respectively to entering the plant when not scheduled to work, interfering with the work of other employees and threatening behavior. The weight of evidence shows that S was threatened by the behavior of the Grievant. There can be no question but what his conduct justified discharge.

The only real question in the case is whether the Company had just cause to believe that the Grievant violated the rules. Its investigation began with S's complaint to his supervisor detailing the threat against him. The investigation found that the statements were supportive of S. Mr. Cain then moved forward and discharged the Grievant. At the grievance hearing on April 2, 1996 the Grievant denied that there was an argument. But, this position contradicted the Ontario police report and the Company denied the grievance.

In support of its version, the Union marshalled a series of collateral attacks, none of which explain why the Grievant told one story at the grievance hearing and another at the arbitration. Unit members were not called by the Union to support the Grievant's version. It must be remembered that the Company's version of the events is not solely dependent on the credibility of S. The statements of the independent witnesses to the Ontario police support the Company version.

To conclude, because the Grievant admittedly violated Plant Rules 15 and 17 and the Company had a legitimate and substantiated belief that Grievant threatened another employee by brandishing a knife in violation of Plant Rule 6, the Company has established just cause for Grievant's discharge. Accordingly, the Company respectfully requests that the arbitrator deny the grievance and sustain the discharge.

The Union Position

The Grievant never saw the plant rule and he couldn't read them anyhow because he cannot read English and can "read very little Mexican". No one ever explained them to him.

When the Grievant asked S for his money, he left the plant when told that S could not pay. He did not use profane language or threaten anybody. No one else has ever been disciplined for entering the plant during non-working hours before. In any event, it is clear that S could stop work for 15 minutes without interfering with production. The Grievant did not have a knife with him during the events in question.

Company Exhibit 1 proved nothing and "is the biggest piece of hearsay evidence . . . ever admitted as evidence, in an arbitration hearing." Most of the other Company exhibits are also hearsay. Where was the statement from S? Evidence produced by the Union and not disputed showed that S was not credible in his dealings with the Union.

The Union proved through its testimony and exhibits that the Grievant is guilty of only one offense, i.e. unknowingly breaking one Company rule, i.e. #15. There has never been enforcement of this rule by the Company. The Company admitted not taking a statement from S and did not check his credibility by looking at his work record before discharging the Grievant. In fact the Company did very little in the way of investigation about this whole incident. There was nothing against the Grievant that deserves a punishment of discharge. Nothing showing that he had a knife. Foreman Lauinger did not testify at the hearing. Neither did the Company make any effort to find S and have him testify. Ditto, the two Ontario, Ohio police officers who investigated.

The Company's entire case was based on hearsay. The Company did not have just cause to terminate the Grievant. The arbitrator should instruct the Company to reinstate the Grievant with full back pay and no loss of seniority and benefits.

V. Discussion

A. Introduction

The present case is a discharge case in which the Grievant is claimed to have entered the plant outside of working hours to collect a Super Bowl bet from a fellow employee, S. When S did not pay up, the Grievant allegedly pulled a knife on S and threatened to "get" him. This was said to violate Plant Rules #15, #6 and #17.

Violence and threats in the work place have always been regarded seriously and are becoming an ever bigger problem. If a proper investigation were made and if the evidence proved sufficient, the conduct ascribed to the Grievant would certainly be sufficient to establish just cause for discharge.

We turn to these matters in the order stated.

B. The Investigation

It is generally held in arbitration that "just cause" requires an adequate investigation prior to the imposition of discipline. E.g. Elkouri and Elkouri, How Arbitration Works, p. 673 (BNA 1985); McCartney's Inc., 84 LA 799, 803-804 (Nelson, Arb., 1985); Otero County Hospital, 85 LA 98, 106 (Finston, Arb., 1984). The parties have adopted the "just cause" language in Article VIII, Section A and Article II, Section A of their agreement, as well as the stipulated issue. In his interpretation of the "just cause" language thrice adopted by the parties, the arbitrator is entitled to apply generally accepted standards concerning the meaning of that language.

Here the incident took place on late Friday afternoon, March 15. It was reported to Manager of Human Resources Charles Cain at his home. Mr. Cain instructed Foreman Lauinger to suspend the Grievant pending investigation. That investigation began on the following Monday morning, March 18.

Mr. Cain interviewed Foreman Lauinger and two unit employees, John Otto and S. According to Mr. Cain's testimony at the arbitration hearing, Foreman Lauinger told him that he did not actually see any of the March 15 incident. S told Mr. Cain that the Grievant had pulled a knife on him and told S that he would "get him". Mr. Otto told Mr. Cain that he had seen part of the incident, namely the Grievant yelling at S and S jumping back. Mr. Lauinger had made a one page handwritten report dated March

15 of his observations. It indicated that still another employee, Ray Freeman had seen the Grievant arguing with S. This statement was available to Mr. Cain on March 18.

Mr. Cain decided not to interview Mr. Freeman and the Grievant as part of his investigation. His reasoning with respect to Mr. Freeman was that his account would not add much to the data that he already had. With respect to the Grievant, Mr. Cain's reasoning was that the Union files grievances over all the discharges at the plant, so that he would have ample time to hear the Grievant's side of the story at the grievance meetings following the discharge. The discharge in fact occurred the following day, March 19.

The most serious elements of the charges against the Grievant were that he pulled a knife on S and threatened to get him. The only witness in the March 18 investigation who said that he saw the knife and heard the threat was S. It was not an open and shut case with five eyewitnesses. Elemental fairness would seem to have dictated that Mr. Cain hear the Grievant's side of the story. Of interest would be whether the Grievant said that he did pull a knife and threaten S and, if he did, whether there were mitigating circumstances such as (for example) S pulling a knife on the Grievant.

As indicated, Mr. Cain's rationale for not interviewing the Grievant was that the Union always files grievances over discharges and he would have a chance to hear the Grievant's side of the story during the grievance meetings. But, it seems to the arbitrator that by the time a grievant has been discharged, a grievance filed and grievance meetings held the situation has fundamentally changed. Management by this time may well feel that they have a position to defend, i.e. that their action in discharging a grievant was correct, i.e. meets just cause standards. Egos may well come into play and it may be difficult to rescind the discharge. At the very least any self-respecting union will probably at that point demand back pay for the period between the discharge and the settlement.

Under the circumstances it seems to the arbitrator that the failure to interview the Grievant as part of the investigation on March 18 prior must be held to have made the Grievant's discharge the following day to have been without just cause.

C. The Evidence Concerning the March 15 Incident

The preceding is the basis of decision in the case. Nevertheless, a few comments may be worthwhile concerning the evidence supporting the offense. The only live testimony at the arbitration hearing by an eyewitness to the March 15 incident was that of the Grievant. He denied pulling a knife, threatening S and/or engaging in an argument with S. Messrs. S, Lauinger, Otto and Freeman did not testify at the arbitration hearing. S was discharged by the Company for absenteeism prior to the arbitration hearing and was in parts unknown. Mr. Lauinger was ill on the day of the hearing, apparently with advanced cancer. There was no particular explanation for not calling Messrs. Otto and Freeman.

As indicated, a one page handwritten statement which was made by Mr. Lauinger on March 15 was placed in evidence. The document bore the signatures of Messrs. Otto, S, and Freeman in various places, but it frankly is rather confusing in form and as to which signatory is verifying which portion of the statement. As indicated, Mr. Lauinger was not available at the hearing to explain the statement.

The foregoing is recounted to indicate that the Company had a certain amount of bad luck in the presentation of its case with respect to the unavailability of witnesses. Nevertheless, the preceding recitation will indicate that this is not a case where the evidence of the Grievant pulling a knife and threatening a fellow employee is overwhelming.

VI. Conclusion

As indicated, the failure to interview the Grievant as part of the investigation is held to have rendered the discharge to have been without just cause. To the extent that it may not otherwise be clear, the stipulated issue, i.e. that concerning just cause is answered in the negative. The award draws its essence from the arbitrator's answer to the stipulated issue and from his interpretation of Article II, Section A and Article VIII, Section A of the parties' agreement.

VI. AWARD

Grievance sustained. Within thirty days of the date of this Award the Company shall offer the Grievant reinstatement to his former position with full seniority and with back pay for the period between March 19, 1996 and the date of his reinstatement. Should the parties be unable to agree on the calculation of the back pay owing under this Award, the arbitrator will reserve jurisdiction over the case until March 14, 1997 to resolve only such disputes.

APPLICATION AND DISCUSSION QUESTIONS

1. Do you agree with HR's decision to not interview the Grievant during the investigation? Why or why not?

2. The Grievant mentioned that he was unaware and unable to read the plant rules. What are your suggestions to the plant for ensuring that this issue is taken care of moving forward?

3. What recommendations, if any, do you have for improving the company's investigation process?

STATE OF FLORIDA DEP'T OF CORRECTIONS AND
INDIVIDUAL GRIEVANT

134 BNA LA 1181 (ABRAMS, 2015)*

Issues

At the hearing the parties stipulated to the following statement of the issues to be resolved:

Did the Department have "just cause" to terminate L? If not, what shall be the remedy?

Facts

A series of arbitration cases arose as a result of discipline issued by the Florida Department of Corrections based on an incident on April 11, 2014, at the Charlotte Correctional Institution in Punta Gorda, Charlotte County, Florida. Inmate Matthew Walker died as a result of the incident. L was one of the Corrections Officers the Department ultimately discharged. Although the record does not include details as to precisely what occurred that day, the parties stipulated that Mr. Walker died as a result of the incident.

* * * *

---

*   14. Reprinted with permission from *Labor Relations Reporter- Labor Arbitration Reports.* 134 BNA LA 1181. Copyright 2015 by the Bureau of National Affairs, Inc. (800-372-1033). http://www.bna.com.

Contentions of the Parties

A. The Agency's Arguments

The Department of Corrections takes its rules regarding the "care, custody and control" of inmates very seriously. It does not tolerate inmate abuse or the use of excessive, unjustified or unreasonable force upon its inmates. The Rules of Conduct provide that no employee shall apply physical force to the person of an inmate or to any other person under his supervision except and only to the degree that it reasonably appears to be necessary in self-defense, to prevent escape, to prevent injury to a person or damage to property, to quell a disturbance, or when an inmate exhibits physical resistance to a lawful command. The Department can reasonably expect that its employees will abide by both the law and the Department's critically important rules.

Although the Department recognizes that it disciplined the Grievant before the FDLE investigation was completed, it could not retain the corrections officers who were involved in this incident. It can hold correctional officers to a higher standard of conduct. That is why the Grievant was dismissed. Once the investigation is completed, if the Grievant is exonerated, he will be reinstated. If he is not exonerated, then the Department's action will stand.

B. The Union's Arguments

The Grievant was discharged without just cause. The Department bears the burden of proof. It simply is unable to prove that Officer L committed any violations of any kind, and it failed to meet the prevailing standard of "clearly convincing" the Arbitrator that just cause existed. The Department never supplied the Grievant with any documents or statements explaining exactly why he was terminated. In fact, it did not provide so much as a "scintilla of credible evidence" that L was involved in the incident in any way. It admits it did not complete its investigation before it acted to terminate the employment of this Corrections Officer.

Terminating Officer L before the investigation was completed and without an opportunity to meet with the Warden was a serious interference with the Grievant's rights. He was not treated fairly and has suffered greatly as a result of the Department's wrongful conduct. Thus, the Department interfered with the Grievant's due process rights. He should be reinstated and made whole.

Discussion and Opinion

This case involves the discharge of a Corrections Officer at Florida's Charlotte Correctional Institution in Punta Gorda, Florida. The Department dismissed Officer L because of his "inappropriate" participation "in a use of force that resulted in the death of an inmate." The Department acknowledges that it bears the burden of proof in this proceeding to establish "just cause." Roger Abrams, Inside Arbitration: How An Arbitrator Decides Labor and Employment Cases (Bloomberg/BNA, 2013).

Although the facts of this case are somewhat different, the core problem with the Department's actions regarding the Grievant is the same as was involved in cases of Corrections Officer Lieutenant Triplett and Corrections Officer Sergeants Grant and Stott already decided by this Arbitrator. Like Grant and Stott, L was placed on paid administrative leave after the incident. For reasons not explained in the record, the Department then dismissed Grant, Stott and L months later but before the completion of the investigation of the incident still being conducted by the Florida Department of Law Enforcement. We are thus left with the same uncertainty as this Arbitrator faced in the prior cases.

As the Arbitrator has explained in the previous cases, under the "just cause" standard contained in the parties' bargaining agreement the Employer must conduct a thorough investigation of an incident before it disciplines or discharges an employee for his alleged misconduct. "A key factor of just cause is a proficient investigation usually carried out by a person not directly involved in the situation. Any investigation must include interviews/questioning of the key players so that the true facts can be determined." BASF Corp., 128 LA 1233 (Arb. Matione, 2011). When employees' lives and employment futures are on the line, "the fullest possible investigation is a matter of necessity." Gowrie Care Center, 127 LA 165 , 172 (Arb. Kravit, 2009). That was not done here. Thus, the resulting discharge of the Grievant cannot stand.

There is an additional reason why Officer L's discharge cannot stand. The Department never gave Officer L (1) "evidence of the reasons" for his termination or (2) "an opportunity to rebut the charges ... furnished to the employee prior to" his dismissal. These critical elements were expressly included in the Department's answer to his grievance at the second step. Under the Florida Administrative Code Section 110.227 (5)(b), the Department can dismiss an employee when the "retention of a career service employee ... would be detrimental to the best interests of the state," but only if he is afforded the due process to which he was entitled under that provision.

In *Dep't. of Veterans Affairs*, 133 LA 1688 , 1695-96 (2014), Arbitrator Michael McReynolds explained the importance of offering an employee an opportunity to rebut the charges that led to dismissal:

> Simply stated, an employee's right to participate in a meaningful investigation of a matter that could result in disciplinary action is fundamental element of the general right to due process. A government employee's right to due process in the disciplinary procedure has been ingrained in this area of the law since the U.S. Supreme Court issued its decision in Cleveland Board of Education v. Loudermill, 470 U.S. 532 [1 IER Cases 424] (1985). Pointing out the critical aspect of the investigation in the disciplinary process, the Court said, "... the only meaningful opportunity to invoke the discretion of the decision maker is likely to be before the [disciplinary action] takes effect." Loudermill, 470 U.S. at 543. In this case, the record evidence establishes that Grievant was effectively deprived of the opportunity to tell [his] side of the story ... This failure to give Grievant any chance to be heard during the decision-making process constitutes an abuse of the Agency's discretion. Such an abuse of discretion is inconsistent with the principles of just cause.

Management is bound to follow the rules it has promulgated. Consider the following situation: management announces a rule that provides for discharge if an employee is tardy six times a quarter. If the employer discharges an employee who has accumulated only five tardies without explaining why the attendance deficiency warranted special treatment, the discharge cannot stand under the "just cause" provision. Management is bound to follow the rules it has promulgated. Here, similarly, the Department denied the grievance based on an administrative rule that contained employee rights that were not afforded to Officer L.

Even without this Code provision, the failure to offer an employee a meaningful opportunity to explain his actions must mean that the termination that results cannot stand. "An employee must be given an adequate opportunity to present his or her side of the case before being discharged." *Graphic Packaging International*, 134 LA 369, 378 (Arb. Wolff, 2014) (quoting Elkouri and Elkouri, How Arbitration Works). See, *Air Canada*, 126 LA 965, 970 (Arb. Abrams, 2009) (company never bothered to ask grievant if she had any explanation for her conduct.)

Situations may arise in a workplace-especially one like a state prison-that require management to remove an employee from the premises for a period of time. The record in this case explains that the Department did remove Officer L from the Correctional Institution for more than five months, but then it terminated him without giving him the opportunity to offer his version of what had happened.

A thorough investigation before separation combined with a statement of charges against an employee and an opportunity to respond to those charges decreases the risk of a wrongful discharge. It must be emphasized that this arbitration award simply returns the Grievant to his prior position. As was the case with regard to the prior arbitration cases arising from the Charlotte CI incident, the remedy does not address the issue whether any discipline that may result from the completed FDLE investigation will satisfy the "just cause" standard.

For these reasons, the grievance must be granted and Officer L returned to his prior positions with no loss of seniority and made whole for his losses.

AWARD

The Department did not have just cause for its dismissal of the Grievant. The Department shall reinstate him to his prior position with no loss of seniority, and it shall make him whole for his lost pay. Under the parties' Agreement, the Department is responsible for the Arbitrator's Bill for services rendered. The Arbitrator shall retain jurisdiction for 60 days to address any issues that might arise concerning the implementation of this Award.

APPLICATION AND DISCUSSION QUESTIONS

1. What key element(s) were missing from the Employer's investigation, resulting in a lack of "just cause" for the Grievent's termination?

2. Based on the facts of the case, what do you think should be included in a "thorough investigation?"

3. The Grievent was held to a higher standard of conduct, resulting in dismissal. Do you think this was a legitimate?

WAS THE INVESTIGATION WAS FAIR?

CITY OF MASON AND MASON PROFESSIONAL FIREFIGHTERS, IAFF LOCAL 4039

134 BNA LA 1165 (TOLLEY, 2015)[*]

Issue

Did the employer terminate the grievant without just cause in violation of the collective bargaining agreement Article 11.2? If so, what is the appropriate remedy?

Facts

Saturday April 5, 2014

Firefighter R while off duty visited his Fire Station 51 with H, arriving shortly after 6 p.m. just as all of the on duty personnel left on an emergency run. On return to the station around 6:30 p.m., the apparatus driver FF Doug Wooland found R's jeep blocking the entry door to the bay and sounded the air H. When R failed to respond, Firefighter Doug Rolph found keys in the jeep and moved it so the fire apparatus could enter the bay.

As the crew washed the vehicle, R entered the bay from the firehouse, joined shortly after by H. R introduced her to members of the crew who noted her very strong perfume scent before she and R left the station.

After entering the firehouse, Rolph and the acting battalion commander Lt. Mark Gerano noted a strong perfume scent in the hallway leading to the bunk rooms; they also detected recent stains and perfume on the mattress pad of R's bunk. Suspecting that the stains were red lip gloss and a woman's makeup, Gerano immediately called R by phone to ask whether his female guest had been on the bunk. R acknowledged that she had been in his bunkroom and denied that she had touched the pad.

Wooland showed Gerano long reddish brown hairs that he found on the pad. Gerano concluded that the situation should be investigated further, secured the hairs

---

[*] Reprinted with permission from *Labor Relations Reporter- Labor Arbitration Reports.* 134 BNA LA 1165. Copyright 2015 by the Bureau of National Affairs, Inc. (800-372-1033). http://www.bna.com.

in a sealed envelope, took a color photo of the stained pad, and sent an e-mail report to R's commanding officer and Deputy Chief Kimble.

* * * *

Employer's Position

The city's post hearing brief argues: The evidence shows beyond any reasonable doubt that R's guest was on or in contact with a bunk bed in the firehouse. Yet R contended throughout the investigation and into this arbitration that his guest was never on and never had contact with the bunk bed.

Section 11.5 of the bargaining agreement expressly provides that during the investigation of alleged misconduct, a member of the bargaining unit must "respond completely and truthfully to all questions asked of him." Similarly, the City has a published policy requiring employees to be honest and forthright with supervisors and in City investigations. Nineteen months before this matter, R received substantial suspension for dishonesty when he reported for work unfit for work due to undisclosed prescription drugs, and then repeatedly and dishonestly denied taking those drugs. The City terminated R here because, for the second time in less than two years, R again responded dishonestly to a City investigation by contending that his guest never had contact with the bunk bed.

The city submitted six cases involving the admissibility of "nose witness" identifications of odors as probative evidence including a decision of the Ohio Supreme Court State v. Moore, 90 Ohio St.3d 47 (2000) and other appellate courts including State v. Gonzales, 2015 WL 502263 (6th Dist. Court of Appeals, 2015). The city also provided eight arbitration awards sustaining dismissal in cases of dishonesty.

The city's investigation was fair and appropriate without taking the steps demanded by the grievant. Further investigation as to: the stains on the mattress pad, whether the air horn could be heard in the bunk room, what H had to say, the hairs found on the pad, whether someone slept on the mattress pad on Sunday night, etc., were not going to change the fact that R was not honest. In addition to the compelling evidence that H's perfume was on the center of the mattress pad, there is also abundant circumstantial evidence supporting the conclusion that something inappropriate happened on the bunk bed.

* * * *

Union's Position

The union's post hearing brief argues: The City did not conduct a fair investigation and as a result did not have evidence that proved H came into contact with the mattress pad or that R was dishonest as charged. The city relied entirely on the olfactory senses of two firefighters to confirm that the mattress pad smelled like H's perfume. These firefighters confirmed the smell on the mattress pad in a room that smelled strongly of that perfume. It is quite possible that the firefighters had grown "nose blind" to the smell and were mistaken. The power of suggestion likely played a role in their belief that the smell was the same.

* * * *

The City did not send the mattress pad to a lab for any testing even after R offered to pay to test the mattress pad. The City refused to speak with H when the Union offered. The City did not bother to speak with Schmidt about the mattress pad. The City refused to test the ability to hear the air horn in the bunk room. Ms. Geiser testified that the only way lipstick could get on the bed was from H and told him that "body fluid stains" on the mattress pad made it "it look as if you and H were messing around on that bed, on that mattress, on Saturday." Geiser had already made up her mind that R was guilty.

H testified that she did not sit on the bed and that nothing happened on the mattress pad. R's wife, B, testified that she adamantly believed nothing happened between R and H. B was aware of the situation early that evening when R called her from the comedy show. B went out with R and H that night and invited H to spend the night in their guest room. The couples remain close friends. If either spouse believed something happened, they would not still be good friends.

The union calls on the arbitrator to sustain the grievance by ordering the reinstatement of R with an award making him whole for all lost wages and benefits.

Discussion

* * * *

Unfair Investigation

Fire department personnel need to preserve the chain of custody for evidence in arson investigations, but did not properly do so in this disciplinary investigation. Lt. Gerrano wrote "I told the other members not to touch anything". He photographed the stained pad and sealed three hairs in a bag but failed to secure the pad on Saturday evening. Prior to Chief Moore securing the pad on Monday afternoon, Andy Schmidt slept on it Sunday evening, and R placed his gear on the pad Monday morning while changing in the bunk room.

When interviewing R on Tuesday April 10, Ms. Geiser noted she had been told no one had slept on the pad. When R informed her that Schmidt had done so, she promised to speak with him, but the city never did so. Geiser accepted as fact that H's perfume was on the pad. The city never questioned Schmidt, an objective witness who had not pre-judged the situation, about any unusual odors or stains he had observed.

On April 10 when R questioned whether the wet, sticky red substance found on the pad was lipstick and requested a lab test. Geiser repeatedly told him it would be sent to a lab for testing). When the city then refused to incur that expense, the grievant offered to pay, but the city again refused. Geiser acknowledged that the red stain had turned brown by the time she saw it on Tuesday, but the city never tested red lipstick to determine whether it would fade to brown after several days.

When R explained that he had not heard the horn and asked the city to test whether or not the air horn could be heard in the bunk room, the employer refused.

In order to establish that "nothing happened" R explained his long friendship with H since their childhood and the close relationship between their two families. The city made only one effort to contact her after Police Chief Moore on April 10 ordered R to provide H's phone number. At the pre-disciplinary hearing the city declined the grievant's offer to arrange for an interview. H's account of April 5 was not heard until she gave deposition testimony for the arbitration hearing.

After hearing R's explanation at the April 10 interview, Geiser shifted from an investigatory to an accusatory approach without affording the accused an opportunity to have a representative. Geiser repeatedly made clear that she did not believe R's explanation and insisted that he must prove H did not have contact with the pad. Geiser's recorded interview clearly revealed pre-judgment when a fair, independent investigation was required. By its own account, the city concluded there was conclusive evidence of R's dishonesty so that no further investigation was required either before or after the pre-disciplinary hearing.

Under the Daugherty test, the city lacked just cause to terminate the grievant by failing to provide a fair investigation of the evidence he offered.

No substantial evidence of guilt

As just cause for discipline, the April 29 termination letter states as substantial evidence: "It is clear that the woman came in contact with the bed. Her perfume, hair and lip gloss were all there." When reviewing R's termination grievance, the City Manager upheld dismissal solely on the grounds of the perfume evidence and prior discipline without making any reference to the lip gloss stain and hair. The city's post hearing arbitration brief argues that the solid perfume evidence in combination with circumstantial evidence including what appeared to be H's hair and lip gloss provide substantial evidence that R lied.

Smell of Perfume (Omitted)

Circumstantial Evidence

Stains

Police Chief Moore produced the discolored pad at the hearing, and the arbitrator noted 17 unidentified dark stains that had been marked during an April 10 ultraviolet. The city offers the observations of Rolph and Gerrano, as circumstantial evidence that H's lip gloss was on the pad. On cross examination, Rolph testified that he initially thought the stain might be blood, but concluded it did not smell like blood. R, his wife, and H, all testified for the first time that the grievant was bleeding from an undetected cut that may have happened when storing his gear prior to the tour, and that his shirt had a blood stain. The city not only failed to demonstrate that red lip gloss turns brown in three days, but did no test whatever of the disputed stain to obtain evidence that would support its case. Nor was there secure custody of the pad after the stain was observed. The city's witnesses also believed that a separate brown stain they observed appeared to be H's make-up. The grievant's witnesses denied that it was her make-up, and no lab test was done that could have resolved the evidentiary dispute.

Hair

As with the stain, the city was unable to provide any evidence beyond conclusory suspicions by its witnesses that the strands came from H's making contact with the pad. Given the age of the pad and break in the chain of custody, the city has no way of using the hair to justify discipline after the grievant established that Schmidt's sister had used the pad and that his mother in law had recently been in the bunk room.

Suspicion of Sexual Activity

The city offers as circumstantial evidence of guilt that "R was alone in the firehouse for about half an hour with an attractive woman not his wife." (Employer Post Hearing Brief). At the initial investigatory interview on April 10 Ms. Geiser told R that "body fluids" were found on the pad, when no one ever reported there had been any such stains. The characterization of H as "an attractive woman not his wife" has no probative value whatever, but instead calls into question the objectivity of city decision makers whose fact finding appears tainted by pre-judgment of the relevant evidence. The grievant testified credibly that he routinely conducted tours of the firehouse for family and friends that included his bunkroom, and that just two weeks previously he had shown the room to his Mother in Law.

H credibly explained in detail how she spent her time on a tour of the stationhouse-helping store R's gear in his locker, drinking a soda, discussing photos on the wall, asking questions in the kitchen, briefly visiting his bunk room and using the restroom. R's wife testified that she had encouraged her husband to take H to the Comedy Club, the three of them went out after she got off work and were photographed together, they invited H to spend the night at the R home where she and the grievant were left alone together on Sunday morning after his wife left for work. Had they been investigated, the long term, close personal friendships and family relationships could have allayed the suspicions aroused by non-probative circumstantial evidence.

Air Horn

In rebuttal to the grievant's claim that he never heard the horn, the city has no basis to rely on circumstantial evidence that he failed to respond after refusing to determine whether the horn can be heard in the bunk room.

As with the perfume smell, the grievant's prior discipline for dishonesty gave the city probable cause to investigate, but does not constitute evidence of guilt in this case.

Under the Daugherty test, the city lacked just cause to terminate the grievant by failing to provide substantial evidence of his guilt. Unrebutted testimony at the hearing by R, and his wife as well as H's unchallenged deposition testimony outweigh the city's unproven accusations that he lied.

Conclusion

The city did not conduct a fair, objective investigation, did not have substantial evidence of guilt, and thus had no just cause for termination of the grievant.

AWARD

The grievant will be reinstated and made whole for all lost wages and benefits. The arbitrator shall retain jurisdiction for 90 days solely for the purpose of resolving any dispute between the parties regarding the meaning, application, or implementation of this award.

APPLICATION AND DISCUSSION QUESTIONS

1. What factors should the arbitrator consider in determining whether any investigation is fair?

2. Reviewing all of the steps taken during the investigation of R, do you agree that the investigation was unfair? Why or why not? The employer refused to conduct various tests required by the union. Is this evidence that the investigation was not completed in a fair manner?

3. The case seemed to turn on the fact that the lipstick turned brown after just 3 days. Do you think the entire outcome of the case would've been different, had this not happened? What is a "nose witness" and should evidence be included in an investigation? Is it reliable evidence? What impact did it have on the decisions that the employer failed to "preserve the chain of custody of the evidence?"

4. What role should prior dishonesty play in determining the legitimacy of future conduct?

Issue

Was the discharge of the Grievant, W, for just cause and if not what is the appropriate remedy?

* * * *

Relevant Contract Provisions (Omitted)

WORKPLACE VIOLENCE PREVENTION POLICY

Policy:

The Company is committed to preventing workplace violence and to maintaining a safe work environment. The Company has adopted the following guidelines to deal with intimidation, harassment, or other threats of (or actual) violence that may occur during business hours or on its premises.

Comments: (Omitted)

Position of the Parties

COMPANY:

The Company's position is that the uncontroverted facts establish a violation of the Workplace Violence Prevention policy. Forcefully pushing a door closed on another employee is an act of violence likely to cause physical harm in an industrial setting. It is both an assault and a battery that cannot be tolerated in the workplace.

The contested facts include evidence of an assault and threatening behavior by the grievant. Both of the co-workers on the shift who were not involved directly in the incident testified that S was visibly upset and afraid of the grievant. The red mark on

---

*   Reprinted with permission from *Labor Relations Reporter- Labor Arbitration Reports.* 133 BNA LA 996. Copyright 2015 by the Bureau of National Affairs, Inc. (800-372-1033). http://www.bna.com.

S's back is physical evidence that a battery had occurred. The Workplace Violence Prevention Policy clearly forbids any actual assault with force strong enough to leave such a mark on S's back.

The Company completed a reasonable investigation by interviewing all four employees who were on the shift that evening. Mr. Blackburn returned to the plant and inspected the marks on S's back and concluded it was a fresh bruise resulting from the incident with the grievant. In addition the Human Resources Manager interviewed all four employees and reduced the comments of S, Ingle and Toler to written statements signed by each employee.

The assault violation of the policy is supported by the testimony of Ingle and Toler who heard the panicked screams from S and saw the bruising on his back. Although the threat to "beat the pulp out of you (S)" was heard only by S, Mr. Ingle testified of threatening remarks from W in the past. In addition, Plant Manager Harris testified that during the investigation of the incident other employees told him of prior threats. Given these facts the Company had no choice but to terminate the grievant to protect the rest of the workforce from violent behavior.

* * * *

UNION:

An allegation of workplace violence is a serious and stigmatizing allegation which requires clear and convincing evidence. The Union argues that the Company's evidence falls far short of establishing that W violated the Workplace Violence Prevention Policy by even a more lenient standard.

The details of the events that occurred on the evening of June 21, 2013 that lead to the discharge of the Grievant do not establish an attempt to threaten harm or injure S. The Grievant merely wanted to get back to work and wanted S to get out of the QC lab so he could resume his work without interruption.

The only testimony presented at the hearing that alleges threatening behavior and physical harm comes from S. S's story has evolved over time and his testimony at the hearing is contradicted by his own written statement, the investigation by Blackburn and the statements and testimony of the remaining co-workers on the shift.

* * * *

The Company relies heavily on the photograph of the red mark on S's back to establish the violation of the Work Place Violence Prevention Policy and to justify the discharge of the Grievant. S never complained of debilitating pain and never sought medical treatment. The red mark looks just as what you would expect to see if one were to press his back against a door frame while pushing the door open against someone pushing it shut.

S's red back is not indicative of any intent to injure or harm. It is the inadvertent result of two stubborn men, one trying to push the door open and the other trying to push it shut. If there was any misconduct both employees were at fault.

The Company failed to produce clear and convincing evidence that the Grievant violated the Workplace Violence Prevention Policy. The investigation was superficial and provided no basis for the discharge of the Grievant while S was not disciplined in any way. The disparity in treatment is unjust.

If any misconduct occurred, discharge was not warranted in light of W's 36 years of seniority and lack of any prior discipline.

The Union requests that the Grievant be reinstated with full back pay and benefits.

Decision and Award

...No one can dispute that the Workplace Violence Prevention Policy is a work rule that is reasonably related to the efficient, orderly and safe operation of the plant. The Company has a duty to provide a safe workplace for its employees and cannot tolerate threats of harm and physical altercations between its employees. The evidence established that the Workplace Violence Prevention Policy was clearly communicated to the employees.

Although violation of the Workplace Violence Prevention Policy could be just cause for discipline up to and including discharge, in the present case the Company failed to establish just cause for discharge.

The Company's investigation was insufficient to justify the discharge of an employee with 36 years seniority and no prior disciplinary record. Statements were taken from the other three employees on the shift and reduced to writing and presented at the hearing. Other than Blackburn's interview the night of the incident the grievant was never afforded the opportunity to present his side of the story in person. Rather a telephone interview was conducted by the Human Resources representative and no record of that conversation was produced at the hearing.

The testimony of S, the only witness present for the alleged threats and assault was inconsistent and not logical. At the hearing S testified he had no problem staying over and that he knew he would have to stay over even before he reported to work. This directly contradicts his own statement given to Human Resources and the testimony of Blackburn, Ingle, Toler and the Grievant.

The allegation that the Grievant threatened to "beat the pulp out of him after everyone left" was not made until thirteen days after the night of the incident. It is hard to believe that something this significant would have not surfaced in Blackburn's investigation on the night of the incident if, it had, in fact occurred.

S's testimony that he returned to the QC Lab to tell W that it was "all a misunderstanding" and that he would be staying over is equally incredible. It is inconsistent with his prior testimony that he knew he would be staying over prior to the start of the shift. There was no need to go to the QC Lab if that was the purpose of the visit. He instead could have used the radio to communicate. More likely the purpose of the visit was to confront the Grievant and vent his frustration with being forced to work overtime on a Friday night.

In contrast, the Grievant's testimony was consistent and made logical sense. S did not want to stay for the overtime. Rather than get into an argument with S, the Grievant called his Supervisor who then informed S he was required to stay. At this point, the Grievant had no reason to be angry or hostile, whereas S had clear motivation.

It is apparent that S returned to the QC Lab to vent his anger at the Grievant. Forcefully closing the lab door by the grievant, if viewed in isolation, is misconduct that should not be tolerated. However, the clear evidence is that S instigated the incident and provoked the Grievant. Provocation is mitigating factor in determining the severity of discipline.

Under Article 19.1 of the Collective Bargaining Agreement "The level of discipline applied for a Rule Violation, whether it be discharge, 1st or 2nd warning level or suspension, will depend on several factors, such as but not limited to, previous discipline administered for the same, similar or different offenses, the seriousness of the offense and consideration of any mitigating factors present."

In determining the level of discipline, the Company failed to consider any mitigating factors. No consideration was given to the Grievant's past record or length of service with the Company. In fact in their post hearing brief the Company argues that length of service is irrelevant. The Grievant had thirty-six years of service with the Company and no prior discipline. There is long standing arbitration precedent that in determining the level of discipline, particularly where discharge is contemplated, an employee's seniority and prior record must be considered. In addition the Company violated the provisions of Article 19.1 in discharging the grievant by failing to consider his prior record and years of service.

At the hearing the Company presented testimony that the Grievant was confrontational in the past and had a temper. Several isolated incidents of this alleged attitude were related but there was no documentation, no prior discipline and the testimony was mainly hearsay. The uncontroverted testimony was that the Grievant was a knowledgeable and dependable employee who for thirty-six years had excellent attendance. Because of his dependability and knowledge he was asked to be the Lead Person on the shift.

* * * *

The evidence presented at the hearing on this case failed to establish misconduct sufficient to warrant the discharge of an employee with thirty-six years of service and no prior disciplinary record. There was however misconduct. An altercation occurred between S and the Grievant. The Grievant admitted closing the door to force S out of the control room and the evidence established that S had a bruise or red mark on his back from being momentarily pinned in the door jam.

However, the preponderance of the evidence points to S as the instigator of the incident. S, an employee with much less seniority, was not issued any discipline whereas the Grievant was discharged. The disparity in the discipline issued to the Grievant and not issued to S is astounding.

AWARD

...The degree of discipline issued is not reasonable given the nature of the incident, the inconsistent and unreliable testimony of the complaining witness and the Grievant's prior record.

Although some misconduct occurred, discharge was not warranted in this situation.

REMEDY

The discharge is hereby converted to a thirty calendar day suspension and the Company is ordered to reinstate the Grievant with full seniority and full back pay and benefits less interim earnings and unemployment compensation benefits.

The arbitrator shall retain jurisdiction to resolve any disputes in carrying out this award.

APPLICATION AND DISCUSSION QUESTIONS

1. What were the major deficiencies in the investigation? Should the employer have given more weight to the Grievant's explanation over an employee with a few years of seniority versus the Grievant's testimony with 36 years of seniority? There were inconsistencies in the witness's testimony, but the employer relied heavily on the testimony to terminate the Grievant. What additional evidence should the employer have collected to support the termination? The arbitrator points out that the employee who alleged he was threatened by the Grievant did not make the allegation until 13 days after the incident. What impact, if any, does the delay in making the claim that he was threatened have on the investigation?

2. Was it right to temporarily suspend the Grievent? Would it have been more fair to also suspend S while the investigation took place?

3. Ultimately, the Grievent was reinstated and placed on a thirty-day suspension. Should there have been any repercussions for S since he not only instigated the situation, but also altered his own testimony?

2007 AAA LEXIS 1475 AMERICAN ARBITRATION ASSOCIATION
DECEMBER 16, 2007, DECIDED*

I. STATEMENT OF FACTS

The facts further indicate that the Grievant has been a special education teacher in the District for six years. She has been a teacher for thirty years. Prior to coming to the District, the Grievant was a regular education teacher and taught every grade from kindergarten through sixth grade.

The Grievant worked as the Disabilities Coordinator for Head Start for eight years. She also worked as the Coordinator for the Even Start Program, a program that assists young mothers that have dropped out of school because of pregnancies. The Grievant received a Master's Degree in special education and applied to the District.

The Grievant was employed by the District and assigned to teach students with Emotional Disturbance at Middle School. However, she transferred and was placed at Elementary School where she completed the 2001-2002 school year and returned for the 2002-2003 school year. It was alleged that the Grievant used acts of corporal punishment against students on three separate occasions in October 2002 (2 incidents), and December 2002. Following a fact-finding hearing and a pre-disciplinary hearing, where the hearing officer determined that the Grievant engaged in actions that violated the District's corporal punishment policy, the Grievant received a 10-day suspension. The Grievant also underwent counseling for anger management. The Grievant successfully completed the counseling and voluntarily continued such counseling for a period of time. The Grievant did not grieve the 10-day suspension.

During the 2004-2005 and 2005-2006 school years, the Grievant was assigned as an "inclusion" teacher at School. In this capacity, she was responsible for special education students included in a regular classroom. The principal of School at the time was Principal. The Grievant was a kindergarten special education inclusion teacher both years at School. She worked in a kindergarten class with a regular education Teacher A, and a Paraprofessional A.

During her first year at School, there was one incident where the Grievant was. The Grievant requested that the child be transferred to another kindergarten room and the request was granted. On January 28, 2005, Principal recommended the Grievant for a continuing contract for the following school year. On April 21, 2005, Principal provided an outstanding evaluation for the Grievant, ranking "excellent" in every category.

During the 2005-2006 school year, there were four incidents that occurred in which the Grievant was charged with using corporal punishment against the students. Following the fourth incident on April 6, 2006, the Grievant attended a fact-finding meeting on April 13, 2006, where she was represented by a Union Chairperson The matter was held in abeyance pending the outcome of an investigation from County Department of Children and Family Services. The Department of Children and Family Services investigated complaints of child abuse and neglect and found that the charges were unsubstantiated. Subsequently, the fact-finding hearing reconvened on August 28, 2006, where the matter was referred to the Legal Department for disciplinary action. A pre-disciplinary hearing was held September 13, 2006, where the hearing officer determined that the District presented sufficient evidence to sustain the four allegations of corporal punishment, and recommended termination. The

Grievant was terminated effective September 14, 2006, due to corporal punishment and conduct unbecoming a District employee.

II. ISSUE

Did the District have just cause to terminate the Grievant, and if not, what is the appropriate remedy?

III. RELEVANT CONTRACT PROVISIONS

Article 18

Section 6. Professional Conduct

A. The District shall have the right to suspend, discipline, demote, or discharge for just cause, under arbitral law.

B. The purpose of discipline is to improve the work performance and conduct of the employee affected. As a result, the District acknowledges its commitment to practice progressive discipline whenever appropriate.

C. Prior to any recommendation regarding discipline, the District will conduct a thorough investigation which shall include a fact-finding hearing. The employee shall meet with the immediate Supervisor, be informed of the specific allegations being investigated, and have the opportunity to respond to the allegations. * * * *

Student Code of Conduct, Section VII, provides in relevant part:
Corporal punishment is defined as inflicting bodily pain upon an individual for the commission or omission of an act. Corporal punishment is prohibited and shall not be used as a form of discipline in the District.

IV. POSITION OF THE PARTIES

A. Union's Position

The Union maintains that the District did not have just cause to terminate the Grievant. The Union further contends that the District did not conduct a fair and impartial investigation into the allegations against the Grievant, thereby depriving her of due process. The Union contends that the District did not put forth sufficient evidence that the Grievant violated its corporal punishment policy.

B. District's Position

The District maintains that it had just cause to terminate the Grievant because she engaged in four acts of corporal punishment against kindergarten students in violation of its policy. The District maintains that it conducted a fair and impartial investigation, substantiating the charges. The District contends that the repeated and severe nature of the Grievant's conduct justifies termination. It is the District's assertion that there are no mitigating factors.

III. DISCUSSION AND ANALYSIS

* * * *

IV.

The Company maintains that it had just cause to discharge the Grievant for the use of corporal punishment against kindergarten students. Despite that it was alleged that the Grievant used corporal punishment on four separate occasions from January to April 2006, the Union maintains that the termination was based solely on the incident involving Little Boy on April 6, 2006. In support of this contention, the Union emphasizes the testimony of Deputy Chief of Human Resources. Deputy Chief of Human Resources testified that he receives recommendations for terminations or suspensions and he confirms those recommendations. He further testified, that in his judgment, the Grievant's termination was based on the last incident that occurred prior to her termination, which is the incident on April 6, 2006, involving the allegation that the Grievant slammed Little Boy's head into the table. He added that the termination wasn't based on the other incidents.

The Arbitrator notes that this testimony supports the Union's position that the termination was based solely on the allegations surrounding Little Boy. However, Deputy Chief of Human Resources also testified that he felt that termination was warranted because, "[a]fter reviewing the documentation that was given to me and given the pattern of corporal punishment, I felt that the consistent pattern warranted termination." He clarified the pattern that he was referring to was the previous incidents of corporal punishment. Moreover, a letter given to the Grievant following a pre-disciplinary hearing states, in relevant part, "District representatives produced narrative and documents to support the charges of alleged corporal punishment and conduct unbecoming of a District employee. Specifically, the allegations concerning four different students on four different occasions." Moreover, the letter further states, "[b]ased on the record and considering that there has been a disciplinary history for similar conduct, I am recommending termination." Subsequently, Deputy Chief of Human Resources concurred with the recommendation of the hearing officer at the pre-disciplinary hearing and terminated the Grievant's employment. Therefore, the evidence demonstrates that the termination was based on a consistent pattern and the history of the Grievant's use of corporal punishment, rather than solely on the incident involving Little Boy. Consequently it is established that the four allegations of corporal punishment formed the basis for the termination. Accordingly, the four separate incidents will be discussed in chronological order. (Omitted)

* * * *

Kindergarten Student A

. . . . the Arbitrator finds that the District provided sufficient evidence to support its conclusion that the Grievant violated its policy against the use of corporal punishment when she "kicked" Kindergarten Student A. Indeed, the Grievant acknowledged, that kicking a student, even if gentle, was a violation of the District's policy against corporal punishment.

Kindergarten Student B

For the reasons mentioned above, the District's evidence was not sufficient to establish that the Grievant engaged in the misconduct that she was charged in relation to Kindergarten Student B.

Kindergarten Student C

The District has met its burden to demonstrate that it had sufficient evidence to conclude that the Grievant violated its policy against the use of corporal punishment in regard to the incident with Kindergarten Student C.

Little Boy

The District maintains that the Grievant slammed a kindergarten student's head on the table, putting a very large knot on the student's head, in violation of its policy prohibiting the use of corporal punishment. In support of its position, the District provided the testimony of Principal. Principal testified that on April 6, 2006, Paraprofessionals C and Paraprofessional B, brought Little Boy into her office and he had a knot on his head. Principal testified that she asked Little Boy how did he get the knot on his head, and he said that the Grievant hit his head on the table. Principal testified that she then took Little Boy to the classroom and asked him to show her what happened. The Grievant was present.

* * * *

The evidence establishes that the principal investigated the matter once it was brought to her attention. She questioned Little Boy and asked him to demonstrate what happened for her. She questioned Teacher A, who according to Principal, didn't see anything, but did confirm that the Grievant worked with Little Boy that day. Principal testified that other children were running up to her asking her if she saw Little Boy's boo-boo and telling her that the Grievant hit his head on the desk. Further, Paraprofessional A also memorialized statements from two kindergarten students. Moreover, the Grievant provided a written statement detailing the incident. Therefore, the Arbitrator finds that the District conducted a fair and objective investigation. Relying on the evidence discovered during this investigation, the District concluded that the Grievant used corporal punishment against Little Boy in violation of its policy.

The District has the burden to demonstrate that sufficient evidence exists to support its conclusion that the Grievant engaged in wrongdoing. The Arbitrator recognizes that the District's case rests primarily with the statements of kindergarten students. Obviously, Principal found Little Boy and the kindergarten student that said the Grievant slammed his head into the table to be credible.

The District was entitled to rely on the statement of the victim and other students that confirmed the Little Boy's account of the incident to reach the conclusion that the Grievant engaged in corporal punishment. See 2006 AAA Lexis 172 (May 31, 2006) where Arbitrator Tillem concluded that the principal had a reasonable basis for concluding the Grievant committed an act of corporal punishment...

In the case at hand, the evidence demonstrates that Little Boy gave a demonstration of what occurred at least twice and has remained consistent when telling the principal, Safety and Security, and his mother about the incident. Additionally, Little Boy told his version and demonstrated the incident for Principal while the Grievant was present. I say this only to point out that many children would be too intimidated to make up a lie on a teacher while in that teacher's presence. Principal testified that other students were coming up to her telling her that the Grievant hit Little Boy's head on table. In addition, the evidence demonstrates that Paraprofessional A memorialized statements from two kindergarten students. The statements are that "Teacher B pulled Little Boy's ears." and "Teacher B 'slammed' Little Boy head on the table." This statement is consistent with Little Boy's account of the incident. Therefore, the District has met its burden to demonstrate that it reasonably concluded that the Grievant slammed Little Boy's head on the table in violation of its policy against corporal punishment.

The Arbitrator notes that the Union argues that Little Boy was on the playground when he was discovered with the injury, and he could have been injured on the playground. The Union also emphasizes that Little Boy was not supposed to be on the playground and therefore he had a reason to make up the story. While this theory is plausible, it is mere speculation.

* * * *

VI. CONCLUSION

The District has met the elements of the just cause standard. The District's position is reasonable. The evidence reveals that the District conducted a fair and impartial investigation prior to the termination. The District's decision to terminate the Grievant was not arbitrary or discriminatory. Moreover, there were no factors that warranted modification of the penalty.

VII. AWARD

The grievance is denied.

APPLICATION AND DISCUSSION QUESTIONS

1. What factors should an arbitrator consider in determining whether an investigation is complete and fair? Should the arbitrator consider the age and mental capacity of the witness?

2. What actions on the part of the principal support the arbitrator's conclusion that the investigation was complete and fair? Were there other witnesses the school should have questioned?

SUBSTANTIAL EVIDENCE IS PRESENT A VIOLATION OCCURRED

THE CITY OF GREEN[*]

I. STATEMENT OF FACTS

The facts indicate that the Union Local, hereinafter (Union) and the City of Green, hereinafter (City) are parties to a collective bargaining agreement, hereinafter (CBA or Agreement), effective September 1, 2004 - August 31, 2007.

The facts indicate that the Grievant received a 30-day suspension involving the theft of the City's ladder. The facts underlying the 30-day suspension are as follows: A City ladder was discovered to be missing. About November 9, 2004, two City employees were working near the Grievant's son's house when a ladder was spotted in the garage that appeared to be the missing ladder. The employees reported the news about seeing the ladder in the Grievant's son's garage to their supervisor. The facts also indicate that the son was previously a city employee. The son's wife, the Grievant's daughter-in-law, was also an employee at the City during this time

---

[*] Unpublished Decision (Floyd D. Weatherspoon, 2005)

period. Two City employees went to the son's residence to identify the ladder. They concluded that the ladder belonged to the City of Green.

The Grievant was placed on paid administrative leave, pending an investigation. Officer O was assigned to investigate the incident. Upon conclusion of his investigation, he submitted a written report. The findings were submitted to the City. The Grievant received a 30-day suspension.

About December 9, 2004, a grievance was filed challenging the Grievant's 30 day suspension. The grievance went through the various stages of the grievance procedure. The grievance was denied. Arbitration was requested pursuant to Article 8 of the CBA.

II. ISSUE

Was the 30 day suspension for just cause? If not, what is the appropriate remedy?

III. RELEVANT WORK RULES AND CONTRACT PROVISIONS
SECTION 5.03

The orderly and efficient operation of the City of Green requires reasonable standards of discipline and conduct. In order to minimize the likelihood of any employee becoming subject to disciplinary action, the following represent the work rules which govern employee conduct.

* * * *

A. Group One

Some serious offense may be deemed to be cause for immediate dismissal. They are:

* * * *

7. Theft or misappropriation of City property (including files and documents), property of employees, or property in the City's custody, including giving false information to be reimbursed for time not worked or for higher pay rates; soliciting or receiving improper

compensation, making copies of confidential information or recording of a private conversation with Administration authorization.

IV. POSITION OF THE PARTIES

A. Union's Position

It is the position of the Union that the City did not have just cause to suspend the Grievant for 30 days. The Union further maintains that the burden is on the City to prove that the Grievant engaged in the misconduct in question. It is the Union's assertion that the quantum of proof necessary in this instance is the clear and convincing standard. The Union contends that the City cannot meet this standard because there is no evidence that the ladder in question was the City's ladder, and there is no evidence that the Grievant had anything to do with the ladder being in his son's garage.

B. City's Position

It is the City's position that it had just cause to suspend the Grievant for theft of the ladder. The City asserts that the correct burden of proof in this case is preponderance of the evidence. The City further contends that the evidence demonstrates that the Grievant had access to the ladder and his son or daughter-in-law would not have had access. The City further acknowledges that it did not have enough information to bring criminal charges against the Grievant, the investigation, nonetheless demonstrates, that the ladder in question was indeed the City's ladder, and that the Grievant took the ladder.

V. DISCUSSION AND ANALYSIS

It is noted at the outset, that the parties have raised procedural issues. The City contends that the instant grievance should be dismissed because the Grievant has filed a verified complaint in Green County Court of Common Pleas. The parties stipulated at the arbitration hearing that the said complaint was filed. The City asserts that pursuant to the CBA, Article 8 Section (Q), the grievance must be dismissed.

Article 8, Section Q, provides,

> This grievance procedure shall be the exclusive-method of resolving grievances. Any employee choosing on his own to pursue other means of resolving a grievance, such as Civil Service appeal, shall be considered to have waived his or her right to the grievance procedure for resolution of the issue.

It was also noted at the arbitration hearing that the complaint was withdrawn. The Union has also submitted a post-hearing attachment indicating that the motion before the Civil Service Board was withdrawn. Therefore, the City's argument is moot.

Having decided that none of the procedural issues raised dispose of the grievance, the Arbitrator will proceed with the substantive issues.

In suspension grievances, typically, the Employer has the burden of demonstrating that the employee was suspended for just cause.

The Grievant testified that he was first notified of the situation regarding the ladder because his daughter-in-law called him when he got off work and asked him to come over to her house because the City was coming to look at the ladder. The Grievant testified that when his daughter-in-law called him, she asked him if the ladder was the City's ladder. The Grievant testified that he replied no, it wasn't. The Grievant testified that his daughter-in-law wanted him there because her husband wasn't home. According to the Grievant, two City employees came to look at the ladder. The Grievant doesn't recall any direct conversation with them. They were talking to his daughter-in-law. The Grievant further acknowledged that he didn't tell either City employee that it wasn't the City's ladder when they came to investigate. He remained silent.

The Grievant testified that after the employees looked at the ladder, they concluded that it was the City's ladder. In response to this conclusion, the Grievant's daughter-in-law showed them that the side of the ladder was marked C&S. The Grievant testified that his son previously owned a business named C&S and that the ladder belonged to the business. The Grievant testified that he went to work the next day and was given a 30 day administrative leave with pay. Although the Grievant testified he wasn't told why he was placed on administrative leave, the evidence reveals he was placed on administrative leave pending an investigation into the theft of the ladder.

During the course of the investigation the Grievant was interviewed by Officer O, and during this time the Grievant raised an issue about possibly resolving the matter. His proposal was that he'd retrieve the ladder in question or buy the City a new ladder, he said he proposed this because this situation was getting out of hand and because he didn't want the City to prosecute his son for receiving stolen property. Officer O presented the Grievant's proposal to the mayor. In response to the

Grievant's proposal, the mayor drafted a memo. When asked whether he bought a new ladder or gave the City a ladder, the Grievant responded, no because Officer O told him not to buy a new ladder and he didn't give the other one back because it wasn't his to give.

[The City also presented the testimony of the employees who saw the ladder is omitted].

The first question to be resolved by the Arbitrator is whether the City met its burden to prove that it had sufficient evidence to conclude the ladder inspected in the Grievant's son's garage was the property of the City of Green.

The Union contends that it did not. The Union points out that six employees were shown photos of the ladder taken in the garage, and they could not identify the ladder as the City's ladder. The City states that the only individuals that had not actually seen the ladder, but were attempting to identify the ladder through photos, were unsure of whether the ladder was the property of the City. Further, the City points out that the ladder was clearly identified by an employee as the City's ladder. Additionally, the City emphasizes that when the employees went to view the ladder, the Grievant made no effort to demonstrate that the ladder did not belong to the City. Lastly, the City also stresses that the employees recognized the notation "C&S" appeared to be shiny and still wet indicating that it was freshly placed on the ladder.

In contrast, the Union presented evidence that the ladder belonged to a business that was formerly owned by the Grievant's son. The City employees testified that Greivant's daughter-in-law said the ladder belonged to C&S and she showed them that the ladder was marked with "C&S". However, they also testified that the markings appeared to be fresh, suggesting that the markings were newly applied to the ladder. Moreover, the evidence also demonstrates that the markings were in black felt pen. The Arbitrator notes that the markings could have been placed on the ladder with relative ease within a matter of seconds. Also noteworthy is the Grievant's testimony his daughter-in-law asked him whether the ladder belonged to the City. This suggests that she wasn't sure if the ladder belonged to the City or to a former business owned by her husband as now claimed.

The ladder was positively identified as City property by two City employees that personally observed the ladder. The Arbitrator acknowledges that the only evidence that the City presented that distinguished the ladder in question from any other similar ladder was the blue tape. While, anyone can put blue tape on a ladder, the City presented sufficient evidence that the tape was in the same location as the tape on the City's ladder. One of the City employees testified that the ladder in question had blue masking tape in the same location as the City's ladder.

Also, somewhat puzzling to the Arbitrator is the Grievant's actions when the City employees came to his son's residence to inspect the ladder. According to the Grievant's testimony he did nothing to indicate to the City employees that the ladder did not belong to the City. He stated he remained silent, even after they concluded that it was the City's ladder, he did not come forth with information that the ladder belonged to his son. In fact, when questioned about why he didn't tell them it wasn't the City's ladder, the Grievant responded, "they was accusing him, he wasn't accusing them." This doesn't seem like logical behavior for someone that could come forward with personal knowledge of facts proving that the ladder was not the City's property.

While none of these factors taken alone would likely be sufficient, looking at the circumstances as a whole, the Arbitrator believes the City provided sufficient evidence that it reasonably determined that the ladder they observed in the Grievant's son's garage belonged to the City of Green.

Having decided that the City met its burden to demonstrate that it reasonably concluded the ladder belonged to the City of Green, the Arbitrator must now decide whether the City met its burden to demonstrate that it reasonably concluded that the Grievant took the ladder.

In support of its position, the City presented testimony from the Director of Public Service for the City of Green for 10 years.

The Director acknowledged that there is no direct evidence that the Grievant took ladder, the ladder was not found on Grievant's property, and several employees could not identify ladder as City's ladder. However, the Director testified that the only employees that couldn't positively identify the ladder were employees that were looking at photos taken of the ladder. The employees that actually went to look at the ladder did positively identify it as the City's ladder.

The Director further testified that the Grievant's daughter-in-law or son would not have had personal access to the ladder. He stated the only way they would have access to the ladder is through the Grievant. The Director clarified that when Officer O gave the findings of his investigation, he specified that while there was not enough evidence for a criminal charge, he believed that the Grievant took the ladder.

The Director based his decision, in part, on Officer O's statement that he believed that the Grievant took the ladder. While Officer O may have believed based on his investigation that the Grievant took the ladder, the question is what the evidence shows. Disciplinary action must be based on proof and not belief. This Arbitrator can believe that the Grievant took the ladder, however, the Arbitrator cannot base his decision on belief, but rather, on evidence and proof in the record. The question for this Arbitrator is did the City provide sufficient evidence to meet its burden of proof to demonstrate that the Grievant took the ladder.

The Arbitrator acknowledges this is a close case, because as I have determined the City provided sufficient evidence that it reasonably concluded that the ladder in question is indeed the City's ladder, the question remains how did the City's ladder get in the son's garage. The City maintains that neither the Grievant's son nor daughter-in-law would have access to the ladder, except through the Grievant. This seems to the Arbitrator to be a logical inference, and that's what makes this case a difficult case. However, as stated previously, the Arbitrator must look at the evidence. There is no direct evidence that the Grievant took the ladder. The ladder was not found in the Grievant's possession. Those facts alone, however, are not detrimental to the City's case. Nevertheless, the most probative and compelling piece of evidence is the City's own investigation into the matter concluded that there is no evidence that the Grievant stole the ladder. Officer O states, "[t]hrough the course of this investigation, I believe there is enough evidence to charge the Grievant's son for receiving stolen property. There is no evidence however to prove who initially stole the ladder." Therefore, while the Director stated that Officer O believed that the Grievant took the ladder, apparently, Officer O concluded there was no evidence to support that belief. The Director based his decision on Officer O's belief that the Grievant took the ladder and the written statement that the ladder was seen in the Grievant's personal truck prior to its disappearance.

As stated above, neither of these factors are sufficient. The Arbitrator recognizes there is a strong inference in this case, however, a strong inference or strong belief is not sufficient to meet a preponderance of the evidence or a clear and convincing standard. Therefore, the City has not met its burden to demonstrate that it had sufficient evidence before it to reasonably determine that the Grievant stole the ladder. Therefore, the City did not have just cause to suspend the Grievant.

VI. CONCLUSION

The City presented sufficient evidence to demonstrate that it reasonably concluded that the ladder identified in the Grievant's son's garage was the property of the City of Green. The City has not met its burden to demonstrate that it had sufficient evidence to reasonably conclude that the Grievant stole the ladder found in the garage.

VII. AWARD

The grievance is sustained.

APPLICATION AND DISCUSSION QUESTIONS

1. Which element of the just cause standard did the City fail to establish?

2. Should a strong influence or strong belief meet the City's burden of proof?

3. Should the burden of proof by a preponderance of the evidence or clear and convincing be the standard?

PEPSI-COLA GENERAL BOTTLERS
117 BNA LA 681 (GOLDSTEIN, 2002)[*]

Statement of the Issue

The parties stipulated to the following issue:

Was there just cause for the termination of the Grievant, P, and, if so, what shall be the remedy?

Pertinent Contractual Provisions and Company General Rules of Conduct

ARTICLE 25
GRIEVANCE PROCEDURE

* * * *

(d) Discharge or Discipline Grievances. No employee shall be discharged except for cause. All grievances relating solely to the discharge or discipline of an employee must be presented within five (5) working days after the occurrence or said grievance shall be deemed abandoned.

---

[*] Reprinted with permission from *Labor Relations Reporter- Labor Arbitration Reports.* 117 BNA LA 681. Copyright 2015 by the Bureau of National Affairs, Inc. (800-372-1033). http://www.bna.com.

* * * *

B. Relevant General Rules of Conduct Provisions

GROUP IV-A

Dishonesty, theft or embezzlement of Company, employee or customer property or funds, or the property or funds of others. This includes making any false injury or illness claims.

* * * *

GROUP IV-S

Failure to turn in to the Company all money, checks and invoices collected or made out that day.

* * * *

Discipline For Violation

Group IV-Violations of Group IV rules are cause for immediate discharge without progressive or corrective discipline.

Factual Background

The Employer, PepsiAmericas, Inc., manufactures and distributes soft drinks including Pepsi, Diet Pepsi, Mountain Dew, Root Beer, Sierra Mist, Aquafina, and Frappaccino. The Pepsi distribution facility involved in the instant matter is in Gurnee, Illinois.

Grievant P began his employment with the Company in 1990. He worked various positions out of the Gurnee facility becoming a route salesman in 1994 or 1995. The subject grievance protests a suspension on December 14, 2000, and subsequent discharge on December 22, 2000, for alleged dishonesty and theft by depositing Company money into his personal account, and for alleged failure to turn in all money to the Employer.

The basis for the discipline involves an Illinois Overweight Ticket and fine of $2,570.00 issued to Grievant for allegedly disregarding a weight limit and driving over a bridge with an overweight truck on January 27, 2000. The police impounded the vehicle with its product cargo. The police refused to release the Grievant or the truck until the fine was paid. As a result, the Gurnee Branch Manager, Marti LaTour, was contacted to arrange for payment of the fine. That same day, Ms. LaTour arranged for a check in the amount of $2,570.00 to be issued and delivered to the police to secure the release of Grievant and the Company vehicle.

Subsequently, LaTour decided to contest the fine in court. The Employer hired an attorney to represent it. On May 8, 2000, the court overturned the fine and ordered that a refund check be issued in the amount of $2,570.00 to the Employer.

* * * *

In mid-June or early July, Employer witness LaTour instructed the Grievant to locate the check in the amount of $2,570.00 that should have been issued to the Employer as a result of the court decision. To assist him, LaTour provided Grievant with her entire file regarding the case. Subsequently, LaTour checked with Grievant as to the status of the check. Grievant replied that he was waiting for responses from others. LaTour further testified that she asked Grievant "a couple of times a month about the check's whereabouts," to no avail.

Manager LaTour further testified that, in December, 2000, the last month to get money credited, she asked Grievant again what happened to the check. She was again told by the Grievant that others were working on it. Deciding she had to get the check, LaTour took the file from the Grievant. She further testified that the next day she called the courthouse and was immediately given the status of the check. At this point, she drove to the courthouse where she was obtained a copy of the check. The refund check had been issued on May 16, 2000, made payable to "P." The check further reflected that it had been endorsed "P" and deposited into his joint checking account on June 9, 2000.

It was the further testimony of LaTour that she returned to her office the same day, contacted her manager regarding the check, and compared the signature on the back of the check with the Grievant's signatures included within his personnel file. In her opinion, the signatures matched. Next, she checked the timecard for June 9, 2000, testifying that Grievant worked that day but did not clock out. As a result of the foregoing, a meeting was held with the Grievant, Branch Manager LaTour and Peter Lebron, Manager of Human Resources, on December 14, 2000.

As noted earlier, Grievant was given a copy of the cashed check. He looked at it and said that it was not his signature, Lebron claimed. Grievant further stated to Lebron and Branch Manager LaTour that "maybe his wife had signed the check and cashed it ..." Grievant, Lebron and LaTour reported in their testimony, in this meeting he emphasized that he did not remember the incident or circumstances regarding the check's being cashed, but he "does not remember exactly. Maybe he did it, but he was on medication, he can't remember for sure."

Based on the statements at the meeting, and the evidence and investigation of the Company to that point, Grievant was told at its conclusion that he was suspended pending investigation. Grievant then told the Company representatives that he was "going to go home and ask his wife if she remembers a check that [if] she had signed it and cashed it."

* * * *

After the Grievant was discharged, the Human Resource Manager Pete Lebron hired a handwriting expert to verify who signed the check at issue. After that expert could not form an opinion, Brother George Searles of the Franciscan Order, a registered document examiner and a Company "expert witness," forwarded two reports to the Employer, concluding the signature on the check belonged to P, not I__. The reports and Company witness Searles' testimony were presented at hearing. Searles gave detailed testimony about his procedure in forming his opinion Grievant endorsed the check. The Union stressed, however, that although Searles had several handwriting examples to work from of Grievant's hand, only a couple of I__'s signatures were available to him for review.

It was on these facts that the case came to me for final resolution.

Contentions of the Parties

A. The Employer

The Employer contends that the Grievant was discharged for violation of two Group IV rules, and that violation of either one by itself results in immediate discharge upon the first infraction. Employees must adhere to the General Rules of Conduct. The General Rules of Conduct are grouped into four levels, with Group IV being the most severe. These General Rules also provide for progressive discipline by Group Level. Any single violation of a Group IV offense carries the penalty of discharge. As Grievant was provided a copy of these Rules of Conduct, the Employer contends the Grievant had notice that discipline, including discharge, would result for rule infractions.

To support the Group IV General Rules of Conduct violations by the Grievant, the Employer relies on the following. Grievant, in the Company's view, was proved to have cashed the Employer's refund check; knowledge that the money belonged to the Employer can be imputed to him, given what he knew of the refund, but also what Branch Manager LaTour credibly says she had told him. LaTour also demanded Grievant trace the check refund for months after Grievant had endorsed it, banked it, and spent its proceeds.

The funds were then deposited into Grievant's bank account, the Ps do not deny. The money was not returned to the Employer, either at the time of receipt of the check or after LaTour asked Grievant about it, which she credibly claimed was on numerous occasions, and at least monthly from June to December, 2000.

* * * *

As to the penalty imposed, in the Employer's view the penalty of discharge should be upheld based upon the clear contract language of the collective bargaining agreement and the teachings of the "Seven Tests." It was also argued that Grievant had a previous disciplinary record and that other employees have been discharged for similar misconduct. Finally, Management submits it has zero tolerance for acts of theft and dishonesty.

4. The Union

* * * *

The Union's final argument involves a failure by the Employer to conduct a timely investigation and to engage in a bona fide investigation of Grievant's account of the facts. The check in question is dated May 16, 2000, yet the Grievant was not approached to explain what happened until December 14, 2000, more than six months later. Therefore, the doctrine of laches should apply to this case, submits the Union. Furthermore, the Union argues that the Employer admitted through Branch Manager LaTour's testimony that no investigation was conducted between December 14, 2000, when Grievant was suspended "pending an investigation" and December 22, 2000, when termination in fact occurred. These failures warrant a reversal of discipline, the Union asserts. See Schaefer's Ambulance

Findings and Discussion

In determining whether or not just cause existed for the discharge of Grievant, the Arbitrator believes the standard of proof required by the Employer is clear and convincing evidence to support the conduct violations of dishonesty and theft, and failure to turn in Company funds. I have ruled in other cases involving fraud and dishonesty that something more than a mere preponderance of the evidence is required where the charge is of a serious nature and results in a greater stigma than in "ordinary" discharge cases. I also note, as cited above, Arbitrator Aaron Wolff's Tower Automotive Award in which Wolff directly stated that the majority of "modern arbitrators find that in cases involving moral turpitude," where burden of proof issues are argued, the most frequently articulated standard is "clear and convincing" evidence, in the sort of case, as here, where a higher standard than "preponderance of credible evidence" is required. Arbitrator Wolff carefully chronicles the "burden of proof" published cases since 1983, finding that "beyond a reasonable doubt" is rarely and more and more infrequently used by arbitrators.

I also believe the proper standard is clear and convincing evidence in this current case, for the reasons I have stated before, as the Union recognizes, and also in line with Arbitrator Wolff's analysis in CTA and ATU Local 308, 110 LA 403 , 409-10 (1997); 98-1 ARB at pp. 5488-9, and I so rule.

Turning to the merits of the case, I find, by clear and convincing evidence, that Grievant knowingly cashed the check at issue here, although he had notice the proceeds were not his to keep, and then converted these proceeds to his own use. Therefore, there was just cause for his discharge.

*   *   *   *

The Union has raised the argument that the Employer failed to timely and thoroughly investigate the Grievant's version of the facts, but I note that LaTour clearly investigated the matter up to December 14, 2000. She then acted to suspend Grievant pending investigation and fired him 8 days later. That is timely action and not evidence of unfair delay, given the totality of evidence presented up to that point, I determine.

Under the facts of record, I also am persuaded, any delay in the investigation of the missing check from mid-June or July to December is attributable to the Grievant's own inaction in not following LaTour's orders to him to investigate what had happened to the refund owed to the Company by the Lake County Court system. LaTour had delegated this task to the Grievant, the record establishes, as I view the evidence. She gave him her file with the relevant information. She testified that since he was currently performing light duty office work and the missing refund had previously paid his fine, she thought locating the refund would be a good task for the Grievant. This is a convincing and sufficient explanation of the time lag, I thus rule.

As to the second part of the Union's contention that the Employer failed to conduct a bona fide investigation of Grievant's assertion, that is, that it waited until after the discharge to hire a handwriting expert, I am persuaded by the testimony that a reasonable investigation had occurred before Grievant was fired. The Employer, through LaTour and Lebron, determined that the Grievant's version of the facts lacked credibility at that point, and they reasonably would do so. Testimony by LaTour and Lebron, after all, reflects that on the December 11, 2000 meeting, the two concluded the story contained too many variables or inconsistencies to be really plausible. Also, the Employer reviewed the 401K hardship withdrawal checks to determine when the checks were issued. That was enough due process, I rule.

This is not a case where the Employer rushed to judgment, without benefit of a fair and complete investigation, I expressly hold. The Employer waited to receive Grievant's explanation as to why, after asking the Grievant what happened to the unaccounted for check refund for six months, the money was found by Branch Manager LaTour to have been deposited into the Grievant's checking account. What Grievant said, and the support he got from this version of the facts did not convince Management, for the reasons detailed above. The fact that the Union disagrees with the credibility assessment made by Management in this factual context does not mean the investigation was actually legally or contractually insufficient, in the sense that it was no more than perfunctory or a sham-the usual factual circumstances where a due process violation is found in this sort of case.

Under all the circumstances of the case, the Company's decision on December 22, 2000 to discharge the Grievant was neither unreasonable, arbitrary or capricious, I therefore am convinced. The fact that a handwriting expert was hired after-the-fact to verify the claims of I__ one last time, cannot cause a finding of a violation of industrial due process under all the circumstances of this case. There is no "bootstrapping" or proffering of evidence discovered post-discharge of pre-removal misconduct. Although I have not overlooked this argument by the Union, I simply believe that there was sufficient evidence for the Employer to act as it did in firing Grievant on December 22, 2000, but that it did have the option to further verify whether I's claims were trustworthy as the grievance was being processed. This is so because there was sufficient evidence to proceed in the first instance, independent of any proofs developed by the handwriting examiner, and I so rule.

The remaining issue is whether discharge was too harsh a penalty, under the circumstances. Having found credible and corroborative evidence in the record to conclude that Grievant's signature was on the missing refund check which was then deposited into his account on June 9, 2000, I must conclude that in mid-June or early July when Branch Manager LaTour asked him to locate the refund check, that Grievant knew what had happened to the check. The check had been deposited into his account. Moreover, prior to his discharge, neither the refund check or the $2,750.00 had been returned to the Employer, I note. Under these facts, I cannot substitute my judgment as to the proper penalty to be imposed.

Therefore, under these facts and circumstances, I find the Employer met its evidentiary burden and that just cause to discipline the Grievant existed. As to whether or not discharge is appropriate under these facts, I find the terms of the General Rules of Conduct are controlling, especially in light of the customary precepts concerning summary discharge as an Employer's option for a "first instance" of theft The clear and undisputed relevant contract and conduct rules provide in the current case that one infraction for dishonesty, theft, and/or failure to turn in Company money or a check is cause for immediate discharge, I also note. I cannot substitute my own sense of justice or grant leniency under these facts, I find.

Accordingly, the grievance must be denied in full. My award to that effect follows.

AWARD

In light of the reasons set forth above and incorporated herein as if fully rewritten, there was just cause for the Grievant's termination and the instant grievance is denied in its entirety.

APPLICATION AND DISCUSSION QUESTIONS

1. What evidence supports the Employer's claim that an investigation was completed before the Grievant was terminated? What is the policy reason for requiring an investigation before terminating an employee?

2. What steps did the Employer take to ensure that the Grievant had a fair and complete investigation? Did the delay in conducting the investigation negatively impact the grievant's ability to present his case?

3. The Union raised issues with the hiring of a handwriting expert after the termination. The Employer insists that there was no "bootstrapping" or proffering of evidence discovered post-discharge of pre-removal misconduct. Do the Unions raise a valid concern with the handwriting evidence being collected after termination?

THERE WAS NO DISCRIMINATION OR DISPARATE TREATMENT

THE GREEN BALLPARK[*]

BEFORE: Floyd D. Weatherspoon, Arbitrator, selected in accordance with the
Federal Mediation Conciliation Services Rules

I. STATEMENT OF FACTS

The facts indicate that the Green Ballpark [hereinafter Employer] and the Employees Union [hereinafter Union] are parties to a collective bargaining agreement, hereinafter (CBA or Agreement) dated March 20, 2004 through March 1, 2007. The facts further indicate that the Employer is engaged in the business of providing food and beverage services at the Green Ballpark in the City of Green. The Employer is also licensed to sell alcoholic beverages.

The Employer has a "Discipline/Violations of Alcohol Service Policy" which strictly prohibits the selling of more than the allowed number of drinks to a patron. According to the policy, a single violation results in "an Associate having their Employment Terminated." In addition to the Alcohol Service Policy, the Employer requires employees to sign an "Alcohol Policy Acknowledgement Commissary" form each day that a vendor reports to work. The form states in part:

> "[i]n vending one beer per sale if fan is unaccompanied (by him/herself) and in posses-
> sion of a beer at the time of purchase." Further, the policy states that "Any violation of
> the Green Ballpark alcohol policy will result in termination. By signing this form you
> understand and will abide by all Green Ballpark alcohol policies."

On June 29, 2006, [the Grievant] was suspended for employment pending an investigation for violating the Employer's Alcohol Service Policy. Specifically, the suspension notice states in part:

> During the 7th inning of the game on June 29, the [Grievant] was vending beer in com-
> missary 6. I observed him make a sale to gentlemen on the concourse near row 140.

---

[*]   Unpublished Decision (Floyd D. Weatherspoon, 2007)

During the entire transaction, the gentleman was holding a bottle of Bud light that was partial full in his hand. As [Grievant] handed the bottle to the gentleman, the gentleman put both bottles in the same hand in clear view to pay the Grievant for the beer and to receive the change back from the sale. As I confronted him about situation, [the Grievant]'s response was that the bottle was empty. When I said that bottle was not empty, he then smiled and said that was only one drink left in the bottle. I advised him to return to the commissary to check out and to give him a call the next day.

The Grievant was subsequently terminated on July 5, 2006 for violating the Employer's Alcohol Service Policy. The Grievant filed a grievance on July 6, 2006, alleging "wrongful termination." The grievance was processed in according with Article III of the CBA.

II. ISSUE

Whether the Grievant was terminated for just cause, if not, what is the appropriate remedy?

III. RELEVANT CONTRACT PROVISIONS AND POLICIES (Omitted)
DISCIPLINE/VIOLATION OF ALCOHOL SERVICE POLICY

A. Single infraction resulting in Associate Having Their Employment Terminated:

Service of more than the allowed number of drinks to a patron; or violation of a rule established by a unit in which associates have signed a written acknowledgement that a single violation will result in termination.

IV. POSITION OF THE PARTIES

A. Employer's Position

The Employer contends that the Grievant was terminated for violating the Discipline/ Violation of Alcohol Service Policy by selling more than the allowed number of drinks to a patron. The Employer indicates that the Alcohol Service Policy prohibits the selling of more than one beer to a patron in a transaction. The Employer further contends that employees are advised that a failure to comply with this policy would result in a termination, even if it was a one-time incident. The Employer also contends that employees have received extensive training on the Alcohol Service Policy as well as repeated notices that they would be terminated for the first violation.

B. Union's Position

The Union does not dispute the fact that on June 29, 2006, the Grievant served a patron more than the allowed number of beers to a patron. Instead, the Union argues that the Grievant did not intentionally or knowingly serve the patron two beers at one time in violation of the Alcohol Service Policy.

The Union contends that the Grievant was distracted when the supervisor approached the Grievant to determine whether he was selling beer in a prohibited area. The Union maintains that the supervisor was present when the Grievant engaged in the transaction and had a duty and an obligation to stop the Grievant from violating the Alcohol Service Policy.

The Union further contends that the incident that occurred on June 29, 2006 as described by the supervisor is not accurate and raises issues of creditability. The Union also alleges that another vendor violated the Alcohol Service Policy by selling more than one drink to a patron was suspended but was not terminated.

V. DISCUSSION AND ANALYSIS

The element of the just cause which is in dispute is whether the Grievant intentionally or knowingly violated the policy. Even with all the testimony, a close reading of the Grievant's own written statement of the incident indicates that the patron "held two beers". The Grievant's argument is that the Supervisor saw him violating the policy and didn't try to stop the infraction. In other words, it appears that the supervisor is the blame for not stopping the transaction.

The General Manager testified that he terminated the Grievant after an investigation was completed and the Grievant gave his explanation of what occurred. According to the General Manager, the Grievant didn't deny that the patrons had another bottle in his hand when he sold him a beer but stated that the container was a "spit cup".

Based on substantial testimony and documentation, there appears to be some factual disputes regarding what the Grievant stated to his supervisor on June 29, 2006 and what he subsequently wrote to support his grievance and his statements that were made during the processing of his grievance. However, the Grievant's own testimony at the hearing resolved this creditability issue for the Arbitrator. The Grievant stated that "I was not paying attention with what I was doing with the fan. I was paying attention [to my supervisor]. I was trying to see what he was doing." The Grievant further testified that he informed his supervisor that he "made an honest mistake." "[He] was not paying attention" and that he "screwed-up." The Grievant acknowledges that he "didn't look to see if the fan had another bottle in his hand." This testimony supports the Employer's position that the Grievant failed to comply with the Employer's well established Alcohol Service Policy.

At this point of the analysis, the Employer has clearly met a majority of the elements of the just cause standard. The employee had notice of the policy, he violated the policy, and there was a fair investigation. The Employer also presented compelling evidence that the policy was reasonable in light of potential liability and the possibility of losing their liquor license. The last element of the just cause standard for the Employer to establish, no disparate treatment, is where their position collapses. The Union presented clear and compelling evidence that another employee engaged in the same infraction was suspended but was not terminated. The Union presented the Record of Associate Counseling for another employee. The relevant portion of the exhibit states:

> During the 2nd inning of the game on July 2, the employee was vending beer in commissary 2. I observed two gentlemen that approached him to buy beer near row 127. At the beginning of the transaction, the employee said something to them about the beers that they had. Both gentlemen started drinking their beer to buy the beers that they ordered. The employee continued with the transaction by opening the two beers and handing them to the two gentlemen. At that point, one of the two gentlemen had finished his beer and put his empty bottle in to the employee's case. However, the other gentleman had placed his beer on the ground between his feet to pay for the second beer and to take possession of his second beer. At that point, the gentleman picked up the beer on the ground and started to drink it as he left the point of sale with two beers in hand. I advised the employee to return to the commissary to check out and give the vending manager a call the next day.

It is not often that the Arbitrator sees evidence of disparate treatment as clear as it is in this grievance. In this grievance, the Grievant and the other employee are both vendors, work in the same department, have the same supervisors, violated the same policy, within the same baseball season, and were written up by the same supervisor. Moreover, the other incident occurred three days before the Grievant was terminated. Similarly, the supervisor completed a Record of Associate Counseling form which stated that the employee sold a beer to a patron who had another beer "between his feet." During the hearing, the Employer presented testimony after testimony that a Vendor could not sell a beer to a patron if they had another beer in their possession. Based on the Counseling Report, the employee was aware that the patron had another beer in his possession. It was not a beer that was on the bench or on the floor; it was between his feet. More importantly, it appears from the supervisor's report, that the vendor witnessed the patron place the beer bottle between his feet. Based on extensive testimony provided by the Employer, it shouldn't have made a difference if the beer was in his hand, on his head, or between two fingers, it would been a violation of the policy. If there were extenuating circumstances to support a legitimate differential, the Employer failed to provide testimony from either the supervisor or the manager who were involved in both incidents. The Employer had an opportunity to call either witness on rebuttal to explain the differential. The Arbitrator is left with compelling evidence of disparate treatment with no valid explanation, other than the Employer's closing argument which summarily dismisses the claim of disparate treatment. Maybe there is a legitimate reason for the differential. However, the Arbitrator can't speculate why the two employees were treated differentially based on very similar facts. It is also interesting to note, but not dispositive of the issue but relevant, that the other vendor was also disciplined the previous year for violating another provision of the Employer's Alcohol Service Policy. The other vendor, however, was not terminated for his second offence of violating the Alcohol Service Policy.

Even if the Arbitrator accepts the Employer's argument that the two incidents are truly different, it still does not explain why the other employee was not terminated. Management provided extensive testimony regarding the enforceability of the policy. The Arbitrator accepted this testimony and relied on it to find that the Employer met the other elements of the just cause standard. If I accept the Employer's argument why the other employee was not terminated it would cause my earlier analysis to weaken. It would also raise serious creditability issues with management's testimony regarding the Alcohol Service Policy. Either the policy is strictly enforced, or not at all, but not selectively.

The Employer also cites the Management Rights clause to justify their right termination employees. This is correct so long as the termination does not violate the just cause standard as cited in the Management Rights clause.

VI. CONCLUSION

The Employer has failed to establish that the Grievant was terminated for just cause. The evidence supports the Union's position that the Grievant was treated differently than another employee who violated the same policy but was not terminated. The

Employer failed to provide any concrete evidence to support a legitimate reason for the differential.

VII. AWARD

The Arbitrator has considered both the conduct of the Grievant and that of the Employer. The Grievant, carelessly violated the Employer's policy and the Employer treated the Grievant differently when issuing discipline. The Grievant is to be reinstated to his position as a Vendor with retroactive seniority. However, the Grievant is denied back pay and all other benefits, except seniority. An award of back pay would reward the Grievant for violating the Employer's Alcohol Service Policy. The failure to reinstate the Grievant would reward the Employer for engaging in disparate treatment among union members who violate the same policies. The Grievant's termination for the 2006 season will serve as a suspension.

APPLICATION AND DISCUSSION QUESTIONS

1. Which party has the burden of proof to establish just cause or no just cause in a termination case?

2. What are the traditional elements of just cause?

3. Which element of just cause did the employer fail to establish and why?

4. Do you agree with the employer's arguments as to why they terminated the Grievant but not the other employee?

5. Do you agree with the remedy award?

Opinion By: Floyd D. Weatherspoon, Arbitrator

I. STATEMENT OF FACTS

The facts indicate that the Union and the Sheriff Department A are parties to a collective bargaining agreement, hereinafter (CBA or Agreement), dated from January 1, 2004 through December 31, 2006. The Facts further indicate that the Grievant, was terminated from the County Sheriff Department A for inmate abuse and use excessive force about September 2, 2005. About September 3, 2005, a grievance was filed challenging the Grievant's termination The grievance went through the various stages of the grievance procedure. The grievance was denied. Arbitration was requested pursuant to Article (7) of the CBA. The parties stipulated that the grievance is properly before the Arbitrator.

II. ISSUE

Was the Grievant terminated for just cause? If not, what is the appropriate remedy?

III. RELEVANT CONTRACT PROVISIONS (Omitted)

IV. POSITION OF THE PARTIES

A. Union's Position

The Union contends that the Sheriff did not establish that the Grievant used unnecessary excessive force. The Union maintains that the incidents in question involved minor injuries that did not constitute excessive force and therefore, there was no just cause to terminate the Grievant. The Union contends that the investigation into the use of excessive force allegations was not initiated within 60 days as required by Article 11 of the CBA. It is the Union's assertion that the two employees that informed the Sheriff's Department that there may have been a problem, had personality differences

---

with the Grievant, and therefore, had an underlying motive to start trouble for the Grievant. The Union contends that the Sheriff did not follow its progressive disciplinary policy and therefore violated the CBA. The Union also maintains that the Sheriff did not comply with the notification requirement under the CBA. Finally, the Union contends that the Sheriff is not consistently applying discipline because other employees were not disciplined in connection with the incidents at issue.

B. Management's Position

It is the Sheriff's position that it had just cause to terminate the Grievant for unnecessary use of excessive force against three inmates. The Sheriff contends that the incident triggering an investigation into this matter was not discovered until late June 2005 and an investigation was commenced within the sixty day period as mandated by the CBA. The Sheriff maintains that there is sufficient evidence that the Grievant used excessive force and that it had just cause to terminate the Grievant. The Sheriff contends that it did not violate the progressive disciplinary policy because this instance merits termination on the first occurrence. The Sheriff contends that it has not acted in a discriminatory manner.

V. DISCUSSION AND ANALYSIS

* * * *

The Sheriff maintains that it had just cause to discharge the Grievant for inmate abuse and excessive use of force in violation of the Sheriff's policy. The Union contends that the Sheriff did not establish that the Grievant used excessive force.

* * * *

A variation in penalty, does not in and of itself denote discrimination. Discrimination is an unfair and unequal treatment of certain employees. Employees have to be treated alike in similar circumstances. In determining whether the employer has discriminated, it is necessary to take the totality of the circumstances into consideration, including, the nature of the misconduct and any mitigating or aggravating circumstances involved. "There is no discrimination, or no departure from the consistent or uniform treatment of employees, merely because of variations in discipline reasonably appropriate to the variations in circumstances." Elkouri, pg. 997, citing *Alan Wood Steel Co.*, 21 LA 843, 849 (Short, 1954).

The Union did not elaborate on why the other employees should have been disciplined. Apparently, the Union believes that the employees' that cooperated during the investigation should have been disciplined because they were a witness to the use of excessive force and didn't report it. The Grievant was terminated for inmate abuse and excessive use of force. There is no evidence that the employees that witnessed the incidents engaged in excessive use of force or inmate abuse in connection with the incidents in question. Even if the employees should have been disciplined for failing to report the incident, the situation is not similarly situated so that the Union can claim that the Sheriff was not applying the discipline in a consistent manner. The Union's argument is not well taken.

VI. CONCLUSION

The Sheriff has met the elements of the just cause standard. The Sheriff demonstrated that the Grievant engaged in wrongdoing, by using excessive force against inmates. The Sheriff's position is reasonable. The evidence reveals that the Sheriff conducted a fair and thorough investigation prior to the discharge. The Sheriff's decision to terminate the Grievant was not arbitrary or discriminatory. Moreover, there were no factors that warranted modification of the penalty.

VII. AWARD

The grievance is denied.

APPLICATION AND DISCUSSION QUESTIONS

1. How does the arbitrator explain the variation of penalties between employees?

2. How do arbitrators determine the existence of discrimination in the issuance of penalties?

3. How do arbitrators determine the "similarly situated" employees when a company issues penalties?

Issue

Did the Employer have just cause to discharge the Grievant, S__; and if not, what is the appropriate remedy?

Statement of the Grievance

This Arbitration arises under the terms of the Work Agreement between TEVA Pharmaceuticals API Division at Mexico, Missouri (hereinafter "Employer" or "Company") and Local International Brotherhood of Teamsters (hereinafter "Union") (CBA).

The Union filed this grievance on behalf of S__ (Grievant) after the Company terminated him for ignoring the requirements of his job. The Union grieved the discharge, claiming Grievant was terminated in violation of Article 9 of the CBA. In their grievance the Union requested that Grievant be made whole for all loses suffered because of his termination. Failing to resolve the dispute in the initial steps of the grievance process, the Union requested arbitration of the matter.

Relevant Contract Provisions

ARTICLE 9
DISCIPLINE AND DISCHARGE

The Employer will not discharge, suspend, or discipline without just cause. All employees shall receive a written copy of the Employer code of conduct, which shall also be posted on the Employer bulletin boards. A shop steward, or designated alternate, shall be present in instances where the Employer is taking this very action against the employee.

Prior to discharge of an employee, the Employer shall give three (3) warning notices of any offense by such employee, in writing, to the employee and the Chief Shop Steward.

---

[*]   Reprinted with permission from *Labor Relations Reporter- Labor Arbitration Reports.* 134 BNA LA 715. Copyright 2015 by the Bureau of National Affairs, Inc. (800-372-1033)

No warning notice need be given to an employee prior to suspension or discharge, if the cause for such suspension or discharge is, for example: theft; assault; threatening/intimidation/ insubordination; falsification of documents; sabotage; negligent or deliberate/careless action which endangers the life or safety of any employee; the sale, possession or being under the influence of intoxicating beverage or control substance while at work; sleeping or possession of a weapon or firearm while on the Employer's property.

*　*　*　*

Position of the Company

The Employer maintains that just existed to discharge Grievant. Evidence submitted by the Company indicated that Grievant, simply ignored (not neglected, ignored) the requirements of his job and then compounded his misconduct by fabricating and falsifying documentation.

*　*　*　*

The investigation that began with Grievant's malfeasance also included the other employees who were similarly interviewed. These operators should have also independently set the Dew Points but did not. According to the Company, their explanation, while flawed, is most assuredly a bit different. By way of example, the same e-mail prepared by Colson (which described his interview with Grievant also described his subsequent interview with G__, the operator who had followed Grievant. That e-mail provided G__'s explanation: "She told me she did not verify the settings. That she looked at the previous Batch Log and wrote down what was on the log thinking that the settings had already been changed."

The Company suspended G__ for three days. The Company did the same for M__ who had followed her and had also explained that his recording too had similarly "followed the leader." Thurman explained that while operators certainly should confirm all settings, that he recognizes there are times when operators do become lax and will rely upon settings recorded by a prior operator on the belief that once the settings are initially set that "will rarely if ever change". Here, these "next" operators relied upon Grievant, obviously not realizing he had not even bothered to try to set the controls and had then simply entered false data. They were wrong in their reliance on Grievant, but in the Company's opinion, not nearly as wrong as Grievant. While the Company does not condone their arguably reasonable reliance on the settings of another operator, it understands that it does occur and distinguished its response to a large extent based upon this apparent difference. Here the other operators would have been fine as likely may have been the case in the past without the Company's knowledge or acknowledgement, except for the fact that they relied upon the wrong person, Grievant who simply didn't even bother to look at any of the settings and then simply made up his numbers.

The Company concluded that the level of culpability was far greater for Grievant than for the others and, based on that business judgment, meted out different discipline. The Company contends that their business judgment in this regard should not be lightly disregarded. There is no evidence of any bias or improper motivation directed only towards Grievant. The Company in the business of manufacturing pharmaceutical products consistent with its standard operating procedures, should be in a position to distinguish between these different levels of wrongdoing.

In summary, the Company contends that they cannot be expected to return an employee like Grievant to the workforce, one regulated by the FDA, and making pharmaceutical ingredients used to help the sick and infirm. Grievant has lost the Company's trust and such an employee really does not deserve a second chance. The Company has established that it had just cause to terminate Grievant and the fact that they did not terminate the other employees who failed to check Grievant's numbers does not and should not change the outcome. The Company requests that the grievance be denied.

Position of the Union

* * * *

Evidence submitted by the Union indicated that all four of the operators were issued discipline for "falsification of documents." G__ received a three (3) day suspension; M__ received a three (3) day suspension; J__ received a written warning; but Grievant was issued the ultimate discipline and was discharged. The Union argues that all four of the operators were guilty of the same offense-noting numbers on a Batch Record without adjusting or checking to see if those numbers matched machine settings.

The Union argues that no matter what level of discipline the employer chose to issue, all four employees should have been given the same penalty. Since the employer believed that issuing a written warning to J__ was an appropriate penalty for the offense, then the other three employees, including Grievant, should have been given written warnings. If the employer had decided that three-day suspensions were appropriate, then all four employees should have been given "staggered" three-day suspensions. The Union chose to use the term "staggered" because the employer raised an issue at the hearing that productivity would suffer if all four operators had been discharged. By staggering suspensions, with no overlapping days, the employer could have avoided the productivity problem according to the Union. The Union argues that just cause simply cannot be established if one employee is discharged and another is given a written warning for the same offense.

Opinion of the Arbitrator

This arbitration centers on whether the Company properly discharged Grievant. In discharge cases, arbitrators determine two factors: (1) proof of wrongdoing; and (2) whether the penalty was reasonable. Elkouri and Elkouri, How Arbitration Works, BNA, Wash. D.C. 6th Ed. (2003) p. 948. On the first factor, the Employer bears the burden to prove that the employee committed the act deserving termination by a preponderance of the evidence. Rock-Tenn Co., 127 LA 390 (Eglit, 2010) (finding that unless the conduct in question was criminal, employers must prove by a preponderance of the evidence that the employee committed the conduct in question).

[1] The first prong of the analysis of just cause is easily resolved in this matter. All of the evidence and testimony in this case, including Grievant's statements during the investigation, clearly establish that Grievant did not comply with Batch Recording procedures by physically checking and documenting the equipment settings for the process on which he was working. Grievant admitted during the investigation that he "just picked the number that was in the range listed on the batch log and put it there," without physically verifying the settings on the equipment. Grievant's admissions in this regard were undisputed at the hearing.

Under the second prong, the Employer must prove that the discipline it administered was reasonable under the totality of the circumstances. *Asset Protection & Security Services*, 127 LA 904 (Whelan, 2010). In a discipline case, the totality of the circumstances test requires the arbitrator to combine all of the variables against the employee and weigh them with the discipline charge. *Proctor & Gamble*, 114 LA 1185 (Allen, 2000); see also *United States Steel Corp.*, 124 LA 1435 (Bethel, 2007) (reasoning that arbitrators regularly evaluate evidence and assign it the proper probative weight by viewing the evidence under the totality of the circumstances). The totality of the circumstances in this case does little to support the position of the Employer.

[2] The evidence and testimony before the Arbitrator clearly establish that Grievant was treated in a disparate fashion when he was discharged for essentially the same offense which was committed by the employees who followed after him running the

same batch. The Company emphasizes that the severe discipline awarded to Grievant was necessary because of FDA requirements and the fact that the manufacturer of pharmaceuticals must be strictly controlled in order to protect the health and safety of the public. Although their argument regarding safety was forceful, the Arbitrator is left to ponder why the other three employees did not receive discipline as serious as that of the Grievant. The Company did present testimony that in their opinion accounted for the disparate treatment.

* * * *

There is merit to the Union's argument that Grievant's actions for which he was discharged do not approximate what is usually encountered in cases involving falsification of company records. The Company may well have overcome the Union's contention in this matter were it not for the very serious issue of disparate treatment of a long-term employee. It is well established in arbitral law in the United States that the enforcement of rules must be exercised in a consistent manner:

It generally is accepted that enforcement of rules and assessment of discipline must be exercised in a consistent manner; all employees who engage in the same type of misconduct must be treated essentially the same, unless a reasonable basis exists for variations in the assessment of punishment (such as different degrees of fault, or mitigating or aggravating circumstances affecting some but not all of the employees). Applying this general rule, one decision recognized, "there must be reasonable rules and standards of conduct which are consistently applied and enforced in a non-discriminatory fashion. It is also generally accepted that enforcement of rules and assessment of discipline must be exercised in a consistent manner; thus all employees who engage in the same type of misconduct must be treated essentially the same." Elkouri and Elkouri, <u>How Arbitration Works</u>, 7th Edition, BNA, Wash. D.C., 2012, p. 15-76 (footnotes omitted).

Each of the Company's arguments when taken separately appears to have merit, but when looked at as a totality their argument simply fails. First, the Company steadfastly stated that they needed to discharge Grievant in order to maintain extremely accurate and high standards in order to meet FDA compliance to protect the public. However, if that pronouncement were completely true, it stands to reason that all employees who failed to check the batch correctly would have been discharged. Secondly, the Company's argument as to why it could not terminate all four employees appears credible. However, in making this argument the Company undermines its previous argument of how serious FDA violations are taken. Quite simply, the Company appears to have placed production ahead of rigid enforcement of their standards to produce a safe product; leading one to believe that the standards are not of sufficient importance to obviate progressive discipline in this matter. The Company treated Grievant in a disparate fashion without any reasonable basis, which as noted supra, is violative of a just cause standard.

In order for a union to prevail on disparate treatment argument, it must be established that the grievant was treated differently than others and that the circumstances surrounding his/her offense were substantively like those of individuals who received more moderate penalties. *Genie Co.*, 97 LA 542, 549 (Dworkin, 1991). In the instant case, the Union has met its burden of proof in proving disparate treatment of Grievant. Arbitral precedent also reveals that:

> Where the union does prove that rules and regulations have not been consistently applied and enforced in a nondiscriminatory manner, arbitrators will refuse to sustain the discharge or will reduce a disciplinary penalty. Elkouri and Elkouri, How Arbitration Works, 6th Edition, BNA, Wash. D.C., (2003) p. 997 (footnotes omitted).

In the instant case, the Union has proved disparate treatment. The just cause standard as referenced by the parties in their Agreement requires that the discipline assessed against Grievant be modified to comport with that given to the other similarly situated employees. Accordingly, it will be ordered that Grievant's discharge be converted to a three (3) day suspension and that he be made whole for all losses he suffered as a result of his discharge. It shall be so ordered.

AWARD

Based upon the analysis supra, the grievance in sustained in part and denied in part. Grievant's discharge is to be converted to a three (3) day suspension and he is to be made whole for all losses he suffered as a result of his discharge. The Arbitrator will retain jurisdiction to rule on any issues related to the remedy that may arise between the parties.

So ordered.

APPLICATION AND DISCUSSION QUESTIONS

1. In determining disparate treatment, the arbitrator must determine whether the grievant and the employee who the grievant is alleging has been treated more favorably are similarly situated. The arbitrator will

typically determine whether the comparable employee works in the same department, whether their misconduct is similar (violated the same rule), length of time employed with the company, and their employment and disciplinary record. Can you add to the list?

2. In this grievance, how did the arbitrator determine which employees were similar to the grievant? Do you agree with the Union that all four employees should have received the same penalty?

THE DEGREE OF DISCIPLINE WAS REASONABLE

In determining whether a penalty is reasonable, arbitrators will often consider the seriousness nature of the offense. See *Capital Airlines*, 25 LA 13 (Stowe 1955). There should also be a correlation to the penalty and misconduct when the employee is terminated for a minor offense the Union has labeled this as "disciplinary overkill." See, *Appleton Paper, Inc.*, 106 LA 11 (Duff 1995). The cases in this section explore whether the disciplinary action is reasonable or punitive in nature.

THE GREEN COMPANY[*]

I. STATEMENT OF FACTS

The facts indicate that the Union and the Green Company (Employer) are parties to a collective bargaining agreement (CBA or Contract) for the period of October 12, 2012 through August 1, 2015.

The Grievant held the position of Journeyman Meat Cutter. The Grievant had been employed with the Green Company for 29 years until he was terminated effective February 22, 2014.

---

[*]   Unpublished Decision (Floyd D. Weatherspoon, 2015)

The record indicates that the Grievant was involved in three disputes with other employees where his comments were interpreted by the Employer as threats of violence and/or violating the company's safety policy. Specifically, the disputes occurred on January 1, 2014, February 10, 2014, and during the week of February 22, 2014, respectively.

After the first incident, the Grievant was given a written warning letter and subsequently transferred to another store. After the third incident, the Employer decided to terminate the Grievant from employment. However, the Grievant initially received a Constructive Advice Record (CAR) on February 22, 2014, that he was suspended pending completion of an investigation. After the investigation was completed, by letter dated March 11, 2014, the Grievant was notified that he was terminated effective February 22, 2014. .

A grievance was filed on February 24, 2014, challenging the termination. The grievance went through the various stages of the grievance process. The grievance was denied. Arbitration was requested pursuant to Article 4 of the CBA. The parties stipulated that the grievance is properly before the Arbitrator and there are no arbitrability issues.

II. ISSUE

Was the Grievant terminated for just cause? If not, what is the appropriate remedy?

III. RELEVANT CONTRACT PROVISIONS AND WORK RULES

Contract Provisions (Text Omitted)
Store Rules: General Employee Conduct

> 4. Harassment of any type by any employee cannot and will not be tolerated and will be just cause for immediate dismissal...

> Violation of these rules may lead to disciplinary action up to and including discharge, based upon the severity of the offense. The Green Co. reserves the right to discharge for the violation of any of the above rules.

> Progressive Discipline Steps
> Some infractions that can lead to disciplinary action up to and including discharge are: Disregard for safety.

IV. POSITION OF THE PARTIES

A. The Employer's Position

The Employer asserts that it had just cause to terminate the Grievant for violating its anti-harassment policy when the Grievant allegedly made threatening statements of a harassing nature. The Employer claims that it also took into consideration that the Grievant had a prior history of making threatening statements. The Employer points out that on January 1, 2014, during an argument with a co-worker, the Grievant allegedly indicated "...words to the effect of it's a new year, I've got six weeks of vacation, and I don't mind spending them in jail. The co-worker understood this as a threat that the Grievant would assault him." In addition to the co-worker perceiving this as threatening, a witness also gave a statement that corroborated the co-worker's concern. The Employer stated that as a result of that incident the Grievant was disciplined in the form of a CAR. The CAR warned the Grievant that "future incidents of that nature would result in additional discipline up to and including discharge."

The Grievant was subsequently transferred to another store that was in need of a meat cutter. The Employer stated that on February 9, 2014, the Grievant was written up for performance issues. The Employer stated that the Grievant did not learn from his previous mistakes when he allegedly went back to the meat department and told a co-worker, that "he [the Grievant] had to give the key to his gun safe to his wife to keep him from having access to his firearms." He also then allegedly stated "that he didn't trust anyone at the Green Company and he would treat them all as terrorists." Management asserts that they took this matter seriously because the Grievant is a military veteran who fought "terrorists" in the Iraq War.

The incident that led to the Grievant's discharge occurred on February 22, 2014 when according to the Employer the Grievant became angry because he had been counseled and according to management the Grievant then made the statement "Do you know how easy it would be to off somebody and get away with it?" The Employer alleged that this statement was made to the co-worker back in the meat department and caused him (co-worker) to be concerned for his safety and the safety of others.

Management then conducted an investigation. The Employer asserts that when the Grievant was questioned, he admitted to making the statements but averred that his statements were taken out of context. Notwithstanding, in an effort to preclude a violence in the workplace situation, the Employer suspended the Grievant and after further investigation, HR recommended that the suspension be converted to a discharge. The Employer contends that there were other employees who were also terminated for making threatening statements; therefore, there was no disparate treatment in this matter. The Employer maintains that the Grievant's past disciplinary record and developing pattern of a violent nature, were factors for aggravation of the penalty, in lieu of mitigation. The Employer asserts that it had just cause to terminate the Grievant's employment.

B. Union's Position

It is the Union's position that there was not just cause to terminate the Grievant. The Union highlights the Grievant's 29 year service history and points out that he had never been suspended prior to the 2014 disciplinary incidents. The Union asserts that the progressive discipline procedure was not followed. The Union also argues that the Grievant's statements that were perceived to be "threatening" were interpreted out of context. The Union claims that the statement about the Grievant giving the key to his gun safe to his wife was to explain that his wife thought he was spending too much money on the weekends going to the gun range, so if she had the key he wouldn't spend as much money. The Union claims that the remark referencing "terrorists" was meant to imply that you should not trust anyone because they could be a like a terrorist; but the Union said the Grievant acknowledged that the remark was "inappropriate" and he "could have used another word." The Union makes a distinction between the Grievant's termination and others who were similarly situated, in that others did not have a lengthy service record comparable to the Grievant's. The Union argues that there was no just cause to terminate the Grievant. Moreover, the Union contends that the Grievant's service time mitigates the penalty.

V. DISCUSSION AND ANALYSIS

* * * *

It appears from the evidence presented by the parties, there are three elements of the just cause analysis at issue. First, is there substantial evidence that the Grievant engaged in the misconduct? Secondly, whether the penalty of termination was reasonable and not punitive in nature? Thirdly, whether any evidence of disparate treatment exists? The Union and the Grievant do not contest that the Grievant used inappropriate language. Therefore, the parties are not in dispute that the Grievant made statements as set forth by The Employer. The factual dispute is whether the statements reasonably can be interpreted to be threats of violence in violation of The Employer's anti-harassment policy. (Omitted Facts on Incidents)

The Grievant tried to explain away the statement he made regarding asking his wife to keep the key to his gun safe by indicating the statement stemmed from his spending too much money going to the gun range. Notwithstanding, the assistant head meat cutter did not take the threatening comments lightly and perceived them as a threat to himself and the safety of others in the store, to include patrons and co-workers.

As stated in *Elkouri*:

> In recent years the issue of workplace violence also has come to the forefront of public and employer concerns. Increased violence in the workplace has prompted employers to implement specific policies to protect workers from both physical harm and threats of physical harm. A sensitivity to the disturbing accounts of workplace violence certainly has contributed to the view that that an employer's obligation to provide a safe working environment requires (1) zero tolerance for [violation of] violence policies, and (2) the discipline or removal of employees who threaten or engage in violence... Violence in the workplace is a serious concern to employers. The law requires that when an employer receives information of threats [of violence], the Employer must respond...Receiving such information directly or by way of hearsay is irrelevant. An employer must act on such information...employees who make threats of physical violence in many cases are subject to the same discipline (i.e., discharge) as for actual workplace assaults." (*Elkouri*, pp. 1020-1021).

Here, the Employer was in a difficult position that involved balancing the utility of a long term employee vs. the gravity of the risk that the Grievant could inflict harm upon his co-workers or shopping customers. It is clear from the record that the employees were fearful of the Grievant and reasonably felt his comments were threatening. One employee stated that he was "freaked out" and scared from the Grievant's comments. It was reasonable for the Employer to take prompt and severe actions. As stated above in *Elkouri*, the Employer [the Employer] had a duty to respond and in a timely manner to threats of violence.

The Arbitrator cannot substitute his judgment for that of the Employer in determining what a terminable offense entails. The Employer's work rules make it clear that the company has a zero tolerance policy for harassment and it is considered an offense that can subject a violator to immediate discharge. Its progressive disciplinary policy also makes it clear that discharge can be an immediate penalty provided that an infraction is severe. The Arbitrator will not cast doubt on the Employer's judgment that the threatening language used by the Grievant was "severe" in light of the potential for impeding the public's safety and the safety of the Employer's employees. Moreover, this was not the Grievant's first offense. Shortly, after being transferred to another store he made statements of a threatening nature to another employee. Additionally, he received warnings that a repeat of such conduct could result in his termination. Notwithstanding the prior warnings, he continued to engage in conduct of a harassing and threatening manner. Although one of the incidents by itself may not warrant termination, the combination of incidents supports a pattern of misconduct.

In reviewing the totality of the circumstances in this case, this Arbitrator finds that there is merit to the Employer's claim that the Grievant had been warned about his threatening conduct. Moreover, the Grievant comments could reasonably be interpreted to be threats of violence. In a business that provides a service to the public, safety is of paramount importance. The Arbitrator also does not concur with the Union's argument that the Employer did not follow its progressive disciplinary procedure. In spite of the Employer's attempts to correct the Grievant's behavior, rehabilitation was not successful. The progressive disciplinary grid allows the Employer to terminate an employee for engaging in threatening conduct, especially when the employee has been warned that they could be terminated if they again engaged in such conduct.

In accordance with the standards articulated in *Grief Bros. Cooperage Corp. and Enterprise Wire Co.,* (Id), the Employer provided advance notice to the Grievant of the disciplinary consequences if his behavior did not improve; the issue of safety and an anti-harassment policy is reasonably related to the efficient and safe operation of running a grocery business; an investigation was conducted and witness testimony plus prior incidents supported management's rationale for terminating the Grievant's employment. There was no evidence of disparate treatment. The degree of discipline was reasonably related to the nature of the offense and the Grievant's past record.

The Employer submitted records of other employees who were also terminated for violation of its workplace violence policy...

Penalty

The only element left under the just cause analysis is the penalty. In determining whether there are mitigating factors which may impact the level of discipline that an employee receives for violating a work rule or policy, arbitrators often consider the employee's work record, service time, gravity of the offense and any other special circumstances. *Paperworks v. Misco, Inc.,* 484 U.S. 29, 41 (1987). Just cause also requires an employer to consider aggravating and mitigating circumstances. The Union proffers the Grievant's long service record of 29 years as a mitigating factor that should be considered in reducing the penalty. Nevertheless, as pointed out in *Elkouri*, workplace violence and even the threat thereof, is a serious matter. I conclude, therefore, that a violation of this policy justifies termination in spite of a long service record. In this grievance, the Grievant's service record is not a compelling factor sufficient to mitigate the penalty of termination.

The Arbitrator acknowledges that he is sympathetic to the fact that the Grievant had a long tenure with the Employer with a record of good performance and a clean disciplinary record prior to the January 1st incident. The Union is correct that the Employer had a number of corrective options it could have used in place of termination, e.g. suspension, last chance agreement, etc. I understand that the Union would want the Arbitrator to direct the Employer to order such a remedy. I am tempted to do so based on the Grievant's record. But I must remind myself and the Union of a very basic arbitration principle from the Supreme Court:

> "[A]n arbitrator is confined to interpretation and application of the collective
> bargaining agreement: He does not sit to dispense his own brand of industrial justice.
> He may of course look for guidance from many sources, yet his award is legitimate
> only so long as it draws its essence from the collective bargaining agreement.

The Arbitrator cannot ignore the evidence and the CBA and *dispense my own brand of justice.* The CBA allows the Arbitrator to mitigate a penalty if it is punitive in nature and consider mitigating factors. Here, the Employer has met its burden of establishing just cause, though marginally, nevertheless by a preponderance of the evidence. The conduct was too severe to be mitigated by his employment record.

VI. CONCLUSION

In this grievance, the Employer has met all of the elements of the just cause standard. Its position in this matter is reasonable. The evidence reveals that the Employer conducted a fair investigation prior to the discharge. The Employer's decision to terminate the Grievant was neither arbitrary nor discriminatory. Moreover, there were no factors that warranted modification of the penalty. The seriousness of the threats to engage in workplace violence supports the Employer's decision to terminate the Grievant.

VII. AWARD

Therefore, the grievance is denied.

APPLICATION AND DISCUSSION QUESTIONS

1. Based on the Supreme Court in *Enterprise Wheel*, the arbitrator refused to modify the penalty. Were there sufficient mitigating factors to modify the penalty without violating *Enterprise Wheel*?

2. The grievant had been employed for almost thirty-two years with good performance and had a clean disciplinary record prior to the three incidents. Should the mitigating factors have been sufficient to reinstate the Grievant?

3. What does the court imply by the statement that arbitrators are not to dispense their own brand of justice?

2008 AAA LEXIS 876

AMERICAN ARBITRATION ASSOCIATION

JANUARY 4, 2008, DECIDED[*]

Opinion By: Floyd D. Weatherspoon, Arbitrator

I. STATEMENT OF FACTS

The facts indicate that Union and School District are parties to a collective bargaining agreement dated January 1, 2006-December 31, 2007, hereinafter (CBA or Agreement). The basic facts in this grievance are not in dispute. Grievant was employed as a bus driver for the School District from April 13, 1992 until she was terminated on March 3, 2007. One of the Grievant's responsibilities was to transport a group of ninth graders from the high school to the junior high school. The students attended the high school during the first two periods then were shuttled by bus to the junior high school building. There were three school buses used to shuttle the students between the schools. On February 12, 2007, the three buses were proceeding on State Route, the Grievant was driving the first bus. As the buses approached the street where the

---

junior high school was located, the Grievant stopped to yield to the on-coming traffic before making the left turn. When the Grievant stopped, the second bus struck the Grievant's bus from the rear. From here, the parties disagree as to what occurred after the accident and whether the Grievant violated the Board's policies and procedures regarding how to handle accidents.

On February 26, 2007, Superintendent, notified the Grievant that he was considering recommending to the Board that she receive a disciplinary action for the following charges:

COUNT ONE
February 12, 2007-Leaving the Scene of an Accident-bus accident involving another school bus on State Route in the school district. You were the bus driver of a lead bus that was making a left hand turn; your turn was stopped before being completed and your bus was struck in the rear by a bus driven by Bus Driver Trainer. The Highway Patrol was not called to report this accident.

COUNT TWO
February 12, 2007-No Check for Injuries-you did not check to see if there were any injuries for the students on your bus.

COUNT THREE
February 12, 2007-Did Not Report an Accident to Transportation Supervisor-You did not report to Transportation Supervisor that there had been an accident. She found out when junior high Principal, called because students were coming to the office saying they were injured on the bus. (Joint Exhibit 2, p. 7).

On March 3, 2007, the Board terminated the Grievant's contract of employment "on the basis of incompetency, inefficiency and neglect of duty" based upon the Superintendent's recommendation.

The Grievant filed a grievance regarding the termination on March 9, 2007. The grievance proceeded through the procedures of the CBA. Thereafter, the Union requested arbitration on April 2, 2007. The arbitration hearing was held on November 29, 2007. The parties stipulated that the grievance was properly before the Arbitrator.

II. ISSUE

Was the Grievant terminated for just cause, if not, what is the appropriate remedy?

III. RELEVANT CONTRACT, OHIO CODE, AND BOARD POLICIES

Article L-Management Rights Clause

On behalf of itself as the representative of the voters, taxpayers, students and parents of students, the Board reserves unto itself rights not abridged by this Agreement including the following:

> 3. Discipline or terminate employees for just cause.
> School Bus Safety Procedures
> School Bus Accident Reporting
> 1. The bus driver shall report accident, involving a school bus to the police agency having jurisdiction where the accident occurs-city police, county sheriff, or State highway patrol.
> 2. The bus driver shall also report, in writing, to the Superintendent's office for insurance purposes and for filing T-10.
> 4. In case of accident, the bus driver shall take steps to list all students who were riding the bus.
> 5. In case of accident, first priority should be given to the attention of the passengers.

> State Preservice School Bus Driver Training Manual, Chapter-9; Safety and Emergency Procedures
> C. Responsibilities and Procedures in the Event of a School Bus Accident
> 3. Reassure children and check for injuries
> 8. Notify School and Law Enforcement Officials:
> a. Contact them by radio or phone (if available)

Ohio Codes 3301-83-15-Emergency and Evacuation Procedures [Omitted]

IV. POSITION OF THE PARTIES

A. Union's Position

The Union contends that the Board did not have just cause to terminate the Grievant. Specifically, the Union argues that the School District failed to establish by clear and convincing evidence that the Grievant violated the School District's policies and procedures in the manner in which she handled and reported the bus accident that occurred on February 12, 2007. The Union also alleges that the School District failed to establish that the policies and procedures that are at issue were made available to the Grievant prior to February 12, 2007.

The Union contends that the investigation conducted by the Board "was seriously flawed" and did not support its claim that the Grievant violated the School District's polices and procedures or/and any state laws. The Union insists that the Grievant handled the incident in a professional manner, followed procedures, and reported the incident within minutes of the occurrence to her supervisor.

The Union claims that that the discipline of discharge was "unreasonable or excessive." Lastly, the Union asserts that the policies and procedures have been inconsistently applied by the Board involving other bus accidents.

B. School District's Position

The School District maintains that after the accident, the Grievant made the left turn and proceeded to the junior high school building. The School District contends that the Grievant failed to report the accident to the transportation supervisor, made no inquiry of whether students were injured, and failed to contact law enforcement.

The School District indicates that once the bus arrived at the junior high school four students complained to their teacher and the Assistant Principal that they were injured. The students were treated by the school nurse. The School District further indicates that three of the students have filed injury claims against the School District with their insurance liability company.

In conclusion, the School District alleges that the Grievant totally ignored policies and procedures on how to handle an accident where injuries or/and damages have occurred. The Grievant also disregarded the safety of the students. Based on these factors the School District asserts that there was sufficient cause to terminate the Grievant.

VI. DISCUSSION AND ANALYSIS

* * * *

It is the seventh element of just cause, the degree of discipline, where the School District's argument is most problematic. The Arbitrator will explore this element in detail to determine if School District established this seventh and final element of just cause.

In determining whether there are mitigating factors which may impact the level of discipline that an employee may receive for violating a work rule or policy, arbitrators often consider the employee's work record, service time, gravity of the offense, and any other special circumstances. Paperworks v. Misco, Inc., 484 U.S. 29, 41 (1987). In this grievance, consideration of all these factors supports the conclusion that the penalty should have been mitigated to something less than termination.

First, the evidence supports that the Grievant's record of performance during her tenure was rated as "good" and in some categories "outstanding". The only negative mark on her performance that is in the record was in 1997, where she received "improvement needed". Not often does the Arbitrator see performance ratings which are consistently good for an extended period of time as in this grievance. Often, arbitrators will reduce penalties based, in part on an employee's extended periods of good performance. Here, the Grievant was employed with the School District for 15 years with good performance evaluations. This clearly should have been a mitigating factor when issuing discipline. The Superintendent testified that he had recommended to the Board that the Grievant receive a suspension, which they rejected. Clearly, the Board has the authority to make the final decision, however, based on the above facts, a suspension would have been more reasonable and in line with the seventh element of the just cause standard.

Secondly, service time which is unblemished with discipline actions and a history of good performance are considered mitigating factors. Here, the Grievant has had 15-years of service with the School District with no evidence of a disciplinary record.

As stated earlier, in determining whether a penalty is reasonable or punitive in nature, arbitrators often will review the gravity or seriousness nature of the offense. *Capital Airlines*, 25 LA 13, 16 (Stowe, 1955). "It is said to be axiomatic that the degree of penalty should be in keeping with the seriousness of the offense. See, Elkouri & Elkouri, How Arbitration Works, 6th ed. pp. 964-966. Here, the Grievant acknowledges that she was involved in an accident involving a school bus that she was driving. However, the seriousness and severity of the accident and the violation of the School District's polices and procedures are questionable.

Typically, arbitrators, give deference to employer's decisions regarding the implementation and enforcement of safety rules, policies and procedures, especially when they appear to be reasonable and related to the safe operation of the business. Without question, the School District has established policies and procedures which are reasonably and directly related to the safe operation of schools buses. A violation of such policies almost always justifies some type of disciplinary action. However, what happened to the Grievant is what the Union correctly describes as "disciplinary overkill," citing *Appleton Paper, Inc.*, 106 LA 11 (Duff 1995). In this grievance, the record clearly shows that there is no correlation to the penalty and the misconduct. Further, a consideration of the mitigating factors as described above would have lessened the penalty from a termination. Based on the School District's failure to consider the compelling mitigating factors in this grievance, the last element of the just cause standard was not established.

VI. CONCLUSION

* * * *

The Arbitrator cannot over emphasize that the safety of students under the supervision of the School District is utmost importance. However, the School District failed to establish that the Grievant's conduct, with consideration of her 15-years of service with the School District, with no disciplinary record, good evaluations, merited termination of her employment. Based on the record, the Arbitrator is reducing the penalty from a termination to a substantial suspension. It is implied in the just case standard that the Arbitrator has authority to modify a disciplinary action where it is determined that the penalty is not reasonable based on mitigating factors.

* * * *

In this grievance, the penalty was clearly not reasonable based upon all the circumstances presented during the hearing. Moreover, the School District barely established elements one and five of the just cause standard.

VII. AWARD

The Grievance is sustained, in part and denied, in part. The Grievant is to be reinstated. The penalty is reduced from a termination to a 30-day suspension. The Grievant is entitled to back pay, less intern earning, and all benefits forfeited from the point of completion of the suspension to her reinstatement. The Arbitrator will retain jurisdiction of this grievance for 30-days for the sole purpose of ensuring the proper implementation of the award.

APPLICATION AND DISCUSSION QUESTIONS

Based on a reading of the above decision, answer the following questions:

1. How does an arbitrator determine whether a disciplinary action is reasonable? What factors are considered? What factors were considered in the above decision?

2. What does the term "disciplinary overkill" mean? How was it applied in the decision?

3. What were the "mitigating factors" that the arbitrator considered in reducing the penalty? How did the arbitrator apply the rule in *Paperwork v. Miso Inc.*, 484 U.S. 29, 41 (1987)?

RECKITT BENCKISER, INC. AND UFCW, DISTRICT UNION LOCAL 2
133 BNA LA 1550 (FITZSIMMONS, 2014)[*]

I. Background

Reckitt Benckiser (hereinafter "Employer") manufactures food products including mustard, hot sauce and barbecue sauce at its facility in Springfield, Missouri. The UFCW, District Union Local 2 (hereinafter "Union") represents approximately 300 bargaining unit members including Grievant, C__. The Employer and Union entered into a Collective Bargaining Agreement (hereinafter "Contract") which was in full force and effect at all relevant times herein. This dispute herein involves Grievant's discharge by the Employer on October 8, 2013. Following that discharge, the Grievant filed the grievance herein.

II. Issue

Was Grievant discharged for just cause? If not, what shall be the remedy?

---

[*]   Reprinted with permission from *Labor Relations Reporter- Labor Arbitration Reports.* 133 BNA LA 1550. Copyright 2015 by the Bureau of National Affairs, Inc. (800-372-1033). http://www.bna.com.

III. Relevant Contract Provisions

ARTICLE III
MANAGEMENT

The Union agrees that the Company shall determine the employees' ability, job skill, competency and other qualifications for the job, and that the management of the plant, the direction of the working forces, including the right to hire, suspend, discharge, promote, demote or transfer or to relieve employees from duty because of lack of work or for other legitimate reasons and to make shop rules for the government of the plant and the right to introduce new production methods or facilities is vested exclusively in the Company, providing, however, that such action by the Company does not conflict with provisions of this agreement.

I. GENERAL RULES AND REGULATIONS
Effective 11/1/89

A. General Regulations. The following are examples of conduct which may result in discipline, up to and including discharge upon the circumstance.
  (2) No articles other than those necessary for the requirements of employment may be brought into the Plant without permission.
  (6) Company premises must be kept clean. No one may cause or contribute to an unsanitary condition.
  (15) Disruptive conduct ... will not be allowed.
  (19) No horseplay will be permitted.

B. In addition to the above, there will be certain cases which may result in immediate discharge. (Partial List Cited)
  (1) Gambling
  (2) The unlawful manufacture, distribution, dispensation, possession or use of a controlled substance in the work place.
  (3) Failure to notify the company within five (5) days of being convicted of a drug statute violation occurring in the work place.
  (4) Possession, consuming or entering the company premises while under the influence of intoxicants.
  (5) Failure to obey the orders of a Supervisor.
  (6) Fighting on Company time or property during or after working hours.

III. GENERAL PLANT SAFETY RULES
Effective 1/1/97

(9) Horseplay will not be tolerated.

IV. Summary Positions of the Parties

A. Employer

That Grievant was discharged for just cause when he brought a live opossum into the Company's cafeteria in violation of the Company's General Rules and Regulations.

B. Union

That Grievant was not discharged for just cause. In the alternative the punishment of discharge was arbitrary and capricious.

V. Summary of the Evidence

Randy Stiles testified he has been employed for six years and presently serves as the Site Manager at the Springfield, Missouri facility. The Employer produces numerous food products including mustard, hot sauce and barbecue sauce at this location. On September 28, 2013 the Employer sponsored an employee appreciation pizza party in the cafeteria during the second shift lunch hour. He was not present at this event. On Monday, September 30, 2013, he learned from Tim Worona and Railene Watson that Grievant brought a live opossum into the cafeteria while employees were eating lunch. He was concerned that this incident could have resulted in an employee being scratched or bitten by the opossum. He was also concerned that the opossum may have brought some type of disease into the facility. The Company is subject to FDA audits and customer external audits because it is a food producer and this incident could have resulted in an adverse finding against the Company.

Stiles instructed Tim Worona, H.R. Manager, to suspend Grievant pending further investigation. Worona investigated the incident and told him that several of the employees were upset about the incident and that Grievant admitted bringing the live opossum into the cafeteria but he did not think it was a "big deal." Worona told him that C__ was attempting to scare fellow employee, Thomas Spoon, with the opossum. On October 8, 2013 he met with Grievant. Grievant apologized and admitted he made a stupid mistake. He determined to terminate Grievant for violating the Employer's Rules and Regulations. He admitted that no one was injured and no disease was introduced into Company facilities as a result of the incident. Nothing extraordinary was done to clean the cafeteria. The opossum did not leave any residue of any kind on the premises.

Jason Salchow, DVM, testified he is a veterinarian who works with large animals in his medical practice. His primary involvement with animals such as raccoons and opossums is to prevent them from contaminating stored feed supply in the cattle and dairy industries. He explained that an opossum can injure a person by a scratch or bite that may cause an infection or bacterial disease. The opossum can cause bacterial disease by its salivary glands or through its feces or urine.

Chad Edelen testified he has been employed for eight months as the H.R. Manager. When he returned from out of town to the Springfield facility on September 30, 2013 Randy Stiles told him about Grievant's incident with the live opossum. He also met with Tim Worona who told him about his meeting with Grievant. He met with Grievant who told him that he caught the opossum and brought it into the cafeteria to scare his friend, Thomas Spoon. Edelen felt this was a clear violation of Company Rules and Regulations. The intentional introduction of wild animals such as the opossum violates multiple provisions of the Missouri Food Code and violates FDA guidelines for food producers. Bringing a live animal into the Company's facility risked contamination and transmission of disease. He, Worona and Stiles met and agreed to terminate Grievant effective October 8, 2013. He admitted that Grievant made a sincere apology to the Company. He also admitted he told Grievant that he probably would make a "great employee" for someone else. Grievant has been employed for three years and has never been disciplined.

* * * *

Grievant testified he has been employed by the Company for three years and works in the warehouse. He works the second shift which works four ten hour days weekly. On September 28, 2013 he was on lunch break during the Company's employee appreciation pizza event. Supervisor Mark Vinyard told him that there was a live opossum outside the cafeteria in the smoking shack. He picked up the opossum by the tail and decided to take it into the cafeteria to scare his friend, Thomas Spoon. He entered the cafeteria and took a step or two towards Spoon and held the opossum three to four feet from Spoon. Spoon reacted by jumping up and moving to the end of his table.

Grievant has handled opossums in this manner on many occasions at his farm in Ava, Missouri. He did not intend to harm anyone and only intended to upset Spoon. He finished his shift and went home. He returned to work on September 30,

2013 and Tim Worona asked him to meet with him to discuss the incident. After he told Worona what occurred, Worona told him he was suspended pending further investigation. On October 8, 2013 he met with Stiles, Edelen and Worona and apologized for his behavior. He told them he made a "stupid" decision and he knew it was wrong, Edelen advised him he was terminated for violation of Company Rules and Regulations. Grievant had never been disciplined in the three years he worked for the Company.

VI. Discussion and Decision

Since this is a discharge case the burden is upon the Employer to prove it had sufficient cause to terminate Grievant's employment. Discharge is the most extreme industrial penalty since the Grievant's job, seniority and other benefits under the Contract are at stake. When applying the principle of just cause to justify the termination of an employee, there are two situations for the Arbitrator to examine. The first is an offense that is the final step in the progressive discipline process. The second is a single incident of very serious misconduct. Midwest Coca-Cola Bottling Co., 94-1 ARB (1993). In the present case, the Arbitrator must decide two issues. First, is the Grievant guilty of the misconduct charged? Second, was the penalty of discharge reasonable under all the circumstances herein?

* * * *

The Company forcefully argues that Grievant's offense merits summary discharge because Grievant's conduct exposed his fellow employees to the risk of bodily harm and disease. The Company further argues that Grievant's intentional conduct was a violation of the Missouri Food Code and the incident could have resulted in a citation from the State of Missouri as well as adverse publicity if the incident became public.

The Company has the right under its Management Rights Clause to manage the work force which includes the right to establish reasonable rules and regulations to enforce employee conduct. The management right to discharge its employees for misconduct is limited to those situations where it has "just cause" to discharge an employee. The principle of just cause when the Company discharges an employee for a single offense requires the arbitrator to examine the entire situation to determine whether the penalty of discharge is reasonable under all the facts of the case. If the arbitrator determines that the punishment is excessive or disproportionate to the facts of the case he may set aside the discharge and reduce the punishment.

The Company utilizes progressive discipline in managing the work force. Progressive discipline is a system of addressing employee behavior over time through escalating penalties. The purpose of progressive discipline is to correct the unacceptable behavior of the employee. The penalty of discharge is reserved for very serious incidents of misconduct and for repeated misconduct. The concept of progressive discipline is based on the idea that both the Company and the employee benefit when an employee can be rehabilitated and retained as a productive member of the work force. Since Grievant was never disciplined during his three years with the Company I must determine if this single incident with the opossum was such a serious offense that it justified discharge.

...There was apparently a feeling of good natured high spirits at the lunch. Grievant took the high spirits of the pizza party too far when he brought the opossum into the lunch room to frighten his friend Thomas Spoon. The Company rightly argues that certain things could have happened but, in fact, nothing happened. No employee was bitten, scratched or became ill. The Company was not required to perform any extraordinary cleaning of the lunch room. There is no evidence that the opossum urinated, defecated or excreted any substance. In fact, the entire incident was brief and lasted less than one minute.

The Company established "General Rules and Regulations" as examples of conduct for which an employee would be subject to discipline. These offenses are minor in nature and include such conduct as: "General Regulations: no parking in restricted areas; notify company of change of address; no soliciting in the plant and other less serious examples of misconduct. Certainly Grievant is guilty of: (15) "Disruptive conduct ... will not be allowed"; and (19) "No horseplay will be permitted." The General Rules and Regulations continue as follows: "B. In addition to the above, there will be certain cases which may result in immediate discharge". In reviewing these examples wherein the Company may decide to immediately discharge an employee there are certain examples included: gambling, distributing controlled substances in the work place; fighting; stealing; punching another employee's; time card; working while intoxicated; and destruction of Company property.

* * * *

I find that the discharge of Grievant was an excessive penalty herein. Grievant was clearly wrong in bringing the opossum into the lunchroom. Although the Company's evidence speculated as to all the adverse events which could have occurred, in fact nothing occurred. Grievant brought the opossum into the lunchroom for less than one minute. Grievant did not chase anyone nor did he release the opossum. I further find that the Company ignored mitigating circumstances when it discharged Grievant. First, Grievant has been described as a good worker by Company and Union witnesses. Chad Edelen, the Company's H.R. Manager, told Grievant he would make someone else "a great employee." Second, Grievant has never been disciplined in the three years he has been employed by the Company.

AWARD

The grievance filed herein is sustained. Grievant's discharge is set aside. The discharge is reduced to a ten work day suspension without pay. The Employer is ordered to make Grievant whole less the ten work day suspension without pay.

I will retain jurisdiction for ninety days in the event there is any dispute in the enforcement of this Award.

APPLICATION AND DISCUSSION QUESTIONS

1. The Employer cites *Midwest Coca-Cola Bottling Co.*, 94-1 ARB (1993) for the proposition that a "single" incident of very serious misconduct can result in the employee being terminated. Is the conduct in this grievance serious enough to justify the termination of the Grievant?

2. Is a ten-day suspension unreasonable for the horseplay incident? Was the incident no "big deal" as the Grievant states? The Grievant has never been disciplined in the three years he worked for the Company. Would a verbal warning have been more appropriate, since he apologized and no one was harmed?

3. Do you agree with the Arbitrator that the discharge was an "excessive penalty"?

Summary of Decision

On February 15 of this year, R hit his then-fiancée, P, in the elevator of an Atlantic City hotel and casino. She hit her head on the rail and fell unconscious to the floor. A surveillance camera captured R dragging her unconscious out of the elevator. R was indicted for felony assault under circumstances evidencing indifference to the value of human life. The criminal proceeding, however, ended with a court ordered pre-trial intervention, an agreement that the case would be dismissed after one year if R satisfactorily completed an anger management course, attended counseling and committed no further crimes.

Thereafter, on June 16, R met with NFL Commissioner Roger Goodell for a pre-discipline meeting. At that meeting, R told the Commissioner that he had hit Mrs. R in the elevator. The NFL knew of the indictment and the results of the criminal proceeding. They had seen the video of R's conduct outside the elevator. They had gathered comparator cases of disciplines given for previous violations of the Personal Conduct Policy based on acts of domestic violence. They believed that there was a second video from a camera inside the elevator. Various sources, including NFL security, had reported its existence. R had received this video in discovery during his criminal case, but it had not been aired publicly, as had the first video. The NFL never asked R for the second video. Approximately one month after the meeting with R, Commissioner Goodell issued a two-game suspension with an additional fine of one week's salary. A firestorm of public criticism followed. In its wake, the Commissioner admitted that he "didn't get it right," and shortly thereafter increased the presumptive penalty for domestic violence for a first-time offender to six-games. Notably, after announcing this increased penalty under the Policy, the Commissioner called R to assure him that the new policy would not affect him-that it was forward looking and his penalty would not be increased.

Then, on September 8, a video from the camera inside the elevator was aired publicly. It captured R hitting Mrs. Rand her hitting her head on the elevator railing and falling to the floor unconscious. It also shows R trying to pick her up and, apparently unable to do so, dropping her, as the elevator doors begin to open. That

---

[*] Reprinted with permission from *Labor Relations Reporter- Labor Arbitration Reports.* 134 BNA LA 61. Copyright 2015 by the Bureau of National Affairs, Inc. (800-372-1033). http://www.bna.com.

same day, alongside a furor of public outcry over the second video, the Commissioner suspended R indefinitely. The NFL justified this increased penalty solely on the basis that the second video was new evidence that showed a "starkly different sequence of events" of what happened in the elevator than what R had said at the June 16 meeting. In this arbitration, the NFL argues that Commissioner Goodell was misled when he disciplined R the first time. Because, after careful consideration of all of the evidence, I am not persuaded that R lied to, or misled, the NFL at his June interview, I find that the indefinite suspension was an abuse of discretion and must be vacated.

* * * *

Applicable Legal Standards

While the parties strongly dispute what standards apply in reviewing determinations of League discipline under Article 46 of the NFL-NFLPA collective bargaining agreement, the legal standards are not outcome determinative in this case, which turns on the facts. Nonetheless, I am persuaded that Article 46 does not contain a just cause provision, either explicit or implied. Where a collective bargaining agreement is silent on just cause, arbitrators often find that such a provision is implied. See *In re J & J Maintenance Inc.* The CBA between the NFL and the NFLPA, however, is not silent on the matter; it explicitly includes just cause in the Club discipline provisions of Article 43. This inclusion demonstrates that the parties knew how to include such a provision when it was bargained for, bolstering the conclusion that it should not be read into Article 46.

Even accepting that Article 46 does not contain a just cause provision and thus is not subject to the attendant standards of industrial due process, such as "double discipline" and "disparate treatment," discipline under the Article must be fair and consistent. The NFL does not dispute this proposition. For me, this means that discipline determinations under Article 46 should be reviewed to determine whether the Commissioner abused his discretion, that is, whether his determination was arbitrary or capricious. Where the imposition of discipline is not fair or consistent, an abuse of discretion has occurred.

The lack of a just cause provision also implicates where the burden of proof lies in appeals of League discipline. Without a just cause standard, the burden of proof lies upon the party challenging the discipline. That is to say, the disciplined employee, which in most instances operates through his certified collective bargaining representative, here, the NFLPA, has the burden of showing that the discipline was arbitrary or capricious.

Discussion

The sole issue in this matter is whether what R told the Commissioner and other League representatives about the assault at their June 16, 2014 meeting was "a starkly different sequence of events" than what was captured on the "inside-the-elevator" video. It was not. In so holding, I find that the NFLPA has carried its burden of demonstrating that R did not mislead the Commissioner at the June 16 meeting and, therefore, that the imposition of a second suspension based upon the same incident, and the same known facts about that incident, was arbitrary.

* * * *

AWARD

Under Article 46, the Commissioner is entitled to great deference in the review of his decisions, but review for abuse of discretion is not a rubber stamp approval. In numerous cases reviewing discipline under Article 46, the hearing officer has decreased the discipline that the Commissioner imposed. An abuse of discretion can be found where the decision maker has acted in an "arbitrary or capricious manner." Because R did not mislead the Commissioner and because there were no new facts on which the Commissioner could base his increased suspension, I find that the imposition of the indefinite suspension was arbitrary. I therefore vacate the second penalty imposed on R__. The provisions of the first discipline-those regarding making continued use of counseling and other professional services, having no further involvement with law enforcement, and not committing any additional violations of League policies-still stand.

APPLICATION AND DISCUSSION QUESTIONS

1. If the just cause provision is omitted from the CBA how do arbitrators analyze such cases? *See, In re J & J Maintenance, Inc.*, 121 BNA LA 847. In this case, how did the arbitrator reach the conclusion that Article 46 did not contain a just cause provision, either explicitly or implied?

2. Why did the arbitrator place the burden on the NFLPA to prove the discipline was arbitrary or capricious? Should the burden have been on the NFLPA?

3. Do you agree with the arbitrator that the indefinite suspension was arbitrary? How did the arbitrator reach this decision?

CITY OF BROOKLYN AND MUNICIPAL FOREMEN AND LABORERS' UNION, LOCAL 1099

134 LA 1066 (J. FULLMER, 2015)[*]

I. Facts

A. Background Facts

The Employer provides the requisite municipal services to the citizens of Brooklyn, Ohio. The Union represents a unit of hourly rated employees in the Service Department and the Recreation Department. One of the classifications inluded is that of Assistant Manager. Up until the events of this case that classification was occupied by the Grievant. The Grievant had worked for the Employer for approximately 23 years and three months. The first 22 years were served in the Employer's Garage. On January 1, 2013 the Grievant was promoted to the position of Acting Assistant Manager and thence to full-fledged Assistant Manager on March 17, 2014. His duties were described as supervising the full time and part time employees in the performance of their cleaning and operational duties at the Ice Rink. The part time employees for the most part are young adults who are otherwise engaged in high school and college studies. One of the part-time employees is Anthony Meehan. He is the son of a Caucasian mother and a African-American father.

The Employer maintains a set of Disciplinary Procedures. The offenses are grouped in the somewhat familiar categories of Group I, II, and III. They are preceded by a group of general misconduct offenses. Group I offenses are the less serious and provide for a five step progression of "Instruction and Cautioning" through "Removal". The Group II offenses are of medium seriousness and provide for a three step progression of "Verbal Instruction" through "Removal". The Group III offenses are the utmost seriousness and provide for "Removal for the first offense.

Among the "general misconduct" offenses are:

---

[*] Reprinted with permission from *Labor Relations Reporter- Labor Arbitration Reports*. 134 LA 1066. Copyright 2015 by the Bureau of National Affairs, Inc. (800-372-1033). http://www.bna.com.

"1. Incompetency"

Among the Group III offenses are:

    25. Willfully demeaning, verbally abusing, and/or humiliating a citizen, employee,
        or other person."

    26. Committing an act of discrimination, sexual harassment, or engaging in conduct
        giving insult or offense on the basis of race, color, sex, age, religion, national
        origin, or disability."

As of the date of the offenses claimed in this case, the Grievant did not have any "live" discipline in his file, or at least none that the Employer was relying upon as the basis for the discipline.

B. Facts Leading to the Grievance

On Monday, March 17, 2014 Anthony Meehan, the previously cited part-time employee, came into the office of Director of Public Service John Verba with his aunt and told him that the Grievant had made several racially charged comments with respect to him. As recorded in Director Verba's contemporaneous memorandum these comments were described by Mr. Meehan in the following terms:

> "Tony claimed that when he jumped over the bleachers during the district hockey
> game at the Recreation Center that P__ said, 'I forgot you are half monkey and do stuff
> like that'".

> "One time Tony made a comment about girls liking him and P__ made a comment that
> the only reason that they like him is that he is half black and has a big dick."

> "On March 11, Tony was painting upstairs in the community room and dropped some
> white paint. P__ made a reference to the fact that he was trying to be white".

(These are referred to subsequently as the "monkey", the "big dick" and "white paint" incidents.)

The matter was thence investigated and the purported witnesses interviewed. The investigation included an interview with the Grievant on March 25, 2014. With respect to the three "incidents", the Grievant's explanation was as follows:

"Monkey" Incident - "... he remembers the incident but did not think that he used the term 'monkey'. He believes that he said that he was able to jump over the bleachers because he is half black."

"Big Dick" Incident - "P__ stated that he never used the word 'dick', but stated that they like him because he is half black."

"White Paint" Incident - P__ admitted to saying something to that effect; however, he thought that it was taken as a joke and he didn't intend on offending anyone.

The Grievant was sent a "Notification of potential disciplinary action" on March 28, 2014. It specified a pre-disciplinary hearing for Wednesday, April 2, 2014. In the wake of that hearing more interviews were held.

Eventually the Employer made the decision to terminate the Grievant, effective April 11, 2014. The letter was over the signature of Mayor Balbier and stated in relevant portion that:

"After carefully investigating this matter and considering your oral response on April 2, 2014 at the pre-disciplinary hearing the city has decided that it is appropriate to proceed with the action of terminating you from your employment. This termination is for cause and is effective April 11, 2014....The City finds that the allegations of policy violations are substantiated. By your actions you have violated 9.4(E)(25), titled 'Wilfully demeaning, verbally abusing, and/or humiliating a citizen, employee, or other person,' which is considered a Group KIIKI Offense; Section 9.4 (E)(26), titled "Committing an act of discrimination, sexual harassment, or engaging in conduct giving insult or offense on the basis of race, color, sex, age, religion, national origin or disability,' which is considered a Group III Offense. Lastly, you are charged with violating Section 9.4(A) (1), titled 'Incompetency,' which is a general category of misconduct. The facts leading up to your termination are as follows. On March 17, 2014, it was brought to our attention that an employee that you directly manage made a complaint alleging that you have made racial and unprofessional remarks to him over the last several months. The Service Director investigated this issue and substantiated the complaint through other employees who heard several racial remarks. On March 25, 2014, you were interviewed and although you did not agree with the exact alleged phrases, you admitted using racial remarks toward a subordinate employee. The City cannot tolerate this behavior from a part of its management team. Your behavior has subjected the City to liability and we feel that due to your actions we have no choice as to terminate you from employment."

On April 14, 2014 the grievance at issue was filed. It stated that:

> "I AM GRIEVING THE ACTIONS TAKEN BY THE CITY AS FAR AS TERMINATION
> FROM THE CITY. I FEEL THAT FROM MY WORK PERFORMED OVER THE
> PAST 23 YEARS OF EMPLOYMENT WITHOUT ANY DISCIPLINARY ACTIONS
> IN MY RECORDS THAT THIS PUNISHMENT WAS SEVERE AND UNFOUNDED.
> I DID NOT IN ANY WAY DEMEAN NOR WAS I VERBALLY OFFENSIVE IN TONE
> TO THE ACCUSATIONS IN QUESTION. I DID ADMIT TO SAYING SOME OF
> THE ACCUSATIONS BUT NOT EXACTLY IN THE WORDS DESCRIBED IN THE
> COMPLAINT. I BELIEVE THE WORDS WERE TAKEN OUT OF CONTEXT BY
> THE EMPLOYEE WHEN THEY WERE SAID IN A JOKING MANNER AND WAS
> NEVER APPROACHED BY THIS EMPLOYEE AS TO HIM TAKING OFFENSE TO MY
> REMARKS. IN FACT ALL WAS DONE WITH HIM LAUGHING AND COMMENTING
> FROM HIM BACK TO ME IN A JOKING MANNER. WHEN I WAS GIVEN THE
> POSITION I WAS NEVER FORMALLY TRAINED IN HANDLING THIS POSITION.
> I AM ASKING THAT I BE REINSTATED WITH A DEMOTION AND SUSPENSION
> AND WOULD BE WILLING TO GO TO ANY CLASSES DEEMED NECESSARY AND
> WOULD WRITE A LETTER OF APOLOGY TO THE EMPLOYEE AND HIS FAMILY."
> (Capitalization from original).

The grievance was then processed through the steps of the grievance procedure to arbitration.

Potentially Applicable Contract Provision

ARTICLE 25
DISCIPLINE

Section 1. Discipline is defined as any verbal or written warning, suspension, discharge or demotion for just cause....

Stipulated Issue

Was the termination of the Grievant, P__, on April 11, 2014 for just cause? If not, what shall be the remedy?

Positions of the Parties

The Employer Position

The Employer maintains that the Grievant committed violations of the parties' agreement and the Policy Manual when he made three racial and insulting remarks to a teenaged part-time employee. The Employer properly investigated the matter and rightfully chose to terminate the Grievant.

* * * *

The Union Position

The Employer bears the burden of establishing that there was just cause for the Grievant's termination. City of N. Royalton v. Urich. Just cause is a significant concept and should be accorded more than lip service. The discipline must be fair and just under the circumstances.

Here the Employer failed to discipline the Grievant within the 5-day period after it learned of the alleged misconduct. See Art. 25, Sec. 1. Such matters have been considered as serious by other arbitrators. There was a clear violation of the provision and the Employer offered no contractual reason to justify the violation.

Beyond this, the Employer failed to establish cause to abandon the contractual progressive discipline system and simply, at first blush, terminate the Grievant's employment. Reference is had to Article 25, Section 4. The Grievant had an indisputable, clean disciplinary record during the contractual look-back period. He had not even progressed to the verbal warning stage. The Grievant's offense, if there was one, was nowhere near the magnitude of the offenses marked out for first offense terminations.

Beyond this there were a plethora of due process violations. The Employer failed to conduct a full and fair investigation of the alleged misconduct. See Goodyear Tire & Rubber Co. The Mayor failed to hear the Grievant before terminating him. The Employer also failed to consider a number of mitigating factors, primary amongst which is the Grievant's unblemished 24 years of service, along with his age, his likelihood of finding alternative employment, his attitude and his expressed remorse.

The arbitrator should sustain the grievance in full and order his reinstatement and make him whole.

Discussion

A. Introduction

The present case is a termination case in which the Grievant was terminated on April 11, 2014 on the basis of several racial remarks he is claimed to have made in March, 2014.

Several aspects of the matter are not in dispute. One is that the Employer has the burden of proof of establishing that the facts exist which indicate that the Grievant's termination was for just cause. A second is that the Employer is proceeding on an "industrial capital punishment basis. In other words it is relying on the current offenses as justifying a termination for the first offense rather than relying on any prior disciplinary offenses. A third is that the "incidents" did in fact take place. A fourth is that the Grievant is conceded to have committed some offense in that the requested remedy, at least at the hearing, was "reinstatement with a long suspension."

What is in dispute are essentially four elements. One is the nuances of the three incidents in question. The second is the extent of the Employer's investigation and whether it meets the standards of just cause. The third is whether the discipline was late under the requirements of Article 25, Section 1. The fourth is whether termination is an appropriate penalty. We turn to these in the order stated.

B. The Nuances of the Grievant's Conduct in the Incidents In Question.
(Omitted)

* * * *

We turn to an overall conclusion on this aspect. Based on the analysis of the evidence set out in the preceding paragraphs it can safely be concluded that the Grievant's remarks in all three of the incidents constituted violations of Rules III 25 and 26. In fact even the Union concedes that such violations existed by only asking at the hearing only that the Grievant be "reinstated after a long suspension".

C. The Investigation. (Omitted)

E. The Appropriateness of the Termination Penalty.

It is usually held that arbitrators are not to substitute their judgment for that of the employer with respect to the severity of disciplinary penalties. Stockham Pipe Fittings Co. 1 LA 160, 162 (McCoy, Arb. 1945).

* * * *

Here there would be no question that the arbitrator would apply this rule were the sole issue that of reinstating the Grievant to his former position as Manager of the Ice Rink. His revealed that he was, and is likely to remain, unsuitable to perform the supervision of the volatile part time work force at the Ice Rink. It is a matter which would justify termination rather than progressive discipline.

But, the unique aspect of this case is that the positions which the Grievant successively occupied at the Ice Rink were management positions. The Grievant's performance as a manager was not up to scratch. Usually industrial "capital punishment" is reserved for those employees who are beyond rehabilitation and who cannot be expected to perform successfully in the workplace. Here the Grievant apparently performed successfully in non-supervisory functions in the Garage for 22 years. There is no record of disciplinary offenses incurred there even though there are presumably minority employees among that work force. Twenty-two years is a long time and there seems to be no reason to expect that the Grievant would fail there if he is returned to a position in the Garage. Accordingly the grievance is going to be granted on the limited basis of providing that the Grievant be offered the next job in the garage that becomes open which involves either no or limited conduct with the public and no supervision of fellow employees. No back pay is provided for.

Conclusion

As set out above, this is a termination case involving the termination of the Grievant, P__, on April 11, 2014 on the basis of several comments he made in March of 2014 to one of the employees he supervised. It is found that the Grievant made the comments charged against him and that they constituted violations of Rules III 25 and 26. The claimed errors concerning the Employer's investigation are held to be not decisive. Nevertheless, the termination penalty is held to be too severe under the circumstances for the reasons set out above.

To the extent that it may not be otherwise clear, the issue, i.e. concerning the merits is answered in the negative, i.e. the termination of the Grievant, P__, on April

11, 2014 was not for just cause. The award draws its essence from the arbitrator's interpretation of Articles 3 and 25 of the parties' agreement and from the terms of the stipulated issue itself.

AWARD

Grievance denied in part and sustained in part.

The Grievant is to be regarded as suspended without pay for the period of April 11, 2014 until he accepts or declines an offer of reinstatement to the next bargaining unit job in the Employer's Garage which becomes open. Should he decline the offer his employment is to be regarded as severed? If he accepts his reinstatement is to be with full seniority dating from his original hire, but not back pay.

APPLICATION AND DISCUSSION QUESTIONS

1. How does the arbitrator define "industrial capital punishment?" Do you agree with the arbitrator's applications of this principle to the facts of this case?

2. What factors did the Arbitrator identify in this case to mitigate the penalty? Was the termination too severe?

3. The arbitrator considered the type of position the Grievant held: supervisor v. non-supervisor in determing the appropriate penalty. Should this have been a distinction in determining the penalty?

GREATER CLEVELAND REG'L TRANSIT AUTH. AND AMALGAMATED TRANSIT UNION, LOCAL 268

135 BNA LA 688 (WEATHERSPOON, 2015)

I. Statement of Facts

The facts indicate that the Amalgamated Transit Union, Local 268 (hereinafter Union) and the Greater Cleveland Regional Transit Authority (hereinafter RTA), are parties to a collective bargaining agreement (CBA or Contract) for the period of August 1, 2011 through July 31, 2014.

The Grievant, B__ (hereinafter the Grievant) held the position of Full-Time Bus Operator. The Grievant began working for RTA on January 3, 1997. He was officially notified of his termination by letter dated August 28, 2014. The letter identified the offense as "... violation of the GCRTA Substance Abuse Policy for Safety Sensitive Employees ... as it relates to Prescription Disclosure." The Grievant had been employed by RTA for approximately 18 years.

The record indicates that on August 12, 2014, the Grievant was driving a RTA bus when he was involved in an accident. As a result of this incident, in accordance with RTA's policy, the Grievant was subjected to a drug and alcohol test. He tested positive for codeine. Operating a bus is a "safety sensitive" position and RTA has a zero tolerance policy regarding testing positive for drugs, to include prescription drugs, unless the employee brings in a doctor's note to inform his or her supervisor that he (or she) is taking a prescription. The Grievant did not inform his supervisor prior to the incident, therefore, RTA decided to discharge the Grievant from employment. The Grievant did not have a prior disciplinary record. Notwithstanding, RTA considered a violation of its substance abuse policy as a serious offense warranting termination because of the safety risk involved in driving a bus.

The Union does not dispute that the Grievant damaged the bus during an accident; that he had been under a prescription for cough syrup containing codeine; and that he did not report that he was taking codeine for a cough to his supervisor until after the accident. Nevertheless, the Union believes that the penalty was too severe in light of the Grievant's prior unblemished record and that he had stopped taking the medicine four days previous to the accident.

The parties were unable to satisfactorily resolve the grievance, therefore, in accordance with the CBA, it was appealed to arbitration. The parties stipulated that the grievance is properly before the arbitrator and there are no arbitrability issues.

II. Issue

Was the Grievant terminated for just cause? If not, what is the appropriate remedy?

III. Relevant Contract Provisions and Work Rules

Contract Provisions: (Sections Omitted)

11.5 Disciplinary Consequences for Prescription Drugs:
  b) When an employee tests positive for a prescription drug which may affect his/
  her ability to perform the employee's job duties, s/he will be discharged unless the
  employee has provided the supervisor with notification from the employee's doctor of
  the use of a prescription drug and an indication of the employee's ability to perform
  his/her job duties without impairment. When the employee's job duties would be
  impaired, the physician must indicate the duration of impairment ... Please be advised
  there is a Prescription Drug Disclosure Form that a physician may complete and is
  located on the GCRTA Intranet ...

Important Prescription Drug Disclosure Notice

If you do not have proper medical documentation on file that you may perform your
safety sensitive duties without impairment while on a prescription drug and you test
positive on a drug test because of the prescription medication; you will be discharged
...

IV. Position of the Parties

A. RTA's Position

RTA terminated the Grievant for testing positive for a prescription drug and not for
providing advance notice to his supervisor that he was at work and operating a bus
while on medication that could impair his ability to perform his job. RTA has a zero
tolerance policy concerning this matter because as a bus operator, the Grievant held a
"safety sensitive" position. Safety is a top priority of the RTA. It is RTA's position that
"When employees violate the substance abuse policies, they put the public in danger."

According to RTA, on August 12, 2014, the Grievant was operating a bus when he
hit a tree branch, causing the mirror to unhinge, thus striking and breaking the door
bus. It is RTA's policy that when an accident occurs, the Grievant should be tested for

drugs and alcohol; he tested positive for codeine. RTA contends that it is undisputed that "... the Grievant did not provide notice of the prescription medication to his supervisor in advance of reporting to work".

B. Union's Position

It is the Union's position that there was not just cause to terminate the Grievant. The Union proffered the following:

> The Grievant acknowledged the awareness of the policy requirement, but due to the fact that the medication was cough syrup, it did not occur to him to provide notice to the supervisor. He began taking the medication not even considering the codeine content. Per the instructions of the doctor, he only was to take the medication at night before going to bed, which he did. He was not prohibited from driving while taking the medication so long as he took the medication at night.

> The Grievant complied with the instructions given. More importantly, the Grievant stopped taking the medication 4 days prior to the accident. He was not taking the medication at the time of the accident, August the 12th, 2014.

The Union also argues that because the policy provides that post-accident testing should occur when a bus "... receives disabling damage ..." and that a broken mirror is not "disabling damage"; that post-accident testing should not have occurred for a "minor accident". The Union stated that post-accident testing was not justified. Moreover, the Union proffers that because the Grievant took the medication at night, he was functionally capable of operating the bus during the next morning.

In light thereof and in consideration of the Grievant's 18 year employment history without any prior disciplinary actions; the Union advocates that the Grievant was terminated without just cause and that the penalty was too severe.

V. Discussion and Analysis

In analyzing this case, it is not in dispute that the Grievant violated RTA's substance abuse policy when he was under prescribed medication for codeine and failed to report that he was taking the medicine to his supervisor. What the Union argues is that because he was taking the medicine only at night and had ceased taking it four days prior to the accident; is that he was not impaired and thus did not present a safety risk on the day of the accident. Notwithstanding, he had to report to work at

5 a.m. and he did test positive when tested. The evidence is clear therefore, that the Grievant violated work rule 11.5 and that the Grievant engaged in the misconduct.

* * * *

In light of the above, the only element remaining in the just cause analysis is whether the degree of discipline was reasonably related to the nature of the offense and the Grievant's past record. The Arbitrator must determine whether the penalty of termination was reasonable and not punitive in nature. In determining the reasonableness of a penalty, that the Arbitrator may consider mitigating factors in determining where the penalty is too severe.

Penalty

In determining whether there are mitigating factors which may impact the level of discipline that an employee may receive for violating a work rule or policy, arbitrators often consider the employee's work record, service time, gravity of the offense and any other special circumstances. Just cause also requires an employer to consider aggravating and mitigating circumstances. RTA maintains that the Grievant's violation of its substance abuse policy is by itself serious enough to warrant termination in light of the safety risk.

When considering mitigating factors, the Arbitrator acknowledges that it is not the Arbitrator's job to substitute his judgment for that of the RTA in determining what constitutes a terminable offense. RTA's work rules and disciplinary policy clearly indicate that a violation of its substance abuse policy is a terminable offense. The Arbitrator recognizes that the RTA takes this matter seriously because of the safety risk to the public in allowing a bus operator to drive while under any type of impairment. Without doubt, the Grievant's offense merits a disciplinary action; but it must be reasonable in light of the offense and not punitive in nature. As stated earlier, the punishment for the infraction should not be arbitrary, capricious or discriminatory. Although it is not within the Arbitrator's discretion to substitute his judgment for RTA's without sufficient evidence of mitigating circumstances; we must still examine whether there were mitigating factors present which impacts the level of discipline.

* * * *

The Arbitrator must acknowledge that having heard numerous grievances involving terminations for misconduct; the mitigating factors in this grievance ... are directly on point. If there is a case where the evidence supports the application of mitigating factors..., it is this grievance.

The Union places major emphasis on the fact that the Grievant had not received any prior discipline in his 18 year employment with RTA. The Union believes that these facts should serve as critical mitigating factors.

* * * *

This Arbitrator finds the Grievant's unblemished service record of 18 years is a compelling factor sufficient to mitigate the penalty of termination. RTA could have enforced its zero tolerance safety and substance abuse policy by still disciplining the Grievant, but imposing a less severe penalty. It is clear that in the present case that RTA did not consider the mitigating circumstances of the Grievant's otherwise satisfactory record and lack of prior disciplinary actions. In light thereof, the ultimate penalty of termination was unreasonable.

This Arbitrator reached a similar decision in 2008 AAA LEXIS 876, AAA (2008), where a school bus operator with 15 years of good service was terminated for a minor safety violation. In that decision, the Arbitrator stated:

> Typically, arbitrators, give deference to employer's decisions regarding the implementation and enforcement of safety rules, policies and procedures, especially when they appear to be reasonable and related to the safe operation of the business. Without question, the School District has established policies and procedures which are reasonably and directly related to the safe operation of schools buses. A violation of such policies almost always justifies some type of disciplinary action. However, what happened to the Grievant is what the Union correctly describes as "disciplinary overkill," citing *Appleton Paper, Inc.*, 106 LA 11 (Duff 1995).

Similar to my earlier award, the termination of the Grievant in the present case could be described as "disciplinary overkill" for violating work rule 11.5. There is no correlation to the penalty and the misconduct. Without some indication there is a relationship to the seriousness of the misconduct and the penalty; the penalty would be considered arbitrary, thus a violation of the just cause standard. Moreover, a failure to consider mitigating factors which have a direct correlation on the appropriate discipline to be issued, violates the reasonableness element of the just cause standard.

*　*　*　*

The Arbitrator has thoroughly considered whether the decision exceeds his authority to modify the penalty. The Arbitrator recognizes that work rule 11.5 specifically states that failure to provide medical documentation that an employee is taking a prescription drug will result in a termination. The language is clear and unambiguous. However, Article 12 includes a just cause provision which cannot be ignored. Here is where the ambiguity exists. The work rule permits RTA to almost automatically terminate an employee for a violation of the rule, but also includes the just cause standard. The Arbitrator's interpretation of work rule 11.5 is based on Article 12. This interpretation does not modify or change the CBA. Indeed, the Arbitrator "draws the essence" of the decision from the just cause provision of the CBA.

This Arbitrator follows the principle that many arbitrators and some courts follow, that where there is no language in the CBA that clearly and unambiguously limits the Arbitrator's authority to apply the just cause standard; the arbitrator has the authority to determine whether a penalty is reasonable. In this grievance, the penalty of termination of a long-term employee without a consideration of whether the penalty is too severe is arbitrary and in violation of the just cause standard.

The Arbitrator cannot over emphasize that he understands RTA's position on safety, especially bus operators. But under the CBA, RTA cannot ignore the just cause provision when terminating employees for violating safety work rules. Here, it was not reasonable to terminate the Grievant for violating work rule 11.5.

VI. Conclusion

In this grievance, RTA has not supported that the ultimate penalty of termination was reasonable under the circumstances. Mitigating factors warrants modification of the penalty.

VII. AWARD

Based on the evidence presented by the parties and the CBA, the grievance is sustained, in part. Recognizing RTA's right to impose discipline for cause; I find that RTA was justified in disciplining the Grievant for not following its policy of reporting that he was taking a prescription drug. However, a thirty day suspension would be more reasonable in light of the mitigating factors. Therefore, RTA is ordered to modify the termination to a thirty day suspension and to reinstate the Grievant with back pay (base salary only), less interim wages. The Grievant is to be credited for all leave and his seniority. The Grievant is required to complete any requirements normally required of bus operators who are returning from an extended leave.

APPLICATION AND DISCUSSION QUESTIONS

1. How did the arbitrator have authority to modify the penalty when the first offense was for violating Workrule 11.5?

2. Is this a case where the arbitrator dispensed his own brand of justice, which the Courts have stated that the arbitrator lacks authority to do so?

3. What are the mitigating facts the arbitrator considered in modifying the penalty?

C. PROGRESSIVE DISCIPLINE AND LAST CHANCE AGREEMENTS

Arbitrators normally take the position that discipline should be corrective and not punitive in nature. Consequently, if the collective bargaining agreement has a progressive disciplinary provision, arbitrators will closely review this provision to determine whether the grievant should have received a lesser penalty; not termination. This will entail a review of the grievant's past disciplinary record. If the grievant's conduct is serious, violates safety policy, and/or is willful, the progressive disciplinary provision may not be applicable. The grievant's conduct may warrant immediate termination.

Employers may also agree to give an employee one last chance to enhance their performance before being permanently terminated. Employers agree to such agreements if they believe the employee can be rehabilitated. Normally the agreement limits the arbitrator's ability to determine a violation of the last chance agreement. Often, that becomes an issue for the arbitrator to initially decide; whether the arbitrator has jurisdiction.

LAST CHANCE AGREEMENTS: HOW MANY CHANCES
IS AN EMPLOYEE ENTITLED TO,

2005 J. DISP. RESOL. 467 (2005)[*]

KATHLEEN BIRKHOFER

Continental Airlines, Inc. v. International Brotherhood of Teamsters

I. INTRODUCTION (Omitted)

II. FACTS AND HOLDING

In March 2003, Continental Airlines, Inc. (Continental) brought action against the
International Brotherhood of Teamsters (IBT) in the Southern District of Texas.
Continental sought to vacate an arbitration award under the RLA, which reinstated
an employee who was terminated for violating a last chance agreement (LCA) after
testing positive for alcohol. The district court granted summary judgment in favor
of IBT and Continental in turn appealed to the U.S. Court of Appeals for the Fifth
Circuit. On appeal, Continental sought to have the arbitration award vacated based
on the following three reasons:

> (1) the district court applied the wrong standard of review under the RLA; (2) the dis-
> trict court erred in upholding the award because the Board exceeded its authority, by
> ignoring the plain language of the agreements and by substituting its judgment for that
> of the EAP director; and, (3) even if the award were otherwise proper, the district court
> should have vacated it as violative of public policy.

In this case, aircraft mechanic Mark Johnson worked at Continental. In August
2000, Johnson was selected for a random alcohol test. Following the test, he was
fired from Continental because he had more than the legal limit of alcohol in his
system. Johnson subsequently filed a grievance contesting his discharge. With the
assistance of IBT, Johnson entered into an LCA with Continental. Johnson was permitted to return to work at Continental provided he satisfied the terms of the LCA.
Per the terms of the agreement, Johnson would be terminated for any use of alcohol. The agreement specifically included mouthwash and any other medications
or substances which might contain alcohol. The only exception was for physician-
prescribed medication. If a physician prescribed medication for Johnson, he was

---

required to inform the Employee Assistance Program (EAP) staff. On March 20, 2001, Johnson left a voice mail message for Continental's EAP director, stating that he was taking over-the-counter cough medicine.' Two days later Johnson was selected for another random alcohol test and again tested positive. Once again Continental terminated Johnson and once again he filed a grievance protesting his termination. The arbitrators, known as the System Board (Board), held an evidentiary hearing on Johnson's grievance. The Board found that Johnson had not violated the LCA agreement and ordered Continental to reinstate Johnson. Following the Board's findings, Continental filed suit in district court, seeking to have the arbitration award vacated.

On appeal, Continental put forth three arguments. First, Continental contended that the district court applied the wrong standard of review under the RLA. Second, Continental argued that the district court erred in upholding the award because the Board exceeded its authority. Finally, Continental alleged that even if the award were otherwise proper, the district court should have vacated it as violative of public policy.

The Fifth Circuit rejected Continental's first argument that the court was not to give deference to the arbitrator's award. Instead, the court held the standard of review to be used was that of deference to the arbitrator, thus upholding the district court's decision. However, as to the second point of argument, the court found that the Board's interpretation of the agreement was not "an arguable construction of the agreement." Therefore, the court found that the Board had exceeded the scope of its jurisdiction and vacated the award. Based on its findings, the court determined it was unnecessary to further address other points which Continental had argued. The court reversed the district court, rendered summary judgment in favor of Continental, vacated the arbitration award and reinstated Continental's discharge of Mark Johnson.

III. LEGAL BACKGROUND

* * * *

Side agreements are also enforceable as part of a collective bargaining agreement. Side agreements include a settlement agreement, a last chance agreement, a second chance agreement, a waiver agreement, a supplemental agreement, and an addendum. The side agreement serves to clarify, add to, or change the collective bargaining agreement in some manner. Thus, the side agreement becomes a part of the original collective bargaining agreement.

The LCA should be regarded as a side agreement to the collective bargaining agreement. LCAs constitute formal contractual agreements of labor disputes, and so the standard of review is no different from that of any other contract. In fact, because the LCA is created after the collective bargaining agreement, it may supersede the collective bargaining agreement in whole or in part. The Eighth Circuit, in *Coca-Cola Bottling Co. of St. Louis*, determined that the arbitrator was required to view the express provisions of the LCA as representing the parties' actual intentions with respect to that individual employee. The Sixth Circuit, in *Ohio Edison*, ruled that an arbitrator does not have the authority to disregard the explicit terms of an LCA. The Fifth Circuit, in *Cooper Natural Resources*, stated that an LCA is considered to form a firm contract between the employer and the employee. It functions as a supplement to the collective bargaining agreement and is binding upon the arbitrator. When an arbitration panel ignores the explicit terms of an LCA, its decision is owed no deference and must be closely scrutinized. The Supreme Court has stated that the arbitrator "does not sit to dispense his own brand of industrial justice." This does not mean however, that an arbitrator's decision interpreting an LCA is entitled to any less deference than one which is interpreting a collective bargaining agreement. In fact, an arbitrator's interpretation of both a collective bargaining agreement and an LCA are entitled to the same high standard of deference.

IV. INSTANT DECISION

In the instant case, the court addresses two issues: (1) determining the appropriate standard of review to be used when reviewing the Board's award; and (2) determining whether the district court erred in upholding the arbitration award. In determining the appropriate standard of review, the court first distinguished between when an arbitration panel interprets an LCA and when it actually ignores the existence of an LCA. The court then determined that a deferential standard of review which applies when an arbitration panel interprets a provision of a collective bargaining agreement, also applies when an arbitration panel interprets a provision of the LCA. However, Continental argued that the court should use a "no deference" standard of review based on the *Cooper Natural Resources* decision. Nevertheless, the court went on to find that there was nothing in the *Cooper Natural Resources* decision which supported a more searching review of an arbitrator's interpretation of an LCA. In this case, the court looked at the Board's interpretation of the LCA, whereas in the Cooper Natural Resources case, the arbitrator did not even attempt to interpret the LCA, but had simply ignored it. The court determined that the standard used to review the arbitrator's interpretation of the LCA was the same standard used for collective bargaining agreements. Therefore, the court held that the standard of review which was applicable in this case was that of deference to the Board's decision. The court adopted the same standard of review the Supreme Court applied in *Misco*. Based on this holding, the court concluded the deference which the lower court gave to the Board's award was proper. In determining whether the district court erred in upholding the arbitration award, this court looked at whether the Board exceeded the scope of its jurisdiction. The court found the Board ignored the plain terms of the LCA. Even though the employee did not adhere to the terms of the LCA, the Board granted him yet another "last chance." The court determined the Board's interpretation was not even an arguable construction of the LCA and therefore, the Board had exceeded the scope of its jurisdiction.

V. COMMENT

In this case, Johnson simply did not follow the terms of the LCA which he signed. The name of the agreement, 'last chance agreement,' indicated that it was Johnson's last chance. The LCA stated that if Johnson did not adhere to the conditions of the LCA, he would be immediately terminated without further proceedings. The LCA Johnson signed had specific requirements which Johnson was required to follow in order to continue working at Continental. Johnson was initially discharged after he tested positive for alcohol in August 2000. However, Continental was willing to give him one more chance, if he agreed to certain specific terms set forth in the LCA. "Johnson agreed to abide by those terms and, on that basis, Continental allowed him to retain his position as a mechanic." Continuing to work for Continental was a privilege for Johnson, not a right. Continental could have refused to permit him to return to work after he tested positive for alcohol. The company elected to give him an opportunity to continue working, albeit under the restrictive terms specified in the LCA.

By its nature, an LCA is more restrictive than a collective bargaining agreement. LCAs typically come into existence when an employee could be fired under the terms of the collective bargaining agreement, but the company agrees to give the employee one more chance. This opportunity is normally based on the employee's agreement to heightened restrictions on their activities.

In this particular case, because Johnson had tested positive for alcohol during a random alcohol test, Continental was concerned about having a drunk mechanic working on its airplanes. In his position as an aircraft mechanic, Johnson's improper actions could potentially affect the lives of hundreds of people through poor maintenance on Continental airplanes. This surely was a factor when Continental drafted an LCA with zero tolerance for alcohol consumption...

Some people may feel sorry for Johnson because the LCA is more harsh than the collective bargaining agreement, but those were the terms agreed to by the parties. It did not matter whether Johnson really was sick and taking the cough syrup or if he was taking it just for the alcohol content. Johnson was well aware of the terms of the LCA, he agreed to be bound by those terms, and it was his responsibility to adhere to those terms. Johnson knew the consequences of not being faithful to the terms of the LCA. He made the decision to take the medicine, knowing that he risked losing his job. If Continental had wanted to continue to adhere to the terms of the collective bargaining agreement only, then they would not have had Johnson sign the LCA. Continental demanded the additional constraints on his activities or they would not have permitted him to return to work.

A. Court's standard of review of the arbitration award

The first issue the appellate court addressed in this case was to determine the proper standard of review when reviewing an award set by the Board. The collective bargaining agreement (CBA) between an airline carrier and its employees is governed by the RLA. The RLA establishes mandatory procedures for the resolution of both major and minor disputes. A minor dispute includes the interpretation or application of agreements covering rules or working conditions. A dispute arising out of the enforcement of an existing CBA is an example of a minor dispute. In this case both Continental and IBT explicitly agreed that this dispute constituted a minor dispute under the RLA. Pursuant to the RLA, because this was a minor dispute it must be resolved through binding arbitration before a board established by the union and the employer. In fact, the RLA expressly mandates that the Board has exclusive jurisdiction to adjudicate these claims in order to achieve the prompt settlement of minor disputes. The RLA provides that judicial review of Board decisions be narrow and highly deferential because of the strong public policy interest in achieving finality in an arbitration proceeding. Furthermore, the Supreme Court has stated in numerous cases that review under the RLA is among the narrowest known to the law. Thus, the Supreme Court affords the utmost deference to the Board's decision.

However, in this case, Continental argued for a "no deference" standard. Continental alleged that the no deference standard was appropriate because this dispute involved an LCA and because the Board ignored an express term of the agreement. The appellate court found the no deference standard to be inappropriate because the issue in this case was still the arbitrator's interpretation of the LCA. Even though the Board appeared to have ignored some of the provisions of the LCA, it did not ignore the LCA itself. The way the Board chose to interpret the LCA was to ignore certain express terms written in it. Even though the Board may have used an incorrect method to interpret the LCA, it was an interpretation nevertheless. Therefore, because it was an interpretation, the appellate court held that the standard of review to be applied was that of great deference to the decision of the Board.

* * * *

B. Did the district court err in upholding the arbitration award?

The next issue the court addressed was whether the district court erred in upholding the arbitration award. Courts will uphold arbitration awards, even if "wrong" or "questionable" as long as it's the arbitrator's interpretation of the contract. Seldom does a court overturn an arbitration award, but this was that rare case.

The arbitrator's responsibility is to uphold the bargain that the two parties agreed to, not to decide what is just or unjust. It does not matter whether the LCA is fair or unfair to the parties involved. It was the bargain that the parties struck. In this particular LCA, the terms were explicitly spelled out. The Board completely disregarded those explicit terms in its interpretation. When the Board chose to disregard clear, unambiguous language in the LCA, it seemed to be applying its "own brand of justice."

Continental contends that the Board exceeded its authority. In order to be within the Board's authority, the award must 'draw its essence' from the LCA. In the LCA, it specifically states that Johnson was not to use anything that contained alcohol, including medications. The ONLY exception was if a doctor prescribed the medication. In that event, Johnson was required to inform the EAP staff of the medication he was taking. Contrary to these unambiguous terms in the LCA, the Board found that a person on the doctor's staff authorizing Johnson to take the over-the-counter cough syrup, "met the letter and spirit" of the agreement. Additionally, the Board found that the EAP director should have called Johnson back and warned him that the use of the cough medicine could potentially violate the agreement.

* * * *

The appellate court was correct in overturning the district court's decision. The Board erred in not upholding the terms of the LCA. Airlines have to balance helping employees who have alcohol problems with other issues such as following Federal Aviation Administration regulations and keeping the public safe when they are flying on their airplanes. The airlines do this by drafting stringent LCAs which retain tight control over the activities of that particular employee. The LCA normally includes such requirements as mandatory rehabilitation programs and random alcohol testing. The employee must comply with these terms, not just to keep the employer happy, but to ensure the safety of those flying on the company's airplanes. The employee knows when he signs the LCA that he will be fired immediately for non-compliance with the terms of the agreement. An airline needs to be able to control the conduct of an employee who has exhibited signs of alcohol problems. An LCA helps an airline do this.

* * * *

The airline industry must be confident that the terms of its LCA agreements will be upheld. This encourages an airline to strive to work with an employee and give him one more chance, rather than simply firing him. Additionally, employees will be more apt to follow the terms of the LCA, if they know that the LCA will be upheld. Therefore, adhering to the terms of LCAs benefits both employees and employers. If the terms of LCAs are not upheld, companies are less likely to use LCAs and more likely to just fire the employee. When an employee in the airline industry has done something that would permit a company to fire him, the terms that the company agrees to bring him back under must be followed. This is critically important because of the many public policy issues at play, the first and foremost of which is the safety of the public. An airline agrees to LCA terms because it feels public safety will not be compromised by allowing the employee to continue to work for the company, as long as the terms of the LCA are followed. Second guessing an airline on this issue could seriously compromise public safety. Therefore, the terms of an LCA must be followed and the LCA should be exactly that for an employee-his "last chance." The LCA is the bargain the two parties struck which both felt they could live with and should be upheld. Airlines should not be forced to compromise safety by being ordered to give an employee yet another chance, an employee who has not been willing to follow the terms which the company felt were necessary in order to keep from compromising public safety.

VI. CONCLUSION

In this case, the Fifth Circuit looked at two issues. The first issue the court addressed was what the appropriate standard of review was for reviewing arbitration awards, specifically in cases governed by the RLA. The court held that the standard of review was one of deference to the interpretation of the arbitrator. Additionally, the court looked at whether the district court erred in upholding the award of the arbitrator. The court held that the district court did err. The court found this particular case was a rare example of an appropriate time for a court to overturn the decision of an arbitrator. The court stated that the Board's interpretation of the LCA was not an arguable construction of it and therefore, the Board had exceeded the scope of its jurisdiction when it determined the award.

APPLICATION AND DISCUSSION QUESTIONS

1. Last Chance Agreements (LCA) are considered "side agreements" to the Collective Bargaining Agreement (CBA). Consequently, they can be enforced through the grievance process. What other types of agreements between parties would be considered "side agreements" to the CBA?

   344

2. As pointed out in the above article, the Courts have provided guidelines for arbitrators in reviewing a LCA. What arbitration principles are set forth by the courts?   345

3. Can a LCA have harsher restrictions than the CBA? Why would the Union agree to such terms? Should an arbitrator uphold the termination of an employee for violating the LCA when there is evidence that when the Union agreed to the LCA, it was highly unlikely that the employee could comply with the agreement?   yes

4. Typically, the Court will give "utmost deference" to an arbitrator's decision. Should the review of a LCA receive the same standard of review by the Court? Should the Court give no deference?

   yes

ISSUE

At the hearing, the parties stipulated that the issue to be decided by the Arbitrator is as follows: "Is Grievant Grievant's discharge grievable and/or arbitrable under the terms of the parties' Last Chance Agreement ("LCA"), dated April 2011?"

issue Q

POSITION OF THE EMPLOYER

The Employer maintains that under the explicit terms of the LCA, its decision to terminate Grievant is neither grievable nor arbitrable. It cites paragraph 5 of the LCA:

ER arg:

At any time within the twelve (12) month period following the date of this agreement, should Grievant violate any Employer rule or regulation, and the violation, in the opinion of the Employer, constitutes a dischargeable offense, such discharge shall be considered for just cause. Neither the issue of whether or not the violation occurred nor the appropriate penalty shall be subject to the grievance procedure or arbitration, and the Union and Grievant agree that no grievance will be filed and no arbitration demanded."

support #

The Employer states that it is well settled that last chance agreements such as the one here, which was voluntarily entered into by both the Union and Grievant and which expressly waived the Union's/Grievant's right to review its determination of just cause for discharge, are routinely enforced by arbitrators. The LCA makes clear that should the Employer decide that Grievant violated an Employer rule or regulation within twelve months of the LCA, neither the question of whether a violation occurred, nor the appropriate penalty, shall be subject to grievance or arbitration. Grievant, in the Employer's reasoned opinion, violated an Employer rule or regulation, when he neglected his duties by failing for one hour and twenty minutes, to respond to the Rd. emergency. That violation constitutes just cause for discharge, as defined by the LCA, and is not subject to the grievance or arbitration process. Accordingly, the Employer's decision to terminate Grievant is neither grievable nor arbitrable.

Here

Finally, the Employer points out that in forming its opinion that a violation occurred, it did so only after conducting an investigation, thus acting reasonably, non-arbitrarily and in full recognition of Grievant's right to due process.

POSITION OF THE UNION

The Union, on the other hand, urges the Arbitrator to find that paragraph 5 of the LCA is not enforceable because it was entered into under duress and its terms are ambiguous. It further argues that the denial of an employee's right to access the grievance and arbitration process provided for in a collective bargaining agreement is arbitrary and capricious and overly broad.

The Union points to the fact that on the day Grievant and his Union representative were provided the LCA for their signatures, they were told that its terms were non-negotiable and that should Grievant fail to sign the LCA by the end of the day, the Employer would withdraw the offer to enter into the LCA, as evidence that the LCA was signed under duress. Specifically, the Union argues, "This take it or leave it proposition provided Mr. Grievant with no alternative but to sign the Agreement if he wanted his job back." This all or nothing approach, in the Union's view, constituted duress sufficient for the Arbitrator to hold the no grievance or arbitration provision of the LCA non-enforceable.

In addition, the Union argues that because the LCA failed to explicitly define the type of conduct which would subject the grievant to termination rendered the LCA ambiguous and invalid. The LCA, which provided that Grievant's violation of "any Employer rule or regulation" would constitute just cause for discharge failed to provide any guidance to Grievant as to what conduct was prohibited and could result in discharge. As such the language is ambiguous and overly broad. In fact, the Union states, "To this date, Mr. Grievant and the Union have waited with baited breath to find out the rule and/or regulation that Mr. Grievant violated."

* * * *

OPINION

This matter presents the Arbitrator with the limited question of whether the Employer's decision to terminate Grievant's employment, under the terms of the LCA, is arbitrable. 1 The Employer points to the express language of the LCA, which states, in relevant part, that "Grievant and the Union understand and agree that Grievant's employment with the Company will cease immediately if he violates any Company rule or regulation at any time within a twelve (12) month period following Grievant's return to work . . and the violation, in the opinion of the Employer, constitutes a dischargeable offense, such discharge shall be considered for just cause. Neither the issue of whether or not the violation occurred nor the appropriate penalty shall be subject to the grievance procedure or arbitration, and the Union and Grievant agree that no grievance will be filed and no arbitration demanded"

* * * *

arb says

The gravamen of the Union's position is that the LCA is unenforceable on the grounds that it was entered into under duress, and that its terms are ambiguous, arbitrary and capricious and overly broad. As to the Union's position that the LCA was entered into under duress, the Arbitrator finds no merit to this argument. While in present- ing the written LCA to Grievant and the Union for signature, the Employer may have taken a hard-line approach, insisting that it would not budge on the terms of the LCA and that it had to be accepted as is by the end of the day, such actions constitute noth- ing more than hard bargaining. If Grievant or the Union were unhappy with those terms, they were free to walk away and simply pursue the matter through the griev- ance procedure to arbitration. The Union and Grievant freely and voluntarily entered into the LCA. There was no duress.

1

As to the Union's argument that the LCA is ambiguous because it failed to cata- logue the conduct prohibited by the Employer's rules and regulations, and that "To this date, Mr. Grievant and the Union have waited with baited breath to find out the rule and/or regulation that Mr. Grievant violated," such argument is disingenuous. Grievant was interviewed, with his Union representative present, on November 10, 2011, regarding the events of the morning of October 28, 2011. More specifically, he was questioned about his failure to respond to the Rd. emergency. He was suspended pending further investigation, the next day. Grievant and his Union representative knew, or reasonably should have known, he was being terminated for failing to do his job, i.e., for failing to respond to the Rd. emergency.

2

blc

The fact that this Employer rule was not spelled out in writing does not make it any less enforceable. It is axiomatic that a fundamental rule of any work place is that employees are required to respond to directions and actually perform the work they are directed to do. In any event, the Union was advised, in writing what Employer rule Grievant violated.

4

Second, parties to collective bargaining relationships routinely place limits on arbitrability. Whether it be by placing time limits on grievance steps, by expressly excluding certain matters from the grievance arbitration process or by narrowly defining the term "grievance" in a collective bargaining agreement, parties can and do place limits on arbitrability.

3

AWARD

[handwritten: derived]

On the substantial and credible evidence of the case as a whole, as to the limited issue presented, the Arbitrator finds that Grievant's discharge is not arbitrable under the terms of the parties' LCA. Accordingly, this matter is dismissed, in its entirety.

APPLICATION AND DISCUSSION QUESTIONS

1. What is the purpose of the last chance agreement? Should arbitrators have the authority to decide if the agreement has been violated?

   [handwritten: last chance— yes]

2. The arbitrator suggested that the Union had the right and the power to not sign the agreement. Do you agree? Was there no duress on the Union to sign the agreement? If the Union had refused to sign the agreement, what options could the Union have taken under the collective bargaining agreement? *[handwritten: yes]*

U.S. TSUBAKI POWER TRANSMISSION LLC [CHICOPEE, MASS.] AND STEELWORKERS, LOCAL #7912

[handwritten: Case]

[handwritten: LCA]

132 BNA LA 1116 (ABRAMS, 2013)

* * * *

II. Issues

[handwritten: issue Q]

Did the Company violate the Collective Bargaining Agreement in discharging T__? If so, what shall the remedy be?

* * * *

IV. Discussion and Opinion

* * * *

Unlike a typical discharge case under the "just cause" standard, this dispute must be resolved under the terms of the last chance agreement in which the Grievant acknowledged that the Company had "just cause" to terminate him the prior December. The arbitrator's job in applying last chance agreements was explained by Arbitrator Matthew Franckiewiez in Eaton Cutler-Hammer Corp., 110 LA 467 , 471 (1998), as follows:

(margin note: LCA)

> In an arbitration proceeding pursuant to a last chance agreement, the arbitrator's first task is normally to examine whether the misconduct alleged is covered by the last chance agreement. If the last chance agreement provides that the employer may discharge an employee for a type of conduct of which the Grievant is accused, the arbitrator's function is usually limited to determining whether in fact the employee engaged in the misconduct alleged. On the other hand, if the arbitrator concludes that the last chance agreement is not applied to the type of misconduct alleged, the arbitrator applies the traditional "just cause" standard, as if there had been no last chance agreement.

(margin note: arb role)

Last chance agreements are common in the workplace, although Jerry Shea testified that to his knowledge this was only the fourth time a last chance agreement has been used at this plant. It gave the Grievant one more opportunity to demonstrate he could safely and reliably fulfill his obligations in moving material in the plant. *Aramark Uniform & Career Apparel,* 131 LA 1370, 1372 (Arb. Brodsky, 2013) (last chance agreement "gives the employee one more chance to redeem himself.") We never know about last chance agreements that actually work and shock an employee into changing his course of conduct and saving his job. We only know about those situations where a last chance agreements fail. See the extensive discussion in Arbitrator Bill Holley's recent decision in Boise White Paper, 132 LA 763 (2013). See generally, Roger Abrams, Inside Arbitration: How An Arbitrator Decides Labor and Employment Cases (Bloomberg/BNA, 2013).

(margin note: Leve)

* * * *

The Grievant's last chance agreement included that statement that T__ acknowledged that he had violated the Company's Rules and "the Company has just cause for discharge." The events of May 7, 2013 triggered that agreement and warranted his discharge.

(margin note: LCA said)

V. AWARD

[handwritten: denied] The Company did not violate the Collective Bargaining Agreement in discharging T__. Therefore, the grievance is denied.

APPLICATION AND DISCUSSION QUESTIONS

1. What was the purpose of the last chance agreement in this case?

2. Based on the last chance agreement in this case, if there was a violation, would the employer still be required to prove cause?

[handwritten: no]

[handwritten: Case]

FLEXSYS AMERICA L.P., A SUBSIDIARY OF EASTMAN CHEMICAL PLANT MONOGAHELA PLANT AND UNITED STEELWORKERS, LOCAL 14693-94

134 BNA LA 1357 (WOOD, 2015)

[handwritten: LCA expired]

For the employer-Thomas A. Smock and Jennifer G. Betts (Ogletree, Deakins, Nash, Smoak & Stewart, P.C.), attorneys.

For the union-James A. Woodward, staff representative.

VI. Discussion and Analysis

A. Introduction

[handwritten: burden] It is well established in labor arbitration that the employer in a discharge case has both the burden of going forward and the burden of proof. National Academy of Arbitrators ("NAA"), The Common Law of the Workplace (2nd Ed. 2005) 190. Here, *[handwritten: just cause req.]* as in most labor contracts, the Company must prove that the discharge was for just cause, the standard contained in Article 8 of the parties' Agreement. The general guidelines used by arbitrators to determine whether discipline of discharge was for just cause involves two essential inquiries:

1. Whether the record establishes that the employee committed the charged misconduct.

2. Whether the penalty imposed was appropriate under the labor contract and the circumstances of the case.

R. Mitlenthal & M. Vaughn, Just Cause: An Evolving Concept, National Academy of Arbitrators Annual Meeting 32-50 (2006). Accord NAA, The Common Law of the Workplace, 169-173; Elkouri & Elkouri, How Arbitration Works (5th Ed. 1996) 884-918.

The majority view of arbitrators is that last chance agreements are supplements to collective bargaining agreements and are binding upon arbitrators. NAA, The Common Law of the Workplace; §6.3 at 173. Further, as argued by the Company, a valid and enforceable last chance agreement defines "what is just cause in respect to the Grievant." Citing *Dresoll-Dresser Pump Co.*, 114 LA 297, 301 (Bickner, 1999). In this case, however, I find for the reasons set forth below that the Last Chance Agreement expired on April 7, 2014, and that the Company's decision to discharge the Grievant on May 15, 2014, is subject to review under the Contract's just cause standard.

APPLICATION AND DISCUSSION QUESTIONS

1. The Company argues that the last chance agreement was enforceable without an expiration date. What is your reason for agreeing or disagreeing?

2. How did the Union determine the Company's intent regarding the last chance agreement?

3. In addition to the last chance agreement, the Personnel Report included a final written warning and a performance improvement plan. Do you think the last chance agreement was effective in reprimanding the employee or could the Company discipline without it?

D. Just Cause Analysis in the Federal Sector: The Douglas Factors

CURTIS DOUGLAS V. VETERANS ADMINISTRATION, ET AL
1981 MSPB LEXIS 886 (1981)

A. Relevant Factors in Assessing Penalties

A well developed body of regulatory and case law provides guidance to agencies, and to the Board, on the considerations pertinent to selection of an appropriate disciplinary sanction. Much of that guidance is directed to the fundamental requirement that agencies exercise responsible judgment in each case, based on rather specific, individual considerations, rather than acting automatically on the basis of generalizations unrelated to the individual situation. OPM's rules on this subject, like those of the Commission before it, emphasize to agencies that in considering available disciplinary actions, there is no substitute for judgment in selecting among them. Further, OPM has specifically counseled agencies that:

> Any disciplinary action demands the exercise of responsible judgment so that an employee will not be penalized out of proportion to the character of the offense; this is particularly true of an employee who has a previous record of completely satisfactory service. An adverse action, such as suspension, should be ordered only after a responsible determination that a less severe penalty, such as admonition or reprimand, is inadequate.... Agencies should give consideration to all factors involved when deciding what penalty is appropriate, including not only the gravity of the offense but such other matters as mitigating circumstances, the frequency of the offense, and whether the action accords with justice in the particular situation.

Section 7513(b)(4) of Title 5 requires that written agency decisions taking adverse actions must include the specific reasons therefore. While neither this provision nor OPM's implementing regulation, 5 C.F.R. 752.404(f), requires the decision notice to contain information demonstrating that the agency has considered all mitigating factors and has reached a responsible judgment that a lesser penalty is inadequate, a decision notice which does demonstrate such reasoned consideration may be entitled to greater deference from the Board as well as from the courts.

Moreover, aggravating factors on which the agency intends to rely for imposition of an enhanced penalty, such as a prior disciplinary record, should be included in the advance notice of charges so that the employee will have a fair opportunity to respond to those alleged factors before the agency's deciding official, and the decision notice should explain what weight was given to those factors in reaching the agency's final decision.

Court decisions and OPM and Civil Service Commission issuances have recognized a number of factors that are relevant for consideration in determining the appropriateness of a penalty. Without purporting to be exhaustive, those generally recognized as relevant include the following:

1. The nature and seriousness of the offense, and its relation to the employee's duties, position, and responsibilities, including whether the offense was intentional or technical or inadvertent, or was committed maliciously or for gain, or was frequently repeated;

2. the employee's job level and type of employment, including supervisory or fiduciary role, contacts with the public, and prominence of the position;

3. the employee's past disciplinary record;

4. the employee's past work record, including length of service, performance on the job, ability to get along with fellow workers, and dependability;

5. the effect of the offense upon the employee's ability to perform at a satisfactory level and its effect upon supervisors' confidence in the employee's ability to perform assigned duties;

6. consistency of the penalty with those imposed upon other employees for the same or similar offenses;

7. consistency of the penalty with any applicable agency table of penalties;

8. the notoriety of the offense or its impact upon the reputation of the agency;

9. the clarity with which the employee was on notice of any [**40] rules that were violated in committing the offense, or had been warned about the conduct in question;

10. potential for the employee's rehabilitation;

11. mitigating circumstances surrounding the offense such as unusual job tensions, personality problems, mental impairment, harassment, or bad faith, malice or provocation on the part of others involved in the matter; and

12. the adequacy and effectiveness of alternative sanctions to deter such conduct in the future by the employee or others.

Not all of these factors will be pertinent in every case, and frequently in the individual case some of the pertinent factors will weigh in the appellant's favor while others may not or may even constitute aggravating circumstances. Selection of an appropriate penalty must thus involve a responsible balancing of the relevant factors in the individual case. The Board's role in this process is not to insist that the balance be struck precisely where the Board would choose to strike it if the Board were in the agency's shoes in the first instance; such an approach would fail to accord proper deference to the agency's primary discretion in managing its workforce. Rather, the Board's review of an agency-imposed penalty is essentially to assure that the agency did conscientiously consider the relevant factors and did strike a responsible balance within tolerable limits of reasonableness. Only if the Board finds that the agency failed to weigh the relevant factors, or that the agency's judgment clearly exceeded the limits of reasonableness, is it appropriate for the Board then to specify how the agency's decision should be corrected to bring the penalty within the parameters of reasonableness.

In considering whether the agency's judgment was reasonably exercised, it must be borne in mind that the relevant factors are not to be evaluated mechanistically by any preordained formula. For example, the principle of like penalties for like offenses does not require mathematical rigidity or perfect consistency regardless of variations in circumstances or changes in prevailing regulations, standards, or mores. This consideration is redolent of equal protection concepts, also reflected in the merit system principle calling for fair and equitable treatment of employees and applicants in all aspects of personnel management. As such, this principle must be applied with practical realism, eschewing insistence upon rigid formalism so long as the substance of equity in relation to genuinely similar cases is preserved. OPM has required that agencies should be as consistent as possible when deciding on disciplinary actions, but has also cautioned that *surface consistency* should be avoided in order to allow for consideration of all relevant factors including whether the action accords with justice in the particular situation. Similarly, agency tables of penalties should not be applied so inflexibly as to impair consideration of other factors relevant to the individual case.

Lastly, it should be clear that the ultimate burden is upon the agency to persuade the Board of the appropriateness of the penalty imposed. This follows from the fact that selection of the penalty is necessarily an element of the agency's decisionwhich can be sustained under Section 7701(c)(1) only if the agency establishes the facts on which that decision rests by the requisite standard of proof. The deference to which the agency's managerial discretion may entitle its choice of penalty cannot have the effect of shifting to the appellant the burden of proving that the penalty is unlawful, when it is the agency's obligation to present all evidence necessary to support each element of its decision. The selection of an appropriate penalty is a distinct element of the agency's decision, and therefore properly within its burden of persuasion, just as its burden includes proof that the alleged misconduct actually occurred and that such misconduct affects the efficiency of the service.

In many cases the penalty, as distinct from the underlying conduct alleged by the agency, will go unchallenged and need not require more than prima facie justification. An agency may establish a prima facie case supporting the appropriateness of its penalty by presenting to the Board evidence of the facts on which selection of the penalty was based, a concise statement of its reasoning from those facts or information otherwise sufficient to show that its reasoning is not on its fact inherently irrational, and by showing that the penalty conforms with applicable law and regulation. When no issue has been raised concerning the penalty, such a prima facie case will normally suffice to meet also the agency's burden of persuasion on the appropriateness of the penalty. However, when the appellant challenges the severity of the penalty, or when the Board's presiding official perceives genuine issues of justice or equity casting doubt on the appropriateness of the penalty selected by the agency, the agency will be called upon to present such further evidence as it may choose to rebut the appellant's challenge or to satisfy the presiding official.

Whenever the agency's action is based on multiple charges some of which are not sustained, the presiding official should consider carefully whether the sustained charges merited the penalty imposed by the agency. In all cases in which the appropriateness of the penalty has been placed in issue, the initial decision should contain a reasoned explanation of the presiding official's decision to sustain or modify the penalty, adequate to demonstrate that the Board itself has properly considered all relevant factors and has exercised its judgment responsibly.

I. APPLICATION TO APPELLANTS

We turn now to the application of these standards to the cases of the individual appellants. In doing so, we shall discuss the relevant facts of each case and the arguments of the parties.

A. Curtis Douglas v. Veterans Administration

Appellant Douglas was employed by the Veterans Administration as a Supply Clerk Dispatcher, GS-4. He was removed from the agency for being absent without leave for thirty minutes, for being away from his assigned duty station without permission, and for selling his employment services to a physically handicapped employee. These charges all arose out of events occurring on January 14, 1979. In selecting the penalty, the agency considered four past disciplinary actions: (1) a February 25, 1977, admonishment for eight hours of being AWOL; (2) a June 3, 1977 reprimand for failure to report for duty on May 28, 1977 and four hours of being AWOL on June 2, 1977; (3) a five-day suspension of June 28, 1977 for a 45-minute period of AWOL; and (4) a 20-day suspension of October 2, 1978 for another period of AWOL.

Upon appeal to the Board, the appellant declined a hearing and the presiding official sustained the action based on the evidence in the record. In his initial decision the presiding official described the facts surrounding the conduct which resulted in appellant's removal, stating:

Here, the record reveals that on January 14, 1979 the appellant was assigned the job of SPD Dispatcher with a tour of duty from 8:00 a.m. to 4:30 p.m. and that at approximately 9:10 a.m. the telephone at the appellant's dispatch station range several times and in his absence was finally answered by the SPD Preparation Area Supervisor, Mr. Edward L. Regan, who, after taking a request for supplies and arranging for their deliverance, became aware that the appellant was absent from his work station without permission. In the meantime, the Ward Supply Clerk Supervisor, Ms. Margaret B. Thomas, was trying to contact the appellant on several occasions at his work site, the Dispatch Office, between 9:00 a.m. and 9:35 a.m. from the wards by use of the executone without success. Consequently, at 9:35 a.m., she asked Mr. Regan of the appellant's whereabouts only to learn that Mr. Regan did not know since the appellant had not requested permission to leave the work station. Thereafter, Ms. Thomas found the appellant on the sixth floor stocking nurservers for physically handicapped Supply Clerk Richard B. Eckert from whom, according to Mr. Eckert, the appellant has solicited $5.00 in payment for helping him do his work and to which the appellant offered that he needed the money.

The presiding official found, after carefully considering appellant's argument to the contrary, that the agency had proven the above facts by a preponderance of the evidence. The record does not contain any evidence which would cause us to change those factual determinations.

Appellant contended that the penalty was too severe. However, he did not explain why he believed the penalty to be too severe, nor did he introduce any evidence to support this contention. In the absence of any specific explanation of this contention from the appellant, we will consider whether, after relevant factors are considered, the penalty of removal was disproportionate to the seriousness of the offense.

The offense in this case was serious. It had a direct impact on the agency's ability to accomplish its mission. According to the agency, appellant's position was "critical to the process of furnishing vital supplies and equipment for emergency as well as routine patient care to all areas of the Medical Center. By being absent from his post, appellant created a situation which could have resulted in serious consequences to a patient who needed equipment or supplies immediately. The seriousness of the offense is compounded by the fact that appellant's absence was intentional and was occasioned by his desire for personal gain.

The record also shows that appellant has been disciplined for unauthorized absence on four previous occasions. This record of progressive discipline demonstrates that appellant was clearly on notice that unauthorized absence from his duty station was a serious offense. It also demonstrates that sanctions less severe than removal have not been successful in curbing appellant's misconduct. On the basis of the above findings, we conclude that the removal penalty was not arbitrary or unreasonable in light of all the circumstances and constituted an appropriate penalty.

Accordingly, the removal action is AFFIRMED.

APPLICATION AND DISCUSSION QUESTIONS

1. What mitigation factors should be considered in determining the appropriate penalty to issue an employee for misconduct? What "aggravating factors" may enhance the penalty?

2. The Court listed a number of factors to consider in determining the penalty. How should the arbitrator weigh the relevancy of each factor?

3. How do arbitrators determine the reasonableness of an agency decision? What is *surface consistency*? What impact does it have on whether a penalty is reasonable?

COUNCIL OF PRISON LOCALS, AFL-CIO, AMERICAN FEDERATION OF GOVERNMENT EMPLOYEES, LOCAL 607 AND U.S. DEPARTMENT OF JUSTICE, FEDERAL BUREAU OF PRISONS, FCI ELKTON, OHIO

(NOVEMBER 11, 2007)

Judge / Administrative Officer: Weatherspoon, Floyd

I. Statement of Facts

The facts indicate that Council of Prison Locals (AFL-CIO) American Federation of Government Employees, Local No. 607 hereinafter (Union) and U.S. Department of Justice, Federal Bureau of Prisons, FCI Elkton, hereinafter (Company) are parties to a collective bargaining agreement, hereinafter (CBA or Agreement).

About June 14, 2006, a grievance was filed challenging the Grievant's 20-day suspension on May 16, 2006. The grievance went through the various stages of the grievance procedure. The grievance was denied. Arbitration was requested pursuant to Article 32 of the CBA. . The parties stipulated that the grievance is properly before the Arbitrator.

The facts further indicate that the Grievant received a twenty day suspension for unprofessional conduct, involving a verbal altercation between the Grievant and another employee, Connie Dysert; the Grievant was also charged with failure to follow policy which involves the Grievant's acceptance of three Cleveland Cavalier tickets from a vendor. The facts indicate that the Grievant was given a proposal letter dated August 22, 2005. The letter informed the Grievant that it was proposed that the Grievant be suspended twenty days for (1) unprofessional conduct and (2) failure to follow policy.

II. Issue

Was the adverse action taken for just and sufficient cause, if not, what is the appropriate remedy?

III. Relevant Contract and Statutory Provisions

5 CFR 2635.202 GENERAL STANDARDS

(a) General prohibitions. Except as provided in this subpart, an employee shall not, directly or indirectly, solicit or accept a gift:

(1) From a prohibited source; or

(2) Given because of the employee's official position.

5 CFR 2635.204 EXCEPTIONS

The prohibitions set forth in § 2635.202(a) do not apply to a gift accepted under the circumstances described in paragraphs (a) through (1) of this section, and an employee's acceptance of a gift in accordance with one of those paragraphs will be deemed not to violate the principles set forth in § 2635.101(b) ...

(b) Gifts based on a personal relationship. An employee may accept a gift given under circumstances which make it clear that the gift is motivated by a family relationship or personal friendship rather than the position of the employee. Relevant factors in making such a determination include the history of the relationship and whether the family member or friend personally pays for the gift.

IV. Position of the Parties

A. Union's Position

The Union contends that the Agency did not have just cause to suspend the Grievant. The Union maintains that the Agency did not prove by a preponderance of the evidence that the Grievant was guilty of unprofessional conduct or failure to follow policy. The Union states, in the alternative, even if the Agency had proven the charges, the level of disciplinary action taken against the Grievant was excessive. It is the Union's assertion that the Grievant was the victim of disparate treatment.

B. Agency's Position

The Agency maintains that it met its burden to prove that the Grievant was guilty of unprofessional conduct and failure to follow policy. Therefore, the Grievant was suspended with just cause. The Agency contends that because the Grievant is in law enforcement, he is held to a higher standard and thus, the penalty was not excessive. The Agency contends that the Union failed to prove the Grievant was the victim of disparate treatment.

V. Discussion and Analysis

* * * *

Charge 1 -- Unprofessional Conduct (Omitted)

* * * *

Charge 2 -- Failure to Follow Policy

The Grievant was also disciplined for failure to follow policy. The behavior underlying this charge involved the Grievant accepting three Cleveland Cavalier tickets from a vendor doing business with the Agency. The Grievant admits accepting the tickets.

The Agency contends that in accordance with 5 CFR 2635.201-205, employees are prohibited from accepting any gift from a ven

* * * *

The evidence demonstrates that Tim Nichols was a vendor with Keefe, with whom the Agency does business. The Union presented the following evidence that the Grievant and Tim Nichols had a personal relationship.

* * * *

The evidence indicates that the Grievant developed a friendship with Mr. Nichols while the Grievant was employed by the Agency and Mr. Nichols was employed by Keefe and did business with the Agency. Other than Mr. Whitesell's belief, the Agency does not provide any explanation to support its premise that when an employee develops a relationship with a vendor, it is not a "personal relationship" as contemplated by the regulation. The Agency has not pointed to anything in the regulation that prohibits employees from establishing personal relationships with vendors. While this may not be the typical personal relationship described by the regulation, it's nonetheless, a personal relationship.

* * * *

The Union has presented sufficient evidence that the Grievant engaged in a personal relationship with Tim Nichols. Further, the Union presented evidence that sufficiently establishes that Mr. Nichols' motivation in giving the tickets was based on the personal friendship rather than the Grievant's position with the Agency. The Grievant's affidavit establishes that Tim Nichols could not attend the Cavaliers game himself, therefore, he gave the tickets to the Grievant. The Arbitrator acknowledges that there are times when it is inappropriate for an employee to accept gifts even when that employee has a personal relationship with a vendor. However, while it may be inappropriate, the CFR doesn't prohibit the acceptance of gifts in this situation. Also strengthening the Union's position that the motivation was based on a personal relationship, rather than the Grievant's position, is Mr. Whitesell's testimony that the Grievant's position doesn't affect the status of the contract between the Agency and the Keefe Company. Therefore, there is no evidence that Keefe Company could have received any advantage by the Grievant's accepting the tickets.

The Agency further contends that receiving tickets from a representative that the Grievant regularly purchases items from is inappropriate behavior that could be perceived by the public and other vendors as preferential treatment.

The Union maintains that the Agency's claim that the Grievant's accepting the tickets gives the impression of impartiality is a double standard given the fact that Mr. Paukstat accepted gratuitous golf outings with the exact same vendor. The Union further points out that Mr. Paukstat did not have a personal relationship with Mr. Nichols. The Union also contends that another management official also provided testimony about receiving a gratuity in the form of a live lobster.

Alvin Paukstat, Trust Fund Supervisor at FCI Elkton, testified that he has been on golf outings with Mr. Nichols twice. He testified that he paid for one golf outing and that Mr. Nichols paid for one. He testified that the value of the golf outing was $9. He added that he did not have a personal relationship with Mr. Nichols. Mr. Paukstat acknowledged that going on a golf outing could have possibly been perceived as preferential treatment toward that vendor.

Additionally, the Union states, "Mr. Whitesell another management official of the Agency and the person responsible for requesting the investigation which led to the disciplinary action against the Grievant provided testimony about receiving a gratuity in the form of a live lobster from a vendor." However, the evidence demonstrates that a lobster was sent to the laundry department and that it was valued at under $20, which is acceptable according to the CFR. According to 5 CFR 2635.204, "an employee may accept unsolicited gifts having an aggregate market value of $20 or less per source per occasion."

The Arbitrator acknowledges that the golf outing appears to be acceptable according to the regulation, as was the acceptance of the tickets. It supports the Union's position, however, that the Grievant's acceptance of the tickets was no less acceptable than Mr. Paukstat's acceptance of the golf outing, as both could be perceived as preferential treatment. Therefore, the Agency did not sufficiently demonstrate that the Grievant engaged in misconduct when he accepted the Cleveland Cavalier tickets from Tim Nichols. Thus, the Agency failed to meet its burden by a preponderance of the evidence that there was a factual basis for sustaining the charge of failure to follow policy against the Grievant.

The Arbitrator has determined that the Agency has met its burden in proving that there was a factual basis for the adverse action in relation to the charge of unprofessional conduct. However, the Agency has not met that burden with the failure to follow policy charge. Now, the Agency must prove that there was a logical relationship between the misconduct and the efficiency of the Service. "In evaluating whether a penalty is merited, however, we examine first and foremost, the nature and seriousness of the misconduct and its relation to the employee's duties, position, and responsibilities, including whether the offense was intentional or frequently repeated." Obviously, when employees engage in a verbal altercation in front of inmates there is an impact on the efficient and safe operation of the prison. Thus, this is an offense that affects the efficiency of Service.

The Agency must next demonstrate that the penalty was within the tolerable limits of reasonableness. In determining whether the selected penalty is reasonable, due deference is given to the agency's discretion in exercising it managerial function of maintaining employee discipline and efficiency, an Arbitrator's function is not to displace management's responsibility, but to assure that management's judgment has been properly exercised. It is not the Arbitrator's role to decide what penalty he would impose, but rather, whether the penalty selected by the Agency exceeds the maximum reasonable penalty.

A penalty will be modified only when it is determined that the agency failed to weigh the relevant factors or that it clearly exceeded the bounds of reasonableness in determining the penalty. The issue in determining whether an arbitrator should exercise its mitigation authority is whether the agency considered the relevant *Douglas* factors and reasonably exercised management discretion in making its penalty determination.

The *Douglas* factors are:

(1) the nature and seriousness of the offense, and its relation to the employee's duties, position, and responsibilities, including whether the offense was intentional or technical or inadvertent, or was committed maliciously or for gain, or was frequently repeated; the Union argues that while law enforcement employees are held to a higher standard, that standard must be applied equitably among similarly situated employees. The Union contends that when all the *Douglas* factors are appropriately considered, the Grievant's discipline is excessive and mitigation is warranted.

(2) the employee's job level and type of past disciplinary record in 3 years of service, he has employment, including supervisory or fiduciary role, contacts with the public, and prominence of the position;

(3) the employee's past disciplinary record;

(4) the employee's past work record, including length of service, performance on the job, ability to get along with fellow workers, and dependability;

(5) the effect of the offense upon the employee's ability to perform at a satisfactory level and its effect upon supervisor's confidence in the employee's ability to perform assigned duties;

(6) consistency of the penalty with those imposed upon other employees for the same or similar offenses;

(7) consistency of the penalty with any applicable agency table of penalties:

(8) the notoriety of the offense or its impact upon the reputation of the agency;

(9) the clarity with which the employee was on notice of any rules that were violated in committing the offense, or had been warned about the conduct in question;

(10) potential for the employee's rehabilitation;

(11) mitigating circumstances surrounding the offense such as unusual job tensions, personality problems, mental impairment, harassment, or bad faith, malice or provocation on part of others involved in the matter; and

(12) the adequacy and effectiveness of alternative sanctions to deter such conduct in the future by the employee or others.

The Agency points out that as a law enforcement officer, the Grievant is held to a higher standard. The a good work record, the Union states that the progressive discipline policy was not followed because there were no prior warnings or reprimands.

The 20-day suspension was based on the Warden's determination that the Grievant engaged in misconduct based on the unprofessional conduct charge and the failure to follow policy charge. However, the Arbitrator concluded that the Agency didn't meet its burden to sustain the failure to follow policy charge; therefore, the Grievant cannot be disciplined for that charge. Thus, the Arbitrator must decide whether the 20-day suspension is an excessive penalty for the Grievant's conduct in engaging in a verbal altercation.

In considering what discipline to impose, the nature and seriousness of the offense is a factor. The Union contends that the altercation between the Grievant and Ms. Dysert was simply a difference of opinion and nothing more. In support of its position, the Union points the testimony of William Meek. Mr. Meek testified that on the day of the incident in question, he and Sam Biafore were in the lobby area on the range. He said that it was evident that the two employees were having a disagreement. He stated that Ms. Dysert's face was red and that the Grievant was saying something to her, but he didn't know what the Grievant was saying. He testified that he didn't believe the disagreement was that serious because they work in a very stressful environment and disagreements take place on a daily basis between staff members. He said that he took notice of the disagreement, but he didn't think that it was really anything out of the ordinary. He further stated that disagreements between employees were very common.

The Union's evidence supports its position that the altercation was not out of the ordinary. However, the evidence establishes that Mr. Sniezek's decision not to mitigate the penalty was based on factors such as: the altercation occurring in front of inmates and the Grievant's comments to Ms. Dysert as she was trying to remove herself from the situation, rather than the severity of the altercation.

The deciding official, Warden Sniezek, testified that he considered the *Douglas* factors when deciding what discipline to impose against the Grievant. Mr. Sniezek testified that one factor he considered in his decision not to mitigate the penalty was that the Grievant was in the military. He explained that in the military you're taught a code on how to conduct yourself, and how to deal with people appropriately. He also considered the Grievant's employment, work record, Ms. Dysert's affidavit, and Mr. Biafore's affidavit. Mr. Sniezek testified that he considered the following facts, surrounding the incident, sufficient to warrant a 20-day suspension: an employee was trying to remove herself from the situation, the Grievant belittled her about her weight, the Grievant made comments that she's a baby in front of inmates. Mr. Sniezek also testified that he considered the Grievant's 15 year work history as a double-edged sword; he explained that even though the Grievant's been there for 15 years with no prior discipline, because he has been there 15 years, he should have known better. Mr. Sniezek also considered that having an altercation in front of inmates is a security concern.

The Arbitrator finds that the deciding official went beyond the bounds of reasonableness when he considered the Grievant's military background and his 13 years of service as aggravating factors. The Grievant is already held to a higher standard because of his status in law enforcement. It is not reasonable to impose a higher level of discipline on the Grievant because he was in the military. The Arbitrator also finds that the warden was not reasonable in his treatment of the Grievant's years of service.

The Warden testified that he considered the Grievant's prior years of service as a double edged sword. Basically, the warden said because the Grievant had 13 years of service with no prior discipline he should have known better. It's not appropriate for employees with one month of service to engage in misconduct anymore that it is for someone that has 30 years of service; however, longtime employment without prior discipline is a mitigating factor, not an aggravating one. The warden exceeded the bounds of reasonableness when he considered these factors to justify a higher level of discipline upon the Grievant.

* * * *

This evidence supports the Union's contention that the Grievant was not disciplined fairly and consistently. The evidence indicates that other employees received lesser penalties for engaging in verbal altercations. The evidence further indicates that the incident involving Mr. Eargle was in front of inmates. Thus, the Union has provided sufficient evidence that the Grievant's level of discipline was not consistent.

The Arbitrator also notes that the parties' CBA provides for progressive discipline. The Arbitrator finds that after reviewing all the relevant evidence and considering the *Douglas* factors that mitigation of the penalty is necessary in this case to bring the level of discipline within the tolerable limits of reasonableness. The factors the warden considered against mitigation were that the Grievant belittled Ms. Dysert as she attempted to remove herself from the situation and that the altercation occurred in front of inmates. The Arbitrator finds this is a relevant consideration on behalf of the Agency. However, these factors must be weighed and balanced against any mitigating factors. The Union has presented sufficient evidence that other altercations occurring in front of inmates were not disciplined so severely. The Arbitrator finds that because the Grievant has received no prior discipline, to be fair and consistent with other similar infractions, the 20- day suspension is mitigated to a letter of reprimand.

VI. Conclusion

Although the Agency met its burden to demonstrate that the Grievant engaged in unprofessional conduct, the Agency did not meet its burden to prove that the penalty was within the bounds of reasonableness. The Union has sufficiently demonstrated that the Grievant was disciplined excessively and that his level of discipline was not consistent with similar penalties of the same nature.

VII. Award

The Grievance is sustained, in part. The penalty is mitigated from a 20-day suspension to a letter of reprimand. The Grievant is entitled to back pay and all benefits forfeited as a result of the suspension. The suspension shall be removed from the personnel file.

The Union states that the Grievant had 13 years of service, while the Agency says 15 years. The Arbitrator doesn't believe the parties are in dispute at to the years of service, the Arbitrator is just pointing out in inadvertent inconsistency in the parties facts.

Application and Discussion Questions

1. The arbitration clause in collective bargaining agreements will outline the process the parties are to follow prior to the arbitration hearing. Often, the parties will be required to share documents related to the grievance. In addition, the parties may be required to exchange their witness list within a certain time period. The exchange of documents and witness lists prior to the hearing, may avoid lengthy delays during the hearing. Where one party fails to comply with the request of documentation, the other party may request the arbitrator to issue a subpoena or to disallow the admission of such evidence. The opposing party may also file a motion to compel a party to comply with the request. What documents are normally presented in disciplinary and issue grievances?

2. Why is there a presumption in favor of arbitration over dismissal of a grievance? Was the failure to provide the witness list prior to the hearing more than a harmless non-prejudicial technical violation? Can you think of a situation where the failure to provide request documentation prior to the hearing could be prejudicial?

3. What limits are placed on the arbitrator when reviewing management's decision to issue discipline? What about the level of discipline?

4. Which *Douglas factor* does the Union primarily rely on to support their position?

5. What is the role of the Arbitrator in determining whether the employer's decisions are "reasonable?"

E. The Burden of Proof in Disciplinary Cases

case

mushroom
theft

MONTEREY MUSHROOMS AND UNITED FARM WORKERS

130 BNA LA 998 (RIKER, 2012)[*]

Issue

Was there just cause for the termination of A__ ("Grievant"), and if not, what is the appropriate remedy?

Background

The Grievant was terminated for taking a Company mushroom product from the Employer's Royal Oak facility on April 21, 2010 without authorization. The Grievant had worked at the Company for 33 years as an equipment operator in what is classified as the Level 700 compost production area. On the day in question two boxes of Portabella mushrooms were found in the compressor room within the Level 700 area by Company supervisors. Storage of such produce in what was described as an inappropriate and unauthorized location had raised suspicion in the minds of the Company supervisors as to who had left the two boxes of mushrooms in that particular place. It was decided to leave them in there and observe the compressor room to see if anyone was going into the location to remove them. At the close of the workday the Grievant was observed entering the compressor room and transferring the two boxes into the trunk of a co-worker's car. In the ensuing stages of the investigation the Grievant admitted to taking part in the physical act of transporting the mushrooms into the automobile. The unauthorized removal of Company property without proper permission was determined by the Employer to have been adequate just cause for discharge and hence the Grievant was terminated. The Grievant argues that there was no intent on his part to steal any mushrooms and that any perception of wrongdoing was based more on circumstantial than factual evidence.

* * * *

Positions of the Parties

UNION

The Employer did not have just cause for discharging the Grievant, as he was a long-term employee with only a single and unrelated disciplinary action in over 30 years. To impose such a severe penalty would require the Employer to prove by clear and convincing evidence that the Grievant not only committed the act of stealing Company property but also had the intent to do so as well. The evidence reveals that at worst the Grievant inadvertently participated in an illegal event committed by another employee and that it was more prompted by an act of chivalry than that of self-interest. An examination of the facts suggests that there are indicators that could imply or give a perception of improper behavior but this is not proof of an intent to take product without authorization. The conditions of just cause were simply not fully satisfied, especially when the Employer attempted to impose an unwritten "zero tolerance policy" in a manner that deduces guilt based on circumstantial evidence. Therefore the Grievant should be reinstated and made whole for all back pay and benefits.

There is precedence requiring employers to have properly established that there was just cause in order to substantiate a termination decision. Discharge is essentially industrial capital punishment in that it imposes a serious, punitive, and final action (General Telephone Co. (1982 Holman) 79 LA 102). When rationalizing a claim of just cause such severity requires clear and convincing evidence that the Grievant committed the act of stealing Company property. To establish this proof requires that the elements of theft would need to be satisfied in the same manner as they would in a criminal theft case or, in other words, there must be proof of specific intent to steal in addition to proof of the actual theft act (American Bakeries Co. (1981 Modjeska) 77 LA 530 , 533 and General Telephone Co., Id. at 105). Specific intent depends on a state of mind and the Employer did not support their charge with "clear and convincing" evidence that the Grievant knowingly stole the property. Also, they did not prove that the Grievant was aware that the mushrooms in the compressor room, which he picked up and transported to the female coworker's car trunk, were indeed stolen. Rather, the facts indicate this particular female coworker was known to regularly buy mushrooms and that it was raining that day. If the compressor room was construed as an unreasonable place to put mushrooms, it would seem equally implausible that the Grievant would blatantly load stolen mushrooms into a car in plain view of supervisors in their nearby office. Hence, the fact that the mushrooms were taken without authorization and that he physically helped move them to a vehicle does not alone prove he had carried out the act of theft-just that he moved some mushrooms another employee had asked him to transport. The evidence only shows that the Grievant thought the mushrooms belonged to the female coworker. Even during the initial query by the observing supervisors there was no specific evidence where the Grievant admitted to taking the mushrooms or even participating in a theft. Further, an assessment that he must have been involved in the event based on his Union role and seniority was deduced by the Company HR Manager, even after knowing that she did not believe the Grievant knew the mushrooms were stolen at the time of the incident. Essentially he was at a crime scene in which he inadvertently participated. This does not qualify as clear and convincing evidence that he was actively participating in a theft event.

* * * *

EMPLOYER

* * * *

The Company met its burden of proof to justify the penalty of discharge on the Grievant. It is acknowledged that in a discharge case the burden of proof typically rests with the Employer. In a discharge case, even if it involves theft, just cause is established if the employer "can show by the preponderance of the evidence, that the employee committed the thefts alleged" (*Square Plus Operating Corp. v. Local 917*, 140 LRRM 2389 (USDC, SDNY, 1992). This precedence establishes that the holding of criminal law standard of "beyond a reasonable doubt" is not the appropriate standard for use in a discharge case. The evidence plainly reveals that the Grievant was a willing participant in the theft or, at the very least, knowingly participated with the unauthorized removal of mushrooms. Without any hesitation, and in a very short period, he quickly and decisively walked straight to a predestined hiding place in the compressor room and transported the two cases of hidden mushrooms to his coworker's car. The fact that he also "grabbed four mushrooms" as he got out of the car clearly implies a "quid pro quo" for his role in a pre-ordained plan and his entitled "pay." This transaction and acceptance indicates that the Grievant was a full and knowing participant in the theft.

* * * *

Discussion and Opinion

A determination as to whether the Employer had just cause to terminate the Grievant due to his alleged failure to comply with Company policy on stealing depends on several factors. The first is whether the policy is appropriate for the effective operations of the business and was it properly conveyed to the workforce so as to ensure that full compliance was in fact achievable. Secondly, were the penalties for the policy fairly and consistently applied in order to ensure that there was no disparate treatment that may have disadvantaged the Grievant. The third factor is determining whether or not the Employer proved that the Grievant was involved in the act of stealing and if there was evidence of clear intent to commit the act. The Employer has the burden to ensure that these factors were properly satisfied to sustain the termination.

factors

The evidence presented in the case indicates that the Company's policy was appropriate for maintaining its successful operations, which had been effectively communicated to the workforce. Clearly, the Company must protect its assets and avoid any behavior that would erode their profitability. A prohibition against any sort of stealing, whether it is company or personal property, is a credible way to convey standards and a spectrum of viable penalties for violations of this policy. This was effectively presented in the Employee Handbook in both English and Spanish. Furthermore, the Company even instituted a more targeted policy with regard to the authorized mushroom purchase policy for its employees. They clearly provided a means for employees to share in the productivity of the plant in a controlled manner that would also protect Company mushroom sales with minimum volume for its market requirements. Packaged within this policy were clear procedures that enabled full visibility of the authorized employee-purchased mushrooms, including a specific allocation per employee and reference to potential discharge penalties if violated. In essence, the Company effectively bounded the conditions benefiting its workforce while maintaining the standards for protecting the resources necessary for its success.

1

The Employer appears to have effectively applied penalties of discharge to violations of the intolerance for stealing policy in a fair and consistent manner. The policy is quite clear in that it cites that violations of said policy can result in discharge. The Employer cited several examples where bargaining unit and non-bargaining unit/salaried employees were terminated for proven theft. This included a long-term foreman of 26 years who was terminated for taking a single basket of white mushrooms and a bargaining unit member who was also discharged for "picking mushrooms after hours". The evidence also establishes that the Grievant's female coworker, who according to the Employer's investigation was determined to have stolen the two

2

boxes of mushrooms, was similarly terminated. Therefore, the finding of the arbitrator is that the penalty application pattern for stolen mushrooms has been fair and consistent.

In examining the third criteria on whether just cause was properly proven in this case it is appropriate to consider the two elements associated with the act of theft. That being, both the act of taking someone else's property without permission and that there was tangible intent on the part of the alleged perpetrator to do so. The arbitrator has determined that these "theft qualifiers" may be applicable to the case even though it is not a criminal proceeding but rather a grievance subject to the terms of the negotiated CBA and the Employer's Handbook relating to employee conduct while at the workplace.

Contrary to the Union's application relating to the levels of proof this issue falls under a level of proof that must be established by at least a preponderance of the evidence. However, in the context of collective bargaining agreement dispute clauses in matters of discipline that are submitted to an impartial arbitrator for a final and binding decision, the arbitrator has to be convinced that the act warrants the severest of penalties that can be applied in the industrial context of just cause. This is because there can be multiple situational variables that if not properly accounted for could lead the governing party to make a decision based on circumstantial or even inconclusive evidence. Inadvertent reliance on such unsubstantiated facts could also enable a decision that could be more influenced by opinion or a bias management agenda. Therefore, it is not unreasonable to ensure that such an aspect of fairness is appropriately applied to protect both the defendant and the workforce perception of the Company's corrective action-centric policies as well.

* * * *

The disparity in this case is not the act but whether or not the Grievant intentionally participated in the event in question. As with the first criteria, the Employer does have the burden of proving that the Grievant knowingly participated with the female coworker in the theft. To demonstrate this proof, the Employer would logically need to show that the Grievant had knowledge either before the event (such as establishing the conditions or conducting the planning) and/or during the event (realizing that a theft was occurring and still continuing his participation versus intervening to stop the activity or report the event). There was no evidence that the Grievant had knowledge before the event, in that there is nothing that cites him as being part of an effort to covertly position the mushrooms in the compressor room or that he helped plan the pick-up and final transport. There is also no evidence that conclusively reveals he knew the act involved a theft and continued with it anyway. The testimony was uncontested that he had been offered a ride by his coworker multiple times and that he had refused the offers. Hence, there is no evidence that this was a mutually planned encounter. It is not implausible that he offered to help load whatever the female coworker needed as the weather was reportedly wet and rainy. Nor, is it implausible that he just loaded what she had requested and then subsequently asked if he could have a few of her mushrooms perhaps, in return for the favor of helping her. The question that arises is if he should have had some spontaneous recognition that something was odd about what the coworker was asking him to do is that it is just simple conjecture. Frankly, it fails to rise to the level of intent on the part of the Grievant to be a co-conspirator in the unapproved removal of the mushroom product from the Employer's property. Rather, the just cause contention by the Employer essentially suggests that a seasoned employee, who also served as a shop steward, should have known that there was something suspicious in this scenario and his continued participation implies guilt. While this could be a theory it is not actual proof that the employee had the intent to participate in the theft.

It is appropriate to also consider if the Grievant was somehow negligent in not being aware enough of the circumstances to deduce that there was a theft event occurring. Acknowledging that his claim of gentlemanly conduct is a plausible excuse, the arbitrator however does not take quarrel with the Employer that it is odd that he did not question why mushrooms were being stored in the compressor room. Again, based on his seniority and his recent role as a shop steward, and routinely counseling another bargaining unit member about rumors of theft, the Grievant should have known better. However, lack of attention and/or negligence standing on its own does not constitute a guilty finding for the seriousness of a theft charge.

Therefore, it is the arbitrator's belief that based on the particular facts of this case and considering the totality of the evidence, in particular recognizing the Grievant's long employment history with the Company, an alternative penalty should have been more appropriately applied. It is the arbitrator's determination that based on the particular facts of this case the severest discipline to be imposed in the industrial sector is found to be inappropriate. Whereas, the more reasonable application of the Employer's discipline policies is to reduce the penalty to a three-month suspension, as well as placing the Grievant on a nine-month Last Chance Agreement that will commence from the day of his re-employment at Monterey Mushrooms, Inc.

DECISION

The termination of A__ is reduced to a three-month suspension with loss of pay and benefits. The Grievant is to be reinstated to his position and made whole for compensation and benefits less the three-month suspension. Likewise, he should be admonished for not being attentive to the conditions leading up to the said theft event, and his use of poor judgment in failing to recognize the obvious signs that would enable him to draw the reasonable conclusion that the female employee was using him to perpetuate her theft.

Finally, the parties will draft and put into place a nine-month Last Chance Agreement in which it states the Grievant fully acknowledges his error and expressing the fact that he will be subject to immediate termination if such negligence/behavior occurs in the future. The arbitrator shall retain jurisdiction for the sole purpose of resolving any disputes that may arise between the parties relating to the application of this decision and award.

It is so ordered.

APPLICATION AND DISCUSSION QUESTIONS

1. This case raises the issue of the standard of proof in disciplinary actions involving theft. The union argues the standard should be clear and convincing and the employer argues the standard is a preponderance of the evidence. The arbitrator points out that the beyond a reasonable doubt standard does not apply in discharge cases. Explain what is required to meet each of the two standards. There is a disagreement among arbitrators as to which standard should apply in these types of cases, but most arbitrators would apply the preponderance of the evidence standard. Which standard do you feel is appropriate? Did this evidence meet the clear and convincing evidence standard or the preponderance of the evidence standard?

2. Citing *Stockham Pipe Fittings, Co.*, LA 160 (1945), Arbitrator Riker stated, "the only circumstances under which a penalty imposed by management can be rightfully set aside by an arbitrator are those where discrimination, unfairness, or capricious and arbitrary actions are proved - in other words where there has been an act of discretion." Which of these standards did the Arbitrator find a violation?

3. What evidence did the employer present that showed the Grievant knowingly participated in the theft? Was the conduct serious enough for the Grievant to receive the "industrial capital" penalty?

4. What is a "Last Chance" agreement and is it appropriate for the Arbitrator to direct the employer and the union to enter into such an agreement?

5. How did the employer show there was no disparate treatment and that the policy was effectively communicated to employees?

SQUARE PLUS OPERATING CORP. V. LOCAL UNION NO. 917
140 L.R.R.M. 2389 (S.D.N.Y. 1992)

case

parking lot theft

FREEH, District Judge

Petitioner Square Plus Operating Corp. ("Square Plus") moves to vacate a November 12, 1989 arbitration award entered in favor of respondent Local Union No. 917, A/W International Brotherhood of Teamsters ("Local 917"), and Jacques Freycinet ("Freycinet"). Local 917 cross-moves to confirm the arbitration award. For the reasons stated at oral argument and below, Square Plus's motion is granted and the arbitration award vacated.

scen

FACTS

Freycinet was discharged by Square Plus in May 1989, allegedly because he had misappropriated parking fees paid to him by customers using one of Square Plus's parking lots in New York City. The collective bargaining agreement between Square Plus and Local 917 provides generally that its "grievance and arbitration procedure . . . shall be the sole and exclusive means for the determination of all disputes, complaints, controversies, claims or grievances whatsoever, including a claim based upon an alleged breach of [the] Agreement." That agreement specifically states, however, that Square Plus may discharge any employee "for theft, pilferage, drunkenness and continued absenteeism without justifiable reason; and such discharge shall not be subject to any grievance procedure as set forth in this Agreement."

issue

CBA

Square Plus agreed to proceed with the arbitration despite its continued protest that the question of Freycinet's discharge was not arbitrable. After conducting a hearing on the issue, the arbitrator concluded that because Square Plus had presented insufficient evidence to establish that Freycinet had engaged in any wrongdoing, the company did not have "just cause" to dismiss him. As a result, the arbitrator ordered Square Plus to reinstate Freycinet, with full back pay with all benefits due between the date of termination and the date of reinstatement.

Square Plus argues that the arbitration award must be vacated because (1) the termination of an employee for theft is specifically excluded from the collective bargaining agreement grievance procedure; (2) the arbitrator applied an erroneous burden of proof in determining that Square Plus had not produced sufficient evidence of theft; (3) the arbitrator failed to consider evidence to which the parties had stipulated; (4) the arbitrator's conduct at the conclusion of the hearing creates an appearance of impropriety; and (5) the relief award is excessive because the arbitrator did not consider whether Freycinet had mitigated his damages. Local 917 disagrees, and argues that the arbitration award should be confirmed in all respects.

DISCUSSION

1. Arbitrability (Omitted)

2. Validity of Arbitration Award

[2] Square Plus correctly argues, however, that the arbitration award must be vacated because of the arbitrator's "manifest disregard of the law" regarding Square Plus's burden of proof. See Merrill, Lynch, Pierce, Fenner & Smith v. Bobker, 808 F.2d 930, 933-34 (2d Cir. 1986) (courts have power to vacate arbitration award in limited circumstance where arbitrator ignores "well defined, explicit, and clearly applicable" rules of law). In finding in favor of Local 917, the arbitrator in this case found that while Square Plus had presented "abundant circumstantial evidence" that Freycinet had misappropriated customer funds, such evidence was insufficient to establish misconduct "beyond a reasonable doubt." According to the arbitrator," [a] suspicion of wrongdoing, however well documented, in the absence of absolute proof of such activity, cannot substitute for rationality." (Id.).

The arbitrator erred in subjecting Square Plus to such a stringent burden of proof. Freycinet was not being criminally prosecuted for theft in this case. Rather, the issue before the arbitrator was simply whether, under the terms of the collective bargaining agreement, Square Plus had just cause to discharge Freycinet. Under these circumstances, Square Plus need not introduce "absolute proof" that Freycinet mis-appropriated customer funds. Just cause for Freycinet's discharge will be established *Standard* if Square Plus can show, by a preponderance of the evidence, that he committed the thefts alleged.

Because we conclude that the arbitration award must be vacated in its entirety, we need not address Square Plus's other grounds for relief. We do note, however, that the arbitrator may have misinterpreted the testimony of Square Plus's handwriting expert, Norman Werling. (arbitration award incorrectly states that handwriting expert did not conclude that Freycinet "has prepared the receipts"). Werling's testimony before the arbitrator, which is consistent with his pre-hearing report and later affidavits, was that Freycinet's handwriting appeared on both the customer receipts. The evidence thus established a strong inference that Freycinet did in fact prepare the receipts at issue.

For the reasons stated above, the November 12, 1989 arbitration award in favor of *vacated* Local 917 is hereby vacated.

SO ORDERED.

APPLICATION AND DISCUSSION PROBLEMS

1. What burden of proof did the arbitrator apply in this case?

2. Even if the court felt the arbitrator made an error, was that sufficient to vacate the award?

V. ISSUE GRIEVANCES

A. The Contract Interpretation Analysis

It is practically impossible for parties to a collective bargaining agreement to negotiate and to agree on terms where there are no gaps, the language is absolute clear, and all are well defined. Indeed, parties may in fact leave some terms left undefined and unclear language in the agreement to reach a final agreement on the entire contract. Consequently there will be disputes over the interpretation of terms and language in the agreement. Arbitrators will be called upon to determine the meaning and interpretation of ambiguous terms.

PRINCIPLES OF CONTRACT INTERPRETATION: INTERPRETING COLLECTIVE BARGAINING AGREEMENTS
16 CAP. U. L. REV. 31 (1986)[*]
JAY E. GRENIG

I. BASIC CONCEPTS

A. Introduction

Contract interpretation requires a determination of just what the parties meant when they adopted certain language or of how the parties would have wanted their language to be applied in specific circumstances. The interpretive process involves giving meaning to the words used by the parties in their collective bargaining agreement.

---

[*]   Reprinted from 16 Cap. U. L. Rev. 31 (1986) with permission from Jay E. Grenig.

Despite the concerns of some arbitrators, over the years many arbitrators have looked to the principles of interpretation for guidance in interpreting collective bargaining agreements. The principles of contract and statutory interpretation serve as guides and are not used as rigid or undeviating rules to be followed as methodically as though labor relations were an exact science. The person interpreting a collective bargaining agreement must rely on his or her total background of experience and expertise in the collective bargaining process with due regard to the relationship of the parties and their presentations in order to provide as practical and realistic an interpretation as is possible. Contract language cannot be viewed or construed in a vacuum, devoid of the background of negotiations and the circumstances and conditions leading up to the ultimate agreement. An arbitrator should not, through a highly technical interpretation of contract language, impose upon the parties conditions that were never agreed to. A true understanding of the collective bargaining agreement may be gained only by giving careful attention to the function it was intended to perform.

B. Intent and Purpose

The primary goal of contract interpretation is to determine the mutual intent of the parties. Many arbitration awards considering issues of contract interpretation are written in the context of the intent of the parties.

The principle of considering the parties' intent is based on the assumption that there is an obligation to construe collective bargaining parties' agreements so that they carry out the intent, real or attributed, of the parties. Because no single principle of interpretation can establish exactly what the parties intended, the determination of intention requires the exercise of judgment.

The parties' intent is generally found in the words which they used to express their intent in the collective bargaining agreement. Although contract language provides a significant indication of what the parties intended, extrinsic evidence found in the bargaining history and the parties' administration of the contract may also be helpful.' The imperfection of language makes it impossible to know what the intention is without inquiring further and seeing what the circumstances were with reference to which the words were used, and what the apparent object the parties had in view. The intent manifested by the parties to each other during negotiations by their communications and by their responsive proposals rather than undisclosed understandings and impressions should be considered in determining the meaning of contract language.

C. Clear and Unambiguous Language

It is frequently stated that arbitrators are bound to give effect to the literal meaning of the language without consulting other indicia of intent or meaning when the language is "plain" or "clear and unambiguous." An arbitrator's failure to follow language which is found to be clear and unambiguous may result in the award being vacated. Language is ambiguous if it is reasonably susceptible of more than one meaning. It has been held that language is not ambiguous if an arbitrator can determine its meaning without any other guide, because the words of the agreement are plain and clearly convey a distinct idea.

An arbitrator may find language to be ambiguous despite both parties' contentions that the language is clear and unambiguous. Language contains a latent ambiguity when the language is clear on its face, but some extrinsic fact makes the language susceptible to more than one interpretation.

It is not always clear whether the words of a collective bargaining agreement are clear and unambiguous. Whether contract language is ambiguous can frequently be determined only after taking into consideration the circumstances existing at the time the contract was adopted and the practice of the parties in applying it. Even where contract language appears unambiguous on its face, it can be rendered ambiguous by its interaction with and its relation to other contract provisions.

D. Strict or Liberal Interpretation

"Liberal interpretation" is often used to describe an interpretation which produces broader coverage or more inclusive application. A liberal construction makes a contract provision applicable to more things or in more situations than would be the case under a so-called "strict construction." A strict interpretation is one which limits the application of the contract provision.

It is sometimes said that remedial provisions should be given liberal interpretation and punitive provisions should be given strict interpretation. Occasionally a contract may expressly provide that it is to "be strictly construed." When an exception is stated as a general principle the exception should be strictly, though properly, construed and applied. If a contract is properly interpreted, it probably serves no useful purpose to describe the interpretation as either "strict" or "liberal."

E. Mandatory or Permissive Interpretation

Ordinarily the use of the word "shall" carries with it the presumption that it is used in the mandatory sense and "may" is used in the permissive sense.

II. INTERNAL STANDARDS

A. Introduction

Initially one must look at the collective bargaining agreement itself for evidence of what the parties intended. Since the words in the con tract are chosen by the parties to express the meaning of the contract, the words are no doubt the most important single factor in ascertaining the parties' intent. When experienced negotiators draft collective bargaining agreements, the presumption must be that they understand what they are doing.

In United Steelworkers of America v. Enterprise Wheel & Car Corp., the United States Supreme Court held an arbitrator is "confined to interpretation and application of the collective bargaining agreement." While the arbitrator may look for guidance from many sources, the Court said the arbitration "award is legitimate only so long as it draws its essence from the collective bargaining agreement." Accordingly, the contract language is the first and most important point of reference when interpreting a contract.

B. Primary Standards

1. Plain Meaning

According to the "plain meaning rule," if a writing appears to be plain and unambiguous on its face, its meaning must be determined from the four corners of the instrument without resort to extrinsic evidence of any nature. The plain meaning rule has been criticized on the grounds that the meaning of words varies with the "verbal context and surrounding circumstances and purposes in view of the linguistic education, and experience of their users and their hearers or readers . . . ."

2. Ordinary and Popular Meaning

a. Generally

It is frequently said that words should be given their ordinary and popular meaning in the absence of anything indicating that they were used in a different sense or that the parties intended sorrie special meaning. The Restatement of Contracts provides:

> In the absence of some contrary indication, therefore, English words are read as having the meaning given them by general usage, if there is one. This rule is a rule of interpretation in the absence of contrary evidence, not a rule excluding contrary evidence. This reflects a concern for the meaning communicated to others by the contract language.

b. Dictionary Definitions

Arbitrators have frequently relied upon the dictionary definitions of words in determining the ordinary and popular meaning. However, one advocate has cautioned that the precise or dictionary meaning of contract language often falls short of expressing fundamental postulates, understandings, assumptions, or policies.

c. Judicial Definitions

The decisions of appellate courts may also provide assistance in determining the meaning of contract terms.

d. Technical Terms

Technical terms should be given their technical meaning, unless the context or usage indicates a different meaning. Some industrial relations terms have acquired special meaning. Technical dictionaries may be useful for ascertaining the meaning of terms used in their technical sense.

3. Construing Contract as a Whole

A primary rule in construing a collective bargaining agreement is to determine the intent of the parties from the instrument as a whole. If one of the asserted interpretations is logically supported by other contract provisions and the other is not, then the former meaning should be upheld.

Dean Harry Shulman recognized the importance of construing a collective bargaining agreement as a whole, declaring, "Though all the parts of the agreement do not necessarily make a consistent pattern, the interpretation which is most compatible with the agreement as a whole is to be preferred over one which creates anomaly."

Language should be construed and harmonized with other provisions so as to give it uniform meaning. A word used by the parties in one sense should be interpreted in the same manner throughout the contract in the absence of countervailing reasons. The use of two different terms probably indicates the parties intended two different meanings. Where the parties have agreed in other provisions to exclude certain items, their failure to exclude those items in the provision in question may indicate the parties did not intend that those items be excluded in that provision.

4. Giving Effect to All Provisions

Because it can be assumed the parties did not intend one provision of the contract to cancel out another provision, if the language is susceptible of two constructions, one which will carry out and the other defeat the object of the contract, the one which will carry out the contract should prevail.

All language should be given meaning and should not be ignored. Effect should be given, if possible, to every word, sentence, and clause in the contract. No words should be rejected as surplusage if any reasonable meaning can be found. Because the parties' use of a word indicates they intended it to have some meaning, an interpretation which gives meaning to every part of the contract is preferred to one that gives no effect to one or more parts. However, when there is an unavoidable conflict between general and specific provisions, the specific provision will prevail.

5. Context

Words must be interpreted with a view to the context in which they are employed. The Restatement of Contracts states:

> Meaning is inevitably dependent on context. A word changes meaning when it
> becomes part of a sentence, the sentence when it becomes part of a paragraph . . . To
> fit the immediate verbal context or the more remote total context particular words or
> punctuation may be disregarded or supplied; clerical or grammatical errors may be
> corrected; singular may be treated as plural or plural as singular.

The language being construed must be considered along with all the other words by which it is surrounded, the history of the parties, the nature of the industry or business, and other relevant circumstances.

In addition to the contractual context, the importance of keeping in mind the labor relations context when interpreting collective bargaining agreements was stressed by Dean Shulman:

> The effects on efficiency, productivity and cost are important factors to be considered. So also are the effects on the attitudes and interests of the employees. The interpretation, no matter how right in the abstract, is self-defeating and harmful to both sides if its day-to-day application provides further occasion for controversy and irritation.

APPLICATION AND DISCUSSION QUESTIONS

1. How are collective bargaining contracts different from traditional contracts? How are the principles of contract interpretation different from interpreting collective bargaining contracts?

2. When interpreting a collective bargaining contract, how does the arbitrator determine the intent of the parties? *words in k, extrinsic evidence*

3. How do arbitrators determine when language in a collective bargaining agreement is clear and unambiguous? How does the author define "liberal interpretation" of contracts? *no other meaning ; broad view*

COLFAX ENVELOPE CORP. V. LOCAL NO. 458-3M, CHICAGO GRAPHIC COMMUNICATIONS INTERNAT'L UNION, AFL-CIO
20 F.3D 750 (7TH CIR. 1994)

POSNER, Chief Judge.

This appeal in a suit over a collective bargaining agreement presents a fundamental issue of contract law, that of drawing the line between an ambiguous contract, requiring interpretation, and a contract that, because it cannot be said to represent the agreement of the parties at all, cannot be interpreted, can only be rescinded and the parties left to go their own ways. Colfax, the plaintiff, is a manufacturer of envelopes. It does some printing of its envelopes, and the seventeen employees who do the printing are represented by the defendant union. Colfax has two printing presses. One prints 78-inch-wide sheets in four colors. The other prints 78-inch-wide sheets in five colors, but most of the time Colfax prints only four-color sheets on it.

Colfax has so few printing employees that it does not bother to participate in the collective bargaining negotiations between the union and the Chicago Lithographers Association, an association for collective bargaining of the other Chicago printing companies whose employees are represented by this union. Instead, whenever the union and the CLA sign a new collective bargaining agreement, the union sends Colfax a summary of the changes that the new agreement has made in the old one. If Colfax is content with the changes, the union sends it a copy of the complete new agreement, which Colfax signs and returns. If Colfax doesn't like the terms negotiated by the CLA, it is free to do its own bargaining with the union.

The collective bargaining agreements specify minimum manning requirements for each type of press used by the printers. The agreement in force between 1987 and 1991 fixed those minima as three men for four-color presses printing sheets 45 to 50 inches wide and four men for four-color presses printing sheets wider than 50 inches. Five-color presses printing sheets more than 55 inches wide required five men unless only four colors were printed, in which event only four men were required. The upshot was that under these agreements, all of which Colfax had signed, Colfax had to man each of its presses (which were 78-inch presses) with four men except on the rare occasions when it printed five-color sheets on its second press, and then it had to add a man.

In 1991 the union negotiated a new agreement with the CLA and sent a summary of the changes to Colfax. The letter enclosing the summary asked Colfax to indicate whether it agreed to the terms in the summary. (This may have been a departure from past practice, in which Colfax signed the complete agreement rather than the summary, but if so neither party makes anything of it.) In a section on manning requirements, the summary lists "4C 60" Press--3 Men" and "5C 78" Press--4 Men." Believing (in part because union members who claimed to be familiar with the new agreement had told Colfax that Colfax would really like the changes in it) that this meant that all presses operated as four-color presses would now require only three men to man them, Colfax's president and majority shareholder, Charles Patten, signed the union's letter, indicating acceptance of the terms in the summary. Later a copy of the actual agreement arrived, but it contained a crucial typo, which supported Patten's understanding of the summary. When a corrected copy of the agreement finally arrived, the manning requirements stated in it were different from what Patten had understood from the summary. Four-color presses between 45 and 60 inches required three men, but all four-color presses over 60 inches required four men. The changes had not benefited Colfax at all, and because it was under competitive pressure, it would have liked to negotiate better terms. Patten refused to sign the agreement but the union took the position that Colfax was bound to it by its acceptance of the summary.

Colfax brought this suit under *section 301* of the Taft-Hartley Act, 29 U.S.C. § 185, for a declaration that it has no collective bargaining contract with the union because the parties never agreed on an essential term--the manning requirements for Colfax's printing presses. The union counterclaimed for an order to arbitrate. The union's position was that Colfax had accepted the new agreement, which requires arbitration of all disputes "arising out of the application or interpretation of this contract." The district judge granted summary judgment for the union, concluding that the reference to the new manning requirement for a four-color 60-inch press in the summary of changes that Colfax had accepted referred unambiguously to 60-inch presses and had no application to any other presses, such as Colfax's 78-inch presses. Colfax has appealed.

One way to describe the issue that divides the parties is that they disagree about the meaning of the term "4C 60" Press--3 Men." Colfax believes that it means four-color presses printing sheets 60 inches and over, while the union believes that it means four-color presses 60 inches and under (down to 45 inches). Remember that the previous agreement had allowed the use of three-man crews on four-color presses between 45 and 50 inches. The union interprets the change as extending the upper bound of the three-man range to 60 inches. Ordinarily a dispute over the meaning of a contractual term is, if the contract contains an arbitration clause, for the arbitrator to decide. But sometimes the difference between the parties goes so deep that it is impossible to say that they ever agreed--that they even *have* a contract that a court or arbitrator might interpret. In the famous though enigmatic and possibly misunderstood case of *Raffles v. Wichelhaus, 2 H. & C. 906,* 159 Eng.Rep. 375 (Ex. 1864), the parties made a contract for the delivery of a shipment of cotton from Bombay to England on the ship *Peerless.* Unbeknownst to either party, there were two ships of that name sailing from Bombay on different dates. One party thought the contract referred to one of the ships, and the other to the other. The court held that there was no contract; there had been no "meeting of the minds." See generally A.W. Brian Simpson, "Contracts for Cotton to Arrive: The Case of the Two Ships *Peerless,*" 11 *Cardozo L.Rev.* 287 (1989).

The premise--that a "meeting of the minds" is required for a binding contract--obviously is strained. 2 E. Allan Farnsworth, *Contracts* § 7.9, at p. 251 (1990). Most contract disputes arise because the parties did not foresee and provide for some contingency that has now materialized--so there was no meeting of minds on the matter at issue--yet such disputes are treated as disputes over contractual meaning, not as grounds for rescinding the contract and thus putting the parties back where they were before they signed it. So a literal meeting of the minds is not required for an enforceable contract, which is fortunate, since courts are not renowned as mind readers.

* * * *

Raffles and *Oswald* were cases in which neither party was blameable for the mistake; *Balistreri* a case in which both were equally blameable, the parents for having failed to read the deed of trust, the lender for having drafted a misleading cover letter. It is all the same. *Restatement (Second) of Contracts* §§ 20(1)(a), (b) (1981). If neither party can be assigned the greater blame for the misunderstanding, there is no nonarbitrary basis for deciding which party›s understanding to enforce, so the parties are allowed to abandon the contract without liability. *Neel v. Lang*, (1920); *Konic International Corp. v. Spokane Computer Services, Inc.*, (App.1985). These are not cases in which one party's understanding is more reasonable than the other's. Compare *Restatement, supra*, § 20(2)(b). If rescission were permitted in *that* kind of case, the enforcement of every contract would be at the mercy of a jury, which might be persuaded that one of the parties had genuinely held an idiosyncratic idea of its meaning, so that there had been, in fact, no meeting of the minds. Cf. Young, *supra*, at 646. Intersubjectivity is not the test of an enforceable contract.

* * * *

Our case is superficially similar. The actual terms of the 1991 agreement were muddied in the summary that the union gave Colfax and that Colfax signed, making it possible that the parties had different understandings. The difference between this case and the others is that Colfax, unlike the hapless promisors in the cases we have cited, should have realized that the contract was unclear. The buyer in *Konic* thought--*really* thought--that he was being quoted a price of $56.20, and no doubt fell off his stool when he discovered that the price was a hundred times greater than he thought. But the expression "4C 60" Press" does not on its face speak to the minimum manning requirement for a 4C 78" Press. The union's interpretation, that the phrase merely extended the upper bound of the old range for three-man four-color presses from 50 to 60 inches, may or may not be correct. The fact that the union restated and clarified the interpretation in the corrected agreement that it sent Colfax is not decisive on the question, because it is the summary rather than the corrected full agreement that is the contract between these parties. But Colfax, if reasonable, could not have doubted from reading the summary that interpretations of the kind that the union and the district judge later placed upon it would be entirely plausible. Colfax had a right to *hope* that its interpretation would prevail but it had no right to accept the offer constituted by the summary on the premise that either its interpretation was correct or it could walk away from the contract. "Heads I win, tails you lose," is not the spirit that animates the principle that latent ambiguity is a ground for rescission of a contract.

It is common for contracting parties to agree--that is, to *signify* agreement--to a term to which each party attaches a different meaning. It is just a gamble on a favorable interpretation by the authorized tribunal should a dispute arise. Parties often prefer to gamble in this way rather than to take the time to try to iron out all their possible disagreements, most of which may never have any consequence. Colfax gambled on persuading an arbitrator that the reference in the summary to the four-color 60-inch press meant what Colfax believes it means. The union gambled on the arbitrator's adopting the meaning that the union later made clear in the full agreement--but, to repeat, if there is a contract it is (the parties agree) the summary, read in light of the collective bargaining agreement that was being modified, that is the contract between these parties.

When parties agree to a patently ambiguous term, they submit to have any dispute over it resolved by interpretation. That is what courts and arbitrators are *for* in contract cases--to resolve interpretive questions founded on ambiguity. It is when parties agree to terms that reasonably appear to each of them to be unequivocal but are not, cases like that of the ship *Peerless* where the ambiguity is buried, that the possibility of rescission on grounds of mutual misunderstanding, or, the term we prefer, latent ambiguity, arises. A reasonable person in Colfax's position would have realized that its interpretation of the term "4C 60" Press--3 Men" might not coincide with that of the other party or of the tribunal to which a dispute over the meaning of the term would be submitted. It threw the dice, and lost, and that is the end of the case. It cannot gamble on a favorable interpretation and, if that fails, repudiate the contract with no liability. Cf. *Prudential Ins. Co. v. Miller Brewing Co.*, (7th Cir.1986).

We would have a different case if the ambiguity were over whether the parties had agreed to arbitrate their disputes. The duty to arbitrate is contractual, and the interpretation of the contract that creates the duty is for the court. *AT & T Technologies,*

Inc. v. Communications Workers of America, (1986). But courts will not allow a party to unravel a contractual arbitration clause by arguing that the clause was part of a contract that is voidable, perhaps because fraudulently induced. *Prima Paint Corp. v. Flood & Conklin Mfg. Co.*, (1967); *Matterhorn, Inc. v. NCR Corp.*, (7th Cir.1985). The party must show that the arbitration clause itself, which is to say the parties' agreement to arbitrate any disputes over the contract that might arise, is vitiated by fraud, or lack of consideration or assent, as in *Three Valleys Municipal Water District v. E.F. Hutton & Co.*, (9th Cir.1991); that in short the parties never agreed to arbitrate their disputes. *Wheat, First Securities, Inc. v. Green*, (11th Cir.1993). Colfax and the union had in a long course of dealing always agreed to submit their contractual disputes to arbitration, so the only question is whether their dispute in this case was a dispute over the meaning of their contract. It was, so it had to be arbitrated, for that was the parties' chosen method of resolving disagreements, whether or not Colfax would have signed on to the 1991 agreement had it realized what the agreement actually meant or could be interpreted to mean. *Matterhorn, Inc. v. NCR Corp.*

We go further: Even if, contrary to our earlier analysis, there was no "meeting of the minds" (in the artificial sense in which the law of contracts uses the term) on the manning requirements in the 1991 agreement, there was a meeting of the minds on the mode of arbitrating disputes between the parties arising from any collective bargaining contract (including a summary of changes in a previous contract) that Colfax signed. Under the Supreme Court's decision in *Prima Paint*, a contract dispute is arbitrable even if one party argues that the contract should be rescinded because it does not express an actual agreement of the parties, for example because it was induced by fraud. All that is important is that the parties have agreed that arbitration rather than adjudication would be the mode of resolving their disputes. A different view would in many cases deprive the arbitrator of an important contract remedy--rescission. This point has implications for the scope of the arbitrator's responsibilities, of which more presently.

We thus affirm the district judge's decision, but point out that her conclusion that the disputed term unequivocally bears the meaning that she assigned to it (which incidentally is not identical to the union's interpretation, for she thought it a point--60-inch presses, period--while the union thought it a range--60-inch presses and down) does not bind the arbitrator. His is the responsibility, subject to the excruciatingly limited right of judicial review of arbitral decisions, to interpret the agreement. It will therefore be open to Colfax to argue to the arbitrator that, under a proper interpretation of the contract, there really was no meeting of the minds over the manning requirements and therefore that the contract should be rescinded after all. The only essential point at this stage of the litigation is that whether or not there was (as we believe, without meaning to bind the arbitrator) such a meeting of minds, there was sufficient mutual understanding to create an enforceable contract to submit the issue to arbitration.

AFFIRMED.

APPLICATION AND DISCUSSION QUESTIONS

1. What contract principle does the Court in *Raffles v. Wichelhaus*, 2 H & C. 906, 159 Eng. Rep. 373 (Ex. 1864) cite to establish the existence of a contract? How might arbitrators cite this case in contract interpretation cases? *"meeting of the minds"; to determine if parties agreed to same thing*

2. The Court also cites Restatement (Second) of Contracts, §20 (1)(A)(5) (1981) when determining whether a contract should be set aside when both parties have a misunderstanding of the terms of a contract provision.

3. If the parties agree to a "patently ambiguous term", how does the arbitrator interpret such terms? *extrinsic evidence, past practice, custom, the more "plain" meaning*

4. Who has the burden of proof in contract interpretation disputes? Arbitrator Bell answers the question in this manner:

"While the Association may be applauded for its creative and resourceful interpretation, placing the "burden of proof" in this proceeding upon the Employer, its efforts fall short of the mark in addressing which party is required by arbitral law to bear that burden, and the weight of the evidence to be borne in a contract interpretation and application arbitral proceeding.

The overall weight of arbitral law in contract interpretation and application proceedings is that the party affirmatively asserting a contract violation by the other party bears the burden of proving, by the preponderance of clear and convincing evidence, that the other party actually committed such violation. As this arbitrator has repeatedly stated, that burden is so placed reflecting the "legal presumption" that both parties to a collective bargaining agreement have faithfully honored and carried out the obligations they respectively undertook when they entered into that agreement. Such placement of the burden of proof also reflects the common sense recognition that it is easier to prove the existence of fact than the absence of fact and that to hold otherwise would encourage conflict grievances by placing the burden on a party to prove they are innocent of alleged violations.... hardly an "objective" of constructive labor/management relations. Where, as here, a party asserts a different placement of that burden, the labor contract must explicitly so state. Such a statement is here lacking. For all these reasons, the burden of proof in these proceedings rests with the Association as the party alleging a violation of the labor agreement."

City of Wadsworth and the Ohio Patrolmen's Benevolent Association, 134 BNA LA 641 (Bell, 2015)

THE PLAIN MEANING RULE

AIR SYSTEM COMPONENTS LP,
125 BNA LA 100 (DILTS, 2008)[*]

Issue

Did the Company violate Article 16 of the parties' 2006 Collective Bargaining Agreement concerning wage increases for certain employees with less than one year of service on August 7, 2006? If so, what shall be the remedy?

Background

Air System Components operates a manufacturing facility in Lebanon, Indiana (herein the Company or Employer). The Company produces air movement components used in the HVAC industry.

* * * *

---

[*] Reprinted with permission from *Labor Relations Reporter- Labor Arbitration Reports*. 125 BNA LA 100. Copyright 2015 by the Bureau of National Affairs, Inc. (800-372-1033). http://www.bna.com.

Shortly after the Agreement was ratified the Union approached the Company concerning "incremental increases" for employees who had not reached the "one year rate" in their respective classifications. The aggrieved employees are those individuals who were employees of the Company as of the effective date of the parties' Collective Bargaining Agreement, but who had not yet achieved one year of service as of that date. These employees did receive a forty cent increase on the effective date of the contract, and then received the "one year rate" contained in Article 16 upon the completion of one year of service. The parties were unable to resolve their differences, and the Union filed a timely grievance alleging a violation of an established practice and Article 16 of the parties' Collective Bargaining Agreement. Management denied the grievance, and its subsequent appeals through the parties' negotiated grievance procedure (Article 6).

Union's Position

The dispute before the Arbitrator arose over employees who were hired prior to August 7, 2006, and who had been hired under then existing system that provided employees with incremental wage increases every two months from the time they hired-in until they reached the "top rate" for their classification. The Company, during negotiations, proposed a "new system" that would require an employee to obtain certain skills, and upon training and obtaining those skills, then the employee would move from a "B" rated classification to the "A" rate, of top of the applicable classification. In contract law, it is common to rule against the drafter when interpreting the proposed language, as in the case here. It is important to understand what was not said, when evaluating what the parties meant. If the Company intended to change the system for current employees, then the Company was required to notify the parties of their intent. Silence, in this matter, should not be rewarded.

Where applicable, because as seen in Article 16, not all classification begin at a "B" level, only those classifications generally thought to require more skill and training are covered under this provision.

The testimony of both witnesses confirms that the Company was proposing new language for a new process for "future" employees. There is nothing ambiguous about the fact concerning the Company's intent in this proposal.

* * * *

As to the Company's assertion that the parties agreed to eliminate "past practices" as delineated in Article 13, Section 8: The Union argues that this citation is not relevant;

in as much as the Union is not asserting a "past practice" but a "claim that the parties had agreed, by their action to a transition from the old system to the new," and therefore, the reason for specifically providing a "cut-off" date in Article 16 of the Agreement. That date, August 7, 2006 specifies that new employees hired thereafter will be under the new system for obtaining the top rate of pay for their respective classification.

The Union believes that the Company's assertion that there is no need for the parol rules to apply is without merit. The meaning of the words "current employees" and the fact that there is a cut-off date included in Article 16 shows that the old system was contemplated by the parties in their negotiations and was being used during negotiations, and subsequently. Company contentions that these matters were not discussed are not credible and must be construed against the Company as it was the author of both pay plans, the old progression, and the new bargained-for plan. The Union is confident that the Arbitrator understands the role he is to play in interpreting and applying the contract and the old pay system in this matter. What occurred during negotiations reflects what the parties' mutual intent was and must be considered by the Arbitrator in this case. The Company suggesting that the plain meaning rule has applicability under these facts and circumstances is utterly without merit and should be rejected by the Arbitrator.

The Union asserts that it has met its burden of proof and the unrefuted testimony of the witnesses, both Company and Union, clearly established the intention of the parties and the meaning of the language that the parties intended to apply during the transition from the old to the new pay system. For all of the foregoing reasons, the Union respectfully requests that the grievance be sustained in its entirety and that the aggrieved employees be made whole for all of their losses.

Company's Position

* * * *

There are several key arbitration principles which apply to this case, all of which support the Company's position. The first principle is that if contract language is clear and unambiguous, an arbitrator is not permitted to give it a meaning other that which is expressed. The recognized treatise How Arbitration Works by the Elkouris notes that an arbitrator may not "ignore clear-cut contractual language" and "may not legislate new language, since to do so would usurp the role of the labor organization and employer."

In the present case, the language of Article 16 is clear and unambiguous. The first paragraph of Article 16 established a uniform rate of pay for employees in various classifications who had completed one year of service as of the effective date of the labor contract. Generally speaking, these individual hold "A" designated jobs, and the one year rate negotiated by the Company and Union represented a forty cent increase for those employees.

The second paragraph in Article 16 covers pay for those employees who are the subject of the instant grievance: employees who were on the payroll on the contract's effective date but who had not yet achieved one year of service. They, too, received a forty cent increase upon the contract effective date, and they then received another increase, to the one year rate for the "A" designated jobs, when the attained one year of service. These two provisions are clear and unambiguous: Bargaining unit employees hired prior to August 7, 2006 who have not completed one year of service as of August 7, 2006 will receive a forty cents ($.40) per hour increase on August 7, 2006 and will receive the rate listed above upon completion of one year of service.

The Union says that regardless of this clear language, the "intent" was to preserve the 2, 4, and 6 month progression increases for these employees. But it is a recognized principle of arbitration that where language is clear and unambiguous, parol evidence is not permitted or appropriate.

Even if parol evidence is improperly considered, the Union has failed in its burden of establishing that the parties agreed to continue the past practice of 2, 4 and 6 month progressions for this group of employees. Union chief negotiator Randy McKay is an experienced negotiator, testifying that he has negotiated 300 to 400 contracts in his career. When asked to produce any proposals from negotiations supporting the Union's position concerning extension of a 2, 4, and 6 month pay progression into the contract, Mr. McKay admitted that he did not have any proposals to support this. When asked whether he could produce any bargaining notes reflecting a discussion or commitment on the subject of maintaining the former pay progression for employees who would not be covered by paragraph two of Article 16, he admitted that he did not have any. Mr. McKay further admitted that the Union read the final draft language of the contract before signing it, that it specifically included the relevant language of Article 16, and that his signature appears on the signature page of the contract.

* * * *

Another principle of contract interpretation is to read provisions in a manner that produces a logical and consistent result. The Company's position in this case meets this test; the Union's position does not.

* * * *

In the end, the Union is attempting to gain through arbitration what it failed to achieve at negotiations. Specifically, the Union is attempting here to gain additional pay for the grievants in this matter to which they are not entitled. It appears obvious that what happened is that after the contract was ratified, employees in the group pushed the Union to get back their progression increases, even though they had received a forty cent increase at contract signing, just like the more senior employees, and even though at the end of one year of employment they began receiving the same one year rate applicable to the more senior employees.

* * * *

Arbitrator's Opinion

* * * *

What is at dispute between these parties is a rather straightforward and simple matter of what is required of the Company with respect to the wage adjustments for employees with less than one year of service as of August 7, 2006. This is a straightforward contract interpretation case. The Company contends that past practices are relied upon by the Union and are not binding in this case, the Union claims it is not relying on practices, but on the mutual understanding of the parties as to what would happen to the employees with less than one year of service during the first year of the contract. Management, claims that Article 16 is clear and complete with respect to these facts and circumstances and that the Union's theory of the case is neither consistent with the agreed-to contract language nor logical. The Arbitrator will examine these competing arguments, in tuna, in the following paragraphs of this opinion, before addressing any remedy that may be due should there be a contract violation.

Past Practice

The Company contends that the plain meaning rule should apply in this matter, and that parol evidence is barred from consideration in this matter. In fact, the plain meaning rule can provide guidance, but it is far from a universal truth that the plain meaning rule bars consideration of parol evidence in matters where otherwise clear language has given rise to competing interpretations-hence in matters where there are competing interpretations of specific contract language and neither is, on its face unreasonable or is shown with a preponderance of evidence to be harsh, absurd, or unreasonable the plain meaning rule must be applied with considerable caution.

Also management contends that Article 13, Section 8 states that past practices "shall not be binding on either party." Such language is also not universally accepted in the arbitration profession as barring consideration of contracts established by the parties through their customs and consistent actions under specific circumstances-even to amend clear and unambiguous contract language. Even so, this Arbitrator does not get the sense that the Union is arguing that a past practice is what they are relying on with respect to their claims concerning this grievance. What the Union argues is that there is a transition period and that the parties' contract recognizes that the old system is applicable to employees with less than one year of service as of August 7, 2006. To this end, testimony concerning the negotiations was entered into this record, and specific language from Article 16 was cited as the Union's authority in this matter.

This Arbitrator is persuaded that past practice could not be an issue in this matter, if for no other reason than this is the initial contract between the parties. How employees are treated under the contract, and the old progression system once the initial contract was negotiated is something for which no evidence of any custom or practice was proffered-nor could it be discovered-by either party. Therefore, practices concerning this specific issue are not found in this record, and are not binding contracts on the parties. More importantly, the party relying on the practice is obliged to prove the practice exists. All that exists here is the Company claiming the Union is alleging a practice exist, and the Union arguing that it is not contending that any such practice is to be found.

Article 16 Language
Article 16, paragraphs 2 and 3 state:

> Bargaining unit employees hired prior to August 7, 2006 who have not completed one
> year of service as of August 7, 2006 will receive a forty cents ($.40) per hour increase

on August 7, 2006 and will receive the rate listed above upon completion of one year of service.

Bargaining unit employees hired on or after August 7, 2006 upon completion of one year of service will receive the following rates of pay. The Company will determine the new hire rate and the 120-day rate for such new hires...

It is the Arbitrator's construction of this language for which the parties bargained and memorialized in Article 6 of their Collective Bargaining Agreement. It is evident from a cursory reading that the second paragraph of Article 16 that the parties intended this paragraph to apply to these aggrieved employees, those with less than a year of service at the time the contract was signed (August 7, 2006). The language is also clear and explicit that these aggrieved employees received a forty cent increase on August 7, 2006-an increase from where their wage was at the time the contract was signed, and that they would receive the specified wage for the classification in which they worked after achieving one year of seniority. Such an arrangement has all the appearances of being the totality of the parties' agreement for those employees with less than a year of service on August 7, 2006. The very next paragraph speaks to what happens to new hire, those employees hired on or after August 7, 2006. In examining the first paragraph of Article 16, the language: "Effective August 7, 2006, the hourly rates of pay for bargaining unit employees who have completed one year of service are as follows:" [emphasis added] Clearly, the parties agreed on a pay scale for those employees with more than a year of service. The remainder of Article 16 provides for wage increases on August 6, 2007, August 4, 2008, and August 10, 2009. At no place in Article 16 could this Arbitrator find any mention of the old pay system providing for 2, 4, or 6 month progressions in pay for the aggrieved employees.

Therefore this Arbitrator is persuaded that on the clear and unambiguous language of Article 16, management must prevail. The Union's contention that ambiguity or incompleteness must be construed against the author of the language is moot in this matter. However, the Union contends that there was an understanding across the table that the progression would continue during the first year of the Collective Bargaining Agreement.

Mr. McKay testified credibly that it was his understanding that the progression would continue as a transition measure to make sure the employees with less than a year of service would be treated fairly. Clearly, Mr. McKay was under the impression that the nonunion pay progression would continue under the Union contract. Mr. Williams, the Company representative, testified that:

Q. And do you recall at any time in the negotiations a proposal or even a discussion of maintaining the old wage progression for certain employees?

A. No, I do not.

On cross examination, Mr. Williams reaffirmed his understanding. Again, this Arbitrator found Mr. Williams to be a credible witness. In other words, two honest men, attending and observing the exact same negotiations came away with two different impressions. However, those negotiations produced a written document which purports to be the agreement of the parties concerning various issues, including wages.

The Arbitrator finds the Company's contentions concerning the logic of the Union's position somewhat strained. Under the Union position it is not at all clear that the aggrieved employees would be entitled to the 120-day increase as argued by the Company, but reserved by the language of the third paragraph of Article 16 to only new hires. Even so, there is a clear logic to the treatment of senior employees, new hires, and those employees with less than a year of service as of August 7, 2006 to be found in Article 16 of the parties initial Collective Bargaining Agreement.

Whether the negotiators had a meeting of the minds seems, ex post facto, subject to debate. However, the language memorializing what they thought they intended on August 7, 2006 is clear, and unambiguous. The product of the negotiations between these parties is best evidence that there was a meeting of the minds. The language of Article 16 may not incorporate all of the impressions testified to at hearing, but it is clear, and unambiguous with respect to application to this grievance. As such, that language is what the Arbitrator has before him which is not subject to recall, or perception and is therefore best evidence here. Without persuasive evidence that a better bargain had been extracted by the Union from management this Arbitrator has no alternative save to deny this grievance in its entirety.

AWARD

For the foregoing reasons, this grievance is denied in its entirety as being without merit.

APPLICATION AND DISCUSSION QUESTIONS

1. The Company cited a number of arbitration principles related to contract interpretation. Explain each of the following principles:

a. "[I]f contract language is clear and unambiguous an arbitrator is not permitted to give it a meaning other than that which is expressed."

Must follow k language – plain meaning

b. "[A]n arbitrator may not 'ignore clear-cut contract language'."

Can't create own meaning

c. The arbitrator "is to read provisions in a manner that produces a logical and consistent result". *pieces must be consistent*

d. A party cannot "gain through arbitration what it failed to achieve at negotiations." *Can't create new terms*

e. "Where language is clear and unambiguous, parol evidence is not permitted or appropriate." *no extrinsic evidence if no ambiguity*

2. The union cites the arbitration principle that where there is ambiguity in a contract, the arbitrator should construe the interpretation against the party who wrote the provision. How does this principle apply in this grievance? *Construe against EE bk they drafted the clause*

3. What is the arbitrator's position on the use of parol evidence when the contract language is clear but there are "competing interpretations of specific contract language"?

permissable

WASHINGTON STATE FERRIES
133 BNA LA 641 (NICKLEBERRY, 2014)[*]

The Washington State Ferries (employer) and the Inlandboatmen's Union of the Pacific (union) are parties to a collective bargaining agreement (CBA) effective from July 1, 2011 through June 30, 2013. The CBA provides for final and binding arbitration of grievances. On October 31, 2012, the union filed a request for grievance arbitration with the Public Employment Relations Commission.

[*]   Reprinted with permission from *Labor Relations Reporter- Labor Arbitration Reports.* 133 BNA LA 641. Copyright 2015 by the Bureau of National Affairs, Inc. (800-372-1033). http://www.bna.com

Issue

I find the issue statement to be: Did the employer violate the CBA when on July 10, 2012, it assigned work to an on call employee rather than a year around employee M? If so, what is the appropriate remedy?

Structure of Contract

It is valuable to note the structure of the CBA. The CBA contains a master contract, also referred to as the general contract. The general contract is made up of rules numbered 1 through 35. The general rules are followed by Appendices A through D which are followed by numerous addendums and letters of understanding. Appendix B applies to the terminal personnel which are the group of employees represented by the union in this arbitration.

The Preamble to Appendix B states that Appendix B rules control over the general contract rules if a conflict exists:

> The following rules are in addition to Rule 1 through Rule 35 and apply to the Terminal
> Personnel only; when there are conflicting Rules resulting from the general contract
> or Appendix B, the Rules in this Appendix shall be the applicable Rule governing
> Terminal Employees.

Relevant Contractual Provisions

The sections of the CBA relevant to this issue are:

RULE 10
MINIMUM MONTHLY PAY AND OVERTIME
10.02 Year round employees, excluding Relief employees, who are called in to work on a scheduled day off and have a minimum of eighty (80) non-overtime compensated hours in the work period will be compensated at the overtime rate of pay. In addition, they will receive three (3) hours of pay at their straight time rate of pay regardless of the length of the overtime shift or the hours actually worked.

10.08 Employees called back to work on their scheduled assigned days off will receive a minimum of eight (8) hours pay at the overtime rate. This section shall not apply to part-time employees.

APPENDIX B
TERMINAL DEPARTMENT

RULE 1
HOURS OF EMPLOYMENT, OVERTIME, AND ASSIGNMENT
   1.02 Overtime for year around employees shall be paid whenever the employee performs work in excess of the scheduled shifts as specified above.

   An employee who wishes to be called for overtime on his/her regularly scheduled day(s) off will submit his/her name to be posted on an overtime availability list in the Terminal Supervisor's office. Employees will be called by seniority when overtime is available, starting with the most senior employee. Once an employee has been dispatched for an overtime opportunity, his/her name will be checked off for that pay period. At the beginning of each pay period, the Supervisor will begin the dispatch starting with the most senior employee on the overtime availability list in accordance with the process set forth.

   1.06 Filling of Temporary Terminal Positions

B. Temporary Positions-Less that Forty-Five (45) Days

Job openings of less than forty-five (45) days will be filled at the affected terminal in the following manner:

   2. Daily Assignments

      a. Daily vacancies will be offered to Part-time and on call employees, by seniority based on their availability schedule as defined in Appendix B, Rule 1.06(B)(1)(b), when the number of hours of the vacancy is greater than their daily hours and will be restricted to one (1) reassignment per day. In the event all Part-time and on call employees refuse the offer, the Supervisor will assign the employee with the least date of hire. Failure of the employee to respond to a call placed by the Supervisor within fifteen (15) minutes will allow the Supervisor to offer the vacancy to the next senior employee in line.

      b. The Supervisor will use their discretion in filling of vacancies that occur outside of the scheduled Supervisor hours or when notified within four (4) hours prior to the start of a shift. If possible, the most senior available unassigned Part-time or on call employee should be notified first.

Background

M, the grievant, has worked for the employer continuously since 1993 and currently holds the position of ticket seller at the Fauntleroy terminal. M holds a year around position which is defined by rule 1.11 of the CBA as "eighty (80) hours of scheduled straight time work within a two (2) week work period, which is expected to exist, during periods of the lowest level of scheduled service." During the summer of 2012, M was scheduled to work Sunday, Monday, Friday and Saturday, ten hours per day.

The employer also has relief employees, part-time employees and on call employees. The position relevant to this arbitration is the on call employee. Rule 1.16 the CBA states: "The term 'on call employee' shall be an employee who may or may not be working on a year around basis, and who is not offered forty (40) hours of straight time pay per week. The employee will be assigned work based on their date of hire and availability."

Employees are allowed to sign up for overtime by indicating on the "Overtime Signup Sheet" which days of the week they would be available to work. If an employee has not indicated a willingness to work overtime on a day of the week the overtime comes available, they will not be called. M had indicated on the overtime sheet for the summer of 2012 that he was available to work any day of the week.

The terminal supervisors maintain a schedule for year around employees for the sailing season. There is also a weekly schedule to fill known absences from the year around positions. There are also daily dispatch shifts that may become available, usually from unknown absences or extra work. A terminal supervisor fills these vacancies with on call employees. If no on call employees are available, the supervisor would hold someone over or go to the overtime list to call someone in to work the hours.

On July 10, 2012, M was on a scheduled day off. The supervisor responsible for daily dispatching during that week was Shawn Vogt. There were four hours of work on the daily dispatch list for July 10, 2012, from 2:30 P.M. to 6:30 P.M. Vogt filled those hours with an on call employee.

On July 17, 2012, the union filed a grievance on behalf of M claiming that the on call employee was called for an overtime shift and M was bypassed although M had signed up for overtime on his scheduled days off and was senior to the on call employee. The employer denied the grievance at earlier steps of the grievance procedure, resulting in this arbitration proceeding.

Principles of Contract Interpretation

A contract term is said to be ambiguous if it is susceptible to more than one meaning, that is, if "plausible contentions may be made for conflicting interpretations." ELKOURI & ELKOURI, How Arbitration Works, 9-8 (7th ed., 2012).

The well-established majority view remains that the existence of an ambiguity must be determined from the "four corners of the instrument" without resort to extrinsic evidence of any kind. This is the so-called "plain meaning rule," which states that if the words are plain and clear, conveying a distinct idea, there is no occasion to resort to interpretation and their meaning is to be derived entirely from the nature of the language used. ELKOURI & ELKOURI, How Arbitration Works, 9-8 (7th ed., 2012).

When contracts are silent or ambiguous about a matter, arbitrators look to other evidence, including the parties' bargaining history and "past practice." ELKOURI & ELKOURI, How Arbitration Works, 9-26 (7th ed., 2012).

The custom or past practice of the parties is the most widely used standard to interpret ambiguous and unclear contract language. It is easy to understand why, as the parties' intent is most often manifested in their actions. ELKOURI & ELKOURI, How Arbitration Works, 12-20 (7th ed., 2012).

Analysis

The union relies on language in Appendix B, Rule 1.02 to support its argument that M should have been called in to work the four-hour shift on July 10, 2012, as overtime. The language of this contract section refers to when and how a year around employee will be called for overtime. It does not address how available hours are categorized as overtime. The union believes the hours in question should be overtime and therefore should have been assigned to M since he has seniority over the on call employee that worked the hours, and M should therefore receive the minimum eight hours overtime pay in Rule 10.08 of the CBA as well as the three-hour straight time call-in pay as stated in Rule 10.02.

The burden of proof that the union has to establish is that the relevant four-hour shift on July 10, 2012, was overtime. The contract is not clear on when hours are declared to be overtime. The only reference is how they are handled when they are overtime and how many hours an employee has to work to qualify for overtime. The CBA is actually silent on how available work hours become overtime except as it relates to the threshold of daily and weekly hours worked by an individual.

As stated above, there are several ways hours get on a schedule. There is the year around seasonal schedule that is bid on by year around employees. There is a weekly schedule that indicates known absences from the year around schedule. Then there is a list of daily dispatch hours of primarily previously unknown absences that need to be covered in the weekly schedule. The weekly schedule and daily dispatch hours are filled in by relief, part-time, and on call employees.

In the absence of clear contract language that outlines when available hours are scheduled as overtime, I must look to the established scheduling practice. The supervisor responsible for scheduling the daily dispatch hours at the Fauntleroy terminal during the time in question was Shawn Vogt. Vogt testified that the practice for the daily dispatch hours since at least 2009 was to look at the weekly schedule, determine who was not working or working fewer hours. He would then look at the on call list for someone to fill those hours. If there were no on call employees available, he would then go to the overtime sign-up list. He stated that he would never go to the overtime sign-up list before the on call list. He did state that sometimes he would ask a year around employee to hold over if they happened to be there when the hours became available.

In analyzing the contract language, when it is silent and/or ambiguous as mentioned above, I must look to the contract language as a whole and the common practice. The hours in question in this case are daily assignment hours. The union business agent, Jay Ubelhart, confirmed that the hours were an "on call" shift. There is no dispute that the hours were daily assignment hours. The contract provision that addresses daily assignments is in Appendix B, Rule 1.06(B)(2).

In a previous arbitration award regarding a grievance filed by John McElhose, the on call employee who worked the shift in dispute, the arbitrator states that McElhose, was called and offered the shift the morning of July 10, 2012. That being the case, I believe the applicable rule would be Appendix B, Rule 1.06(B)(2)(b), which allows the supervisor discretion to fill the shift with the most senior available unassigned part-time or on call employee. That also seems to reflect the practice described by Vogt.

The union contends that the hours were overtime hours because the McElhose arbitration awarded the grievant overtime for those hours. Actually the arbitrator in that case awarded overtime for the fact that McElhose worked forty-four hours in that week, not because he worked four hours on July 10, 2012. McElhose did not reach the overtime threshold until the end of the work week.

APPLICATION AND DISCUSSION QUESTIONS

1. How does the arbitrator determine when a contract term is ambiguous? How does the arbitrator apply the "four corners of the instrument" rule?

2. What is the "plain meaning rule" and how does the arbitrator apply this rule in this case? *See* |

3. When a contract is silent or ambiguous, what basic principles of arbitration will the arbitrator apply? Did the arbitrator apply the "custom" or "past practice" rule?

history / practice / custom?

yes, Vogt's past practice when assigning

AMBIGUOUS V. UNAMBIGUOUS CONTRACT LANGUAGE

NATIONAL BASKETBALL ASSOCIATION AND PLAYERS' ASSOCIATION
52 BNA LA 702 (TURKUS, 1969)[*]

PLAYER TRADE

The issue presented for determination in this arbitration is as follows:

"Whether a player may be required to play more than 82 regularly scheduled season games, and if so, upon what terms and conditions, if any, shall said player play such additional games?"

The resolution of the issue involves the construction of the 1968 Memorandum of Understanding of the parties. Paragraph 11 thereof provides:

"Each member [Club] agrees that in no event will it play more than 82 regularly scheduled season games."

---

[*] Reprinted with permission from *Labor Relations Reporter- Labor Arbitration Reports*. 52 BNA LA 702. Copyright 2015 by the Bureau of National Affairs, Inc. (800-372-1033). http://www.bna.com.

The basic facts are not in the area of controversy. The scheduled basketball season extends over some 160 days between the middle of October and the middle of March the following year. There are 14 teams or clubs in the National Basketball Association and approximately 155 players. Although each club has 82 regularly scheduled season games, it would be sheer happenstance if all, or indeed if many of the clubs had actually played the same number of games on any given day during the scheduled season because of the diverse factors effecting the scheduling of games.

As a consequence, on December 9, 1968, when the New York Knickerbockers and the Detroit Pistons consummated a trade which brought David De Busschere to the Knickerbockers and Walter Bellamy and Howard Komives to the Pistons, the Knickerbockers had completed 35 games of their regular season schedule of 82 games while the Pistons had played only 29 games (of their regular season schedule of 82 games) at the time of the trade.

In the National Basketball Association, as in professional sports generally, the number of players permissible on the active roster of each club is limited. The rules permit unlimited substitutions and contemplate that every able-bodied player on each roster will be available to play in every game. Thus if the three (3) players involved in the trade play in all regularly scheduled games, at the end of the season De Busschere will have played in 76 games while Bellamy and Komives will have played in 88.

The Players are concerned with the "additional" six (6) games to be played by Bellamy and Komives-not with the six (6) games less than 82 which De Busschere will be required to play-interpreting Paragraph 11 of the Memorandum of Understanding as requiring any player to play no more than 82 regularly scheduled season games; and seek a determination that the players be permitted to "sit out" any games in excess of 82 regularly scheduled games or in the alternative be given additional compensation for any games played in excess of 82.

The club owners on the other hand, maintain that the language and meaning of Paragraph 11 of the 1968 Memorandum of Understanding is clear and unambiguous to wit, that each club owner has agreed to schedule no more than 82 games; that the Players are seeking in arbitration to change that provision to read that "no player will be required to play in more than 82 regularly scheduled season games; that the arbitrator has no authority to change or amend that provision, nor may he under the guise of interpretation apply a construction which would do violence to its clear language and meaning; that any award which would purport to provide for additional compensation or authorize players to "sit out" any games would alter and amend other provisions of the agreement of the parties; would be entirely inconsistent with the principles of any team sport and would exceed the scope and authority of the arbitrator's jurisdiction which is limited to the settlement of disputes involving differences "as to the meaning or application of the provisions of this Memorandum. . .", to wit, Paragraph 11 of the 1967 Memorandum of Understanding which the 1968 Memorandum of Understanding amends and extends.

The primary rule in the construction of a written agreement is to determine, not alone from a single word, phrase or paragraph, but from the instrument as a whole, the true intent of the parties and to interpret the meaning of the questioned part with regard to the connection in which it is used, the subject matter, and its relation to all other parts and provisions of the agreement. A section or portion cannot be isolated from the rest of the agreement and given construction independently of the purpose and agreement of the parties as evidenced by the agreement in its totality. (See, "How Arbitration Works," Revised Second Edition, Elkouri and Elkouri, BNA, Inc., 1960, and the reported cases therein cited.)

The language of Paragraph 11 of the 1968 Memorandum of Understanding is clear and unequivocal-"Each member [club] agrees that in no event will it play more than 82 regularly scheduled season games." No club has scheduled more than 82 games, and it is conceded that there has been no violation of the provision in that respect.

During the negotiations leading to the execution of the 1968 Memorandum of Understanding, the Players sought a reduction in the number of regularly scheduled games. Because of the increase in the number of teams in the league, the club owners sought to increase the schedule from 78 to 84 games to accommodate team travel and scheduling problems. The Players opposed any increase above the 78 game schedule of the previous season, and the parties finally compromised on 82 games. No question whatsoever was raised throughout the negotiations respecting the number of games to be played by any individual player.

The Uniform Player Contract is an integral part of the Memorandum of Understanding between the parties. (See, Exhibits A and B attached to the 1967 Memorandum and Paragraph 10 thereof which is perpetuated in the very first paragraph of the 1968 Memorandum and remains binding as if restated therein.) Players are compensated on an annual and not a "per game" basis. Paragraph 2 of the Uniform Player Contract provides for compensation to be paid "in twelve equal semi-monthly payments." Paragraph 4 of the 1968 Memorandum prescribes minimum annual salaries for rookies and second year players. There are no provisions in either the Memorandum or the Uniform Player Contract which expresses an owner's pecuniary responsibility in terms of games. (Indeed, the apportionment of responsibility for traded players' salaries between transferor and transferee clubs is made on the basis of days spent with each club rather than games played for each as specified in Section 3.07 of the By-Laws of the National Basketball Association).

Paragraph 10 of the Uniform Player Contract gives each club "the right to sell, exchange, assign or transfer" the contract and the "Player agrees to accept such sale, exchange, assignment or transfer and to faithfully perform and carry out this contract with the same force and effect as if it had been entered into by the Player with the assignee club instead of with this (assignor) club."

The very next paragraph of the Uniform Player Contract, to wit, Paragraph 11 thereof, provides that traded Players are entitled to certain specific and express payments from the assignee club, to wit, "all reasonable expenses incurred by the Player in moving himself and his family from the home city of the (assignor) club to the home city of the (assignee) club. . .". No other payment as the result of a trade (in excess of the fixed and agreed salary of the player) is prescribed; no other or additional payment was intended nor may be justly implied to either club.

Parties to a collective bargaining agreement are charged with full knowledge of its provisions and of the significance of its language. In the 1967-1968 season there were a total of 9 trades or sales involving 14 players. During the current season there have been 11 trades or sales involving 19 players, two (2) of which occurred prior to the commencement of the 1968-1969 scheduled season.

The parties were fully cognizant when they entered into the 1968 Memorandum of Understanding that in all reasonable likelihood some trades or sales would occur at a time when an unequal number of games had been played by the clubs involved.

It was manifest that in consequence thereof under the clear and unequivocal language of the Memorandum of Understanding and the Uniform Player Contract (Paragraph 1) which obligates the player to play "the games scheduled for the club's team during the schedule of the Association. . .", that although each club has but 82 regularly scheduled season games:

1. Some players, as for example De Busschere, would be required to play less than 82 games without any diminution in the agreed salary because players are not compensated on a "per game" basis but on an annual basis (with the apportionment of the fixed and agreed salary of players traded on the basis of days spent with each club not games played for each); and,

2. Some players, as for example Bellamy and Komives, would be required to play more than 82 games without any increased compensation since players, as stated, are compensated on a fixed and agreed annual basis not on a "per game" played basis, with the set and agreed salary for players traded, apportioned between the clubs on the basis of days spent with each club not for games played for each.

The parties entered into the 1968 Memorandum of Understanding with full knowledge of its provisions and the impact thereof on trades or sales. If traded or sold the player is assured that he will be paid his agreed annual compensation "in toto" regardless of whether as a result thereof he may be required to play a lesser or greater number of games than if he had remained with his original team or club for the entire season.

To read into the parties' agreement under the guise of interpretation a provision that if as a result of a trade or sale, the player, who under its terms is contractually obligated to play a greater number of games than if he had remained with his original club for the entire season, may either "sit out" the excess number or be paid extra compensation for each such game played, is to rewrite the agreement of the parties by doing violence to the very meaning of the agreement which the parties themselves made-while at the same time preserving the integrity and vitality of their agreement only when the player as a result of the trade or sale is required to play a lesser number of games than if he had remained with his original club.

The function of the arbitrator is to construe, apply and give effect to the contract which the party themselves have made, not to "legislate" or rewrite the agreement for them. If the existing agreement in the light of experience fairly and realistically requires revision of its clear meaning and impact with respect to a trade or sale of players, the appropriate forum for its achievement is not through resort to the arbitral process, but the bargaining table-at which the parties are currently due to meet.

AWARD

A player may be required to play more than 82 regularly scheduled season games. In situations involving the transfer of players, those affected may be required to play either more or fewer than 82 regularly scheduled games without an increase or decrease in compensation provided, however, that no club has scheduled more than 82 regularly scheduled games during the season.

APPLICATION AND DISCUSSION QUESTIONS

1. How did the players and the club owners interpret the contract as to whether a player can be required to play more than 82 regularly scheduled season games? What are the functions and limits of the arbitrator in interpreting the agreement?

players: no more than 82 per player

teams: . . . per team

arb can't legislate, can only interpret what parties intended

2. Was the contract language clear and unequivocal? How does the arbitrator propose the true intent of the parties is determined? *yes; meaning within context/full text* *(words)*

3. Why did the arbitrator indicate he would be "legislating" or rewriting the agreement between the parties if he found in favor of the players' interpretation of the contract? Do you agree?

   b/c would require changing member (club) to player ... yes

PAROL EVIDENCE

CVS PHARMACY, 11-03561-A11/060
2012 BNA LA SUPP. 147419 (E. GOLDSTEIN, 2012)[*]

GRIEVANCE NO. 2565

(Issue of whether oral agreement to interpret Section 4.2 of parties' collective bargaining agreement was an enforceable meeting of minds; parol evidence rule; parties' mutual assent by entire course of conduct).

II. ISSUE

The parties stipulate that the issue to be decided is:

- Was there a Settlement of Grievance 2033 during a telephone conversation on March 9, 2011 between John Iaderosa, Vice President of Labor Relations for CVS, and Carmen Olmetti, Business Representative for Local 727?

- If so, did CVS breach that settlement?

* Reprinted with permission from *Labor Relations Reporter- Labor Arbitration Reports.* 2012 BNA LA Supp. 147419. Copyright 2015 by the Bureau of National Affairs, Inc. (800-372-1033). http://www.bna.com

RELEVANT CONTRACT PROVISIONS
(some articles omitted)

ARTICLE 3

Section 4.2: Extra Work-Full-Time Pharmacists

A pharmacist who is required to perform extra work shall be compensated at an hourly rate, which will be equal to their base weekly salary divided by their base weekly hours. Any pharmacist who is required to perform extra work beyond 44 hours in a work week will be compensated an additional $6/hr for such work.

Each regular full-time employee who has worked a basic workweek as defined in Section 3.1 who reports for work on a sixth (6th) or seventh day (7th) of a workweek shall be guaranteed a minimum of one-half (1/2) day of work. The compensation for all such work and for time work in excess of the basic workweek within workweeks as set forth in Section 3.1.

There shall be no mandatory overtime in excess of the maximum workday or standard workweek except for vacation coverage and emergencies. Moreover, when mandatory overtime in these situations would pose an undue hardship, the Employer may, at its option, assign management personnel who are registered pharmacists to perform such work.

IV. STATEMENT OF THE CASE

The case arises from the Union's assertion that the parties settled a grievance about pay for immunization training during a brief telephone call on March 9, 2011, through a subsequently submitted grievance form drafted by the Union and then by the Parties' subsequent course of conduct. As a result, the core issues in this case are whether the parties reached an agreement during that telephone call and whether such oral agreement and later course of conduct established a binding contract of settlement to pay all CVS pharmacists for time spent in training sessions in 2011.

From the Union's perspective, the Employer and the Union settled their dispute regarding payment for immunization training and that settlement was memorialized in writing by the Union. Then, the Employer began performing the terms of the settlement by printing paychecks for the training time. According to the Union, the Employer backed out of the above settlement agreement only when certain CVS managers complained about the cost of that settlement. Moreover, the Union urges, only when these complaints arose did the Employer assert that the settlement was conditioned on the immunization training's being mandatory. As a result, the Union asserts that the settlement was binding and that all pharmacists should be compensated for their time spent at immunization training in 2011 at their respective pay rates.

The Employer, however, contends that no such settlement to pay for training for pharmacists for immunization training was reached on March 9, 2011 or otherwise. There thus was no mutual agreement between the parties regarding pay for voluntary training, it quickly adds. Rather, the alleged March 9th agreement was based on the Union Representative's erroneous statement to Vice President Iaderosa that a Company memorandum indicated the immunization training was mandatory. According to the Employer, the Union cannot prove that Vice President of Labor Relations John Iaderosa then or ever agreed that CVS would pay for immunization training even if such training was voluntary. The Union has proved neither an enforceable grievance settlement nor a breach of such a settlement, CVS concludes. As a result, the Employer asserts that the grievance should be denied in its entirety.

* * * *

VII. DISCUSSION AND FINDINGS

As this is a case of contract interpretation, it is the Union's burden to establish that its interpretation of the contract is correct. As the Arbitrator in this dispute, my function in turn is to be the parties' "contract reader," that is, to determine and apply the intent and understanding of the parties themselves concerning the contractual issue in dispute. Moreover, as I see it, the issue in this case is whether there was a binding settlement agreement between the Company and this Union, primarily based on a telephone conversation between CVS Vice President of Labor Relations Iaderosa and the Union Business Representative Olmetti on March 9, 2011, detailed above, and based on the course of conduct of these parties as to how settlements of disputes over contractual issues are handled by these parties, too, I note.

In order for a contract to be formed, there must be a meeting of the minds between the parties, I remind the Parties. Elkouri & Elkouri, How Arbitration Works. In this case, the evidence shows that the Company and the Union did not have a mutual understanding of their alleged settlement agreement. The record reveals that on March 1, 2011, Business Representative Olmetti received a CVS document from Zaraitis, a Union pharmacist, regarding the upcoming training. Subsequently, Employer witness Iaderosa recalls that during the March 9, 2011 telephone conversation between Iaderosa and Olmetti, Olmetti stated that he had a CVS document stating that immunization training "was mandatory."

I also point out that the instant matter does not represent a circumstance where there is no underlying contractual section to be interpreted or where the parties are attempting to add a new term or condition of employment to their CBA. Simply put, Section 4.2 of the Parties' labor contract, set out above, provides for payment when "extra work" is required for full-time pharmacist. This provision is clear and unambiguous in its terms, as they apply to this case, I find.

This is not a case where the underlying contractual provision meaning is sought to be proved by parol evidence, but whether a settlement of the parties' dispute of a particular fact pattern arising under the terms of Section 4.2 was intended to be a binding contract. Thus, many of the arguments the parties pressed on me in this case, such as the parol evidence rule and cases involving "secret side deals" are inapplicable, I hold.

It is certainly clear, from my above detailed recitation of the facts in this case, that there indeed was some sort of agreement between Iaderosa and Olmetti on March 9, 2011. However, a settlement was never resolved or finalized, I find. Whether the misunderstanding that ensued could be called a mutual mistake over the issue of "Was there a mandate to train or not?" or whether the telephone agreement was conditioned on the Company's requiring training for all its bargaining unit pharmacists is unclear from the conversation itself. What is clear from the remainder of the facts, however, is that the Employer never actually required pharmacists to attend immunization training sessions, but instead, as it had the year before, had a goal to get as many of the employees as possible to go to the sessions.

For example, the email sent by Olmetti to Burau on the evening of March 9, 2011 actually stated that Olmetti was "capturing" a conversation with Iaderosa in which Iaderosa said the pharmacists would be paid for attending training. Burau further sent Iaderosa an email that same evening to say she would handle the grievance, which is indicative of the fact that there was no earlier binding settlement, I find. It is also important that Burau testified her routine when a grievance is filed, she conducts an investigation and then reports her findings to Olmetti in a letter on CVS letterhead. She would either deny the grievance as she did in her June 24, 2011 letter to Olmetti in this case, or she would agree to a settlement as she did in her March 29, 2011 letter in response to Grievance 2025, the facts show. No such letter was sent in this case. Nor is there an email indicating that the grievance was "resolved" like the email sent to Olmetti after the parties met to discuss the August, 2010 immunization grievance, as Management notes. This is of critical significance to the correct resolution of the current dispute, I hold.

Regarding Business Representative Olmetti's assertion that Burau told him on March 29 that the pharmacists would be paid for 12 hours of training, the Employer contends that Burau never made such a statement. Equally important, in addition to Burau's denial, the facts on this record indicate that the parties did not document the resolution of Grievance 2033 as a result of that meeting. Other Grievances that Olmetti and Burau discussed that day were documented in writing and Grievance 2033 was not, I stress. There also was no express mention of a settlement of the actual underlying dispute, namely, whether both voluntary or mandatory attendance at the subject immunization training would be provided the affected pharmacists, I emphasize.

Third, like the Employer, I find that Business Representative Olmetti's testimony regarding the March 9, 2011 conversation with Vice President Iaderosa confirms that the understanding between the parties was specifically conditioned on the immunization training being mandatory. I point to Olmetti's testimony that he "had expressed to [Iaderosa] my concern and referenced the internal document that the pharmacists had to register for training and they would not be paid for their time." (Emphasis mine.) The record makes clear that Olmetti stated to Iaderosa that pharmacists who were not already immunizers "had to register for immunization training," and thus, the context of whether or not Section 4.2 applied to require payment was always conditioned on the mandatory or non-mandatory issue, I hold.

* * * *

Fourth, in my judgment, there exists a lack of credibility in the Union's argument that Vice President Iaderosa agreed on March 9, 2011 to pay pharmacists to attend training, which was not required by the CBA and particularly by Section 4.2 thereof, merely because Olmetti "requested it." Rather, the most reasonable explanation for why Iaderosa, who knew that pharmacists had not been paid for attending immunization training in 2010, would agree to pay the pharmacists in 2011 was because Olmetti told Iaderosa that he had a Company document stating that training was mandatory. That is the nub of this case, I hold.

Further, it is undisputed that immunization training in 2011 as it played out was not mandatory. The only change from the 2010 to the 2011 immunization program was an increased goal of 2 immunizers per store, the facts reveal. The non-mandatory nature of the training is confirmed by the actions of pharmacists Zuraitis and his wife Stephanie, who signed up for training but did not attend once they discovered the training would be unpaid, I am persuaded. Stephanie never attended training and suffered no adverse consequences, as the Company was quick to point out.

* * * *

In sum, the testimony presented at the instant hearing revealed that no settlement agreement ever existed. There was never a written or oral statement from any company official to indicate that the Company would proceed in the fashion to mandate immunization for all bargaining unit pharmacists. According to the Company, the most the Union can point to is Iaderosa's agreement with Olmetti that if it was Management's plan to "make training mandatory" Section 4.2 applied. There was no meeting of the minds on March 9, 2011 in Olmetti and Iaderosa's telephone conversation to settle because, as the Employer has correctly argued, the Union's evidence that the Immunization Program was in fact designed to be mandatory was incorrect, I rule.

VIII. AWARD

For the reasons set forth above and incorporated herein as if fully rewritten, the grievance is denied.

IT IS SO ORDERED.

APPLICATION AND DISCUSSION QUESTIONS

1. How does the arbitrator define the term "contract reader"? How would you define the role of the arbitrator in contract interpretation disputes? Was this a "mutual mistake" between parties? *determine & apply intent + understanding of parties; an analyst; no union made mistake of saying it mandatory*

2. May arbitrators rely on an oral agreement between the parties and subsequent conduct of the parties to interpret contract language? What did the parties specifically agree to during their telephone conversations regarding payment of time for attending the training?

yes if language is ambiguous and parol evidence doesn't contradict it; EE would pay if sessions were mandatory

B. Pattern, Practices and Custom Cases

The custom or past practice of the parties is the most widely used standard to *is it?* interpret ambiguous and unclear language. See, Mittenthal, Past *Practice and the Administration of Collective Bargaining Agreement*, 59 Mich L. Rev. 1017 (1961). The parties' intent is often manifested in their actions. *Elkouri* Pg. 623. The essence of a past practice is that the practice is the understood and accepted way of doing things. In order for a custom and past practice to be binding, it must have clarity, mutuality, it must be consistent and repetitive. The term clarity embraces the element of *)A* uniformity. Mutuality says that the assumptions and expectations of one party do not establish a binding practice. Both sides have reasonable cause to believe what has been done in the past will be continued in the future. Fairweather's Practice and Procedure in Labor Arbitration, 3rd Ed, Pg. 183. Consistency involves the element of repetition. The practice is followed with such consistency that employees rely on and reasonably expect such behavior to continue.

PAST PRACTICE AND THE ADMINISTRATION OF COLLECTIVE BARGAINING AGREEMENTS

PROCEEDINGS OF THE 14TH ANNUAL MEETING OF THE NATIONAL ACADEMY OF ARBITRATORS, 30 (1961)[*]

RICHARD MITTENTHAL

Past practice is one of the most useful and hence one of the most commonly used aids in resolving grievance disputes. It can help the arbitrator in a variety of ways in interpreting the agreement. It may be used to clarify what is ambiguous, to give substance to what is general, and perhaps even to modify or amend what is seemingly unambiguous. It may also, apart from any basis in the agreement, be used to establish a separate, enforceable condition of employment.

* * * *

The Nature of a Practice

Sum In short, something qualifies as a practice if it is shown to be the understood and accepted way of doing things over an extended period of time.

What qualities must a course of conduct have before it can legitimately be regarded as a practice?

First, there should be *clarity* and *consistency*. A course of conduct which is vague and ambiguous or which has been contradicted as often as it has been followed can hardly qualify as a practice. But where those in the plant invariably respond in the same way to a particular set of conditions, their conduct may very well ripen into a practice.

Second, there should be *longevity* and *repetition*. A period of time has to elapse during which a consistent pattern of behavior emerges. Hence, one or two isolated instances of a certain conduct do not establish a practice. Just how frequently and over how long a period something must be done before it can be characterized as a practice is a matter of good judgment for which no formula can be devised.

Third, there should be *acceptability*. The employees and the supervisors alike must have knowledge of the particular conduct and must regard it as the correct and customary means of handling a situation. Such acceptability may frequently be implied from long acquiescence in a known course of conduct. Where this acquiescence does not exist, that is, where employees have constantly protested a particular course of action through complaints and grievances, it is doubtful that any practice has been created.

One must consider, too, the *underlying circumstances* which give a practice its true dimensions. A practice is no broader than the circumstances out of which it has arisen, although its scope can always be enlarged in the day-to-day administration of the agreement. No meaningful description of a practice can be made without mention of these circumstances. For instance, a work assignment practice which develops on the afternoon and mid night shifts and which is responsive to the peculiar needs of night work cannot be automatically extended to the day shift. The point is that every practice must be carefully related to its origin and purpose.

And, finally, the significance to be attributed to a practice may possibly be affected by whether or not it is supported by *mutuality*. Some practices are the product, either in their inception or in their application, of a joint understanding; others develop from choices made by the employer in the exercise of its managerial discretion without any intention of a future commitment.

* * * *

Clarifying Ambiguous Language

The danger of ambiguity arises not only from the English language with its immense vocabulary, flexible grammar and loose syntax but also from the nature of the collective bargaining agreement. The agreement is a means of governing "complex, many-sided relations between large numbers of people in a going concern for very substantial periods of time." It is seldom written with the kind of precision and detail which characterize other legal instruments. Although it covers a great variety of subjects, many of which are quite complicated, it must be simply written so that its terms can be understood by the employees and their supervisors. It is sometimes composed by persons inexperienced in the art of written expression. Issues are often settled by a general formula because the negotiators recognize they could not possibly foresee or provide for the many contingencies which are bound to occur during the life of the agreement

* * * *

Implementing General Contract Language

Practice is also a means of implementing general contract language. In areas which cannot be made specific, the parties are often satisfied to state a general rule and to allow the precise meaning of the rule to develop through the day-to-day administration of the agreement.

* * * *

Modifying or Amending Apparently Unambiguous Language

What an agreement says is one thing; how it is carried out may be quite another. A recent study at the University of Illinois revealed that differences between contract provisions and actual practice are not at all unusual. Thus, an arbitrator occasionally finds himself confronted with a situation where an established practice conflicts with a seemingly clear and unambiguous contract provision. Which is to prevail? The answer in many cases has been to disregard the practice and affirm the plain meaning of the contract language.

* * * *

As a Separate, Enforceable Condition of Employment

Past practice may serve to clarify, implement, and even amend contract language. But these are not its only functions. Some times an established practice is regarded as a distinct and binding condition of employment, one which cannot be changed without the mutual consent of the parties. Its binding quality may arise either from a contract provision which specifically requires the continuance of existing practices or, absent such a provision, from the theory that long-standing practices which have been accepted by the parties become an integral part of the agreement with just as much force as any of its written provisions.

Duration and Termination of a Practice

It is a well-settled principle that where past practice has established a meaning for language that is subsequently used in an agreement, the language will be presumed to have the meaning given it by practice. Thus, this kind of practice can only be terminated by mutual agreement, that is, by the parties rewriting the ambiguous provision to supersede the practice, by eliminating the provision entirely, etc.

* * * *

Conclusion

Through past practice, the arbitrator learns something of the values and standards of the parties and thus gains added insight into the nature of their contractual rights and obligations. Practices tend to disclose the reasonable expectations of the employees and managers alike. And as long as our decision is made within the bounds of these expectations, it has a better chance of being understood and accepted.

The ideas expressed in this paper may be useful as a general guide to the uses of past practice in administering the collective agreement. They do not provide an easy formula for resolving disputes; they are no substitute for a thorough and painstaking analysis of the facts. In the problem areas of past practice, there are so many fine distinctions that the final decision in a case will rest not on any abstract theorizing but rather on the arbitrator's view of the peculiar circumstances of that case.

No matter how successful we may be in systematizing the standards which shape arbitral opinions, we must recognize that considerable room must be left for "art and intuition," for good judgment. Perhaps an IBM computer may someday be able to write this kind of paper, but I doubt that it will ever be able to exhibit the kind of good judgment arbitrators have shown in answering complex grievance disputes.

APPLICATION AND DISCUSSION QUESTIONS

1. Under what circumstances would an arbitrator review the parties' past practices to reach a decision? *usually when language is ambiguous & a practice exists*

2. What elements are required to prove the existence of past practices? *clarity mutuality consistency and repetitiveness*

3. How does Arbitrator Mittenthal describe why there will be ambiguous language in the collective bargaining agreement? How are past practices used to resolve issues of ambiguity in contracts? Are there any limits on the use of past practices to clarify ambiguous terms in the contract? *English language + complexity of CBAs; past practice shows intent of parties (see readings p. 425-26); yes, limit is that arb still needs to do full analysis and use his own good judgment*

THE PROBLEM OF PAST PRACTICES OF SHIFT ASSIGNMENTS

A multi-campus university awarded a maintenance and service contract to the Alpha Company in 2004. At the time Alpha assumed the contract, electrical technicians worked 12-hour rotating shifts. In 2005, the Alpha Company and the Union signed a Letter of Agreement confirming use of the rotating 12-hour shift and their 2007 successor agreement confirmed it again.

In 2011, the Alpha Company was replaced by the Beta Company. The Beta Company agreed to comply with the terms and conditions already in place under the University's agreement with Alpha. Beta and the Union signed a Letter of Understanding memorializing the 12-hour rotating shift practice. The 2012-2016 CBA between the Beta Company and the Union contains a Work Shift Provision indicating employees will have regular starting and stopping times; 12-hour shifts will be filled through job posting based on seniority; and mutual agreement between the Union and the Company is required to change work schedules. The Company continues to use rotating 12-hour shifts and the jobs are not posted.

The Union filed a grievance in 2014 alleging the Company violated the CBA. The Company's position is that rotating 12-hour shifts is a long-standing past practice. The Company further asserts the schedule rotation is an implied term of the CBA, substantiated by the fact that the Union has never asserted it was a violation until the 2014 grievance.

How should the arbitrator rule?

[handwritten: the past practice is clean appears mutual given the lack of complaints, its consistent, Q is, is it repetitive — is 2 years long enough? yes?]

WPLG-TV AND I.A.T.S.E. PHOTOGRAPHERS LOCAL 666

1993 BNA LA SUPP. 102771 (R. ABRAMS, 1993)

[handwritten margin: case-newsroom seniority]

[handwritten margin: issue]

On October 10, 1991, Photographers Local 666 I.A.T.S.E. filed a grievance complaining about WPLG-TV's "unilateral and unlawful creation of a separate seniority list with respect to the newsroom on Biscayne Boulevard and Broward bureau." Two Grievants, Linda Vasquez and Helen Moore Harbeson, "were wrongfully denied the use of their seniority when they requested assignment to the Broward bureau," according to the Union. The Company denied their grievance.

* * * *

I. ISSUE

At the hearing, the parties could not agree on a statement of the issue to be resolved. They requested that the Arbitrator state the issue. The issue is as follows:

[handwritten margin: Q]

Did the Employer violate the Agreement when it denied the request of two employees to use seniority to bump more junior employees assigned to the Employer's Broward bureau?

* * * *

III. BACKGROUND FACTS

WPLG-TV, Channel 10 in Miami, and Photographers Local 666 I.A.T.S.E. have been parties to collective bargaining agreements for more than twenty years. Periodically, the photographers represented by the Union select their work schedules using their seniority. This dispute concerns assignments to the Company's Broward bureau that was established during the early 1970's.

In the early days of the Broward bureau, the Company had some difficulty getting photographers to go up to "the wilds" of Broward. Almost all the photographers lived in South Dade County. The Union tried to assist the Company. According to the Union, the members of the bargaining unit reached an internal "gentlemen's agreement" that employees would not use their seniority to bump employees who were working in Broward. This would give stability to the workforce in Broward, something the Company wanted.

[handwritten margin note: union internal agreement]

* * * *

IV. CONTENTIONS OF THE PARTIES

A. The Union's Argument

The Company violated the Agreement when it created a separate seniority list for its Broward bureau when the clear and unambiguous language of the Agreement provided for a single seniority list. During negotiations, the Company specifically sought to eliminate the contractual right to use seniority in selecting shifts. It failed in this attempt; it cannot now succeed in this arbitration.

The Company must bear the burden of proving any past practice that might supersede the explicit language of the Agreement. The evidence shows there was no mutuality as to the "gentlemen's agreement," which was only internal to the Union. "The fact that the Union and the Company had different rationale but arrived at the 'same place' filling shifts does not create an understanding or a past practice." It would be "patently ridiculous" to find a practice here. There is no evidence the parties acted on any alleged practice, and the evidence of the negotiations support the Union's position. Therefore, the grievance should be granted.

B. The Company's Argument

The Union failed to rebut the existence of a binding past practice under which the Company appropriately denied the Grievants' requests to bump Broward news photographers. The parties 1989-91 negotiations did not change this practice. Although the Company proposed abolition of all practices through a zipper clause, the Union adamantly refused.

* * * *

V. DISCUSSION AND OPINION

This case presents two fascinating questions: (1) Can a union unilaterally create a practice that is binding on the parties? and (2) How does a past practice end? Past practices are an important part of any collective relationship. See, Mittenthal, "Past Practice and the Administration of Collective Bargaining Agreements," Proceedings of the 14th Annual Meeting of the National Academy of Arbitrators, 30 (1961). Parties have long recognized that the "agreement" is not simply the written words of the little booklet that used to fit in your back pocket. Parties can create binding arrangements by the way they behave towards one another over time. Normally, it is management that creates a practice, because normally it is management that "acts" and the union "reacts."

The Union here claims that there was no binding practice at all. The members of the Union agreed internally not to use their seniority rights to displace Broward photographers. What was created internally can be abolished at will, according to the Union. When the Union decided it would no longer be bound by any such "gentlemen's agreement," it was over and done.

In order to resolve this grievance, the Arbitrator must first determine whether there was a past practice binding on the parties, and then, based on the evidence in the record, determine what effect the 1989-90 negotiations had on the practice, if any.

The Union appropriately reminds the Arbitrator that the Agreement speaks for itself. It states rather plainly that preference is a matter of seniority, provided the employee is capable of performing the work required to be done. If there was strong evidence of a practice that modified this express contract rule, that could be binding on the parties. The Company would have to demonstrate both that there was a practice and that it survived the most recent negotiations.

A. Was There a Past Practice?

The first issue is whether there was any practice prior to negotiations that was binding on the parties. Arbitrators regularly address the issue of the establishment of a past practice. The tests are well known. Normally, practices arise when management acts in a certain known way concerning particular circumstances over and over again, to the benefit of the union or the employees. In order to be binding, a practice must be clearly understood and based on conduct that is repeated over time. A consistent past practice is as binding as a contract clause. Past practice can be used to interpret contract language and, in some instances, even to modify or negate a contract clause.

The Union argues that there can be no practice here because the Agreement's provisions are clear and unambiguous. Article V does say: "Preference shall be given to employees, as regards schedules, based upon seniority...." It is not unusual in arbitration for a party to argue that the contract language is clear and, of course, it is favorable to its side. (Often both parties see the same language as clear and favoring their side.)

The important thing to remember is that the Arbitrator must determine the parties' intent. What the parties say in their Agreement is the most important evidence of that intent, but it is not the only evidence of their understanding. On some occasions, what they say in the words of their Agreement is not their whole understanding. On other occasions, what they say is not even what they mean.

There is no particular reason why a union cannot create a practice binding on the parties to a collective relationship, although that is an unusual scenario. In some industries, for example in construction, printing, and the media, unions traditionally play an important role in assignment and attendance matters. If a union decides to enforce a contract right in a certain manner that benefits management and, through its members, repeatedly behaves in a certain manner, it plants the seed for a practice. The practice ripens when management reasonably relies and acts upon it on a number of occasions. In effect, the union "offers" to modify the contract and the company "accepts" by its conduct. It is useful if behavior is accompanied by some communication between the parties recognizing the practice.

The Union argues that the "gentlemen's agreement" was only an internal union matter among the affected employees. Every practice starts as the internal matter of one party or the other, typically of management. One important thing to remember about practices is that they are not created through negotiation across the bargaining table. They are created by conduct by both parties or conduct by one party and reasonable reliance by the other party.

The evidence here shows that the protection for photographers at the Broward bureau arose within the Union to assist the Company in staffing the new bureau. If that was all that happened, perhaps this would not constitute a practice, but there was more. Repeatedly during the 1980's, Company officials acted pursuant to this "gentlemen's agreement." It was repeatedly applied. When the Company created new shifts in Broward, they were filled "from the street" or by Broward photographers, not by seniority as the Agreement would have required.

repetition + consistency

* * * *

clarity + mutuality

The practice was also well understood by representatives of both parties. Union Business Representative Larry Gianneschi testified: "I'm sure that over time -- if not originally, over time anyway management became aware of it (the "gentlemen's agreement") and more than likely probably assumed it, either assumed it or tried to co-opt it." 6 Management witnesses, as might be expected, specifically recalled the practice and its application.

* * * *

consistency + repitition

There is another critical factor here that supports the finding of a practice. We must remember this is the unusual case of a practice created by a union. The practice originated with an internal "gentlemen's agreement." Every week (and now every two weeks) employees bid on schedules, exercising their seniority. The employees -- the people who had created the practice by their internal agreement -- continued over sixteen years to bid for assignments consistent with the practice. They all knew what the deal was. They knew, as the Union's fine attorney said in his opening statement in this case explaining the "gentlemen's agreement," "that once you were in Broward you were there even if someone more senior than you wanted to take your position." The Union, through its members, consistently reaffirmed the practice by their bidding. Management relied on this understood practice, and it acted accordingly.

there was PP

Considering the evidence as a whole, the Arbitrator must conclude that there was a past practice.

Q2

B. Did the Practice Survive Negotiations?

In its written proposal to the Union, the Company sought to abolish all seniority preference in the assignment of shifts. The Union flatly rejected that proposal. The Company also proposed abolishing all prior practices through the zipper clause. The

Union rejected that as well. The parties negotiated long and hard about the issue of assignments. They reached an agreement that included, with two minor changes, the same language as the predecessor Agreement concerning seniority preference in assignments. There was nothing in the Agreement about the "gentlemen's agreement" or about prior practice in general. There was no zipper clause. What does all this negotiation behavior mean with regard to the prior practice?

There must be some way for parties to abolish a binding practice. As explained above, a practice arises by mutual conduct. It can be terminated by mutual conduct. Is it sufficient for one party to a practice to simply say it no longer exists? That would certainly not be sufficient with regard to a practice during the term of the collective bargaining agreement. Once an agreement expires and is renegotiated, prior practices continue unless "something" happens. What is the "something" that must happen?

Certainly, parties in their new agreement could expressly negate a prior practice (or all prior practices). If the contract says a practice is abolished, then it is gone. Will something less suffice? At one point during negotiations, a Union witness says their spokesperson denied they were bound by any understanding with regard to protecting the status of Broward people. Curiously, neither set of bargaining minutes included this important comment. An unconditional repudiation of a practice during negotiations would seem sufficient to terminate it. If that was all we had (and the Arbitrator is not sure we even have that), it might be concluded that the practice disappeared. The record of what actually happened is far more complicated.

* * * *

By their conduct under prior collective bargaining agreements, the parties gave a particular, special, and well understood meaning to the scheduling preference language. Under that prevailing and binding practice, the contract language meant, in fact, "preference except with regard to Broward assignments." The parties worked diligently in negotiations to develop an alternative system, but they failed. They tinkered around the corners with the junior-person-special-project exception. The heart of their agreement on shift assignment remained unchanged, however. That understanding included the Broward exception created by the prior binding practice.

neg didn't change agreement

* * * *

Had the Union agreed to the Company's zipper clause -- and who would have known what that would have meant] -- it could argue forcefully that the grievance must be granted because the prior practice (if any) was abolished. It vehemently opposed that clause. The parties did negotiate over alternatives, but they did not reach closure. Then after full and exhausting collective bargaining, they returned to the status quo ante language. The practice lived on as part of that preference language. The continuing practice protects the Broward photographers from bumping by seniority. The continuing practice required -- and allowed -- the Company to deny the Grievants' requests to use their seniority to bump Broward photographers.

PP cont'd

This all means that the grievance must be denied. The Company was within its rights based on the prior practice in denying the request of the two senior Dade photographers to be reassigned to Broward.

grievance denied

VI. AWARD

The Company did not violate the Agreement by denying the two employees the use of their seniority to be reassigned to the Broward bureau. The grievance is denied.

APPLICATION AND DISCUSSION QUESTIONS

It is well established in labor arbitration jurisprudence that for a custom or past practice to be binding on the parties, the following elements must be established:

PP req.

> The past practice must be "(1) unequivocal; (2) clearly enunciated and acted upon; (3) readily ascertainable over a reasonable period of time as a fixed, and established practice accepted by both parties." Elkouri, How Arbitration Works, 6th Edition, pp. 607-608.

1. What evidence did the Union present to support their position that there were no past practices? What evidence did the employer present to show the existence of past practices? *ER relied + 16 years+ clear* *U=internal agreement, not mutual*

2. When and how do parties end past practices? How can parties use the negotiation of a new contract to end past practices? What is the zipper clause and how does it impact past practices? *practice stops for long time; explicitly in agreement/ negotiations*

3. Why did the union establish internal past practices? What was the "gentleman's agreement"? Who has the burden of proving the existence of past practices? *agreement among members — no seniority in Broward Party claiming it*

ALPENA GEN. HOSP. AND LOCAL 204, UNITED STONE
AND ALLIED PRODUCTS WORKERS
50 BNA LA 48 (JONES, 1967)[*]

On January 4, 1967, the Kitchen or Dietary Department employees submitted the following grievance which is the issue in this dispute:

> Kitchen employees now have to pay for their meals. This was provided in the past for years. Union contends that Hospital cannot unilaterally change this practice since it has the effect of at least 10¢ per hour decrease in wages.

issue

On January 24, 1967, the Hospital replied to the grievance as follows:

> Rejected by the Board of Trustees on 1/23/67 for the reason that the dietary personnel have now been brought up to the same salary level as comparable workers in other departments. To allow them to continue receiving free meals would simply perpetuate a differential which is felt to be unjustified in relation to the comparative skills required.

reply

The grievance was thereupon processed to arbitration. At the hearing the Hospital raised a question as to the arbitrability of the grievance. The Hospital agreed, however, to present evidence and testimony on the merits of the grievance following the presentation of argument on the arbitrability question.

The contractual provisions applicable to this dispute are: (Omitted)

Background

Prior to January 1958, all Hospital employees received one free meal per day. This practice was discontinued at that time for all employees except those in the Kitchen or Dietary Department; those employees who no longer received a free meal were given a $5.00 per pay period (50 cents per day) salary increase. Although the Kitchen employees at that time were limited to a 50 cent meal, the "special," during the recent past this restriction has not been observed.

Until 1966 the employees of the Hospital were not organized; at that time the Union won representation rights. The current and first contract between the parties

---

was negotiated in the summer of 1966. Negotiations began in June and ended in September when the agreement was signed.

Kitchen employees continued to receive free meals for some three months following the consummation of negotiations. On December 27, 1966, the Hospital notified all Kitchen employees that effective December 28, 1966, they would be required "to pay for cafeteria meals in the same manner as other hospital personnel." A notice to all employees posted on the same date announced the discontinuance of the 50 cent special and the pricing of all food items on an a la carte basis more closely approaching the Hospital's cost of providing the food. The notice stated further that although the Hospital had been providing food at a substantial loss, increased food and labor costs made it necessary to end this practice. On January 4, 1967, the Kitchen employees submitted the grievance quoted in full herein above.

The Hospital contends that this grievance is not arbitrable because it does not involve the application or interpretation of any provision of the agreement, and the matter grieved is not a working condition under Section A(1) of the Grievance Procedure. The Union claims that the matter is arbitrable because it is a working condition inasmuch as it is a form of compensation and is a part of the total working situation, Section A(1) was included in the agreement to cover such matters as this, and the question of arbitrability was not raised until the hearing; therefore, it is untimely.

The Union urges in regard to the merits of the grievance that the Hospital's unilateral action in discontinuing the long established practice of providing a free meal effectively lowered the compensation of the Kitchen employees and that such an action cannot be taken without negotiations and the consent of the Union. The Union asserts that the parties were fully aware of the practice during negotiations and if the Union had known the practice would be changed, it would have altered its contractual proposals. The Union also points out that the practice was in effect prior to negotiations and continued after negotiations were concluded. The Union requests that the practice be reinstated and the grievants be compensated at the rate of 80 cents per day for the meals for which they had to pay. This amount, claims the Union, is a reasonable figure based upon the food prices in effect since December 28, 1966. The Union cites in support of its basic position *Luthern Medical Center*, 44 LA 107.

The Hospital contends that although there has been a practice of providing Kitchen employees with a free meal, the Hospital had the right to discontinue the practice for the following reasons. First, the basis for the practice has disappeared. The Kitchen employees, urges the Company, were permitted to continue receiving a free meal in lieu of a wage increase; this in turn resulted in a salary differential between the Kitchen and other employees with comparable skill (Laundry and Housekeeping), and this differential was maintained until the agreement between the parties was negotiated. The negotiations resulted in a $1.65 minimum for the lowest rated people with comparable skill and actually resulted in the largest increase for the Kitchen employees; thus, the differential was eliminated and the purpose for providing the free meal no longer existed. To continue providing the free meal, claims the Hospital, creates a differential in favor of the Kitchen employees that is unfair to other employees of comparable skill. The Hospital also urges that because of the increased labor costs as a result of the negotiations, it was necessary to take every action possible to reduce costs.

Second, the Hospital urges that a practice in a new relationship is not the same as in a continuing relationship and that all practices cannot be regarded in the same manner. The Hospital also points out that it did raise during the negotiations the question of whether the free meal should be continued in view of the wage increases but the Union did not pursue the matter and insist that provision for it be included in the contract. On the other hand, the Union insisted that certain other practices concerning medications, X-rays, laundry of uniforms, etc., should be specifically included in the agreement (Article XVII).

* * * *

In rebuttal, the Union urges that when the Hospital raised the question of whether the free meal should be discontinued, the Union voiced an objection and there was no further discussion of the matter; the Union thus believed the Hospital intended to continue the practice. The Union further contends that the evidence indicates the gap between the wages of the Kitchen employees and the employees in the Laundry and Housekeeping departments had been closed prior to negotiations and that in fact there was no effort to make interdepartmental comparisons during negotiations.

Discussion

* * * *

II. It is generally accepted that certain, but not all, clear and long standing practices can establish conditions of employment as binding as any written provision of the agreement. There is no question that the practice of providing a free meal to employees of the Kitchen department was of long standing; it had been in existence for several years prior to the time the parties negotiated their first agreement and was continued subsequent to negotiations. Even though this was the first agreement between the parties, it would seem, on its face, that this is the kind of practice which should be held binding for the life of the agreement unless there is mutual agreement to the contrary. The Hospital urges, however, that there are reasons why this should not be so.

* * * *

There is color in the Hospital's position. A practice of the kind here in dispute to have a binding quality must rest upon mutual consent. It is not only the fact that there is a practice which is important, but also the fact that it is known and agreed to by the parties either explicitly or by acquiescence. When a fully known and accepted practice is not repudiated by either party during the course of negotiations, then it is generally held that the practice must continue for the life of the agreement. If the practice is repudiated during negotiations, however, and there is no longer mutual consent, then it would seem as a general proposition that the party desiring the practice to continue does have an obligation to obtain, contractual or otherwise, agreement to continue the practice.

The Hospital did interject during the course of the wage negotiations the matter of the free meals. Although the testimony is very unsatisfactory on this score, it would seem that Mr. Chipman for the Hospital did raise a query as to whether the practice should be continued in view of the wage increase being granted the Kitchen employees. Apparently, the Union took the position that it should. The matter was then dropped with little or no further discussion.

If indeed the Hospital had placed the Union on notice that the practice would be discontinued because of the wage increase, then the Union would have been obligated, in this instance, to pursue the matter and to obtain agreement from the Hospital to continue the practice. But this was not the case. The proof does not indicate that there was a repudiation of the practice and the Union placed on notice that it would be discontinued. Instead, it would seem that the Hospital simply made a tentative proposal and when the Union objected to it, the Hospital dropped the matter and concurred in the Union's position. This is also indicated by the fact that the Hospital continued the practice for some 3 months following the consummation of negotiations.

* * * *

In view of the foregoing, I must hold that the Hospital must continue the practice of providing a free meal to the Kitchen employees and to compensate them for the meals which they have lost.

granted

* * * *

AWARD

(1) The practice of providing the employees of the Dietary or Kitchen Department with one free meal per day at a cost not to exceed 50 cents shall be reinstituted. If the cost of the meal exceeds 50 cents, the employee shall bear that part of the cost in excess of 50 cents.

(2) The employees of the Dietary or Kitchen Department shall be reimbursed for all meals lost since December 28, 1966, at the rate of 50 cents per day.

APPLICATION AND DISCUSSION QUESTIONS

1. What factors were considered by the arbitrator to determine whether there was a past practice? *Clear & long standing*

2. How did the arbitrator determine a past practice has ended? How do parties end a past practice? *repudiation in negotiation*

3. How might the outcome have been different, if the Hospital had placed the Union on notice? *grievance denied*

4. For a detailed discussion of past practices, see, Richard Mittenthall, *Past Practices and the Administration of Collective Agreements,* 59 Mich. L.Rev. 1017 (1961).

THE PROBLEM OF PAYMENT FOR TRAVEL TIME AND
PATTERN AND PRACTICE

A company installs and maintains commercial and residential security systems. Employees begin the workday at home, travel from home to various locations to perform work, and return home at the end of the workday. Sometimes employees travel from home to the Company's branch offices. The 2012-2015 Collective Bargaining Agreement has a provision indicating employees will receive pay for drive time over 45 minutes to and from the first and last job site of the day. The prior 2009-2012 CBA contained the same language.

In 2013, the Company installed a new electronic payroll system. Under the old system, employees manually entered hours worked and were paid for all commute time to customer locations and to branch offices that exceeded 45 minutes. However, the new electronic payroll system automatically calculates travel time and does not include hours or pay for travel time to branch offices.

The Union filed a grievance contending the language of the CBA is clear and unambiguous, which is further substantiated by the Company's 4 year practice of paying for travel time from employees' homes to branch offices. The Company's position is also that the CBA language is clear and unambiguous. The term "job site" refers to a customer work location, not a branch office. Therefore, commute time to branch offices is not compensable. Prior payments were made because of a glitch in the old payroll system.

How should the arbitrator rule?

grievance granted b/c PP indicates "job site" included branches for a year; but maybe 1 year not repetitive enough

VI. VARIOUS TYPES OF SUBJECTS IN ARBITRATION

A. MANAGEMENT RIGHTS

2014 AAA LEXIS 168[*]
AMERICAN ARBITRATION ASSOCIATION
(WILLIAM E. LONG, 2014)

[handwritten: Case discharge for misconduct]

ISSUE

Where, as here, the contracting parties have expressly recognized that the Employer may immediately discharge an employee for certain misconduct, does the Arbitrator have authority to alter the severity of the penalty the Employer assessed when such misconduct is established?

RELEVANT CONTRACT PROVISIONS (Omitted)

EMPLOYER POSITION

The Employer's position is that the CBA contains several provisions that limit the Arbitrator's authority to alter the discipline penalty assessed by the Employer. The Employer refers to Article 2, the Management Rights clause, and says it reserves to the Employer the right to direct and require its work force to comply with policies, rules and regulations and includes language giving the Employer the exclusive

[handwritten: Man. rights]

right to exercise these rights "and all other rights subject only to clear <u>and express</u> <u>restrictions governing the exercise of these rights as are expressly provided for in</u> <u>this Agreement."</u>

CBA

The Employer acknowledges that Article 13.1A does address express restrictions governing the exercise of the Employer's rights as it relates to discipline, just cause and due process. Article 13.1A states:

> Discharge, demotion, suspension or any other disciplinary action applied to a non-probationary member shall be made only for reasonable and just cause and shall offer due process. Any such action shall be in accordance with the policies and provisions of this agreement.

But the Employer's position is that Article 13.1A language becomes inapplicable when the Employer is confronted with identified misconduct that permits the Employer to immediately discharge an employee as provided in Article 13.2 entitled "Discipline Steps." The Employer refers to the following language in Article 13.2:

> "13.2. Discipline Steps
> All Bargaining unit member discipline shall be applied according to the following progressive steps except when the offense may require a more severe penalty.
> Step 1. Formal Counseling
> Step 2. Formal Written Reprimand
> Step 3. Suspension
> Step 4. Discharge

Except that the following offenses on the Employer's premises or worksites may lead to immediate discharge:

> a. Theft
> b. Intoxication
> c. Drug impairment
> d. Gross insubordination, e.g. willful refusal to perform work duties/responsibilities
> e. Willful destruction of property
> f. Deliberate falsification of records
> g. Willful injury to others
> h. Physical fighting"

The Employer's position is that the evidence in this case will show that the Grievant engaged in theft, gross insubordination (the willful refusal to perform work duties/responsibilities), and deliberate falsification of records. Therefore, the Employer says, Article 13.2 provides the Employer the authority and the discretion to immediately discharge the Grievant.

[handwritten margin note: El arg here]

UNION/GRIEVANT POSITION

The Union/Grievant position is that the CBA contains clear and unambiguous language that provides the Arbitrator jurisdiction to determine whether or not the Employer had reasonable cause to terminate the Grievant. The Union/Grievant position is that if the Arbitrator determines the Employer did not have reasonable and just cause for termination, there is no CBA language restricting his right to fashion an appropriate remedy based upon the case in its entirety, considering all aspects of reasonable and just cause.

The Union, similar to the Employer, points to several provisions in the CBA in support of its position. The Union notes that Article 2, Management Rights, does indicate that "the Employer has and retains the exclusive right to take any and all action as it may deem proper with respect to the management of its business ... and all other rights subject only to clear and express restrictions governing the exercise of these rights as are expressly provided in this agreement" (Emphasis added). The Union argues that other provisions in the CBA, pertinent to this case, provide clear and express restrictions with regard to the rights of management.

The Union argues that the Employer's position that Section 13.2 restricts the Arbitrator from modifying the severity of the penalty imposed by the Employer is in error. The Union notes that the word "may" is used in two key phrases within Section 13.2, i.e. "All bargaining unit member discipline shall be applied according to the following progressive steps except when the offense may require a more severe penalty," and "Except that the following offenses on the Employer's premises or worksites may lead to immediate discharge:" (emphasis added). The Union points out that Section 13.1 requires that discharge shall be made only for reasonable and just cause and shall offer due process. The Union says Section 13.2 does not contain any language indicating the Arbitrator is limited from modifying the penalty with regard to the offenses for which there may be discharge.

[handwritten margin note: "may"]

[handwritten margin note: U arg]

DISCUSSION AND FINDINGS

In any arbitration proceeding the Arbitrator must be guided by the provisions of the CBA. Excerpts from the relevant contract provisions in the CBA in this case are:

* * * *

My review is, therefore, based on the specific language within the CBA and "draws its essence" from the CBA.

I find the Employer's management rights granted in Article 2 are subject to the clear and express restrictions governing the exercise of those rights specified in Article 13.1. In carrying out its actions involving discipline, which can include discharge, demotion, suspension or any other discipline, Article 13.1 requires that such action taken by the Employer shall be made only for reasonable and just cause and shall offer due process. Therefore, the answer to question 2 is yes -- the Employer's disciplinary action in this case must be shown to have been only for reasonable and just cause and to have offered due process. And the answer to question 3 is no -- the language in Article 13.2 does not remove the restriction on the Employer specified in Article 13.1 to exercise disciplinary action only for reasonable and just cause and to offer due process.

Upon close review of Article 13 in its entirety, and the cases cited by the parties, I conclude the language of Article 13 does not support the Employer's position that the language of Article 13.1 becomes inapplicable when the Employer exercises its right to immediately discharge an employee as authorized in 13.2. The Article title is -- Discipline. Article 13.1 is titled "Just Cause and Due Process." Article 13.1A specifies certain standards the Employer must comply with when exercising discipline and Articles 13.1B and 13.1C describe specific procedures to be followed when determining and applying discipline. Article 13.1 D makes clear that the question of whether an Employer's exercise of its authority to discipline was without reasonable and just cause or without due process is subject to review by an Arbitrator. And if the Arbitrator finds discipline is justified, the Arbitrator has the authority to order a level of discipline different from the discipline administered by the Employer if the Arbitrator finds the discipline administered by the Employer was without reasonable and just cause or without due process.

Article 13.2 is titled "Discipline Steps." It is not divided into subsections. The first part of Article 13.2 mandates certain procedural/progressive steps that must be followed when exercising discipline, but also includes language that allows exceptions to the requirement that those steps be followed (emphasis added) when certain specified offenses on the Employer's premises or worksites (identified in the second part of Article 13.2) occur. I interpret the intent of the language in Article 13.2 is to remove the requirement that the Employer follow the progressive disciplinary steps listed in the first part of Article 13.2 and provide the Employer the ability to take action to immediately remove an employee from the workplace and immediately discharge the employee for behaviors listed in the second part of Article 13.2. *13.2*

I find nothing in the language of Article 13.2 that removes the Employer from the requirements established in Article 13.1. I believe the intent of the language in Article 13.2 is merely to allow the Employer to bypass the progressive steps normally required for discipline and discharge an employee for the specific offenses listed. The language in Article 13.2 does not remove the requirement that the disciplinary action of the Employer must be made only for reasonable and just cause (13.1A), or prohibit review in an arbitration proceeding of the question of whether the level of the discipline administered was with or without reasonable and just cause or without due process (13.1D). *13.1+2 thus*

* * * *

In this case, there is no language in the CBA that "clearly and unambiguously" mandates discharge; there is no clear and unambiguous language reserving to the Employer the exclusive right to determine the degree of discipline to impose; and there is no clear and unambiguous language restricting the Arbitrator from determining whether just cause for discipline exists and, if so, the appropriate level of discipline. *here*

* * * *

For the reasons stated in this Interim Opinion and Order the Arbitrator finds that the Arbitrator does have the authority to alter the severity of the penalty the Employer assessed when such misconduct is established. *thus*

APPLICATION AND DISCUSSION QUESTIONS

1. What was the original intent of Article 13. 2 and in what instances does it apply? *to allow discipline when there is just cause*

2. When does the Arbitrator have the authority to order discipline different from the discipline ordered by the Employer?

When ER discipline is w/out reasonable & just cause and due process

3. When does the Employer have the right to bypass the "discipline steps" outlined in the CBA? What language could the parties have negotiated to have limited the authority of the arbitrator to review the disciplinary action?

When misconduct;

added terms like "shall" or "ER at its sole discretion"

Case custodian seniority at school

BRENTWOOD SCHOOL DISTRICT
134 BNA LA 1173 (FELICE, 2015)[*]

Issue

Did the District violate Article 11 Section C of the CBA when it failed to award open positions on the daylight shift at the elementary schools to the most senior interested custodians? If so, what shall be the remedy?

Pertinent Contract Provisions

ARTICLE 11
WORK FORCE CHANGES

Section C - Vacancies

1. Any new job or any vacancy in existing job classifications (due to resignation, death, or dismissal for cause) may be filled initially by the employer on a substitute basis.

2. Such vacancies shall be posted on all bulletin boards for not less than ten (10) working days. The posting shall begin immediately after the employer realizes the vacancy if it is the intention of the School District to fill the vacancy. Such position shall be filled within thirty

---

[*] Reprinted with permission from *Labor Relations Reporter- Labor Arbitration Reports.* 134 BNA LA 1173. Copyright 2015 by the Bureau of National Affairs, Inc. (800-372-1033). http://www.bna.com.

(30) days of the initial date of posting unless the filling of such a vacancy requires the hiring of a new employee.

3. Current employees desiring to apply for such jobs shall submit an application in writing to their immediate supervisor. Seniority and qualifications will be considered.

4. If no active employee applies within ten (10) days of the posting, the employer shall contact all employees on the lay-off list who meet the qualifications of the position, in the order of their seniority, and offer the position to each of them within the next ten (10) days.

Background

The Association on August 29, 2014, filed grievance No. 2014-15-1 as a group grievance alleging that the District failed to post openings for daylight custodial positions at two elementary schools and failed to place the most senior interested employees into those positions in violation of the CBA and past practice. The Association requests the immediate posting of the positions and placement of the most senior interested custodian employees into the daylight custodian positions, together with a Make Whole Remedy.

issue

After reviewing the matter, the District denied the grievance. When the parties were unable to resolve the dispute by means of the grievance procedure, they submitted the matter to the undersigned arbitrator for final and binding disposition.

Contentions of the Parties

The Association contends that the District violated the CBA when it failed to post openings for daylight custodial positions and failed to place the most senior interested employees into those positions. The Association also asserts that the resolution of a previous grievance involving essentially the same factual circumstances was granted by the prior superintendent. Accordingly, the Association requests that the grievance be sustained.

U arg

The District contends that it has the right to assign custodial employees as needed. It further asserts that no custodial postings specify time, location or work shift. The District further contends that under the Management Rights Clause the District has a right to direct the staff of employees unless otherwise provided in the CBA. The

ER arg

District asserts that it has the right to assign custodial employees without reference to seniority.

Findings and Conclusions

The testimony offered by the District and the Association is totally antithetical as to the parties' interpretation of Article 11, Section C of the CBA. The Arbitrator is confronted with the task of applying a reasonable construction and interpretation of said article and section.

On or about August 29, 2014, Association representative Martin McGeever filed a grievance claiming the District "failed and/or refused to post openings for daylight custodian positions at the two elementary schools, and has failed and/or refused to place the most senior interested employees into those positions in violation of the Collective Bargaining Agreement and past practice." The remedy requested by the Association was to "immediately post the position openings, place the most senior interested maintenance/custodian employees into the daylight custodian positions in the elementary schools, make the grievants whole in every way, and provide such other relief as may be deemed appropriate by an arbitrator."

The action which precipitated the instant grievance occurred when the District Director of Facilities Management Joseph Kozarian issued a memo to maintenance and custodial staff on August 15, 2014, setting forth the assignments for the 2014-15 school year. Custodians assigned to the morning shift at the Elroy and Moore elementary schools had less seniority than custodian grievant McGeever who was assigned to a 3 to 11 p.m. evening shift.

By memo dated September 3, 2014, District Superintendent Amy Burch denied the grievance on several grounds, more particularly that the District had the right under the CBA not to post vacancies if it intended not to fill them and the District had the right to assign maintenance and custodial employees as needed.

At the threshold, the Association argues that a previous grievance resolution involving custodian Peggy Orman which was resolved by the prior District Superintendent is dispositive of the issue raised in the instant case. In that previous case, the District transferred Orman, who was not the most senior custodian, to a daylight position at Moore Elementary School without regard to seniority and without bargaining. The Association filed a grievance in June 2011 protesting the transfer and alleging "the District has failed and/or refused to post an opening for a daylight custodian position and failed and/or refused to place the most senior interested employee into that position in violation of the Collective Bargaining Agreement and past practice." The relief sought was to place the most senior interested maintenance/custodian employee into the daylight custodian position and make the grievants whole in every way and provide such other relief as may be deemed appropriate by the arbitrator.

Thereupon, Superintendent Dr. Ron Duffala granted the grievance, stating, "The District will take the actions agreed upon during the June 14, 2011 meeting and discussion attended by Martin McGeever, Cynthia Dilla, Joe Kozarian, Joe Ferris and Dr. Ron Duffala." As a result of the resolution, Orman was moved out of the daylight elementary position and a more senior custodian was placed in the daylight elementary position.

During the hearing in instant case, the Association also referred to another grievance which was filed on March 4, 2013, in which McGeever claimed he was improperly displaced from his position as a daylight custodian without allowing him to exercise his seniority and bump a less senior employee in the job classification in violation of the CBA. However, after considering the factual circumstances surrounding that particular grievance, the Arbitrator finds that it is not dispositive of the dispute in the instant case.

The thrust of the District's case centers on its assertion that Kozarian exercised his management right to transfer Orman into the daylight shift at Moore Elementary School. Kozarian also testified he was unaware of the prior grievance and had no knowledge of the remedy granted by Dr. Duffala, notwithstanding that he was noted as being present at the meeting where the resolution was discussed. However, in the hearing, Kozarian denied ever attending that meeting. Orman was assigned to the evening shift after the June 2011 grievance was granted. She remained in that position through the 2011-2012 school year, however, her assignment in the 2013-2014 school year triggered the instant grievance.

Kozarian testified that under the Management Rights Clause in Article 2, Section B of the CBA, he had discretion to make assignments based on need, particularly to ensure safe and clean buildings for students and school personnel. He testified that he never assigned positions based on seniority even after the number of positions in each building changed according to needs.

The essence of Kozarian's testimony is that the CBA does not refer to shiftwork in particular buildings and the posting of positions by job title do not specify shift times. Kozarian contends that the number of maintenance or custodial personnel assigned to a building on a particular shift fluctuates from year-to-year and, at times within a year that he must prioritize and maximize his resources.

In an effort to bolster its case, the District referred to the Mary Pauletich Grievance when she was assigned to daylight duties at Moore Elementary School near the end of the 2011-2012 school year. Pauletich had difficulty performing some aspects of the custodial work during the day and after meeting with the Association officers in

October 2012 the District and the Association agreed that Pauletich would be reassigned to an evening shift. However, the Pauletich grievance resolution is not dispositive of the issue raised in the instant case since it did not involve applying for an open position which is the subject of the instant grievance before the Arbitrator.

There is no dispute that the District has the right to establish a set number of custodians or other maintenance personnel to employ, to fill vacant positions and the right to assign work to employees on their shifts. However, with respect to open positions, the District under Article 11, Section C (2) and (3), is obligated to post open positions and interested employees may submit their applications in writing for those positions and their seniority and qualifications must be considered.

[margin handwritten: CBA]

If the arbitrator were to accept the District's position in the instant grievance, it would be tantamount to vitiating the posting of open positions and the consideration of seniority, engrained in Article 11, Section C (2) and 3) of the CBA.

In the instant case, the District violated Article 11, Section C (2) and (3) of the CBA when it failed to post the disputed daylight open positions and denied interested employees the opportunity to apply for such positions and to have their seniority and qualifications considered. There was no evidence adduced that any economic loss was incurred by the grievant or any other employee.

[margin handwritten: thus]

AWARD

On the basis of the foregoing and after evaluating and reviewing the testimony and evidence presented in the hearing and the post hearing briefs filed by the parties, the grievance is sustained. The District is hereby ordered to post the disputed open positions on the daylight shift at the two elementary schools and to fill said positions with the most senior qualified custodial employees who apply for the positions. There is no economic or other relief ordered by the Arbitrator.

[margin handwritten: sustained]

APPLICATION AND DISCUSSION QUESTIONS

1. How might the Custodian's performance affect his ability to remain on the daylight shift? *[handwritten: If poor, wouldn't want him on day shift]*

2. Does the "opportunity to apply" mean that the School must hire the current and most senior employee? *[handwritten: no]*

3. What happens if after the posting has been up for ten (10) days, no current employee applies? Is it required to be posted for additional time?

No, 11 CC(4) kicks in

THE PROBLEM OF THE SCOPE OF A MANAGEMENT RIGHTS CLAUSE

A police officer in a small municipal police department always knew he wanted to pursue a law degree. Prior to joining the department, the Chief of Police gave the officer general information about the tuition reimbursement benefit, although the officer did not mention his intent to attend law school at that time. The officer also discussed the tuition reimbursement benefit with the city's finance director and a sergeant in the department a few days before he was hired and discussed his plan to attend law school. Both indicated tuition reimbursement requests had to be approved by the Chief, but it shouldn't be a problem as long as the courses were job related.

The officer completed his first year of law school and submitted his request for reimbursement. Much to his surprise, the Chief denied the request indicating the coursework did not meet the criteria that coursework must be job related. The chief previously approved tuition reimbursement requests for three police officers who were pursuing a bachelor's degree in criminal justice, even though a bachelor's degree was not a requirement for the position. The Chief also denied a request for reimbursement of expenses for a computer science degree. When the officer questioned the Chief about the denial, the Chief stated, "If I approve your request, other officers will want to go to law school and the department would never be able to pay for it. Besides, your job is to enforce the law, not to practice it!"

The Collective Bargaining Agreement (CBA) contains a Tuition Refund Clause that gives the Chief of police authority to approve requests for tuition reimbursement, but does not provide criteria. The CBA also contains a Management Rights Clause, which indicates the City retains the full right and responsibility to direct the operations of the department and otherwise exercise the prerogatives of management. The union contends the discretion afforded under the Management Rights Clause is not unbridled discretion and must be reasonable. The Union alleges that the Chief's denial of the tuition reimbursement request was an unreasonable abuse of management discretion.

How Should the Arbitrator Rule?

deny grievance b/c ER had broad discretion & it wasn't unreasonable to deny reimbursing tuition for a J.D.
?

B. SENIORITY RIGHTS

*Case
disability
& seniority* (handwritten)

INTERNAT'L BROTHERHOOD OF TEAMSTERS, LOCAL 120 AND
UNIVERSITY OF ST. THOMAS

2010 WL 805003 MN BMS (A. BEENS)

SUMMARY

Sum (handwritten)

A university did not violate a collective bargaining agreement (CBA) by removing an employee from its seniority list and posting his position after the employee had been on disability leave for more than six months. Although the CBA contained provisions for the preservation of seniority rights, it also allowed the employer to terminate an employee for legitimate business reasons such as the inability of the employee to perform his job.

* * * *

ARBITRATION OPINION AND AWARD

ISSUE

The parties deferred formulation of the Issue to the Arbitrator. I conclude it can be stated as follows:

> Does the collective bargaining agreement compel Employer to hold
> Grievant's job open and continue recognition of his seniority when he has
> been on disability leave for more than six months?

FACTUAL BACKGROUND

Grievant was employed for 24 years as a Building Service worker at the University of St. Thomas and a member of Local 120. He was, by all accounts, an excellent employee with no disciplinary history. As a result of several adverse health conditions, Grievant was placed on Short Term Disability ("STD") on October 20, 2008. Six months later, on April 11, 2009, Grievant was still unable to return to work. The

Employer had advised that it would no longer hold his current position open, and that it would be posted and filled as soon as a qualified candidate is hired. After six months on STD, Grievant was transferred to Long Term Disability ("LTD"), removed from the Employer's seniority list and, in effect, terminated.

Article Two of the CBA governs the acquisition and exercise of seniority rights by bargaining unit members. A sentence within Section 7 of Article Two states, "Inability to work because of proven illness or injury shall not result in loss of seniority rights." The CBA also provides that full-time Union members will be covered, at Employer's expense, by both the Employer's STD and LTD Programs. The STD plan is funded and administered by the Employer. It provides 100% of pre-disability salary during the 1st to 60th day of disability, 80% during the 61st to 120th day and 60% during the 121st to 180th day The LTD plan was purchased by Employer from Unum Life Insurance Companyssuming continued disability, it provides for payment of 60% of the employee's pre-disability salary from the 181st day through the recipient's Social Security Retirement age.

As of March, 2009, Grievant was 15th on an 85 employee seniority list. The Employer removed Grievant from the next Building Service Worker seniority list it published in October, 2009. In reposting Grievant's job and removing him from their seniority list, St. Thomas was relying on a provision contained in their Short-Term Disability Plan and its reiteration in their Employee Handbook which provides,

> "Positions for employees on an approved short-term disability leave will be held for at least 12 weeks but not longer than 6 months. If an employee not released to work before the end of the period, their position will be posted and filled..."

The Union grieved the Employer's action, arguing that the University had violated a seniority provision in the CBA.

At this point, Grievant remains disabled. Whether or not he can ever again physically perform his prior job is unknown. However, Grievant has neither resigned nor been formally terminated from employment at the University.

UNION POSITION

It is the Union's position that the employer is obligated under the terms Article Two, Section 7 of the CBA to continue recognition of Grievant's seniority and hold his job open until such time as he is able to return to work or formally resigns his University employment. Second, the Union contends removal of Grievant's name from the seniority list is a de facto termination in violation of the CBA provision relating to discipline and discharge.

EMPLOYER'S POSITION

The University contends it is simply following the provisions of a Short Term Disability Plan which was specifically agreed to by the Union in Article Ten, Sections 3, 4, and 5 of the CBA. Under that plan, the employer is only obligated to hold open Grievant's job for the six months he is on STD. If not released for a return to work within the six month period, the plan provides the employee's job will be posted and filled. The Employer denies any termination of Grievant under the Discharge and Discipline sections of the CBA.

RELEVANT CONTRACT AND DISABILITY PLAN PROVISIONS

Collective bargaining agreement provisions:
ARTICLE TWO, Section 7:

An employee desiring a leave of absence from the job shall secure written permission for the leave from the Employer and shall register same with the Union. Failure to comply with this provision shall result in a complete loss of seniority rights of the employee involved. The leave of absence shall not be in excess of ninety (90) days, but may be renewable by mutual written agreement between the Employer and Union up to a maximum of one (1) year. Inability to work because of proven illness or injury shall not result in loss of seniority rights. Employees on leave of absence shall accrue seniority rights during the absence.

ARTICLE TEN:
Section 3:

All full-time Bargaining Unit Employees shall be covered under the Employer's Short Term Disability Program, at the Employer's expense. (For qualifications, refer to Article Thirteen, Section 4.)

Section 4:

All full-time Bargaining Unit Employees shall be covered under the Employer's Long Term Disability Program, at the Employer's expense. Eligibility begins on the first of the month following six (6) months of full time employment.

Short Term Disability Plan provision:

Positions for employees on an approve STD leave will be held for at least 12 weeks but no longer than 6 months. If an employee is not released to work before the end of this period, their position will be posted and filled. If an employee receives a medical release after this 6 month period, the employee is eligible to apply for any open position at the University for which they are qualified. The University cannot guarantee re-employment.

DISCUSSION

Resolution of this grievance entails the single most important function of a labor arbitrator, interpreting the parties' collective bargaining agreement. Undoubtedly the parties to the current CBA negotiated and entered into their contract willingly and in good faith. However, no negotiator, whether labor or management, is prescient enough to envision every situation or context to which contract language might be considered applicable. In this case the arbitrator is asked to determine the meaning of some portions of the collective bargaining agreement. While he may refer to sources other than the collective bargaining agreement for enlightenment as to the meaning of various provisions of the contract, the arbitrator's essential role is to interpret the language of the collective bargaining agreement with a view to determining what the parties intended when they bargained for the disputed provisions of the agreement. When reviewing the contract, it must be read as a whole. Interpretation that tends to nullify or render part of the contract meaningless is to be avoided. Indeed, the validity of the award is dependent upon the arbitrator drawing its essence from the language of the agreement. It is not for the arbitrator to fashion his or her own brand of workplace justice nor to add to or delete language from the agreement.

The sentence principally at issue in this grievance is contained in the Seniority section of the CBA: "Inability to work because of proven illness or injury shall not result in loss of seniority rights." The Grievant contends this provision is in conflict with and superior to Article Ten, Sections 3, 4, and 5. They, in essence, allow the employer to repost the job of an employee who has been on Short Term Disability for six months or more. The net effect of this action is to terminate the employee and strip his seniority. The Union contends the Employer actions violate the most basis protections of the CBA's seniority clause. For a variety of reasons discussed below, I disagree.

Seniority is a negotiated right appropriately treasured by bargaining unit members. It provides tenured workers job security and protection from preferential treatment of favored employees by the employer. It adds predictability to employee job assignments, promotions and layoffs. These factors result in a more stable workplace. All seniority systems are, to one degree or another, limits on managerial discretion. Work assignments which are normally management prerogatives can become problematic. Administration of seniority rights can be a time consuming, complex process for the employer. These competing union-management interests are usually balanced at the bargaining table. Pure seniority clauses, where longevity is the sole determinant, are extremely rare. Most collective bargaining agreements contain modified seniority provisions which attempt to meet the needs of both union and employer. When each party makes some concessions, a reasonable balance of employee job security and management operational efficiency can result.

In this instance, the Union relies on the premise that specific provisions in a contract prevail over general provisions. Consequently, they argue, Grievant's job must be held open and his seniority retained so long as he is out with "proven illness or injury." They contend the specific language of Article Two, Section 7 overrides the general inclusion of a contrary provision only alluded to in Article Ten, Sections 3, 4, and 5. The latter incorporate the Employer's disability plans into the CBA by reference. The actual plan provisions are not spelled out within the contract. However, incorporation by reference is a common contract drafting device. It promotes efficiency by avoiding repetition of massive amounts of information already available to the parties in other documents. There is no evidence the parties did not understand his concept when agreeing to Article Ten.

The chief fallacy in the Union's argument lies in taking the Section 7 phrase completely out of context. An arbitrator cannot ignore clear contract language or legislate new contract interpretations. When an arbitrator can ascertain the principal purpose of a contract provision, that purpose must be given greater weight in interpreting the words of the provision. The language upon which they rely, "Inability to work because of proven illness or injury shall not result in loss of seniority rights," is contained in Article Two, Section 7 of the CBA. Article Two outlines seniority rights. Section 7 deals specifically with seniority rights where an employee has requested and received a leave of absence. Section 7 leaves of absence and STD leaves entail two different procedures in this CBA. The former can be granted for any numbers of reasons, including "proven illness or injury," while the latter results solely from physical disability. The former is customarily unpaid, while the latter is specifically design to provide employee income. Read in that context, the plain meaning of the phrase is that an employee doesn't lose seniority while on an approved Section 7 leave of absence due "to proven illness or injury" -- no more, no less. Section 7 does not limit leaves of absence to reasons of disability. Leaves could be granted for reasons unrelated to physical disabilities such as education, travel, or family care. In fact, there are no CBA limitations on reasons for leaves of absence so long as the employee complies with the provision of Section 7. Adoption of the Union's view of Section 7 would render Article Ten, Section 5 meaningless. In order to give effect to both provisions, the Section 7 language must be limited to leaves of absence due to "proven illness or injury" specifically granted under that section.

The Union disregard for context is demonstrated by the lack of compliance with other provisions in Section 7. There is no evidence Grievant even attempted to comply with requirements contained in Section 7. There is no evidence he secured written permission for a leave of absence from the Employer or registered the same with the Union. He neither requested a simple 90 day leave nor sought a written agreement between Employer and Union to extend a leave to one year. In fact, Section 7 specifically provides that, "Failure to comply with this provision shall result in a complete loss of seniority rights of the employee involved."

here

* * * *

In summary, when the contract is read as a whole, Article Two sets out and preserves seniority rights in great detail. However, it is irrational to believe the parties agreed that an employee retains seniority forever, irrespective of his long term ability to do his job. Management's right to terminate a worker who cannot perform his job for an extended period is preserved in Article Ten. They have an equally compelling interest in maintaining a modicum of efficiency and continuity in their operations. In my view, Articles Two and Ten, as they are written, strike a reasonable balance between competing union-management interests.

thus

AWARD

The grievance is DENIED.

denied

APPLICATION AND DISCUSSION QUESTIONS

1. The arbitrator explains that "no negotiator, whether labor or management, is prescient enough to envision every situation or context to which contract language can be considered applicable." Why is this statement true? But in this case, why didn't the parties see that they were negotiating a seniority provision that might be in conflict with other provisions of the CBA?

bk we cant foresee everything
diff understandings?

2. What is the purpose of the seniority clause? How does this clause benefit both the Union and Management? What are the conflicting interests on both sides in negotiating a seniority clause? Why are "pure seniority clauses" rarely negotiated into contracts?

ER wants control, U wants security

3. The arbitrator provided guidance on how to analyze contract provisions when the primary purpose of the provision is ascertained. Why does the arbitrator suggest that when determining the meaning of a provision the purpose of the provision is given more weight than the words in the provision? How does the arbitrator apply this principle in this case?

Uses context / whole CBA to show purpose outweighs words

case police nepotism vs. seniority

CITY OF WADSWORTH AND THE OHIO PATROLMEN'S, BENEVOLENT ASSOCIATION,

134 BNA LA 641 (BELL, 2015)[*]

Issue

Q

Does Wadsworth's Police Department's Nepotism Policy constitute "good cause" under Section 42.4 of the parties' collective bargaining agreement to override bargaining unit members' Section 42.3 seniority based selection of shifts under the record facts of this case? If not, what is the appropriate remedy?

Selected Contract Provisions

ARTICLE 11
SENIORITY

SECTION 11.1 DEFINITION. Unless otherwise defined in this agreement seniority shall be defined as an employee's length of continuous full-time employment within a specific classification with the Employer from the last date of hire. A lay-off of one-hundred eighty (180) days or less shall not constitute a break in service for the purposes of calculating seniority.

---

[*] Reprinted with permission from *Labor Relations Reporter- Labor Arbitration Reports.* 134 BNA LA 641. Copyright 2015 by the Bureau of National Affairs, Inc. (800-372-1033). http://www.bna.com.

SECTION 11.2 TIE BREAKERS. In cases where two (2) or more employees wish to take time off at the same time, preference shall be granted to the most senior employee except in cases where such preference would adversely affect the operation of the Department. If employees have the same date of hire, seniority will be determined by the employees' civil service test scores. The employee with the higher score is placed above the employee with the lower score on the seniority list. In cases of promotion where employees have the same date of promotion, seniority in rank will be determined by department seniority.

SECTION 42.4 ADMINISTRATIVE FILL. The employer reserves the right to reserve shift slots for all employees who are ineligible pursuant to Section 42.3 above. The employer agrees to indicate those reserved shift slots on the shift selection document used in the shift selection process outlined in this Article. Employer agrees that selection of days off for these reserve shifts shall take place after all eligible bargaining unit employees have made their day off selections within any given shift.

For good cause shown, the Employer shall have the right to administratively fill or reassign any bargaining unit employee should it determine that the effective operation of the Police Department dictates that seniority not be the determining factor for shift assignment and shift rotation.

The employer may temporarily change employee shifts due to temporary staffing needs caused by illness, injury or emergencies. Such changes shall affect members in reverse order of seniority.

Relevant Wadsworth Police Dept. Nepotism Policy
Policy 1050

Wadsworth Police Department Policy Manual

Nepotism and Conflicting Relationships
1050.1 PURPOSE AND SCOPE
The purpose of this policy is to ensure effective supervision, safety, security, performance, assignments and discipline while maintaining positive morale by avoiding actual or perceived favoritism, discrimination or other actual or potential conflicts of interest by or between members of this department.

* * * *

1050.2 RESTRICTED DUTIES AND ASSIGNMENTS

While the Department will not prohibit personal or business relationships between employees, the following restrictions apply:

(a) Employees are prohibited from directly supervising or being directly supervised by any other employee who is a relative or with whom they are involved in a personal or business relationship. However, an employee may be permitted to work in the same "chain of command" unless the Director of Public Safety determines the terms and conditions of employment could be adversely influenced.

   1. At times circumstances may require that such a supervisor/subordinate relationship exist temporarily, the supervisor shall make reasonable efforts to defer matters involving the involved employee to the employee's direct supervisor or another uninvolved supervisor.

   2. When personnel and circumstances permit, the Department will make reasonable efforts to avoid placing employees in such supervisor/subordinate situations. The Department reserves the right to transfer or reassign any employee to another position within the same classification as it may deem necessary in order to avoid conflicts with any provision of this policy.

(b) Employees are prohibited from participating in, contributing to or recommending promotions, assignments, performance evaluations, awards, transfers or other personnel decisions affecting an employee who is a relative or with whom they are involved in a personal or business relationship.

* * * *

Nepotism

The City of Wadsworth permits the employment of qualified relatives of employees of the same household or immediate family so long as such employment does not, in the opinion of the appointing authority, create a conflict of interest or otherwise violate Ohio Ethics Law.

An employee is permitted to work in the same City department as another employee in his/her immediate family provided that no supervisor-to-subordinate relationship exists.

The City retains the right to deny an appointment to a person in the same department where his/her relationship to another employee in his/her immediate family has the potential for creating an adverse impact on supervision, safety, security or employee morale.

* * * *

For the purposes of this policy, immediate family is defined as a spouse, child, parent, sister, brother, grandparent, grandchild, aunt, uncle and corresponding in-law, "step" relation or any member of the employee's household.

Introduction

The City of Wadsworth, Ohio is located in Medina County in northeastern Ohio. It has a population of approximately 21,000 residents and a full compliment of city departments serving its populace, including its police department. This department consists of a Chief, a Lieutenant, five Sergeants including a Detective Sergeant, and some twenty patrol officers.

As with any police department of this size, little flexibility exists with respect to the scheduling and supervision of patrol officers given the need for 24-7 coverage of the safety and security of the City's residents. During 2015 the department issued a directive making its shift assignments as follows:

* * * *

The Parties' Positions

The positions of the parties are rather straight forward. The Association takes the position that the language of Section 42.4 of the labor agreement that gives the Employer "the right to administratively fill or reassign any bargaining unit employee should it determine that the effective operation of the Police Department dictates that seniority not be the determining factor for shift assignment and shift rotation" requires the employer to first show "good cause" before rejecting seniority based shift assignments-thus placing the burden of proof upon the Employer in these proceedings.

Effectively, the Association asserts that seniority dictates shift assignment and rotation unless the Police Department can "prove" that to do so will render its operation ineffective. It goes on to assert that the denial of seniority based rights to these two grievants constitutes an unjust "penalty," in the absence of any "wrong" done by them, simply because of their marital status or that of another member of their family violates the subject policy-a status pre-dating the promulgation of the subject policy and its subsequent caused denial of their seniority rights.

Conversely the Employer responds that the function, purpose, and intent of the department's nepotism policy is to pro-actively address potential conflicts before they occur and not to reactively address such conflicts after their occurrence. Such a policy is clearly authorized under Section 4.1, 5) and 6) of its contractual "management rights." Moreover, the spirit and intent of such policy is to do more than prevent "actual" conflicts of interest but to also to avoid the "appearance" or "perception" of favoritism, discrimination or other conflicts of interest so as to maintain and enhance the community's support for the department and the carrying out of its mission in the absence of such conflicts.

* * * *

Analysis, Findings & Conclusions

Aside from expressed economic benefits, there is no more cherished bargaining unit right than seniority based rights impacting the family lives of bargaining and members. Generally speaking, when all other factors are considered equally in the selection of bargaining unit members for promotions, assignments, shift selections, etc., it is not uncommon for labor agreements to decree that seniority is to be considered-if not be controlling-in the final determination. So it is with the instant agreement and its Section 11.2, Tie Breakers...

D. Article 42 and The Nepotism Policy

With the foregoing as a given, the issue here presented is the seeming conflict between Section 42.3 and 42.4 of the parties' collective bargaining agreement, and whether the employer's unilaterally promulgated "nepotism policy," standing alone, constitutes the "good cause" of Section 42.4 not to use seniority as the determining factor for shift assignment and shift rotation.

Commencing as he must with the expressed language of Section 42, Seniority Shift Bidding and its several subsections, it is axiomatic that all of the subsections should be read in such a manner as to give effect to all those subsections. Such a reading reveals that seniority is a relevant factor in the shift bidding selection process and not the determining factor in the actual assignment of shifts and rotation. For instance Section 42.1 limits the employees eligible to participate in the shift bidding selection process to only non-probationary bargaining unit employees with three or more year of continuous full time employment from the last date of hire. Section 42.2 of the labor agreement requires the employer to annually post shifts available for seniority based selection and choice of shift days off by November 1st, without indicating exactly which shifts are to be made available for seniority based selection.

Section 42.3 further limits the bidding process by stating that "all eligible employees shall not be permitted to bid on the same shift more than five consecutive years." And the final two subsections of Section 42 place restrictions on seniority based bidding should the shift bidding involve "specialized assignments" (42.5) or should the employer demonstrate good cause that seniority based assignments not be followed because the effective operation of the police department dictates otherwise (42.4). Stated differently, each of the foregoing subsections place contractually agreed to restrictions on the use of seniority as a basis for shift assignment and shift rotation. The ultimate question here presented is whether this employer's "nepotism policy," standing alone, constitutes "good cause shown" for not using seniority as a determining factor for shift selection and shift rotation of these grievants.

It is to be observed at the outset that the Association did not in these proceedings at any time challenge the employer's Nepotism Policy as being arbitrary, capricious, or as being unjust or unreasonable in any manner. The essence of the Association's challenge is that such a policy is not necessary for the "effective operation of the police department" as neither the grievants or the police department as a whole has experienced conflicts of interest such as to warrant the adoption of such a policy at odds with bargaining unit members' seniority based rights.

Herein lies the fatal flaw in the Association's otherwise meritorious case. The nepotism policy at issue herein was not created out of the "whole cloth" of this department's imagined conflicts of interest, but instead culled from a best practices manual used by police departments all over the country. As here applied and grieved by these two police officers, the policy mirrors that of the City of Wadsworth's nepotism policy in its application to all city employees-both members of bargaining units and those in management positions as well. Moreover, as here applied and grieved, this departmental nepotism policy is identical in its application to state law and the State of Ohio's Ethic's Commission Guidelines.

* * * *

This Arbitrator is not unmindful of the potential adverse effects such a policy has upon law enforcement officers such as the grievants, but it is not unlike other adverse effects they are potentially subject to as a result of their chosen vacation. In some respects it is not unlike the ethics constraints placed upon lawyers, as officers of the Courts, to avoid even the appearance of impropriety in both their professional and personnel lives... constraints not found in many vocations.

With the expiration of their current collective bargaining agreement in December of this year perhaps the parties can craft a contractual solution to avoid the hardships potentially caused by this policy. Until then this Arbitrator is powerless to reform the current agreement so as to address this issue.

AWARD

denied

Reluctantly, the subject grievance is denied for the reason the employer possessed "good cause shown" under Section 42.4 to not follow seniority based shift selections of these grievants.

APPLICATION AND DISCUSSION QUESTIONS

1. Do you agree with the arbitrator's conclusion that the nepotism policy is a "good cause" to circumvent a seniority system?

   Yes

2. Was it an error by the Union in not challenging the nepotism policy as being "arbitrary, capricious, or as being unjust or unreasonable in any manner"? *Yes*

3. The arbitrator suggests that the parties negotiate a contract provision to avoid hardship on employees when enforcing the policy. What language would you suggest be negotiated into the agreement?

   nepotism policy only counts as good cause if there is actual wrongdoing & not mere concern

CARGILL MEAT SOLUTIONS
133 BNA LA 1528 (BONNEY, 2014)[*]

Issue

This case involves a grievance filed by George Alexander ("the grievant") regarding the processing of his vacation requests by Cargill Meat Solutions ("Company" or "Cargill"). At the hearing, the parties stipulated that this case presents no issue of arbitrability, either substantive or procedural, and that the following issue is properly before me for decision:

> Did the Employer violate the collective bargaining agreement (CBA) by refusing to allow the grievant to schedule vacation preferences based upon warehouse department seniority and, if so, what shall the remedy be?

Findings of Fact

Cargill operates a meat processing plant in Marshall, Missouri. The bargaining unit at the Marshall plant includes about 500 workers, and the CBA's seniority provision divides those employees among eight departments. The Beef and Warehouse Departments are relevant to this grievance. According to seniority lists in evidence, the Beef Department has over 100 employees, and the Warehouse Department has about ten employees.

The grievant works as a Cardboard Compactor Operator on the first shift at the Marshall plant and is listed as a Forklift Operator in the Warehouse Department on all of the seniority lists in evidence. He is the most senior employee in the Warehouse Department. Of the people working the first shift, 106 have seniority in the Beef Department and two or three employees have seniority in the Warehouse Department. Sometime in 2013, the Company switched the grievant from the Warehouse Department to the Beef Department. In May 2013, Mr. Alexander filed a grievance protesting his move to the Beef Department. On October 3, 2013, the parties signed a settlement agreement, drafted by the Company, which provided as follows: "It is the Company's position that who a person reports to and what department they follow for scheduling purposes is a 'management right'. The Company will agree that for purposes of departmental seniority the Cardboard Compactor position

* Reprinted with permission from *Labor Relations Reporter- Labor Arbitration Reports.* 133 BNA LA 1528. Copyright 2015 by the Bureau of National Affairs, Inc. (800-372-1033). http://www.bna.com.

will have seniority rights in the Warehouse Department." Despite that settlement agreement, however, the Company has continued to require the grievant to schedule his vacation through the Beef Department rather than through the Warehouse Department. According to Operations Lead Jay Grantham, a management employee, the grievant's "seniority is with the beef department for scheduling purposes. His overall seniority is with the warehouse." Mr. Grantham explained that this means that, if the grievant requests non-prescheduled vacation days in a week in which five Beef Department employees on first shift are already scheduled to be on vacation, management will deny his request even if no other Warehouse Department employee on first shift is on vacation that week.

The grievant spends most of his shifts outdoors operating the cardboard compactor that serves the Beef Department's operations. The compactor is located partly inside the plant and partly outside. Another Warehouse Department employee, Danny Hays, works inside the Beef Department where he loads cardboard into the compactor. Although, like the grievant, Hays is shown on the seniority lists as a Forklift Operator, his job title is actually Cardboard Compactor Operator. Once Hays loads cardboard into the hopper, the machine compacts the cardboard into bails which emerge in the grievant's work area outside the plant. Once a bail has been compacted, the grievant shuts down the machine, ties the cardboard bail with wire, and uses a forklift to transport the bail to another part of the plant for storage. Occasionally, the grievant must go inside the building to load cardboard into the compactor or to perform other duties.

The CBA provides vacation time for employees who have completed at least one year of service with the Company. Employees with twenty full years of service-including the grievant-are entitled to four weeks of paid vacation each year, which must be used during the year and cannot be carried over to the next year. The CBA provides two ways for employees to schedule vacation. "Employees may sign up for vacation preferences by seniority from March 1 through March 31" by indicating their vacation preferences on the calendar that is posted or made available to employees for that purpose. The Company uses that sign up calendar to prepare the annual vacation schedule by April 15 of each year. In addition to this pre-selection process, employees can request vacation on an ad hoc basis at any time of year by submitting a Vacation Request form. Such ad hoc vacation requests are considered on a first-come, first-served basis without regard to seniority. All vacation requests are subject to approval by the Company "in order to insure regular and efficient production." Management has adopted a rule limiting the number of employees in each department who can be on vacation in a particular work week. For instance, on the first shift, management permits only five Beef Department employees and one Warehouse Department employee to be on vacation at one time.

The grievant did not submit any vacation pre-selection requests during March 2013 but submitted one such request in March 2014, which the Company approved. During 2013 and 2014, moreover, the grievant submitted several Vacation Request forms in which he requested the following days off: October 14 through 18, 2013; December 9 through 13, 2013; December 16 through 20, 2013; December 30 and 31, 2013, and January 1 through 3, 2014; January 6 through 10, 2014; March 24 through 28, 2014; November 24 through 28, 2014; December 29 through 31, 2014, and January 1 and 2, 2015; and January 5 through 9, 2015. The Company apparently approved all of the grievant's requested vacation days except the week of December 16 through 20, 2013. That week is crossed out and noted as "Full" on the Vacation Request form dated December 3, 2013. Based on Mr. Grantham's testimony that the Company considers the grievant to have seniority in the Beef Department for scheduling purposes and requires the grievant to take his vacation days through the Beef Department, I find that the supervisor denied the grievant's December 16 through 20, 2013 vacation request because five Beef Department employees were already scheduled to be on vacation that week.

* * * *

Positions of the Parties

Union:

The Union argues that the grievant has seniority in the Warehouse Department. Thus, because the CBA's vacation provision allows employees to pre-select vacation time by departmental seniority during March each year, the Company must allow the grievant to pre-select his vacation each year in the Warehouse Department. Regarding vacation requests the grievant submits in months other than March, the Union argues that the parties have a well-established past practice of evaluating such ad hoc vacation requests within the department in which the employee maintains seniority. Thus, the Company must schedule the grievant's ad hoc vacation requests within the Warehouse Department.

Company:

The Company contends that it did not deprive the grievant of any right to preschedule his vacations during March and that there is no reasonable likelihood that it will ever deny any prescheduling request submitted by the grievant because he is the most senior Warehouse Department employee and the second most senior employee in the Beef Department. Thus, because the grievant has suffered no actual harm, the grievance should be denied. The Company further argues that, even if the CBA provides a right to schedule vacation preferences based on the grievant's Warehouse Department seniority, management retains discretion to approve or deny any vacation request "to insure regular and efficient production."

Opinion

* * * *

By contract and past practice, there are two distinct ways for employees at the Marshall plant to request and schedule vacation time. On one hand, employees can preschedule vacations during March of each year. On the other hand, employees can request vacation time by submitting a Vacation Request form at any time of year. I will treat each type of vacation request separately.

Article 11, §4 of the CBA grants employees the right to preschedule vacation by indicating their vacation preferences on the posted vacation calendar during March of each year. Once employees have indicated their vacation preferences on that calendar during March, the CBA obligates the Company to prepare and post a vacation schedule by April 15. The CBA further provides that "Employees will be given their preference of vacation based on departmental seniority provided the choice is made prior to April 1."

The Company argues that the Union has failed to prove a violation of the labor agreement in this case because the grievant never requested to preschedule his vacation in either March 2013 or March 2014 and because the Company never denied and would never deny any request the grievant might submit since he is a very high seniority employee. But the Company's arguments fail to acknowledge the testimony of management employee Grantham, who unequivocally stated that, for the past two years, the Company has required the grievant to schedule all vacation days-both prescheduled and ad hoc-through the Beef Department. According to the settlement agreement signed on October 3, 2013 and all of the seniority lists in evidence, the grievant maintains his seniority in the Warehouse Department. Thus, requiring the grievant to preschedule his vacations in the Beef Department violates the plain and unambiguous language of Article 11, §4 of the CBA, which specifically provides that "Employees will be given their preference of vacation based on departmental seniority provided the choice is made prior to April 1."

* * * *

Notwithstanding these considerations, however, I find that the Company's decision to consider the grievant's requests for prescheduled vacation time in the Beef Department deprived the grievant of a valuable contractual right to have those requests considered in the department where he has seniority, specifically the Warehouse Department. Thus, I find this grievance ripe for review and arbitrable under the parties' CBA.

Next, I will consider the much closer issue of whether the Company violated the CBA when it considered the grievant's ad hoc vacation requests. First, it is true that, under Article 11, seniority-departmental or otherwise-plays no role in an employee's entitlement to schedule ad hoc vacation time. Based on the parties' well-established and consistent past practice, those requests are determined on a first-come, first served basis, and-as with all vacation requests-the Company has the right to approve ad hoc requests "in order to insure regular and efficient production." Insuring regular and efficient production means that-in considering the grievant's ad hoc vacation requests-management can consider the schedules and availability of any Beef Department employees who would need to cover the shifts the grievant would miss due to his vacation. But that does not mean that management can deny the grievant's ad hoc vacation requests simply because five Beef Department employees are already on vacation in the week in which the grievant has applied for ad hoc vacation time.

The grievant has seniority in the Warehouse Department, and-in applying the Company's automatic exclusionary rules-his ad hoc vacation requests should be considered in reference to whether one other Warehouse Department employee is already scheduled for vacation in the same week. The grievant should not be lumped in with Beef Department employees for that purpose. The well-established past practice is to consider ad hoc vacation requests with regard to the other employees in the department in which the employee applying for vacation time maintains seniority. Most relevant to the grievant's situation is Danny Hays, the other Cardboard Compactor Operator on first shift. The grievant and Hays both work on the same machine, on the same shift, and both maintain seniority in the Warehouse Department. But the Company only considers the grievant's ad hoc vacation requests with regard to the

Beef Department. That is unfair and not in keeping with the practice applied to all other employees.

For that reason, I find that the Company also violated the CBA when it considered the grievant's ad hoc vacation requests with regard to the Beef Department. Specifically, the Company violated the CBA when it rejected the grievant's request for vacation time from December 16 through 20, 2013, based only on the fact that five Beef Department employees were already scheduled to be on vacation that week. Rather than applying that automatic exclusion to the grievant as if he maintained seniority in the Beef Department, management should have considered the schedules and availability of any Beef Department employees who would have covered the shifts the grievant would have missed due to his vacation as one factor in assessing the overall impact of the grievant's vacation request on the Company's interest in regular and efficient production.

AWARD

The grievance is sustained. In keeping with the parties' stipulation, I will retain jurisdiction over the remedy in this case-if any-for a period of thirty days.

APPLICATION AND DISCUSSION QUESTIONS

1. Explain the employer's position that the grievance "was not ripe for review"? How did the arbitrator resolve this issue? Was the Grievant ever harmed by how the seniority system was implemented?

2. How is seniority used to determine vacation? Which department's seniority should apply to the Grievant?

3. How did the arbitrator use past practices to resolve the seniority issue?

THE PROBLEM OF SENIORITY RIGHTS V. MANAGEMENT RIGHTS

A liquor distillery plant produces, bottles and warehouses over 1,500 different types of rums, tequilas, bourbons, and blended whiskeys. The facility operates 3 shifts to produce 13 million cases of spirits annually, though production demands vary based on the month and the season. Overtime may be required when a process started on one shift must be completed on another shift due to equipment problems or scheduling changes. Under the CBA, departmental seniority lists determine the choice of shift within each department in accordance with other provisions in the Agreement.

For the last 12 years, the plant has used temporary agency employees in entry level positions to manage seasonal fluctuations in production demands and as a result, has been able to prevent lay-offs of bargaining unit employees during non-peak production periods. The CBA limits the number of temporary agency employees to 30 in the plant at any given time. Agency employees have no rights under the CBA, are not given any preferences regarding shifts, and may not work overtime. Each week the company notifies the employment agency of how many temporary employees it needs on each shift. A mix of bargaining unit employees and temporary agency employees are scheduled for each shift.

An entry level bargaining unit employee with low seniority did not receive her preferred shift and was assigned to work second shift, while some temporary agency employees were assigned to work first shift. She filed a grievance alleging that the company violated her seniority rights under the CBA by assigning temporary agency non-bargaining unit employees to first shift instead of granting her preferred shift request.

The Union asserts that the work performed by the grievant and temporary employees is the same and requires no special training or skills. By reserving slots on each shift for temporary agency employees, the company is denying bargaining unit employees a contractual seniority right to work on their preferred shift. The company argues that even though the CBA has no management rights clause, the practice of scheduling agency employees on all shifts is an implicit management right that gives the company the right to effectively operate its business.

How should the arbitrator rule?

Sustain grievance, EE had
seniority & was denied it
+ no MR clause
?

C. Hiring and Filling Vacancies

Ohio Association of Public School Employees
OAPSE/AFSCME, AFL-CIO
013 LA supp. 149983 (f.weatherspoon, 2013)[*]

I. STATEMENT OF FACTS

The facts indicate that the Ohio Association of Public School Employees OAPSE/ AFSCME Local __/AFL-CIO and its Local # __ (hereinafter, Union) and M__ City School District Board of Education (hereinafter, Board) are parties to a collective bargaining agreement, effective from June 30, 2011 through June 29, 2014 (hereinafter, CBA or Agreement).

The current grievance arises from the Board's decision to fill a vacant Maintenance Specialist with an Air-Conditioning Emphasis position. The announcement of the vacant position was posted on January 16, 2013. The Grievant and two other bargaining unit employees applied for the position. The Union and the Board presented slightly different facts as to what occurred after the employees applied for the position. The Union indicated that management advised all three applicants that they did not meet the job requirements for the position. Management then proceeded to consider external candidates for the position. After considering outside candidates, management once again considered the internal applicants, which included the Grievant, for the position. The internal candidates were requested to submit additional documentation regarding their skills and qualifications for the position. Even though there are different versions of what occurred after the applicants applied for the position, it is not dispositive of the issue before the Arbitrator. It is clear that at the end of the process, the decision was between the Grievant and another bargaining unit employee.

After reviewing the additional documentation and informally verifying their experience with previous employers, the Board selected an employee with less seniority than the Grievant. The facts are undisputed that at the time of the selection, the Grievant had more than ten (10) years of seniority with the M__ School District,

---

whereas the selectee had less than a year with the Board, and was on probation as a bus driver when the decision was posted.

On March 15, 2013, S__ (hereinafter, Grievant) filed a grievance alleging the Board violated Article 5, Section 5.04 of the CBA. The grievance went through the various stages of the grievance process. The grievance was denied. Arbitration was requested pursuant to Article 7 of the CBA. The remedy requested by the Grievant is to be offered the position with monetary losses.

II. ISSUE

Whether Article 5, Section 5.04 was violated when the Board denied the Grievant the Maintenance Specialist with Air-Conditioning Emphasis position, and if so, what is the appropriate remedy?

III. RELEVANT CONTRACT PROVISIONS

Article 5 Seniority-Bid Procedure, Section 5.04, states:

> The position shall be awarded to the most senior employee within the vacant clas-sification who bids the job and meets the minimum job qualifications. If no one applies from the same classification as the vacancy, the job shall be awarded to the most senior employee from within the same classification series in which the vacancy exists who bids the job and meets the minimum job qualifications.
>
> Additionally, if no employee from within the classification or from within the same classification series bids the job, the job shall be awarded to the most senior employee who bids and meets the qualifications listed on the job description for the classification in which the vacancy exits.
>
> A provisional appointment shall be made within ten (10) working days of the close of the posting period and receipt of the testing scores subject to confirmation by the Board. The Board will assume 100% of the cost of the initial job-screening test required by the administration. Any employee wishing to improve their initial scores may do so at their cost in accordance with guidelines of the job related testing service. Employees may retest at the Board's cost after two years from the initial test date should a vacancy be posted. The minimum passing score on any test, as determined by the job related testing service shall be accepted as a passing score for this provision. If no one meets the qualifications set out in the job description, and the qualifications of two or more employees are equal, seniority shall be the determining factor in awarding the position.

IV. POSITION OF THE PARTIES

A. Union's Position

The Union maintains that the Grievant had more seniority than the selectee and met the qualifications for the Maintenance Specialist with Air-Conditioning Emphasis position. The Union states that in accordance with Article 5, Section 5.04 the Grievant should have been selected because no employee within the classification or same classification series bid for the position, and the Grievant was the most senior employee who bid and met the qualifications for the position, as listed in the job description. Likewise, the Union insists that the failure to select the Grievant was clearly a violation of Section 5.04 of the CBA because the Grievant met all the listed minimum job qualifications on the job posting and job description. In addition, the Union raised the procedural issue at the hearing. The Union also alleged that the Board violated Article 5, Section 5.04 by failing to make a provisional appointment within ten (10) days of the close of the posting period for the position.

* * * *

B. Board's Position

The Board maintains that it did not violate Article 5, Section 5.04 when it selected another bargaining unit employee to fill the Maintenance Specialist with Air-conditioning Emphasis position. The Board contends that although the selectee had less seniority than the Grievant, the selectee met the minimum qualifications for the position, whereas the Grievant did not. Specifically, the Board claims that the selectee had the perquisite maintenance skills to perform the duties as outlined in the job description.

With regard to the issues raised at the hearing, the Board acknowledges that Article 5, Section 5.04 requires a provisional appointment as the Union contends. However, the Board claims that the President of the OAPSE granted an extension of time to make an appointment.

V. DISCUSSION AND ANALYSIS

In contract interpretation cases, the grieving party has the burden of persuading the arbitrator that its position is the correct one. [3] Therefore, in this grievance, the burden is on the Union to prove a violation has occurred. The Union must demonstrate that the actions taken by the Board is inconsistent with the CBA. The Union must provide sufficient evidence that the Board violated the contract.

* * * *

The facts indicate that no one applied from the same classification or the same classification series as the vacancy, thus the Board was required to select the most senior employee from those who bid on the position and met the qualifications listed on the job description. There is no dispute that the Grievant had more seniority than the selectee. Indeed, the parties stipulated that the Grievant had more than ten (10) years seniority and the selectee had less than a year and was on probation in his position as a bus driver.

The principle of seniority is a cornerstone provision in most collective bargaining agreements. The expectation of the Union and bargaining unit employees is that the most senior employee will have the opportunity to fill a position before less senior employees. Employers and Unions who negotiate a seniority clause will often have what is often called a modified seniority clause. As in this CBA, the senior employee will be selected if they meet the minimal qualification for the position.

* * * *

The Arbitrator must acknowledge that it is difficult to ignore the fact that the Board selected an employee with less than a year's seniority over an employee with ten (10) years of seniority. Moreover, it appears that the Grievant is a dedicated employee with a good work record. For example, his performance evaluations rating were rated Good" to "Excellent." Nevertheless, the CBA requires that the person selected must meet the qualification for the position and not just have the most seniority. Thus, the Arbitrator is limited by the CBA. The Arbitrator will review the evidence and testimony to determine whether the Union can meet its burden of proving the Grievant had the prerequisite skills to perform the job.

A review of the selectee's resume and supporting documentation indicate that he met the qualifications as outlined in the job description.

The Union must present concrete evidence which clearly supports its claim that the Grievant met the minimum qualifications of the position by having the prerequisite skills cited in the job posting and job description. This is a difficult task for the Union to meet this burden because the evidence must be more than just the Union's affirmation that the Grievant could perform the duties. In non-selection disputes, the Union has the burden of providing persuasive evidence that the Grievant had the relevant experience and skills to perform the position. Moreover, the Arbitrator's role is not to second-guess management's personnel decisions but to determine whether their decision violated the CBA. This will entail reviewing the Grievant's qualifications and prior work experiences to determine whether he met the requirements of the maintenance position.

The starting point in analyzing the evidence presented by the parties is a review of the Maintenance Specialist with Air-Conditioning Emphasis job description. The following minimum qualifications are listed on the job description: (Omitted)

$$* \quad * \quad * \quad *$$

During the hearing, the parties stipulated that the Grievant completed high school and had a valid Ohio Driver license, he could obtain a valid Ohio Low Pressure Boiler Operator's License within in a reasonable amount of time, and he had the ability to lift 75 lbs of dead weight.

The parties adamantly disagree as to whether the Grievant met the minimum qualifications for items 3 and 5 of the position. To determine whether the Grievant met the minimum requirements as outlined in items 3 and 5 of the job description, the Arbitrator has closely reviewed the testimony of the selecting official, Mr. D__, Director of Facilities. Mr. D__'s testimony sets forth legitimate business reasons why the Maintenance Specialist with Air-Conditioning Emphasis position required mechanical and electrical skills. D__ testified that having an employee perform some of these duties would reduce the need to outsource work to a contractor. He further explained that having experience with HVACs was crucial.

The Union presented a number of the Grievant's certificates of training, reference letters, and a summer appointment memo to prove that the Grievant met the minimum requirements of the job. As stated earlier, the Grievant has a lengthy record of training. However, the Union failed to show how this experience is related specifically to the maintenance, repair and instillation of air conditioners. For example, the Grievant received training certificates from FEMA the State Fire Marshall, Ohio Peace Officer, and the Association of Safety Communication Officers. The Grievant also received a Certificate of Recognition from the Washington County Career Center. Most impressive was a reference letter submitted by the Chief of Police of a local community regarding the fine work the Grievant did as an Auxilliary Police Officer. However, there is no mention of the Grievant performing any type of maintenance work as an officer. All of these trainings and the recognition are important, and the Grievant should be proud of these accomplishments, but these trainings failed to support the Union's claim that the Grievant met the minimum qualifications for the position. There is no evidence that his trainings related to the repair and instillations of air conditioning.

* * * *

In addition to failing to establish that the Grievant met the minimum qualifications for the position, the Union also failed to establish that the Grievant could perform the responsibilities listed in items 2 and 4 of the following position description:

1. Position substitutes in all buildings for custodians and assumes their responsibilities.

2. Position is capable of making "skilled" level repairs to air conditioning, electrical and mechanical equipment.

3. Position performs installations, replacements and repairs to district buildings and grounds in safe and professional manner consistent with applicable buildings and safety codes.

4. Licensed to purchase and install "F__" Refrigerant".

There was extensive testimony from both sides regarding the Grievant's training and certification regarding refrigerants. The record shows that the Grievant completed an on-line certification related to this function. As stated above, the Board stated "this type of certification limits the holder to working only on small appliances (i.e., those with 5 lbs. or less of refrigerant). Mr. D__ testified that the District has air conditioning equipment much larger than small appliances referenced with Type I certification."

5. Position may order/purchase parts and materials as required to complete a specific job.

6. Position supervises/trains maintenance helper, substitute and casual labor personnel.

As stated above, the Union provided a wealth of material regarding the Grievant's record of trainings and certifications, but failed to show a correlation between such experience and the requirements and responsibilities of the job. Specifically, there was no verifiable evidence that the Grievant repaired air conditioning, electrical and mechanical equipment. The job requirements and responsibilities emphasized the need to have this type of training and experience.

VI. CONCLUSION

The Union has failed to provide sufficient evidence that the Board violated Article 5, Section 5.04 of the CBA when it denied the Grievant the position of Maintenance Specialist with an Air-Conditioning Emphasis position. The Grievant has an extensive record of training and work experience but not related to the repair and installation of air conditioning, as the job requires.

VII. AWARD

The grievance is denied.

APPLICATION AND DISCUSSION QUESTIONS

1. When is seniority the absolute determinative factor in awarding a position? For a description of the Sufficient Ability Clause, see Elkouri & Elkouri, How Arbitration Works, 2nd ed. (2012) pp. 14-48.

2. Who in this case and in similar cases, has the burden of proving the validity of their position to the Arbitrator?

3. What was the grievant lacking that made him unqualified for the position? For a discussion of the burden of proof in arbitration, see Elkouri & Elkouri, How Arbitration Works, 2nd ed. (2012) pp.1524; Fairweather's Practice and Procedure in Labor Arbitration, 3rd ed. P. 192.

THE PROBLEM OF HIRING AND FILLING VACANCIES

School District A has a successful athletic program, but faced fiscal challenges when the last school levy failed. The Collective Bargaining Agreement indicates all coaching positions will be posted and filled annually and provides the process for selection. If there are multiple applicants, a committee consisting of the Athletic Director, an administrator, and an appointed faculty member will select the most qualified applicant based on the criteria of coaching certification, overall experience, and coaching experience within the district, subject to superintendent and board approval.

To contain costs and to continue to provide students with an opportunity to participate in a football program, School District A merged their football program with School District B's football program starting with the 2013 – 2014 school year. Practices, games, and expenses were split between the districts. School District A did not appoint anyone to any coaching positions for the 2013 – 2014 school year.

Mr. G. has been in various football coaching positions in District A for the last 23 years. Mr. G. received a voicemail from the District B Athletic Director informing him that he had been hired as the coach of Freshman Football in the newly merged District A/B Football Program and would be compensated using District B's pay scale. Mr. G declined the offer, because he believed he would have been appointed to the higher level Assistant Varsity Coach's position if the hiring protocol under District A's Collective Bargaining Agreement had been followed. Mr. G. filed a grievance alleging District A violated the CBA's contractual requirement that all coaching positions will be posted and filled annually.

How should the arbitrator rule?

D. SUBCONTRACTING

ANHEUSER-BUSCH, INC. AND INTERNATIONAL BROTHERHOOD OF TEAMSTERS, LOCAL 6

132 BNA LA 945 (FITZSIMMONS, 2013)[*]

[handwritten: Case]
[handwritten: window cleaning]

I. Background

Anheuser-Busch, Inc. is an American brewing company which operates breweries in the United States. The International Brotherhood of Teamsters, Local 6 is the sole and exclusive bargaining agent for the Company's bottlers. The Company and Union are parties to a Collective Bargaining Agreement which was in force at all relevant times herein. Robert Granda filed the grievance herein claiming non-bargaining unit personnel performed bargaining unit work when the Company hired outside contractors to wash the interior windows in the Bevo Building.

[handwritten: Issue]

II. Issue

[handwritten: Q]

Did the Company violate the Contract by subcontracting bargaining unit work when it hired an outside contractor to wash the interior windows in the Bevo Building?

Relevant Documents Renewed for the Term of the 2008 Contract

Memorandum of Understanding Non-Core Business Functions

The Company's resources, including human resources, are the greatest value when committed to its core business of brewing, packaging, and shipping beer. The parties recognize, however, that not every job performed by every employee consists solely of core duties. Nevertheless, like core duties, non-core duties best serve the core business when they are performed in an efficient and cost effective manner. To that end, the parties agree to cooperate in identifying and improving operations through a more economically efficient delivery of non-core services.

The parties have agreed that the following non-core duties may be contracted ~~Out~~
outside the bargaining unit.

- Carton Make-up
- Beer Dumping
- Forktruck Washing
- Custodial Work in non-production areas in the Bevo, Warehouse and MRB*

*The Bottlers identified on the roster in Exhibit A shall remain employed by the Company subject to normal attrition (e.g. retirement, resignation, death, or termination) and assigned to Building Cleaning. Beginning immediately, the Company shall have the right to assign or subcontract custodial work in non-production areas in the Bevo, Warehouse and MRB.

> (CLARIFICATION: The Company's core business is brewing, packaging and shipping beer. However, the Company recognizes not all jobs consist of core duties. We expect to transition to contracting the items noted in the final offer. One part concerns work which the Company has identified in the proposal that it may want to subcontract. Before the Company subcontracts that work, however, we have committed that we will meet with the Union to discuss our plans and reasons. We also will consider any ideas which the Union may have regarding alternative methods).

The parties agree to the continued improvement of all processes involving employees represented by Local 1187, Bottlers. To that end, whenever the Company identifies opportunities where improvement can be accomplished as contemplated by this provision, the Company will so notify the Union in writing and will provide information supporting the Company's conclusion. The parties shall continue to work together to achieve a good faith method for implementing an improvement plan and the Union shall not arbitrarily reject the Company's efforts to achieve the goals consistent with this Memorandum. (CLARIFICATION: If future events give us cause to consider other tasks as non-core, we will notify the Union in writing and provide related documentation. Our expectation is that the Union will not arbitrarily reject our effort to perform such work in an efficient and cost-effective manner.)

IV. Summary Positions of The Parties

A. Company

That the Company had the right to subcontract to an outside contractor the window washing of the Bevo building as this work was a non-core business function not directly related to the brewing, packaging and shipping beer.

B. Union

That the Company violated the MOU when it subcontracted the washing of the interior windows which was bargaining unit contractual work.

V. Summary of the Evidence

Denver Washburn testified he has been employed by the Company for 35 years and now works in the Building Cleaning Department. He also serves as a Union Trustee. He is familiar with the MOU and understands that the Company may contract out certain non-core work. He agreed that the employees listed in of the MOU were "grandfathered" so they could continue to do custodial work in non-production areas of the Bevo building. All but one of those employees has retired. He considered production areas to include any place bottlers work while doing production. He was aware that the Company used King Cleaning to clean non-production areas as the employees listed in retired. Employees in the Bevo building are involved in production with bottle lines and can lines. At the direction of his supervisor, Craig Baggett, he used a high pressure hose to clean interior windows, screens and sills on four occasions since 2009. He has observed other bottlers cleaning interior windows in the same manner. He never observed outside contractors cleaning interior windows until 2012...

Robert Granda (Grievant) testified he has been employed by the Company for thirty-five years and works in the Material Receiving department. He explained that the windows get dirty due to dust and aluminum and glass dust. On March 6, 2013 he observed two Icon employees cleaning the interior windows in the Bevo building. He was aware the Company contracted out the exterior window cleaning but he had never observed outside contractors cleaning the interior windows.

Terry Spink testified he retired from the Company on May 19, 2010 after working as a bottler for 35 years. He has used a high pressure hose to clean interior screens and windows. On May 15, 2010, four days before he retired, he cleaned the interior

Bevo windows and screens using a telescopic pole, mop and squeegee. Craig Baggett told him to clean interior windows once in 2008. He never observed outside contractors cleaning interior windows. On cross-examination he admitted that Baggett told him to clean the interior windows in 2008 because VIPs were coming on a tour on short notice. He has observed outside contractors cleaning the exterior windows through the years.

* * * *

Dave Mulherin began working at the Company in 1986 in labor relations including contract negotiations. He was the author of the MOU involved in this dispute. He compared this MOU to the prior MOU. The only change was the inclusion of "custodial work" as work the Company could contract out in the current MOU. He explained that the 2003 MOU was negotiated by the Company in an effort to reduce the high costs at the St. Louis brewery compared to the costs of some of the Company's sister breweries. The Company wanted to work more efficiently and be more flexible in producing beer. The Company was trying to move its employees out of non-core business functions such as grass cutting, bar tending, assembling cardboard boxes and window washing. The Company desired to subcontract work to augment the work force including situations where the Company didn't have the equipment or skill set to do the work. The interior window washing done by bargaining unit members was "touch-up" in nature and was not comparable to the Company's use of outside contractors such as Icon who performed a thorough inside and outside window cleaning.

When he negotiated the MOU with the Union he told them that the Company wanted to concentrate on its core function of brewing, packaging and shipping beer. The Company emphasized that bargaining unit members would continue cleaning production equipment including fillers, packers and palletizers and the immediate areas adjacent to that production equipment. The interior and exterior window washing was always considered custodial work in non-production areas. He has advised Union officials that bargaining unit members will still occasionally do quick cleanups of a few inside windows but the Company will contract out window washing if it is part of an overall inside and outside window cleaning project. On cross-examination he confirmed that the Company would not use outside contractors to clean production equipment and the areas immediately adjacent to that equipment such as floors. The Company already uses outside contractors to clean offices, hallways and break rooms.

* * * *

Jeff Stanford testified he is the President of Icon Window Cleaning Company and his company has periodically cleaned the interior and exterior windows of the Bevo building. He described in detail how his employees use power lifts and ladders to wash the exterior windows while coordinating with employees washing the interior windows and screens. He estimated that it takes three Icon employees one month to wash all the Bevo windows interior and exterior. Icon employees participate in regular safety programs due to safety issues related to washing exterior windows on power lifts at great heights, using ladders, and assessing fall risks. Icon employees wash each window using cleaning solution, strip washer, sponges, brushes and squeegees...

* * * *

VI. Discussion and Decision

The issue to be decided by the Arbitrator is whether the Company violated the Memorandum of Understanding related to non-core business functions in the Contract when it subcontracted the cleaning of the interior and exterior windows in the Bevo building. The Company core business is the brewing, packaging and shipping beer. The Company's position is that window washing is not part of the Company's core business and such work can be more skillfully and economically performed by outside contractors. The Union contends that the Company violated the Memorandum of Understanding by subcontracting the interior window washing which was bargaining unit work in that it was custodial work in a production area of the Bevo building.

In contract interpretation cases, the Arbitrator's primary task is to determine the mutual intent of the parties as expressed in the language of the Contract. If the disputed contractual language is clear and unambiguous, the Arbitrator will interpret the Contract according to its plain meaning. The language in dispute in this case is contained in the parties MOU. The MOU states in part:

> "The parties have agreed that the following non-core duties may be Contracted outside the bargaining unit.
> ... Custodial work in non-production areas in the Bevo...
> ... Beginning immediately the Company shall have the right to assign or subcontract custodial work in non-production areas in the Bevo...."

The evidence in this case proved that the Company determined to reduce its expenses by contracting out some of its non-core business functions. The Company considered its core business functions to be the brewing, packaging and shipping beer. The Company and Union entered into a MOU on November 25, 2003 which allowed the Company to contract out certain non-core duties. These included carton make-up, beer dumping and forktruck washing. The Company and Union later agreed on the MOU which is at the heart of the current dispute. The only change from the previous MOU was the addition of the sentence:

only change

"Custodial work in non-production areas of the Bevo...."

The Union does not contend that the washing of the exterior of the 412 windows in the Bevo building is bargaining unit work as Union members do not have the equipment or skills to do this work. The Union also does not contend that other custodial work including the cleaning of break rooms, offices and hallways is bargaining unit work. The crux of the Union's grievance is that the cleaning of the interior windows in the Bevo is custodial work in a "production area" of the Bevo as the Union contends that the entire floor is a production area.

U arg

The MOU does not define "non-production areas." The Arbitrator finds that the phrase: "non-production areas" is ambiguous. A term is considered ambiguous if plausible contentions may be made for conflicting interpretations of the disputed language. The burden is upon the Union to prove its interpretation of the MOU language is correct since its grievance contends that the entire floors of the Bevo are "production areas" including the interior windows. The Arbitrator will look at other aids of contract interpretation including bargaining history and past practice of the parties to determine the intent of the disputed language in the MOU.

U burden

PP+BH

The Union failed to produce any evidence regarding the bargaining history in the implementation of the 2003 MOU. The only testimony on bargaining history came from Company witness Dave Mulherin who drafted the 2003 MOU. Mulherin testified that the Company's focus was not to subcontract custodial work in the production areas of the Bevo but to continue to have Union workers perform all the custodial work in the areas immediately adjacent to the production equipment. The windows were as far as possible from the production areas. The interior and exterior window washing was custodial work in a non-production area of the Bevo. Mulherin testified further that the meaning of "production area" in the MOU did not include the 412 windows of the Bevo building.

U fail BH

A

The past practice of the parties is an established technique utilized by arbitrators to interpret contractual provisions. For a past practice to be enforced by the

PP?

arbitrator it must be long standing and relied upon by the parties; unequivocal; and readily ascertainable over a reasonable period of time as a fixed and established practiced accepted by both parties and not waived or abandoned by the party seeking to enforce the practice.

In reviewing all the testimony presented at the Hearing by the Union as to Union employees washing the interior windows of the Bevo the Arbitrator finds that Union testimony was not persuasive. Witness Washburn testified that his supervisor directed him to use a high pressure hose to touch up the screens and windows on four occasions. Washburn used only water to hose down the windows. He did not use soap, squeegee or rags to wipe down the windows. Witness Spink testified that he has used a high pressure hose on occasion to clean the screens and interior windows and that he sometimes used pole, mop, or squeegee. Witness Pelizarro testified that on one occasion in 2007 he cleaned the interior windows using a power hose and water and used a squeegee and rags to wipe down the window sills and floors. These Union witnesses testified they had observed other Union employees cleaning the windows in the same manner through the years.

The Company's evidence was persuasive that the Union workers cleaning of the interior windows was touch up in nature which involved hosing down the windows usually at the direction of a Company supervisor...

The Arbitrator finds that the Union's evidence only proved that Union employees occasionally performed touch up cleaning of the interior windows of the Bevo building. The Union failed to prove that its members ever performed thorough interior window cleaning. The Union has failed to prove any long standing, unequivocal past practice that would prevent the Company from subcontracting professional window cleaning of the entire 412 windows in the Bevo building as the Company evidence proved it had done on numerous past occasions.

The Company's evidence was persuasive that it desired to operate its business core functions of brewing, packaging and shipping beer more efficiently and to utilize bargaining unit employees to support its core functions. Window washing is not a core function of the Company's business. The Company continues to utilize bargaining unit members to perform custodial cleaning in the production areas where beer is brewed, packaged and shipped. The Arbitrator finds that the Union has failed to prove that the Company violated the 2003 MOU when it contracted out periodic professional interior and exterior window cleaning at the Bevo building. This periodic use of an outside contractor was for a legitimate business purpose. There was no proof that the Company desired to violate the Contract or weaken the bargaining unit. No bargaining unit employees were laid off or lost their jobs as a result of the Company's periodic use of professional window cleaners.

VII. AWARD

The grievance is denied.

APPLICATION AND DISCUSSION QUESTIONS

1. How did the Arbitrator decide the role of the arbitrator in contract interpretation cases? If the language is clear and unambiguous, how should the arbitrator interpret the contract? Was the language in the MOU clear or ambiguous? *determine mutual intent of Prs; follow K; ambiguous*

2. What role does bargaining history have on determining the intent of the parties when negotiating the bargaining agreement? Was the bargaining history helpful to the Arbitrator in determining the meaning of the MOU? *helped interpret; yes - for EK*

3. How are past practices used to interpret contract provisions? How does the arbitrator define past practices? *als. helps interpret intent; see p. 486 top*

UNIVERSITY OF THE PACIFIC PHYSICAL PLANT AND GENERAL TEAMSTERS LOCAL 439

131 BNA LA 619 (RIKER, 2012)[*]

Case
fire extinguish
Maintenance

RIKER, Arbitrator

Issue

Did the Company violate Section 1(B) of the Collective Bargaining Agreement when it sub-contracted the fire extinguisher work or portion thereof? If so, what is the appropriate remedy? *Q*

Applicable Provisions of the Collective Bargaining Agreement

[*] Reprinted with permission from *Labor Relations Reporter- Labor Arbitration Reports*. 131 BNA LA 619. Copyright 2015 by the Bureau of National Affairs, Inc. (800-372-1033). http://www.bna.com.

SECTION 1. RECOGNITION

(margin handwritten: CBA)

Section 1(B) SUB-CONTRACTING

Should a department be proven to be an unreasonable financial hardship to the University, the Union and the University would meet to attempt to resolve the financial problems, and that sub-contracting should be the last resort? Nothing in the foregoing shall restrict, qualify or limit the Employer's right to maintain its past practices of sub-contracting where, in the Employer's judgment, such practice is desirable.

Background

(margin handwritten: issue)

The dispute in this case is centered on a work activity and the Union's contention that the Employer, pursuant to the terms of the CBA, had the obligation to abide by the conditions of the CBA to continue to service the tasks at hand. On September 12, 2011 the Union filed a grievance alleging that the Employer violated the 2010-2013 CBA by their decision to subcontract the servicing and maintaining of approximately 900 fire extinguishers that were in numerous locations throughout UOP's campus:

> "As you know from our meeting this morning the Union believes that Scott Heaton blatantly violated Section 1(B) (Subcontracting) of our Collective Bargaining Agreement. Mr. Heaton maintained that the University subcontracted out the work because of a financial hardship but never gave the Union an answer as to not notifying us due to his unilateral decision to subcontract the work. Our agreement states in part ... the Union and the University would meet to attempt to resolve the financial problems. This meeting never took place due to the fact that Mr. Heaton maintained there was no obligation on his part to notify the Union.
>
> Therefore, this is a formal grievance against Scott Heaton's blunt contractual violation of our agreement, and we demand to meet and discuss how we can resolve the financial hardship that he has declared."

(margin handwritten: violation?)

Positions of the Parties

The arbitrator summarizes the positions of the parties as follows:

UNION

U arg

PP

The Company cannot evade its contractual obligation to properly assign work as required under the terms and conditions of the CBA. For 20 years the bargaining unit personnel have consistently accomplished the work of the inspecting and servicing of fire extinguishers located throughout the University's campus. In May of 2011, when the Employer subcontracted duties relating to certain fire extinguishers that had been serviced and maintained by bargaining unit members to an outside vendor, they did so in plain violation of the Collective Bargaining Agreement.

CBA

The CBA clearly specifies instances in which the University is permitted to contract out work at the campus. One of those instances may be if one of the University's departments is faced with an unreasonable financial hardship, in which case the Union and the University would then meet and attempt to resolve the financial problems. Secondly, that subcontracting should be considered as a last resort. In addition to the above, there is also an opportunity for the University to contract out work when they can identify that it is being done pursuant to an existing past practice....

Violation

In the matter before the arbitrator the evidence that was presented at the hearing by the University shows that they failed to meet these conditions in all respects. They did not establish that the Physical Plant Department was faced with a financial hardship. Even if they had done so they have the obligation, under Section 1(B) of the CBA, to first meet with the Union to discuss their actions of why they deem it would be necessary to subcontract bargaining unit work.

The arbitrator is also asked to take note that the University had not presented any substantive evidence to establish that subcontracting of the fire extinguishing service was the last resort available. The testimony is that when the University subcontracted out the inspecting and servicing of the fire extinguishers they did so without meeting any of the pre-conditions noted above.

* * * *

EMPLOYER

ER arg

* * * *

In essence, the contract language is clear and unequivocal, and the need to resort to interpretation is not required as the meaning can be derived entirely from the language of Section 1(B). As specifically written, the language of the CBA's "Recognition" clause limits the Union's jurisdiction to two distinct forms of subcontracting. Those are, if an entire department is going to be subcontracted then such subcontracting will only be allowed if the department is in an unreasonable financial hardship, and that the University and Union must first confer over whether the hardship can be resolved. Secondly, in conformity with past practice, the University has sole judgment to decide if subcontracting any work that affects less than the entire department is desirable.

The evidence presented at the hearing proved that the subcontracting of the fire extinguisher work falls within the second category, as an entire department was not affected by the University's decision. Therefore, the University determined that in their judgment subcontracting the retrofitting was desirable. All of the factors discussed during the course of the hearing: such as the subcontractor having the mobile equipment thus allowing maintenance to be done on site; that the work in question could be completed quicker by the contractor; removal of the retrofit equipment (that occupied the work space) allowed for the office space to be expanded. This led to the analysis that determined it was productive and desirable to subcontract rather than continue to perform the retrofitting with UOP employees. In addition, there is the fact that not even one employee, covered by the CBA, was laid off because of the subcontracting of the fire extinguisher work.

All of these factors contributed to saving thousands of dollars for the University while increasing the ability to perform in-house work. To reiterate, in 2007 the contract language in Section 1(B) provided that the University agreed not to subcontract work presently performed by the Physical Plant employees. That restrictive language was deleted from the terms and conditions of the CBA. In addition, the arbitrator is also asked to recognize the University has the discretion to subcontract work based on UOP's past practices. The evidence, as presented through testimony and relevant exhibits, is that there is a history of subcontracting various services including but not limited to fire extinguisher work. The only remaining restriction on the part of the University is if an entire department's services are subcontracted, which is not at issue nor is it one that has been presented to the arbitrator.

In summary, the University exercised good faith rationale when they determined that the subcontracting of the retrofit work was desirable. Therefore, for all the reasons noted during the course of the hearing, and as presented in the University's post-hearing brief, the arbitrator is asked to deny the grievance in its entirety.

Discussion and Opinion

...it is the arbitrator's finding that this unilateral decision on the part of UOP violated the terms of the CBA. The negotiated agreement must be considered as a whole and when reviewed with the action taken by Mr. Heaton, who fully admitted he had never discussed his concerns with the Union before determining he would remove the servicing and maintaining of the more than 800 fire extinguishers from bargaining unit employees, he stepped over the line by violating the terms of the negotiated agreement. It was a decision that ignored the accountability and responsibility of the UOP and Teamsters Local 439, which is contained in the current CBA. There can be no issue as to the fact that there was a long-standing past practice of utilizing bargaining unit employees to perform the service required on the campus. Section 1(B) is clear in that the "University and Union would meet to attempt to resolve the financial problems, and that subcontracting should be the last resort."

The arbitrator has considered the Employer's arguments relating to Section 1(B) and the meaning of the word "department" in the paragraph at issue. However, the arbitrator finds that throughout the terms of the CBA, in addition to the adversarial role of the UOP and Union inherently there is recognition in the meaning of "partnership," which obligates the parties to meet and confer before taking any action that negatively impacts the employees working under the terms and conditions of the negotiated agreement. In this regard, it is acknowledged that under the terms of the CBA managerial discretion regarding matters of work assignments including subcontracting is appropriate. However, that authority is not absolute, particularly when the evidence had identified that for the past two decades bargaining unit members have performed the services that UOP elected to subcontract, and the fact is that they did so without any meaningful discussion with the Union. Frankly, upon the arbitrator's review of the record including the testimony of the principal UOP and Union protagonists, it all boils down to a matter between two experienced and senior professionals who simply failed to recognize their responsibilities as chief spokespersons for the administration of the CBA. They failed in their responsibility to those salaried employees, and to the hourly bargaining employees who are required to comply with the CBA. The result was that instead of seeking solutions that would benefit the common good of the facility, they elected to throw down the gauntlet and take an attitude of "no prisoners." The issue, in the considered opinion of the arbitrator, is far more complex and goes beyond the servicing of fire extinguishers. The UOP and members of the bargaining unit would expect that two level-headed experienced professionals should work together for the common good of their respective constituencies to resolve significant concerns that impact both the Physical Plant

Department and the Union, as well as all those employees who may be affected by the subcontracting of bargaining unit work at UOP.

* * * *

In summary, the Union was persuasive when they identified that the University did not even consider alternatives when subcontracting the work out of the bargaining sunit, such as training the unit member who already had the preliminary know-how and fire extinguisher experience, by only temporarily subcontracting the work while training occurred.

violation

Under the terms of the CBA the subcontracting of all fire extinguisher services is a violation of the CBA, as it directly violated the clear language and intent of the parties. The action by the Employer to diminish the bargaining unit's work and to unilaterally subcontract work that had not been proven to be a financial hardship without first meeting with the Union to consider utilizing alternative options violates Section 1(B) of the Collective Bargaining Agreement and therefore the grievance is sustained.

The final question is what the remedy shall be, since the University has removed from the campus all the necessary equipment that is needed for bargaining unit members to resume their traditional work relating to the servicing and maintenance of the more than 800 extinguishers that are at issue.

The arbitrator, who has been given the authority to frame a remedy based on the particular facts of this case, believes that imposing a mandatory remedy at this point with the expectation that it would bring the dispute to closure, would; however, leave the parties no better off than when the grievance was filed in 2011. Therefore, it is the considered opinion of the arbitrator that the final step in the arbitration process is best served by holding in abeyance any monetary or other award. Thus, Local 439 and UOP are to be offered the opportunity of having a 60-calendar day window in which to return to the table. The intent being not only to bring the matter at issue to closure but to find ways in which to go forward and resolve any further issues that may impact both the Employer and Union.

* * * *

DECISION

sustained

The grievance is sustained.

The Employer violated Section 1(B) of the Collective Bargaining Agreement when it subcontracted the fire extinguisher work or portion thereof.

The arbitrator will retain jurisdiction for 60-calendar days from the date of this award.

It is so ordered.

APPLICATION AND DISCUSSION QUESTIONS

Based on the Arbitrator's decision in the above arbitration decision, respond to the following questions:

1. What language in the CBA did the arbitrator rely on to find that the employer subcontracted out bargaining unit work in violation of the CBA? Is the Arbitrator's decision in conflict with the "management's prerogatives" to assign work? *"meet to resolve"; & no*

2. Did the CBA require the employer to consider other alternatives before contracting out bargaining unit work? How did the arbitrator address this question? *yes; said ER failed to find other alts (see top of p. 492)*

3. What remedy did the arbitrator issue in this grievance and was it logical? If the parties wanted to resolve this issue prior to arbitration, why send them back to negotiation after arbitration? *told Ps to negotiate for 60 days; now they have guidance*

ALLIANT ENERGY
134 BNA LA 1217 (A. WOLFF, 2015)[*]

Case "reclosers" oh "one-shot"

Background Facts

Interstate Power & Light, a subsidiary of Alienate Energy [at times referred to as "IPC," "Alienate" or the "Company"] and International Brotherhood of Electrical Workers, Locals 204 and 949 at times referred to as "Local 204," "Local 949," "Locals 204 & 949," the "IBEW" or the "Union"] submitted to arbitration two grievances dated

[*] Reprinted with permission from *Labor Relations Reporter- Labor Arbitration Reports.* 134 BNA LA 1217. Copyright 2015 by the Bureau of National Affairs, Inc. (800-372-1033). http://www.bna.com.

Q

August 1 and 12, 2013 involving the same issue: whether the Company could use outside contractors to put "reclosers on 'one-shot,' inside of substations," which the Union claims had been exclusively bargaining unit work.

Most of the facts are not in dispute. The contractual language, the meaning of which is in dispute and has a long history that must be considered, appears in the 2012-2015 Collective Bargaining Agreement [the "CBA"] as follows:

CBA

Article II

Employment-Union Membership

Section 5. Contractors

(c) Contractor Switching-The Company agrees that contractors shall not perform, except when it is necessary to protect life and property, substation or transmission line switching on the system owned and operated by Alienate Energy/IPL (former IPC). For purposes of this agreement, contractors do not include employees of Alienate Energy/ IPL (former IES), Alienate Energy/WP&L, Municipals, REC's and/or joint operating agreements.

(d) Distribution line switching, or de-energizing of lines (outside of substations) may be performed by contractor personnel under the following conditions:

1. Prior Alienate Energy/IPL (former IPC) approval using Alienate Energy/IPL (former IPC) switching and hold card procedures.

2. Notification of circuit conditions to appropriate standby/call-out personnel on a daily basis.

3. Contractor switching shall be limited to the immediate job site, and shall not be requiring paralleling of substations.

4. Any unscheduled outages are referred to appropriate Alienate Energy/IPL (former IPC) bargaining unit and non-bargaining unit personnel.

5. Contractors may put reclosers on "one shot" when required for their immediate job and when proper notice is given.

* * * *

The first labor agreement attained in 1999 was between IES, and different members of Local 204, known as the "204 Large Group IES" contract [the "IES" contract]. Its "recloser" language was also in the IPC contract. However, Union business manager David George testified that in 2002 Local 204 filed a grievance under the IES contract protesting what the Union understood was IES' use of a contractor's putting a recloser on one-shot inside a substation. The grievance was later settled, he said, by moving the sentence in Article VIII, §3 [c] that contractors may put reclosers on "one shot" when required for their immediate job and when proper notice is given in §3[c] to a "stand-alone second paragraph in the contract, so that allowed them to put reclosers on 'one-shot' under all circumstances." However, the IES contract is not at issue here.

The unamended 1999-2012 IPC contracts, all of which still contain the parenthetical phrase in §5(d) "(outside of substations)" meant, according to Mr. George, that contractors could not put reclosers on one shot inside substations. However, he testified that in 2008 and again in 2012, the Union sought to amend the CBA by deleting §5(d)5 from the IPC CBA, which, he said, would bar IPC from using contractors to put reclosers on one shot outside of substations. These proposals were either rejected by IPC or withdrawn. Asked why it was withdrawn, he replied:

> "because of the fact that our position was consistent with the current language. The contractors can only enter substations to switch to protect life or property, which is an emergency, not for routine work on a regular basis."

* * * *

Contentions of the Parties

The Union: The Union contends, first, that the contract's words are "clear and unambiguous" and must be given their "plain meaning." In this respect it says:

> Art. II, Sec. 5 (c) states that substation line switching work belongs to bargaining unit members "except when it is necessary to protect life and property." Jt. Ex. 1 at 6. The language presumes this is bargaining unit work unless "necessary" to use a contractor. Alienate cannot demonstrate that it is "necessary" to use contractors to put reclosers on one shot inside of substations in routine situations, or situations in which bargaining unit linemen are available.

* * * *

It then invokes the "useful rule" of contract interpretation, "espresso units est exclusio alterius" in order to argue:

> By including "(outside of substations)" in 5(d), the implication is that the following five numbered statements of rights do not apply to situations inside of substations. When read in conjunction with the presumption in 5 (c) that substation line switching-work done inside of substations-is bargaining unit work, the clarity is reinforced that Alienate's right to use contractors outside of substations does not extend to inside of substations.

in vs. Out

The Union also deems unpersuasive Alienate's attempt to introduce ambiguity with regard to the term "line switching." ...

Next, the Union responds to what it considers Alienate's "two primary arguments," that §5[c] enabled it to use contractors to "protect life and property" and that putting reclosers on one shot is not line switching. In this respect it states:

> The Employer's interpretation of Art. II, Sec. 5 (c) is unreasonable as it would render the statement of the union's rights moot. Under the Employer's interpretation of the "life and property" clause, life and property would always need protecting thereby Alienate would always be empowered to utilize contractor employees. In short, the exception would swallow the rule.

no PP

The Union also contends that the record shows no evidence that Alienate had a past practice of using contractors to put reclosers on one-shot inside substations before 2010 and only minimally before the grievance was filed in 2013...

The Union also contends that the bargaining history supports its interpretation of the CBA...

* * * *

ER arg

The Company: The Company's central argument is that it has the right to allow contractors to put reclosers on "one shot" inside or outside of substations "to protect life and property." Stated succinctly, its argument runs:

protect ...

> "First, the Agreement provides that contractors can perform 'substation or transmission line switching' "when it is necessary to protect life and property." (* * * *§5(c)).

Second, it provides that contractors may perform the recloser work as part of [d]istribution line switching, or de-energizing of lines (outside of substations).> (* * * *§5(d)(5)). Each time a recloser is put on one shot inside of a substation, it is done so to protect life and property. Therefore, the exception in Article II, Section 5(c) applies to this dispute. Likewise, the one-shot provision under the second subsection (§5(d)(5)) should be read to apply whether the work is being done inside or outside of the substation.»

* * * *

The Company also believes that "negotiating history" is useful to clarify ambiguous contract terms. It notes that "on December 1, 1999, the Union introduced the 'life and property' language as well as the separate sentence that became Section 5(d)(5) regarding putting reclosers on one shot 'when required for the immediate job and with proper notice is given.'" Accordingly, IPC holds that "Any ambiguity should be construed against the author, the Union."

IPC also contends that if the CBA's language is ambiguous, past practice may be an interpretive guide...

* * * *

Finally, the Company contends that in 2008 contract talks the Union made a proposal to eliminate §5(d)5 that permitted contractors to put reclosers on one-shot under specified circumstances. This request was rejected by the Company, although the language was modified in certain other respects. But, IPC contends, that since the right to use contractors to put reclosers on one shot remained in the CBA, the Union cannot obtain in arbitration what it failed to receive in negotiation, citing New Britain Mach. Co., 45 LA 993 , 995-96 (1965).

Discussion

After careful review of the record and the parties' arguments, I find that these grievances must be denied. My reasoning follows.

First, I find that Section 5(c) of the CBA is not ambiguous and supports the Company. It plainly permits contractors to perform substation or transmission line switching when necessary to protect life and property. The record shows that when a contractor [or unit employee] is switching power lines carrying high voltage, the work is dangerous. In order to protect life and property in the event of a fault on a line, a recloser must be placed on "one shot" so that power to the line can return only once instead of three times. In sum, it is undisputed that in order for a contractor to perform line switching or de-energizing lines, it is essential that the contractor place a recloser on one-shot so as to protect life and property. Section 5(c) does not limit this requirement to outside or inside of substations; it covers all substations.

Section 5(d) does not require a different result. It places certain conditions on contractors who are engaged in distribution line switching or de-energizing of lines outside of substations, but it does not expressly bar contractors from working inside substations. The requirement of §5 (c) covers all substations and the need to place reclosers on one-shot to protect life and property when hot lines might come in contact with unit linemen or contractors or whoever is working on them.

Even if it could be said that either §5(c) or (d) is ambiguous, it would have to be construed against the Union, the party who proposed them. As was said long ago by Arbitrator Alex Elson in *Universal Milking Machine Co.*, 2 LA 399 , 403 (1946): "If there are any doubts about the language in this contract, the rule of law would require that the doubts be resolved against the person drawing the contract." In that case it was the employer, but here §5(c) and (d) were proposed by the Union. See also: *Georgia-Pacific Corp.*, 87 LA 217, 221 (1986); *Mesker Industries, Inc.*, 85 LA 921, 929 (1985); and F. & E. Elkouri, How Arbitration Works, (6th Ed. 2003), p. 477.

An additional ground for denying the grievances is that the record reveals a past practice of allowing contract employees to place reclosers on one-shot inside substations. Local 204 filed a grievance under the IES contract in 2002 seeking to end that practice and settled the grievance by providing that "Contractors will continue to put reclosers on 'one shot' in substations when required for the their immediate job. Proper notice will be given and Interstate Power and Light hold card procedures for contractors will be followed." The practice that became part of the IES contract has been followed by IPC and Locals 204 and 949 for years.

*   *   *   *

There is still another ground for denying the grievances. In 2008 and 2012 bargaining the Union sought to amend the contract by deleting §5(d)5. That would have withdrawn IPC's contract right to use contractor employees to place reclosers on one-shot. IPC rejected that proposal and the Union withdrew it. Arbitrators have long considered such actions as barring a party from obtaining in arbitration what it failed to achieve in collective bargaining. [Elkouri (6th Ed.) p. 454; Elkouri (7th Ed.) p. 9-27].

For any or all of the above reasons, the grievances must be, and are, denied.

AWARD

For the reasons set forth in the Opinion, which Opinion is incorporated by reference *denied* in this Award, the grievances are denied.

APPLICATION AND DISCUSSION QUESTIONS

1. Define the term "espresso unitis est exclusio alterius" and how does the *exclusion?;* Court use this term to interpret the contract language in dispute? *Mentioning out means doesn't apply to in — doesn't use*

2. What is the specific contract language that the employer and the union disagree on? Is the language clear as to whether the work can be contracted out? *protect life & property; — no*

3. Is there any "clear and unambiguous" evidence of a past practice of having contractors perform certain work? What arguments do the parties present to support their respective positions? *no*

4. How does the union attempt to use bargaining history to prove their position? What conclusion does the arbitrator use regarding bargaining history? *in vs. out; ER rejected U proposal*

5. To support the finding, the arbitrator cites the following basic arbitration principle:

    "If there are doubts about the language in this contract, the rule of law would require that the doubts be resolved against the person drawing the contract..."

    The arbitrator cites the following cases for this principle: *Universal Milking Machine Co.*, 2 LA 399,403 (1946); *Georgia-Pacific Corp.*, 87 LA 217, 221 (1986); *Mesker Industries, Inc.*, 85 LA 921, 929 (1988). In this case, which party does the arbitrator find proposed the contract provision? *ER*

6. Explain the arbitration principle that "a party cannot do in arbitration what they failed to do in negotiation", citing Elkouri (7th Ed.) p. 9-27. *failed to negotiate for a right so can't get it via arb...*

A pharmaceutical distributor operates a facility in Honolulu, Hawaii that delivers pharmaceuticals and over-the-counter products to retail pharmacies and grocery stores. The company uses non-bargaining unit employees on four of six delivery routes that are considered "irregular", such as routes requiring deliveries to other islands. The company uses union employees on the other "regular' delivery routes. For years, if a union employee on a regular route was absent due to illness or on an extended leave, the company's practice was to outsource the work by using temporary replacement drivers.

A bargaining unit employee on one of the regular routes retired. To control costs and address liability concerns, the company did not post the position, but instead outsourced the driver work. When another driver on a regular route voluntarily transferred to a different department the following year, the company again outsourced the driver work. The union filed a grievance alleging the Company violated the Collective Bargaining Agreement by outsourcing bargaining unit work.

The Company argues the CBA does not have a subcontracting provision and it saves money and reduces liability exposure by outsourcing the work as much of its national operation outside of Hawaii does. Therefore, the company contends the broad Management Rights Clause in the CBA empowers it to manage and direct its operation, so there was no violation.

How should the arbitrator rule?

no violation b/c allowed to outsource in similar context

E. SOCIAL MEDIA

The term social media includes social networking, Facebook, Twitter, Web Sites, Blogs, text, Instagram, and Myspace. The use of social media has become a part of most employees' daily lives. The question that arbitrators are being asked to determine is whether the employer had just cause to take disciplinary actions against an employee for inappropriately using social media.

WHEN WORLDS COLLIDE:
AN ARBITRATOR'S GUIDE TO SOCIAL NETWORKING
ISSUES IN LABOR AND EMPLOYMENT CASES
66-JAN DISP. RESOL. J. 20
NOVEMBER, 2011-JANUARY, 2012*
ROBERT L. ARRINGTON, AARON DUFFY, ELIZABETH RITA

SOCIAL NETWORKING SITES Like Facebook, Twitter, MySpace, and linked-In have exploded in popularity in the last few years. Facebook alone has more than 800 million active users, meaning that if Facebook were a country, it would be the third largest in the world, behind only china and India. As social networking grows, the worlds of social networking and arbitration inevitably will collide with ever-increasing frequency.

Since social networking is ubiquitous, evidence from social media will undoubtedly find its way into labor and employment cases, but it could be involved in almost any kind of case. For this reason, arbitrators need to become familiar with all kinds of social networking platforms, learn how to deal with this kind of evidence, and understand the applicable statutory and case law. This article presents an overview of social networking, the evidentiary issues they raise, and a short primer on the law that could apply to social networking activity. This discussion is intended to provide some guidance for employers that wish to regulate social networking by employees, as well as introduce arbitrators to the social networking phenomenon, so that they are not "flummoxed" by it, even if, by being so, they may consider themselves in good company.

Social Networking at a Glance

Social networking involves posting personal information and other content on Web sites like Facebook, and MySpace and sharing some or all of that information with other people. Users of these Web sites typically have some control over the people who may access the content they post. For example, a user may share his or her profile and postings with all other users of the Web sites, or restrict viewing to family, close friends, or only one or two people. The kinds of content typically shared on social networking sites include vacation photographs, comments about the user's day, and lists of the user's favorite bands, movies, and authors, among other things. However, postings on social networking site are not limited to such items.

People who put content on Facebook and similar sites rarely consider the legal consequences of their postings, although they should. Say, for example, that the user posted a gleeful tweet about catching the "Yankees cremating the Red Sox" on a day when she called in sick to work. The user ends up being called as a witness in an arbitration arising out of injuries sustained during a Red Sox-Yankees fan altercation, where she testifies that she was sick all day and did not observe relevant events. The tech-savvy lawyer for the adversary mines all social networking sites, finds this posting, and introduces it as evidence. The witness never envisioned her post being used in a dispute resolution forum. This example demonstrates that social networking activity can play a role in all types of disputes, from those involving personal injury and divorce, to labor and employment claims

Arbitral Discovery and Social Media

Suppose one party to an arbitration wants to view the other party's Facebook page, which is restricted to "friends," and the other party refuses, citing privacy concerns. What should the arbitrator do? The arbitrator has discretion to allow discovery under most arbitration rules, unless the parties have otherwise agreed Suppose the arbitrator has decided to allow discovery and has determined the requested information is discoverable (i.e., it is relevant and not privileged). This situation raises two questions. Should privacy concerns control the arbitrator's decision? If not, then how can the arbitrator secure the needed information?

While reasonable minds can differ on the privacy question, most of the courts that have addressed the issue do not treat privacy as controlling. These courts reason that, as long as the information is relevant, social networking postings by a party are discoverable because they are essentially party admissions. In colloquial terms, these courts are effectively saying "you posted it, so now you have to live with it."

We suggest that an arbitrator who is not comfortable with this view consider reviewing the social networking posting in camera in order to decide whether any information in the posting would be unduly embarrassing, and therefore should be redacted before it is released to the other party, or is entirely irrelevant to the matter at issue, and should not be admitted.

The next question is how to gain access to the material if access to it has been restricted to certain users of the Web site. The obvious way to do so would be for the arbitrator to issue a subpoena directed to the Web site host. But the obvious solution is no solution at all. It simply won't work.

First, if the governing statute is the Federal Arbitration Act, or a state statute based on the original (1955) Uniform Arbitration Act, the arbitrator probably lacks the power to subpoena third parties or their documents for discovery purposes. Most courts limit the arbitrator's subpoena power to requiring the third party's appearance at a hearing. Commentators have suggested that this need not be the final hearing on the merits, as long as an arbitrator is in attendance.

The Revised Uniform Arbitration Act provides the arbitrator with authority to issue third-party discovery subpoenas. But even if the RUAAA applies, the enforcement of such a subpoena could be limited because the arbitrator may have no direct authority over the third party. Further, the party seeking enforcement of the subpoena by a federal court must demonstrate that the court has federal question or diversity jurisdiction over the case and that it has personal jurisdiction over the subpoenaed entity.

But the real difficulty with gaining access to information on social networking sites via a subpoena lies in the Stored Communications Act (SCA). In general, the SCA prohibits access to stored electronic communications without the consent of the communicator. This prohibition means social networking providers like Facebook may not release a user's information without the user's permission. Accordingly, social networking sites have taken the position that subpoenas for such information are ineffective as applied to them. The courts that have faced this issue have tended to agree.

A number of courts, however, have enabled discovery of information on social networking sites by treating the issue as a request for inspection of documents or things in the possession or control of the party who has used the social networking Web site, and ordering inspection under Rule 34 of the Federal Rules of Civil Procedure (or the state equivalent), rather than issuing a subpoena under Rule 45. These courts have ordered the party who has the social networking page to make that page, and all archived information, available for inspection by the opposing party.

Where does that leave the arbitrator? Fortunately, the most widely used arbitration rules, those of the American Arbitration Association (AAA), give the arbitrator authority to order the parties to produce the requested information. Rule 9 of the AAA Employment Arbitration Rules provides that "[t]he arbitrator shall have the authority to order ... discovery, by way of deposition, interrogatory, document production, or otherwise, as the arbitrator considers necessary to a full and fair exploration of the issues in dispute, consistent with the expedited nature of arbitration." Rule 28 of the AAA Labor Arbitration Rules states that the parties "shall produce ... evidence as the arbitrator may deem necessary to an understanding and determination of the dispute." Rule R-31 of the AAA Commercial Arbitration Rules gives the arbitrator the same authority.

Rather than ordering production of social networking material, some courts have taken the approach of requiring the parties to give the court or opposing counsel access to their Face book page by "friending" them. While this is an efficient means of gaining access to the parties' social networking sites, "spoliation" issues should be considered. Has any party deleted or altered any potentially damaging material from his or her social networking page or archive? Accordingly, the better practice is to require the parties to produce an archive report of their social networking activity, which will show any material that has been deleted. If a party refuses to provide the requested information, the arbitrator could draw appropriate negative inferences.

Social Networking and the Law

Social networking implicates many laws that arbitrators are likely to face, including the National Labor Relations Act (NLRA), off-duty conduct laws, invasion of privacy laws, anti-discrimination laws, the Genetic Information Nondiscrimination Act (GINA), and the SCA.

APPLICATION AND DISCUSSION QUESTIONS

1. Arbitrators, particularly labor arbitrators, tend to be "baby boomers" or older, with little to no social media experience. How should the parties present social media type evidence to arbitrators who acknowledge they have limited experience with this type of evidence?

2. What factors should arbitrators consider in the admissibility of social networking evidence? Should the arbitrator review networking postings in camera as suggested by the authors?

3. What import, if any, does the Uniform Arbitration Act have on the admissibility of social media evidence and Rule 34 of the Federal Rules of Civil Procedures?

4. How could arbitrators address the issue of social media evidentiary challenges under AAA rules?

THE CITY OF ADA AND INTERNATIONAL ASSOCIATION OF FIREFIGHTERS, LOCAL 2298

134 BNA LA 702 (LUMBLEY, 2014)[*]

Issue

* * * *

Having now had the opportunity to consider the entire record in this matter, while I see little substantive difference between the parties' statements of the issue in light of the language of the Agreement, I have decided to frame the issue as follows:

1. Did the termination of the Grievant violate the Agreement?

2. If so, what is the appropriate remedy?

* * * *

Relevant Provisions of the Agreement

The relevant provisions of the Agreement are:

Background

* * * *

The series of incidents that led ultimately to the Grievant's termination commenced on April 24, 2013. At approximately 9:30 p.m. on that date the car in which the Grievant's wife was a passenger was stopped by Ada Police Department (hereinafter "APD") Officer R__ for investigation of an illegal turn. During the stop, both the driver of the vehicle and the Grievant's wife were administered field sobriety tests. During this procedure, the Grievant arrived on scene after being notified of the stop by his wife via cell phone. The Grievant protested and attempted to convince R__

[*] Reprinted with permission from *Labor Relations Reporter- Labor Arbitration Reports.* 134 BNA LA 702. Copyright 2015 by the Bureau of National Affairs, Inc. (800-372-1033). http://www.bna.com.

to let his wife go home with him. After R__ refused and instructed the Grievant a number of times to return to his vehicle, the Grievant responded to R__ in a profane fashion but eventually returned to his own vehicle. R__ ultimately arrested both the driver and the Grievant's wife, the latter for public intoxication.

R__ then took both arrestees to the Ada Justice Center for booking. The Grievant also showed up at the Justice Center and spoke to APD Sergeant P__, R__'s shift supervisor. During this confrontation, the Grievant called R__ profane names, threatened to "knock his fucking ass off" and made clear to Potter his unhappiness with both R__ and the APD. He also promised to "smear this shit all over the place." It is undisputed that he kept that promise commencing the following day via his public Facebook account.

Thus, between April 25 and the date of the Grievant's termination on May 13, he made scores of posts disparaging R__, P__ and the APD generally. The posts ranged from general observations that the APD "is completely out of control" and that the City "is infested with leeches" as well as questions such as "who picks these morons out" to specific comments directed at R__ and P__. Those directed at R__ included the following, among others:

- I will not miss a single day of trying to bust you to a cart pusher where you belong. I'm not one to turn the other cheek you prick. I'm coming to make you miserable you incompetent son of a bitch.

- I don't know where you live and don't have your number R__. But I will. You take from me and I'll take from you. I'll have my say.

- I want your job R__.

- You take my wife and I'll take your head.

- So go fuck yourselves you incompetent Barney fife sob.

- Come pick on me. I got one mean bone in my body and R__ found it.

* * * *

As regards P__, the Grievant posted the following, "Where's P__? You got nothing to add? For [sic] your [sic] going to [sic] boss. If anything I can do your [sic] going too.

You took up for your corrupt desk jockey. You [sic] either with me or against me. I know where you stand now. Your [sic] one of them."

Examples of the Grievant's expressions of anger toward APD and other institutions included the following:

- And ada pd do not park across the street from my house for your speed trap. I don't want to be associated with your corruption. Stay away or I'll push you down the street.

- It's no wonder people are bombing and shooting everyone. People are getting TIRED of this bull shit. You can only push so far before somebody busts your head.

* * * *

The Grievant's interaction with R__ and P__ was brought to the attention of Fire Chief H__ on April 25. After H__ was advised on April 30 that the Grievant had been arrested, he assigned the Grievant to desk duties with pay. Thereafter, on May 3, during a meeting between H__, the Grievant, the Grievant's supervisor Ross and a Union representative concerning the Grievant's use of sick leave on April 24, the Grievant was issued a verbal reprimand for inappropriate use of sick leave.

Later that morning, H__ and the Grievant met in H__'s office without Union representation at the Grievant's request to talk about the evening of his wife's arrest. The Grievant advised H__ that he had taken to Facebook because he believed his wife had been wronged and H__ advised the Grievant that he needed to stay off Facebook, that he should consider hiring an attorney and that his termination for harassment of another City employee was being considered.

On the same date, i.e. May 3, after the aforementioned meeting with the Grievant and after reviewing the Grievant's arrest affidavit and receiving input from P__ as well as Assistant APD Chief Crosby who reported that R__ was concerned for his safety, H__ wrote City Manager Holcomb requesting that the Grievant be terminated for "numerous violations of workplace harassment." Although Holcomb had already been aware of the events of April 24, he waited until after he had received H__'s May 3 recommendation before determining to assign Fire Marshall Priest to investigate the allegations of workplace harassment leveled against the Grievant.

* * * *

On May 13, after Priest had completed his investigation, Holcomb decided to approve H__'s request that the Grievant be terminated. Holcomb's letter of that date to H__ stated, in relevant part, "In regards to your request in the letter dated May 3, 2013, the investigative report as well as other information provided to me, I approve your request for termination of S__." Holcomb, with whom the ultimate authority regarding termination from the Fire Department rests, testified that he reached his decision on the basis of the Grievant's activities on and after April 24 and gave no consideration to any previous discipline appearing in the Grievant's record.

* * * *

The Union grieved the Grievant's termination on May 30, alleging the Grievant had been terminated without due process and seeking reinstatement and a make whole remedy. H__ denied the grievance in writing on June 4. IAFF moved the grievance to the next step in writing on June 7. A hearing subsequently was held with Holcomb on June 18 as required by Article VII, Section 3D of the Agreement and was attended by City Attorney Stout and Union President Haines. The Grievant did not attend, testifying he was not told about the meeting. Holcomb responded by letter dated June 27, noting, in relevant part, "It is determined that the City of Ada did not violate any provisions of the contract or City Handbook in its termination of S__." The parties processed the grievance through the remaining steps of the grievance-arbitration procedure without success. The Union then invoked arbitration and the dispute came on for hearing before the undersigned as set forth above.

Discussion and Analysis

Position of the Employer

The Employer contends the termination of the Grievant occurred for just cause as required by the Agreement. In support of that basic position, it asserts the Grievant interfered with R__'s traffic stop and undertook an extensive campaign of harassment against R__ and APD that interfered irreparably with the working relationship between APD and the Ada Fire Department. In the City's view, not only did the Grievant not deny the conduct of which he was accused, the Grievant admitted at the hearing that he was aware of the City's policy against harassment and that his conduct amounted to harassment. Thus, according to the Employer, discharge was a reasonable, appropriate response to offenses that showed a severe lack of good judgment and caused interdepartmental conflict within the City.

* * * *

Position of the Union

The Union asserts the discharge of the Grievant was not for just cause as required by Article V, Section 2C of the Agreement. * * * *

* * * *IAFF asserts the Facebook activities of the Grievant were engaged in during office-duty hours and should have First Amendment protection since they were aimed at expressing dissatisfaction with the APD and its officers. It notes in this connection that the Grievant was acquitted of both the felony and misdemeanor charges brought against him in criminal court and it argues that consideration should weigh in favor of overturning the Grievant's termination.

Decision of the Arbitrator

Having now had the opportunity to consider the entire record in this matter, including the arguments of the parties voiced at the hearing and on brief as well as the numerous arbitral and legal decisions cited, I have determined to agree with the City that the termination of the Grievant did not violate the Agreement. Although I have studied the entire record in this matter carefully and considered each argument and authority cited, the discussion that follows will address only those considerations I found either controlling or necessary to make my decision clear.

* * * *

Events of the Evening of April 24

As to these events, I understand and can empathize with the Grievant's emotions on the evening of April 24 since I believe a reasonable person would not find it pleasant to witness his or her spouse being arrested for public intoxication, particularly if he/she was not known to be a heavy drinker, as the Grievant claims was the case. However, Officer R__ had a job to do, a job that included enforcing Section 50-101 of the Ada Municipal Code prohibiting public intoxication. In this regard, there is absolutely no showing in the record that R__ was going about that duty inappropriately at the time the Grievant arrived on scene...

These actions of the Grievant on April 24 were, in and of themselves, worthy of some discipline. Because the Grievant was not independently disciplined for those activities, it is unnecessary to determine what level of discipline would have been appropriate. However, I agree with the City that it was proper to include them within the conduct for which the Grievant was ultimately disciplined.

Facebook Posts

* * * *

Clearly, some of his posts, such as that the City is "infested with leeches," were merely inane and unprofessional. Others, embodying opinions such as that unnamed department heads leave work early, officials don't do their job and city buildings are in shambles, even without supporting details, touch on matters of public interest, as the Union notes, and, absent a showing they were knowingly false or recklessly made, were arguably protected. *Pickering v. Bd. of Ed.* Others, however, are both 1) lacking as regards the public concern test since they exhibited the Grievant's personal anguish over his wife's arrest and 2) constitute personal attacks on R__, P__ and others that had the effect of disrupting the workplace and thus were not protected. As the Elkouris note in *How Arbitration Works*, BNA (7th Ed., 2012):

> In determining if the exercise of First Amendment rights constitutes just cause for discipline, courts often adhere to the following principle: speech that is disruptive of the workplace or demoralizing and reflects the expression of a private complaint is not protected speech, whereas commenting on a matter of public interest is protected speech, but must be balanced against the government's interest in the effective and efficient fulfillment of its responsibilities to the public.

Example of those falling within this category are cited at the bottom of page 6 and the top of page 7 of this Opinion.

Still others, including many of those quoted at the bottom of page 5 and the top of page 6 of this Opinion, contain what I believe a reasonable person would consider to be threats uttered directly at R__. In particular, posts threatening to find out where R__ lives, to take R__'s head, to take R__'s wife and to break R__'s hands are beyond merely troublesome. Indeed, R__ testified that, after becoming aware of the posts, he feared for his and his girlfriend's safety and he varied his drive home at night and started carrying a firearm when he mowed his grass in response to them. In similar vein, P__ testified that he commenced carrying two firearms while off duty, showed the Grievant's picture to his family and instructed them to contact him if they were to see him approach after seeing the Grievant's posts directed at him.

* * * *

In view of all the above, I find that the discharge of the Grievant occurred for just cause as required by Article V, Section 2C of the Agreement. That is to say I find the City has established that the Grievant engaged in behavior warranting discipline and that, in light of all the circumstances, the discipline imposed was appropriate. International Union of Operating Engineers Local No. 351, AFL-CIO and CP Kelco US, Inc., Okmulgee Facility, citing Elkouri and Elkouri, *How Arbitration Works*, BNA (6th Ed. 2003) at p. 948. Thus I must find that the discharge of the Grievant did not violate the Agreement.

AWARD

I. It is the Award of the Arbitrator that the termination of the Grievant did not violate the Agreement.

II. It is therefore ordered that the grievance be, and it hereby is, dismissed.

APPLICATION AND DISCUSSION QUESTIONS

1. In public sector off-duty types of cases, the arbitrator will consider the interest of the employer and the private rights of the employee. The arbitrator will attempt to balance the interests of both parties as outlined by the arbitrator.

2. The Union contends that the Grievant's Facebook activities were off-duty and protected by the First Amendment. Does the Union have a valid argument?

3. The arbitrator cites *Connick v. Meyers*, 461 U.S. 138 (1983) and *Pickering v. Bd. of Education*, 391 U.S. 563 (1968) to support his conclusion. How do these cases support each parties' argument?

SELECTED CASES INVOLVING SOCIAL MEDIA

Review the following cases and identy the form of social media at issue. Do you agree with the arbitrator's analysis and conclusion?

2014 AAA LEXIS 65 (2014)

The employee was terminated for violating the employer's policy regarding the use of the state owned computers and other IT equipment. The employee used the computer to access a social networking site where there were "sexually explicit photographic images." In analyzing the case, the Arbitrator stated "[t]his Arbitrator does not claim to be an IT expert, not by any stretch of the imagination. However, based on the evidence... I am not able to conclude that the grievant in fact was spending many hours of work time surfing around, looking at displayed images, writing emails, posting ads..." The Arbitrator concluded "that the punishment of summary termination was excessive with regard to the magnitude of the proven offense, violated the concept of progressive discipline..."

2013 AAA LEXIS 480 (2013)

Police Office terminated in part for posting rude and insulting remarks on his Facebook account. The officer mistakenly thought his postings were private. The officer made negative comments of citizens and a defendant in a criminal trial. In reducing the termination to a suspension, the arbitrator considered the young age of the officer. The arbitrator stated "we need to grant some slack to today's young people which I define as those under 30. It is for this reason that the Township should develop and publish a social media policy. I believe we need to recognize that young people today need more time to grow up and become responsible members of society." The Arbitrator also held that "many posts were contained in a single pool; thus the conduct was not ongoing.

2013 AAA LEXIS 634 (2013)

The Grievant, a teacher, received a written reprimand for inappropriate posts made on Facebook to a parent. The Grievant alleged that his posting was in response to the parent threatening him. The Arbitrator acknowledged that the Employer had a legitimate reason to address the electronic communication. However, the Arbitrator determined that the penalty was "overly punitive" and reduced the written reprimand to a verbal warning.

UNAP, LOCA
LA SUPP. 148221 (ARB. 2013)

This arbitration decision arises from a Hospital termination of an employee for misconduct related to HIPPA violations as a result of posting the death and cause of a patient on a social media site. The Union contended that "the Use of Electronics in the Workplace policy has not been enforced with regularity or consistence." The Union argued that the termination was a violation of the CBA. The Hospital argued that the nurse violated Hospital policies related to HIPPA, the social media policy and a breach of standards of professional conduct. The Arbitrator determined that the nurse's termination violated the collective bargaining agreement under either the arbitrary and capricious standard of Article 13 or the just cause standard. Specifically, the Arbitrator determined that "pictures are often taken of patients on Unit 6- with Santa, the Easter Bunny or in Halloween costumes... and are posted in the Unit for all to see." In addition, other employees had violated HIPAA and received lesser discipline. The remedy is that she is reinstated to former position and made whole for lost wage and benefits.

POLICE DEPARTMENT AND POLICE ASSOCIATION
2013 LA SUPP. 148178 (ARB. 2013)

This arbitration decision arises from alleged misconduct of a Police Officer who not only failed to include all pertinent information in two specific reports, but also made rude and offensive posting on a social media site concerning the police work he was involved in. As a result of the action, the officer was accused of violating the Employer Code of Ethics. After an investigation he was eventually discharged. One question presented was whether the Officer engaged in conduct unbecoming of a Police Officer by publishing the many post on his social media account. The arbitrator was reluctant to uphold the penalty concerning the post because there was no evidence of ongoing misconduct. The Arbitrator reduced the penalty to a suspension without pay for the entire period of time.

The Union filed a grievance alleging that a police officer was discharged without just cause due to the officer's social media postings. The City argued the grievance was not arbitral because termination cases were required to be processed through the City's Civil Service Commission not the grievance process. The City also argued that it had just cause to terminate the officer for his use of the "N word on his social media page. This action, according to the City, violated a number of City polices. The City insisted that the Officer was "not absolved of responsibility for his actions because it occurred while he was off duty." The Union argued that the discharge was not subject to civil service laws. Moreover, the alleged rule violations were "overbroad, unenforceable, and procedurally deficient." The Union also argued that the rules could not be applied equally and the City would "rarely have sufficient knowledge to enforce them with any type of regularity or consistency." The Arbitrator concluded that the grievance was not arbitral because the language in the CBA was clear and unequivocal on its face. Consequently, the Arbitrator did not rule on the merits of the case, however, the case raised a number of issues that Arbitrators will have to resolve in grievances involving social media.

SUMMARY OF ANALYSIS OF SOCIAL MEDIA ARBITRATIONS

- Arbitrators must become familiar with social media terminology.

- The Arbitrator must determine if there was a social media policy and whether it was effectively communicated to employees.

- Did the employee consistently take disciplinary actions when the policy was violated?

- How serious was the violation of the social media policy.

- Other forms of communication may be reviewed to determine if there is disparate treatment, e.g., emails, postings on boards.

- Arbitrators may face discovery challenges when requested to issue a subpoena for social media documents that are private.

- Arbitrators may have to review the NLRA if there are postings allegedly relates to Section 8 rights.

APPLICATION AND DISCUSSION QUESTIONS

1. In a termination case, how might the grievant establish the element of disparate treatment involving the inappropriate usage of social media in the workplace? Can you think of a fact pattern where an arbitrator has to determine whether the employer violated Title VII (employment discrimination), GINA (genetic information), or the ADA (disability statute), when it took disciplinary action against an employee for posting information on Facebook or a blog?

2. Can an individual waive their attorney-client privilege if they post information regarding conversations they had with their attorney on Facebook, blogs, etc.? See *Lenz v. Universal Music Corp.* from the Northern District of California.

THE PROBLEM WITH SOCIAL MEDIA AND OFF-DUTY CONDUCT

A firefighter's union filed a grievance alleging that the following policy was an unreasonable interference with their constitutional and employment rights:

The Objectionable Provisions of the Social Media Policy[*]

Paragraph A: Department personnel are free to express themselves as private citizens on social media sites to the degree that their speech does not impair working relationships of this Department for which loyalty and confidentiality are important, impede the performance of duties, impair discipline and harmony among coworkers, discuss

---

[*] Reproduced with permission from *Labor Relations Reporter-Labor Arbitration Reports*, 134 BNA LA 276 (Sept. 22, 2014). Copyright 2014 by The Bureau of National Affairs, Inc. (800-372-1033) http://www.bna.com.

the home addresses of Departmental personnel, or negatively affect the public perception of the Department.

Paragraph C: Department personnel shall not post, transmit, or otherwise disseminate any information to which they have access as a result of their employment without written permission from the Public Safety Director or their [sic] designee.

Paragraph E: When using social media, Department personnel should be mindful that their speech becomes part of the worldwide electronic domain. Therefore, adherence to the Department's code of conduct is required in the personal use of social media. In particular, Department personnel are prohibited from the following:

1. Speech containing obscene or sexually explicit language, images, or acts and statements or other forms of speech that ridicule, malign, disparage, or otherwise express bias against any race, any religion, or any protected class of individuals.

2. Speech involving themselves or other Department personnel reflecting behavior that would reasonably be considered reckless or irresponsible.

3. Personnel shall not publicly criticize or ridicule the Department, its guidelines, or other personnel by speech, writing, or other expression, where such speech, writing or other expression undermines the effectiveness of the Department, interferes with the maintenance of discipline, or is made with reckless disregard of the truth.

Paragraph K: Reporting violations-any employee becoming aware of or having knowledge of a posting or updating website or web page in violation of the provision of this policy shall notify his or her supervisor immediately for follow-up action.

How should the arbitrator rule?

F. Benefits

THE GREEN TRANSIT AUTHORITY
AMERICAN ARBITRATION ASSOCIATION
(FLOYD D. WEATHERSPOON 2010)[*]

I. STATEMENT OF FACTS

The facts indicate that the Union and the the Green Transit Authority, hereinafter (Company or Authority), are parties to a collective bargaining agreement, hereinafter (CBA or Agreement).

The facts are basically not in dispute. It is undisputed that the Authority changed the definition of dependent eligibility, effective February 1, 2008. The Authority changed the definition of dependent by discontinuing coverage at ages 19-23, unless the dependent was enrolled full-time in an accredited college or university.

During the hearing the parties stipulated that as of February 1, 2008, dependents between the ages of 19 and 23 must be enrolled full time in school, but prior to February 1, 2008, full time enrollment into school was not a requirement for a dependent to be eligible for healthcare benefits.

The parties agree that the Healthcare Committee, which includes members of the Union, discussed the change of eligibility as a cost containment. Beyond these facts, the parties have different positions on whether the Company could change the definition of dependent eligibility, the authority of the Healthcare Committee, and whether there was an established past practice of providing coverage for dependents between the ages of 19-23, regardless of whether they were full time students.

A class action grievance was filed on January 2, 2008 and processed in accordance with the CBA grievance procedures. The arbitration hearing was held on June 29, 2008. The parties stipulated that the grievance was properly before the arbitrator.

II. ISSUE

The parties stipulated to the following issue: Whether the Company violated the CBA by unilaterally changing the definition of employee dependant from 19 to 23 to be

---

[*]   Unpublished Decision (Floyd D. Weatherspoon, 2010).

eligible for health coverage by requiring they be full time students, if so, what is the appropriate remedy?

A. RELEVANT CONTRACT PROVISIONS AND POLICIES

ARTICLE 17. Benefits
Section 3. Health Care Benefits

    A. The Authority will continue to provide a level of benefits comparable to those now in effect for the duration of the Agreement.

    C. An eligible employee and that employee's dependent (s) shall not be covered under more than one plan of health care benefits offered by the Authority.

    Section 4. Health Care Committee
    A health care committee with an equal number of Authority and Union representatives shall be established to discuss the implementation of cost containment options, such as second opinions for surgical procedures.

IV. POSITION OF THE PARTIES

A. Union's Position

The Union contends that the unilateral change of definition of dependent eligibility, without negotiation between the parties is a violation of the CBA. The Union states that the parties negotiated healthcare benefits into the CBA, which creates a legal obligation to negotiate the change of benefits.

The Union acknowledges that the CBA does not define what constitutes dependent eligibility. However, the Union insists that "the past practice between the parties have always defined the term as constituting those dependents between the ages 19-23."

The Union maintains that the parties have mutually accepted the practice of including 19-23 as eligible dependents without a requirement that they be full-time students for thirty years. The Union insists that a procedure established by a past practice cannot be changed, unless the parties negotiate such a change.

The Union also asserts that the "[t]he Healthcare Committee was without contractual authority to make the change. The Committee was vested by the [CBA] with authority to discuss cost saving ideas and nothing more". The Union acknowledges that the Committee discussed the issue of dependent eligibility of 19-23 year old, but the Union never negotiated or gave the Authority approval for a change in the definition of eligibility.

B. The Authority's Position

The Authority states that effective February 1, 2008, the definition of dependent for healthcare benefits was changed due to health care cost containment. The Authority insists "that the (CBA) was not violated and it had the right to define dependent eligibility." According to the Authority, the definition of dependent was changed in the Authority's Personnel Policies & Procedures Manual which was approved by the Board of Trustees. The Authority states that "[t]he change in definition of dependent was contained in the [Personnel Policy & Procedures Manual] was a cost containment measure that allowed the Authority to provide the additional benefits to employees without increasing the monthly employee contribution amount. The Authority states that the term "dependent" is not defined in the CBA but in the Personnel Policy & Procedures Manual, which the Company has the right to define.

The Authority contends that Article 17 of the CBA permits the Authority to make changes to the healthcare insurance plan so long as the plan provided "a level of benefits comparable to those now in effect for the duration of this Agreement." The Authority further contends that the change in the definition of dependent eligibility did not lessen the level of benefits.

The Authority insists "that no past practice existed because the language defining a dependent for healthcare coverage has been contained in the Transit Authority's Personnel Policy & Procedures Manual."

The Authority also contends that the Union was aware of its intent to change the definition because the change was discussed during the 2006 and 2007 Labor Management Healthcare Committee meetings, which consisted of union and management employees. Moreover, the Authority alleges that the Health care Committee early as 2006 recommended limiting coverage for dependent 19-23 as a cost containment.

1. DISCUSSION AND ANALYSIS

* * * *

Grievances regarding healthcare benefits under health insurance plans are often complex and raise technical issues. The issue of dependent eligibility in this grievance is both complex and technical. Both parties presented plausible arguments as to how the Arbitrator should resolve this issue. Consequently, the Arbitrator has conducted extensive research on this issue, as well as thoroughly analyzing the evidence submitted by the Parties.

The Arbitrator has determined that the following basic principles of labor relations and labor arbitration apply to the present grievance. First, an employer is required to negotiate mandatory subjects such as wages, hours, and terms and conditions of employment. Healthcare insurance would be considered a term and condition of employment. Thus, an employer is required to negotiate insurance plans. Secondly, once a healthcare plan has been negotiated, an employer is prohibited from unilaterally making substantial changes in the healthcare plan without first negotiating such changes with the Union, unless waived by the Union.

Thirdly, the mere discussion of healthcare cost containment measure by a Healthcare/Insurance Committee, where Union members participate, is insufficient to prove that union officials agreed with the changes in the healthcare benefits plan by an employer.

Based on these principles of labor arbitration, the Authority violated the CBA when it failed to negotiate the change of dependent eligibility prior to unilaterally making such a substantial change in the definition of dependent eligibility. The Union presented compelling evidence that the change of the definition of dependent eligibility lessened the level of benefits. Therefore, the change in definition equaled a change in benefits. The Union further established the existence of a past practice. Additionally, the Union demonstrated that the Healthcare Committee lacked authority to bind the Union. The Arbitrator has set forth the following analysis and reasoning for this conclusion:

Comparable Level of Benefits

Article 17, Section 3 of the CBA states that the Authority would continue to "provide a level of benefits comparable to these in effect for the duration of this agreement." In this grievance, the Authority changed the definition of dependent eligibility which directly impacted healthcare benefits. The Arbitrator has to review the healthcare plan before the change and after the change to determine whether they are comparable. "[W]hen an arbitrator is forced to make a judgment whether a plan is 'comparable,' there is no uniform definition or interpretation regarding 'comparable coverage.'" See, *In re Village of Ballston Spa*, 124 Lab. Arb. Rep. 104 (Lobel, 2007).

The Authority's decision to change the eligibility requirement to qualify for health-care benefits resulted in a substantial loss of healthcare benefits for bargaining unit employees who have dependents aged 19-23, who are not full time students. The requirement that dependents between the ages 19-23 be enrolled in college has the potential to disqualify an entire class of dependents.

Testimony was provided by the Union that it advised the Authority it objected to such a change. Nevertheless, the Authority unilaterally changed the definition.

The Authority attempts to justify its action by contending that the change of the definition of dependent eligibility was no more than a plan design; not a change in the level of comparable healthcare benefits. This is mere semantics. This is not a *de minimis* change but a substantial change in healthcare benefits. On one hand the Authority is correct that the level of benefits did not change. For example, those employees who dependents ages are 19-23 and in college, full time, receive the same level of benefits, thus, the level of comparable benefits did not change. But on the other hand, those employees who dependents ages are 19-23 but not in college will lose all their healthcare benefits. Clearly, the total loss of health benefits couldn't be considered comparable benefits, as Article 17 requires.

The line of demarcation between changing a definition within the health care plan design and changing eligibility may be unclear. But what is clear is that some bargaining unit employees will lose substantial benefits for their dependent coverage. Regardless of how the Authority frames its actions, the result is still the same, a loss of benefits has occurred. Therefore, the level of benefits is not comparable.

The Authority contends that the definition of dependent eligibility, which is defined in the Personnel and Procedural Manual and not in the CBA, permits the Authority to unilaterally make changes to the plan. This is correct so long as the changes are not in conflict with Article 17 of the CBA. The changes in the definition of dependent eligibility in the Personnel and Policy manual results in a loss of benefits for Union members.

An employer can implement new policies and procedures to efficiently operate their business, however, those policies must be reasonable and not in conflict with the CBA. Based on this principle, the Authority can legitimately continue to issue new policies and procedures in the healthcare plan, as well as modify terms or even enhance benefits. The Authority, however, must be conscious of the fact that changing terms, must not have the effect of reducing benefits as prohibited by Article 17.

In reaching this conclusion, the Arbitrator cannot over emphasize that the Authority is not required to consult or negotiate every change in its healthcare insurance plan. It is only those changes that reduce the level of healthcare benefits which results in a violation of Article 17.

Health Care Committee [omitted]

Past Practices

Even if the Arbitrator had decided that Article 17 was not violated, the Union would still prevail based on the principle of customs and past practices. The Union contends that the CBA does not define what constitutes "dependent eligibility." However, the Union presented convincing evidence that the past practice between the parties has always defined the term as constituting those dependents between the ages 19-23. Moreover, the Union presented sufficient evidence to support its claim that the parties have mutually accepted the practice of including dependents between the ages of 19-23 as eligible dependents without a requirement that they be full-time students.

* * * *

VI. CONCLUSION

In conclusion, the Union has met its burden that the authority violated Article 17 when it unilaterally changed the definition of eligibility of dependents that are between the ages of 19-23.

VII. AWARD

The grievance is granted. The Authority is to reinstate the definition of dependent eligibility as it relates to dependents 19-23 years old in effect prior to February 1, 2008. The Authority shall reimburse all employees who incurred additional healthcare cost/ expenses as a result of the change of policy on February 1, 2008. The Arbitrator recognizes that this award may have an impact on the cost of healthcare benefits to the Authority as well as the Union. The Arbitrator has no control over the cost of healthcare benefits, but the parties have the flexibility to reach an agreement to resolve this issue to meet the interests of both parties. The Arbitrator shall retain jurisdiction for the limit purpose of resolving disputes arising out of this award for a period of sixty days from the date of this award.

APPLICATION AND DISCUSSION QUESTIONS

1. What are mandatory subjects? Can the employer unilaterally make changes in providing benefits? How did changing the definition of "dependants" impact employees' wages?

2. What elements must be established to support the principle of "past practices"? What impact, if any, did the Health Committee's meeting have on ending past practices?

3. Why does the arbitrator retain jurisdiction? Should the arbitrator consider the cost of benefits if the grievance is granted?

STANLEY BLACK & DECKER AND AFL-LOCAL UNION NO. 6433
128 LA 1639 (F.WEATHERSPOON, 2011)[*]

Opinion By:
WEATHERSPOON, Arbitrator.

I. Statement of Facts

The facts indicate that United Steelworkers, AFL-CIO-CLC-Local Union No. 6463, hereinafter (Union) and The Stanley Works, hereinafter (Company) are parties to a collective bargaining agreement, dated October 31, 2007 through October 31, 2011, hereinafter (CBA or Agreement).

On January 13, 2010, the Company met with the employees to announce the terms of the Closure Agreement. Meetings were held during each shift. Basically, during the meeting, Mr. Bryan read the Closure Agreement verbatim. The facts indicate that the facility was closed in phases, beginning in March 2010 and ending June 2010. Exit interviews were conducted for all employees as their position was eliminated. Marty Bailey, Eric Esquibel and Kenny Bryan were present in every exit interview. The facts further indicate that in April 2010, Marty Bailey approached Eric Esquibel and

*   Reprinted with permission from *Labor Relations Reporter- Labor Arbitration Reports.* 128 LA 1639. Copyright 2015 by the Bureau of National Affairs, Inc. (800-372-1033). http://www.bna.com.

made an inquiry regarding his own pension eligibility. Mr. Bailey's main concern was whether he had the required 25 years of service to qualify for the early retirement option. Mr. Esquibel sent Mr. Bailey's request to the pension department. Mr. Bailey received his pension estimate through the mail. When Mr. Bailey received his pension estimate, he was informed that he had the required number of service years, but that he was going to receive a reduced pension. Mr. Bailey felt that this was inconsistent with the terms of the Closure Agreement and approached Mr. Esquibel. Mr. Esquibel notified Mr. Tallaksen (V.P. ___ and Employee Relations) of Mr. Bailey's concern. Mr. Tallaksen stated that the pension estimate was consistent with the Closure Agreement because at the time of the request, Mr. Bailey was not 60 with 25 years of service. It was at this point that it was discovered that the Union and the Company disagreed as to the interpretation of the Closure Agreement.

The evidence indicates that upon Mr. Bailey's actual retirement, he met the criteria of the CBA, because he turned 60 on his last day of work, and he had 25 years of service. Therefore, he received an unreduced pension benefit.

About April 13, 2010, a grievance was filed challenging the Company's implementation of the early retirement window of the CBA. The grievance went through the various stages of the grievance procedure. The grievance was denied. Arbitration was requested pursuant to Article 10 of the CBA.

II. Issue

The parties stipulated that the issue before the Arbitrator is: Did paragraph 15 of the Closure Agreement modify Section 21.2 of the October 31, 2007 - October 31, 2011 Collective Bargaining Agreement by allowing employees to qualify for unreduced pension benefits if they turned 60 years of age with 25 years of service after their last day of work/termination date but before October 31, 2011?

III. Relevant Contract Provisions

Article
Miscellaneous—Notices

Section 21.2

For the life of this Agreement, the Company is opening up a special 'early retirement window.' Effective for employees retiring on or before October 30, 2011, instead of waiting until age 65, terminated vested employees who are at least 60 years of age with at least 25 years of service on their date of termination shall be eligible for an early unreduced retirement benefit (in such cases—eliminates the current reduction rate of .4% per month from age 65 down to the date of the benefit distribution). In addition, the Plant shall pay anyone who qualified for such an early retirement, a subsidy of $160 per month for the lesser of thirty-six months or until they become eligible for Medicare/Medicaid.

Closure Agreement

15. The Company will continue to honor the early retirement provisions contained in Article 21.2 of the current labor agreement for any employee who retires—or has already retired—on or before October 31, 2011.

IV. Stipulations

The parties stipulated to the following:

> The third paragraph of Section 21.2 of the Collective Bargaining Agreement was added during the 2003 labor negotiations for the first time.
> The third paragraph of Section 21.2 of the Collective Bargaining Agreement was extended in the 2007 labor negotiations.
> The intent of the third paragraph of 21.2 of the Collective Bargaining Agreement was that anyone who was 60 years old and with 25 years of service at the time of their last day of work or termination was entitled to an unreduced benefit under the early retirement window.
> Section 21.2 also allowed employees who qualified for the early unreduced retirement benefit to receive a subsidy of $160 per month for up to three years.
> The Company met with Union leadership on January 6, 2010 to announce the closing of the Sabina facility.
> The Company met with Union leadership on January 12, 2010 to engage in effects bargaining over the decision to close the Sabina facility.

V. Position of the Parties

A. Union's Position

The Union maintains that the parties agreed at the effects negotiations to allow employees with 25 years of service and that turned 60 after their last day worked, but before October 31, 2011 were eligible for an unreduced pension. The Union contends that Company communicated this intent to the employees during a January 13, 2010 meeting as well as in employee exit interviews. The Union maintains that paragraph 15 modified the CBA, otherwise there would be no need to include paragraph 15 in the Closure Agreement.

B. Company's Position

The Company contends that the parties did not modify the early retirement criteria set forth in the CBA. The Company maintains that under the CBA and the Closure Agreement an employee had to have 25 years of service and turn 60 years old on his/her last day of work. The Company acknowledges that it hesitantly included paragraph 15 in the Closure Agreement, but that it was not intended to modify the early retirement criteria.

VI. Discussion and Analysis

* * * *

It is further noted that my role as Arbitrator is to interpret the bargained for agreement. The rights the Union seek to enforce must draw its essence from the CBA or the Closure Agreement. As Arbitrator, I have no authority to add, subtract, or modify the contract as written between the parties. My job is to ascertain the intent of the parties. In order to ascertain the intent, I am guided by the language used by the parties. Any inferences must clearly and logically follow from the language used.

* * * *

The question before the Arbitrator is whether paragraph 15 of the Closure Agreement modified the early retirement criteria set forth in the CBA.

* * * *

The Arbitrator finds that Paragraph 15 is ambiguous. As emphasized by the Union and acknowledged by the Company, typically only changes to the CBA are included in a closure agreement; therefore, the Union maintains if there were no modification, there would be no need for the inclusion of paragraph 15. Moreover, the Arbitrator finds the addition of the language "for any employee who retires—or has already retired—on or before October 31, 2011" in the Closure Agreement causes ambiguity, especially the date, because the implication is that employees could retire up to October 31, 2011. Therefore, the provision is subject to different interpretations. A general aid to the interpretation of ambiguous contract provisions is the parties' pre-contract negotiations, or in this case, the effects negotiations.

* * * *

The Arbitrator wants to make it known that both Mr. Bailey and Mr. Tallaksen seemed to be credible witnesses. Indeed, Mr. Tallaksen acknowledged that Mr. Bailey was an honorable guy. However, given the above parameters, the Arbitrator finds that the Company's version of the events to be the more credible, that is not to say Mr. Bailey was purposely untruthful. However, the Arbitrator found Mr. Bailey's testimony to be vague, confusing, inconsistent at times, and generally hard to follow. Additionally, Mr. Bailey seemed to confuse material terms of the contract, which likely attributed to some of the disconnect between the parties. For example, Mr. Bailey testified that he asked Jim Tallaksen to honor the original contract, not to change it. This seems to be consistent with the Company's contention. Because, the Company contends that it did honor the CBA. However, it appears that Mr. Bailey's interpretation of "honor" the agreement is something different. For instance, Mr. Bailey went on to explain that he interpreted "honor" as allowing employees to retire if they are 60 by October 31, 2011 with unreduced benefit. This is a perfect example of what could lead to a misinterpretation, the parties clearly attribute a different meaning to the word "honor". However, the Arbitrator believes that Mr. Bailey's interpretation is flawed. To "honor" the agreement, does not suggest a change in the necessary criteria to be eligible for an unreduced pension benefit, as outlined in the CBA. However, according to the Union's interpretation, there is clearly a change in the criteria. On the other hand, Jim Tallaksen provided precise, clear and consistent testimony. Further, the Company's version of events is reasonable and logical. Indeed, the Company provided compelling rationale and foundational background that supports its version of events. Specifically, Mr. Tallaksen testified that he had previously negotiated 12-15 closure agreements for Stanley Black & Decker. Mr. Tallaksen testified that the Company has never modified or even discussed modifying a pension plan during a closure agreement.

* * * *

When these factors are taken into consideration, it doesn't seem reasonable or logical that the Company would agree to modify the pension. It further seems illogical that such a decision would be made in one-day of negotiations. Moreover, the evidence suggests that Mr. Tallaksen didn't have authority to make such a modification. The evidence indicates that such a modification would increase the closure budget by 50%, which doesn't seem reasonable, given that the Company's purpose is to stream-line, not increase its budget. Further, the evidence indicates that a union's negotiating power is minimal during an effects negotiation, therefore, there is no incentive for the Company to make such a drastic increase of its budget. Thus, the evidence supports the Company's contention that Paragraph 15 of the Closure Agreement did not modify the CBA. Therefore, an employee had to meet the criteria as negotiated under the CBA to be eligible for an unreduced benefit. Specifically, an employee had to have 25 years of service and be 60 years of age on their last day of work.

January 13, 2010 meeting and Exit Interviews

The evidence establishes that the Company held exit interviews with all the union employees. The evidence demonstrates that Eric Esquibel, Kenny Bryan, and Marty Bailey was present at each bargaining unit employee's exit interview. The Union maintains, that even though, the Company denies it, Eric Esquibel did in fact tell employees that they would receive their pension unreduced if they met the criteria by October 31, 2011.

On January 13, 2010, the Company met with all of the employees to explain the negotiated document. The Union contends that there were questions regarding pension. The Union presents evidence that pension was discussed at the January 13, 2010 employee meeting as well as in various exit interviews. Specifically, Marty Bailey testified that there were pension questions in the January 13 meeting and Kenny Bryan specifically said that an employee would get unreduced pension benefit if he/she turned 60 by October 31, 2011, with no objection from Eric Esquibel.

* * * *

Lastly, the Union provided the testimony of Lois Steiner. Ms. Steiner was an employee of Stanley for 35.5 years. She was a Financial Officer and Grievance person for the Union. She has been on the negotiating committee for approximately ten contracts. She was present at the Effects bargaining. Ms. Steiner testified that she was at the second shift meeting held with the employees, she testified there was a question asked about pension and Kenny's answer was consistent with the Union's interpretation that you would not receive reduced benefits, if you turned 60 by October 31, 2011.

Ms. Steiner had her exit meeting on March 8, 2010. Ms. Steiner was on worker's compensation at the time. She asked about how her worker's compensation would impact her severance or her pension. She testified that she was told by Eric that it would not be impacted. Ms. Steiner testified that she did not have to accept layoff at that time because of her union position. Ms. Steiner testified that she didn't want to draw her pension, and receive her severance pay, while she was receiving worker's compensation because she felt as if she would be double dipping. She further testified that she asked if she would get her full pension if she waited to retire, because she turned 60 in 21 days and she didn't have to accept the layoff. She reiterated that she was assured that if she waited until her severance ran out to draw her pension, that she would receive her full pension under the terms of the Closure Agreement. In other words, her pension would be unreduced. Mr. Bailey confirmed that Ms. Steiner was told that she would not get a reduced benefit because she turned 60 before October 31, 2011.

The evidence also demonstrates that Ms. Steiner was eligible for an unreduced early retirement benefit under the terms of the Closure Agreement if she did not accept the layoff on March 8, because she turned 60, March 29, 2010. Specifically, Union Exhibit 7, provides, in relevant part, "[y]ou are currently eligible for an early unreduced retirement."

Again, the evidence presented by the Company is substantially different from the evidence presented by the Union. The Company provided the testimony of Eric Esquibel. Mr. Esquibel testified that the issue of reduced or unreduced pensions was never brought up in any exit interview, including Lois Steiner's interview or in the January 13 meeting with the employees. Mr. Esquibel further testified that he never agreed with the Union's interpretation of the Closure Agreement. Additionally, Mr. Bryan testified that the issue of reduced or unreduced pensions never came up in any of the exit interviews or in the January 13 meeting with the employees.

* * * *

However, as determined above, the Closure Agreement does not modify the contract and it does not change the criteria required for early retirement. Likewise, a management employee's misinterpretation or misinformation also does not change the terms of a contract. In other words, a management employee's erroneous communication does not change the terms of the contract. Thus, despite any information to the contrary, the employee must have turned 60, with 25 years of service, on the last day worked as provided in the CBA.

However, there is one exception. The Union provided compelling testimony from Lois Steiner and compelling evidence that she was eligible for early retirement and an unreduced pension. The evidence was overwhelming that Ms. Steiner relied on Management's erroneous information to her detriment. Ms. Steiner was credible and convincing. She was precise and detailed. The Company has not put forth any evidence to dispute Ms. Steiner's claim that she didn't have to accept the layoff, on March 8, 2010, before she turned 60. Ms. Steiner turned 60 on March 29, 2010. The evidence establishes that Ms. Steiner's exit interview was on March 8, 2010, which was also calculated to be her last day worked. Ms. Steiner received vacation pay until April 30, 2010 and separation pay until October 29, 2010. Moreover, the evidence indicates that Ms. Steiner applied for her pension benefits around September 2010. Therefore, the Arbitrator believes that Ms. Steiner was told that she would still receive an unreduced pension if she waited to apply for her pension. Nothing else makes sense. Under a detrimental reliance or a promissory estoppel exception, "[a] promise which the promisor should reasonably expect to induce action or forbearance on the part of the promissee or a third person and which does induce such action or forbearance is binding if injustice can be avoided only by enforcement of the promise." Elkouri, pg. 928. The evidence indicates that Ms. Steiner relied on the promises of management to her detriment. Otherwise, it doesn't make sense that Ms. Steiner accepted the layoff date of March 8, when she would have been 60 years old, 21 days later and eligible for an unreduced benefit. If Ms. Steiner waited 21 days and accepted retirement, she would have been 60 years old with over 25 years of service, and thus eligible for an unreduced pension benefit. However, she believed that she would still be eligible for unreduced retirement based on promises from management. Thus the elements of promissory estoppel apply, and this injustice can only be avoided by enforcement of the promise. Thus, the Union has provided sufficient evidence that Lois Steiner is entitled to an unreduced pension benefit.

VII. Conclusion

The Union has not provided sufficient evidence that the intent of Paragraph 15 of the Closure Agreement was to change the early retirement criteria set forth in the CBA. The Union did not provide sufficient evidence that the parties agreed to modify the Agreement so that an employee that turned 60 before October 31, 2011 and had 25 years of service was entitled to an unreduced pension benefit. The Union did provide sufficient evidence that bargaining unit employees were given the impression that they would receive an unreduced benefit under the aforementioned circumstances. However, that does Steiner detrimentally relied on Management's promise that she would receive an unreduced pension. Thus, Ms. Steiner is entitled to an unreduced pension.

VIII. AWARD

The grievance is denied, in part, and sustained in part. Specifically, the grievance is sustained only as it pe not change the criteria set forth in the CBA. However, the Union provided compelling evidence that Lois rtains to Lois Steiner. Lois Steiner's entitled to an unreduced pension to be retroactive to the time she initially began receiving pension benefits. The Arbitrator retains jurisdiction for 60 days for the limited purpose of resolving any dispute about the monetary amount owed to Lois Steiner.

APPLICATION AND DISCUSSION QUESTIONS

1. How does the arbitrator describe his role, authority, and limits in interpreting the CBA?

2. The arbitrator determined that part of the contract language in the Closure Agreement was ambiguous. The arbitrator indicates that a review of "effects negotiation" would provide guidance in understanding the parties' intent. What is "effects negotiation"?

3. The witnesses have conflicting testimony on what the parties agreed to during negotiation. In determining the credibility of witnesses, the arbitrator cites *Duke University*, 103 LA 289, 290 (Basiskin, 1994) for guidance. Arbitrator Basiskin cites the following factors in assessing the credibility of witnesses:
   (1)the demeanor of each witness; (2) the manner in which the testimony was given; (3) the presence of internal inconsistencies in the testimony; (4) the witnesses' ability to perceive, recollect and communicate; (5) the reasonableness of the witnesses' testimony in light of the other evidence presented; and (6) the interest of each witness in the outcome of the arbitration.

4. Can a Closure Agreement modify benefits which are outlined in the CBA?

5. Why did the arbitrator apply the "promissory estoppel" rule in this grievance to grant the employee full early retirement benefits?

MODIFYING EMPLOYEE BENEFITS

Company A is an organization comprised primarily of bargaining unit employees. Under the agreement between Company A and the Union, the employees are offered two (2) options for healthcare: a traditional health insurance plan or compensation for *not* enrolling in the plan. According to Article 1 of the bargaining unit agreement, Company A cannot make any changes that will result in a substantial decrease in benefits to the bargaining unit employees, without giving the Union at least six (6) months advance notice. Furthermore, under Article 2 of the bargaining unit agreement, Company A agrees to not eliminate past practices in an arbitrary or capricious manner.

Company A has abruptly eliminated the cash incentive program for its employees opting out of the insurance. This unilateral change was not communicated to the Union beforehand and left many of the bargaining unit employees without any healthcare coverage or monetary compensation. The Union is arguing that this change is in violation of both Article 1 and Article 2 to of the Agreement.

How Should the Arbitrator Rule?

G. WAGES AND HOURS

2004 AAA LEXIS 244
AMERICAN ARBITRATION ASSOCIATION
(FLOYD WEATHERSPOON, 2004)[*]

Case
lift truck
operator
wages

Opinion By: Floyd D. Weatherspoon, Arbitrator
AWARD: The grievance is denied.

I. STATEMENT OF FACTS

The Grievant is a Lift Truck Operator. The grievance alleges that the Grievant performed duties of a Lead Checker, a higher classification. The grievance seeks to adjust
the wages to the Lead Checker rate of pay. The grievance went through the various
stages of the grievance procedure. The grievance was denied at each stage.

grievance

II. ISSUE

The Union frames the issue as: Has the company violated the CBA when it has a
lower rated classification doing the work of a higher classification at the lower rate
of pay? The Company frames the issue as: Was the Grievant entitled to set up pay at
the Lead Checker rate of pay?

U says

Based on the hearing, the Abitrator has determined that the issue is whether the
Lift Truck Operator classification was performing the duties of a Lead Checker clas-
sification such that the Lift Truck Operator should receive the higher classification
Lead Checker rate of pay?

III. RELEVANT CONTRACT PROVISIONS

Article 3, Management Rights

Section 1.

It is agreed that the parties have fully bargained about the rights of the Management of the Company and that, except as otherwise expressly limited by this Agreement and by law, the Company retains the full and exclusive right to fully manage and conduct its business affairs, which rights include specifically, but are not limited to the following: * * * * to introduce * * * * job procedures; to establish classification; to determine the size and scope of its work force and all crews; * * * * and to generally manage the Company's operations and business as it deems; best.

IV. STIPULATIONS

The parties stipulated to the following:

1. The grievance is properly before the Arbitrator.

2. The Plant operated 12 hours, 7 days a week at the time of the grievance.

V. POSITION OF THE PARTIES

A. Union's Position

It is the position of the Union that the Company has violated the Collective Bargaining Agreement. The Union maintains that the Lift Truck Operator performs duties that entitle the Lift Truck Operator to the Lead Checker rate of pay. The Union next contends that the Company upgraded the Roll Truck Operator position to Lead Checker following a similar grievance, therefore, the same logic should apply. Finally, the Union contends that the plant operates 24 hours a day, and there is no Lead Checker on the night shift, therefore, the Lead Checker duties are being performed by the Lift Truck Operator on second shift.

B. Management's Position

The Company maintains that there is some overlap between the functions of the two classifications, however, simply removing pallets from a trailer rather than the storage area does not entitle Lift Truck Operator to Lead Checker pay. The Company maintains this is a routine duty of the Lift Truck Operator and of the Lead Checker. The Company further contends that upgrading the Roll Truck Operators to Lead Checkers is not factually similar to this grievance. The Company contends that the Roll Truck Operators upgraded because of a new system and they were given more responsibility.

The Company maintains that the Union presented no evidence that this grievance involved a Lift Truck Operator being asked to load outbound shipments of finished goods, nor that the Grievant, in fact loaded any outbound shipments during the time in question.

VI. DISCUSSION AND ANALYSIS

It is clear from the evidence presented that the duties of the two classifications overlap. It is not unusual to find duties and tasks that may properly fall within two or more separate job classifications. Elkouri 6th ed., pg. 702. As the Company points out, when duties overlap, or has been performed by two or more classifications in the past, management has been given considerable leeway in assigning work and has not generally been limited to assigning it to exclusively to one classification. See Elkouri, at 703.

The evidence demonstrated that both the Lift Truck Operator and the Lead Checker handle pallets and from time-to-time corrugated material. Moreover, the evidence also demonstrates that the duties at issue only comprise a small portion of the Lead Checker duties. According to management the Lead Checker duties are representative of two major areas, inbound and outbound finished goods shipment. The Company presented evidence that the majority of the Lead Checker duties, approximately 90 - 95% relate to outbound shipment, compared to the other 5 -10% inbound material. The Company maintains that the 5 -10% inbound duties are the duties at issue dealing with the pallets and corrugated material.

This is also corroborated by the testimony of Union's witness where he acknowledged the Lead Checker is mainly responsible for loading product onto trucks and getting an outbound shipment ready. The evidence also demonstrates that the Lead Checker's primary duties are related to outbound and the duties brought into question by the Union fall under the Lead Checker's inbound duties, which, according to testimony, only comprise a small fraction of the duties performed by the Lead Checker.

Taking skids or pallets off trucks and putting down corrugated when the Lead Checker is not on duty, does not qualify the Lift Truck Operator to the Lead Check rate of pay. Further, Union's witness testified that if no Lead Checker is available this is a duty of the Lift Truck Operator. Therefore, although the two classification are very similar, it appears that the majority of the Lead Checker's duties are getting the product ready for outbound shipment whereas, the duties at issue relate to inbound shipment. The duties in question are only a small portion of the Lead Checker's duties. The Union has not met its burden of showing that the Lift Truck Operator is performing the duties of a Lead Checker, entitling the Lift Truck Operator to the Lead Checker rate of pay.

The Union next argues that the Roll Truck Operator was upgraded to the Lead Checker classification under similar circumstances, therefore the same rationale should apply here. The Union maintains that one of the factors considered in upgrading the Roll Truck Operators to the Lead Checker position was that the SAP shipping and receiving system was implemented. The Union notes that this same system applies to the Lift Truck Operator.

The Company maintains that situation is not in any way similar to this grievance. Terry Lehman testified that the Roll Truck Driver was upgraded to the Lead Checker classification because there was an increase in the workload and responsibility, and the SAP shipping and receiving system was added. The Company acknowledges the new SAP system also applied to the Lift Truck Operator. However, Plant Manager, testified that the Roll Truck Driver was upgraded to Lead Checker because it was decided that the Roll Truck Drivers were responsible for unloading all rolls coming into the plant. The Roll Truck Drivers also dealt directly with the truck drivers themselves, and were responsible for quality. Plant Manager testified that the circumstance that lead to the upgrade of the Roll Truck Driver does not resemble the situation in this grievance where two different classifications are simply performing some of the same duties.

The Company states that there is a procedure provided for in the CBA whereby, the Union can ask for a rate change if it is believed that the classification of a position has changed. The Company maintains that the Union has not utilized this procedure. The Union maintains that the similar change in classification of the Roll Truck Drivers was handled through the grievance procedures. Therefore, it should be changed by the grievance in this instance. The Company acknowledges that the change in classification was the result of a grievance, however, the Company maintains that the grievances do not resemble one another. The Company maintains that the instant grievance asks the Arbitrator to require the Company to grant the Lift Truck Operator "set-up" pay, for performing duties they have been assigned for many years. In contrast, the Company maintains the grievance involving the Roll Truck Driver classification requested that a job be reclassified because of substantial changes to the job classification.

The Union seems to rely heavily on the premise that the addition of the SAP shipping and receiving system's implementation also applied to the Lift Truck Operators. However, this, without more, does not justify a change in classification. As stated earlier, the duties of the two classifications overlap. Therefore, it is logical that the SAP system would affect both classifications. Further, the Company presented evidence that the duties of the Roll Truck Driver changed such that a change in classification was warranted. The Union is not arguing or has not presented any evidence that the Lift Truck Operator duties have changed such that it should become a different classification. Rather, the Union is contending that the same duties the Lift Truck Operator has always performed entitle it to Lead Checker pay. As stated earlier, the Union has not met its burden demonstrating that the Lift Truck Operator is performing Lead Checker duties. Finally, the Union maintains that the Plant operates 24 hours a day, but the Lead Checker only works from 7:00 am to 7:00 pm. The Union maintains the Lift Truck Operator solely performs the Lead Checkers duties on the second shift. The Company maintains that the Union presented no evidence that this grievance involved a Lift Truck Operator being asked to load outbound shipments of finished goods, nor that the Grievant, in fact loaded any outbound shipments during the time in question.

* * * *

VII. CONCLUSION

The Union has not met its burden to prove that the Lift Truck Operator is performing the duties of the Lead Checker. The evidence demonstrates that the duties at issue were intended to be performed by both classifications. The Union has not established that the previous grievance in which the Roll Truck Driver was upgraded to the Lead Checker classification is applicable to this grievance.

VIII. AWARD

The grievance is denied.

APPLICATION AND DISCUSSION QUESTIONS

1. What must the Union prove to show that the Lift Operator was performing duties of the Lead Checker?

   duties changed or a large portion overlapped

2. The plant is open 24/7. How did the Union use this information to argue their position?

   no lead for 12 hrs

3. What role did past practices play in this case?

   past practice = lift truck operator did these duties for years

2004 AAA LEXIS 1490
AMERICAN ARBITRATION ASSOCIATION
(F. WEATHERSPOON, 2004)*

Case
teacher job change, exp. ignored

I. STATEMENT OF FACTS

The facts indicate that Union and District are parties to a collective bargaining agreement, hereinafter (CBA or Agreement) dated from 2003-2005.

griev.
On August 26, 1998, Grievant was hired by District as a Magnet Professional in the Center for Performing and Visual Arts at High School. The facts indicate that Grievant was hired as a Stage Manager. This is an unlicensed position. In 2003, District changed the position of Stage Manager to Theatre Teacher/ Stage Manager and required that the position be filled by someone holding a valid State teacher's license in speech and drama or speech, communication, and theater. Grievant received a limited license and was awarded the position of Theatre Teacher. Grievant was placed on the teacher salary schedule with zero years experience as a teacher. Grievant requested the credit for teaching experience while in his position of Stage Manager. District denied this request.

A grievance was filed May, 17, 2004, alleging that District violated Article 9, Section 5, when it denied him credit for his teaching position of Stage Manager at District. The grievance went through the various stages of the grievance procedure. The grievance was denied. Arbitration was requested pursuant to Article 19, Sec (2)(c).

*   Reprinted with permission 2004 AAA Lexis 1490. Copyright 2015 by the American Arbitration Association. (800-778-7879). https://adr.org.

II. ISSUE

Was Grievant properly placed on the teacher's salary schedule in accordance with Article 9, Section 5 of the CBA, or did District violate Article 9, Section 5 when it failed to grant Grievant full-credit on the salary schedule for full-time outside school teaching experience? If so, what is the appropriate remedy?

[handwritten: Q]

III. RELEVANT CONTRACT PROVISIONS

Article IX: Professional Compensation

> Section 5: All teachers shall receive full credit on the salary schedule for full-time out-side school-teaching experience in pre-K to 12 accredited schools completed after the teacher received a Bachelor's degree. No teacher shall be employed in excess of credit authorized by this schedule.

[handwritten: CBA]

IV. POSITION OF THE PARTIES

A. Union's Position

[handwritten: U arg / CBA met, deserves credit for 5 years]

The Union maintains that District is in violation of Article 9, Section 5 by denying Grievant credit on the salary schedule for his previous five years of teaching experience. The Union contends that Grievant was required to teach classes in his position as a Stage Manager. The Union maintains that Grievant has a Bachelor's Degree as required, he was not required to have a license to teach by District and therefore, he is entitled to the credit. The Union maintains that Article 9, Section 5 does not require a teaching license to receive credit. Further, the Union maintains that since obtaining a license, Grievant performs substantially the same duties as a Teacher with District as he did prior to obtaining a license.

B. Company's Position

[handwritten: ER arg]

According to District, Grievant was properly placed on the teacher salary schedule as a teacher with zero years of experience. District maintains that Article 9, Section 5 is not applicable to this situation because Section 5 applies to "outside" teaching experience. District maintains that if Article 9, Section 5 does apply, Grievant is not entitled to credit because Article 9, Section 5 credits "full-time" teaching experience. District maintains that Grievant did not teach on a full-time basis, and therefore is

[handwritten: CBA not met b/c not "outside" exp + not full-time]

not entitled to the credit. Lastly, District maintains that Grievant was not a Teacher at High School, but rather Grievant was hired under the non-licensed classification of Educational Support Personnel.

V. DISCUSSION AND ANALYSIS

The Union alleges that District is in violation of Article 9, Section 5 of the CBA by denying Grievant credit on the salary schedule for his previous five years of teaching experience. District maintains that Grievant was properly placed on the teacher salary schedule as a teacher with zero years' experience.

In contract interpretation grievances, typically, the Union has the burden of demonstrating that the Employer violated the collective bargaining agreement. See, generally, Fairweather, Practice and Procedure in Labor Arbitration, 3rd. ed. (1991) pp. 192- 193. Therefore, in this grievance, the Union has the burden of proving by a preponderance of the evidence that District violated Article 9, Section 5 of the CBA.

Article 9, Section 5 provides:

> All teachers shall receive full credit on the salary schedule for full-time outside school-teaching experience in pre-K-12 accredited schools completed after the teacher received a Bachelor's degree. No teacher shall be employed in excess of credit authorized by this schedule.

My role as the arbitrator is to review the language in Section 5 and to give the words their plain meanings, unless there is evidence to the contrary. Unless there is some ambiguity in this provision of the CBA, with few exceptions, the parties must comply with its meaning.

To meet their burden of proof, the Union presented evidence that requirements of the Stage Manager position included the "ability to teach stage design class to theatre magnet students" and to "possess a genuine desire to teach students how to behave in a professional manner when using the stage." Further, Grievant testified that he was required to attend teacher meetings as well as participate in professional development , as were the other teachers. Grievant also testified that he was required to develop and submit lesson plans Grievant also testified he submitted grade cards. Although not hired as a Licensed Teacher in 1998, the Union has sufficiently established that Grievant taught classes from 1998 and continues to teach as a licensed Teacher presently. However, the mere fact Grievant performed teaching duties does not change his status as a Stage Manager.

District maintains that although in his position as Stage Manager, Grievant taught classes related to stagecraft, he was not a teacher and he is not entitled to credit as a Teacher under Section 5. In support of its position that Grievant was not considered a teacher, District presented the following: Grievant was not hired as a certified teacher in 1998 and did not perform as a certified teacher from 1998 -- 2002. Grievant was hired under the classification of an Educational Support Personnel. This classification is used to describe employees that are not licensed teachers who support the education process. District notes that Grievant did not enter into a teacher's contract prior to the 2003-2004 school year. He was paid an hourly wage, whereas, teachers are paid salary. He was not a member of the Union that represents the teachers. Pension contributions were not made on his behalf to the teacher's retirement fund. He was not evaluated using the instrument used to evaluate teachers; rather he was evaluated as an Educational Support Personnel. District notes that since being hired into a licensed position, Grievant has signed a teacher's contract, he is covered by the collective bargaining agreement governing teachers, and contributions are made on his behalf to the teacher's retirement fund. This evidence overwhemhley supports District's position that Grievant was not hired as a classified teacher and was not considered a teacher by District. To overcome this wealth of evidence, the Union must set forth compelling evidence to discount this evidence or at least provide some other evidence to contradict District position. The Union did not present any compelling evidence to refute District contentions. Instead, the Union submitted substantial documents to support.

APPLICATION AND DISCUSSION QUESTIONS

1. What standard of proof is the Union subject to? What does it require?

2. What role did Contract Law play in this case?

3. What were the key arguments made by the District to refute the Grievant's complaint?

[handwritten: Case]

[handwritten: OT equalization]

LITHONIA HI TEK – VERMILION AND LOCAL 998, INTERNATIONAL BROTHERHOOD OF ELECTRICAL WORKERS

109 BNA LA 775 (FRANCKIEWICZ, 1997)*

EQUALIZATION

Contract Provisions Involved

The Facts (Omitted)

Analysis and Conclusions

Although the facts in this case are undisputed and fairly straightforward, the questions raised by the parties' arguments are complex, and require fairly detailed discussion.

* * * *

II. The Standard of Proof

[handwritten: issue]

I am satisfied that the Union has sustained its burden of proof in this case. The Union's statistical approach demonstrates disparities in overtime among employees in the same classification. Its method addresses a number of considerations which are implicit in the overtime equalization provision.

[handwritten: req.]

First is that overtime need not be equalized on a daily or weekly basis. No contract violation occurs if the Company temporarily permits some employees to exceed others in overtime assignments, so long as the disadvantaged employees are later permitted to catch up. But if the Company fails to even out the overtime opportunity over a reasonable period of time, a contract violation has occurred. I conclude that a

[handwritten: held]

year is a reasonable time within which the Company should accomplish the equalization. This is especially appropriate given the parties' prior history, which suggests a mutual understanding that a contract year (from July to July) is the appropriate measuring period.

[handwritten: reas?]

The second notion that is inherent in the overtime equalization provision, and taken into account in the Union's statistical method, is that exact mathematical precision is not to be expected in overtime distribution. Even if two employees had

*   Reprinted with permission from *Labor Relations Reporter- Labor Arbitration Reports*. 109 BNA LA 775. Copyright 2015 by the Bureau of National Affairs, Inc. (800-372-1033). http://www.bna.com.

identical overtime accounts as the end of the contract year approached, the need to have a single employee work overtime on a Saturday for eight hours could create an eight hour imbalance. Factors such as special skills and availability could account for some degree of disparity. (In this regard, however, the large number of different classifications at the facility suggests that skill differentials may be more apparent across different classifications than within a given classification. Further, the practice of charging employees for declined overtime should minimize the importance of availability in accounting for overtime disparities.) Given that overtime is normally assigned in increments of one to four hours (with up to eight hours on Saturdays), I conclude that the Union, by demonstrating a variation of over eight hours among the employees in a classification on the same shift, has sustained its burden of proof, at least to the extent of shifting to the Employer the burden of coming forward with evidence to explain the disparity. Since the Employer is in the best position to present the evidence of why it assigned overtime to one employee over another, it is appropriate to shift the burden to it, once the Union has demonstrated that a disparity of over eight hours has occurred.

The third proposition inherent in the overtime equalization provision (or perhaps it is only a special case of the second) is that a greater degree of disparity between employees on different shifts may fairly be expected. Considerations which do not obtain in the within shift situation may affect the assignment of overtime to employees on one shift rather than another shift, for example the need to complete a "rush" assignment quickly, or limitations on equipment or work stations which may make it infeasible on some occasions to assign work to employees on one shift or the other. The Union's statistical method, utilizing a standard of in excess of 16 hours disparity in cross shift situations, addresses this issue. I conclude that by showing disparities of over 16 hours in cross shift situations, the Union has sustained its burden of proof, at least to the extent of shifting to the Company the burden of producing evidence to explain the disparity.

Since the Company has not offered evidence to explain the disparities in either the within shift or cross shift situations, I conclude that the Union has demonstrated violations of the agreement.

III. The Remedy

Arbitrators differ as to the appropriate remedy in overtime situations. One text summarizes the holdings as follows.

Where it has been found that an employer has improperly distributed overtime assignments in violation of the agreement or a past practice (as opposed to the situation where management simply neglects to call in an employee on overtime), the reported *remedy* cases indicate that arbitrators either award monetary compensation for the opportunity lost or issue quasi-injunctive relief providing the employee the opportunity to work overtime at some later date.

While a majority of the arbitrators prefer a monetary award rather than a "make-up" remedy for improper distribution of overtime, a study of the reported cases indicates that the remedy has varied depending upon the specific context of the violation. The most important variable in the arbitrator's decision to award monetary damages is the relevant contractual provision at issue. In many instances the contract will explicitly provide the remedy. . .

Where the remedy is not specified, the cases indicate that arbitrators are more likely to award monetary relief where the parties' contract or past practice provides for distribution of overtime on a strict seniority basis, as opposed to the situation where the agreement compels distribution of overtime on an equalization basis.

* * * *

here My own view, regardless of whether I am in the majority or the minority, is that in this case, an award of make-up overtime is appropriate (with certain additional considerations discussed in more detail below).

Where there has been a contract violation, I believe that an arbitrator's role is to place all involved where they would have been had there been no violation. In this case, if overtime had been distributed more evenly, certain employees would have received more money. But they would also have worked more hours. To simply award them money without requiring them to do the work which otherwise would have been the prerequisite to earning that money, would make them more than whole, since it would place them in a better position than they would have enjoyed had there been no violation. (In this regard I note that at least some overtime is voluntary. Some employees prefer not to work overtime. An employee who would have declined additional overtime if it had been offered lost nothing by virtue of the Company's failure to equalize overtime. For such an employee, a monetary remedy would be simply a windfall.) A make-up remedy only postpones, but does not deprive, the employees of the overtime (and earnings) which they should have received earlier. Arguably, this delay should entitle the employees to some additional consideration. Conceivably the employees should receive interest from the time they should have received the overtime, until it is actually offered to them. But interest is not customarily awarded in arbitration, and computation of interest in this case would be problematical, since, as the Union's statistical method implicitly acknowledges, there is no fixed point (other than the end of the contract year) to use for the beginning of the period. Further such potential interest is roughly counterbalanced by the fact that the employees will receive their make-up overtime in a later contract year, at a higher rate of pay.

* * * *

In my view, an arbitrator's role is not to punish an employer for its transgressions. Rather the arbitrator's role is to apply the agreement, and to restore, to the greatest extent feasible, all involved to the situation in which they would have been if the agreement had been followed. As noted above, where there have been repeated or willful violations (which themselves would implicate the duty of good faith implicit in all agreements), more stringent remedies may be called for. But bad faith or a need for deterrence should not be presumed.

Some arbitrators have expressed the view that the employees who failed to receive assignments were entitled to their overtime at the time it arose, and not later. Some have expressed the view that monetary compensation represents the "damages" for this type of contract violation. To me such reasoning only begs the question. The real question is how best to restore the parties to the positions in which they should be under the agreement. In my view, since the employees who were disadvantaged by the failure to equalize overtime should have been given the opportunity to perform additional work for premium pay, the appropriate remedy is to now restore to them that work opportunity, with appropriate compensation for the work performed.

Finally, some arbitrators have analogized to the situation of an improperly discharged or laid off employee, who normally receives backpay for time not worked. To me, this suggests exactly the opposite conclusion than reached in the cited case. It is generally accepted that an improperly discharged or laid off employee has the obligation to seek interim employment, and his backpay can be reduced if he fails to do so. Further, if he obtains such employment, the interim earnings are deducted from backpay. Thus the correct proposition seems to be that the employer's obligation to restore lost earnings is balanced by the employee's obligation to work.

Accordingly in this case, given the nature of the violation and the specific agreement involved, as elucidated by the parties' prior grievance settlements, as well as the fact that such a remedy can be accomplished without unduly harming other employees, I believe that a make-up remedy is generally appropriate. Nonetheless, this remedy is not possible in all cases.

It appears that some employees have left the Company's employment. As to them, offering make-up overtime would not be feasible, and the only remedy possible is a monetary payment. Other employees are no longer in the same classifications they occupied during the contract year covered by the grievance. In this situation, I also consider a monetary remedy necessary. It might be possible to temporarily return these employees to their former classifications for the purpose of make-up overtime, but doing so might cause havoc with the provisions of Article 9 of the collective bargaining agreement, covering seniority, job posting and bidding, and temporary transfers. An arbitrator should be most reluctant to apply a remedy which itself vandalizes other provisions of the parties' agreement.

* * * *

In summary, I conclude that the appropriate remedy in this case is a monetary payment to employees who have left the Company, or no longer occupy the same classification they held during the 1995-1996 contract year, but only if they meet the following criteria: 1) the employee was in the appropriate classification for the entire 1995-1996 contract year, and 2) the employee was more than 4 hours below the average overtime for the classification in a within shift situation, or more than 8 hours below the average overtime for the classification in a cross shift situation. Other employees, who occupy the same classifications as they did during the 1995-1996 contract year, are entitled to make-up overtime assignments. In as much as an additional contract year has now passed, and the parties are now in the final year of the current collective bargaining agreement, the precise method by which these employees are to catch up on overtime assignments is best left to the parties for discussion. I shall retain jurisdiction in case they are unable to resolve this or any other questions which may arise under this award.

One final point deserves mention. As noted, the parties are now in the final year of the current collective bargaining agreement. Depending on economic factors, it may not be possible during this final contract year to provide sufficient overtime opportunities to remedy the disparities for all employees affected. In addition, new disparities may arise in this final contract year. This award does not address the question of whether a monetary payment is the appropriate remedy for overtime equalization disparities which can no longer be remedied through make-up overtime before the expiration of the current collective bargaining agreement. This award should not be taken as expressing any view as to the appropriate remedy under those circumstances.

AWARD

The grievance is sustained. The Company shall take remedial action as set forth above. Jurisdiction is retained for the limited purpose of resolving any disagreements which may arise in connection with this award.

[handwritten: sustained]

APPLICATION AND DISCUSSION QUESTIONS

1. How would you define overtime equalization? How does the Arbitrator determine whether an employer fails to "even out the overtime opportunity" among employees? What is a reasonable time period for an employer to accomplish equalization? *[handwritten: EEs get similar OT hours; fails if 8+ hr diffs or 16+hrs for cross-shift; 1 year]*

2. The Arbitrator determined that an "exact mathematical precision is not to be expected in overtime distribution." Why is it difficult to have a precise mathematical method to determine overtime equalization? What factors do arbitrators consider in determining overtime equalization? *[handwritten: seniority, skill, shift, need, OT rejection]*

3. What are the different remedies available in overtime situations? Can you think of any that were not listed in the case? Would you order a "make-up" remedy or monetary award? *[handwritten: make-up or $]*

4. What's the most important consideration in determining the award for overtime issues? Do you agree with the Arbitrator's position that the employer should not be punished for the error? *[handwritten: make parties whole; yes]*

5. What criteria must be met for former employees or employees in different classifications to receive a monetary payment for the lack of overtime opportunities? Do you think this is sufficient? *[handwritten: See p. 546]*

THE PROBLEM WITH WORK HOURS

Employer has a Collective Bargaining Agreement permitting it to hire part-time or seasonal employees who can work up to 1800 hours in a calendar year. If an employee works more than 1800 hours without interruption in a calendar year, the position will be considered a full-time bargaining unit position. The provision has been a negotiated part of the CBA since the 1990's. The Union filed a grievance asserting an employee worked more than 1800 hours in the 2014 calendar year and in accordance with the plain language of the CBA the employee's position should be made into a full-time bargaining unit position, which the employer refused to do.

The employer contends that the employee worked less than 1800 hours during the applicable period. The employer based its calculations on actual payroll hours worked in a calendar year, starting with the employee's January 1, 2014 pay, which included pay for hours the employee worked during the last two weeks of 2013. The employer did not include hours that the employee worked during the last 2 weeks of 2014, because the hours were not paid until the following calendar year on the January 1, 2015 payroll. The employer argues it has used the payroll method of calculating hours worked in a calendar year for several years, reported it to the Union, and there were no complaints.

How should the arbitrator rule?

H. Safety Policies

CARRIER CORPORATION, MCMINNVILLE, TENNESSEE AND SHEET METAL WORKERS INTERNATIONAL ASSOCIATION, LOCAL 483
110 BNA LA 1064 (IPAVEC, 1998)*
SAFETY GLASSES

Grievance

* * * *

On 6/26/97 the Company unjustly terminated T for violation of four (4) different rules within a twelve month period when in fact T did not violate four (4) different rules within a twelve month period of time. The action requested by the Union was that:

To be reinstated and made whole.

The final answer given by the Company to the foregoing grievance was as follows:

The termination is a result of his violation of the labor agreement on Article XXXII, Section 5 "Employees may be discharged when four different rules have been violated within a twelve month period."

Issue

The issue which has been presented to the arbitrator, in this case may be stated as follows:

Did the Company violate the Agreement between the parties when it terminated the employment of the Grievant, T.

* Reprinted with permission from *Labor Relations Reporter- Labor Arbitration Reports.* 110 BNA LA 1064. Copyright 2015 by the Bureau of National Affairs, Inc. (800-372-1033). http://www.bna.com.

Contract Provisions

The following provision of the Agreement between the parties is deemed to be central to the issue involved in this case.

ARTICLE XXXII--PLANT RULES AND DISCIPLINE

Section 1. It is agreed that the employees covered by this Agreement shall be governed by the Plant Rules listed in Section 6 herein, agreed upon by the parties, effective as [of] the date of this Agreement.

* * * *

Section 4. If an employee keeps his record clear of all violations of plant rules for a period of twelve months, such prior violations will not be considered when administering discipline in the event of a subsequent violation.

Section 5. Employees may be discharged when four (4) different rules have been violated within a twelve (12) month period.

Section 6. Reasonable rules of conduct are necessary for the orderly and efficient operation of any organization. It is mutually agreed that the plant rules are stated herein and the penalties as related to violations are necessary for the orderly and efficient operation of the plants; that the plant rules will not be used in capricious manner by the Company. Any infraction of these rules shall constitute just cause for the disciplinary action.

e) Violating and disregarding safety rules and common safety practices or contributing to unsanitary and unhealthy conditions:

f) Deliberate falsifying of production counts or other Company records:

g) Attendance will be tracked and disciplinary action given in accordance with the M-1 Absentee Point System as shown in the back of the contract book.

j) Failure to meet accepted work standards for quality or failure to perform work in a quantity commensurate with the ability of a normal employee to perform the work assigned:

k) Habitual failure to scan badge for time reporting purposes:

Decision

The Company alleged that the employment of the Grievant was terminated because, four or more different Plant Rules had been violated by the Grievant within a twelve month period. Specifically the Grievant violated Rule (k) on November 5, 1996; Plant Rule (f) on February 12, 1997; Plant Rule (g) on February 18, 1997; Plant Rule (j) on April 17, 1997 and Plant Rule (e) on June 23, 1997. In addition the Grievant also violated Plant Rule (g) on two other occasions, April 25, 1997 and April 30, 1997.

The Union has alleged that the Company has not met the just cause requirement for termination by merely stating that the Grievant had violated four Plant Rules within a twelve month period in that a greater explanation must be given to the Grievant and to the Union as to the specifics of the alleged Plant Rule violations. The Collective Bargaining Agreement provides that the Company may discharge an employee for legitimate reasons and the arbitrator is urged to apply the concept of just cause to determine if the reasons for discharge were legitimate.

The evidence presented at the hearing showed that the Grievant was originally hired on May 4, 1992 and after a short lay-off was returned to employment in March of 1996. The Grievant was terminated on June 26, 1997. From November 5, 1996 through June 24, 1997 the Grievant had been given discipline in the form of three written warnings, two one day disciplinary suspensions and one three day disciplinary suspension and then as a result of the Grievant not wearing his safety glasses in the plant on June 23, 1997 the Grievant was notified that he had violated Plant Rule (e) and such violation then triggered the termination on June 24, 1997.

The evidence presented at the hearing showed a series of documents setting forth each violation of the Plant Rules and the discipline imposed for each such violation. The evidence showed that as to each of the disciplines imposed upon the Grievant prior to June, 1997, that no grievance was filed concerning such discipline, therefore, in the opinion of the arbitrator, each of the disciplinary actions taken by the Company between November 5, 1996 and April 30, 1997 are deemed to be a proper notation upon the employment record of the Grievant.

There was no allegation made or evidence presented that the Company violated Section 2 of Article XXXII wherein it is provided that, in the event of discipline or discharge of an employee that the Union representative at interest was not notified within one (1) normal working day. From the evidence presented the arbitrator may conclude that the Grievant was made aware of each discipline imposed upon him and the Union was informed of such disciplinary action, so that both the Grievant and the Union knew of each Plant Rule violation and knew that four or more different Plant Rules had been violated by the Grievant from November 5, 1996 to June 23, 1997 all within less than one year.

On June 18, 1997, Grievance Number 230190 was filed on behalf of the Grievant alleging that the Company was using Plant Rules in a capricious manner plus discrimination against said employee; in addition on June 24, 1997, Grievance Number 231092 was filed on behalf of the Grievant alleging that the Company was saying T not wearing safety glasses. Neither of the two foregoing grievances filed on behalf of the Grievant are part of the case presented to the arbitrator in that the only grievance which is the subject matter of this case is the allegation that the Company unjustly terminated the Grievant, T, however, the Plant Rule violation documented on June 23, 1997, of Plant Rule (e) did result in the termination of the Grievant and the action of the Grievant which precipitated such discipline was failure to wear safety glasses.

Prior to June 23, 1997, the Grievant was observed by supervision as not wearing safety glasses on Monday, June 16, 1997 and on Tuesday, June 17, 1997; and on each occasion was instructed by each supervisor to "get his glasses on". The next observed violation of Plant Rule (e) on Monday, June 23, 1997 resulted in discipline for such violation and because such violation was four or more different Plant Rule violations within; one year, the employment of the Grievant was terminated.

Although the Grievant had given the Company cause to terminate for violation of Article XXXII, Section 5, on April 17, 1997 which was the occasion of the fourth violation of four different Plant Rules; the Company chose to keep the Grievant within their employment and it was not until June 24, 1997 that the Company terminated the Grievant for violating Company Plant Rule (e), which was triggered by the Company's allegation that the Grievant was not wearing safety glasses so that technically Grievance Number 230192 because it deals with a single incident which triggered the termination of the Grievant may also be reviewed by the arbitrator. The Grievant subjected himself to being disciplined for not wearing safety glasses on three occasions in close succession.

[1] The termination of the Grievant was not triggered by a violation of Plant Rule (e), on June 23, 1997, standing alone, but rather the Grievant was disciplined under such Plant Rule (e) because he had been observed not wearing safety glasses on June 23, 1997, June 17, 1997 and June 16, 1997; which in the opinion of the arbitrator shows a habitual disregard for such Plant Rule.

[2] The evidence showed that the Grievant had a great propensity for not wearing his safety glasses within the Plant in compliance with the requirements of the Company. The Union attempted to show that the rule requiring wearing safety glasses within the Plant is continually being violated by many employees of the Bargaining Unit. Several employees testified on behalf of the Grievant that they did not wear safety glasses nor did other employees wear safety glasses, so that in fact the Grievant was not acting any differently than all other employees.

The Company admitted that they had been lax in enforcing the safety glass requirement in the past, however, in several months prior to the time the Grievant was terminated without wearing the safety glasses the Company had been impressing upon the employees the need to wear safety glasses and to that extent the Grievant had been warned a number of times just prior to June 23, 1997 that he must wear his safety glasses and on June 23, 1997 when the Grievant was again observed not wearing the safety glasses and the Company concluded that the Grievant was incorrigible and that he was more of a detriment to the Company rather than a benefit and the decision was made to terminate the Grievant.

In the opinion of the arbitrator the Company has a duty to protect the eye sight of all of its employees, and of all visitors to the plant. The required wearing of safety glasses is the attempt of the Company to perform such duty. Each person entering the plant, employee or visitor should wear safety glasses for their own protection and also should an injury occur to an eye or eyes, that they would not be found to have contributed to the cause for the injury because they refused to wear safety glasses. For the Bargaining Unit employees the Union should stress the importance of wearing safety glasses.

[3] The Grievant is a short term employee therefore, in the opinion of the arbitrator, his length of service with the Company is not a mitigating factor in this case. In addition the fact that the Grievant violated five different plant rules shows that the Company tried to rehabilitate him and help him to become an acceptable employee. Further, when the Grievant violated Plant Rule (f), the Company opted to impose only a one day disciplinary suspension upon him whereas such Plant Rule (f) calls for discharge on the first violation of such rule. Taking into consideration all of the evidence presented at the hearing concerning the conduct of the Grievant in relation to following the plant rules set forth by the Company and the lenience of the Company to encourage the Grievant to establish a mode of conduct which would be acceptable, the arbitrator can find no mitigating circumstances which could be relied upon to reduce the disciplinary penalty of termination; accordingly then the arbitrator finds that the Company had a legitimate reason for terminating the Grievant, T.

AWARD

The Grievance filed by T concerning his termination of employment, is denied and such termination is upheld.

APPLICATION AND DISCUSSION QUESTIONS

1. What plant rule did the Grievant continuously violate? Was this rule alone enough to terminate him?

2. What more could the company have done to honor its duty to protect employees and visitors, especially if they were aware of so many employees violating the plant rules?

3. Do you agree with the Arbitrator's decision? If you think the employee should have been reinstated, why?

ONCOR ELEC. DELIVERY CO., LLC AND ELECTRICAL WORKERS IBEW

134 BNA LA 1264 (MOORE, 2015)[*]

Stipulated Issues

Whether there was just cause for the termination of the Grievant, and if not, what should be the remedy? If there is a remedy, should laches be considered? Should the arbitrator retain jurisdiction in case there is a dispute as to the remedy?

Background

The Company is a transmission and distribution operation that services about two-thirds of the State of Texas with electrical power. It manages and transports electrical

---

*   Reprinted with permission from Labor Relations Reporter- Labor Arbitration Reports. 134 BNA LA 1264. Copyright 2015 by the Bureau of National Affairs, Inc. (800-372-1033). http://www.bna.com.

energy from source generators to residential and business customers. The Company employs approximately 3,400 people.

The Grievant began work for the Company on September 19, 2005, as a meter reader and later enrolled in the Company apprenticeship program. The program consists of six steps culminating in the position of journeyman lineman. The Grievant was in his sixth level that qualified him to work without supervision.

Applicable Collective Bargaining Provisions (In part.)
ARTICLE II

Section 2, Paragraph (G)

"Functions of Management: Discharge employees for cause and lay off employees because of lack of work or for other reasons."

Paragraph (F) "Make reasonable rules and regulations governing the operation of its business and the conduct of its employees, and revise and modify such rules and regulations from time to time as conditions may require."

Applicable Safety Rules (In part.)

Section 107-Suitable Clothing:

A. Employees shall wear clothing suitable for the job being done and weather conditions.

C. Employees shall wear long sleeve flame resistant flame retardant or 100% Cotton shirts when contacting treated wood products or herbicides.

D. Electrical employees who work on energized lines and apparatus and/ or are exposed to flames or electric arcs shall wear clothing approved for the Hazard Class of the work to be performed.

Section 108-Work Gloves

Suitable work gloves shall be worn where there is a likelihood of hand injury.

Section 109 H.

Hard hats shall be worn in and around all areas where the potential of head injury exists.

Section 111 A

Employees shall wear appropriate protective footwear (except for employees working in offices) when working in areas where there is a danger of foot injuries due to falling or rolling objects.

Section 112 A

Safety glasses meeting ANSI Z87.1 Standards and approved by Business Unit Function Management, shall be worn when the wearing of a hard had is required.

Facts

On Saturday, October 6, 2012, the Grievant was called out after regular working hours to respond to an outage in one of the Company's electrical lines. He was being compensated at his double time rate of pay. The Grievant investigated the problem by inspecting the line and concluded that birds were causing one line to sag onto another line, which caused the outage. The Grievant relieved the problem by removing and replacing an overhead fuse box with an extension pole. The Grievant left the area and returned to his home changing from his work clothes into a jogging suit. While performing this task, on his first visit to the area, the Grievant testified that he was wearing the prescribed Personal Protective Equipment (PPE), which consists of steel-toed boots, fire-retardant jeans and shirt, hardhat, safety glasses, and leather gloves.

Thirty minutes later, he was called out again to the same location. Another crew was dispatched to the area to correct the sagging line which was at a point at a distant from the fuse. The Grievant returned to the location dressed in his jogging suit, with his Personal Protective Equipment (PPE) in his truck and did not change into his PPE. The Grievant inspected the line in his jogging suit without wearing any PPE. The Grievant waited in his truck until a crew arrived. It was the Grievant's responsibility to use an extension pole to close the overhead fuse. Which he did while wearing his jogging suit.

After performing his task, the Grievant walked back to where the crew was working on another pole. It was then that two journeymen/linemen noticed that the Grievant was not wearing any Personal Protective Equipment (PPE). They commented to the Grievant on his attire and reported the matter to their supervisor who was in the truck completing paper work.

The crew supervisor reported the matter to the Grievant's supervisor the following regular workday (Monday). The Grievant's supervisor reported the matter to the District Manager who commenced an investigation that involved several meetings that included interviewing the two journey/linemen, the Grievant, his Union Representative, the crew supervisor, and the Labor Relations Manager. The Grievant admitted that he did not wear his Personal Protective Equipment on his second trip to the call out.

Two months prior to the above-described incident, the Grievant drove a "bucket truck" into a tree while talking on his cell phone. He was placed on a Step 2 discipline, that was effective for 12 months and he was advised that future discipline could lead to further discipline, up to and including termination. No Grievance was filed regarding this discipline. The Company terminated the Grievant which is the reason for this arbitration hearing. A Grievance was timely filed by the Union on November 29, 2012. But, due to periphery litigation and scheduling conflicts the case was no heard until December 2, 2014.

Company's Position

The Company points out that safety is a top priority and all employees are trained to wear appropriate Personal Protective Equipment (PPE). The transmission and distribution of electricity is dangerous and proper precautions must be taken to protect employees. Employees are taught from the first day they come to work that they are to wear PPE. This is emphasized during weekly meetings. The Company further points out the Grievant acknowledged that he was trained to wear his PPE and that he had it available

The Company maintains that the Company policies and procedures require that appropriate clothing be worn when reporting to work. The appropriate PPE for closing a fuse require that the Grievant should have worn steel-toed boots, fire-retardant jeans, fire retardant shirt, hardhat, safety glasses and leather gloves. The Company points to the specific provisions contained in the Safety Handbook.

The Company argues that the conduct displayed by the Grievant warranted termination because it has shown during the hearing that the Grievant committed the act, that he knew of the consequences of his actions, and that the Company rules regarding PPE are reasonable. Further, the Company asserts that the Company conducted a prompt, fair and objective investigation to determine whether the Grievant had in fact failed to wear the required PPE to report to work when he closed the fuse. Also, the Company opines that violation of the Safety Rules in this situation warrants termination for the first-time offense.

Additionally, the Company disputes the Union's assertion that other employees were assessed lesser degrees of discipline. Disputing that, the Company points out that this was the Grievant's second violation of Safety Rules within a two-month period of time and the number of PPE items that the Grievant chose not to wear are distinguishing from other cases. The Company maintains that termination of the Grievant is warranted.

Union's Position

The Union argues that the punishment in this case did not fit the crime. It is pointed out that the Grievant may have made a mistake, but it was not blatant or flagrant. The Union asserts that the termination of the Grievant is based on serious misunderstanding of the facts, the Company's failure to consider management's and co-workers fault in the incident, the failure to adhere to progressive discipline and the failure to consider mitigating facts. The Grievant was merely performing a quick task.

Further, it is asserted that the Company does not have a zero tolerance policy for safety violations, pointing out that employees are not terminated for exceeding driving speed limits or even instances involving serious injuries. The Company has demonstrated disparate treatment between represented and non-represented employees.

The Union points to the Grievant's fine work record prior to his first discipline and his supervisors considered him as a great employee, who had a good attitude and worked hard.

The Union requests that the Grievant be reinstated with full back pay and benefits, including overtime he would have earned, plus interest thereon and any moving expenses the Grievant has incurred or incurs as result of the unjust termination and that no laches be applies.

Opinion

Electrical power serves humankind's needs and pleasures, but it is dangerous. As brought out by the witnesses' testimony during the hearing there are more than 1500 rules contained in the Company's Safety Rules. When disciplining an employee for a violation of one or more safety rules the rule(s) must be reasonable and clearly conveyed to the employee. The Company has the burden of proof to show that the employee committed the violation and there were no mitigating circumstances warranting the violation. In contrast, an employee may refuse to carry out a direction of a supervisor if the employee believes that the order is dangerous or violates a safety rule.

The Grievant showed up at the worksite wearing jogging trousers and tennis shoes. This was the second time that evening he had been at the work site. On the first occasion, he was wearing his Personal Protective Equipment (PPE), which consisted of the required hardhat, glasses, gloves, cotton shirt and trousers, and steel-toed shoes. These are reasonable and practical items required by the Company Safety Rules. The Grievant acknowledged and demonstrated that he knew of the Safety Rules pertaining to the wearing of PPE for the task he was performing. On both occasions he was required to close in a fuse, which required that he manipulate a heavy object over head on the end of an extension pole. By his own admission, and the testimony of two fellow employees he was observed on the second occasion, performing the job without any Personal Protective Equipment (PPE), although he had the PPE readily available in his truck.

The Grievant's actions of not wearing his PPE occurred merely two months into a one-year probation for another safety violation involving talking on a cell phone while backing up the truck he was driving, which resulted in damage to the bucket truck. After that occasion, the Grievant acknowledged that any other violation of Company Rules could lead to termination. (Company Exhibit No. 1) The Company's action in this case is not an example of zero tolerance for violation of Safety Rules.

The Union argues on behalf of the Grievant that there was no progressive discipline shown the Grievant. Absent a specific provision in the Collective Bargaining Agreement, flagrant violations of reasonable and practical Safety Rules do not warrant progressive discipline. The Safety Rules are in place to protect the employee, other employees, the public and the Company. Once an employee commits a flagrant violation, without mitigating circumstances, as the Grievant has done in this case, progressive discipline is not warranted.

The Union also argues on behalf of the Grievant that other employees were not terminated for violations of Safety Rules. Those instances reflect that those cases were not of the severity of the Grievant's actions. The Grievant was terminated for deliberate violation of simple standard and practical Safety Rules. His good behavior of admitting his conduct and over all good work did not give him a license to violate Safety Rules. Further, the Grievant's conduct was investigated and reviewed by a committee and was not merely the decision of one person.

*　*　*　*

AWARD

The Grievance is denied.

APPLICATION AND DISCUSSION QUESTIONS

1. Was there sufficient evidence that the Grievant was aware of the safety rules he violated? Was the safety rule reasonable? Should arbitrators evaluate employers' rules to determine if they are reasonable?

2. Do you agree with the Union that termination was too severe and progressive discipline would have been more appropriate? What about management's rights to implement safety rules and policies?

3. How could the Employer have acted differently in handling the Grievant's policy violation?

THE PROBLEM OF SAFETY OF EMPLOYEES AND THE PUBLIC

A city employee, while working as a bus driver, has pled guilty to aggravated criminal sexual abuse, which is a felony. As a result of the conviction, the bus driver is sentenced to four years' probation, during which he cannot be in the presence of minors without another adult being present. The driver never intended to disclose this information to the city, but has recently been suspended and ultimately discharged after the city anonymously received a copy of his sex offender registration page. Although there is a policy to protect the safety of the public, the city transportation authority does not have a policy that a conviction for a felony automatically results in discharge. The union has just filed a grievance challenging the driver's discharge.

How Should the Arbitrator Rule?

I. SCHEDULES AND TELEWORK

KEYSTONE STEEL & WIRE AND INDEPENDENT STEEL ALLIANCE
954 (M. SUARDI, 2013)[*]

* * * *

The arbitration pertains to a July 26, 2009, grievance involving the scheduling of work in the Company's Fabric Department. The "Statement of Grievance" as set forth on the grievance form is as follows:

Fabric Committee grieves on behalf of Fabric Department that the management in implementing new sign-up procedures violates seniority of employees who are forced to work by allowing younger employees to volunteer to work, and placing them ahead of senior employees, who are being forced to work. When the parties were unable to amicably resolve the grievance, it proceeded to arbitration before the undersigned Arbitrator.

Background

The Company is a manufacturer of steel products with a facility in Peoria, Illinois, The Union represents various employees at the facility, including production and maintenance employees. Under the Agreement, seniority covers various aspects of work and the assignment thereof. Notably, the assignment of work on a sixth (6th) day or when overtime pay is involved is offered to employees with the most departmental seniority (experience and ability being reasonably equal), except in emergency situations (covered elsewhere) and where written rules or past practice agreements to the contrary are in effect. Article XIV, Section 14.1.

The Fabric Department manufactures specialty wire products. It also maintains "Fabric Department Rules" (the "Rules"). The cited Rules carry a date of June 22, 1998. Rule No. 15 and Rule No. 21 state as follows:

---

15. Fabric bids, rules, seniority, working conditions, installation of new or changed jobs or equipment and practices are protected under the provisions of the May 3, 1996 or the Labor Agreement currently in effect.

21. Scheduled overtime (e.g. sixth day or Sunday) will be filled from a sign-up sheet based on seniority and qualification.

    Insofar as practical, a sign-up sheet for Saturday and Sunday overtime will be posted on or before Wednesday at 1:00 p.m. It is each individual's responsibility to indicate on the sign-up sheet his/her desire to work on Saturday and/or Sunday. The job and shift priority will be indicated. The sign-up sheet will be removed Friday, at or around 9:00 a.m.

Openings created by operational changes made after Friday, 9:00 a.m., will be filled by seniority and bid. The Company will make a reasonable attempt to notify each individual in the department of any schedule changes after the sign-up sheet has been posted.

As indicated in Rule No. 21, scheduled overtime on a sixth day or on a Sunday is scheduled through use of a sign-up sheet based on seniority and qualification. In situations where an insufficient number of employees sign up for work, the Company can require mandatory overtime. These mandatory assignments ("forced overtime") go in reverse order of seniority (i.e. "the youngest qualified employee(s) in seniority shall be required to do the work"). Article VIII, Section 8.01. To the extent problems occur with forced overtime, the parties have adopted Memorandum of Understanding #14 (MOU) which states as follows:

> In a department where there is a problem with forced overtime, the Seniority Committee, Department Committee, and Management will work out a workable solution for that department. However, if a solution cannot be made, they will follow paragraph 8.01 of the Contract.

A typical sign up sheet for Sunday overtime was presented at the hearing. The sheet includes columns for an employee's number, name, whether overtime was desired, desired jobs (by number) and whether a double shift was acceptable. The sheet also includes a circled "F" in the case of employees who would work "if forced."

    Prior to the current Agreement, employees could not be forced to work Sunday overtime. Now they can be forced. On July 21, 2009, the Company posted a notice announcing changes to the filling of scheduled weekend overtime. The Notice states as follows:

> NOTICE 7/21/09
> Changes have been made on the filling of scheduled weekend overtime. They are as follows:
>
> 1) Volunteers will first be placed on the schedule according to bid preference. Forced employees will fill open positions only. No bumping will occur. You will still be allowed to put an "F" for "If Forced" and a bid preference, but that bid will only apply to open positions.
>
> 2) 7 day work will not be allowed. This applies to both forced or voluntarily.
>
> 3) There will be one sign up sheet for both Sat. and Sun. since it will all be the 6th day work.
>
> Thank you,
> Jeff Klokkenga

Union testimony at the hearing indicated that the prospect of scheduling employees seven (7) days per week generated a protest based on state law prohibiting the same. The upshot of the protest was that seven (7) day scheduling did not occur (as the Notice indicates). However, Union witness Martindale stated that some Union members believed the protest prompted the Company change in "if forced" scheduling. Company witness Klokkenga denied that the scheduling change was prompted due to the protest.

Much of the remaining testimony at the hearing concerned the origins of the "if forced" sign-up procedure, which side originally suggested it (Company or Union), the efficiency and inefficiency of scheduling work under the prior system, the nature of emergency assignments and whether mandatory overtime on Sunday ever occurred prior to the "if forced" procedure. There was also testimony and a demonstration as to the time needed to schedule and re-work the overtime schedule under the "if forced" policy.

Issue

The parties submitted differing statements of the issue presented in the case. The Arbitrator frames the issue as follows:

Is the Company's July 21, 2009, notice regarding scheduled weekend overtime enforceable? If not, what shall the remedy be?

Cited Contract Provisions (Omitted)

Union Contentions

The seniority provisions of Section 6.41 of the Agreement are clear. Seniority controls the assignment of Sunday overtime absent written rules or past practice agreements to the contrary. The past practice at issue supports the Union's position, and there is no past practice or written rule to the contrary to override seniority.

The disputed past practice meets all the criteria of a binding practice. Most importantly, the parties mutually agreed to adopt the forced Sunday overtime scheduling procedure in 2002 or 2003. Thereafter, Management consistently prepared a Sunday overtime schedule pursuant to the Agreement. There were no objections voiced to the procedure and no grievances filed. Neither was there any mention of changing the procedure when the parties discussed the new collective bargaining agreement and related Fabric Department Rules.

The assignment procedure which the Union wants reinstated was clear, and it was applied consistently. There is no ambiguity or inconsistency in the practice, and it is of long duration. Equally important, the Sunday overtime scheduling procedure does not conflict with any language in the Agreement. It merely fills a gap insofar as there is no express language on the topic.

Even the Company admits that the second paragraph of Fabric Department Rule No. 21 controls the situation. There, employees are allowed to express their desire to work on Saturday and/or Sunday. How individual employees indicate their desire is left unstated. Accordingly, while employees may simply write a 'yes or no,' it is equally reasonable to assume—as the practice had been applied—that employees could state a desire to work, not work, or to work certain jobs, if forced. To this extent, both of the above-described Sunday scheduling methods comply with Rule No. 21, and both allow for seniority to control.

Had the Company desired to change the procedure allowing employees to exercise seniority if forced to work Sunday overtime, the proper place to discuss the matter would have been during contract negotiations, not through unilateral mid-term action. Further, mere convenience is not a proper ground to repudiate a binding past practice.

The right of senior employees to select overtime assignments should be honored. The past practice at issue recognized this principle, and it filled a gap in the Agreement by allowing senior employees to exercise seniority when forced on Sunday overtime. By contrast, if the Company's position is sustained, it would require forfeiture of the recognized seniority rights of senior employees in some circumstances.

The grievance should be sustained. The previous Sunday overtime scheduling procedure should be reinstated on a interpretive, prospective-only basis.

Company Contentions

The management rights provisions of Section 2.3 of the Agreement are clear. The Company has the exclusive right to cease utilizing a past practice if the past practice is not covered by the Agreement. The Arbitrator must apply the clear and unambiguous language found in Section 2.3, as written.

The discretionary authority set forth in Section 2.3 allowed the Company to switch back to the two-step method provided for in Fabric Department Rule No. 21. Further, the Union's witness admitted that Rule No. 21 does not permit employees who do not wish to work weekend overtime to designate a preferred position if they are forced to work. Absent a designated third "if forced" category, the Company's two-step procedure for scheduling sixth day overtime complies with Rule No. 21. As such, the current two-step procedure is "covered by" the Agreement, and it can be properly applied by the Company.

The disputed "if forced" method of scheduling weekend overtime did not amount to a binding past practice. There was no mutual commitment by both sides to establish the procedure as a practice, only an agreement to try the procedure. For this reason, whatever practice may have arisen was merely a present way of doing things, not a prescribed way.

Both sides recognized that the trial period of the "if forced" system would not create a binding past practice. Accordingly, when the trial became problematic, the Company exercised its right to reinstate the two-step procedure described in Rule No. 21.

Even if the "if forced" method was a past practice, the Company had a right to change back to the two-step method. On this point, Section 2.3 of the Agreement allows the Company to take "reasonable steps to improve the efficiency and economy of its operation...." Here, even the Union agrees that the most efficient method of scheduling would be to force the fewest number of employees and, as shown at the hearing, the Union's method actually increased the number of forced employees. Finally, there are absolutely no facts or evidence to support a Union theory that the Company's decision to switch back to the two-step method was retaliatory.

The grievance should be denied.

Discussion

The Arbitrator's role in this matter is to determine the parties' common intentions with respect to the assignment of weekend overtime on a scheduled sixth day of work. So far as appears, the physical aspects of the sign-up process (i.e. when the list is posted, how names are entered, when it is taken down and when assignments are announced) are not at issue. Rather, the grievance turns on how those who sign up are selected and what role seniority plays in the selection process when forced overtime is involved.

* * * *

Without doubt, the Company maintains exclusive authority over operations. But such authority is subject to a companion duty to "abide by and comply with the provisions of this Agreement." Article II, Section 2.0. Among the other provisions of the Agreement is Section 2.3.

In Section 2.3, the parties concede the impracticality of listing all past practices recognized as established conditions of employment. Section 2.3 goes on to permit Management the right to change or eliminate past practices in effect and not covered by the Agreement, subject to an employee's right to grieve. Here, Management asserts that the two-step process for scheduling weekend overtime is "covered by" the Agreement through the Fabric Department rules. The desired inference is that elimination of the "if forced" method of scheduling—a matter not covered by the Agreement—could be accomplished within its exclusive discretion. The Arbitrator disagrees with this argument.

For one thing, the elimination of past practices "not covered by the Agreement" is conditional. Under Section 2.3, an affected employee may file a grievance with respect to such elimination. In fact, unlike many agreements Section 2.3 goes into great detail explaining *how* a grievance can be initiated and subsequently processed. Any fair reading of the criteria set forth in Section 2.3 requires an aggrieved employee to establish the existence of a past practice as a condition of employment, at which point Management is required to justify the change it has made. Thereafter,

Section 2.3 admittedly states that Management may take reasonable steps to improve efficiency and economy. But this right, too, is qualified by language indicating that whatever action Management takes cannot work an undue hardship on employees.

As for the Union's proof of a past practice regarding use of the "if forced" overtime schedule, it matters little—to the Arbitrator at least—who may have proposed the initiative. The point here is that there *was* an agreement to use the "if forced" procedure and, crediting Mr. Martindale, "it worked very well." To this extent, the agreed-upon "if forced" procedure amounted to a "workable solution" for purposes of MOU #14. Also, there is virtually no dispute that the "if forced" sign-up procedure was consistently applied over a period of some six (6) years, all without complaint (as noted above). From this, the Arbitrator concludes that the Union established a past practice amounting to a condition of employment, thus shifting the burden to Management to justify its action in eliminating it.

* * * *

AWARD

The grievance is sustained. The "if forced" method of scheduling weekend overtime shall be reinstated in the Fabric Department on a prospective basis.

APPLICATION AND DISCUSSION QUESTIONS

1. What evidence did the Union present to establish a past practice of how overtime is scheduled?

2. As discussed earlier, a past practice may be used to fill-in a gap in the Collective Bargaining agreement. How was this principle applied in this grievance?

THE PROBLEM OF SHIFT CHANGES

The town provides firefighter services twenty-four hours per day, seven days per week to protect the community and therefore requires a shift of firefighters to be on duty at all times. Article X of the agreement specifically says that the schedule of working firefighters will average forty-two hours per week with consecutive two ten-hour day shifts and two fourteen-hour night shifts. The union has recently proposed a new schedule that would have the firefighters working two twenty-four hour shifts with two days in between. This new schedule would not change the number of hours each firefighter would work or the assignments. The town is opposing this change, because it believes this to be an issue outside of the collective bargaining agreement.

How Should the Arbitrator Rule?

J. OFF-DUTY CONDUCT

idea

Public and Private employers have policies and work rules which place limitations on employee's off-duty conduct. The typical issues involve life-styles, criminal activities, domestic abuse, and drug use.In unionized organizations, an employee may file a grievance if they receive a disciplinary action because of off-duty misconduct.

procedure

Arbitrators will normally review the policy to determine whether the policy is reasonable. If the policy is reasonable, the arbitrator will normally explore whether the employee's off-duty conduct or behavior negatively impacts the employee's performance. The arbitrator may also explore whether the employe's conduct sheds a negative image on the employer's image or reputation. For public sector employees, their right of privacy may raise constitutional issues, especially First Amendmnet rights. The Arbitrator will balance the interest of the employe's to engage in off-duty conduct and the government need to regulate off-duty conduct.There must be a clear link between the employee's conduct and their job with the employer.

In determining whether reinstatement is an approach remedy, arbitrators will consider whether it will damage the employers reputation, the impact of co-workers and the ability of the terminated employee to perform their duties with a record of off-duty conduct.

Case

*vehicular
assault by
city ee*

Introduction

Issues

Upon review of the separate issue statements submitted by the parties, the arbitrator formulates the issues for arbitration as follows:

1. Are the grievances arbitrable?
2. If so, did the City have just cause to suspend and terminate G?
3. If not, what is the appropriate remedy?

Qs

Facts

G was hired by the City of Seldovia in October 2007 to work in facilities maintenance. His job duties included building maintenance, snow removal, road grading work, harbor maintenance, street sweeping, and maintenance of water and sewer lines. His normal work hours were Monday through Friday from 8 a.m. to 5 p.m. Prior to the events leading to his suspension and termination, he had not received any disciplinary action from the City.

record

In 2012 G became engaged to his fiancée W, who he had known for about 30 years and had been dating for several years. On the evening of January 21, 2013, after work hours, G and W went to a local establishment to celebrate W's rental of a new home for herself and her three children. During the course of the evening G and W got into a verbal argument and W asked to G to take her home in his truck. Because W's house was at the bottom of a steep hill and road conditions were slippery, W told G to let her out at the top of the hill, which he did. As W walked in front of the truck to go down to her house, G attempted to back out but his vehicle, which had experienced mechanical issues in the past, suddenly lurched forward, hit W and knocked her to the ground. W's children came running out of the house and one of them called 911. G stayed with W at the scene until the ambulance arrived and took her to the clinic. At the same time, a Seldovia police officer arrived at the scene and took G into custody to test him for driving under the influence. After the test, however, G was not

harm

* Reprinted with permission from *Labor Relations Reporter- Labor Arbitration Reports.* 133 BNA LA 1593. Copyright 2015 by the Bureau of National Affairs, Inc. (800-372-1033). http://www.bna.com.

accident arrested or charged with DUI and was released. At arbitration, both G and W testified they believed the incident was an accident and was not intentional.

The next day G went to work as usual. At the end of his work day, he was called to the police station where an Alaska state trooper was there to investigate the previ-*arrested* ous evening's incident. As a result of the investigation G was arrested, charged with felony assault, and was incarcerated. On January 24, 2013, after appearing in court, G was released upon posting a $500 bond. The court's release order included a number of conditions, one of which was that G not have any contact directly or indirectly with W. At arbitration W testified that she did not want to press charges against G and did not ask for a "no contact" order, but the court nevertheless imposed the no-contact order.

suspended On January 27, 2013, City Manager Tim Dillon suspended G's employment without pay until the pending criminal assault case against him was resolved. Dillon's suspension memorandum stated that the reasons for G's suspension were (1) the charges in the criminal case, and (2) Dillon's belief that G had been operating municipal vehicles without valid licenses. The memorandum further warned G that if he violated any of the conditions in the court's order of release, his employment would be terminated immediately. G signed for receipt of the suspension memorandum.

City Manager Dillon notified the Union's business representative, Pam Cline, of G's suspension. On February 5, 2013, Cline filed a Union grievance on behalf of G. The grievance asserted that G's conduct took place while he was off duty; that he had not violated any City work rules, regulations or policies; and that he should be reinstated to his job with back pay and benefits.

In a memorandum to G dated February 26, 2013, Dillon stated that due to a delay in the criminal proceedings on G's assault charge until April 2013, the City would return him to work effective February 27, conditioned on his compliance with the CBA and the terms of the court's release order. A copy of the memorandum was sent *suspension lifted* to Union representative Cline. G returned to work on February 27 and resumed his usual job duties.

G and W, who were still engaged, both wanted the court's no-contact order against G to be lifted so they could communicate and spend time with each other. On July 9, 2013, G's attorney filed a motion to modify the court's conditions of release to have *no-contact removed* the no-contact order removed. Both G and W testified that they spoke to the attorney and came away with the understanding that the no-contact order had been removed and they were now free to see each other. A few days later, G and W made plans to go camping and fishing together. On the evening of July 19, as they rode out of town on G's four-wheeler, they were stopped by a Seldovia police officer who said he was *pulled over* going to arrest G for violating the no-contact order in his conditions of release. G responded that the no-contact order had been lifted, and the officer then called G's attorney who confirmed that papers had been filed with the court to remove the no-contact order. The officer permitted G and W to continue on their planned excursion, but warned G that he might be arrested upon his return if he was found to be in violation of the court's order of release. During the following week the officer contacted the prosecutor in G's criminal case who advised that a motion had been filed to remove the no-contact order but the court had not yet acted on the motion, whereupon the officer arrested G for violating the court order. After a brief incarceration, G was released and went back to work on or about August 1.

[margin note: arrested & released]

On September 6, 2013, City Manager Dillon, having learned of G's second arrest, notified him in writing that he was suspended from work without pay for violating the court's order of release. Dillon's memorandum further stated that it was the City's intent to terminate G's employment unless he showed cause by September 9 why he

[margin note: suspended]

should not be terminated. A copy of the City's notice was sent to Union representative Cline. In a letter of response on G's behalf dated September 9, Cline noted that G had only been charged with, not convicted of, violating the terms of the court's release order. Cline also reiterated that the issues in G's criminal case related to off-duty conduct and were totally unrelated to work. Cline asserted that G should not be suspended or terminated, and that the City should return him to his job and make him whole.

In a memorandum dated September 9, Dillon informed G that he was still suspended but that the City would hold in abeyance its decision to terminate his employment "until we learn of the results of the current legal proceedings against you and further investigate other possible violations of the January 27, 2013 memorandum concerning suspension of your employment." On September 17 the Union filed a second grievance on behalf of G, asserting that an "indefinite suspension is unreasonable and extremely punitive considering the multitude of unsubstantiated concerns and actions surrounding this dispute, as well as the untimeliness of the suspension/pending termination." Over the ensuing weeks, Dillon and Cline continued to communicate regarding the status of G's criminal case and the two Union grievances. Among other things, they agreed to suspend processing of the grievances until the end of November.

On December 6, 2013, as part of a plea agreement, the prosecutor dismissed the felony assault charge against G and G pled guilty to the misdemeanor charge of violating the no-contact order in his January 2013 conditions of release. He was sentenced to 90 days in jail with 70 days suspended.

[margin note: legal proceeding]

On December 20, 2013, upon confirming G's conviction for violating the conditions of his release, the City terminated G's employment, retroactively effective to September 6, 2013.

[margin note: terminate]

* * * *

Discussion

(A. Arbitrability Omitted)

B. Just Cause for Suspension and Termination

Article 1.10 of the CBA authorizes the City to "[t]ake disciplinary action, including termination for just cause [.]" Likewise, Article 7.6 provides: "No Employee will be discharged except for cause." Article 4.6 sets forth the grounds for disciplinary action in relevant part as follows:

> City Employees are expected to conduct themselves in a manner befitting the public service in which they are employed. Grounds for disciplinary action, up to and including discharge, include, but are not limited to the following:

> (k) Proof or conviction of a misdemeanor or felony crime when such social misconduct will have a demonstrably adverse effect upon the ability of the City to perform its functions in relations with the public or its employees.

The City argues that it could discipline G for misconduct, including misconduct while not on duty; that the City Manager's suspension memorandum of 1/27/13 clearly indicated the misconduct for which G could be disciplined, namely any violation of his court-ordered conditions of release; and that G clearly engaged in the misconduct for which he had been advised his employment would be terminated. The Union responds that the City did not have just cause to suspend or terminate G; that G's alleged offenses occurred off duty and had no nexus to the employer; that the City's investigation did not produce substantial evidence or proof that G committed all the offenses it listed as the reasons for his discipline; that the City's investigation was not conducted fairly and objectively; and that the degree of discipline imposed was not reasonably related to the seriousness of G's alleged offenses and his employment record with the City.

* * * *

Under well-established principles developed by arbitrators in collective bargaining arbitration, the general rule is that an employer cannot discipline an employee for off-duty conduct unless there is a "nexus" or connection between the off-duty conduct and the employer's legitimate business interests. The employer may demonstrate such a nexus in several ways: (1) conduct involving harm or threats to supervisors, co-workers, customers, or others with an actual or potential business relationship with the employer; (2) conduct that could seriously damage an employer's public image; (3) conduct that reasonably makes it difficult or impossible for supervisors, co-workers, customers, or others with an actual or potential business relationship with the employer to deal with the employee; or (4) public attacks by the employee on the employer, supervisors, or the employer's product. The connection between the off-duty misconduct and the injurious effect on the employer's business must be reasonable and discernible and not merely speculative. In cases where an employee is arrested or charged with a crime for off-duty conduct, a leading treatise states:

> The general rule followed by arbitrators is that an employer has just cause to suspend an employee for off-duty conduct that leads to an arrest, and to convert the suspension to discharge following the employee's conviction, where the employer has made its own good faith investigation into the alleged misconduct, the charge gives rise to a legitimate concern for the safety of employees or property, and the employer determines that the misconduct disqualifies the employee from directly rendering his or her services, impairs his or her usefulness to the employer, or is likely to have an adverse effect on the employer's business.

Applying the terms of the CBA and the foregoing arbitral principles to the facts of this case, I conclude that the City has failed to demonstrate any nexus between G's off-duty conduct and the City's legitimate business interests. It is undisputed that the conduct for which G was disciplined took place after business hours and away from the workplace. As to the alleged vehicular assault in January 2013, the criminal charges against G were ultimately dismissed by the prosecutor. As to G's subsequent arrest in July 2013 for violating the no-contact order in his conditions of release, G pled guilty to a single misdemeanor charge even though both he and his fiancée were under the mistaken impression from his attorney that the no-contact order had been removed. The City admittedly did not do its own investigation of either incident but simply relied on the criminal charges against him and the subsequent proceedings in court.

Moreover, the City made no showing, as required by Article 4.6 (k) of the CBA, that G's off-duty arrests or misdemeanor conviction had any "adverse effect upon the ability of the City to perform its functions in relations with the public or its employees." There was no evidence of any harm or threats to any supervisors, co-workers or others doing business with the City. There was no evidence that G's off-duty conduct made it difficult or impossible for him to perform his maintenance job or deal with supervisors, co-workers or members of the public. Nor was there any evidence that his off-duty conduct received any publicity or otherwise damaged the City's reputation or public image. City Manager Dillon further acknowledged that G's off-duty conduct did not cause any financial harm to the City. In short, the City failed to prove that it had any grounds for disciplinary action against G under Article 4.6 of the CBA or any of the recognized exceptions to the general rule that an employee may not be disciplined for off-duty conduct. Therefore the City did not have just cause to suspend, terminate or otherwise discipline G for either incident of alleged off-duty misconduct in 2013.

AWARD

Sustained The grievances are sustained. The City of Seldovia did not have just cause to suspend or terminate the employment of G for alleged off-duty misconduct. As a remedy, the City shall reinstate G to his former position and shall make him whole for lost wages and benefits, less any interim earnings. The arbitrator retains jurisdiction for 60 days in the event of any dispute regarding the remedy or the implementation of this award.

In accordance with the grievance procedure, the City is designated as the losing party and shall be responsible for payment of the arbitrator's fees and expenses.

APPLICATION AND DISCUSSION QUESTIONS

1. Were the standards of conduct ambiguous, especially the terms "common sense" and "values"? Are the terms sufficiently clear to give adequate notice to employees regarding the limits of off-duty conduct?

2. What is the "nexus requirement" to determine if an employer has just cause for disciplinary action based on an employee's off-duty conduct?

3. Why did the employer fail to establish just cause for the discharge?

4. Would the result have been different if the grievant was a police officer for the city? What if the grievant was a 911 Emergency Operator?

*case
firefighter
rapper*

Issue

Did the City of Philadelphia have just cause for the suspension and dismissal of J Q Firefighter J; if not, what shall the remedy be?

Background

This matter presents for review as the result of the following facts and circumstances, *facts* many of which are undisputed:

1) The Grievant began his musical activities as a "rapper" while attending high school; while a teenager he was signed to a recording contract with Rough Rider Recordings, an entertainment entity specializing in the production and marketing of "hard core" rap music-he adopted A as his nom de plume.

2) Before becoming a firefighter in May of 2003 the Grievant's contractual relationship with Rough Rider terminated and he established his own company, Larsiny Records, and A continued to produce and perform rap music much of which was "hard core"; it dealt with violent street scenes and language.

3) The Fire Department became aware of the Grievant's musical talent and at some point in the summer of 2005 he was approached about the possibility of utilizing that talent to produce musical material supporting the Department's fire prevention program. That resulted in his creation of a rap music video entitled "Take it Outside"; the video was used in the City's fire prevention program and widely distributed out side of Philadelphia.

4) In the conversations between the Grievant and the Fire Commissioner concerning "Take it Outside" it was observed that the Grievant had

* Reprinted with permission from *Labor Relations Reporter- Labor Arbitration Reports.* 127 BNA LA 1384. Copyright 2015 by the Bureau of National Affairs, Inc. (800-372-1033). http://www.bna.com.

not complied with the Departmental regulation requiring prior approval for outside employment-his activities with Larsiny Records. When informed of his non-compliance he requested approval, and on November 1, 2005 his request for outside employment with Larsiny Records was approved.

* * * *

6) On or about April 13, 2007 broadcast and print media began to exploit comparisons of the Grievant and talk show host Don Imus; according to the record that comparison first arose on "Dome Lights", a cyberspace bulletin board where public safety personnel may anonymously post comments regarding current and past events. We are told Dome Light posts asked if Imus was taken off the air because of his racially provocative remarks about African American female college basketball players, why the Grievant should not be fired when his Sin City CD rapped about "... turning pigs into bacon bits", by luring police into a building set to explode into flames.

issue

* * * *

9) In response to the media storm following initial publication of the Sin City extract dealing with police in a burning building, the Fire Department reassigned the Grievant to a location where the media was unlikely to confront him, lessening the prospect of fire service interruptions by picketing off-duty police, and the crowds occasioned by media frenzy. Days after the interview and the reassignment, on April 18th, pursuant to Law Department advice, the Fire Department instructed the Grievant to "... cease any business activity with his outside music endeavors until the investigation was completed"; he complied. On April 23rd the Grievant met with the Department's Special Investigations Officer, and others, accompanied by Union representation. At that meeting he was advised that the Commissioner might permanently revoke approval for his outside employment, suspended on April 18th, as well a s imposing some discipline.

reassigned

investigation

further

* * * *

11) On May 14, 2007 the Grievant was mailed a "NOTICE OF DISMISSAL"; *dismissed* that document Charges the Grievant with "Conduct Unbecoming A Member, Neglect of Duty, Disobedience of Orders, Violation of the Mayor's Statement of Policy and Civil Service Regulations". Appendix A is the full text of the Specifications accompanying those Charges. Firefighters Local 22 filed a grievance asserting that "The 30 day suspension and dismissal of FF J was unjust and unfair". The parties' inability to resolve that dispute led to the selection of this arbitrator.

Positions of the Parties

City of Philadelphia

We are told this dismissal must be upheld because the Grievant's Sin City song: *ER arg*

> "... advocating violence against police created a public outcry, brought disrespect upon the Fire Department, and negatively impacted the Department's relationship with the Police Department."

Furthermore, when offered at least three opportunities to quell the storm he created, by fulfilling his promise to write an apology to the FOP, and promising to desist from performing and/or writing similar songs in the future, he refused. This Grievance must be denied in its entirety.

Union

The Grievant was fired for artistic activities undertaken while off-duty, when he utilized his stage name A; nothing in Sin City identifies the performer as J, the Firefighter. *U arg*

> "The City's failure to distinguish between advocating for violence and acting out a role as an artistic character led it to wrongly conclude that FF J advocates violence against the police."

Additionally, the Union argues that the City dismissed the Grievant in contravention of his First Amendment rights to freedom of speech; that a disciplinary action in violation of the law is, ipso facto, without just cause. In support of that proposition the Union cited decisions the U.S. Supreme Court, U.S. Circuit Courts of Appeal, and several arbitrators. We are told the City has not borne its burden of proving the *1st amend*

Grievant did something wrong, when he performed as an artist; this Grievance must be sustained with a make whole remedy.

Discussion and Analysis

* * * *

The Charges

issue here

Appendix A. to this Opinion and Award contains the Charges and Specifications that are the City's basis for the Grievant's dismissal. I find that "Violation #5 Civil Service Regulations" addresses the gravamen of this matter because it deals with "Outside Employment", and the Grievant's 2005 off-duty performance as a rap singer is really what this ease is about; that, and his refusal of the City's demand that he cut all ties to the record company he created before becoming a firefighter.

That being so, the numerous City exhibits showing the media's exploitation of the Fire Department's belated discovery of the Sin City CD tend more toward inflammation and prejudice than probative value.

Nexus

city rules

[1] The City has the reserved management right to make and enforce rules governing what work an employee may engage in off-duty, however, those rules must be reasonable and reasonably enforced-an essential characteristic is that they must be designed to assure the affected employee's physical, mental and ethical capacity to effectively perform their primary City job: that is the principal element in the nexus, the connection, between the jobs.

here

The best evidence that the Grievant's production of Sin City-where the objectionable language lasts approximately 5 seconds-did not intrinsically affect his ability as a firefighter is his continued performance of those duties, without incident, for approximately 18 months after the Sin City CD was produced. Similarly, the City produced no evidence that other firefighters or police officers are reluctant to work with the Grievant, in that connection we have the following testimony: (omitted)

The preceding sworn testimony shows the only nexus the City has proven between the Grievant's outside employment-producing and performing hard-core rap music-and its interests, is the avoidance of negative reactions from those who do not like his music. Whether it is traditional work, or "work" involving "speech", enforceable employer attempts to curtail that off-duty conduct must prove the presence of nexus, and the absence of intrusion into areas protected by the First Amendment to the United States Constitution.

First Amendment

Among the numerous cases cited by the parties in support of their arguments, the one that provides the best guidance for our consideration of the "free-speech" element in this matter is *Berger v. Battaglia.* That case involved a white police officer performing in the persona of Al Jolson, as follows:

precedent

> "The employee, while an officer with the department, performed a musical act off-duty, which included an impersonation using blackface makeup.
>
> After being disciplined once, he did not receive money for his act, nor did he hold himself out as an "officer. After some members of a minority group took offense to the act, the department ordered the employee to cease public performances wearing the makeup. The department also denied permission to perform for pay, allegedly for disciplinary reasons for past performances. The district court found that the department's interests concerning the threat of future disruptions of racial harmony outweighed the employee's artistic rights. The (Appeals court) held that the performance in blackface was constitutionally protected speech and the department was not justified in taking disciplinary action for the employee's performance or in any way chilling his continuation of the conduct. The only threat of disruption was to external operations, and the threat was not caused by the employee's conduct, *but was a threatened reaction by those offended by the performance.* Therefore, the district court erred ..." (Emphasis added)

The similarities in that case and ours are inescapable; and as the Union argues, the demonstrations and disruptions feared by the Fire Department never occurred, and while some overtime costs arose as the result of the Grievant's reassignment, that cost was dwarfed by the expense associated with reassigning tactical crowd control personnel in the ease cited above-yet there the performing artist's First Amendment rights were confirmed.

here

Conclusions

This case is about the Department's over-reaction to the belated discovery that the Grievant, someone the Commissioner says was held out as a Departmental "spokesperson" for rapping in Take it Outside, also performed darker art. That discovery resulted in the overly broad "indictments" shown in Appendix A, as well as the over-reaching demand that he not only cease performing and producing arguably inflammatory rap music, but that he essentially dissolve Larsiny Records, the corporate entity he had created before becoming a fighter.

A at fault too

However, the Fire Department does not hold a monopoly on unreasonable reactions in this matter; the Grievant had alternatives he did utilize: Rather than his piqued refusal to tender a written FOP apology, he could have done so, despite what he perceived as Eddis' bad faith.

Similarly, he refused to sign proffered Department agreements that he cease and desist from further "inflammatory" recordings and performances-while Berger v. Battalia seems to support that stance, that is law from a different Circuit, and not dispositive of my arbitral authority.

Additionally, he and the Union failed to propose a less restrictive covenant, one permitting the Grievant to remain active with Larsiny records outside of the Philadelphia area spotlight; that failing, he could have agreed and grieved the coerced "agreement", an alternative to his "self-help" refusal. Furthermore, the posting of the Daily News' full page "Rapper Rouses FOP Fury" on his MySpace webpage was an act of defiance, consistent with the image associated with hard-core rappers, rather than that of an apologetic short-term firefighter who wanted his job back.

* * * *

AWARD

Held

[3] The Grievant shall be reinstated with back pay for all time off the job before his posting of the "Rapper Arouses FOP Fury" Daily News piece on his and/or Larsiny. Records' web pages. The City shall provide, and the Grievant shall sign, a written agreement with the Fire Department saying:

The Grievant may maintain all present financial and artistic involvement with Larsiny Records, except that he shall not appear as A and/or J in any audio or visual productions where Police or Firefighters are shown or referred to directly, or by inference.

APPLICATION AND DISCUSSION QUESTIONS

1. The Court relied on *Berger vs. Battaglia*, 779 F2d. 992 (4th Cir 1985), to find that the employee's off-duty conduct was protected speech. Do you agree with the arbitrator's analysis? Can the two cases *Berger and City of Philadelphia* be distinguished?

2. How did the Arbitrator analyze the First Amendment Claim? Did the arbitrator violate the employee's freedom of speech by limiting his activities in certain productions? Does the arbitrator have authority to limit the grievant's off-duty conduct as a perquisite to be reinstated?

SUMMARY OF CASES ON OFF-DUTY CONDUCT

Do you agree with the arbitrators' awards in the following decisions? Explain your reasoning in each decision.

VULCAN ASPHALT REFINING COMPANY,
78 LA 1311 (1982).

The employer terminated the employee for participating in off-duty drug activity. The employee was discharged for selling a small amount of marijuana to an old friend from high school and the friend just happened to be working as an undercover agent. The employer terminated the employee on grounds that his actions tainted the company's reputation. The union argued that his arrest and sentence did not unreasonably harm the company's reputation nor did it reflect an incapacity for the employee to perform his original duties. The employee was reinstated.

ELYRIA BOARD OF EDUCATION
862 A. 921 (1985)

The board terminated the counselor off-duty activity relating to drugs. The counselor's house was being used for drug trafficking. The board argued that the conviction of drug-related offenses was just cause for termination. The union agreed, because the counselor's conduct related directly to her advising on drug abuse.

Yes

LIFE-STYLE ACTIVITIES: ALLIED SUPERMARKETS
41 LA 7113 (1963)

The employer terminated the employee for a personal choice to be pregnant. The employee was a single mother and the store fired her after her second child was born. The employer argued that her presence might deter parents from allowing their teenage daughter to work there. The union argued that the employee's personal choice did not make her a bad influence on female employees. She was reinstated.

Yes

OFF-DUTY CRIMINAL ACTIVITIES: HILTON HAWAIIAN VILLAGE
76 LA 347 (1981)

The employer terminated a bellhop for participating in criminal activity. While off duty, the bellhop sold a stolen gun to an undercover agent and pleaded guilty. The employer claims that this type of position requires a high level of trust, because the bellhop has access to guests' room and the trust was now diminished. The union agreed.

Maybe

COMMONWEALTH OF PENNSYLVANIA
65 LA 280 (1975)

The employer terminated the store clerk for his off-duty criminal conduct. In response to a physical altercation the store clerk was having with his wife, an elderly woman intervened and he beat her to death. The employer claimed there was just cause for his termination, because of the danger her posed to the store and customers. The union agreed on the grounds that the publicized assault by the store clerk would likely create a sense of danger in the customers, causing them to be hesitant in dealing with him and/or the store.

Maybe

POTOMAC ELECTRIC POWER CO.,
83 LA 449 (1984)

The employer terminated the employee for off-duty misconduct. The employee was discharged for making inappropriate phone calls to the daughter of a customer. The employer claims that the duty is considered misconduct even though the calls were made while off-duty. The union argued that there was actually a lack of company policy on off-duty conduct, the caller's identify was not certain, and the employee had a satisfactory work record for over 20 years. The employee was reinstated.

no, affects business

GOULD, INC.
76 LA 1187 (1981)

The employer terminated the employee for off-duty misconduct. The employee harassed his former supervisor by pouring a load of dirt in his driveway, putting his house up for sale, and calling the paramedics to the house for a false emergency. The employer claimed that the "pranks" resulted in deterioration of the supervisor's *no,* work. The union argued that the evidence did not show a direct correlation between *affect* the hoaxes and the work duties. The employee also had a clean history with the *relationship* organization, except for one minor incident. The employee was reinstated.

Arbitrators may be faced with the issue of how to analyze cases involving the use of marijuana in states where it is legal to use but violates an employer's workplace policy. For example, in Coats v. Dish Network. Brandon Coat filed a claim against his former employer Dish Network, regarding state-legal marijuana and the drug free workplace. Specifically, the issue in this case was whether or not Brandon's use of legal marijuana, which he used for medical purposes, was legal ground for his termination. The Colorado statute in question was C.R.S. 24-34-402.5 "Unlawful prohibition of legal activities as a condition of employment." This statute specifically states that a termination is a "discriminatory or unfair employment practice" if the employee is fired for "engaging in any lawful activity off the premises of the employer during nonworking hours."

The plaintiff argues that "lawful activity" for purposes of section 24-34-402.5 refers only to state, not federal and his medicinal use of marijuana is legal in the state of Colorado. However, the labor laws in the United States are established by the federal government and work environments are subject to both state and federal laws. This dispute over the meaning of "lawful activity" is what led the court to turn to the legislative intent. Concluding that the intent of section 24-34-402.5 was to protect employees, the Court of Appeals held that Mr. Coats' state-licensed use of medical marijuana was not "lawful activity" within the meaning of the Lawful Activities Statutes and is prohibited by federal law, therefore making Dish Network's decision to terminate him, legal. *Coats v. Dish Network, L.L.C.*, 2013 COA 62, 303 P.3d 147 cert. granted sub nom. *Coats v. Dish Network, LLC*, No. 13SC394, 2014 WL 279960 (Colo. Jan. 27, 2014) and aff'd sub nom. *Coats v. Dish Network*, LLC, 2015 CO 44.

THE PROBLEM OF OFF-DUTY CONDUCT

While off duty, a correctional officer connects with a former inmate and agrees to share the cost of a bag of heroin. After giving the former inmate the money, the correctional officer suspects that the inmate did not actually purchase the heroin. After asking for the money back several times, the officer hits the former inmate in the face with a hammer, knocking out his front teeth. The two parted ways, but while leaving the hospital, the correctional officer is attacked by the former inmate and later arrested. He's been charged with assault with a deadly weapon, which is a felony, but continues to work at the jail in a different capacity not involving inmates. He eventually accepted a plea bargain for a lessor charge, but has recently received a letter stating that an adverse action to remove him from his job has been initiated.

How should the arbitrator rule?

reinstate b/c
no hexuos?

K. INTEREST ARBITRATION

UNIVERSITY OF CINCINNATI AND INTERNATIONAL UNION
OF OPERATING ENGINEERS, LOCAL 20
133 LA 1658 (F.WEATHERSPOON, 2014)*

I. Statement of Facts

The facts indicate that the International Union of Operating Engineers (IUOE), Local 20 (hereinafter Union) and the University of Cincinnati (hereinafter Employer), are parties to a collective bargaining agreement (CBA) for the period of August 1, 2013 to July 31, 2015. The bargaining unit of approximately 68 members is comprised of tradesmen (carpenters, painter-plasterers, plasterers, plumber-pipefitters, underground pipeline technicians, pipefitter-welders, mason-cement workers, insulation technicians, building trades helpers, carpenter/painters and building trades leaders); stationary steam engineers (chief stationary engineer, stationary engineer, lead stationary engineer and boiler repair worker); and maintenance (builder trades leader).

The issue in this case involves an alleged breach of a grievance settlement agreement calling for the parties to conduct and retroactively implement the results of a market wage survey for the job classification of Carpenter (Journeyman), Carpenter-Painter (Journeyman), Painter-Plasterer (Journeyman), and Plasterer (Journeyman). The parties' prior CBA expired on July 31, 2012. A new CBA was not reached prior to the expiration date, however, negotiations continued. In August 2012 the Employer prepared a market wage survey proposing new rates of pay. Negotiations continued for another year until the parties reached a new CBA with a term of August 1, 2013 through July 31, 2015.

In pertinent part the newly agreed upon CBA stated that "... [t]he university and the union will conduct and implement the results of a market wage survey for carpenters and painters in July 2013...." The parties basically utilized the Employer's August 2012 market wage survey to establish initial wage rates under the new CBA and the initial salary increases were made retroactive to October 2012. Notwithstanding, some job classifications did not receive an initial wage increase. The job classifications

* Reprinted with permission from *Labor Relations Reporter- Labor Arbitration Reports.* 133 LA 1658. Copyright 2015 by the Bureau of National Affairs, Inc. (800-372-1033). http://www.bna.com.

of journeyman carpenters, carpenter-painters, painter-plasterers and plasterers were included in the group that did not receive salary increases. In light thereof, the parties agreed to conduct and implement a joint market wage survey in July 2013.

The Union alleges that the parties did not "jointly conduct and implement the results of a follow-up market wage survey for these job classifications...." As a result, on September 25, 2013 the Union filed a grievance challenging the Employer's alleged failure and refusal to conduct a joint market wage survey. The Employer produced a market wage survey purportedly demonstrating that the affected job classifications were not entitled to a wage increase. In light thereof, the Employer denied the grievance. The Union, therefore, moved the dispute to arbitration. This matter was scheduled for arbitration on May 7, 2014. However, prior to arbitration the parties reached a settlement agreement on May 6, 2014. The agreement stipulated that the parties were "jointly" to conduct and retroactively implement a market wage survey for the four job classifications referenced above. In accordance with subject agreement, this matter was submitted to a third-party neutral for final and binding arbitration because the parties were unable to reach a majority consensus upon determination of the appropriate labor market.... This arbitrator was selected by the parties as the neutral to determine the appropriate labor market.

II. Issue

What is the appropriate market in which to conduct the wage market survey for the job classifications of Carpenter (Journeyman), Carpenter-Painter (Journeyman), Painter-Plasterer (Journeyman) and Plasterer (Journeyman)?

III. Relevant Contract Provisions and Grievance Settlement

Contract Provisions

Article
Wages (0mited)

IV. Positions of the Parties

A. Employer's Position

The Employer is a large public university located in Southwestern Ohio. It employs around 14,000 persons. The Union represents employees that maintain the Employer's power plants and that provide semi-skilled labor to maintain the buildings on campus. In the parties' Collective Bargaining Agreement (CBA), Article 18.B states in pertinent part "[t]he university and the union will conduct and implement the results of a market wage survey for carpenters and painters in July 2013". The parties were unable to reach agreement on the conduct of the survey, so the Union filed the grievance that is the subject of this matter. The parties agreed to a settlement outlining the steps for conducting and implementing the wage survey.

The Employer indicates that their Human Resources Office's compensation and classification analysts established the appropriate wage rate. The Employer further indicates that the wage assignment was determined by conducting a survey of the appropriate and relevant job market. The Employer's analysts determined the appropriate and relevant job market by considering such factors as geography, industry and employer size. The Employer proposes that the market be defined as the greater Cincinnati area because the competition for employees in the affected classifications does not extend beyond the greater metropolitan area of Cincinnati. The Employer insists that applicants for the classifications at issue largely are selected from the local metropolitan area.

The Employer proposes that "education, government and nonprofit organizations" are the appropriate comparable. The Employer contends that "[o]ther options, such as financial services, media or healthcare" are not appropriate in determining wages in this case. According to the Employer, their total compensation packages are more appropriately compared to other public institutions than to retail or industrial organizations where wages may be higher at the expense of inferior fringe benefits. In assessing the appropriate employer size, the Employer proposes the market be defined as fifty to one hundred employees to reflect the size of the bargaining unit.

B. Union's Position

It is the Union's position that the appropriate market is accurately based on labor agreements from "... 3 local public employers, 1 'private' employer, and 1 regional public employer, all with comparable journeyman job classifications." The Union contends that the Employer's market data is based upon "regional employers reflected in data derived from private data service Kenexa, as well as the [Federal government's] Bureau of Labor Statistics [BLS], both apparently based upon entry level job classifications."

The Union asserts that its proposed market wage survey data was based upon journeyman job classifications, in lieu of "entry level" positions. Additionally, the Union states that its market wage survey was "... based upon the collective bargaining agreements of 3 local public employers (City of Cincinnati, Cincinnati City School District, and the Hamilton County Board of Commissioners); regional public employer (City of Dayton); and 1 local 'private sector' employer (University of Cincinnati Medical Center)." According to the Union, the UC Medical Center is included because until about 1997, when the UC medical Center went 'private', it was encompassed by the Union's University of Cincinnati bargaining unit.

The Union and the Employer were unable to reach majority consensus upon what constituted the "... appropriate market for the affected job classifications and that issue is now submitted for final and binding determination by the Arbitrator."

The Union asserts that it is inappropriate for the Employer to rely upon entry-level wage rates because they are lower than the higher journeyman trade classifications that the Union proposed. The journeyman rates are based on "skilled journeyman trade classifications" with specific skill requirements. The Union also contends that its proposed market is based upon its own wage survey which was limited to the Greater Cincinnati market. The Unions states that all but one of the proffered comparable are located within the City of Cincinnati and all but one of these are public employers, and the sole "private" employer utilized was UC Medical Center. The Union indicates that the Medical Center "once was encompassed by the University of Cincinnati bargaining unit (and remains represented as a separate bargaining unit by the Union)." The Union concludes that its proposed market is more relevant than the Employer's, and is more adequately reflected as the appropriate "comparables".

V. Discussion and Analysis

This case involves an interest dispute over wages. The Arbitrator's role here is to carefully review each of the parties' positions on this issue of the appropriate jurisdictional market for determining the wage survey of affected job classifications. Each party has provided contrasting views of the appropriate geographical area to assess the size of the market under consideration. The Union proposes a slightly broader area than that of the Employer, whereas, the Employer proposes a more limited area to survey. The Arbitrator must determine the most logical and reasonable conclusion as it relates to this matter.

Typically, interest disputes are complex because in many cases there are no set guidelines or standards to follow, unless the parties have agreed on a specific set of standards. In most wage disputes, there are always different paths the parties can take in determining the appropriate wage standard which can result in a wide divergence of different wage rates. Arbitrator Seinsheimer said it best that "[i]n an interest dispute the standards are very hazy unless the parties agree beforehand on some sort of standards under which the Arbitrator is expected to operate. No such standards were agreed upon by the parties in [this] dispute...." Similarly, the parties in this dispute failed to establish guidelines as to the number and type of employers to survey. In determining the appropriate wage rate, closely analyzing the "comparable competitive operations" in a given geographical area is the starting point. The ending point of the analysis is where the parties often disagree.

Moreover, in determining the appropriate comparable an assessment of jobs that have a similar range of duties and levels of experience is crucial. Consequently, the positions at issues should be evaluated at the same level of experience and perform similar work. [2] Normally, if assessing local levels, the most germane salary comparisons come from other organizations in the same area, city or town. However, reliable salary comparisons can also be obtained from a different city or town with similar labor market characteristics and a comparable cost of living.

The elements or factors considered in conducting a wage survey are easily stated. Indeed, the parties cited many of the following factors to consider: skill level of employees, location of comparable, the type of business, private vs. public employers, local, regional, and national operation of the employer, type of duties performed by employees, the size of the public, etc. All of these factors may be considered in determining the appropriate market to survey.

The Employer maintains that the market should be defined as the "greater Cincinnati area." The Employer insists that the competition for employees "... in the affected classifications does not extend beyond the greater metropolitan area of Cincinnati..." The Employer maintains that "[a]pplicants selected for these classifications are generally from the local area...." The Union maintains that the market data proposed by the Employer was based largely on "entry level" job classifications. In contrast, the Union asserts that its proposed market wage survey data was based upon "journeyman classifications." The Union also based its market wage survey upon collective bargaining agreements from "... 3 local public employers (City of Cincinnati, Cincinnati City School District, and the Hamilton County Board of Commissioners); regional public employer (City of Dayton); and 1 local 'private sector' employer (University of Cincinnati Medical Center)."

The Employer states that in determining the appropriate industry, that "education, government and nonprofit be the appropriate standard." Interestingly, it appears this is exactly what the Union based its survey on: an educational institution, i.e. the Cincinnati School District; governmental organizations (i.e., the City of Cincinnati, the Hamilton County Board of Commissioners, and a regional nearby public employer—the City of Dayton); and a nonprofit (University of Cincinnati

Medical Center that once was part of the University of Cincinnati bargaining unit and remains represented as a separate bargaining unit by the Union).

Based on the evidence submitted by the parties, with a couple of modifications, the Union's proposal is reasonable considering that its wage market survey was more applicable to that of other public institutions doing comparable work with similar job classifications. Moreover, the Union's proposal is more reasonable considering that the employees in the Union's bargaining unit in the select job classifications are journeyman not entry level employees. The Union's market survey included like major job duties; similar requirements for job classifications; nearby geographical locations; similar organizational entities; and comparable size of bargaining units for affected job classifications.

The Employer indicates that applicants are primarily from the Cincinnati area. As Arbitrator Ruben commented in another wage survey dispute "... ideally comparable communities [Employers] ought to be located nearby in the same labor market and county; be of similar territorial size and population density; draw upon similar resources and tax bases...." and have the financial means to pay the appropriate rate increase, if any. The local market should be the focus of a wage survey if that is where applicants are located. The Union's proposed wage survey is primarily based upon employers who are in the local Cincinnati metropolitan area. This is exactly what the Employer requested the market survey include. The only exception is the comparable for the City of Dayton.

The Union's rationale for including the City of Dayton in the wage survey is based on the City of Dayton's "geographic proximity, its utilization of comparable job classifications," and the fact that the Employer included Dayton in a previous survey. All of these factors would be legitimate reasons for including Dayton in the survey but for the fact that there are a number of comparable public employers in the Cincinnati metropolitan area that can be included in the survey. If there were a limited number of comparable public sector employers in the Cincinnati area to compare wages with the Employer, it would have been reasonable to include the City of Dayton. But here, the Union has provided three comparable public sector employers in the Cincinnati area who can be included in the wage survey. The same rationale for excluding the private sector employer in the wage survey also applies here as well. Again, the Union provided a rational reason for including the private employer. Had there been a shortage of comparable public sector employers in the Cincinnati area to include in the wage survey, the private sector employer could have been included in the survey.

Except for the City of Dayton and the private sector comparables, the Union's data is in accordance with the factors commonly considered for local market surveys as outlined above. There appears to be no significant differences in the relative skills, ability or types of tasks performed by the journeyman carpenters, carpenter-painters, painter-plasterers and plasterers employed by Employer and those performed by the public institutions that the Union used in its comparability market wage survey. The Employer failed to present evidence that the Union's proposal is out of line with how wage surveys are conducted. The Employer failed to establish that their wage surveys conducted by BLS and the Human Resource Department compared the Employers' skilled journeyman positions with their comparable.

The prevailing practice that should be used for the comparison is that of the employer's competitors, whether within or without the area, or that of other firms or industries so situated that there is a sufficient similarity of interests between them and the employer in question for it to be reasonable to use their practice as the standard. [4] The Union's market survey has a more relevant "similarity of interest" in light of the fact that the Union utilized data from organizations that were public governmental entities and a school district. The Union's survey of journeyman positions is more germane to the skill level of the positions at issue. The Employer primarily relied upon data that was provided by a private data service, BLS data and the interpretation of its own Human Resources' classification specialists. The data provided by the Employer lacks evidence that it was based on the wages of the aforementioned occupations at the journeyman rates.

Often Employers rely on the Federal government's Bureau of Labor Statistics (BLS) which has Occupational Compensation Surveys for most geographical areas. The Arbitrator acknowledges that the BLS data is relevant because it reflects data in geographical areas pertinent to specific occupational classifications or wages for specific jobs in the given area. But this data is not dispositive of the issue before the Arbitrator. A consideration of BLS' survey still requires a review of other factors as well, such as the specific skill levels of employees. In addition, the Arbitrator does not intend to marginalize the Employer's Human Recourses Compensation survey. However, the Union's survey appears to come closer to identifying the most appropriate comparable and skill level of employees to compare.

VI. Conclusion

In this grievance the Employer has not supported the rationale for its position concerning the appropriate market for determining compensation rates and concluding that the affected job classifications were not entitled to a wage increase. The Arbitrator finds that the Union appropriately conducted a market survey based on three comparable public employers' data. As previously indicated, the Arbitrator does not accept the wage data for the private sector employer and the City of Dayton. It appears that the parties are awarded what they asked the Arbitrator to order. The wage survey is based on the Cincinnati metropolitan area, as requested by the Employer. However, the determination of wage rates must be at the journeyman level, as requested by the Union.

A method of determining a remedy in this matter, is to compute the "... the mean, or average values" of the comparison group and then applying that average to determine the appropriate wage increase." [5] In light thereof, the Arbitrator hereby order the parties to reconvene in good faith to determine an appropriate wage increase based on the average salary increases as depicted in the three public employers proposed by the Union. Elkouri, *id.*

VII. AWARD

The parties are to conduct a wage survey for the position in question based upon the three public employers: the City of Cincinnati, Cincinnati City School District, and the Hamilton County Board of Commissioners. The wage rate should be based on journeyman level positions. In addition, wages increases must comply with Article 18B of the CBA and is retroactive to August 1, 2013. The Arbitrator hereby exercises his discretion to retain jurisdiction for sixty (60) days for the limited purpose of resolving any issues related to the wage survey and the determination of the appropriate wages.

APPLICATION AND DISCUSSION QUESTIONS

For a discussion of factors arbitrators consider in resolving wage disputes, *see Cummins Sales*, 54 LA 1071 (Seinsheimer, 1970); Elkouri, How Arbitration Works, 7th Ed., p. 22-71; *City of Willowick, OH*, 110 LA 1150 (Ruben 1998).

1. What is an interest dispute and why is this type of dispute complex?

2. What factors did the arbitrator consider to resolve the wage dispute?

3. Why did the arbitrator find that the Union's survey of market wages had a more relevant "similarity of interest" than the employer's survey?

128 LA 1550 (F.WEATHERSPOON, 2011)*

This Interest Arbitration arises pursuant to 24 V.I.C. Section 376 between the Virgin Islands Government Hospitals (Hospital) and the Association of Employed Physicians (Association or AHEP), Floyd D. Weatherspoon was selected to serve as the impartial Arbitrator, whose report is issued below.

The Interest Arbitration Hearing was held on December 6, 2010. The parties submitted post-hearing briefs on December 20, 2010. The parties identified the following issues as being unresolved. (Selected sections are included)

1. Article I - Recognition Clause (Omitted)
2. Article II, Section 1 - Rights of the Employer
3. Article II, Section 2 - Rights of the Employer (Omitted)
4. Article V, Section 4 - Grievance & Arbitration Procedure (Omitted)
5 Article X, Section 1 - Professional Development (Omitted)
6. Article XIII, Section 1 - No Individual Contracts
7. Article XIII, Section 6 - Job Descriptions (Omitted)
8. Article XV - Work Assignments (Omitted)
9. Article XVI, Section 2 - Staffing Levels and Recruitment. (Omitted)

* * * *

(24 V.I.C. Section 376 requires the atbitrator to consider the following factors)

1. The financial ability of the public employer to meet the costs of any proposed settlement;

2. The interests and welfare of the public;

3. A comparison of the wages, hours and conditions of employment of the employees involved in the arbitration proceedings with the wages, hours and conditions of employment of other employees performing similar services and with other employees generally in public employment in

---

the same community and in comparable communities and in private employment in the same community and in comparable communities.

4. A comparison of peculiarities of employment in regard to other trades or professions, including (i) hazards of employment; (ii) physical qualifications; (iii) educational qualifications; (iv) mental qualifications; and (v) job training skills;

5. The overall compensation presently received by the public employees including direct wages and fringe benefits;

6. The average consumer prices for goods and services, commonly known as the average cost of living;

7. Stipulations of the parties;

8. Changes in any of the foregoing circumstances during the pendency of the arbitration proceedings;

9. Such other factors, not confined to the foregoing, which are normally or traditionally taken into consideration in the determination of wages, hours, and conditions of employment through voluntary collective bargaining, mediation, or otherwise between the parties, in the public service or in private employment.

Issue 1. Article 1 (Recognition Clause) (Omitted)

Issue 2. Article II, Section 1 (Rights of the Employer)

The parties' CBA currently provide:
The Government as Employer shall have the right to establish and execute public policy, subject to the provisions of this Agreement by:

A. Directing and supervising the employees covered by this Agreement;

B. Determining qualifications and standards for hiring new physicians;

C. Hiring, promoting, assigning, retaining, disciplining, suspending, demoting, or discharging physicians subject to the terms of this Agreement.

D. Maintaining efficiency of operations;

E. Determining methods, means and personnel by which the Employer's operations are to be conducted, subject to the terms of this Agreement;

F. Taking such actions as may be necessary to carry out the mission of the public employer in times of emergency;

G. Any departmental or managerial function not limited by the terms of this Agreement is reserved to the Employer.

Association's Proposal

The Association's proposal is two-fold: first, the Association seeks to add language to the current provision that would acknowledge that the Hospital's Management Rights are limited by the Medical Staff Bylaws, the national and local standards of care applicable to each physician's area of practice, the laws and regulations of both the United States and the Virgin Islands and the Constitution of the United States. Second, the Association proposes adding language that essentially requires the Hospital to enter into a dialogue with the Association as to what the qualifications and standards should be for new physicians.

Hospital's Position

The Hospital opposes the Association's proposal and submits its own proposal to change the current language. The Hospital contends that its proposed language mirrors the Virgin Islands Code, Title 24, Chapter 14, Section 374(b) and it is included in almost every other collective bargaining agreement with the Government of the Virgin Islands. It is noted, however, that the Hospital's proposal would remove the current limitations in the CBA which explicitly subjects the Management's Rights Clause to the provisions of the Agreement.

Discussion

As a threshold matter, the Arbitrator recognizes that because of the nature of the Association and the members, i.e. physicians, the situation presents some very unique considerations for the parties and the Arbitrator. As noted by the Association, physicians are not typically a group that is represented by a union. Therefore, special consideration has to be given to the relationship between the self-governance of the profession as well as the Medical Staff Bylaws that relate to patient care as well as the CBA. Of course, as always the collective bargaining agreement must adhere to local, state, and federal laws. The Arbitrator notes that because of this uniqueness there is a certain amount of interplay involved between these relationships that do not exist in the typical union-management relationship. The Arbitrator is sensitive of this relationship when making his Findings. The Arbitrator will discuss both aspects of AHEP's proposal below.

Association's Bylaw Proposal

First, the Arbitrator notes that, at the hearing, it was his understanding that the Hospital did not oppose the inclusion of the Medical Bylaw language. Nevertheless, the Association has provided sound rationale for including the language that the Management Rights are limited by the Medical Bylaws. The CBA already provides that in the event of a conflict between it and the Bylaws, the provisions of the Bylaws govern. Additionally, the evidence indicates that the Bylaws deal more with the practice of medicine and the standards of care that physicians must adhere to when dealing with patients. However, the current language of the CBA only deals with situations involving a conflict between the Bylaws and the CBA, as opposed to recognition of the Bylaws in a general sense. Further, the Association gave an example of why the Bylaws needed more recognition. Dr. Mavis Matthew, testified that she helped to develop the Bylaws now in effect. She explained the reason that the CBA needed to give the Bylaws more recognition. She testified that when developing the Bylaws, there were eight defined Departments or Services and in the process of developing Chiefs of Service as leaders or supervisors of the areas, the medical staff elected to defer to the organizational structure as defined in the CBA. Ms. Matthew stated that this caused some of the Chiefs of Service to be demoted and lose their status as Chief because only the eight positions defined in the CBA were recognized as Chiefs. Therefore, the Association has provided justification for the proposed addition.

Moreover, the Association provided evidence that the physicians are required to follow standards of care. Therefore, the Association's proposal to include the language limiting management's rights to the standards of care are not unreasonable. Further, the parties are required to adhere to the laws of the Virgin Islands and the United States, therefore, adding this language will not impact the management's rights clause.

Association's Collaboration Proposal

The Association's proposal for adding language that the Hospital collaborate with it about determining the qualifications and the the standards for hiring replacement or additional physicians is not as persuasive.

A standard feature of collective bargaining is that if a provision is contained in a contract and one party wishes to modify or delete the provision, that party must offer a quid pro quo or a compelling reason. The same principle applies when one party wants to add contract language. Another way to convince a neutral of the need to delete a provision from a contract is to show that the provision is either unique or not needed. Therefore, the Association must provide a sufficient reason to add the language to the contract.

The only rationale provided by the Association was that it thought that there should be a dialogue regarding the qualifications and standards for new physicians. Again, the Arbitrator acknowledges the uniqueness of this situation. However, the Association didn't provide any evidence that this was typical in the industry or that most employers and unions collaborate in the determination of the qualification and standards of skill for new employees. Moreover, the Hospital provided evidence that the Medical Director is involved in hiring staff positions. Even though the Association, stated that the Medical Director would not necessarily know the intricacies of the specific needs or standards of care of a particular specialty, the Association has not provided sufficient justification for its proposed change.

Hospital's Proposal

Basically, the Hospital's proposed language mirrors the Virgin Islands Code, Title 24, Chapter 14, Section 374(b). It is noted that the Hospital's proposal would remove the current language of the CBA which explicitly subjects the Management's Rights Clause to the limitations of the Agreement.

In reviewing the Hospital's proposed language versus the current language of the CBA, the Arbitrator notes that the Hospital's proposal includes the language, "[n]o contract or other instrument of agreement between the public employer and an exclusive representative shall be valid to the extent such contract or agreement unduly interferes with the right of the public employer to establish and execute public policy by:* * * *" The remaining parts of the provision are substantially similar to the current language. The current language begins with "[t]he Government as Employer shall have the right to establish and execute public policy, subject to the provisions of this Agreement by:* * * *" This language would be removed under the Hospital's proposal.

Therefore, the current CBA limits the Hospital's management rights to the provisions set forth in the Agreement, whereas, the proposed language has no limitation and emphasizes the employer's rights over any contract that unduly interferes with the employer's right to establish and execute public policy. The Arbitrator believes that the two concepts are not inconsistent with one another. While the current CBA provision provides limitations, the Code provides that no contract can unduly interfere with the employer's right to establish and execute public policy. This is true, regardless of the contractual language. Therefore, whether the provision proposed by the Hospital is in the contract or not, the employer's rights are not impacted.

Moreover, it is typical for an agreement to contain a provision which states that management reserves rights unless specifically limited by the agreement. "It is a well recognized arbitral principle that the Collective Bargaining Agreement imposes limitations on the employer's otherwise unfettered right to manage the enterprise." See, generally, Elkouri & Elkouri, How Arbitration Works, 6th Ed. pg. 638.

Finding

I accept the Association's proposed language as it relates the the Medical Staff Bylaws, the national and local standards of care, and the laws and regulation language. I do not accept the Association's language about collaboration. I do not accept the Hospital's proposal.

New Language to go in the Contract Provisions

The parties shall draft the new contract provisions to include the following language:

The Government as Employer shall have the right to establish and execute public policy, subject to the provisions of this Agreement, the Medical Staff Bylaws at the Juan F. Luis Hospital and Medical Center and the Roy L. Schneider Hospital and Medical Center, the national and local standards of care applicable to each physician's area of practice, the Medical Staff Bylaws adopted at each of the Hospital and Medical Centers, the laws and regulations of the United States Virgin Islands and the Constitution, laws and regulations of the United States by:

A. Directing and supervising the employees covered by this Agreement;

B. Determining qualifications and standards for hiring new physicians;

C. Hiring, promoting, assigning, retaining, disciplining, suspending, demoting, or discharging physicians subject to the terms of this Agreement.

D. Maintaining efficiency of operations;

E. Determining methods, means and personnel by which the Employer's operations are to be conducted, subject to the terms of this Agreement;

F. Taking such actions as may be necessary to carry out the mission of the public employer in times of emergency;

G. Any departmental or managerial function not limited by the terms of this Agreement, law, regulation, or the Medical Staff Bylaws is reserved to the Employer.

* * * *

Issue 6. Article XIII, Section 1 -- No individual Contracts

The parties' current contract provides,

"[t]here shall be no individual contracts relating to terms and conditions of employment between the Employer and any physicians covered by this Agreement."

Association's Proposal

The parties acknowledge that the Hospital has entered into individual contracts with physicians. AHEP recognizes the need for the Hospital to enter into individual contracts in rare exceptions. AHEP proposes language that would allow the Hospital to enter into contracts in certain circumstances.

The Association's proposal requires the Hospital to obtain AHEP's approval prior to entering into any individual contract with a physician regarding the terms of employment. The proposal is written so that AHEP will give approval in rare instances in which it deems an emergency situation exists in order to meet the healthcare needs of the public. The Association's proposal provides that any such contract will not have a duration longer than nine months. The Association's proposal also seeks specific information regarding the prospective contract, such as loan forgiveness, other benefits, relocation expenses, etc. The proposal also specifies that this provision is subject to binding arbitration under the rules and procedures of the Voluntary Labor Arbitration Rues of the American Arbitration Association.

Hospital's Proposal and Position

The Hospital proposes that it be allowed to enter into individual contracts under certain circumstances. The Hospital contends that has had to enter into individual contracts with physicians because of certain factors including the hiring freeze and the non-competitive pay scale under the current agreement.

The Hospital's proposal allows it to enter into individual contracts where it believes it is required. The Hospital's proposal does not require the approval of AHEP. The Hospital contends that the hiring of physician's is within its managements rights. The Hospital maintains that the Union's proposal would unduly interfere with its duty to provide quality healthcare. The Hospital emphasizes that it statutory duty to provide quality healthcare prevails over the employee's rights under the CBA, when the two conflict. The Hospital agrees to notify AHEP of such a contract. The Hospital agrees to limit the individual contract to one-year. At the end of one-year, the physician will be placed into the Association pay scale.

Discussion

The Arbitrator believes both parties' proposals display a spirit of compromise. The contract expressly forbids individual contracts, yet the Association recognizes the special circumstances that give rise to the need for the Hospital to enter into individual contracts so that the healthcare needs of the Virgin Islands do not suffer. The evidence indicates that the Hospital has had difficulty recruiting physicians due to the government-wide hiring freeze. Additionally, the Hospital provided evidence that the wages under the collective bargaining agreement were not competitive. Because of these factors, the Hospital entered into individual contracts with physicians. The Association recognizes this and has expressed a sincere desire to further the public interest, without unduly hindering healthcare, while maintaining the fairness to its members. However, the Association's proposal as written, is overly broad and encroaches upon management's prerogative. As cited by the Hospital, the public welfare prevails over the public employee's collective bargaining rights when the two conflict. *District 2A v. Gov't of the Virgin Islands*, 794 F.2d 915, 919 (3d Cir. 1986). It is unreasonable for the Hospital to be required to get approval from AHEP before it hire a physician. It is further unreasonable for AHEP to have sole authority to withhold approval subject to its determination that an emergency situation exists that is necessary to meet the health care needs of the Virgin Islands.

Finding

I accept the Hospital's proposal as written.

New Language to go in the Contract Provisions

The parties shall draft the new contract provisions to include the following language:

A. There shall be no individual contracts, whether formal or informal, written or oral, relating to terms and conditions of employment between the Employer and any physicians covered by the Agreement.

B. Except in the event the Employer believes conditions require offering or providing pay or benefits, of whatever form, including by not limited to salary, incentive, benefits, office space, insurance, services, personnel, supplies, or referral services to any physician, which pay or benefits is different than that provided for pursuant to the terms and conditions of the Agreement, the Employer shall notify the Association of such agreement. In no event shall such agreement provide for such different pay and benefits for a period longer than one (1) year from the date of the Agreement. At the expiration of one (1) year period, the physician shall be slotted into the Association's pay scale. The physician will pay Association dues. Copies of the Agreement submitted to the Association in the same manner in which NOPA's are transmitted.

In accordance with 24 V.I.C. Section 376, the Arbitrator's decision is final and binding.

Respectfully submitted and issued this 20th Day of January 2011.

APPLICATION AND DISCUSSION QUESTIONS

1. What factors listed under the statute does the arbitrator rely on to reach a finding in each issue discussed? Were there factors that the arbitrator did not discuss that were relevant to the issues?

2. The Employer cites *District 2A v. Gov't of the Virgin Islands,* 794 F.2d 915 (3rd Cir. 1986) to support its position on the impact that the Union's position has on the public. Was the Employer's argument persuasive? Do you agree with the arbitrator's finding?

3. In resolving public sector interest arbitration, state laws will set forth the criteria arbitrators are required to consider in resolving contract disputes. For example in Ohio, see Ohio Revised Code 4117-9-05 and in Michigan Comp Laws §423.239 [2011 Act 312].

FRATERNAL ORDER OF POLICE QUEEN CITY LODGE, NO. 69 AND CITY OF CINCINNATI
OHIO STATE EMPLOYMENT RELATIONS BOARD
CASE NUMBER: 08-MED-07-0743; 08-MED-07-0744 (2009)

This fact finding arises pursuant to Ohio Revised Code Section 4117.14 between the Fraternal Order of Police, Queen City Lodge No. 69 (Union) and, the City of Cincinnati, (City), Floyd D. Weatherspoon was selected to serve as the impartial Fact Finder, whose report is issued below.

The Fact Finding Hearing was held on February 18, 2009. The parties identified the following issues, and/or contract provisions as being unresolved: (Selected Sections Included)

The Ohio Public Employee Bargaining Statute sets forth the criteria the Fact Finder is to consider in making recommendations. The criteria are set forth in Rule 4117-9-05. The criteria are:

1. Past collectively bargained agreements, if any.

2. Comparison of the unresolved issues relative to the employees in the bargaining unit with those issues related to other public and private employees doing comparable work, giving consideration to factors peculiar to the area and classification involved.

3. The interest and welfare of the public, and the ability of the public employer to finance and administer the issues proposed, and the effect of the adjustments on the normal standards of public service.

4. The lawful authority of the public employer.

5. Any stipulations of the parties.

6. Such other factors, not confined to those listed above, which are normally or traditionally taken into consideration in the determination of issues submitted to mutually agreed-upon dispute settlement procedures in the public service or private employment.

Issues (Selected Issues Included)

Article VII, Section 1. Appendix A Wages

Union Position:

The Union proposes a wage increase of 3.75% for both years of the contract. The Union emphasizes that other bargaining units within the City of Cincinnati that are receiving wage increases in 2009.

The Union uses Akron, Cleveland, Columbus, Dayton, and Toledo for its comparable cities. The Union contends that its proposal for increase is reasonable and would keep Cincinnati within the average with regard to pay in the compared cities.

The Union maintains that the City has the funds in its budget for an increase for 2009. In support of this assertion, the Union presented Attachment 5, showing that 3% has been budgeted city wide for cost of living adjustments for 2009. The Union also puts forth evidence that the recommended budget included a 3% cost of living adjustment for the non-represented employees for 2009 and 2010, as well as a merit increase of 2% in 2009 for the non-represented employees.

The Union presented the City Manager's Budget Message for 2009/2010 which assumes that employees under an existing labor contract for 2009 will receive a 3% salary increase, this specifically includes the FOP. The budget message also states that employees not under an existing labor contract are budgeted for a 2% increase in 2009 and 2010.

The Union contends that the evidence indicates that the City has a history of hiding funds and subsequently redirecting funds to give the false impression that it has no funds for a reasonable wage increase. The Union submits several newspaper articles where the City announced budget cuts to services and layoffs. The Union suggests these strategies by the City are tactics attempting to paint a bleak financial picture during negotiations so that the City can claim that it cannot afford any wage increases. It is the Union's contention that the City has a history of making exaggerated claims of insisting that it is experiencing severe financial problems during each set of negotiations for many years. According to the Union, the City always manages to find and spend money excessively, immediately following the conclusion of the negotiations. The Union submits evidence that the City's behavior has become so disingenuous that a previous neutral has acknowledged a lack of credibility in the City's claimed lack of funds.

The Union also notes that the final budget approved by City Council on December 17, 2008 increased the budget for several offices. The Union states that these increases were made despite the City's alleged bleak financial picture.

The Union also notes that the members of the Cincinnati Police Department have been performing at an exemplary level that warrants an increase on merit alone.

City Position:

The City proposes a lump sum increase of $650 in the first two years of the contract, and a 2% increase to the base wage in a proposed third year of the contract.

The City emphasizes the grim economic picture that has swept the nation and has largely impacted the entire financial system. The City highlights that this state of economic turmoil impacts government funding at all levels. The City outlined budget reduction and decline since 2000 in most departments, other than police and fire. The City further outlined many additional cuts and reductions to its current General Fund budget proposed by City Manager Dohoney.

The City points out that in June 2008, a financial forecast projected a structural deficit of $14.4 million in 2009 and $15.1 million in 2010, not including the "carry-over" balance. The City emphasizes that the nation's economy has all but collapsed since the June 2008 forecast. The City states that with the economy plummeting from

June through December 2008, the forecast deficits are even more alarming. The City states that its budget office should be using a budget assumption of a yearly income tax growth increase of 1% rather than the 3%.

Due to the worsening economy, in negotiations since 2007, the City has proposed lump sum adjustments as opposed to an increase in base salary. The following groups received lump sum payments: AFSCME agreed to $1,750 lump sum per bargaining unit employee, unrepresented employees will received a lump sum equivalent to 2% of the employee's base salary, and CODE employees received a lump sum payment equivalent to 3% of the employee's base salary.

The City lists Ohio jurisdictions and nearby cities with a population more than 150,000 as its comparison group. The City includes Akron, Columbus, Cleveland, Dayton, Indianapolis, Louisville, Pittsburgh and Toledo. The City states that Cincinnati police pay ranks high in comparison to these cities. Under the City's comparison charts, only Columbus exceeds Cincinnati pay levels. The City notes that officers also receive training pay at a rate of 2% of the top step and certification pay of 4% of the top step.

The City indicates that the police wage increases during the past five contracts exceed the CPI for the Cincinnati Standard Metropolitan Statistical Area by over 14%.

The City submits that as an internal wage comparison only the Fire Department has received wage increases close to the Police increases over the past five contracts or 10 years. The chart presented by the City indicates that the police officers received increases of 36%, while the firefighters received 37%, management received 24.5% and AFSCME received 24%.

Lastly, the City submits that its agreement to roll the 4% OPOTA (Ohio Peace Officer Training Academy) certification required by state law, and the 2% training allowance into the two year contracts negotiated by the parties.

Discussion

As with all levels of government, the City of Cincinnati is also facing the decreased revenues and decreased funding that has impacted the nation. And, it will certainly impact the City's economic budget and financial forecast. This fact is hard to deny. However, the City is willing to give the Union members a lump sum increase the first and second year of the contract as well as a 2% base wage increase in a third year.

The Union is against the lump sum increase instead of a base wage increase. The Union states that with the cost of living for the Cincinnati-Hamilton metropolitan area rising, the FOP members effectively earn less today than they did 4 years ago based on wage and insurance increases. The Union states the lump sum scheme fails to account for the cumulative negative effect of inflation from year to year on real wages. Indeed, this is exactly what is attractive about the lump sum option to the City, because it only impacts the budget once.

Although both parties used the same cities as its comparables. The parties' charts utilize different figures, and place Cincinnati in different places in comparison to the other comparable cities. For instance, Under the City's comparison charts, only Columbus exceeds Cincinnati pay levels. The City uses the police specialist as its highest pay level, when not all police officers obtain this classification. Whereas, the Union's charts shows that Columbus, Dayton, and Toledo exceed Cincinnati pay levels. The Union also provided an in-depth comparison of the total compensation package. The Union's calculations also project a 3% increase for those cities that are in negotiations for a new contract.

The Union also emphasizes other bargaining units within the City of Cincinnati that are receiving wage increases in 2009. However, most of these contracts appear to have been previously negotiated with a increase for 2009.

Thus, while there is clearly a budget issue, the City has already budgeted for a 2% increase for the parties not represented by a union, and 3% for parties that are represented.

Recommendation

A 2% base wage increase both years, not including the OPOTA pay and training pay that are going to be rolled into the base pay as agreed to by the City.

Article XI- Service Record Availability Section 1. Expungement, Inspection Notice

The City has a proposal under this section and the Union has two proposals under this section.

City Proposal:

The City proposes changes to its expungement of discipline provision. Under the parties' current contract, a suspension of 30 days or more can be expunged after 5 years. A suspension of less than 30 days can be expunged after 3 years.

The City proposes that a suspension of 10 days or more stay on the employee's record permanently, and will not be expunged for any reason. The City further proposes that a suspension of 5-9 days be eligible for expungement after 6 years if there is no intervening discipline of suspension, and a suspension of 4 days or less be eligible for expungement after 4 years.

The City recognizes that these proposals are drastic changes from the current contract language. The City states, however, that it feels very strongly that arbitrators have had a false sense of a grievant's work record due to the current generous expungement provisions.

Union position:

The Union is against the City's proposal to increase the retention period. The Union contends that the Cincinnati Police Department retains service records of discipline in the member's service records longer than any of the Big Six comparison contracts (Akron, Cleveland, Columbus, Dayton, Toledo, and Cincinnati). Discussion:

The City contends that it cannot introduce evidence of that a grievant was suspended for similar conduct over three years ago. The fact finder is sympathetic to the City's concern. Indeed, typically in arbitration cases, consideration is generally given to the past record of any disciplined or discharged employee. See *Elkouri & Elkouri, How Arbitration Works*, (6th Edition), pg. 983.

However, the comparison jurisdictions do not support the City's proposal. According to the City's comparison numbers, Cleveland removes oral/written reprimands after 6 months, and all other discipline after 2 years; Dayton removes oral/written reprimands after 2 years and suspensions after 4 years; Toledo removes suspensions in excess of 30 days after 5 years, and all other discipline after 4 years; and Akron has no expungement provisions. Consequently, the City's expungement provision leaves suspensions on the record similar to the comparison contracts. Likewise, the City's internal contracts all have expungement provisions of 6 years or shorter. Therefore, I cannot recommend the drastic changes proposed by the City.

Recommendation:

I recommend the current expungement provision timeline.

Union Proposal:

1. The Union proposes to add language into the current provision that states that all records pertaining to "administrative insights" will be removed from the employee's file after three years. The Union states that administrative insights are not grievable or disputable. The Union states that the administrative insights stay in an employee's

record for his/her entire career. The Union states that the City categorizes administrative insights as non-discipline, therefore, it should not be treated more serious than discipline and remain in the file permanently. The Union states that the number of administrative insights has drastically increased in the past several years.

City Position:

The City contends that administrative insights are not discipline, thus their removal has no place in a collective bargaining agreement. The City also states that the administrative insights serve a valid management purpose in that if the same performance issues occur time and time again, would be hard to detect and correct if administrative insights are removed after three years. The City contends that it doesn't appear that any such provision appears in any of the other nine cities' contracts.

Discussion

Both parties have reasonable positions with regard to this issue. However, the City has demonstrated that a mechanism exists for members to request for an administrative insight to be removed from the file. Therefore, there doesn't appear to be a compelling need to have an automatic expungement after three years.

Recommendation:

I do not recommend the Union's proposal.
1. The Union also proposes to add language that the City shall request permission from the State of Ohio Records' Commission to purge disciplinary records consistent with Article _?

XI. City Position:

The City maintains that it needs to retain expunged disciplinary records in the event the City is sued by disgruntled citizens because of misconduct by police officers. The City contends that destroying the records would render it unable to prove the prior discipline and thus would not have a defense against such a lawsuit.

Discussion:

The Union has not demonstrated that disciplinary records need to be destroyed in a time frame that is consistent with Article XI. The evidence demonstrates that the records can be expunged from an employees file after 3 years and cannot always be used against that employee in the event of subsequent discipline. Moreover, the City has a valid concern in that it needs to be able to show that it disciplined an employee in case of a lawsuit that alleges a pattern of misconduct. Thus, I recommend the current retention schedule.

Recommendation:

I do not recommend the Union's proposal.
Respectfully submitted and issued this 23rd day of April, 2009.

APPLICATION AND DISCUSSION QUESTIONS

1. What factors did the Fact Finder consider in making recommendations to the parties?

2. Ohio Revised Code 4117-9-05(6) indicates that the Fact Finder may "consider such other factors, not confined to those listed above, which are normally or traditionally taken into consideration..." What additional factors would you suggest the Fact Finder consider in making recommendations?

3. Compare the criteria listed in Ohio Revised Code Section 4117-9-05 and V.I.C. Section 376. What are similarities and differences between the statutes?

VII. ARBITRATION OF EMPLOYMENT DISPUTES
IN LABOR ARBITRATION

The Supreme Court has issued two decisions that sanctioned the use of mandatory arbitration provisions in collective bargaining agreements (CBA). First, in 1998, the Supreme Court in *Wright v. Universal Maritime Service Corp.* paved the way for employers and unions to negotiate a waiver provision within the CBA, which prohibits employees from litigating an individual statutory claim in court. Although the Court did not uphold the waiver provision in *Wright*, the Court held that such a provision is valid, if the language is "clear and unmistakable". Next, in 2009, the Supreme Court issued the second case, *14 Penn Plaza LLC v. Pyett*, which held that a mandatory arbitration clause in the CBA was valid and enforceable. The waiver clause in *Pyett* specifically stated that the "grievance and arbitration procedures" were the sole and exclusive procedures for processing statutory claims. Prior to *Wright* and *Pyett*, the Supreme Court had issued the decision in *Alexander v. Gardner-Denver which* related to mandatory arbitration of employment claims in the grievance procedures. As you read these three cases, consider whether the Supreme Court's legal anaysis is sound.

A. SUPREME COURT DECISIONS

ALEXANDER V. GARDNER-DENVER CO.
415 U.S. 36 (1974)

Mr. Justice POWELL delivered the opinion for a unanimous Court.

This case concerns the proper relationship between federal courts and the grievance-arbitration machinery of collective-bargaining agreements in the resolution and enforcement of an individual's rights to equal employment opportunities under Title VII of the Civil Rights Act of 1964, 78 Stat. 253, 42 U.S.C. s 2000e et seq. Specifically, we must decide under what circumstances, if any, an employee's statutory right to a trial de novo under Title VII may be foreclosed by prior submission of his claim to final arbitration under the nondiscrimination clause of a collective-bargaining agreement.

I.

In May 1966, petitioner Harrell Alexander, Sr., a black, was hired by respondent Gardner-Denver Co. (the company) to perform maintenance work at the company's plant in Denver, Colorado. In June 1968, petitioner was awarded a trainee position as a drill operator. He remained at that job until his discharge from employment on September 29, 1969. The company informed petitioner that he was being discharged for producing too many defective or unusable parts that had to be scrapped.

On October 1, 1969, petitioner filed a grievance under the collective-bargaining agreement in force between the company and petitioner's union, Local No. 3029 of the United Steelworkers of America (the union). The grievance stated: 'I feel I have been unjustly discharged and ask that I be reinstated with full seniority and pay.' No explicit claim of racial discrimination was made.

Under Art. 4 of the collective-bargaining agreement, the company retained 'the right to hire, suspend or discharge (employees) for proper cause.'1 Article 5, s 2, provided, however, that 'there shall be no discrimination against any employee on account of race, color, religion, sex, national origin, or ancestry,'2 and Art. 23, s 6(a), stated that '(n)o employee will be discharged, suspended or given a written warning notice except for just cause.' The agreement also contained a broad arbitration clause covering 'differences aris(ing) between the Company and the Union as to the meaning and application of the provisions of this Agreement' and 'any trouble aris(ing) in the plant.'3 Disputes were to be submitted to a multistep grievance procedure, the first four steps of which involved negotiations between the company and the union. If the dispute remained unresolved, it was to be remitted to compulsory arbitration. The company and the union were to select and pay the arbitrator, and his decision was to be 'final and binding upon the Company, the Union, and any employee or employees involved.' The agreement further provided that '(t)he arbitrator shall not amend, take away, add to, or change any of the provisions of this Agreement, and the arbitrator's decision must be based solely upon an interpretation of the provisions of this Agreement.' The parties also agreed that there 'shall be no suspension of work' over disputes covered by the grievance arbitration clause.

The union processed petitioner's grievance through the above machinery. In the final pre-arbitration step, petitioner raised, apparently for the first time, the claim that his discharge resulted from racial discrimination. The company rejected all of petitioner's claims, and the grievance proceeded to arbitration. Prior to the arbitration hearing, however, petitioner filed a charge of racial discrimination with the Colorado Civil Rights Commission, which referred the complaint to the Equal Employment Opportunity Commission on November 5, 1969.

At the arbitration hearing on November 20, 1969, petitioner testified that his discharge was the result of racial discrimination and informed the arbitrator that he had filed a charge with the Colorado Commission because he 'could not rely on the union.' The union introduced a letter in which petitioner stated that he was 'knowledgeable that in the same plant others have scrapped an equal amount and sometimes in excess, but by all logical reasoning I . . . have been the target of preferential discriminatory treatment.' The union representative also testified that the company's usual practice was to transfer unsatisfactory trainee drill operators back to their former positions.

On December 30, 1969, the arbitrator ruled that petitioner had been 'discharged for just cause.' He made no reference to petitioner's claim of racial discrimination. The arbitrator stated that the union had failed to produce evidence of a practice of transferring rather than discharging trainee drill operators who accumulated excessive scrap, but he suggested that the company and the union confer on whether such an arrangement was feasible in the present case.

On July 25, 1970, the Equal Employment Opportunity Commission determined that there was not reasonable cause to believe that a violation of Title VII of the Civil Rights Act of 1964, 42 U.S.C. s 2000e et seq., had occurred. The Commission later notified petitioner of his right to institute a civil action in federal court within 30 days. Petitioner then filed the present action in the United States District Court for the District of Colorado, alleging that his discharge resulted from a racially discriminatory employment practice in violation of s 703(a)(1) of the Act, 42 U.S.C. s 2000e—2(a)(1).

The District Court granted respondent's motion for summary judgment and dismissed the action. 346 F.Supp. 1012 (1971). The court found that the claim of racial discrimination had been submitted to the arbitrator and resolved adversely to petitioner.[4] It then held that petitioner, having voluntarily elected to pursue his grievance to final arbitration under the nondiscrimination clause of the collective-bargaining agreement, was bound by the arbitral decision and thereby precluded from suing his employer under Title VII. The Court of Appeals for the Tenth Circuit affirmed per curiam on the basis of the District Court's opinion. 466 F.2d 1209 (1972).

We granted petitioner's application for certiorari. 410 U.S. 925, 93 S.Ct. 1398, 35 L.Ed.2d 586 (1973). We reverse.

II and III (omitted)

The actual submission of petitioner's grievance to arbitration in the present case does not alter the situation. Although presumably an employee may waive his cause of action under Title VII as part of a voluntary settlement, mere resort to the arbitral forum to enforce contractual rights constitutes no such waiver. Since an employee's rights under Title VII may not be waived prospectively, existing contractual rights and remedies against discrimination must result from other concessions already made by the union as part of the economic bargain struck with the employer. It is settled law that no additional concession may be exacted from any employee as the price for enforcing those rights. J. I. Case Co. v. NLRB, 321 U.S. 332, 338—339, 64 S.Ct. 576, 580—581, 88 L.Ed. 762 (1944).

Moreover, a contractual right to submit a claim to arbitration is not displaced simply because Congress also has provided a statutory right against discrimination. Both rights have legally independent origins and are equally available to the aggrieved employee. This point becomes apparent through consideration of the role of the arbitrator in the system of industrial self-government. As the proctor of the bargain, the arbitrator's task is to effectuate the intent of the parties. His source of authority is the collective-bargaining agreement, and he must interpret and apply that agreement in accordance with the 'industrial common law of the shop' and the various needs and desires of the parties. The arbitrator, however, has no general authority to invoke public laws that conflict with the bargain between the parties:

'(A)n arbitrator is confined to interpretation and application of the collective bargaining agreement; he does not sit to dispense his own brand of industrial justice. He may of course look for guidance from many sources, yet his award is legitimate only so long as it draws its essence from the collective bargaining agreement. When the arbitrator's words manifest an infidelity to this obligation, courts have no choice but to refuse enforcement of the award.' *United Steelworkers of America v. Enterprise Wheel & Car Corp.*, 363 U.S. 593, 597, 80 S.Ct. 1358, 1361, 4 L.Ed.2d 1424 (1960).

If an arbitral decision is based 'solely upon the arbitrator's view of the requirements of enacted legislation,' rather than on an interpretation of the collective-bargaining agreement, the arbitrator has 'exceeded the scope of the submission,' and the award will not be enforced. Ibid. Thus the arbitrator has authority to resolve only questions of contractual rights, and this authority remains regardless of whether certain contractual rights are similar to, or duplicative of, the substantive rights secured by Title VII.

IV.

* * * *

Arbitral procedures, while well suited to the resolution of contractual disputes, make arbitration a comparatively inappropriate forum for the final resolution of rights created by Title VII. This conclusion rests first on the special role of the arbitrator, whose task is to effectuate the intent of the parties rather than the requirements of enacted legislation. Where the collective-bargaining agreement conflicts with Title VII, the arbitrator must follow the agreement. To be sure, the tension between contractual and statutory objectives may be mitigated where a collective-bargaining agreement contains provisions facially similar to those of Title VII. But other facts may still render arbitral processes comparatively inferior to judicial processes in the protection of Title VII rights. Among these is the fact that the specialized competence of arbitrators pertains primarily to the law of the shop, not the law of the land. *United Steelworkers* of *America v. Warrior & Gulf Navigation Co.*, 363 U.S. 574, 581–583, 80 S.Ct. 1347, 1352–1353, 4 L.Ed.2d 1409 (1960).18 Parties usually choose an arbitrator because they trust his knowledge and judgment concerning the demands and norms of industrial relations. On the other hand, the resolution of statutory or constitutional issues is a primary responsibility of courts, and judicial construction has proved especially necessary with respect to Title VII, whose broad language frequently can be given meaning only by reference to public law concepts.

Moreover, the factfinding process in arbitration usually is not equivalent to judicial factufinding. The record of the arbitration proceedings is not as complete; the usual rules of evidence do not apply; and rights and procedures common to civil trials, such as discovery, compulsory process, cross-examination, and testimony under oath, are often severely limited or unavailable. And as this Court has recognized, '(a)rbitrators have no obligation to the court to give their reasons for an award.' United Steelworkers of America v. Enterprise Wheel & Car Corp., 363 U.S., at 598, 80 S.Ct., at 1361. Indeed, it is the informality of arbitral procedure that enables it to function as an efficient, inexpensive, and expeditious means for dispute resolution. This same characteristic, however, makes arbitration a less appropriate forum for final resolution of Title VII issues than the federal courts.

* * * *

We think, therefore, that the federal policy favoring arbitration of labor disputes and the federal policy against discriminatory employment practices can best be accommodated by permitting an employee to pursue fully both his remedy under the grievance-arbitration clause of a collective-bargaining agreement and his cause of action under Title VII. The federal court should consider the employee's claim de novo. The arbitral decision may be admitted as evidence and accorded such weight as the court deems appropriate.

The judgment of the Court of Appeals is reversed.

Reversed.

APPLICATION AND DISCUSSION QUESTIONS

1. From a policy perspective, why is it important for individuals to bring their own private discrimination action under Title VII outside of the collective bargaining agreement?

2. What evidence did the Court rely on to find out that individuals do not forfeit their right to bring a separate claim under Title VII if they pursue a grievance under the collective bargaining agreement?

3. What were the reasons the lower court refused to permit the Grievant to proceed in federal court?

WRIGHT V. UNIVERSAL MAR. SERV. CORP.
SUPREME COURT OF THE UNITED STATES
525 U.S. 70 (1998)

Judges: SCALIA, J., delivered the opinion for a unanimous Court.
Opinion by: SCALIA

Opinion
JUSTICE SCALIA delivered the opinion of the Court.

This case presents the question whether a general arbitration clause in a collective-bargaining agreement (CBA) requires an employee to use the arbitration procedure for an alleged violation of the Americans with Disabilities Act of 1990 (ADA), 104 Stat. 327, 42 U.S.C. § 12101 *et seq.*

I

In 1970, petitioner Ceasar Wright began working as a longshoreman in Charleston, South Carolina. He was a member of Local 1422 of the International Longshoremen's Association, AFL-CIO (Union), which uses a hiring hall to supply workers to several stevedore companies represented by the South Carolina Stevedores Association (SCSA). Clause 15(B) of the CBA between the Union and the SCSA provides in part as follows: "Matters under dispute which cannot be promptly settled between the Local and an individual Employer shall, no later than 48 hours after such discussion, be referred in writing covering the entire grievance to a Port Grievance Committee . . . ." If the Port Grievance Committee, which is evenly divided between representatives of labor and management, cannot reach an agreement within five days of receiving the complaint, then the dispute must be referred to a District Grievance Committee, which is also evenly divided between the two sides. The CBA provides that a majority decision of the District Grievance Committee "shall be final and binding."

a. If the District Grievance Committee cannot reach a majority decision within 72 hours after meeting, then the committee must employ a professional arbitrator.

Clause 15(F) of the CBA provides as follows:

The Union agrees that this Agreement is intended to cover all matters affecting wages, hours, and other terms and conditions of employment and that during the term of this Agreement the Employers will not be required to negotiate on any further matters affecting these or other subjects not specifically set forth in this Agreement. Anything not contained in this Agreement shall not be construed as being part of this Agreement. All past port practices being observed may be reduced to writing in each port.

Finally, Clause 17 of the CBA states: "It is the intention and purpose of all parties hereto that no provision or part of this Agreement shall be violative of any Federal or State Law."

Wright was also subject to the Longshore Seniority Plan, which contained its own grievance provision, reading as follows: "Any dispute concerning or arising out of the terms and/or conditions of this Agreement, or dispute involving the interpretation or application of this Agreement, or dispute arising out of any rule adopted for its implementation, shall be referred to the Seniority Board. The Seniority Board is equally divided between labor and management representatives. If the board reaches agreement by majority vote, then that determination is final and binding. If the board cannot resolve the dispute, then the Union and the SCSA each choose a person, and this "Committee of two" makes a final determination.

On February 18, 1992, while Wright was working for respondent Stevens Shipping and Terminal Company (Stevens), he injured his right heel and his back. He sought compensation from Stevens for permanent disability under the Longshore and Harbor Workers' Compensation Act, 44 Stat. 1424, as amended, 33 U.S.C. § 901 *et seq.*, and ultimately settled the claim for $ 250,000 and $ 10,000 in attorney's fees. Wright was also awarded Social Security disability benefits.

In January 1995 Wright returned to the Union hiring hall and asked to be referred for work. (At some point he obtained a written note from his doctor approving such activity.) Between January 2 and January 11, Wright worked for four stevedoring companies, none of which complained about his performance. When, however, the stevedoring companies realized that Wright had previously settled a claim for permanent disability, they informed the Union that they would not accept Wright for employment, because a person certified as permanently disabled (which they regarded Wright to be) is not qualified to perform longshore work under the CBA. The Union responded that the employers had misconstrued the CBA, suggested that the ADA entitled Wright to return to work if he could perform his duties, and asserted that refusing Wright employment would constitute a "lock-out" in violation of the CBA.

When Wright found out that the stevedoring companies would no longer accept him for employment, he contacted the Union to ask how he could get back to work. Wright claims that instead of suggesting the filing of a grievance, the Union told him to obtain counsel and file a claim under the ADA. Wright hired an attorney and eventually filed charges of discrimination with the Equal Employment Opportunity Commission (EEOC) and the South Carolina State Human Affairs Commission, alleging that the stevedoring] companies and the SCSA had violated the ADA by refusing him work. In October 1995, Wright received a right-to-sue letter from the EEOC.

In January 1996, Wright filed a complaint against the SCSA and six individual steve-doring companies in the United States District Court for the District of South Carolina. Respondents' answer asserted various affirmative defenses, including Wright's failure to exhaust his remedies under the CBA and the Seniority Plan. After discovery, respon-dents moved for summary judgment and Wright moved for partial summary judgment with respect to some of respondents' defenses. A Magistrate Judge recommended that the District Court dismiss the case without prejudice because Wright had failed to pursue the grievance procedure provided by the CBA. The District Court adopted the report and recommendation and subsequently rejected Wright's motion for reconsid-eration. The United States Court of Appeals for the Fourth Circuit affirmed* * * * We granted certiorari, 522 U.S. 1146 (1998).

II

In this case, the Fourth Circuit concluded that the general arbitration provision in the CBA governing Wright's employment was sufficiently broad to encompass a statu-tory claim arising under the ADA, and that such a provision was enforceable. The latter conclusion brings into question two lines of our case law. The first is repre-sented by *Alexander v. Gardner-Denver Co.,* 415 U.S. 36, 39 L. Ed. 2d 147, 94 S. Ct. 1011 (1974), which held that an employee does not forfeit his right to a judicial forum for claimed discriminatory discharge in violation of Title VII of the Civil Rights Act of 1964, 78 Stat. 253, as amended, 42 U.S.C. § 2000 et seq., if "he first pursues his griev-ance to final arbitration under the nondiscrimination clause of a collective-bargain-ing agreement." 415 U.S. at 49. In rejecting the argument that the doctrine of election of remedies barred the Title VII lawsuit, we reasoned that a grievance is designed to vindicate a "contractual right" under a CBA, while a lawsuit under Title VII asserts "independent statutory rights accorded by Congress. The statutory cause of action was not waived by the union's agreement to the arbitration provision of the CBA, since "there can be no prospective waiver of an employee's rights under Title VII." *Id.,* at 51. We have followed the holding of Gardner-Denver in deciding the effect of CBA arbitration upon employee claims under other statutes.

The second line of cases implicated here is represented by *Gilmer v. Interstate/Johnson Lane Corp., supra,* which held that a claim brought under the Age

Discrimination in Employment Act of 1967 (ADEA), 81 Stat. 602, as amended, 29 U.S.C. § 621 *et seq.*, could be subject to compulsory arbitration pursuant to an arbitration provision in a securities registration form. Relying upon the federal policy favoring arbitration embodied in the Federal Arbitration Act (FAA), 9 U.S.C. § 1 *et seq.*, we said that "statutory claims may be the subject of an arbitration agreement, enforceable pursuant to the FAA."

There is obviously some tension between these two lines of cases. Whereas *Gardner-Denver* stated that "an employee's rights under Title VII are not susceptible of prospective waiver," 415 U.S. at 51-52, Gilmer held that the right to a federal judicial forum for an ADEA claim could be waived. Petitioner and the United States as amicus would have us reconcile the lines of authority by maintaining that federal forum rights cannot be waived in union-negotiated CBAs even if they can be waived in individually executed contracts -- a distinction that assuredly finds support in the text of *Gilmer*, see 500 U.S. at 26, 35. Respondents and their amici, on the other hand, contend that the real difference between *Gardner-Denver* and *Gilmer* is the radical change, over two decades, in the Court's receptivity to arbitration, leading *Gilmer* to affirm that "questions of arbitrability must be addressed with a healthy regard for the federal policy favoring arbitration," 500 U.S. at 26 (internal quotation marks and citation omitted); *Gilmer,* they argue, has sufficiently undermined *Gardner-Denver* that a union can waive employees' rights to a judicial forum. Although, as will appear, we find *Gardner-Denver* and *Gilmer* relevant for various purposes to the case before us, we find it unnecessary to resolve the question of the validity of a union-negotiated waiver, since it is apparent to us, on the facts and arguments presented here, that no such waiver has occurred.

III

In asserting the existence of an agreement to arbitrate the ADA claim, respondents rely upon the presumption of arbitrability this Court has found in § 301 of the Labor Management Relations Act, 1947 (LMRA), 61 Stat. 156, 29 U.S.C. § 185. In collective bargaining agreements, we have said, "there is a presumption of arbitrability in the sense that 'an order to arbitrate the particular grievance should not be denied unless it may be said with positive assurance that the arbitration clause is not susceptible of an interpretation that covers the asserted dispute.'

That presumption, however, does not extend beyond the reach of the principal rationale that justifies it, which is that arbitrators are in a better position than courts to interpret the terms of a CBA. See *AT&T Technologies,* 475 U.S. at 650; *Warrior & Gulf,* 363 U.S. at 581-582. This rationale finds support in the very text of the LMRA, which announces that "final adjustment by a method agreed upon by the parties is declared to be the desirable method for settlement of grievance disputes arising over the application or interpretation of an existing collective bargaining agreement." 29 U.S.C. § 173(d). The dispute in the present case, however, ultimately concerns not the application or interpretation of any CBA, but the meaning of a federal statute. The cause of action Wright asserts arises not out of contract, but out of the ADA, and is distinct from any right conferred by the collective-bargaining agreement. See *Gilmer*, 500 U.S. at 34; *Barrentine*, 450 U.S. at 737; *Gardner-Denver*, supra, 415 U.S. at 49-50. To be sure, respondents argue that Wright is not qualified for his position as the CBA requires, but even if that were true he would still prevail if the refusal to hire violated the ADA.

Nor is the statutory (as opposed to contractual) focus of the claim altered by the fact that Clause 17 of the CBA recites it to be "the intention and purpose of all parties hereto that no provision or part of this Agreement shall be violative of any Federal or State Law." App. 47a. As we discuss below in Part IV, this does not incorporate the ADA by reference. Even if it did so, however -- thereby creating a contractual right that is coextensive with the federal statutory right -- the ultimate question for the arbitrator would be not what the parties have agreed to, but what federal law requires; and that is not a question which should be presumed to be included within the arbitration requirement. Application of that principle is unaffected by the fact that the CBA in this case, unlike the one in Gardner-Denver, does not expressly limit the arbitrator to interpreting and applying the contract. The presumption only extends that far, whether or not the text of the agreement is similarly limited. It may well be that ordinary textual analysis of a CBA will show that matters which go beyond the interpretation and application of contract terms are subject to arbitration; but they will not be presumed to be so.

IV (omitted)

We hold that the collective-bargaining agreement in this case does not contain a clear and unmistakable waiver of the covered employees' rights to a judicial forum for federal claims of employment discrimination. We do not reach the question whether such a waiver would be enforceable. The judgment of the Fourth Circuit is vacated, and the case is remanded for further proceedings consistent with this opinion.

14 PENN PLAZA LLC, ET AL. V. PYETT, ET AL.

556 U.S. 247; 129 S. CT. 1456; (2009)

OPINION BY: THOMAS

The question presented by this case is whether a provision in a collective-bargaining agreement that clearly and unmistakably requires union members to arbitrate claims arising under the Age Discrimination in Employment Act of 1967 (ADEA), 81 Stat. 602, as amended, 29 U.S.C. § 621 *et seq.*, is enforceable. The United States Court of Appeals for the Second Circuit held that this Court's decision in *Alexander* v. *Gardner-Denver Co.*, 415 U.S. 36, 94 S. Ct. 1011, 39 L. Ed. 2d 147 (1974), forbids enforcement of such arbitration provisions. We disagree and reverse the judgment of the Court of Appeals.

I

Respondents are members of the Service Employees International Union, Local 32BJ (Union). Under the National Labor Relations Act (NLRA), 49 Stat. 449, as amended, the Union is the exclusive bargaining representative of employees within the building-services industry in New York City, which includes building cleaners, porters, and doorpersons. See 29 U.S.C. § 159(a). In this role, the Union has exclusive authority to bargain on behalf of its members over their "rates of pay, wages, hours of employment, or other conditions of employment." *Ibid.* Since the 1930's, the Union has engaged in industry-wide collective bargaining with the Realty Advisory Board on Labor Relations, Inc. (RAB), a multiemployer bargaining association for the New York City real-estate industry. The agreement between the Union and the RAB is embodied in their Collective Bargaining Agreement for Contractors and Building Owners (CBA). The CBA requires union members to submit all claims of employment discrimination to binding arbitration under the CBA's grievance and dispute resolution procedures:

> "30. NO DISCRIMINATION "There shall be no discrimination against any present
> or future employee by reason of race, creed, color, age, disability, national origin,
> sex, union membership, or any characteristic protected by law, including, but not
> limited to, claims made pursuant to Title VII of the Civil Rights Act, the Americans
> with Disabilities Act, the Age Discrimination in Employment Act, the New York
> State Human Rights Law, the New York City Human Rights Code, . . . or any other
> similar laws, rules, or regulations. All such claims shall be subject to the grievance and

arbitration procedure (Articles V and VI) as the sole and exclusive remedy for violations. Arbitrators shall apply appropriate law in rendering decisions based upon claims of discrimination."

Petitioner 14 Penn Plaza LLC is a member of the RAB. It owns and operates the New York City office building where, prior to August 2003, respondents worked as night lobby watchmen and in other similar capacities. Respondents were directly employed by petitioner Temco Service Industries, Inc. (Temco), a maintenance service and cleaning contractor. In August 2003, with the Union's consent, 14 Penn Plaza engaged Spartan Security, a unionized security services contractor and affiliate of Temco, to provide licensed security guards to staff the lobby and entrances its building. Because this rendered respondents' lobby services unnecessary, Temco reassigned them to jobs as night porters and light duty cleaners in other locations in the building. Respondents contend that these reassignments led to a loss in income, caused them emotional distress, and were otherwise less desirable than their former positions.

At respondents' request, the Union filed grievances challenging the reassignments. The grievances alleged that petitioners: (1) violated the CBA's ban on workplace discrimination by reassigning respondents on account of their age; (2) violated seniority rules by failing to promote one of the respondents to a handyman position; and (3) failed to equitably rotate overtime. After failing to obtain relief on any of these claims through the grievance process, the Union requested arbitration under the CBA.

* * * *

In May 2004, while the arbitration was ongoing but after the Union withdrew the age-discrimination claims, respondents filed a complaint with the Equal Employment Opportunity Commission (EEOC) alleging that petitioners had violated their rights under the ADEA. Approximately one month later, the EEOC issued a Dismissal and Notice of Rights, which explained that the agency's "'review of the evidence . . . fail[ed] to indicate that a violation ha[d] occurred,'" and notified each respondent of his right to sue. *Pyett v. Pa. Bldg. Co.*, 498 F.3d 88, 91 (CA2 2007).

Respondents thereafter filed suit against petitioners in the United States District Court for the Southern District of New York, alleging that their reassignment violated the ADEA and state and local laws prohibiting age discrimination. Petitioners filed a motion to compel arbitration of respondents' claims pursuant to §§ 3 and 4 of the Federal Arbitration Act (FAA), 9 U.S.C. §§ 3, 4. The District Court denied the motion because under Second Circuit precedent, "even a clear and unmistakable union-negotiated waiver of a right to litigate certain federal and state statutory claims in a judicial forum is unenforceable." App. to Pet. for Cert. 21a. Respondents immediately appealed the ruling under § 16 of the FAA, which authorizes an interlocutory appeal of «an order . . . refusing a stay of any action under section 3 of this title» or «denying a petition under section 4 of this title to order arbitration to proceed.» 9 U.S.C. §§ 16(a)(1)(A)-(B).

The Court of Appeals affirmed. 498 F.3d 88. According to the Court of Appeals, it could not compel arbitration of the dispute because *Gardner-Denver*, which "remains good law," held "that a collective bargaining agreement could not waive covered workers' rights to a judicial forum for causes of action created by Congress."

* * * *

The Court of Appeals attempted to reconcile *Gardner-Denver* and *Gilmer* by holding that arbitration provisions in a collective-bargaining agreement, "which purport to waive employees' rights to a federal forum with respect to statutory claims, are unenforceable." As a result, an individual employee would be free to choose compulsory arbitration under *Gilmer*, but a labor union could not collectively bargain for arbitration on behalf of its members. We granted certiori, to address the issue left unresolved in *Wright*, which continues to divide the Courts of Appeals, and now reverse.

II A

The NLRA governs federal labor-relations law. As permitted by that statute, respondents designated the Union as their "exclusive representativ[e] . . . for the purposes of collective bargaining in respect to rates of pay, wages, hours of employment, or other conditions of employment." 29 U.S.C. § 159(a). As the employees' exclusive bargaining representative, the Union "enjoys broad authority . . . in the negotiation and administration of [the] collective bargaining contract." *Communications Workers* v. *Beck*, 487 U.S. 735, 739, 108 S. Ct. 2641, 101 L. Ed. 2d 634 (1988) (internal quotation marks omitted). But this broad authority "is accompanied by a responsibility of equal scope, the responsibility and duty of fair representation." *Humphrey* v. *Moore*, 375 U.S. 335, 342, 84 S. Ct. 363, 11 L. Ed. 2d 370 (1964). The employer has a corresponding duty under the NLRA to bargain in good faith "with the representatives of his employees" on wages, hours, and conditions of employment. 29 U.S.C. § 158(a)(5); see also § 158(d).

In this instance, the Union and the RAB, negotiating on behalf of 14 Penn Plaza, collectively bargained in good faith and agreed that employment-related discrimination claims, including claims brought under the ADEA, would be resolved in arbitration. This freely negotiated term between the Union and the RAB easily qualifies as a "conditio[n] of employment" that is subject to mandatory bargaining under § 159(a).

* * * *

Respondents, however, contend that the arbitration clause here is outside the permissible scope of the collective-bargaining process because it affects the "employees' individual, non-economic statutory rights." See *Post*, at 281-283, 173 L. Ed. 2d, at 425-426 (Souter, J., dissenting). We disagree. Parties generally favor arbitration precisely because of the economics of dispute resolution. See *Circuit City Stores, Inc.* v. *Adams*, 532 U.S. 105, 123, 121 S. Ct. 1302, 149 L. Ed. 2d 234 (2001) ("Arbitration agreements allow parties to avoid the costs of litigation, a benefit that may be of particular importance in employment litigation, which often involves smaller sums of money than disputes concerning commercial contracts"). As in any contractual negotiation, a union may agree to the inclusion of an arbitration provision in a collective-bargaining agreement in return for other concessions from the employer. Courts generally may not interfere in this bargained-for exchange. "Judicial nullification of contractual concessions . . . is contrary to what the Court has recognized as one of the fundamental policies of the National Labor Relations Act--freedom of contract." *NLRB* v. *Magnavox Co.*, 415 U.S. 322, 328, 94 S. Ct. 1099, 39 L. Ed. 2d 358 (1974) (Stewart, J., concurring in part and dissenting in part) [**1465] (internal quotation marks and brackets omitted).

* * * *

B

The CBA's arbitration provision is also fully enforceable under the *Gardner-Denver* line of cases. Respondents interpret *Gardner-Denver* and its progeny to hold that "a union cannot waive an employee's right to a judicial forum under the federal antidiscrimination statutes" because "allowing the union to waive this right would substitute the union's interests for the employee's antidiscrimination rights." Brief for Respondents 12. The "combination of union control over the process and inherent conflict of interest with respect to discrimination claims," they argue, "provided the foundation for the Court's holding [in *Gardner-Denver*] that arbitration under a collective bargaining agreement could not preclude an individual employee's right to bring a lawsuit in court to vindicate a statutory discrimination claim." *Id.*, at 15. We disagree.

The holding of *Gardner-Denver* is not as broad as respondents suggest. The employee in that case was covered by a collective-bargaining agreement that prohibited "discrimination against any employee on account of race, color, religion, sex, national origin, or ancestry" and that guaranteed that "[n]o employee will be discharged . . . except for just cause." 415 U.S., at 39, 94 S. Ct. 1011, 39 L. Ed. 2d 147 (internal quotation marks omitted). The agreement also included a "multistep grievance procedure" that culminated in compulsory arbitration for any "differences aris[ing] between the Company and the Union as to the meaning and application of the provisions of this Agreement" and "any trouble aris[ing] in the plant." *Id.*, at 40-41, 94 S. Ct. 1011, 39 L. Ed. 2d 147 (internal quotation marks omitted).

* * * *

We recognize that apart from their narrow holdings, the *Gardner-Denver* line of cases included broad dicta that were highly critical of the use of arbitration for the vindication of statutory antidiscrimination rights. That skepticism, however, rested on a misconceived view of arbitration that this Court has since abandoned.

First, the Court in *Gardner-Denver* erroneously assumed that an agreement to submit statutory discrimination claims to arbitration was tantamount to a waiver of those rights. See 415 U.S., at 51, 94 S. Ct. 1011, 39 L. Ed. 2d 147 ("[T]here can be no prospective *waiver* of an employee's rights under Title VII" (emphasis added)). For this reason, the Court stated, "the rights conferred [by Title VII] can form no part of the collective-bargaining process since waiver of these rights would defeat the paramount congressional purpose behind Title VII."

Second, *Gardner-Denver* mistakenly suggested that certain features of arbitration made it a forum "well suited to the resolution of contractual disputes," but "a comparatively inappropriate forum for the final resolution of rights created by Title VII."

These misconceptions have been corrected. For example, the Court has "recognized that arbitral tribunals are readily capable of handling the factual and legal complexities of antitrust claims, notwithstanding the absence of judicial instruction and supervision" and that "there is no reason to assume at the outset that arbitrators will not follow the law."

* * * *

Third, the Court in *Gardner-Denver* raised in a footnote a "further concern" regarding "the union's exclusive control over the manner and extent to which an individual grievance is presented." 415 U.S., at 58, n. 19, 94 S. Ct. 1011, 39 L. Ed. 2d 147. The Court suggested that in arbitration, as in the collective-bargaining process, a union may subordinate the interests of an individual employee to the collective interests of all employees in the bargaining unit.

* * * *

The conflict-of-interest argument also proves too much. Labor unions certainly balance the economic interests of some employees against the needs of the larger work force as they negotiate collective-bargaining agreements and implement them on a daily basis. But this attribute of organized labor does not justify singling out an arbitration provision for disfavored treatment. This "principle of majority rule" to which respondents object is in fact the central premise of the NLRA. *Emporium Capwell Co. v. Western Addition Community Organization*, 420 U.S. 50, 62, 95 S. Ct. 977, 43 L. Ed. 2d 12 (1975). "In establishing a regime of majority rule, Congress sought to secure to all members of the unit the benefits of their collective strength and bargaining power, in full awareness that the superior strength of some individuals or groups might be subordinated to the interest of the majority."

* * * *

In any event, Congress has accounted for this conflict of interest in several ways. As indicated above, the NLRA has been interpreted to impose a "duty of fair representation" on labor unions, which a union breaches "when its conduct toward a member of the bargaining unit is arbitrary, discriminatory, or in bad faith." *Marquez v. Screen Actors*, 525 U.S. 33, 44, 119 S. Ct. 292, 142 L. Ed. 2d 242 (1998). This duty extends to "challenges leveled not only at a union's contract administration and enforcement efforts but at its negotiation activities as well." *Beck*, 487 U.S., at 743, 108 S. Ct. 2641, 101 L. Ed. 2d 634 (citation omitted). Thus, a union is subject to liability under the NLRA if it illegally discriminates against older workers in either the formation or governance of the collective-bargaining agreement, such as by deciding not to pursue a grievance on behalf of one of its members for discriminatory reasons. See *Vaca v. Sipes*, 386 U.S. 171, 177, 87 S. Ct. 903, 17 L. Ed. 2d 842 (1967) (describing the duty of fair representation as the "statutory obligation to serve the interests of *all* members without hostility or discrimination toward any, to exercise its discretion with complete good faith and honesty, and to avoid arbitrary conduct" (emphasis added)). Respondents in fact brought a fair representation suit against the Union based on its withdrawal of support for their age-discrimination claims. Given this avenue that Congress has made available to redress a union's violation of its duty to its members, it is particularly inappropriate to ask this Court to impose an artificial limitation on the collective-bargaining process.

In addition, a union is subject to liability under the ADEA if the union itself discriminates against its members on the basis of age. See 29 U.S.C. § 623(d); see also 1 B. Lindemann & P. Grossman, Employment Discrimination Law 1575-1581 (4th ed. 2007) (explaining that a labor union may be held jointly liable with an employer under federal antidiscrimination laws for discriminating in the formation of a collective-bargaining agreement, knowingly acquiescing in the employer's discrimination, or inducing the employer to discriminate); cf. *Goodman* v. *Lukens Steel Co.*, 482 U.S. 656, 669, 107 S. Ct. 2617, 96 L. Ed. 2d 572 (1987). Union members may also file age-discrimination claims with the EEOC and the National Labor Relations Board, which may then seek judicial intervention under this Court's precedent. See *EEOC* v. *Waffle House, Inc.*, 534 U.S. 279, 295-296, 122 S. Ct. 754, 151 L. Ed. 2d 755 (2002). In sum, Congress has provided remedies for the situation where a labor union is less than vigorous in defense of its members' claims of discrimination under the ADEA.

III

*   *   *   *

IV

We hold that a collective-bargaining agreement that clearly and unmistakably requires union members to arbitrate ADEA claims is enforceable as a matter of federal law. The judgment of the Court of Appeals is reversed, and the case is remanded for further proceedings consistent with this opinion.

It is so ordered.

DISSENT BY: STEVENS; SOUTER

Justice Souter's dissenting opinion, which I join in full, explains why our decision in *Alexander* v. *Gardner-Denver Co.*, 415 U.S. 36, 94 S. Ct. 1011, 39 L. Ed. 2d 147 (1974), answers the question presented in this case. My concern regarding the Court's subversion of precedent to the policy favoring arbitration prompts these additional remarks.

* * * *

Today the majority's preference for arbitration again leads it to disregard our precedent. Although it purports to ascertain the relationship between the Age Discrimination in Employment Act of 1967 (ADEA), the National Labor Relations Act, and the Federal Arbitration Act, the Court ignores our earlier determination of the relevant provisions' meaning. The Court concludes that "[i]t was Congress' verdict that the benefits of organized labor outweigh the sacrifice of individual liberty" that the system of organized labor "necessarily demands," even when the sacrifice demanded is a judicial forum for asserting an individual statutory right. *Ante*, at 271, 173 L. Ed. 2d, at 418. But in *Gardner-Denver* we determined that "Congress' verdict" was otherwise when we held that Title VII does not permit a CBA to waive an employee's right to a federal judicial forum. Because the purposes and relevant provisions of Title VII and the ADEA are not meaningfully distinguishable, it is only by reexamining the statutory questions resolved in *Gardner-Denver* through the lens of the policy favoring arbitration that the majority now reaches a different result.

* * * *

Justice Souter, with whom Justice Stevens, Justice Ginsburg, and Justice Breyer join, dissenting.

The issue here is whether employees subject to a collective-bargaining agreement (CBA) providing for conclusive arbitration of all grievances, including claimed breaches of the Age Discrimination in Employment Act of 1967 (ADEA), 29 U.S.C. § 621 *et seq.*, lose their statutory right to bring an ADEA claim in court, § 626(c). Under the 35-year-old holding in *Alexander v. Gardner-Denver Co.*, 415 U.S. 36, 94 S. Ct. 1011, 39 L. Ed. 2d 147 (1974), they do not, and I would adhere to *stare decisis* and so hold today.

* * * *

Finally, we took note that "[i]n arbitration, as in the collective-bargaining process, the interests of the individual employee may be subordinated to the collective interests of all employees in the bargaining unit, *ibid*," 415 U.S. 36, n. 19, 94 S. Ct. 1011, 39 L. Ed. 2d 147, a result we deemed unacceptable when it came to Title VII claims. In sum, *Gardner-Denver* held that an individual's statutory right of freedom from discrimination and access to court for enforcement were beyond a union's power to waive.

APPLICATION AND DISCUSSION QUESTIONS

1. The Supreme Court raised a number of questions regarding the use of labor arbitration to resolve statutory employment claims. How does the Court respond to the following issues and do you agree with the Court's response?

   a. Is the arbitration clause outside the permissible scope of the collective-bargaining process?

   b. Is the Courts's holding in *Gardner-Denver* broad enough to cover the issue in the present case?

   c. Did the employees waive their rights under various Federal statutes?

   d. Is the Court decision in contradiction with the holding in *Gardner-Denver*?

   e. Did Gardner-Denver mistakenly suggest that arbitration may be an inappropriate forum for resolution of the federal statutory claims?

   f. Would the Union's exclusive control over employees' statutory rights create a conflict-of-interest? As a policy issue, should employees' individual non-economic statutory rights be outside the scope of arbitration clauses? What would the dissent's response be?

2. After reading *Gardner-Denver*, do you agree with Thomas' analysis or the 2nd Circuit Court's decision? Is the Court of Appeals' attempt to reconcile *Gardner-Denver* and *Gilmer* more rational than Thomas' analysis?

3. How is the mandatory arbitration provision in *Penn Plaza* different from the typical arbitration provision in a labor contract?

4. Justice Thomas states that union members can bring a "duty of fair representation" claim against the Unions "when its [union] conduct toward a member of the bargaining union is arbitrary, discriminatory, or in bad faith," citing *Vaca v. Sipes*, 386 U.S. 171, 177 (1967). What challenges will the individual union member face who brings such a claim?

5. Could the *Pyett* decision benefit employees in vindicating their employment claims? See Sarah Cole *Let the Grand Experiment Begin: Pyett Authorizes Arbitration of Unionized Employees' Statutory Discrimination Claims*, Lewis & Clark L. REV. 141 (2010).

6. In employment arbitration cases, it is not unusual for the arbitrator to respond to various motions filed by the parties, especially motions for summary judgment, and motions to compel. This requires the arbitrator to be familiar with the Federal Rules of Civil Procedure, as well as other external laws. What impact will these decisions have on labor arbitration, if employment claims are processed through the grievance procedure? What impact will the decision have on the selection of labor and employment arbitrators to hear statutory claims that are processed under the collective bargaining procedures?

B. LOWER COURT APPLICATION OF PENN PLAZA

SHIPKEVICH V. STATEN ISLAND UNIVERSITY HOSP.
2009 WL 1706590 (E.D.N.Y. 2009)

MEMORANDUM AND ORDER

BLOCK, Senior District Judge.

Yemelyan Shipkevich ("Shipkevich") has filed an Amended Complaint which alleges discrimination in violation of Title VII of the Civil Rights Act of 1964; the New York Human Rights Law ("NYHRL"), N.Y. Exec. Law §§ 290–301; and the New York City Human Rights Law ("NYCHRL"), N.Y.C. Admin. Code §§ 8–101 to—131.1. Defendants Staten Island University Hospital ("the Hospital") and Aramark, Inc. ("Aramark") move to dismiss pursuant to Federal Rule of Civil Procedure 12(b)(6) for failure to state a claim and under Rule 12(b)(1) for lack of subject matter jurisdiction.

The defendants do not contend that Shipkevich has failed to allege the facts necessary to state a claim of employment discrimination based on his status as a Russian–American Jew born in Moldova, see *Ashcroft v. Iqbal,* –––U.S. ––––, ––––, 129 S.Ct. 1937, 1949, 173 L.Ed.2d 868, –––– (2009) (stating plausibility standard for deciding motions to dismiss); rather, they contend that the Amended Complaint should be dismissed for the following reasons: (1) the Hospital argues that a mandatory arbitration provision in the agreement governing Shipkevich's employment requires that he arbitrate his claims against the Hospital; (2) Aramark argues that it cannot be liable for discrimination because it never employed Shipkevich; both Aramark and the Hospital argue (3) that Shipkevich waived his discrimination claims by instituting an action under New York's whistleblower law, which includes an election-of-remedies provision; and (4) that Shipkevich's claims are preempted by federal labor law. For the reasons explained below, the defendants' motions are denied.

I. Mandatory Arbitration

The Hospital argues that the suit against it should be dismissed because "[t]he CBA, to which both [Shipkevich] and the Hospital are bound, mandates the arbitration of [Shipkevich's] claims against the Hospital." The CBA that governed Shipkevich's employment prohibits discrimination: "Neither the Employer nor the Union shall discriminate against or in favor of any Employee on account of race, color, creed, national origin, political belief, sex, sexual orientation, citizenship status, marital status, disability or age." Arbitration is contemplated if the CBA's grievance procedure does not resolve the dispute: "A grievance ... which has not been resolved [under the grievance procedure] may, within thirty (30) working days after completion of ... the grievance procedure, be referred for arbitration by the Employer or the Union...."

Subsequent to the parties' submissions, the Supreme Court held, in a suit alleging discrimination in violation of the Age Discrimination in Employment Act ("ADEA"), "that a collective-bargaining agreement that clearly and unmistakably requires union members to arbitrate [statutory anti-discrimination] claims is enforceable as a matter of federal law." *14 Penn Plaza LLC v. Pyett,* ––– U.S. ––––, ––––, 129 S.Ct. 1456, 1474, 173 L.Ed.2d 398 (2009). The CBA at issue in 14 Penn Plaza "require[d] union members to submit all claims of employment discrimination to binding arbitration under the CBA's grievance and dispute resolution procedures," id. at 1461; it listed several anti-discrimination statutes, including the ADEA and Title VII, and noted that all claims of discrimination "shall be subject to the grievance and arbitration procedures ... as the sole and exclusive remedy for violations," id.(quoting the CBA). The Supreme Court noted that it "has required ... that an agreement to arbitrate statutory antidiscrimination claims be 'explicitly stated' in the collective-bargaining agreement." Id. at 1465 (quoting Wright v. Universal Mar. Serv. Corp., 525 U.S. 70, 80, 119 S.Ct. 391, 142 L.Ed.2d 361 (1998)). Although *14 Penn Plaza* was an ADEA case, the Court's reasoning applies equally well to Title VII claims, *see 14 Penn Plaza LLC*, 129 S.Ct. at 1478 (Stevens, J., dissenting) ("[N]either petitioners nor the Court points to any relevant distinction between the two statutes."); indeed, much of the precedent the Court looked to for guidance concerned Title VII.

It is clear from the Court's discussion in *14 Penn Plaza* that the content of the CBA is determinative. Discussing a series of decisions holding that arbitration pursuant to a CBA does not preclude subsequent litigation of Title VII claims in federal court (beginning with *Alexander v. Gardner–Denver Co.*, 415 U.S. 36, 94 S.Ct. 1011, 39 L.Ed.2d 147 (1974)), the Court took pains to note that the CBA in each of these prior cases "did not expressly reference the statutory claim at issue," unlike the CBA at issue in 14 Penn Plaza. Id. at 1466–69 ("*Gardner–Denver* and its progeny thus do not control the outcome where, as is the case here, the collective-bargaining agreement's arbitration provision expressly covers both statutory and contractual discrimination claims.").

Contrary to the Hospital's argument, the CBA does not mandate arbitration of Shipkevich's claims because it does not "clearly and unmistakably require" arbitration of statutory anti-discrimination claims. Id. at 1474.Nowhere in the CBA is there an explicit statement that such claims are subject to mandatory arbitration. On the contrary, the CBA here is more similar to the one at issue in *Gardner–Denver* than the one in 14 Penn Plaza: The CBA in *Gardner–Denver* prohibited discrimination with a list of protected characteristics and did not mention any statutes. See 415 U.S. at 39 n. 2 ("The Company and the Union agree that there shall be no discrimination against any employee on account of race, color, religion, sex, national origin, or ancestry."). It contained a broad definition of the events that could trigger the grievance procedure, see id. at 40 n. 3 ("Should differences arise between the Company and the Union as to the meaning and application of the provisions of this Agreement, or should any trouble arise in the plant, ... an earnest effort shall be made by both the Company and the Union to settle such differences promptly."), and provided that disputes not settled by the grievance procedure "may be referred to arbitration," id. Despite this broad language, *Gardner–Denver* held, as explained in *14 Penn Plaza*, that the "collective-bargaining agreement did not mandate arbitration of statutory antidiscrimination claims."129 S.Ct. at 1467. Thus, *14 Penn Plaza* requires the same result in the present case: the CBA does not require arbitration of Shipkevich's discrimination claims.

* * * *

V. Conclusion

The defendants' motions to dismiss are denied.
SO ORDERED.

APPLICATION AND DISCUSSION QUESTIONS

1. What language in the arbitration clause of the CBA would you have recommended to the Employer and the Union to be included to be in compliance with *Penn Plaza*?

2. Apply the rulings in *Gardner-Denver*, *Wright*, and *Penn Plaza* to the facts in this case.

3. What type of claims did the employee file and what actions did the employer file?

VOLPEI V. COUNTY OF VENTURA
221 CAL. APP. 4TH 391, 163 CAL. RPTR. 3D 926 (2013)

An employee is a member of a union whose collective bargaining agreement provides that the union may submit a grievance to arbitration. Here we conclude that this provision does not preclude the employee with a statutory grievance against his employer from filing a judicial action.

The County of Ventura (County) appeals from an order denying its petition to compel arbitration of Mark D. Volpei's claims for retaliation, harassment and discrimination under the California Fair Employment and Housing Act (FEHA). (Gov. Code, § 12940 et seq.) We conclude that Volpei is not bound to arbitrate his claims under the terms of a memorandum of agreement (MOA) between the County and his bargaining representative, the Ventura County Deputy Sheriffs' Association (Association), because the MOA does not provide for a clear and unmistakable waiver of Volpei's right to a judicial forum for his statutory discrimination claims. We affirm.

FACTUAL AND PROCEDURAL BACKGROUND

In 1994, Volpei was an investigator for the Ventura County District Attorney's office. The Association entered into an MOA with the County governing Volpei's conditions of employment.

In April 2011, Volpei filed a complaint against the County for retaliation, harassment, disability discrimination, and other claims pursuant to the FEHA. Among other things, he alleged that the County harassed him because he disclosed that the district attorney's office had abused its authority and violated the law. He alleged the County also harassed him because he testified for a co-worker in his co-worker's sexual harassment claim against the County. He also alleged that the County failed to accommodate his physical disability and that it violated the Public Safety Officer's Procedural Bill of Rights Act. (Gov.Code, §§ 3300–3312.)

In its answer to Volpei's complaint, the County asserted 20 affirmative defenses, none of which invoked an agreement to arbitrate. It conducted written discovery, moved for summary judgment, and entered into stipulations concerning the trial date.

In July 2012, the County filed a petition to compel arbitration of Volpei's claims, citing a provision of the MOA. Article 30 of the MOA sets forth a "Grievance Procedure." A "grievance" is defined to include employee disputes over the terms of the MOA or "a complaint of illegal discrimination because of the charging party's sex, [or] physical disability." (MOA, § 3003.) The grievance procedure begins with an informal complaint and then entails a three-step formal complaint process. (MOA, § 3006.) "A grievance unresolved in the steps enumerated above may be submitted to arbitration by the Association by submitting a letter requesting that the grievance be submitted to arbitration to the Director–Human Resources within fourteen (14) calendar days after the Department Head renders a decision." (MOA, § 3007(A), italics added.) The MOA provides that the decision of the arbitrator "shall be final and binding upon the County, [the Association] and the employee affected, subject to judicial review." (MOA, § 3007(D).) It also provides that "[a]t any step of the grievance procedure the employee may represent himself." (MOA, § 3004.)

The trial court denied the petition to compel arbitration because the arbitration provision was unilateral and permissive and did not clearly and unmistakably waive Volpei's right to a judicial forum for his statutory discrimination claims. The court did not decide Volpei's alternative argument that the County waived arbitration by participating in litigation for more than a year.

DISCUSSION

Upon petition of a party, the trial court shall compel arbitration if it determines that an agreement to arbitrate the controversy exists, unless the petitioner has waived the right to compel arbitration. (Code Civ. Proc., § 1281.2.) Strong public policy favors arbitration and courts will indulge every intendment to give effect to an agreement to arbitrate. (*Moncharsh v. Heily & Blase* (1992) 3 Cal.4th 1, 9.) The policy in favor of arbitration applies to arbitration provisions in collective bargaining agreements, and contractual claims are generally presumed arbitrable. (*Posner v. Grunwald–Marx, Inc.* (1961) 56 Cal.2d 169, 180; *Vasquez v. Superior Court* (2000) 80 Cal.App.4th 430, 434.) This presumption does not apply, however, when an employee seeks to litigate a statutory claim. The arbitration provision for such claims must be "particularly clear." (*Wright v. Universal Maritime Service Corp.* (1998) 525 U.S. 70, 79; *Vasquez*, at p. 434.) An employee is bound to arbitration as the exclusive forum for statutory claims only if the union "clearly and unmistakably" waived his or her right to a judicial forum. (*14 Penn Plaza LLC v. Pyett* (2009) 556 U.S. 247, 274 (*14 Penn Plaza*); *Wright*, at p. 80.)

We consider de novo the question whether an agreement to arbitrate exists. (*Molecular Analytical Systems v. Ciphergen Biosystems, Inc.* (2010) 186 Cal.App.4th 696, 707.) We conclude that the provision that an unresolved grievance "may be submitted to arbitration by the Association" is not a clear and unmistakable agreement to arbitrate Volpei's statutory claims against the County.

The MOA in the instant case is unlike the MOA in *14 Penn Plaza*, supra, 556 U.S. 247. In *14 Penn Plaza*, a union clearly and unmistakably waived employee rights to a judicial forum for federal statutory age discrimination claims with this language: "claims made pursuant to Title VII of the Civil Rights Act [and] the Americans with Disabilities Act shall be subject to the grievance and arbitration procedure as the sole and exclusive remedy for violations." (Id. at p. 252.)

By contrast, the MOA here provides that unresolved grievances "may be submitted to arbitration by the Association." The provision is permissive and unilateral. The Association is not a party to the present controversy and did not submit the grievance to arbitration. Moreover, the MOA defines a grievance to include a "complaint of illegal discrimination," but does not refer to the FEHA or any other statute. It does not, like the *14 Penn Plaza* agreement, "expressly cover both statutory and contractual discrimination claims." (*14 Penn Plaza*, supra, 556 U.S. at p. 264.) Even if we construed the grievance definition to implicitly include statutory claims, the provision that unresolved grievances "may be submitted to arbitration by the Association" does not clearly and unmistakably require an employee to submit a grievance to arbitration as the "sole and exclusive remedy" for a statutory violation. (Id. at p. 252.)

The County argues that the arbitration provision applies to Volpei (not just the Association) because the MOA allows employees to prosecute grievances individually. (MOA, § 3004.) That Volpei could have submitted his claims to arbitration if the Association refused to, is beside the point. It is neither clear nor unmistakable that he was so required. The County cites no authority holding that a provision similar to the one here requires an employee with a statutory grievance to submit to arbitration.

The County argues that the word "may" has been construed in two other cases to make arbitration mandatory. (*Ruiz v. Sysco Food Services* (2004) 122 Cal.App.4th 520; *International Assn. of Bridge etc. Workers v. Superior Court* (1978) 80 Cal.App.3d 346.) Neither case involved an employee's statutory claims. In Ruiz, an employee was required under a collective bargaining agreement to arbitrate defamation and tort claims that arose from the terms of the collective bargaining agreement and were "inextricably intertwined" with his previously arbitrated contractual claims. (*Ruiz*, at p. 531.) In dicta, the court construed the following language to be mandatory: "the matter may be referred to arbitration." (Id. at p. 527.) But it also stated that "Ruiz's contention that there was no mandatory agreement to arbitrate appears to be a new argument on appeal, which is not properly addressed here." (Id. at p. 532.) *International Assn. of Bridge*, concerned an employer's contractual claims against a union for violating a no strike clause in the collective bargaining agreement. Because it did not concern statutory claims, the court did not consider whether the provision that the employer and association "may refer [unsettled disputes] to an agency mutually agreeable" was a clear and unmistakable wavier of employees rights to a judicial forum. (*International Assn. of Bridge*, at p. 353.)

The word "may" does not create a clear and unmistakable waiver here. It is permissive, or at least susceptible of a permissive meaning, particularly where "shall" is used elsewhere in the same provision. (MOA, § 3007(B) ["Arbitrator shall be selected by mutual agreement"]; § 3007(C) ["Costs of the Arbitration shall be shared equally."]) More is required to waive an employee's right to a judicial forum for statutory claims. Even in Vasquez, where the arbitration provision was "mandatory" and "binding," the individual employee's right to a judicial forum was not waived because "grievances" were not explicitly defined to include statutory discrimination claims. (*Vasquez v. Superior Court*, supra, 80 Cal.App.4th at pp. 433–434.) The employee in Vasquez claimed that his discharge violated the FEHA. A collective bargaining provision required "mandatory, binding arbitration" (id. at p. 433) for disputes arising over "the interpretation or application of any of the terms of this Agreement, including discharge." (Ibid.) Because the provision did not specifically identify statutory discrimination claims, it did not clearly and unmistakably waive his right to a judicial forum. (Id. at p. 436; see also *Wright v. Universal Maritime Service Corp.*, supra, 525

U.S. at p. 82 [a union did not waive employee rights to a judicial forum for statutory claims because the grievance procedure was limited to contractual disputes].)

Similarly, in *Mendez v. Mid–Wilshire Health Care Center* (2013) 220 Cal.App.4th 534, our colleagues in Division Seven recently concluded that an MOA did not clearly and unmistakably waive a health care worker's right to a judicial forum for her FEHA claims. The MOA did not specifically identify statutory claims and provided that a party "may appeal the grievance to arbitration." (Id. at p. 539.)

Volpei's bargaining representative did not clearly and unmistakably waive his right to a judicial forum. The provision may have required arbitration of contractual claims, and may have permitted Volpei to voluntarily arbitrate his statutory claims, but it did not unambiguously require arbitration as the sole and exclusive remedy for his statutory discrimination claim.

DISPOSITION

The order is affirmed. Costs awarded to respondent on appeal.
GILBERT, P.J.

We concur: YEGAN, J.PERREN, J.

APPLICATION AND DISCUSSION QUESTIONS

1. What is the *Penn Plaza* "test" for determining whether or not an employee is bound to arbitration?

2. Although this case is similar to *Penn Plaza v. Pyett*, why was the outcome so different?

3. Did this case appropriately apply the *Penn Plaza* "test"?

4. What are your recommendations to the employer to ensure that the contract language in the future clearly and unmistakably requires union members to arbitrate?

INCORPORATING MANDATORY ARBITRATION EMPLOYMENT CLAUSES INTO COLLECTIVE BARGAINING AGREEMENTS: CHALLENGES AND BENEFITS TO THE EMPLOYER AND THE UNION

38 DEL. J. CORP. L. 1025 (2014)*

FLOYD D. WEATHERSPOON

I. Introduction

* * * *

Clearly, there are benefits to both the employer and the union to incorporate a mandatory employment arbitration clause into the CBA. Simultaneously, there are disadvantages to both parties in incorporating an arbitration provision into the CBA. Consequently, both parties must balance their interests against one another, including the employee's decision to negotiate such a provision in the CBA.

* * * *

III. What Are the Challenges to Incorporating Mandatory Arbitration of Statutory Claims Into the CBA?

A. The Union Has to Convince its Membership of the Benefits

A waiver provision might not be acceptable to all members of the bargaining unit. Unions may find it difficult to convince its members that advocating for members' individual rights may also protect the rights of all members. The union must persuade its members that by advocating for individuals' rights, all members will benefit. Moreover, the union can claim that arbitration will allow it to combat discrimination against its members and violations of other employment laws.

* * * *

A. "The Simplicity, Informality, and Expedition of Arbitration"

The average time from filing an employment claim in federal court until it is dismissed or settled is approximately two and a half years, whereas the typical time frame for an employment arbitration claim may take 8.6 months. Bringing closure to employment disputes in a shorter period of time also benefits the employer because its employees are not being deposed, investigated, or made to testify in a lawsuit. This may permit the workplace to return to some normalcy and enhanced worker productivity.

It should be pointed out that arbitrating statutory disputes is normally faster and less protracted than in court, but not faster than labor arbitrations. There is little to no motion practices or complex case law to be analyzed. Advocates for unions, in particular, will have to adjust their processes and expand their knowledge for defending the various types of employment claims, if they take on the defense of such disputes. The union and the employer may also find it necessary to incorporate strict arbitration procedures into the CBA, such as limiting motion practice. This will benefit both the union and employer by expediting the processing of complex employment claims.

B. Less Exposure to Juries Awarding Significant Monetary Damages [omitted]

C. Limited or No Judicial Review

An arbitrator's award is normally final, binding, and receives little or no judicial review. The award is presumed valid unless it can be shown that it violated the Federal Arbitration Act (FAA). Courts have repeatedly stated that the scope of judicial review of an award is extremely limited.

* * * *

D. Avoid Public Disclosure of a Finding of Discrimination (No Dirty Laundry)

Maintaining the confidentiality of employment arbitration awards is possibly the most important factor for the employers to consider when negotiating mandatory arbitration of employment disputes into the CBA. Employers and, to a lesser extent, employees strongly favor non-disclosure of the award. In court, however, the public has a right to know about allegations of discrimination and violations of other laws. Normally, the employment arbitration award remains confidential unless the parties give permission to distribute or to publish the decision in a legal reporter.

In labor arbitration, the employer or the union may object to publication of arbitration awards, unless the employer is a governmental entity. Generally, in labor arbitration, the parties are not concerned if the decision is published, thus leaving the decision up to the arbitrator. However, employers will normally request that employment arbitration awards remain confidential. Thus, cases involving egregious claims of race and gender harassment that would normally be made public if in court, will remain confidential or filed away in arbitration.

A finding by a court that an employer has violated an employment law, especially Title VII's prohibition against racial or sexual harassment, will be widely published on social media, legal publication, and the general news outlets. Such publicity may negatively impact a company's reputation and product brand. Normally, employers will avoid such publicity by requiring awards to remain confidential. The employer will most likely negotiate such language into the CBA, to prohibit the publication of employment arbitration awards, or deny permission for awards to be published.

* * * *

V. What Are the Employer's Disadvantages of Incorporating Mandatory Arbitration of Statutory Claims Into the CBA?

A. No Opportunity to Appeal Adverse Arbitration Decisions

As stated earlier, the employer will have limited authority to appeal an arbitrator's decision in court. The authority to overturn an arbitrator's decision is very limited and narrow, even if the arbitration award appears to be unreasonable. The Federal Arbitration Act (FAA) provides limited provisions to set aside an arbitrator's decision. Even if the employer challenges the decision under the FAA, the cost of litigation may be prohibitive, especially where the likelihood of the court setting the award aside is very limited. In most cases, the federal court will reject the employer's request to vacate the award; therefore, the time invested and the litigation costs may not have been merited.

B. Arbitrators Less Likely to Grant Motion for Summary Judgment

Employers have a number of advantages by incorporating a waiver provision into the CBA. However, in exchange for the waiver employers may lose their major legal arsenal-the motion for summary judgment, which is routinely granted in federal court. Title VII claims, especially, are often dismissed in federal court once a motion for summary judgment is filed. Arbitrators, on the other hand, tend to be more conservative in granting a motion for a summary judgment without having a full hearing on the merits of the case.

* * * *

VI. What Are the Union's Benefits of Incorporating Mandatory Arbitration of Statutory Claims Into the CBA?

A. "The Simplicity, Informality, and Expedition of Arbitration" (omitted)

B. Bargain For Other Substantial Benefits (i.e. Wages, Benefits)

Companies have whole-heartedly embraced the use of arbitration in employment, consumer, commercial, and labor disputes. Employers believe that arbitration, unlike the courts, will reduce the cost and length of time for resolving disputes. Due to the benefits of utilizing arbitration to resolve labor and employment disputes in lieu of litigation, employers will be highly motivated to negotiate this clause with the union into the CBA. In exchange, the union will seek additional benefits for its members.

This negotiation will be an opportunity for unions to make demands for benefits that they have found difficult in the past to negotiate; the union may propose increases of benefits, wages, insurance, and pensions. Unions will be inclined to agree to a waiver of individuals' rights to proceed with a statutory claim for benefits of all members.

* * * *

VII. What Are the Union's Disadvantages of Incorporating Mandatory Arbitration of Statutory Claims Into the CBA?

A. The Potential Increase in Duty of Fair Representation (DFR) Claims

Unions may undoubtedly face an increase in claims that they breached their duty of fair representation, especially if there is an alleged statutory violation and the union refuses to process the grievance to arbitration. To prove a claim that the union breached its duty of fair representation, the employee must establish that the union's conduct was "arbitrary, discriminatory, or in bad faith."

Unions cannot possibly proceed with every statutory claim raised by employees, and will have to make the difficult decision of which claims will proceed to arbitration. Applying the Supreme Court decision in *Vaca v. Sipes*, the union is given discretionary authority in deciding which cases will be processed through the grievance procedures, and which cases, if any, will proceed to arbitration. Consequently, as employees file grievances related to alleged violations of a state or federal statute or common law, the union may legitimately decide not to pursue the claim all the way through each step of the grievance process and onto arbitration. In determining whether to pursue the claim to arbitration, the union will be forced to review the "legal landscape" of a particular area to determine whether to proceed to arbitration.

*　*　*　*

B. Increase Number and Cost of Arbitrations

1. Increase in the Number of Demands for Arbitration From Union Members

There will likely be increased demand by union members for the union to process their statutory claims through arbitration because the CBA may limit their ability to proceed to state or federal court. If the union becomes entirely responsible for the cost of providing members with representation in the arbitration of employment disputes, the demand for arbitration will increase substantially. Employees will take the position that because they are paying union dues, and because there is a mandatory waiver in the CBA that prohibits them from filing a lawsuit, the union has a duty to represent them in arbitration.

The potential financial burden and lack of expert knowledge of substantive state and federal employment statutes may discourage the union from negotiating a waiver into the CBA. There is, consequently, a major increase in the number of complaints filed with the EEOC.

2. Cost of Arbitration Impacts Union Dues

A major disadvantage to the union will be a substantial increase in the cost of arbitrating statutory claims. Increased union dues may be necessary to cover the cost of representing members in employment arbitration cases. The daily rate for arbitrators in employment disputes is substantially higher than in labor disputes.

*　*　*　*

E. Possible Conflict Between the Union and Women or Minorities Over the Processing of Gender and Race Claims

There has been a long history of discrimination by unions against women and minority groups. Clearly, as a result of federal laws prohibiting unions from engaging in discrimination against union members, the relationship has improved substantially. Indeed, minorities and women have a more dominant role in certain unions. Nevertheless, if a union refuses to proceed with a grievance where a race or gender claim of discrimination is raised, the union may face a claim of a breach of the duty of fair representation.

The union's interest in pursuing a discrimination claim against the employer may be in conflict with the union's efforts to improve or maintain collaborative relationship with the employer. The individual claim of discrimination may become subordinate to the interest of the union's goals and objectives, especially during the negotiations of the CBA.

F. Potential Conflict Between Individual and Collective Rights

The union's decision to pursue individual statutory claims with union's limited resources will, without a doubt, engender conflict with the collective body of union members. Employment statutes generally permit an individual to file a claim when one employee has allegedly been favored over another employee because of their immutable characteristics. This will result in claims filed by one union member against another union member over employment benefits. Such claims will be a difficult balancing act for the union to manage. The principle of majority rule will ultimately conflict with individual rights provided by federal and state statutes.

VIII. Conclusion

Unless Congress places limitations on incorporating mandatory arbitration provisions in a CBA, employers in particular will continue to pressure unions to negotiate these provisions into the CBA. Even if the union rejects such a provision, the employer may have the legal authority to implement the provision once the parties have negotiated in good faith but reached impasse.

* * * *

APPLICATION AND DISCUSSION QUESTIONS

1. Can you suggest other advantages and disadvantages to the parties incorporating mandatory arbitration clauses into CBA's?

2. What are some policy considerations that both parties should consider?

3. Does the public have an interest in knowing employment claims have been filed against an employer? What about enforcement agencies? Should they demand a copy of an arbitration award when the allegation is that a federal employment law has been violated?

VIII. REMEDIES

Arbitrators have broad authority to award a wide range of remedies, unless limited by the agreement. In disciplinary type of grievances, arbitrators have reinstated terminated grievants, with or without back pay. Grievants have been placed on probation and/or on a last-chance agreement.

[margin note: ★ wide range]

Arbitrators have also awarded interest on back pay, reduced a termination to a substantial penalty, such as a 30-day suspension. Grievants who have been reinstated after an extended absence, may be required to be drug tested, complete a new applications, take a physical examination, and have a background check.

An arbitrator's authority to award a variety of remedies are limited by the federal labor policy set forth by the Supreme Court's decisions in the trilogy cases. The Court placed two major limits on remedies ordered by arbitrators. First, the award must "draw its essence" from the agreement. Secondly, arbitrators are also prohibited from modifying a penalty based on the arbitrator's personal view of industrial justice. In addition, an arbitrator's awards may not violate public policies. If the remedy ordered by the arbitrator violates a public policy, the courts can vacate the award.

[margin note: ★ limits ① ② ③]

A. Reinstatement With No Backpay

In labor arbitration, if the arbitrator finds there is no just cause in disciplining the grievant, the arbitrator will normally order back pay, less interim wages. Arbitrators may limit or deny back pay when the employee has an extensive disciplinary record, their testimony during the hearing was not credible or questionable, the grievant was not totally innocent of the alleged misconduct, or the grievant was not cooperative during the investigation of the misconduct.

[margin note: backpay?]

Similarly, in employment cases, if the arbitrator rules in favor of the claimant, normally the arbitrator will order a make whole remedy, which includes back pay. However, the arbitrator also has the discretion to deny a request for full back pay.

Case

racist lab tech

STATEMENT OF FACTS

work

The Grievant held the position of Lab Technician (a.k.a., IT Help Desk Technician), in the Office of the Chief Information Officer. The Grievant held this position from February 4, 2008 until he was terminated effective February 22, 2012

issue

The record indicates that on February 16, 2012, the Grievant was in a verbal altercation with a Co-op student where he admittedly told the student to "shut up and sit [her] black ass down." The Grievant subsequently apologized for his comments. As a result of this incident, the Grievant was put on administrative leave for the College to "conduct a formal disciplinary review to determine the appropriate disciplinary sanction." During the review of the Grievant's personnel record, it was determined that the Grievant had noted on his application that he had been convicted of a felony but there was no information in the file explaining the details of the conviction.

terminated

On March 18, 2012, the Grievant received a memorandum from the Labor and Employee Relations Manager terminating the Grievant for cause. The disciplinary action charged the Grievant with "failure of good behavior – inappropriate comments"; and "falsification and/or fraudulent misrepresentation of information with respect to the nature and extent of prior felony convictions during the hiring process and in the course of a disciplinary review." In essence, the Grievant was charged with failure to provide complete information regarding his convictions for what he

crimes

believed and reported was the charge of "statutory rape". The evidence indicates that in 2000, the Grievant pled guilty to multiple counts of felonious conduct including third degree felony rape, third degree felony sodomy, third degree felony sexual assault and one felony count of possession of a dangerous ordinance [a gun clip].

U says

The Union filed a grievance on March 23, 2012 alleging that the Grievant was terminated without just cause in violation of Article 23 of the CBA.

* * * *

The parties were unable to satisfactorily resolve the grievance, therefore, in accordance with the CBA, it was appealed to arbitration. The parties stipulated that the grievance is properly before the arbitrator and there are no arbitrability issues.

---

[*]   Unpublished Decision (Floyd D. Weatherspoon, 2014)

II. ISSUE

Was the Grievant terminated for just cause? If not, what is the appropriate remedy?

* * * *

IV. POSITION OF THE PARTIES

A. University's Position

The University hired the Grievant as a Co-Op student in July 2005 to work in its IT Department on the Help Desk team. The Grievant was then a student at the University of Green. At the time he completed his application, he checked the block on the application indicating that he had "...been convicted of a felony within the last 10 years." The application noted that "[c]onviction will not necessarily disqualify applicant from employment."

While employed as a Co-op student, the Grievant submitted an application for full-time employment on October 30, 2007. On that application he again checked the block showing that he had been "convicted of a felony within the last 10 years." By letter dated January 17, 2008, the then Director of HR, notified the Grievant that the Interim President had approved the recommendation to hire Grievant for a full-time Laboratory Technician/Help Desk position effective February 4, 2008.

On February 21, 2012, the Grievant received a memo from the then Organizational Development and Legal Compliance Director notifying him that "...due to a racially derogatory and offensive remark..." that Grievant made to a Co-op student, the University's HR Office would conduct a formal disciplinary review to determine the appropriate disciplinary sanction. Meanwhile, the Grievant was placed on administrative leave. A disciplinary conference was scheduled for March 6, 2012. By memo dated February 27, 2012, the Organizational Development and Legal Compliance Director ("OD & L Director") notified the Grievant that the disciplinary conference would address the charges of "failure of good behavior – inappropriate comments" and "falsification and/or fraudulent misrepresentation of information with respect to the nature and extent of prior felony convictions during the hiring process and in course of a disciplinary review." He was also notified that his termination was proposed. By memo dated March 18, 2012, the University notified Grievant that the final decision was termination for cause.

U arg

B. Union's Position

1

It is the Union's position that the University violated the CBA because it issued excessive discipline. The Union pointed out that the Grievant was severely over-punished for a first time disciplinary offense. The Union also contends that the University did not comply with the principles of progressive discipline. Moreover, the Union disputes that the Grievant falsified his employment application or fraudulently misrepresented the nature of his prior felony convictions. The Union contends that the University violated Article 24 of the CBA because it did not have "just cause" to terminate the Grievant.

2

VI. DISCUSSION AND ANALYSIS

* * * *

The heart of this grievance surrounds the Grievant's conviction record. It is also the most difficult part of the analysis because both sides have raised valid arguments. HR interviewed the Grievant and then asked him about his felony conviction. He responded that when he was interviewed by the President in 2008, he explained that the felony referenced in his application involved a statutory rape conviction for having a sexual relationship with an under-age minor. HR asked Grievant whether this information was complete; he then admitted that he had a separate conviction for possession of a dangerous ordinance (a gun clip) during a search related to the rape conviction. He acknowledged that he had not disclosed this separate conviction to the President prior to his employment.

* * * *

The Union contests the charge of falsification and/or fraudulent misrepresentation of information regarding the nature and extent of prior felony convictions. Although the Grievant acknowledges that during his interview with the President that he disclosed he was convicted of "statutory rape" for having a sexual relationship with a minor girl; the Union argues that Grievant does not have a legal knowledge of the statutory offenses for which he was convicted, and in Grievant's mind and understanding, all three felony convictions related to that incident were for "statutory" rape.

fraud claim → U

The Arbitrator agrees with the Union regarding the Grievant's understanding of his convictions. All his convictions are directly or indirectly related to the rape, of which he informed the University. Had there been charges unrelated to the rape, the University's argument would be more persuasive.

The University had a duty to investigative the convictions, if there were concerns regarding his employment at the University. The record indicates that one of the University's highest officials approved the Grievant's employment, with HR's approval. There is no evidence in the record that a background inquiry was conducted to obtain the details of the Grievant's criminal record. The Arbitrator finds that the evidence in the record does not support the University's claim that Grievant "falsified" his application about the felony conviction. Instead, the record supports the Grievant's claim that he advised the College of his conviction on his applications and during his interview.

no fraud

* * * *

The Arbitrator clearly understands and empathizes with the University's concern with reinstating the Grievant to work among employees and students with a felony record and the racial incident. The Arbitrator has labored over the concern that the Grievant mere's presence would create a hostile work environment and safety concerns. However, the evidence in the record does not support the The University's position. This one incident of making inappropriate racial comments and the existence of a felony record, of which he gave notice on two occasions; is insufficient to deny the Grievant reinstatement. In other words, the The University failed to establish that the Grievant met the element of just cause, which requires theUniversity to establish that the Grievant intentionally engaged in "falsification and/or fraudulent misrepresentation of information". In addition, the termination of the Grievant for the racial incident violates the principle of just cause, which requires that the penalty be reasonable. The University's arguments to terminate the Grievant fail to meet the just cause standard required by the CBA. The University failed to establish that there is "substantial" evidence that supports the falsification/ fraudulent charge against the Grievant.

concern

but

★

ER failed burden

Penalty

The only element left under the just cause analysis is the penalty. The Union maintains that the University ignored the principles of progressive discipline and failed to apply an appropriate level of discipline. In determining whether there are mitigating factors which may impact the level of discipline that an employee may receive for violating a work rule or policy; arbitrators often consider the employee's work record, service time, gravity of the offense, and any other special circumstances. Just cause also requires an employer to consider aggravating and mitigating circumstances. It is clear that in the present case that the University did not consider the mitigating circumstances of the Grievant's otherwise satisfactory record, including average performance evaluations and lack of prior disciplinary actions. The one incident of making an inappropriate racial comment would not support a termination, but would support a severe disciplinary action. This is based on the University's progressive disciplinary procedures. The ultimate penalty of termination from employment, however, was unreasonable.

penalty wrong

With regard to the charge of "falsification and/or fraudulent misrepresentation", the mitigating factor is that Grievant provided compelling, uncontroverted testimony that he advised the University President, the highest level of authority with approval to hire employees, and the Chief of Security, the details of his felony convictions when he was initially hired almost four years earlier. Again, the Grievant disclosed his understanding of his felony convictions at his administrative meeting. His felony convictions all stem from the charge of rape.

* * * *

The Arbitrator is amazed that on two occasions the Grievant clearly indicated he had a felony record, but the University failed to investigate or document the extent of the felony charges. The evidence in the record supports the Union's claim that the University was aware of the details of the Grievant's felony conviction, but at the time of termination claims it never had detailed knowledge. Nevertheless, the University failed to provide any credible testimony or evidence to support such a claim. The Arbitrator is only left with the uncontradicted testimony of the Grievant.

EK knew of felony

VI. CONCLUSION

After reviewing all the evidence in the record, this Arbitrator concludes that the University had sufficient evidence to charge the Grievant with "failure of good behavior – inappropriate comments". The Union and the Grievant admit that the Grievant committed this infraction. On the other hand, the Arbitrator does not find the University's argument persuasive pertaining to the falsification/fraudulent misrepresentation charge. The University failed to provide sufficient evidence that the Grievant engaged in such conduct. Under the just cause analysis, the Employer must establish that the Grievant actually engaged in misconduct by violating a specific policy. The University must establish this element of the just cause analysis.

charge 1 good

charge 2 bad

The University has failed to support its position that the Grievant was terminated for just cause.

VII. AWARD

Therefore, the grievance is sustained in part. There is a range of remedies that can be considered, including reinstatement with appropriate back pay and modification of the termination to a suspension; to not reinstating the Grievant but providing back pay retroactive to the effective date of his termination up until the date of this decision.

Recognizing the University's right to impose discipline for just cause, I find that the University was justified in disciplining the Grievant for using racially derogatory language in the workplace. However, based on the CBA's progressive disciplinary provision, a thirty day suspension would be more appropriate in light of the afore-mentioned circumstances. The Arbitrator has thought long and hard on what should be the appropriate remedy in this grievance. Based on the record, the following corrective actions are ordered: *suspension instead*

1. The University is ordered to modify the termination to a thirty day suspension. *remedy 2*

2. The Grievant's personnel record shall reflect a thirty day suspension for the racial comment but not the falsification/fraudulent charge.

3. The Grievant is to be immediately reinstated to the same position or a comparable position.

4. The Grievant is denied any back pay and/or benefit.

5. The Grievant is to be credited for the time he was off for purposes of calculating future leave, vacation, sick leave, etc., but not competitive leave.

6. The Grievant must submit an up-to-date application prior to being reinstated, which includes a record of his employment during the time he has been off. In completing the application, the Grievant is ordered to include the details of his felony convictions on or attached to the application.

The Arbitrator hereby exercises his discretion to reserve jurisdiction for 60 days following this decision. The University is requested to provide a status report to the Arbitrator within thirty (30) days on the status of this award.

APPLICATION AND DISCUSSION QUESTIONS

1. Do you agree with the Arbitrator that the racial comments made by the Grievant were egregious, however, the "conduct, separate and distinct from other allegations of misconduct, could justify a disciplinary action" but not termination? What principles of arbitration did the Arbitrator apply to reach this conclusion?

2. What factors did the Arbitrator consider in modifying the penalty? Were those factors compelling in this grievance? Which provision of the Collective Bargaining Agreement does the Arbitrator cite to support modification of the penalty? What concerns did the Arbitrator express regarding the Grievant reporting his convictions to University personnel?

3. Analyze each corrective action outlined in the Award. Does the Arbitrator's conclusion support the remedy ordered? Why is backpay denied in this case?

B. Rightful Position

FOP, OHIO LABOR COUNCIL V. WRIGHT STATE UNIVERSITY
2011 LA SUPP. 119780 (FLOYD D. WEATHERSPOON, 2011)[*]

AWARD:

The grievance is sustained.

I. STATEMENT OF FACTS

The facts indicate that the Fraternal Order of Police, Ohio Labor Council, Inc., hereinafter (Union) and Wright State University, hereinafter (University) are parties to a collective bargaining agreement, effective from July 1, 2008 through June 30, 2011, hereinafter (CBA or Agreement).

The Grievant, Marcus Wyatt, is employed with Wright State University as a Sergeant. On June 29, 2009, Sergeant Wyatt was terminated from his employment with the University. Mr. Wyatt filed a grievance and was ultimately reinstated to his former position. The evidence indicates that the Grievant worked third shift immediately prior to his termination and he was serving in a "special assignment" as the Investigations Supervisor. The Grievant was returned to work on June 7, 2010. On June 4, 2010, the Grievant learned that he woould be working first shift (7:00 a.m. - 3:00 p.m.) as the Directed Patrol Supervisor. The Grievant spoke to Lieutenant Ratliff and requested that he be returned to third shift. Lieutenant Ratliff instructed the Grievant to submit a bid preference. The Grievant complied. On June 9, 2010, the Grievant was notified that he would remain on first shift, but his title changed to Investigations Supervisor and he would be acting as court liaison.

On June 11, 2010, a grievance was filed challenging the University's refusal to return the Grievant to third shift. The grievance went through the various stages of the grievance procedure. The grievance was denied. Arbitration was requested pursuant to Article 12 of the CBA.

II. ISSUE

The parties stipulated that the issue before the Arbitrator is: Did the Employer violate articles 41, 4, 14, or 39 of the Collective Bargaining Agreement when the Grievant was reinstated on June 7, 2010? If so, what is the appropriate remedy?

III. RELEVANT CONTRACT PROVISIONS

Article 3 Management Rights

Unless expressly provided to the contrary by a specific provision of this Agreement, the University reserves and retains solely and exclusively all of its rights to manage the operation of the Police Department.

These rights shall include, but are not limited to, the right of the University to:

* * * *

B. direct, supervise, evaluate, or hire employees: * * * *

Article 41 - Scheduling

Section 1. Guiding Principles. The University in its sole discretion shall establish the work schedule for its employees consistent with Article 21. In all cases, the University's need for effective law enforcement staffing shall have first priority in scheduling. Once these needs are met, employee preference will be given consideration. * * * *

Section 2. Shift Preference. The following shift preference procedure shall be applicable to the assignment of employees:

1. Eligible employees shall submit a written request including their top three shift preferences to the Chief of Police or designee. Requests for shift preference shall be submitted every six months by November 1, and May 1, annually. 2. Shift preference requests shall be determined by time in service with the Police Department, unless waived or agreed to by both parties, or unless the Chief of Police or designee determines that the operational needs of the department will require different shift assignments. * * * *

IV. POSITION OF THE PARTIES

A. Union's Position

The Union maintains that the University violated Article 41, Section 2 of the CBA when it refused to return the Grievant to third shift. The Union contends that the University did not demonstrate a legitimate operational need to have the Grievant on first shift. The Union maintains that the University's so-called need for the Grievant to serve as a court liaison is a sham intended to deny him of his right to work the third shift. The Union maintains that prior to the Grievant's termination, he worked as the Investigations Supervisor on third shift. The Union contends that other officers were available to serve as the court liaison. The Union argues that University's actions toward the Grievant are in retaliation because the Grievant pursued his termination to arbitration and was subsequently reinstated.

B. University's Position

It is the University's position that it has sole discretion to establish work schedules and that the operational needs of the University overrides any shift preference rights of an employee. The University contends that it had a legitimate operational need for the Grievant to serve as court liaison and work the first shift. The University maintains that while the Grievant worked the third shift immediately prior to his termination in June 2009, for the majority of the time, the Grievant worked the first shift. The University contends that the Grievant was the officer best qualified to serve as the Investigations Supervisor and court liaison.

V. DISCUSSION AND ANALYSIS

* * * *

The Arbitrator notes that the University argues that it had the sole discretion to determine work schedules according to its operational needs. The University cites *International Assn. of Machinists & Aerospace Workers, Dist. 154 Local Lodge No. 2770,* 958 F.2d 154 (6th Cir. 1992), in support of this position. The Arbitrator agrees, that Article 41 gives the University the sole discretion to establish the work schedules. However, Article 41 also requires the University to give consideration to employee preference when scheduling, subject to the operational needs of the department.

Thus, a senior employee's preference shall be honored unless an operational need requires a different assignment.

The evidence establishes that prior to his termination, the Grievant worked day shift as the Patrol Shift Commander with a special assignment as the Investigations Supervisor and concurrently, the Grievant worked many overtime hours on third shift. The evidence further establishes that for several months immediately preceding the Grievant's termination in 2009, the Grievant worked as an Investigations Supervisor on the night shift. Therefore, the question becomes did the University have a legitimate operational need to place the Grievant on first shift, instead of his preference of third shift.

According to the University's interpretation of Joint Exh 7, the Grievant worked 106.25 hours on third shift in the month of March 2009, as opposed to 64.25 hours on day shift; and the Grievant worked 139.25 hours on night shift as opposed to 85.25 hours on day shift in April 2009. Additionally, the evidence establishes that the remaining months leading up to the Grievant's termination in June 2009, he worked the night shift.

The Union acknowledges that Article 41, Section 2 allows the University to require a different shift assignment, other than the employee's preference, when it is done for the operational needs of the Department. However, the Union maintains that such a need must be a justified and legitimate operational need. The Union further asserts that the University cannot simply claim an operational need without demonstrating its necessity. It is the Union's position that the University failed to establish a legitimate operational need for denying the Grievant's shift request.

The University maintains that upon the Grievant's reinstatement, it had a legitimate operational need for the Grievant to work on the first shift. In support of this position, the University presented the testimony of Chief Michael Martinsen. Chief Martinsen testified that upon the Grievant's reinstatement he reassigned the Grievant to the Investigations Supervisor and court liaison. Chief Martinsen testified that due to concerns and issues there became a clear need for there to be a court liaison which would be responsible for maintaining a close relationship with the prosecutor, the Municipal court and the county court.

The University explains in its brief that the Investigations Supervisor is the natural choice to act as the court liaison because the Investigations Supervisor necessarily involves interaction with the Greene County Prosecutor's Office in order to transition investigations into criminal prosecutions. However, this explanation as to why the duties were assigned to the Investigations Supervisor was not emphasized at the arbitration hearing.

According to Chief Martinsen this was a demand made of the prosecutor because of various issues, including problems with investigations and handling of cases, improvement in officer testimony in court, and evidence retention issues.

* * * *

Arbitrator Stanton concluded that the Sheriff's actions were arbitrary and capricious when he denied the Grievant's shift preference despite his 22 years seniority. Arbitrator Stanton looked at the circumstances as a whole and based this conclusion on the Grievant's unrebutted statement that he was told by the new Chief Deputy that he was placed on third shift, to "take him out of the loop.'; the fact that the Grievant was issued a written warning for 'mis-spelled words' in an Accident Report; and the timing of the shift change in relation to the Grievant's request for arbitration. Under the rationale set forth in this case, the University's actions were arbitrary. Specifically, when looking at the timing of the emails and the change in the Grievant's title from Directed Patrol Supervisor to Investigations Supervisor supports the Union's claim.

In conjunction with this contention the Union maintains that the University's failure to return the Grievant to third shift is discrimination in violation of Article 4. The Union contends that the University discriminated against the Grievant based on the previous arbitration outcome which reinstated the Grievant. The Union maintains that in addition to all the reasons mentioned above, the discriminatory action is evidenced when the Grievant asked to be relieved of his assignment of the Investigations Supervisor so that he could work on third shift, Chief Martinsen responded by emailing FOP representative Mark Scranton seeking clarification as to whether the Grievant's email was a letter of resignation. The Union states that this email is indicative of the University's desire to rid itself of the Grievant. Chief Martinsen testified that he sought clarification from the Grievant because the Grievant did not have the option to decline a special assignment. The University contends that the Union has not presented any evidence that it treated the Grievant differently because he is a union member or because he won his previous arbitration. While the Arbitrator is not willing to conclude that the University engaged in discriminatory conduct, for the reasons that follow below, the Arbitrator finds that the University abused its discretion when it denied the Grievant's third shift preference.

VII. AWARD

The grievance is sustained.

APPLICATION AND DISCUSSION QUESTIONS

1. What evidence in this case suggests that the Employer's refusal to assign the grievant to the shift he worked prior to his termination/reinstatement may have been discriminatory?

2. What evidence in the case suggests the conclusion that the management decision was "arbitrary and capricious"?

3. Review Article 41 of the CBA, which states that management has the "sole discretion" to establish work schedules. Does this provision allow the Employer to schedule the grievant to any shift, even if for discriminatory, arbitrary, or capricious reasons?

IX. DEVELOPMENT OF EMPLOYMENT ARBITRATION

In 1991, the Supreme Court made it absolutely clear in *Gilmer v. Interstate/Johnson Lane* that mandatory arbitration and employment contracts were valid and legal. To eliminate any doubts that mandatory employment arbitration was legal and would be enforced by federal courts, the Supreme Court issued its decision in *Circuit City Stores, Inc. v. Adams*, which held that §1 of the Federal Arbitration Act applied to employment arbitration. Prior to *Circuit City stores, Inc.*, a number of lower federal courts held that §1 of the FAA which states that "contracts of employment of seamen, railroad employees, or any other class of workers engaged in foreign or interstate commerce" were exempted employment contracts. The Supreme Court held that a plain reading of the FAA only exempted transportation workers, not all workers who engaged in interstate commerce. This interpretation opened the floodgates for employers, especially private-sector employers, to require their employees to agree to resolve their employment disputes through arbitration, not in court.

A. Compulsory Arbitration

GILMER V. INTERSTATE/JOHNSON LANE CORP.
111 s. ct, 1647 (1991)

Justice WHITE delivered the opinion of the Court.

The question presented in this case is whether a claim under the Age Discrimination in Employment Act of 1967 (ADEA), 81 Stat. 602, as amended, 29 U.S.C. § 621 *et seq.*, can be subjected to compulsory arbitration pursuant to an arbitration agreement in a securities registration application. The Court of Appeals held that it could, 895 F.2d 195 (CA4 1990), and we affirm.

I.

Respondent Interstate/Johnson Lane Corporation (Interstate) hired petitioner Robert Gilmer as a Manager of Financial Services in May 1981. As required by his employment, Gilmer registered as a securities representative with several stock exchanges, including the New York Stock Exchange (NYSE). His registration application, entitled "Uniform Application for Securities Industry Registration or Transfer," provided, among other things, that Gilmer "agree[d] to arbitrate any dispute, claim or controversy" arising between him and Interstate "that is required to be arbitrated under the rules, constitutions or by-laws of the organizations with which I register." *Id.*, at 18. Of relevance to this case, NYSE Rule 347 provides for arbitration of "[a]ny controversy between a registered representative and any member or member organization arising out of the employment or termination of employment of such registered representative."

Interstate terminated Gilmer's employment in 1987, at which time Gilmer was 62 years of age. After first filing an age discrimination charge with the Equal Employment Opportunity Commission (EEOC), Gilmer subsequently brought suit in the United States District Court for the Western District of North Carolina, alleging that Interstate had discharged him because of his age, in violation of the ADEA. In response to Gilmer's complaint, Interstate filed in the District Court a motion to compel arbitration of the ADEA claim. In its motion, Interstate relied upon the arbitration agreement in Gilmer's registration application, as well as the Federal Arbitration Act (FAA), 9 U.S.C. § 1 *et seq.* The District Court denied Interstate's motion, based on this Court's decision in *Alexander v. Gardner-Denver Co.,* 415 U.S. 36, 94 S.Ct. 1011, 39 L.Ed.2d 147 (1974), and because it concluded that "Congress intended to protect ADEA claimants from the waiver of a judicial forum." The United States Court of Appeals for the Fourth Circuit reversed, finding "nothing in the text, legislative history, or underlying purposes of the ADEA indicating a congressional intent to preclude enforcement of arbitration agreements." 895 F.2d, at 197. We granted certiorari, 498 U.S. 809, 111 S.Ct. 41, 112 L.Ed.2d 18 (1990), to resolve a conflict among the Courts of Appeals regarding the arbitrability of ADEA claims.

II.

* * * *

It is by now clear that statutory claims may be the subject of an arbitration agreement, enforceable pursuant to the FAA. Indeed, in recent years we have held enforceable arbitration agreements relating to claims arising under the Sherman Act, 15 U.S.C. §§ 1-7; § 10(b) of the Securities Exchange Act of 1934, 15 U.S.C. § 78j(b); (Case citations omitted). In these cases we recognized that "[b]y agreeing to arbitrate a statutory claim, a party does not forgo the substantive rights afforded by the statute; it only submits to their resolution in an arbitral, rather than a judicial, forum." *Mitsubishi,* 473 U.S., at 628, 105 S.Ct., at 3354.

Although all statutory claims may not be appropriate for arbitration, "[h]aving made the bargain to arbitrate, the party should be held to it unless Congress itself has evinced an intention to preclude a waiver of judicial remedies for the statutory rights at issue." *Ibid.* In this regard, we note that the burden is on Gilmer to show that Congress intended to preclude a waiver of a judicial forum for ADEA claims. See *McMahon,* 482 U.S., at 227, 107 S.Ct., at 2337. If such an intention exists, it will be discoverable in the text of the ADEA, its legislative history, or an "inherent conflict" between arbitration and the ADEA's underlying purposes. See *ibid.* Throughout such an inquiry, it should be kept in mind that "questions of arbitrability must be addressed with a healthy regard for the federal policy favoring arbitration." *Moses H. Cone, supra,* 460 U.S., at 24, 103 S.Ct., at 941.

III.

Gilmer concedes that nothing in the text of the ADEA or its legislative history explicitly precludes arbitration. He argues, however, that compulsory arbitration of ADEA claims pursuant to arbitration agreements would be inconsistent with the statutory framework and purposes of the ADEA. Like the Court of Appeals, we disagree.

A.

* * * *

As Gilmer contends, the ADEA is designed not only to address individual grievances, but also to further important social policies. See, *e.g., EEOC v. Wyoming,* 460 U.S. 226, 231, 103 S.Ct. 1054, 1057-1058, 75 L.Ed.2d 18 (1983). We do not perceive any inherent inconsistency between those policies, however, and enforcing agreements to arbitrate age discrimination claims. It is true that arbitration focuses on specific disputes between the parties involved. The same can be said, however, of judicial resolution of claims. Both of these dispute resolution mechanisms nevertheless also can further broader social purposes. The Sherman Act, the Securities Exchange Act of 1934, RICO, and the Securities Act of 1933 all are designed to advance important public policies, but, as noted above, claims under those statutes are appropriate for arbitration. "[S]o long as the prospective litigant effectively may vindicate [his or her] statutory cause of action in the arbitral forum, the statute will continue to serve both its remedial and deterrent function." *Mitsubishi, supra,* 473 U.S., at 637, 105 S.Ct., at 3359.

We also are unpersuaded by the argument that arbitration will undermine the role of the EEOC in enforcing the ADEA. An individual ADEA claimant subject to an arbitration agreement will still be free to file a charge with the EEOC, even though the claimant is not able to institute a private judicial action. Indeed, Gilmer filed a charge with the EEOC in this case. In any event, the EEOC's role in combating age discrimination is not dependent on the filing of a charge; the agency may receive information concerning alleged violations of the ADEA "from any source," and it has independent authority to investigate age discrimination. See 29 CFR §§ 1626.4, 1626.13 (1990). Moreover, nothing in the ADEA indicates that Congress intended that the EEOC be involved in all employment disputes. (Case citations omitted). Finally, the mere involvement of an administrative agency in the enforcement of a statute is not sufficient to preclude arbitration...

Gilmer also argues that compulsory arbitration is improper because it deprives claimants of the judicial forum provided for by the ADEA. Congress, however, did not explicitly preclude arbitration or other nonjudicial resolution of claims, even in its recent amendments to the ADEA. "[I]f Congress intended the substantive protection afforded [by the ADEA] to include protection against waiver of the right to a judicial forum, that intention will be deducible from text or legislative history." *Mitsubishi,* 473 U.S., at 628, 105 S.Ct., at 3354. Moreover, Gilmer's argument ignores the ADEA's flexible approach to resolution of claims. The EEOC, for example, is directed to pursue "informal methods of conciliation, conference, and persuasion," 29 U.S.C. § 626(b), which suggests that out-of-court dispute resolution, such as arbitration, is consistent with the statutory scheme established by Congress. In addition, arbitration is consistent with Congress' grant of concurrent jurisdiction over ADEA claims to state and federal courts, see 29 U.S.C. § 626(c)(1) (allowing suits to be brought "in any court of competent jurisdiction"), because arbitration agreements, "like the provision for concurrent jurisdiction, serve to advance the objective of allowing [claimants] a broader right to select the forum for resolving disputes, whether it be judicial or otherwise." *Rodriguez de Quijas, supra,* at 483, 109 S.Ct., at 1921.

B.

In arguing that arbitration is inconsistent with the ADEA, Gilmer also raises a host of challenges to the adequacy of arbitration procedures. Initially, we note that in our recent arbitration cases we have already rejected most of these arguments as insufficient to preclude arbitration of statutory claims. Such generalized attacks on arbitration "res[t] on suspicion of arbitration as a method of weakening the protections afforded in the substantive law to would-be complainants," and as such, they are "far out of step with our current strong endorsement of the federal statutes favoring this method of resolving disputes." *Rodriguez de Quijas, supra,* at 481, 109 S.Ct., at 1920. Consequently, we address these arguments only briefly.

Gilmer first speculates that arbitration panels will be biased. However, "[w]e decline to indulge the presumption that the parties and arbitral body conducting a proceeding will be unable or unwilling to retain competent, conscientious and impartial arbitrators." *Mitsubishi, supra,* 473 U.S., at 634, 105 S.Ct., at 3357-3358. In any event, we note that the NYSE arbitration rules, which are applicable to the dispute in this case, provide protections against biased panels. The rules require, for example, that the parties be informed of the employment histories of the arbitrators, and that they be allowed to make further inquiries into the arbitrators' backgrounds...

Gilmer also complains that the discovery allowed in arbitration is more limited than in the federal courts, which he contends will make it difficult to prove discrimination. It is unlikely, however, that age discrimination claims require more extensive discovery than other claims that we have found to be arbitrable, such as RICO and antitrust claims. Moreover, there has been no showing in this case that the NYSE discovery provisions, which allow for document production, information requests, depositions, and subpoenas...

A further alleged deficiency of arbitration is that arbitrators often will not issue written opinions, resulting, Gilmer contends, in a lack of public knowledge of employers' discriminatory policies, an inability to obtain effective appellate review, and a stifling of the development of the law. The NYSE rules, however, do require that all arbitration awards be in writing, and that the awards contain the names of the parties, a summary of the issues in controversy, and a description of the award issued...

It is also argued that arbitration procedures cannot adequately further the purposes of the ADEA because they do not provide for broad equitable relief and class actions. As the court below noted, however, arbitrators do have the power to fashion equitable relief...

C.

An additional reason advanced by Gilmer for refusing to enforce arbitration agreements relating to ADEA claims is his contention that there often will be unequal bargaining power between employers and employees. Mere inequality in bargaining power, however, is not a sufficient reason to hold that arbitration agreements are never enforceable in the employment context...

IV. (Omitted)

V.

We conclude that Gilmer has not met his burden of showing that Congress, in enacting the ADEA, intended to preclude arbitration of claims under that Act. Accordingly, the judgment of the Court of Appeals is *Affirmed.*

Justice STEVENS, with whom Justice MARSHALL joins, dissenting.
Section 1 of the Federal Arbitration Act (FAA) states:

> "[N]othing herein contained shall apply to contracts of employment of seamen,
> railroad employees, or any other class of workers engaged in foreign or interstate commerce." 9 U.S.C. § 1.

The Court today, in holding that the FAA compels enforcement of arbitration clauses even when claims of age discrimination are at issue, skirts the antecedent question whether the coverage of the Act even extends to arbitration clauses contained in employment contracts, regardless of the subject matter of the claim at issue. In my opinion, arbitration clauses contained in employment agreements are specifically exempt from coverage of the FAA, and for that reason respondent Interstate/ Johnson Lane Corporation cannot, pursuant to the FAA, compel petitioner to submit his claims arising under the Age Discrimination in Employment Act of 1967 (ADEA), 29 U.S.C. § 621 *et seq.,* to binding arbitration.

I and II (omitted)

Not only would I find that the FAA does not apply to employment-related disputes between employers and employees in general, but also I would hold that compulsory arbitration conflicts with the congressional purpose animating the ADEA, in particular. As this Court previously has noted, authorizing the courts to issue broad injunctive relief is the cornerstone to eliminating discrimination in society...

IV.

When the FAA was passed in 1925, I doubt that any legislator who voted for it expected it to apply to statutory claims, to form contracts between parties of unequal bargaining power, or to the arbitration of disputes arising out of the employment relationship. In recent years, however, the Court "has effectively rewritten the statute",1 and abandoned its earlier view that statutory claims were not appropriate subjects for arbitration. See *Mitsubishi Motors v. Soler Chrysler-Plymouth, Inc.,* 473 U.S. 614, 646-651, 105 S.Ct. 3346, 3363-3367, 87 L.Ed.2d 444 (1985) (STEVENS, J., dissenting). Although I remain persuaded that it erred in doing so,2 the Court has also put to one side any concern about the inequality of bargaining power between an entire industry, on the one hand, and an individual customer or employee, on the other. See *ante,* at 1655-1656. Until today, however, the Court has not read § 2 of the FAA as broadly encompassing disputes arising out of the employment relationship. I believe this additional extension of the FAA is erroneous. Accordingly, I respectfully dissent.

APPLICATION AND DISCUSSION QUESTIONS

Gilmer involved the interpretation of the Federal Arbitration Act, which was enacted in 1925. The FAA was reenacted and codified in 1947.

1. What was Congress' goal in enacting the FAA?

2. What are the major provisions of the FAA? Which employees are covered and which are excluded?

3. What are *Gilmer's* primary arguments as to ADEA claims that should be excluded from compulsory arbitration agreements?

4. The Court addresses a number of "challenges to the adequacy of arbitration procedures". What are the Court's responses to the following challenges and do you agree?

    a. Arbitration panels will be biased.

    b. Discovery is more limited in arbitration than in court.

    c. Arbitrators will not issue written decisions.

    d. Only limited equitable relief is available in arbitration.

    e. There is an unequal bargaining power between employees and employers, when negotiating arbitration clauses.

5. Arbitrators who hear arbitration disputes should be aware of the National Academy of Arbitrators' Professional Responsibility Standards in Employment Arbitration. See http://naarb.org/Guidelines_for_standard. asp. The Guidelines provide guidance on such topics as post-hearing conduct, post-award conduct, disclosure, public standards, etc.

CIRCUIT CITY STORES, INC. V. ADAMS
532 U.S. 105, 121 S.CT. 1302 (2001)

Justice KENNEDY delivered the opinion of the Court.

Section 1 of the Federal Arbitration Act (FAA or Act) excludes from the Act's coverage "contracts of employment of seamen, railroad employees, or any other class of workers engaged in foreign or interstate commerce." 9 U.S.C. § 1. All but one of the Courts of Appeals which have addressed the issue interpret this provision as exempting contracts of employment of transportation workers, but not other employment contracts, from the FAA's coverage. A different interpretation has been adopted by the Court of Appeals for the Ninth Circuit, which construes the exemption so that all contracts of employment are beyond the FAA's reach, whether or not the worker is engaged in transportation. It applied that rule to the instant case. We now decide that the better interpretation is to construe the statute, as most of the Courts of Appeals have done, to confine the exemption to transportation workers.

I

In October 1995, respondent Saint Clair Adams applied for a job at petitioner Circuit City Stores, Inc., a national retailer of consumer electronics. Adams signed an employment application which included the following provision:

> "I agree that I will settle any and all previously unasserted claims, disputes or controversies arising out of or relating to my application or candidacy for employment, employment and/or cessation of employment with Circuit City, *exclusively* by final and binding *arbitration* before a neutral Arbitrator. By way of example only, such claims include claims under federal, state, and local statutory or common law, such as the Age Discrimination in Employment Act, Title VII of the Civil Rights Act of 1964, as amended, including the amendments of the Civil Rights Act of 1991, the Americans with Disabilities Act, the law of contract and [the] law of tort." App. 13 (emphasis in original).

Adams was hired as a sales counselor in Circuit City's store in Santa Rosa, California. Two years later, Adams filed an employment discrimination lawsuit against Circuit City in state court, asserting claims under California's Fair Employment and Housing Act, Cal. Govt.Code Ann. § 12900 *et seq.* (West 1992 and Supp.1997), and other claims based on general tort theories under California law. Circuit City filed suit in the United States District Court for the Northern District of California, seeking to enjoin the state-court action and to compel arbitration of respondent's claims pursuant to the FAA, 9 U.S.C. §§ 1–16. The District Court entered the requested order. Respondent, the court concluded, was obligated by the arbitration agreement to submit his claims against the employer to binding arbitration. An appeal followed.

While respondent's appeal was pending in the Court of Appeals for the Ninth Circuit, the court ruled on the key issue in an unrelated case. The court held the FAA does not apply to contracts of employment. See *Craft v. Campbell Soup Co.*, 177 F.3d 1083 (C.A.9 1999). In the instant case, following the rule announced in *Craft*, the Court of Appeals held the arbitration agreement between Adams and Circuit City was contained in a "contract of employment," and so was not subject to the FAA. 194 F.3d 1070 (C.A.9 1999). Circuit City petitioned this Court, noting that the Ninth Circuit's conclusion that all employment contracts are excluded from the FAA conflicts with every other Court of Appeals to have addressed the question. (citation omitted)

II

A

Congress enacted the FAA in 1925. As the Court has explained, the FAA was a response to hostility of American courts to the enforcement of arbitration agreements, a judicial disposition inherited from then-longstanding English practice. See, e.g., *Allied–Bruce Terminix Cos. v. Dobson*, 513 U.S. 265, 270–271, 115 S.Ct. 834, 130 L.Ed.2d 753 (1995); *Gilmer v. Interstate/Johnson Lane Corp.*, 500 U.S. 20, 24, 111 S.Ct. 1647, 114 L.Ed.2d 26 (1991). To give effect to this purpose, the FAA compels judicial enforcement of a wide range of written arbitration agreements. The FAA's coverage provision, § 2, provides that "[a] written provision in any maritime transaction or a contract evidencing a transaction involving commerce to settle by arbitration a controversy thereafter arising out of such contract or transaction, or the refusal to perform the whole or any part thereof, or an agreement in writing to submit to arbitration an existing controversy arising out of such a contract, transaction, or refusal, shall be valid, irrevocable, and enforceable, save upon such grounds as exist at law or in equity for the revocation of any contract." 9 U.S.C. § 2.

B

1

Respondent, at the outset, contends that we need not address the meaning of the § 1 exclusion provision to decide the case in his favor. In his view, an employment contract is not a "contract evidencing a transaction involving interstate commerce" at all, since the word "transaction" in § 2 extends only to commercial contracts. See *Craft*, 177 F.3d, at 1085 (concluding that § 2 covers only "commercial deal[s] or merchant's sale [s]"). This line of reasoning proves too much, for it would make the § 1 exclusion provision superfluous. If all contracts of employment are beyond the scope of the Act under the § 2 coverage provision, the separate exemption for "contracts of employment of seamen, railroad employees, or any other class of workers engaged in ... interstate commerce" would be pointless. See, *e.g.*, *Pennsylvania Dept. of Public Welfare v. Davenport,* 495 U.S. 552, 562, 110 S.Ct. 2126, 109 L.Ed.2d 588 (1990) ("Our cases express a deep reluctance to interpret a statutory provision so as to render superfluous other provisions in the same enactment"). The proffered interpretation of "evidencing a transaction involving commerce," furthermore, would be inconsistent with *Gilmer v. Interstate/Johnson Lane Corp.,* 500 U.S. 20, 111 S.Ct. 1647, 114 L.Ed.2d 26 (1991), where we held that § 2 required the arbitration of an age discrimination claim based on an agreement in a securities registration application, a dispute that did not arise from a "commercial deal or merchant's sale." Nor could respondent's construction of § 2 be reconciled with the expansive reading of those words adopted in *Allied–Bruce,* 513 U.S., at 277, 279–280, 115 S.Ct. 834. If, then, there is an argument to be made that arbitration agreements in employment contracts are not covered by the Act, it must be premised on the language of the § 1 exclusion provision itself.

Respondent, endorsing the reasoning of the Court of Appeals for the Ninth Circuit that the provision excludes all employment contracts, relies on the asserted breadth of the words "contracts of employment of ... any other class of workers engaged in ... commerce." Referring to our construction of § 2' s coverage provision in *Allied–Bruce*—concluding that the words "involving commerce" evidence the congressional intent to regulate to the full extent of its commerce power—respondent contends § 1's interpretation should have a like reach, thus exempting all employment contracts. The two provisions, it is argued, are coterminous; under this view the "involving commerce" provision brings within the FAA's scope all contracts within the Congress' commerce power, and the "engaged in ... commerce" language in § 1 in turn exempts from the FAA all employment contracts falling within that authority.

This reading of § 1, however, runs into an immediate and, in our view, insurmountable textual obstacle. Unlike the "involving commerce" language in § 2, the words "any other class of workers engaged in ... commerce" constitute a residual phrase, following, in the same sentence, explicit reference to "seamen" and "railroad employees." Construing the residual phrase to exclude all employment contracts fails to give independent effect to the statute's enumeration of the specific categories of workers which precedes it; there would be no need for Congress to use the phrases "seamen" and "railroad employees" if those same classes of workers were subsumed within the meaning of the "engaged in ... commerce" residual clause. The wording of § 1 calls for the application of the maxim *ejusdem generis,* the statutory canon that "[w]here general words follow specific words in a statutory enumeration, the general words are construed to embrace only objects similar in nature to those objects enumerated by the preceding specific words." 2A N. Singer, Sutherland on Statutes and Statutory Construction § 47.17 (1991); see also *Norfolk & Western R. Co. v. Train Dispatchers,* 499 U.S. 117, 129, 111 S.Ct. 1156, 113 L.Ed.2d 95 (1991). Under this rule of construction the residual clause should be read to give effect to the terms "seamen" and "railroad employees," and should itself be controlled and defined by reference to the enumerated categories of workers which are recited just before it; the interpretation of the clause pressed by respondent fails to produce these results.

* * * *

In sum, the text of the FAA forecloses the construction of § 1 followed by the Court of Appeals in the case under review, a construction which would exclude all employment contracts from the FAA. While the historical arguments respecting Congress' understanding of its power in 1925 are not insubstantial, this fact alone does not give us basis to adopt, "by judicial decision rather than amendatory legislation," *Gulf Oil, supra,* at 202, 95 S.Ct. 392, an expansive construction of the FAA's exclusion provision that goes beyond the meaning of the words Congress used. While it is of course possible to speculate that Congress might have chosen a different jurisdictional formulation had it known that the Court would soon embrace a less restrictive reading of the Commerce Clause, the text of § 1 precludes interpreting the exclusion provision to defeat the language of § 2 as to all employment contracts. Section 1 exempts from the FAA only contracts of employment of transportation workers.

* * * *

For the foregoing reasons, the judgment of the Court of Appeals for the Ninth Circuit is reversed, and the case is remanded for further proceedings consistent with this opinion.

It is so ordered.

Justice STEVENS, with whom Justice GINSBURG and Justice BREYER join, and with whom Justice SOUTER joins as to Parts II and III, dissenting.

Justice SOUTER has cogently explained why the Court's parsimonious construction of § 1 of the Federal Arbitration Act (FAA or Act) is not consistent with its expansive reading of § 2. I join his dissent, but believe that the Court's heavy reliance on the views expressed by the Courts of Appeals during the past decade makes it appropriate to comment on three earlier chapters in the history of this venerable statute.

I

Section 2 of the FAA makes enforceable written agreements to arbitrate "in any maritime transaction or a contract evidencing a transaction involving commerce." 9 U.S.C. § 2. If we were writing on a clean slate, there would be good reason to conclude that neither the phrase "maritime transaction" nor the phrase "contract evidencing a transaction involving commerce" was intended to encompass employment contracts.

The history of the Act, which is extensive and well documented, makes clear that the FAA was a response to the refusal of courts to enforce commercial arbitration agreements, which were commonly used in the maritime context. The original bill was drafted by the Committee on Commerce, Trade, and Commercial Law of the American Bar Association (ABA) upon consideration of "the further extension of the principle of *commercial* arbitration." Report of the Forty-third Annual Meeting of the ABA, 45 A.B.A. Rep. 75 (1920) (emphasis added). As drafted, the bill was understood by Members of Congress to "simply provid[e] for one thing, and that is to give an opportunity to enforce an agreement in *commercial* contracts and *admiralty* contracts." 65 Cong. Rec.1931 (1924) (remarks of Rep. Graham) (emphasis added). It is no surprise, then, that when the legislation was first introduced in 1922, it did not mention employment contracts, but did contain a rather precise definition of the term "maritime transactions" that underscored the commercial character of the proposed bill. Indeed, neither the history of the drafting of the original bill by the ABA, nor the records of the deliberations in Congress during the years preceding the ultimate enactment of the Act in 1925, contain any evidence that the proponents of the legislation intended it to apply to agreements affecting employment.

* * * *

Justice SOUTER, with whom Justice STEVENS, Justice GINSBURG, and Justice BREYER join, dissenting.

Section 2 of the Federal Arbitration Act (FAA or Act) provides for the enforceability of a written arbitration clause in "any maritime transaction or a contract evidencing a transaction involving commerce," 9 U.S.C. § 2, while § 1 exempts from the Act's coverage "contracts of employment of seamen, railroad employees, or any other class of workers engaged in foreign or interstate commerce." Whatever the understanding of Congress's implied admiralty power may have been when the Act was passed in 1925, the commerce power was then thought to be far narrower than we have subsequently come to see it. As a consequence, there are two quite different ways of reading the scope of the Act's provisions. One way would be to say, for example, that the coverage provision extends only to those contracts "involving commerce" that were understood to be covered in 1925; the other would be to read it as exercising Congress's commerce jurisdiction in its modern conception in the same way it was thought to implement the more limited view of the Commerce Clause in 1925. The first possibility would result in a statutory ambit frozen in time, behooving Congress to amend the statute whenever it desired to expand arbitration clause enforcement beyond its scope in 1925; the second would produce an elastic reach, based on an understanding that Congress used language intended to go as far as Congress could go, whatever that might be over time.

In *Allied–Bruce Terminix Cos. v. Dobson*, 513 U.S. 265, 115 S.Ct. 834, 130 L.Ed.2d 753 (1995), we decided that the elastic understanding of § 2 was the more sensible way to give effect to what Congress intended when it legislated to cover contracts "involving commerce," a phrase that we found an apt way of providing that coverage would extend to the outer constitutional limits under the Commerce Clause. The question here is whether a similarly general phrase in the § 1 exemption, referring to contracts of "any ... class of workers engaged in foreign or interstate commerce," should receive a correspondingly evolutionary reading, so as to expand the exemption for employment contracts to keep pace with the enhanced reach of the general enforceability provision. If it is tempting to answer yes, on the principle that what is sauce for the goose is sauce for the gander, it is sobering to realize that the Courts of Appeals have, albeit with some fits and starts as noted by Justice STEVENS, *ante,* at 1316–1317 (dissenting opinion),1 overwhelmingly rejected the evolutionary reading of § 1 accepted by the Court of Appeals in this case. See *ante,* at 1306–1307 (opinion of the Court) (citing cases). A majority of this Court now puts its *imprimatur* on the majority view among the Courts of Appeals.

The number of courts arrayed against reading the § 1 exemption in a way that would allow it to grow parallel to the expanding § 2 coverage reflects the fact that this minority view faces two hurdles, each textually based and apparent from the face of the Act. First, the language of coverage (a contract evidencing a transaction "involving commerce") is different from the language of the exemption (a contract of a worker "engaged in ... commerce"). Second, the "engaged in ... commerce" catchall phrase in the exemption is placed in the text following more specific exemptions for employment contracts of "seamen" and "railroad employees." The placement possibly indicates that workers who are excused from arbitrating by virtue of the catchall exclusion must resemble seamen and railroad workers, perhaps by being employees who actually handle and move goods as they are shipped interstate or internationally.

Neither hurdle turns out to be a bar, however. The first objection is at best inconclusive and weaker than the grounds to reject it; the second is even more certainly inapposite, for reasons the Court itself has stated but misunderstood.

APPLICATION AND DISCUSSION QUESTIONS

1. The arbitration agreement cited examples of employment claims covered by the agreement. Is that sufficient to prohibit employees from filing claims under employment statutes which are not cited, for example, the Family Medical Leave Act or the Fair Labor Standard Act? How should an arbitrator rule if an employer files a motion to compel an employee to file their FMLA and FLSA claims through the arbitration process and not federal court?

2. The Ninth Circuit held in *Craft v. Campbell Soup Co., 177 F.3d 1083 (C.A. 1999)* that the FAA does not apply to contracts of employment. Every other Court of Appeals has reached a different conclusion. The Supreme Court reversed the Ninth Circuit. As you read the Supreme Court's contract construction analysis, do you agree with the conclusion?

3. How does the Court resolve the issue of whether employment contracts are not a contract involving interstate commerce? How does the Court apply the term *ejusdem generis?* How do arbitrators use this contract principle when analyzing disputes?

E.E.O.C. V. WAFFLE HOUSE, INC.
534 U.S. 279 (2002)

Justice STEVENS delivered the opinion of the Court.

The question presented is whether an agreement between an employer and an employee to arbitrate employment-related disputes bars the Equal Employment Opportunity Commission (EEOC) from pursuing victim-specific judicial relief, such as backpay, reinstatement, and damages, in an enforcement action alleging that the employer has violated Title I of the Americans with Disabilities Act of 1990(ADA), 104 Stat. 328, 42 U.S.C. § 12101 *et seq.* (1994 ed. and Supp. V).

I

In his application for employment with respondent, Eric Baker agreed that "any dispute or claim" concerning his employment would be "settled by binding arbitration." As a condition of employment, all prospective Waffle House employees are required to sign an application containing a similar mandatory arbitration agreement. See App. 56. Baker began working as a grill operator at one of respondent's restaurants on August 10, 1994. Sixteen days later he suffered a seizure at work and soon thereafter was discharged. *Id.,* at 43–44. Baker did not initiate arbitration proceedings, nor has he in the seven years since his termination, but he did file a timely charge of discrimination with the EEOC alleging that his discharge violated the ADA.

After an investigation and an unsuccessful attempt to conciliate, the EEOC filed an enforcement action against respondent in the Federal District Court for the District of South Carolina, pursuant to § 107(a) of the ADA, 42 U.S.C. § 12117(a) (1994 ed.), and § 102 of the Civil Rights Act of 1991, as added, 105 Stat. 1072, 42 U.S.C. § 1981a (1994 ed.). Baker is not a party to the case. The EEOC's complaint alleged that respondent engaged in employment practices that violated the ADA, including its discharge of Baker "because of his disability," and that its violation was intentional, and "done with malice or with reckless indifference to [his] federally protected rights." The complaint requested the court to grant injunctive relief to "eradicate the effects of [respondent's] past and present unlawful employment practices," to order specific relief designed to make Baker whole, including backpay, reinstatement, and compensatory damages, and to award punitive damages for malicious and reckless conduct. App. 38–40.

Respondent filed a petition under the Federal Arbitration Act (FAA), 9 U.S.C. § 1 *et seq.,* to stay the EEOC's suit and compel arbitration, or to dismiss the action. Based on a factual determination that Baker's actual employment contract had not included the arbitration provision, the District Court denied the motion. The Court of Appeals granted an interlocutory appeal and held that a valid, enforceable arbitration agreement between Baker and respondent did exist. 193 F.3d 805, 808 (C.A.4 1999). The court then proceeded to consider "what effect, if any, the binding arbitration agreement between Baker and Waffle House has on the EEOC, which filed this action in its own name both in the public interest and on behalf of Baker." *Id.,* at 809. After reviewing the relevant statutes and the language of the contract, the court concluded that the agreement did not foreclose the enforcement action because the EEOC was not a party to the contract, and it has independent statutory authority to bring suit in any federal district court where venue is proper. *Id.,* at 809–812. Nevertheless, the court held that the EEOC was precluded from seeking victim-specific relief in court because the policy goals expressed in the FAA required giving some effect to Baker's arbitration agreement.

* * * *

The Court of Appeals based its decision on its evaluation of the "competing policies" implemented by the ADA and the FAA, rather than on any language in the text of either the statutes or the arbitration agreement between Baker and respondent. 193 F.3d, at 812. It recognized that the EEOC never agreed to arbitrate its statutory claim, *id.,* at 811 ("We must also recognize that in this case the EEOC is not a party to any arbitration agreement"), and that the EEOC has "independent statutory authority" to vindicate the public interest, but opined that permitting the EEOC to prosecute Baker's claim in court "would significantly trample" the strong federal policy favoring arbitration because Baker had agreed to submit his claim to arbitration. *Id.,* at 812. To effectuate this policy, the court distinguished between injunctive and victim-specific relief, and held that the EEOC is barred from obtaining the latter because any public interest served when the EEOC pursues "make whole" relief is outweighed by the policy goals favoring arbitration. Only when the EEOC seeks broad injunctive relief, in the Court of Appeals' view, does the public interest overcome the goals underpinning the FAA.

If it were true that the EEOC could prosecute its claim only with Baker's consent, or if its prayer for relief could be dictated by Baker, the court's analysis might be persuasive. But once a charge is filed, the exact opposite is true under the statute—the EEOC is in command of the process. The EEOC has exclusive jurisdiction over the claim for 180 days. During that time, the employee must obtain a right-to-sue letter from the agency before prosecuting the claim. If, however, the EEOC files suit on its own, the employee has no independent cause of action, although the employee may intervene in the EEOC's suit. 42 U.S.C. § 2000e–5(f)(1) (1994 ed.). In fact, the EEOC takes the position that it may pursue a claim on the employee's behalf even after the employee has disavowed any desire to seek relief. Brief for Petitioner 20. The statute clearly makes the EEOC the master of its own case and confers on the agency the authority to evaluate the strength of the public interest at stake. Absent textual support for a contrary view, it is the public agency's province—not that of the court—to determine whether public resources should be committed to the recovery of victim-specific relief. And if the agency makes that determination, the statutory text unambiguously authorizes it to proceed in a judicial forum.

* * * *

Even if the policy goals underlying the FAA did necessitate some limit on the EEOC's statutory authority, the line drawn by the Court of Appeals between injunctive and victim-specific relief creates an uncomfortable fit with its avowed purpose of preserving the EEOC's public function while favoring arbitration. For that purpose, the category of victim-specific relief is both overinclusive and underinclusive. For example, it is overinclusive because while punitive damages benefit the individual employee, they also serve an obvious public function in deterring future violations. See *Newport v. Fact Concerts, Inc.,* 453 U.S. 247, 266–270, 101 S.Ct. 2748, 69 L.Ed.2d 616 (1981) ("Punitive damages by definition are not intended to compensate the injured party, but rather to punish the tortfeasor ..., and to deter him and others from similar extreme conduct"); Restatement (Second) of Torts § 908 (1977). Punitive damages may often have a greater impact on the behavior of other employers than the threat of an injunction, yet the EEOC is precluded from seeking this form of relief under the Court of Appeals' compromise scheme. And, it is underinclusive because injunctive relief, although seemingly not "victim-specific," can be seen as more closely tied to the employees' injury than to any public interest. See *Occidental,* 432 U.S., at 383, 97 S.Ct. 2447 (REHNQUIST, J., dissenting) ("While injunctive relief may appear more 'broad based,' it nonetheless is redress for individuals").

The compromise solution reached by the Court of Appeals turns what is effectively a forum selection clause into a waiver of a nonparty's statutory remedies. But if the federal policy favoring arbitration trumps the plain language of Title VII and the contract, the EEOC should be barred from pursuing any claim outside the arbitral forum. If not, then the statutory language is clear; the EEOC has the authority to pursue victim-specific relief regardless of the forum that the employer and employee have chosen to resolve their disputes. Rather than attempt to split the difference, we are persuaded that, pursuant to Title VII and the ADA, whenever the EEOC chooses from among the many charges filed each year to bring an enforcement action in a particular case, the agency may be seeking to vindicate a public interest, not simply provide make-whole relief for the employee, even when it pursues entirely victim-specific relief. To hold otherwise would undermine the detailed enforcement scheme created by Congress simply to give greater effect to an agreement between private parties that does not even contemplate the EEOC's statutory function.

V

It is true, as respondent and its *amici* have argued, that Baker's conduct may have the effect of limiting the relief that the EEOC may obtain in court. If, for example, he had failed to mitigate his damages, or had accepted a monetary settlement, any recovery by the EEOC would be limited accordingly. See, *e.g., Ford Motor Co. v. EEOC,* 458 U.S. 219, 231–232, 102 S.Ct. 3057, 73 L.Ed.2d 721 (1982) (Title VII claimant "forfeits his right to backpay if he refuses a job substantially equivalent to the one he was denied"); *EEOC v. Goodyear Aerospace Corp.,* 813 F.2d 1539, 1542 (C.A.9 1987) (employee's settlement "rendered her personal claims moot"); *EEOC v. U.S. Steel Corp.,* 921 F.2d 489, 495 (C.A.3 1990) (individuals who litigated their own claims were precluded by res judicata from obtaining individual relief in a subsequent EEOC action based on the same claims). As we have noted, it "goes without saying that the courts can and should preclude double recovery by an individual." *General Telephone,* 446 U.S., at 333, 100 S.Ct. 1698.

But, no question concerning the validity of his claim or the character of the relief that could be appropriately awarded in either a judicial or an arbitral forum is presented by this record. Baker has not sought arbitration of his claim, nor is there any indication that he has entered into settlement negotiations with respondent. It is an open question whether a settlement or arbitration judgment would affect the validity of the EEOC's claim or the character of relief the EEOC may seek. The only issue before this Court is whether the fact that Baker has signed a mandatory arbitration agreement limits the remedies available to the EEOC. The text of the relevant statutes provides a clear answer to that question. They do not authorize the courts to balance the competing policies of the ADA and the FAA or to second-guess the agency's judgment concerning which of the remedies authorized by law that it shall seek in any given case.

Moreover, it simply does not follow from the cases holding that the employee's conduct may affect the EEOC's recovery that the EEOC's claim is merely derivative. We have recognized several situations in which the EEOC does not stand in the employee's shoes. See *Occidental,* 432 U.S., at 368, 97 S.Ct. 2447 (EEOC does not have to comply with state statutes of limitations); *General Telephone,* 446 U.S., at 326, 100 S.Ct. 1698 (EEOC does not have to satisfy Rule 23 requirements); *Gilmer,* 500 U.S., at 32, 111 S.Ct. 1647 (EEOC is not precluded from seeking classwide and equitable relief in court on behalf of an employee who signed an arbitration agreement). And, in this context, the statute specifically grants the EEOC exclusive authority over the choice of forum and the prayer for relief once a charge has been filed. The fact that ordinary principles of res judicata, mootness, or mitigation may apply to EEOC claims does not contradict these decisions, nor does it render the EEOC a proxy for the employee.

The judgment of the Court of Appeals is reversed, and the case is remanded for further proceedings consistent with this opinion.

It is so ordered.

Justice THOMAS, with whom THE CHIEF JUSTICE and Justice SCALIA join, dissenting.

The Court holds today that the Equal Employment Opportunity Commission (EEOC or Commission) may obtain victim-specific remedies in court on behalf of an employee who had agreed to arbitrate discrimination claims against his employer. This decision conflicts with both the Federal Arbitration Act (FAA), 9 U.S.C. § 1 *et seq.,* and the basic principle that the EEOC must take a victim of discrimination as it finds him. Absent explicit statutory authorization to the contrary, I cannot agree that the EEOC may do on behalf of an employee that which an employee has agreed not to do for himself. Accordingly, I would affirm the judgment of the Court of Appeals.

*   *   *   *

III

Rather than allowing the EEOC to undermine a valid and enforceable arbitration agreement between an employer and an employee in the manner sanctioned by the Court today, I would choose a different path. As this Court has stated, courts are "not at liberty to pick and choose among congressional enactments, and when two statutes are capable of co-existence, it is the duty of the courts, absent a clearly expressed congressional intention to the contrary, to regard each as effective." *Pittsburgh & Lake Erie R. Co. v. Railway Labor Executives' Assn.,* 491 U.S. 490, 510, 109 S.Ct. 2584, 105 L.Ed.2d 415 (1989). In this case, I think that the EEOC's statutory authority to enforce the ADA can be easily reconciled with the FAA.

Congress has not indicated that the ADA's enforcement scheme should be interpreted in a manner that undermines the FAA. Rather, in two separate places, Congress has specifically encouraged the use of arbitration to resolve disputes under the ADA. First, in the ADA itself, Congress stated: "Where appropriate and to the extent authorized by law, the use of alternative means of dispute resolution, including settlement negotiations, conciliation, facilitation, mediation, factfinding, minitrials, and *arbitration, is encouraged to resolve disputes arising under this chapter.*" 42 U.S.C. § 12212 (emphasis added). Second, Congress used virtually identical language to encourage the use of arbitration to resolve disputes under the ADA in the Civil Rights Act of 1991. See Pub.L. 102–166, § 118, 105 Stat. 1081.13

The EEOC contends that these provisions do not apply to this dispute because the Commission has not signed an arbitration agreement with Waffle House and the provisions encourage arbitration "only when the parties have consented to arbitration." Reply Brief for Petitioner. Remarkably, the EEOC at the same time questions whether it even has the statutory authority to take this step. See Brief for Petitioner 22, n. 7. As a result, the EEOC's view seems to be that Congress has encouraged the use of arbitration to resolve disputes under the ADA only in situations where the EEOC does not wish to bring an enforcement action in court. This limiting principle, however, is nowhere to be found in § 12212. The use of arbitration to resolve all disputes under the ADA is clearly "authorized by law." See Part I, *supra.* Consequently, I see no indication that Congress intended to grant the EEOC authority to enforce the ADA in a manner that undermines valid and enforceable arbitration agreements.

Given the utter lack of statutory support for the Court's holding, I can only conclude that its decision today is rooted in some notion that employment discrimination claims should be treated differently from other claims in the context of arbitration. I had thought, however, that this Court had decisively repudiated that principle in *Gilmer.* See 500 U.S., at 27–28, 111 S.Ct. 1647 (holding that arbitration agreements can be enforced without contravening the "important social policies" furthered by the ADEA). For all of these reasons, I respectfully dissent.

APPLICATION AND DISCUSSION QUESTIONS

1. Is it logical that an employee agrees to resolve all discrimination claims through arbitration but the courts hold that the agreement does not apply to SCCH claims? How does the court reach this conclusion?

2. The Court typically cites the FAA to require employment claims to be processed through arbitration. How did the Court distinguish Gilmer which stated the FAA required arbitration and the decision in Waffle House?

3. If the court had prohibited the EEOC from bringing such claims, would it have effectively limited their enforcement powers? Does the public have an interest in the EEOC pursuing such claims?

OPINION

CLIFTON, Circuit Judge:

Defendant Ralphs Grocery Company appeals the district court's denial of its motion to compel arbitration. Plaintiff Zenia Chavarria filed an action alleging violations of the California Labor Code and California Business and Professions Code §§ 17200 et seq. She asserted claims on behalf of herself and a proposed class of other Ralphs' employees. Ralphs moved to compel arbitration of her individual claim pursuant to its arbitration policy, to which all employees acceded upon submitting applications for employment with Ralphs. The district court denied the motion, holding that Ralphs' arbitration policy was unconscionable under California law and therefore unenforceable.

Ralphs argues that its policy is not unconscionable under California law and in the alternative that the Federal Arbitration Act ("FAA") preempts California law. The FAA provides that arbitration agreements must be enforced except "upon such grounds as exist at law or in equity for the revocation of any contract." 9 U.S.C. § 2. The FAA preempts a contract defense, such as unconscionability, that may be generally applicable to any contract but disproportionately impacts arbitration agreements. AT&T Mobility LLC v. Concepcion.

We affirm. We conclude that Ralphs' arbitration policy is unconscionable under California law, and that the state law supporting that conclusion is not preempted by the FAA.

I. Background

Plaintiff Zenia Chavarria completed an employment application seeking work with Defendant Ralphs Grocery Company. Chavarria obtained a position as a deli clerk with Ralphs and worked in that capacity for roughly six months. After leaving her employment with Ralphs, Chavarria filed this action, alleging on behalf of herself and all similarly situated employees that Ralphs violated various provisions of the California Labor Code and California Business and Professions Code §§ 17200 et seq. Ralphs moved to compel arbitration of her individual claim pursuant to an arbitration policy incorporated into the employment application. Chavarria opposed the motion, arguing that the arbitration agreement was unconscionable under California law.

* * * *

I. Discussion

Ralphs argues that the district court erred when it held that the arbitration policy was unconscionable under California law. Ralphs also contends that federal law requires that the policy be enforced in accordance with its terms, even if the policy is unconscionable under California law, and that therefore the district court was required to compel arbitration. We review de novo the denial of a motion to compel arbitration.

The FAA provides that any contract to settle a dispute by arbitration shall be valid and enforceable, "save upon such grounds as exist at law or in equity for the revocation of any contract." 9 U.S.C. § 2. This provision reflects both that (a) arbitration is fundamentally a matter of contract, and (b) Congress expressed a "liberal federal policy favoring arbitration." Concepcion (citation and internal quotation marks omitted). Arbitration agreements, therefore, must be placed on equal footing with other contracts.

* * * *

A. Unconscionability under California Law

Under California law, a contract must be both procedurally and substantively unconscionable to be rendered invalid. Armendariz. California law utilizes a sliding scale to determine unconscionability—greater substantive unconscionability may compensate for lesser procedural unconscionability. *Id.* Applying California law, the district court held that the arbitration agreement in this case was both procedurally unconscionable and substantively unconscionable. We agree.

1. Procedural Unconscionability

Procedural unconscionability concerns the manner in which the contract was negotiated and the respective circumstances of the parties at that time, focusing on the level of oppression and surprise involved in the agreement. *Ferguson v. Countrywide Credit Indus., Inc.*; *A & M Produce Co. v. FMC Corp.* Oppression addresses the weaker party's absence of choice and unequal bargaining power that results in "no real negotiation." A & M Produce. Surprise involves the extent to which the contract clearly discloses its terms as well as the reasonable expectations of the weaker party. Parada v. Super. Ct.

The district court held that Ralphs' arbitration policy was procedurally unconscionable for several reasons. The court found that agreeing to Ralphs' policy was a condition of applying for employment and that the policy was presented on a "take it or leave it" basis with no opportunity for Chavarria to negotiate its terms. It further found that the terms of the policy were not provided to Chavarria until three weeks after she had agreed to be bound by it. This additional defect, the court held, multiplied the degree of procedural unconscionability.

Ralphs argues that the policy is not procedurally unconscionable because Chavarria was not even required to agree to its terms. Ralphs bases this contention on a provision in the employment application that provides, "Please sign and date the employment application ... to acknowledge you have read, understand & agree to the following statements." The word "please," Ralphs contends, belies any suggestion of a requirement. Ralphs argues that Chavarria could have been hired without signing the agreement.

Ralphs' argument ignores the terms of the policy itself, which bound Chavarria regardless of whether she signed the application. The policy provides that "[n]o signature by an Employee or the Company is required for this Arbitration Policy to apply to Covered Disputes." That Ralphs asked nicely for a signature is irrelevant. The policy bound Chavarria and all other potential employees upon submission of their applications.

* * * *

2. Substantive Unconscionability

Chavarria must also demonstrate that Ralphs' arbitration policy is substantively unconscionable under California law. A contract is substantively unconscionable when it is unjustifiably one-sided to such an extent that it "shocks the conscience."

The district court found that several terms rendered Ralphs' arbitration policy substantively unconscionable. First, the court noted that Ralphs' arbitrator selection provision would always produce an arbitrator proposed by Ralphs in employee-initiated arbitration proceedings. Second, the court cited the preclusion of institutional arbitration administrators, namely AAA or JAMS, which have established rules and procedures to select a neutral arbitrator. Third, the court was troubled by the policy's requirement that the arbitrator must, at the outset of the arbitration proceedings, apportion the arbitrator's fees between Ralphs and the employee regardless of the merits of the claim. The court identified this provision as "a model of how employers can draft fee provisions to price almost any employee out of the dispute resolution process." The combination of these terms created a policy, according to the court, that "lacks any semblance of fairness and eviscerates the right to seek civil redress.... To condone such a policy would be a disservice to the legitimate practice of arbitration and a stain on the credibility of our justice system."

* * * *

Ralphs also argues that there is nothing of concern in its cost allocation provision because it simply follows the "American Rule" that each party shall bear its own fees and costs. Ralphs misses the point. The troubling aspect of the cost allocation provision relates to the arbitrator fees, not attorney fees.

The policy mandates that the arbitrator apportion those costs on the parties up front, before resolving the merits of the claims. Further, Ralphs has designed a system that requires the arbitrator to apportion the costs equally between Ralphs and the employee, disregarding any potential state law that contradicts Ralphs' cost allocation.

* * * *

The significance of this obstacle becomes more apparent through Ralphs' representation to the district court that the fees for a qualified arbitrator under its policy would range from \$7,000 to \$14,000 per day. Ralphs' policy requires that an employee pay half of that amount—\$3,500 to \$7,000—for each day of the arbitration just to pay for her share of the arbitrator's fee. This cost likely dwarfs the amount of Chavarria's claims.

The district court focused its substantive unconscionability discussion on these terms, and it was correct in doing so because the terms lie far beyond the line required to render an agreement invalid. We therefore need not discuss at length the additional terms in Ralphs' arbitration policy, such as the unilateral modification provision, which we have previously held to support a finding of substantive unconscionability.

3. The Sliding Scale of Unconscionability

Excessive procedural or substantive unconscionability may compensate for lesser unconscionability in the other prong. But here we have both. Ralphs has tilted the scale so far in its favor, both in the circumstances of entering the agreement and its substantive terms, that it "shocks the conscience." Accordingly, Ralphs' arbitration policy cannot be enforced against Chavarria under California law.

B. Preemption by the FAA

Federal law preempts state laws that stand as an obstacle to the accomplishment of Congress's objectives. Accordingly, the FAA preempts state laws that in theory apply to contracts generally but in practice impact arbitration agreements disproportionately.

California's unconscionability doctrine applies to all contracts generally and therefore constitutes "such grounds at law or in equity for the revocation of [a] contract." 9 U.S.C. § 2. But specific application of rules within that doctrine may be problematic.

In this case, California's procedural unconscionability rules do not disproportionately affect arbitration agreements, for they focus on the parties and the circumstances of the agreement and apply equally to the formation of all contracts. The application of California's general substantive unconscionability rules to Ralphs' arbitration policy, however, warrants more discussion.

III. Conclusion

The arbitration policy imposed by Ralphs on its employees is unconscionable under California law. That law is not preempted by the FAA. We affirm the decision of the district court denying Ralphs' motion to compel arbitration, and we remand for further proceedings.

AFFIRMED and REMANDED.

APPLICATION AND DISCUSSION QUESTIONS

1. As pointed out by the Court, "Under California law, a contract must be both procedurally and substantively unconscionable to be rendered

invalid". How does the Court define the two types of unconscionability in contracts? Give an example of each type.

2. How can the cost of arbirtration, especially the cost-shfting provision, be considered unconscionable? What was the estimated cost of arbitration an employee would be liable for if they lost their case?

3. How did the Court avoid a conflict with the FAA and the state laws on arbitration? Were they not in conflict?

4. See, *Arnold v. Burger King*, 2015-Ohio-1639, 31 N.E.3d 687, where the court held the mandatory arbitration agreement was unconscionable. The employee, Shannon Arnold, was raped by her Supervisor in the men's bathroom at a Burger King restaurant while she was cleaning the restrooms as part of her regular work duties. Arnold's employment was subject to her signing a mandatory arbitration agreement in which she agreed to submit to a national arbitration association, "any and all disputes, claims or controversies for monetary or equitable relief arising out of or relating to [Arnold's] employment." The agreement also covered "claims or controversies relating to events outside the scope of your employment." The issue in this case is whether or not the trial court erred in ruling that an employer cannot require an employee who signed a mandatory arbitration agreement, to arbitrate a claim if the agreement was unconscionable. To understand the theory behind Ohio's public policy, the appellate court referenced *Taylor Building Corporation of America v. Benfield* stating that arbitration agreements are "valid, irrevocable, and enforceable, except upon grounds that exist at law or in equity for the revocation of any contract."

In addition, the court identified two elements of unconscionability: (1) unfair and unreasonable contract terms and (2) an absence of meaningful choice on the part of one of the parties. In applying this test, the court concluded that there was clearly a "disparity in bargaining power" for many reasons, such as Arnold's inability to alter the terms of the agreement or continue the employment process without signing the agreement, and Burger King misleading its employees regarding the cost and timeliness of the arbitration process. After confirming that Arnold met the two-prong test for unconscionability, the appellate court affirmed the trial court's decision.

B. DISCRIMINATION CLAIMS

2010 AAA EMPLOYMENT LEXIS 105[*]

Employment Arbitration Tribunal

* * * *

Summary of Facts

The facts further indicate that several incidents involving the Claimant occurred with the department, for instance, on April 28, 2008, Compliance Manager received an email from an employee, Employee A, about the Claimant, stating, "[y]ou better get her under control. She is dawgin you out." Another incident occurred on July 17, 2007, in an email exchange between the Claimant and a coworker, Employee B, the Claimant wrote, "I told you Employee B- I don't play the games -- I just sit back and watch and listen. Never a token always an individual."(Compliance Manager stated that Employee B, who is also African-American was very emotional and offended by the comment. Compliance Manager counseled the Claimant, and told her that there was a strong implication underlying the email, and that she felt Employee B was legitimately upset, then the Claimant became visibly defiant.

The facts indicate that Compliance Manager had observed the Claimant angry and unpleasant on occasion as well as very rude and confrontational on several occasions, and her behavior included crossing her arms and rolling her eyes. Compliance Manager observed that the Claimant was disrespectful and unpleasant in response to her 2007 performance review, in response to Compliance Manager's discussion with her about her violating the dress code, in response to her February 2008 performance review, in the April 30 CAP meeting. Additionally, Compliance Manager had to intervene and have a discussion with the Claimant because of her harsh tone and inappropriate conduct during a conversation she was having about a file with Employee B.

On May 1, 2008, Compliance Manager met with Employee C and Employee A, who informed Compliance Manager that they were confronted earlier that morning by the Claimant. They then proceeded to inform Compliance Manager of several other complaints regarding the Claimant's behavior. Compliance Manager gave them options, including telling them to submit their complaints in writing. By the end of the day, Compliance Manager received written complaints from four of her workers all complaining about the Claimant's behavior and statements made by the Claimant. Compliance Manager emailed Director A, Director of Financial Operations, regarding the complaints. She also contacted HR Officer of HR Services Contractor, a contractor providing HR services for Respondent, for guidance on how to handle the situation. The Claimant was on FMLA until May, 19, 2008. When she returned, Compliance Manager and Director B, Director of Account Management, met with the Claimant to discuss the written complaints. The Claimant denied making any of the statements attributed to her in the written complaints. Compliance Manager did not believe the Claimant and terminated her employment.

The Claimant filed a demand for arbitration in which she contends that Respondent terminated her in retaliation for her taking FMLA, and discrimination based on race, age, and gender.

Prior to the hearing, the Respondent filed a motion for summary judgment which was denied on May 17, 2010, At the arbitration hearing which was held May 24-26, 2010, the Claimant's FMLA claims were dismissed, the discrimination claims remain.

Issue

Whether the Claimant was discriminated against on the basis of race, African-American; age, over 40; gender, female when she was terminated on May 19, 2008.

Analysis of the Issues

The Claimant contends that Respondent terminated her employment based on her age, gender, and race. When reviewing a discrimination claim, a plaintiff may make out a prima facie case of discrimination in one of two ways. A plaintiff may use direct evidence of discrimination which shows that the employer was motivated by discriminatory intent in the discharge of the employee. Discriminatory intent must be proven. *Mauzy v. Kelly Services, Inc.,* (1996) 75 Ohio St. 3d 578.

Under the direct evidence method, an employee must prove a causal link or nexus between evidence of a discriminatory statement or conduct and the prohibited act of discrimination. *Byrnes v. LCI Communication Holdings Co.*, 77 Ohio St.3d 125 (1996). The Claimant does not rely on this method.

A plaintiff may also use indirect evidence by satisfying the four-part burden-shifting analysis set forth in *McDonnell Douglas Corp. v. Green*, 411 U.S. 792, 802-803 (1973). If the Claimant succeeds in this burden, then the employer has the burden to provide a legitimate, nondiscriminatory reason for the plaintiff's discharge. If the employer succeeds at this burden, the plaintiff has the ultimate burden to show by a preponderance of the evidence that the reasons for which the defendant articulated for the discharge were merely a pretext for unlawful discrimination.

In order to establish a *prima facie* case of discrimination, the Claimant must prove that: (1) she was in a protected class; (2) she suffered an adverse employment action; (3) she was qualified for her job and (4) she was replaced by an employee not in the protected class, or that similarly-situated employees not in the protected class were treated more favorably.

The Respondent recognizes that the Claimant can establish the first three prongs of the *prima facie* case. The Respondent states that the Claimant cannot establish the fourth prong by showing that she was replaced by someone outside her protected class, therefore, she must prove the fourth prong by showing that similarly-situated employees not in the protected class were treated more favorably.

In order to establish the fourth prong of the *prima facie* case, the Claimant must demonstrate that a comparable non-protected person was treated better.

The relevant factors for consideration when making a determination whether employees are similarly situated often include the employee's supervisors, the standards that the employees had to meet, and the employee's conduct. But the weight to be given to each factor can vary depending on the particular case.

It is the Claimant's contention that multiple co-workers exhibited performance problems or interpersonal conflict similar to herself and was not terminated by the Respondent. Specifically, the Claimant emphasizes performance weaknesses recognized on a 2007 job evaluation of a coworker named Employee D.

* * * *

...However, the Arbitrator finds that the Claimant has not demonstrated that Employee D's situation was similarly-situated to the Claimant's.

Next, the Claimant, again emphasizes performance related issues of another coworker, Employee E. The Claimant stresses Employee E's weaknesses that were noted on his April 2007 performance evaluation. Again, Employee E is not similarly-situated, because the Claimant was not terminated for performance issue. Again, his race, gender or age is not an issue.

Lastly, the Claimant maintains that she is similarly-situated to another employee, Employee A. Employee A is a Caucasian male, under the age of 40. The evidence indicates that Employee A was placed on a Corrective Action Plan (CAP), in May 2006 after having a "highly emotional, loud, and disruptive" conversation with a co-worker that was similar to a behavioral issue that Employee A had a few days prior. Additionally, Employee A was observed engaging in a heated debate with his supervisor, Compliance Manager, during an Appeals Coordinator meeting. The evidence further indicates that Compliance Manager noted that Employee A was still unsatisfactorily immature in his handling of conflict.

The Respondent maintains that Employee A is not similarly-situated to the Claimant. The Respondent acknowledges that Employee A was placed on a CAP for behavior in 2006 for engaging in a loud emotional conversation with a coworker. The Respondent further acknowledges that Employee A engaged in a heated debate with Compliance Manager over a work-related matter. Lastly, the Respondent acknowledges that Employee A's comments on his March 2009 performance review stated that he needed to handle conflict more maturely and that he reacted to disagreements on a personal level. However, the Respondent contends that the Claimant engaged in different, more frequent, and for more egregious misconduct than Employee A.

However, the Respondent appears to expand the instances of misconduct beyond the complaints that were memorialized in the May 1 statements given to Compliance Manager. Indeed, the Respondent isolates confrontations that would appear to be already incorporated into the written complaint of the coworker. For instance, the Respondent lists a "verbal confrontation with Employee B (August 2007)" as one of the inappropriate incidents from the Claimant. While the confrontation is not mentioned in Employee B's written complaint, it, nonetheless, most likely played a part in the environment described by Employee B and thus, was taken into account when she wrote the complaint. Additionally, the Respondent includes instances where it says that the Claimant reacted rudely and inappropriately to Compliance Manager. However, the Arbitrator believes the proper comparison is for the specific conduct complained about in the May 1, 2008 statements given to Compliance Manager. The Arbitrator will look at each complaint individually.

(Employee B, Employee C, Employee D omitted)

Employee A

* * * *

The evidence establishes that both employees were previously placed on CAPS for behavior related issues, by previous supervisors. The evidence establishes that both employees still exhibited behavioral issues. Specifically, the evidence indicates that the behavior complained of by the Claimant includes comments regarding Compliance Manager's inability to manage, that she probably went home and smacked her son because Employee A challenged her in a heated debate. The statements also convey that the Claimant would not accept responsibility for her actions and became offensive when an error was brought to her attention. In regards to Employee A, the evidence demonstrates that he engaged in a heated debate with Compliance Manager which challenged and upset her. The evidence also indicates that he handles conflict immaturely and disagreements on a personal level. Therefore, the evidences supports the Claimant's contention that Employee A engaged in similar behavioral issues and was not terminated for this behavior. The Arbitrator notes that the Respondent contends that the cumulative effect of the Claimant's multiple instances of misconduct must be taken into consideration, the Arbitrator agrees that the misconduct as a whole must be considered under the pretext analysis, but for purposes of the *prima facie* case, the Claimant has met her burden.

Employer's Burden to Articulate a Legitimate, Non-Discriminatory Reason for Its Action

Under the burden-shifting paradigm set forth in *McDonnell Douglas*, because the Claimant met her burden of establishing a *prima facie* case, the burden shifts to the Respondent to articulate a legitimate, non-discriminatory reason for its action.

* * * *

The Respondent contends that it terminated the Claimant because of the written complaints by her coworkers, and the Claimant's failure to offer any explanation to the comments that were attributed to her. Therefore, the Respondent has met its burden to articulate a legitimate non-discriminatory reason for its action. Now, the Claimant must show that the articulated reason is but a mere pretext for unlawful discrimination.

PRETEXT

The Claimant maintains that she can establish that the Respondent's articulated reason is a pretext for unlawful discrimination. A plaintiff can show pretext, "by showing that the proffered reason (1) has no basis in fact, (2) did not actually motivate the Defendant's challenged conduct, or (3) was insufficient to warrant the challenged conduct."

No Factual Basis

* * * *

The Respondent maintains that Compliance Manager had an "honest belief" that the coworkers' complaints against the Claimant were true. The Respondent further contends that the Claimant's flat denials are not credible against four of her coworkers. In support of its position, the Respondent states that in the May 19th meeting when asked about the statements, the Claimant's response was to simply say ask her coworkers. The Respondent emphasizes that Compliance Manager's "honest belief" is further bolstered by evidence that demonstrates that the Claimant has engaged in numerous acts of dishonesty and has not told the truth about her own behavior on many occasions.

An employer's "honest belief" in the articulated non-discriminatory reason for the adverse action is not pretext. The "honest belief" rule provides that if an employer honestly believed in the reason given for its employment action, then the employee cannot establish pretext even if the employer's reason is ultimately found to be mistaken, foolish, trivial or baseless. *Smith v. Chrysler Corp.*, 155 F.3d 799, 807 (6th Cir. 1998). As the *Smith* Court explained the rationale underlying the rule is that the focus of a discrimination suit is on the intent of the employer. When the employer honestly, even if mistakenly, believes in the non-discriminatory reason it relied upon, then, the employer arguably lacks the necessary discriminatory intent. However, in order for an employer to demonstrate that it had an honest belief, the employer must establish its reasonable reliance on the particularized facts that were before it at the time the decision was made. Even then, an employee has the opportunity to produce evidence to the contrary.

The question for the Arbitrator is whether Compliance Manager had an "honest-belief" that the coworkers statements were true. When making a determination that the employer had an "honest-belief", courts look to whether the employer can establish its 'reasonable reliance' on the particularized facts that were before it at the time the decision was made. *Braithwaite a The Timken Co.*, 258 F.3d 488, 494 (6th Cir, 2001) quoting *Smith v. Chrysler Corp.* 155 F.3d 799, 807 (6th Cir. 1998). A plaintiff must put forth evidence which demonstrates that the employer did not "honestly believe" in the proffered non-discriminatory reason for its adverse employment action. *Geiger a Kroger Co.* 2008 U.S. Dist. LEXIS 91237 citing *Braithwaite* at 494. A court's job is not to second guess an employer's business judgment, rather to evaluate "whether the employer gave an honest explanation of its behavior." Id. The Arbitrator also agrees that it is not his job to second guess an employer's business judgment.

Compliance Manager had written complaints from four of her workers complaining about the Claimant. The complaints ranged from making snide remarks about Compliance Manager's management style to the Claimant's statements that she had Director A in her back pocket, to calling Compliance Manager names, to reacting angrily and negatively when an error in her work was brought to her attention. Several of the complaints claim that the Claimant made the work environment intolerable. In response to these written statements, Compliance Manager contacted Director A and HR Services Contractor for guidance. The evidence indicates that she worked with HR Services Contractor on a plan to address the concerns. Consequently, a meeting was held giving the Claimant an opportunity to explain the comments. The Claimant denied making the statements. Compliance Manager didn't believe the Claimant's denials and chose to terminate. Thus, it appears that Compliance Manager's reliance on the statements was reasonable.

Therefore, the Claimant has not established that the Respondent's legitimate non-discriminatory reasons were a pretext for unlawful discrimination.

After Acquired Evidence

The Respondent contends that the Claimant is not entitled to reinstatement, backpay, or frontpay based on "after-acquired evidence" that would have resulted in her termination upon discovery. Although not really relevant here since the Claimant has not established that she was terminated based on illegal discriminatory motives, the Respondent puts forth evidence that it would have terminated the Claimant based on "after-acquired evidence". Specifically, the Respondent contends that the Claimant's failure to disclose a felony theft conviction on her applications was cause for termination. "Where an employer seeks to rely upon after-acquired evidence of wrongdoing, it must first establish that the wrongdoing was of such severity that the employee in fact would have been terminated on those grounds alone if the employer had known of it at the time of discharge." *McKennon a Nashville Banner Publishing Co.*, 513 U.S.

352 (1995). At the arbitration hearing, the Claimant admitted to having a felony theft conviction resulting from her stealing checks from a prior employer, Claimant's Prior Employer. Although the Claimant states that she told the interviewer that she had been in previous trouble with the law, the evidence indicates that the Claimant did not disclose this conviction on her application to Respondent. The evidence further indicates that upon discovery of this information, the Claimant would have been terminated. Therefore, the Claimant would not be entitled to reinstatement, backpay or frontpay.

Conclusion

The Claimant established a *prima facie* case of discrimination. The Respondent met its burden to articulate a legitimate non-discriminatory reason for its action. However, the Claimant did not establish that the Respondent's reason was a pretext for illegal discrimination. The evidence demonstrates that the Respondent terminated the Claimant based on written complaints that were received by the Claimant's coworkers. The evidence further demonstrates that Compliance Manager reasonably relied on these complaints in making her decision to terminate the Claimant.

APPLICATION AND DISCUSSION QUESTIONS

1. What is "after acquired evidence" and should the arbitrator consider such evidence?

2. What was the "after acquired evidence" in this case? Should this evidence deny the claimant all possible remedies?

3. Did the claimant establish a "prima facie case"? Which element was at issue?

4. What was the employer's legitimate reason for terminating the claimant? If the employer is asked to show a legitimate reason, the claimant can argue "pretext". How is the claimant to prove "pretext" and how is it normally established?

5. What is the "honest belief test" and how was it applied in this case?

6. What facts did the arbitrator consider in determing the "similarly situated" person?

GREEN MORTGAGE BANK, INC. [*]

II. ISSUE

Whether the Claimant was terminated based on his age. If so, what is the appropriate remedy?

III. POSITION OF THE PARTIES

A. Claimant's Position

It is the Claimant's position that he was terminated based on his age. The Claimant contends that he can establish that persons outside of the protected class were treated more favorably than he was, and this is evidence of age discrimination. The Claimant further maintains that the three incidents of discipline are merely pretexts for unlawful age discrimination. The Claimant contends that the work environment at Green was fostered to attract younger employees and discriminate against older employees.

B. Green's Position

It is Green's position that it did not discriminate against the Claimant and that it had a legitimate, non-discriminatory reason to terminate the Claimant. Green asserts that the Claimant developed a pattern of angry behavior at work against his co-workers that could not be tolerated. Green maintains that it treated employees substantially younger than the Claimant similarly. Green acknowledges that it encouraged a "fun" work environment because this environment encouraged innovation and low employee turnover. Green further contends that the Claimant failed to provide make a causal connection between the work environment and his termination.

---

*   Unpublished Decision (Floyd D. Weatherspoon, 2007)

IV. DISCUSSION AND ANALYSIS

Green paints the portrait of an angry, overbearing, domineering person that strikes fear into coworkers. The Claimant paints the picture of a gentle, soft-spoken and caring man that is a poet and author that publishes children's books.

In order to establish a prima facie case of age discrimination, the plaintiff must demonstrate that: (1) he is a member of a statutorily protected class; (2) that he suffered an adverse employment action; (3) that he was qualified for the position; and (4) either that he was replaced by or that his discharge permitted the retention of a person of a substantially younger age.

Once the plaintiff establishes a prima facie case, the burden shifts to the employer to articulate a non-discriminatory reason for the action. *McDonnell Douglas,* 411 U.S. at 802. If the employer meets this burden, the burden shifts back to the plaintiff to establish that the reason offered by the employer was merely a pretext for discrimination. Pretext can be established by showing: the proffered reason has no basis in fact, the proffered reason did not actually motivate the defendant's challenged conduct, the proffered reason was insufficient to warrant the challenged conduct, or the employer acted contrary to a written company policy prescribing the action to be taken by the employer under the circumstances. The ultimate burden of the plaintiff in an age discrimination case is to prove he or she was discharged because of age.

It is undisputed that the Claimant meets the first two prongs of the prima facie case. The Claimant is a member of the protected class, he is over 40 years of age. The Claimant's employment was terminated; therefore, he suffered an adverse employment action. Green contends that the Claimant cannot meet the last two prongs of the prima facie case.

Green maintains that an employee is not qualified where it is shown that he or she was not meeting the employer's legitimate expectations. Green asserts that the Claimant was not qualified for the position because of his angry outbursts. However, the ability to perform the required job duties in a satisfactory manner is what determines whether an employee is qualified for the position. Because an employee becomes subject to disciplinary action does not automatically render that employee unqualified to perform the duties required of the job. Green has not provided sufficient evidence that the Claimant was unable to do the duties required in a satisfactory manner. This evidence established that the Claimant was qualified for his position.

For the fourth prong of the prima facie case, the Claimant must demonstrate that his discharge permitted retention of a substantially younger person. To meet this requirement the Claimant maintains that persons outside the protected class were treated more favorably than he was and that this is evidence of age discrimination.

Specifically, the Claimant asserts that Eric W. was not disciplined for engaging in the same type of behavior for which he was disciplined.

The Arbitrator finds that the Claimant has sufficiently met the elements of a prima facie case. "To say that a plaintiff has established a *prima facie* case is simply to say that he has produced sufficient evidence to present his case to a jury. * * * * Further, there must be at least a logical connection between each element of the prima facie case and the illegal discrimination for which it establishes a legally mandatory, rebuttable presumption." Under the burden shifting paradigm set forth in *McDonnell Douglas*, once the plaintiff establishes a prima facie case of discrimination, the burden shifts to the employer to articulate a legitimate, non-discriminatory reason for its action. The Employer meets this burden by stating that the Claimant engaged in a pattern of angry behavior that could not be tolerated at the workplace. Green maintains that the Claimant developed a pattern of angry behavior as evidenced by the three incidents of angry outbursts. The Claimant maintains that this is merely a pretext for age discrimination. The Claimant contends that in looking at the individual incidents of discipline and the workplace environment, age discrimination is established.

The evidence establishes that the Claimant was disciplined and eventually terminated for three separate incidents. In analyzing the Employer's theory that the Claimant developed a pattern of angry behavior and the Claimant's theory that this is merely a pretext to age discrimination, a review of the incidents leading to the termination is necessary. The Arbitrator will analyze each of the three separate incidents and the parties' arguments.

* * * *

Similarly Situated

The Claimant contends that this is nothing more than a pretext for unlawful discrimination because it is undisputed that Eric W. engaged in the same behaviors for which the Claimant was disciplined, "i.e., using foul language in anger, and that Ron's and W.'s supervisor did nothing to address W.'s behavior."

Green maintains that the focus of the Claimant's discipline in this instance was his use of foul language while angry. It was not the use of profanity that was the issue. Green contends that the evidence demonstrates that Eric W. used profanity in the office, but not in an angry manner. Therefore, it was not the same behavior. Moreover, Green contends that the Claimant acknowledged at the hearing that it was not inappropriate for him to get disciplined regarding this incident. The Claimant testified that he crossed the line when he used that language toward Eric W. However, the Claimant provided evidence that Eric W. did use profanity in anger. In support of his argument, the Claimant points to the testimony of Pam E. Pam E. testified that she heard Eric W. use profanity in the office while he was angry. The question becomes are the employees and situations similarly situated, as to show that Green engaged in different treatment of the employees?

A similarly situated employee is one who is "directly comparable to [the plaintiff] in all material respects." In order to be considered similarly-situated for comparison purposes, two employees must be virtually identical, in that they must "have dealt with the same supervisor, been subject to the same standards, and engaged in the same conduct without any mitigating or distinguishing circumstances."

The evidence establishes that the Claimant was disciplined for using foul language in an angry manner. As Green pointed out, the Claimant acknowledged that he crossed the line and he further acknowledged that his being disciplined was appropriate in this situation. The evidence presented demonstrates that Eric W. used profanity regularly in the office. There was also evidence that Mr. W. used profanity while angry. However, there is no evidence that any of these incidents were brought to Joe's attention. It was Joe that decided to discipline the Claimant for use of foul language in an angry manner. According to Joe, Mr. W. wasn't disciplined because he didn't receive complaints about him. Indeed, the Claimant contends that Pam was aware and did not discipline Mr. W. However, she is not the one that disciplined the Claimant for use of foul language. Therefore, the situations are not similarly situated. Thus, the Claimant has not shown discriminatory animus.

To the extent that the Claimant maintains that Green based its decision to discipline on previous undocumented conduct that did not occur, again, the argument is without merit. As stated, this incident, alone, is sufficient to warrant discipline.

Final Warning [Facts Omitted]

As a result of this incident, the Claimant received a "final warning" stating, "Claimant demonstrated insubordination in his actions and words toward a supervisor. This is the second occurrence claimant has been written up for regarding actions towards another employee on the floor." Under his expectations, it states, "because of the disruptive nature of his actions, claimant must respect every person he encounters and must maintain a harmonious work environment. Any further outbursts or disrespectful behavior will result in termination."

The Claimant did provide sufficient evidence that this was not an angry outburst. However, the evidence established that the Claimant's behavior in this instance was definitely inappropriate. The evidence indicates there was sufficient reason for Green to discipline the Claimant regarding this incident. The Claimant has not demonstrated that this was a pretext for age discrimination.

Termination (Omitted)

* * * *

The Claimant was terminated May 19, 2004. Employer Exhibit 18, proides despite previous warnings and coaching, claimant continues to communicate in a manner which is intimidating to others. His supervisor reported the conversation between her and claimant to include comments by claimant that were insubordinate, questioning Tina's practices that are consistent with company policy, and standing over her in what she described as "an intimidating manner". The evidence reveals that Green had sufficient reason to terminate the Claimant after three incidents of misconduct. The Claimant had received two previous warnings. The Claimant was put on notice that after the "final warning" that any further misconduct would result in termination.

* * * *

Environment at Green

The Claimant contends that Green intentionally created a youthful environment and maintained a separate culture. The Claimant states that this environment when viewed in light of the other evidence demonstrates that age was a deciding factor in the decision to terminate the Claimant.

The Claimant testified regarding the work environment at Green. He testified, "there were many, many toys added, the motorcycles were added, there was much more encouragement to be involved with the toys and the play games and the music." He further testified, "there was at least one pogo stick that I recall. There were dart guns, the dart games, all types of little soft Nerf ball-type things. And it started out with small water pistols, and over a period of time escalated into these monster water guns, and people would be running through the office and squirting each other, and that was pretty constant. The Claimant testified that the employees were encouraged by Joe to engage in use of the toys by announcing it over the loudspeakers, e-mails, and one-on-one conversations. He further stated that he was personally encouraged by Joe to get involved with the toys. He responded he didn't care to. According to the Claimant, Joe didn't seem to care one way or another, and didn't pursue the issue at that point.

Green acknowledges that it attempted to create a "fun" environment. Joe testified the reason for this was, "we tried to create a culture that resulted in innovation and in an atmosphere that kept people wanting to come back to work and resulted in low turnover." Joe further testified that he wanted to bring in older employees to diversify the workforce. It was Joe's belief that such an environment had several benefits. It fostered an attitude of innovation and creativity, and encouraged good customer service. Joe also felt that having a fun work environment would result in low employee turnover.

The Claimant asserts that this environment was fostered to attract young people. However, Joe testified that he thought this environment would attract "people that wanted a place that they could go that felt a little less like work when they went there and wasn't mundane for them, so that even though they had to work hard all day long, they had something that broke up the monotony for them."

In support of his position, the Claimant cites *Ahern v. Ameritech Corp.*, 137 Ohio App.3d 754 (8th Dist. 2000), for the proposition that "age discrimination was found to exist based on management's fostering a youthful, playful environment." The Claimant asserts that the evidence of a youthful environment is much more compelling in this case, than that of *Ahern*. The Claimant contends that Joe created a work environment that "encouraged game-playing (e.g. chair-racing, darts, water pistols and super soakers, pogo sticks and electric mini-motorcycles) in order to foster an environment of thinking and acting young."

However, *Ahern* is distinguishable. Initially, it is noted that unlike the facts in *Ahern* the "fun" environment fostered by Joe existed prior to the Claimant's employment at Green. In *Ahern* the work environment changed significantly under the new general manager. Another distinction is that Joe is the one that made the decision to hire the Claimant.

* * * *

V. CONCLUSION

The Claimant met the elements of a prima facie case. The Employer met its burden to articulate a non-discriminatory reason for its conduct. Specifically, the Employer provided sufficient evidence that the Claimant was terminated for three separate incidents of misconduct. The Claimant did not prove that this was merely a pretext for unlawful termination based on age. Moreover, the Claimant did not prove that he was treated less favorably than other similarly-situated employees. While the evidence demonstrates that a "fun" work atmosphere was encouraged by Green, this is not sufficient evidence of age discrimination.

Each party is to bear his own cost for attorney's fees.

VI. AWARD

The grievance is denied.

APPLICATION AND DISCUSSION QUESTIONS

1. Did the Claimant establish a claim/prima facie case of age discrimination? Was the Claimant successful in presenting evidence that the Employer's claims were a "pretext" to discrimination? How does the arbitrator define "pretext"?

2. Was there sufficient evidence to terminate the Claimant? Were the claimant and Mr. W "similarly situated", in that their conduct was similar? How does the arbitrator define "similarly situated"? Does the record support the Claimant's claim that a younger employee was permitted to engage in misconduct (used profanity), but was not disciplined?

3. The Claimant argues that the "youthful" environment at Green supports his claims of age discrimination. What conduct by other employees did the climant point to that created a "youthful environment"? The Claimant cited *Ahern v. Ameritech Corp.* to support his claim of age discrimination. How does the arbitrator distinguish the case?

4. As the arbitrator, would you have reached the same or a different conclusion in this case?

C. CONTRACT DISPUTES

2004 AAA EMPLOYMENT LEXIS 141

AMERICAN ARBITRATION ASSOCIATION

AUGUST 25, 2004, DECIDED*

Employment Arbitration Tribunal

* * * *

I. STATEMENT OF FACTS

The facts indicate that Claimant and Respondent A and Respondent B (Respondent/ Firm) entered into a contractual agreement effective January 1, 2001. (Claimant's Exh. A) Pursuant to the agreement, Respondent/Firm joined Claimant in an "of counsel" relationship with the intention to merge its existing law practice. Under the agreement Claimant paid Respondent/Firm an annual base compensation. The relationship terminated August 31, 2002. At the termination of the relationship, there were outstanding accounts receivables that were to be billed on the August 2002 billing cycle.

The Claimant, seek the following claim in arbitration pursuant to Section 15 of the agreement between the parties. The Claimants seek relief for Respondent/Firm' failure to remit fees earned while Respondent/Firm was still in an "of counsel" relationship, but collected from clients after the relationship terminated. Respondent/Firm contend they were responsible for the servicing of their own clients and worked the cases. Therefore, they are entitled to the accounts receivables in question. Respondent/ Firm filed a counterclaim seeking relief for Claimant's breach of the agreement.

Respondent/Firm contend that Claimant breached the agreement and terminated the relationship without the required thirty day notice.

II. ISSUE

Whether there was a breach of the contractual agreement between the parties dated December 29, 2000, if so, what is the appropriate remedy?

III. STIPULATIONS (Omitted)

IV. RELEVANT CONTRACT PROVISIONS

1. Compensation

a. Annual Base Compensation

We propose to set each of your base compensation at $175,000 per year, payable at the rate of $7,291.67 on the 15th and last day of every month. In order to accommodate our cash flow considerations, you agree to defer the first two months of this compensation. The January, 2001 deferred compensation will be paid in January 2002 (in addition to your then current compensation), provided that your combined originated billings for 2001 and your combined originated collections for 2001, on an annualized basis, are reasonably close to $ 650,000. Respondent B's February 2001 deferred compensation will be paid in March 2002, provided that your combined originated billings and collections through February 2002, on an annualized basis, are reasonably close to $ 650,000. Respondent A's February 2001 deferred compensation will be paid around the same time in 2002, assuming the same criteria are met and we are able to come to an agreement on a reduced compensation schedule for Respondent A during the balance of 2002 to accommodate his anticipated reduced billable work effort, of which we are supportive and feel sure we can arrive at a satisfactory arrangement.

4. Partnership.

We agree to consider Respondent B for admission as a partner in the firm effective January 1, 2003. We will give Respondent B feedback on this subject at least every six months.

12. Transition of Clients

In order to avoid any issues regarding whether payments received from clients transitioned to our firm belong to you or tot he firm, all fees collected by us after the effective date of our relationship will belong to the law firm. You should arrange for payments for work prior to joining the law firm to be made other than to Claimant. You will record and bill all of your work commencing January 1, 2001, on our time-keeping/billing system.

16. Termination

While we anticipate our association will be of long duration, we acknowledge that either of you or we will have the right to terminate this agreement upon thirty days advance written notice to the other; however, the firm shall have the right to immediately terminate this agreement in the event the firm reasonably determines that the ongoing association is not in the firm's best interests, provided you shall be entitled to a payment equal to one month's base compensation (and all deferred compensation if the expressed criteria for that have been met) in the event of such immediate termination after one year. All client files shall be the property of the firm and shall not be removed from the business premises of the firm, except in accordance with firm policies and procedures pertaining to, among other things, client consent and payment of outstanding balances owed.

V. POSITION OF THE PARTIES

A. Claimant's Position

Claimant maintains that upon termination of the agreement between the parties, the Respondent/Firm asserted ownership of outstanding receivables owed to Claimant. Claimant maintains that the accounts receivables were earned prior to the termination of the relationship while the Respondent/Firm were being paid by Claimant. Claimant contends that Respondent/Firm took all responsibility for collecting the outstanding accounts receivables. Claimant maintains that in addition to collecting $ 65,790 on these receivables, Respondent/Firm wrote-off $ 99,007, without any consultation with Claimant.

Respondent A & Respondent B' Position

Respondent/Firm maintain that Claimant breached several provisions of the agreement including: failing to pay the deferred compensation, failing to consider Respondent B for admission as a partner in Claimant, and failing to pay one month's severance compensation for termination of the agreement without thirty days written notice. Respondent/Firm maintain they are entitled to the accounts receivables. They maintain that the agreement requires Claimant to "collect" the accounts receivables to have an entitlement. Respondent/Firm maintain that Claimant's failure to pay the deferred compensation was improper because they came "reasonably close" to the collections goal of $ 650,000. Respondent/Firm maintain that Claimant terminated the agreement with its failure to adhere to the agreed terms.

VI. DISCUSSION AND ANALYSIS

* * * *

The evidence demonstrates that after the termination of the relationship, Claimant collected $ 53,060. Respondent/Firm collected $ 65,790 and wrote off
$ 99,007. Claimant concedes that $ 40,159 was a legitimate write-off, but maintains that the remaining write-offs were not authorized by Claimant. Respondent/Firm contend that Claimant is attempting to hold Respondent/Firm responsible for amounts that cannot be collected. Witness testified that the accounting department refers any write offs to the finance or executive committee for approval. Respondent/Firm demonstrated they remained responsible for the fee arrangements and billing decisions for its clients. Respondent/Firm reviewed all bills and made the decision whether to write-down or write-off. Respondent A testified that Claimant never questioned Respondent/Firm' billings. Claimant has not sufficiently demonstrated that the remaining write-offs were not legitimate.

Claimant maintains that Respondent/Firm owe $124,639 for the accounts receivables. Respondent/Firm wrote off $99,007. Claimant concedes that Respondent/Firm legitimately wrote-off $40,159 leaving $58,849 remaining due. Respondent/Firm also collected $ 65,790 of the outstanding accounts receivables due to Claimant. As stated above, the write-off amount of $99,007 was legitimate. Therefore, Claimant is entitled to $65,790, the amount that Respondent/Firm collected of the outstanding receivables.

VII. COUNTERCLAIM

Respondent/Firm filed a counterclaim against Claimant. Respondent/Firm maintain that Claimant breached several provisions of the agreement including: failing to pay the deferred compensation, failing to consider Respondent B for admission as a partner in Claimant, and failing to pay one month's severance compensation for termination of the agreement without thirty days written notice.

Partnership

Section 4 of the agreement provides;

> "We agree to consider Respondent B for admission as a partner in the firm effective January 1, 2003. We will give Respondent B feedback on this subject at least every six months."

Exhibit G, a memo to the Respondent/Firm from the Executive Committee at Claimant, dated August 20, 2002, establishes Claimant's intention to postpone Respondent B consideration for partnership until January 1, 2004. Respondent/Firm contend this is a clear violation of the agreement.

The evidence indicates that Claimant delayed consideration of Respondent B for partnership until January 1, 2004 based upon the postponement and uncertainty' of several conditions including: the integration of the practice, along with the retirement/winding down of Respondent A, and the Respondent/Firm' apparent dissatisfaction with the status quo. While the Arbitrator acknowledges that several factors came into play in this decision to delay consideration for partnership, such as: whether Claimant provided assistance with the integration, Respondent A's transition of work and reduction of hours, etc. These considerations were not listed in the agreement as prerequisite conditions for the consideration of partnership, and therefore, do not justify the delay.

Claimant maintains that the executive committee considered Respondent B for partnership and the decision was made to wait. However, the evidence establishes that the typical process for becoming a partner entails that the executive committee review the performance and make a recommendation to the partners to consider whether to let the person in and what percentage of profits to assign. The partners vote.

However, the evidence establishes that the executive committee did not adhere to the typical process of allowing the partners to vote. Instead the executive committee decided to wait until the practice was integrated because they needed some indication to determine what Respondent B's profit share would be as partner.

Although the Arbitrator recognizes that Claimant was in a precarious situation, I have no choice but to find Claimant violated the plain language of the agreement. The agreement clearly required Claimant to consider Respondent B for partnership effective January 1, 2003. It did not require Claimant to make Respondent B a partner, but just consider him. However, the evidence supports that Claimant was not going to consider Respondent B for partnership effective January 1, 2003, even if the relationship had not terminated prior to this date. The Arbitrator finds Claimant violated Section 4 of the agreement.

Deferred Compensation

* * * *

Respondent/Firm contend that "deferred compensation" means that the payment is deferred until a later time, not that the payment of the compensation is conditional. Respondent A testified it was his understanding that the compensation was established at $ 175,000, and not contingent upon any factor. Respondent/Firm maintain that the deferred compensation was put into the agreement to accommodate Claimant's cash flow problems. It was never an issue of "if the compensation would be paid", the issue was "when the compensation was to be paid."

Claimant maintains that Respondent/Firm was not "reasonably close" to annualized collections of $ 650,000 and therefore are not entitled to the deferred compensation.

It is noted at the outset that "reasonably close" is not defined in the agreement and the parties agree that it was not discussed. It is further noted, the contractual language is written ambiguously. The provision specifies that the base compensation is $ 175,000 per year, with part of the first year's base pay being deferred for a time. With the ambiguity of the written language, it is not easy to ascertain the intent of the parties, since clearly Respondent/Firm believe the intent was a timing of payment issue and Claimant believes the intent was to make the payments contingent upon reaching the reasonably close to $ 650,000 requirement.

The Respondent/Firm emphasize that the deferred compensation provision was put in the agreement to accommodate cash flow considerations. This is supported and specified, in the agreement, "[i]n order to accommodate our cash flow considerations, you agree to defer the first two months of this compensation." This statement postpones or delays the first two months of compensation, it does not predicate the compensation upon some further consideration. The agreement, further, states, "[t]he January, 2001 deferred compensation will be paid in January 2002 (in addition to your then current compensation), provided that your combined originated billings for 2001 and your combined originated collections for 2001, on an annualized basis, are reasonably close to $ 650,000. Reading this language, the "reasonably close" requirement can be viewed as a timing of the payment issue or as a condition as to whether the payment will be made at all issue. However, given the other language in the provision, the reasonable and practical interpretation of this ambiguous provision is that the compensation is to be paid, and the "reasonably close" criteria determines when the compensation is to be paid.

The language of the agreement is worded such that it supports the conclusion that the "reasonably close" to $ 650,000 determined when the Respondent/Firm would be paid the compensation, not if they would be paid the compensation. In *Merriam-Webster Dictionary of Law*, 1996 Merriam-Webster, Inc. the definition of "deferred compensation" is current compensation deferred until a later time. The agreement does not specify what happens if the billings and collections do not come reasonably close to $ 650,000 (i.e. another date that the compensation will be paid). This gives credence to Claimant's interpretation that the "reasonably close" to $ 650,000 was intended to be a prerequisite to receiving the deferred compensation. However, the agreement clearly establishes the base compensation at $ 175,000 and clearly defers payment of the first two months of the compensation to a later date. The agreement did not make the yearly base pay of $ 175,000 contingent upon billings and collections coming reasonably close to $ 650,000. Therefore, to say that you will get $ 175,000 per year and defer the payment of the first two months, but you will only get the deferred payment if you bill and collect reasonably close to $ 650,000 is not consistent.

Moreover, even if, the "reasonably close" requirement was a contingency for the payment of the compensation, the evidence supports that Respondent/Firm was generating approximately $ 550,000 per year. The Arbitrator finds that this is reasonably close. Respondent/Firm did not dispute the method of calculation to determine whether they met the annual goal. The evidence supports that the Respondent/Firm met the billings goal, therefore, the collections are at issue. The evidence suggests that the annual collections were averaging near $ 555,000 or 85% of the $ 650,000 goal. As noted above, the parties failed to define "reasonably close". Respondent A testified that this was in line with the other "of counsel" attorneys collections. Further, the evidence supports that Respondent/Firm received the January 2001 deferred compensation payment. The evidence supports that annualized collections through 2001 were $ 551,068 and actual collections through February 2002 were $ 530,122. While Claimant contends that it paid one month as a compromise, the Arbitrator believes that the standard was met for the payment of both months. Further, the agreement provides that the target for billings and collections are to be reasonably close to $ 650,000. The evidence established that it is unlikely to collect 100% of billings, therefore, it should be anticipated that the collections will be smaller than the billings. Therefore if the goal of the billings is $ 650,000, it would be anticipated that the collections would be less. Nonetheless, the Arbitrator concludes that collecting 85% of your goal is reasonably close. Respondent/Firm is entitled to deferred compensation in the amount of $ 29,166.68.

Termination of Agreement without 30 days notice (Omitted)

VIII. CONCLUSION

Claimant demonstrated that it is entitled to the accounts receivables. Claimant is entitled to $ 65,790, the amount that Respondent/Firm collected of the outstanding receivables. Respondent/Firm demonstrated that Claimant breached the agreement when it did not consider Respondent B for partnership effective January 1, 2003, and its failure to pay the deferred compensation. Respondent/Firm is entitled to $ 29,166.68. Respondent/Firm also demonstrated that Claimant terminated the agreement without 30 days written advance notice and therefore, Respondent/Firm is entitled to $ 29,166.68.

Claimant is entitled to a total of $ 65,790. Respondent/Firm is entitled to a total of $ 58,333.36. Claimant is owed the difference between the two amounts. Therefore, Respondent/Firm owes to Claimant $ 7,456.64.

The above sums are to be paid on or before 30 days from the date of this Award. The administrative fees and expenses of the American Arbitration Association ("the Association") and the compensation of the arbitrator totaling [Number redacted] shall be borne equally by the parties. These amounts reflect all payments made to date.

This Award is in full settlement of all claims and counterclaims submitted to this Arbitration. All claims not expressly granted herein are hereby, denied.

APPLICATION AND DISCUSSION QUESTIONS

1. Unlike labor arbitration, in employment disputes, the employer may file counterclaims against the employee who has requested arbitration. In the

above case, what counterclaim did the Respondent/Firm file against the Claimant?

2. How did the arbitrator resolve the issue of the meaning of terms in the agreement? How would you have resolved the issue?

GREEN STATE UNIVERSITY
(FLOYD D. WEATHERSPOON, 2007)[*]

Summary of Facts

The facts indicate that the Claimant was appointed the Head Coach the Green State University's (GSU) Men's basketball team on May 22, 2000. The term of the contract was from May 22, 2000 through March 31, 2004. The Claimant and GSU renegotiated and extended the terms of the contract on October 2, 2002. The term of the contract was extended through March 31, 2008. By letter dated March 15, 2006, GSU President notified the Claimant that he was being reassigned to the Department of University Advancement pursuant to Section 6 of the October 2 Contract. The Claimant reported to the Department of University Advancement on Monday, March 20, 2006.

By letter dated May 5, 2006, Steve Forest, the Claimant's attorney, notified GSU of the Claimant's belief that his duties at the Department of University Development were not commensurate with his education, training and experience as required under Section 6 of the October 2 contract.

Summary of the Issues Presented

The Claimant contends that GSU did not reassign him to a position that was commensurate with his education, training and experience as required by the contract. The Claimant maintains that GSU's failure to properly reassign him amounted to a breach of the contract, resulting in a constructive termination. Therefore, the Claimant states that he is entitled to the balance of his contract for termination without cause as permitted under Section 9(c). The Claimant maintains that his job experience has been as a basketball coach and he was reassigned to assist with the

---

*   Unpublished Decision (Floyd D. Weatherspoon, 2007)

University's fundraising efforts. The Claimant maintains that he has no prior experience as a fundraiser or sales representative. The Claimant further maintains that a plain reading of the contract leads to the conclusion that the University was required to reassign the Claimant to a position consistent with his background and job history as a basketball coach.

GSU maintains that the contract allowed it to reassign the Claimant to a position in University Advancement. GSU contends that the Claimant agreed to this language knowing that the positions in University Advancement involved fundraising and were not related to basketball. GSU contends that the skill set developed by the Claimant as a basketball coach, mainly, good communication skills, organization, and experience establishing personal relationships, are transferable to a job in University Advancement. GSU further contends that there is a lot of overlap between coaching and development work because both are building relationships with others.

Analysis of Issues Presented

This is a case of contract interpretation. The goal is to determine the intent of the parties at the time of execution. In determining the intent of the parties, the language chosen by the parties is given its plain and ordinary meaning.

Section 6 of the October 2002 contract, provides in relevant part,

> It is understood by the parties, however, that the University retains the right to reassign the coach to other faculty and/or professional personnel positions with different duties, within the Department of Intercollegiate Athletics or University Advancement, during the term of this appointment. In no event, however, will the Coach be assigned to any position that is not commensurate with his educational training and experience.

The language at issue here is "[i]n no event, however, will the Coach be assigned to any position that is not commensurate with his educational training and experience."

GSU maintains that pursuant to Section 6 of the Claimant's employment contract, it was permitted to reassign the Claimant to the Department of Intercollegiate Athletics or University Advancement. Therefore, the Claimant's reassignment to University Advancement was within the scope of this provision. GSU states that the Claimant expressly agreed that his reassignment could be to a professional position with different duties in University Advancement. GSU further contends that when the Claimant agreed to this, he knew generally that University Advancement was the University's fundraising department and that the jobs there were not related to basketball. The Claimant testified that his attorney and agent negotiated his contract with GSU. The Claimant testified as to his understanding of the reassignment clause. "I would say that it probably protects both parties and allows the University to make a change, which is their right, and at the same time to make a change that is commensurate with your educational training and your experience." He testified that commensurate with your educational training and experience means "that they are things that I already possess, things that I've already done, my experiences."

The Claimant testified that he knew that Advancement did fundraising to some degree. He admits that he knew the jobs in Advancement were not related to teaching, the administration of, or the coaching of basketball.

The Claimant's attorney and agent testified that he negotiated the contract on behalf of the Claimant. He testified that his intent in drafting the provision at issue was to make sure that if the Claimant was reassigned, he was going to be put in a position that he was capable of doing, that it was commensurate with what the Claimant did for the past 20 or 22 years. He clarified, "[w]ell, my client is a basketball coach. So it was to be a reassignment to a position that corresponded either to being a basketball coach or something where his experience of being a basketball coach would fit." The attorney testified he attempted to restrict the language so that the Claimant could only be reassigned to the Department of Athletics; he further added that he felt that he client was protected by the sentence that states that he would not be assigned to any position not commensurate with his educational training and experience. According to Claimant's atttorney, that meant his reassignment could only be a position that the Claimant was qualified to do, that his experience lends itself for him to do. Claimant's atttorney also admitted that he knew at the time that the contract was executed that the essence of University Advancement involved fundraising.

The evidence establishes that Section 6 permitted the University to reassign the Claimant to University Advancement. The evidence further demonstrates that the primary function of University Advancement is fundraising. The evidence also indicates that the Claimant agreed that he could be assigned to University Advancement; and that he was aware that the primary duty in University Advancement was fundraising. The plain language of the contract permits GSU to place the Claimant in University Advancement. Both the Claimant and his attorney acknowledged that they were aware that University Advancement's primary function was fundraising, and that the positions in University Advancement were not related to basketball. Therefore, it was foreseeable that the Claimant would be placed in a position not related to basketball.

The Arbitrator must now decide whether or not GSU's reassignment of the Claimant to the position of Director of Development–Special Initiatives was commensurate with the Claimant's educational training and experience. In line with the rules of contract interpretation, contract terms are given their plain and ordinary meaning. The issue turns on the phrase, "commensurate with the educational training and experience." In this context, the Arbitrator finds that commensurate means "corresponding in size, extent, magnitude, amount or degree: proportionate: having a common measure." See *Dictionary.com; see also, Merriam-Webster Dictionary.* Thus, the question becomes does the educational training and experience the Claimant obtained as a coach correspond or have a common measure to the experience and skills necessary for a Director of Development position.

GSU contends that the skills and experience obtained by the Claimant as a basketball coach are transferable to the position of Director of Development and therefore, the reassignment was commensurate with the Claimant's educational training and experience.

The Claimant contends that GSU failed to properly reassign him to a position that was commensurate with his educational training and experience pursuant to its obligation under Section 6 of the October 2002 contract. The Claimant testified that he had no experience soliciting individuals for donations or gifts. He further testified that he never worked in any type of sales capacity.

* * * *

The evidence clearly demonstrates that the Claimant's background and experience primarily involved coaching basketball. The Claimant contends that a plain reading of the sentence leads to the conclusion that the University was required to reassign the Claimant to a position consistent with his background and job history as a basketball coach. The Claimant states that he was assigned to assist with the University's fundraising efforts, despite that he had no prior experience as a fundraiser or sales representative. Therefore, this position was not commensurate with his education, training and experience as a basketball coach.

* * * *

GSU put forth evidence that there is sufficient overlap between the job of coaching and the job of Director of Development whereby, the skill set of a coach is transferable to that of a Development Officer because both deal with establishing relationships. Specifically, the Vice President of Advancement, testified, "[p]robably the biggest task the Development Director has is to represent the university and to establish a relationship with the prospective donors, whether it be an alumnus or a friend or a corporation, AT&T, you may be dealing with them here. There's always kinds of ways to learn about them, and the research provides that for you. The real role of the Development office is to take that research and establish the relationship. He further testified the following about how the Claimant as a Head Coach represented the University, "he was heavily involved in recruiting. Obviously he is a person who is used to dealing with families and establishing a relationship where they have confidence in him. I mean, there is a lot of overlap between recruiting and Development because they are both about relationships, and they're both about trying to establish if this is a fit, and if it is a fit, how does it fit." This testimony clearly supports the University's position that both the job of coaching and the Director of Development role involve establishing relationships with people.

* * * *

Therefore, GSU presented sufficient evidence that the skill set that is typically developed as a coach, specifically recruiting and establishing relationships, as well as good communication skills culminated in a skill set or experience that is transferable to that of a Development Officer. Now, the Arbitrator must focus on whether the Claimant developed the skill set or experience that lends itself or is transferable to the duties of a development officer.

In support of its position that the Claimant possesses the necessary skill set of a Director of Development position, GSU points to the following factors:

a. The Claimant's eleven years at GSU in a high profile job with continuing alumni contact gave him exceptional name recognition among the base he would be expected to cultivate and solicit for major donations.

b. The Coach's undergraduate degree was in communications.

c. The coaching jobs required him to make speeches and presentations to alumni and community service groups.

d. He was responsible for supervising a number of staff members in the basketball program and for motivating them.

e. The Advancement job would involve travel, as had his coaching positions.

f. He worked without daily supervision.

g. The job of coaching required the essential skill of effective recruiting, which requires selling the recruit on the school, just as the Director of Development requires selling donors on the reasons they should support the school. (GSU's pre-hearing brief pg. 9).

* * * *

While the evidence establishes that the Claimant had no prior experience in fundraising or in the Department of Advancement; the evidence overwhelmingly demonstrates that the experience that the Claimant developed as a coach was transferable to a Director of Development position. The evidence establishes that the Claimant had experience establishing relationships, had excellent communication skills, and was highly organized. The Claimant admits that he has strong communication skills and that he is a good communicator. The Claimant also testified that he is highly organized.

The evidence further indicates that a Director of Development identifies, cultivates, and successfully solicits individuals, corporations, and foundations for major and annual gifts. They coordinate relationships and development activities with other administrative areas, campus units, peer development officers and departmental leaders. They manage donor relationships. The evidence also indicates that the essence of recruiting involves establishing and maintaining a relationship. Indeed, the Claimant testified that when recruiting potential athletes, he emphasized the relationship building. While fundraising is not related to basketball, the Claimant's training and experience is broader than basketball. Indeed, the Claimant admitted that his reassignment didn't have to relate to basketball, it just had to be commensurate with his educational training and background. The Claimant further admits that the educational training is broader than basketball.

Also significant, the Claimant agreed that his reassignment could be to the Department of University Advancement. As stated previously, the Claimant knew that University Advancement was the fundraising department and the jobs were not related to basketball. Thus, the Arbitrator is compelled to conclude that the Claimant agreed that he could be placed into a fundraising position. The Arbitrator cannot ignore this compelling and indisputable language. A cardinal rule of construction is that contracts should be construed so as not to render any words, phrases, or terms ineffective or meaningless. *Bicknell Minerals, Inc. V. Tilly*, 570 N.E.2d 1307, 1316 (Ind. Ct. App. 1991). Therefore, the Claimant knew or should have known and therefore agreed that he could be reassigned to a position involving fundraising. Thus, the Arbitrator finds that the reassignment to the Director of Development position was commensurate with the Claimant's educational training and experience as a basketball coach.

* * * *

The evidence supports the University's position that the reassignment did not violate the terms of the parties' contract. Section 6 permitted the University to assign the Claimant to the Advancement Department and assign him different duties. The University established that the Claimant's communication skills and experience at establishing relationships that he developed in his position as a basketball coach is commensurate with the skills and experience necessary as a Development Officer.

APPLICATION AND DISCUSSION QUESTIONS

1. Do you agree that the contract was not violated? Would you have determined the meaning of the term "commensurate"? Do you agree that the coach's skills are transferrable to another position?

2. What contract principle did the arbitrator apply in this case? The Arbitrator cites the cardinal rule of construction "that contracts should be construed so as not to render any words, phrases, or terms ineffective or meaningless". How did the Arbitrator apply this rule to the facts? Is the term "commensurate" ambiguous?

3. Are abitrators practicing law when they interpret state law in a state where they are not licensed?

THE GREEN CITY BANK[*]

Summary of the Facts

Mr. W, the Claimant, filed a grievance against The Green City Bank, on September 18, 1978. In 1995, the Claimant was promoted and transferred to an affiliated company in New York. He returned to Evansville in November 2001. The Claimant was terminated March 31, 2002.

---

[*] Unpublished Decision (Floyd D. Weatherspoon, 2007)

Summary of Issues Presented

The Claimant contends that The Green City Bank terminated his employment in violation of Indiana law. The Claimant contends that he was terminated because he complained to management about illegal accounting practices and therefore engaged in protected activity. The Claimant states that he was considered a good employee until he began complaining about the accounting irregularities. Thus, a causal connection between the complaining and his termination was established. The Claimant maintains that the reasons given by The Green City Bank for his termination do not make sense and are a pretext. The Claimant contends that The Green City Bank doesn't terminate employees without following its three-step policy, which was not followed in this case, establishing the company's wrongful motives.

The Green City Bank contends that the Claimant was not engaged in protected activity under Indiana law. The Green City Bank contends that it had valid reasons to terminate the Claimant because of his lack of trust and credibility and his inability to lead the decommissioning efforts of RMST. The Green City Bank maintains that the Claimant did not complain about illegal accounting, but rather internal warehouse reports. The Green City Bank states that the Claimant was the executive in charge of RMST and as such was to mitigate all losses, he failed to do this and so he was terminated. The Green City Bank contends that the Claimant continued to act outside of his authority, which resulted in a $1.2 million deficiency to The Green City Bank.

Analysis of Issues Presented

The Claimant and the Respondent were involved in an employee-at-will relationship. Under an employee-at-will doctrine, both the employer and the employee can terminate the employment at any time for a "good reason, bad reason, or no reason at all." The Indiana Supreme Court has recognized some limited exceptions to the employment at will doctrine. One such exception is a cause of action for retaliatory discharge when an employee is discharged solely for exercising a statutorily conferred right. The courts will also recognize a cause of action when an employee-at-will is allegedly fired for refusing to commit an unlawful act for which he/she would be personally liable.

The issue in the present case is whether the Claimant engaged in protected activity under Indiana law, and if so, whether this protected activity had a causal connection to his termination. The Claimant contends that because he complained about accounting problems that he deems as "accounting irregularities" and/or "illegal accounting practices", he engaged in protected activity. The Claimant maintains that his termination falls within the carved out exception to the employment at will doctrine because he was terminated for his refusal to commit an unlawful act for which he could be personally liable. Specifically, the Claimant contends that he complained about accounting practices regarding how the company was listing certain loans in the warehouse.

It is the Claimant's contention that he complained that the company was booking a $1,230,147.48 loss as an asset on its books.

The courts clearly recognize a cause of action when an employee is fired for refusing to commit an illegal act for which he or she would be personally liable. However, in researching the cases that allowed this exception, two common themes arose; the employees clearly refused to follow their employer's instructions to commit illegal acts and the employees would potentially face personally liability for committing such acts.

The Indiana courts have found the public policy exception to be "limited and strictly construed" The courts have steadfastly refused to extend the exception past the narrow boundaries of wrongful discharge if a clear statutory expression of a right or duty is contravened.

In *McGarrity* and similar cases where the employee met the necessary elements to qualify for the exception, the employee was directly involved with the unlawful act. Here, the Claimant was not responsible for preparing the financial records of RMST. The Claimant also does not allege that he was responsible for the reporting of the company. Significantly, the Claimant has not demonstrated that he was asked or in some way was expected to perform an unlawful act.

The Claimant testified that the $1 million reflected deficient loans for which he had no responsibility. These loans came into the warehouse from a rogue underwriter, they were defective and had market value below what was advanced for them, and was not his responsibility. His responsibility was to clean out the warehouse.

The Claimant contends that there is a causal connection between his complaining about the accounting irregularities and his termination. This causal connection argument is only relevant if the Claimant was able to prove that he engaged in protected activity. As stated above, the Claimant failed to meet his burden that complaining about the accounting practices of The Green City Bank fell into the protected activity category. Nonetheless, the claimant's causal connection argument is not persuasive. The Claimant contends that he began complaining about the accounting irregularities during the first week of March, and twenty-seven days later, he was fired.

The Company submitted persuasive evidence the claimant was terminated for legitimate reasons.

The Claimant has not established a casual connection between his complaining and his termination. The Claimant cannot establish that he refused to commit an unlawful act that would subject him to personal liability. The Claimant's objection is not persuasive.

Conclusion

The Claimant has not demonstrated that he was terminated while engaging in protected activity in violation of Indiana law. The Green City Bank has articulated valid reasons for the Claimant's termination, and the Claimant cannot establish that these reasons are a pretext.

This Award is in full settlement of all claims and counterclaims submitted to this Arbitration. All claims not expressly granted herein are hereby, denied.

APPLICATION AND DISCUSSION QUESTIONS

1. What arguments did the claimant attempt to prove?

2. Why did the arbitrator find in favor of the company?

3. What is the employment-at-will doctrine?

4. What are the exceptions to the employment-at-will doctrine?

D. EMPLOYMENT STATUTES

Family Medical Leave Act (FMLA)

THE GREEN BUILDING COMPANY[*]

Summary of Facts

Mr. B. was employed by The Green Building Company from September 2001 through April 15, 2005. The Claimant worked as a CEFLA Sander on the CEFLA line. The CEFLA operated an A, B, and C line. In 2003, the Claimant was diagnosed with a shoulder impingement. Effective February 19, 2003, the doctor imposed no lifting with his left arm restrictions on the plaintiff. He worked on the A line with these restrictions. He took a period of approved FMLA medical leave from March through June 2003. The Claimant returned to work June 16, 2003, with the same "no lifting" with his left arm restriction. The Claimant continued to work on A line. The Claimant subsequently presented a doctor's note with the restrictions of occasional lifting of no more than 5 lbs and rotating between block and power sanding. The Claimant continued to work on the A line.

In November 2003, the Claimant was diagnosed with a bulging disk, unrelated to the shoulder injury. Effective January 9, 2004, the Claimant was to continue his light duty with occasional lifting of no more than 5 lbs and rotate between block and power sanding. The Clamant took a three-day approved FMLA leave February 2-5, 2004. He returned to work with medical restrictions. The Claimant was on FMLA in March 2004. On April 15, 2004, the Claimant began a medical leave for the treatment of his back. On June 11, 2004, the Claimant submitted a return to work slip and was told that Green Building could not meet his restrictions. The Claimant did not return to work by April 15, 2005 and his employment was terminated for failure to return to work within a year.

The parties stipulated that the issue is whether the company violated the FMLA when it denied the Claimant the right to return to work June 11, 2004, and thereafter?

---

[*]   Unpublished Decision (Floyd D. Weatherspoon, 2007)

Summary of the Issues Presented

Green Building contends that the essential functions of a CEFLA Sander has always been to perform the duties on all three lines of the CEFLA 3 line. The Claimant contends that it was not essential for every CEFLA Sander to rotate through all positions of A, B, and C of any CEFLA line prior to his medical leave. Green Building contends that while the Claimant worked with medical restrictions he could not perform the essential functions of the job and therefore, essentially worked in a "light duty" position. The Claimant contends that he performed the essential functions of the job when he worked with medical restrictions and therefore he was not in a "light duty" position.

There is a dispute about whether the Claimant was capable of performing the essential functions of the job when he sought restoration rights in June 2004. Green Building maintains that the Claimant exhausted all of his restoration rights by June 2004 when he requested reinstatement. The Claimant contends that even if he has no entitlement to restoration under the FMLA, he should have been reinstated pursuant to Green Bulding's medical leave policy.

Analysis of Issues Presented

Pursuant to the Family Medical Leave Act (FMLA), an eligible employee is granted a total of 12 workweeks of unpaid leave during any 12-month period because of a serious health condition that makes the employee unable to perform functions of the employee's position. Upon return from FMLA leave, employees must be restored to their original position or to an equivalent position with equivalent pay, benefits, and terms and conditions of employment.

29 U.S.C. ξ 2614(a), Section 104(a), provides in relevant part:
[omitted]

Green Building cites the Department of Labor's regulations as additional guidance regarding an employee's rights when returning to work after an FMLA leave. It is Green Building's contention that the regulation specifies that the employee is not entitled to return to his/her original position unless he/she can perform all of its essential functions. The FMLA states in part: [omitted]

It is Green Building's contention that the Claimant had no restoration rights under the FMLA when he attempted to return to work June 2004, because he could not perform the essential functions of a CEFLA Sander. The Claimant contends that he could perform the essential functions of a CEFLA Sander. The Claimant contends that it was not an essential function for every CEFLA Sander to rotate through all positions on A, B, and C of any CEFLA Line prior to his medical leave.

Green Building maintains that as a CEFLA Sander, it has always been expected that the employees be able to perform sanding and related work at any location along the three components of a CEFLA operation, Lines A, B, and C. Green Building contends that the Claimant acknowledges as much when he testified, "I did the block sanding, the power sanding. I worked over on B line. I worked on C line, at the repair area, the loading table."

Therefore, Green has sufficiently demonstrated that it was an essential function that a CEFLA Sander be able to perform the functions of all three lines. The evidence reveals that when the Claimant attempted to return to work June 2004, his restrictions allowed him to only do "block sanding."

Nonetheless, the evidence reveals that despite Green Building's contention that it was an essential function of a CEFLA Sander to perform the functions of all three lines; Green Building, allowed the Claimant to work with medical restrictions where he did not rotate to the other lines, but only worked on Line A. It is Green Building's assertion that this was a "light duty" position. Green Building further contends that employers' have no FMLA obligation to offer light duty work, and an employee cannot transform temporary light duty into a permanent position, to which FMLA restoration rights would apply, by taking an FMLA covered leave after being assigned light duty.

This regulation provides that an employee that is unable to perform an essential function of his/her position has no right to restoration to another position. This supports Green Building's contention that the FMLA imposes no obligation upon the employer to restore the employee to another position, light duty or otherwise, if the employee is unable to perform the essential functions of the position after 12 weeks.

It is Green Building's contention that when the Claimant sought reinstatement in June 2004, he still could not perform the essential functions of a CEFLA Sander and therefore he had no entitlement under the FMLA. The evidence reveals that the Claimant was given a return to work date of June 11, 2004 by his doctor with a maximum 8 hour work day, no lifting, no bending, and a restriction to do only block sanding. As already decided, Green Building has demonstrated "block sanding" is only one aspect of the functions of a CEFLA Sander. Therefore, the evidence supports Green Building's position that the Claimant was not able to perform all the essential functions of a CEFLA Sander and therefore, had no restoration entitlement under the FMLA as of June 2004.

Green Building next contends that even if the Claimant could show that he could perform the essential functions of a CEFLA Sander as of June 2004, he had already exhausted his FMLA entitlement to restoration, as a matter of law, prior to his June 2004 reinstatement demand. It is Green Building's contention that the Claimant began exhausting his 2004 FMLA restoration rights from the beginning of 2004 because he started the year subject to doctor's restrictions that precluded him from performing essential functions of a CEFLA Sander - Line B and Line C work. Essentially, it is Green Building's contention that because the Claimant was not capable of performing all the functions on lines B, and C, he was working a "light- duty" position. Green Building maintains that his time working with medical restrictions, or a "light-duty" position counted toward his 12 week restoration right under the FMLA.

* * * *

Green Building uses this regulation to support its position that the FMLA distinguishes between "leave" rights and "restoration" rights. Green Building contends that any light duty assignment that is taken because of a FMLA qualifying incapacity, is a substitute for taking FMLA leave, for the purpose of restoration rights. Green Building maintains, "[i]f the employee chooses to continue working by accepting a light duty position instead of taking FMLA leave from his/her original position, the employee retains all his FMLA leave rights, except that the employee begins to exhaust the annual 12 weeks of FMLA entitlement to be restored to his original (non-light-duty) position or to a substantial equivalent position."

In further support, Green Building, relies on the Department of Labor's Opinion Letter FMLA-55, which states:

> If an employee on FMLA leave voluntarily accepts a light duty assignment, the final
> regulations have been amended at 29 CFR 825.220(d) to provide that such an employee
> retains rights under FMLA to job restoration to the same or an equivalent position
> held prior to the start of the leave for a cumulative period of up to 12 workweeks. This
> "cumulative period" would be measured by the time designated as FMLA leave for the
> worker's compensation leave of absence and the time employed in a light duty assign-
> ment. The period of time employed in a light duty assignment cannot count, however,
> against the 12 weeks of FMLA leave.

Green Building contends that in applying the aforementioned provisions, courts have held that an employee's voluntary acceptance of a light duty assignment is counted as part of the 12-week leave entitlement under the FMLA.

The Claimant has not demonstrated that he was able to perform the major functions of the CEFMLA Sander position as of June 2004, when he sought reinstatement.

Additionally, Green Building has sufficiently demonstrated that the Claimant exhausted his restoration right under the FMLA prior to his June 2004 reinstatement request. Therefore, the Claimant has not demonstrated that he had any entitlement under the FMLA.

Therefore, the evidence reveals that all lines started rotating in April 2004. This essentially means that Green Building was no longer assigning employees to one particular position only. In June 2004, the Claimant was restricted to "block sanding" only, thus, Green Building could not accommodate this restriction.

Conclusion

Green Building did not violate the FMLA when it denied the Claimant the right to return to work June 11, 2004, and thereafter. Green Building sufficiently demonstrated that the Claimant had no FMLA restoration rights in June 2004. Moreover, the Claimant has not demonstrated an entitlement to a "light duty" position under Green Building's medical leave policy.

APPLICATION AND DISCUSSION QUESTIONS

1. What are the parties' primary arguments regarding the application of the FMLA? Why are employment arbitrators required to be familiar with various employment statutes? Analyzing the various claims by the parties will require a review of court cases in the jurisdiction where the claim arose.

2. How does the arbitrator resolve these issues?

2011 AAA EMPLOYMENT LEXIS 232
AMERICAN ARBITRATION ASSOCIATION
(A.MCKISSICK, 2011[*]

Employment Arbitration Tribunal
OPINION AND AWARD: Dr. ARBITRATOR

AWARD

Claimant, who filed a discrimination claim via § 1981, has not proved her prima facie case, as required. Accordingly, this race discrimination claim must be denied for the aforementioned reasons. Thus, this Arbitrator finds that the prevailing party is the Respondent. Based upon the Arbitration Agreement, Joint Exhibit I, the Claimant shall receive no damages nor shall she receive attorney's fees due to her signed waiver, dated June 6, 2005.

STATEMENT OF FACTS

Claimant, commenced her employment with Respondent, on June 20, 2005 as a Sales Agent. She was assigned to District 131 which is comprised of: Washington, DC; Maryland; Alexandria, VA; and other surrounding Virginia areas. She remained an agent with United until her termination on July 5, 2010.

Although the Claimant alleges race, gender, and place of origin discrimination on the basis of Title VII of the Civil Rights Act of 1964, as amended, 42 USCA § 2000(e) and § 1981 of the Civil Rights Act of 1886, as amended, as well as the Immigration Reform and Control Act of 1986 (IRCA), 8 USC § 1254-1357, thus only the 42 USCA § 1981 action is presently viable.

The Respondent was awarded a partial grant regarding the Motion to Dismiss on September 13, 2010 due to the exclusion of Claimant's Title VII time-based claims. Specifically, the Claimant via her first former attorney failed to file her Demand for Arbitration, dated April 26, 2010, within the required ninety (90) days of receiving a Notice of Right to Sue letter from the Equal Employment Opportunity Commission

---

(EEOC). Thus, actions connected with Title VII such as: race discrimination and retaliation are now time-barred and excluded from this arbitration. Similarly, the Claimant's allegation of Age Discrimination in Employment Act (ADEA) as well as hostile work environment fell outside of the three hundred (300) day limitation period for the filing of the Equal Employment Opportunity Commission charge. In addition, the Tort of Negligent Infliction of Emotional Distress as well as claims involving IRCA were dismissed in the Motion. The Claimant's second former counsel withdrew from this arbitration. The current counsel, the Claimant's third attorney, was then hired on February 1, 2011. During the administrative conference call, a stipulation was made by Gladys Weatherspoon, Esq. to withdraw these monetary claims related to the omission of the release of the Health Insurance Portability and Accountability Act of 1996 (HIPAA) records. Accordingly, the Claimant withdrew her claim for emotional distress, as noted. Thus, a solo claim limited to back pay is at issue for damages.

Currently, the Claimant alleges race discrimination via § 1981 due to the Respondent's failure to promote her to a Staff Manager position on two (2) occasions on March 5, 2008 and May 12, 2008.

The record reflects that Employee A, who is from Bangladesh, was promoted to replace Staff Manager who resigned in March, 2008. Still further, the record reveals that Employee B, who is from Iran, was also promoted to a Staff Manager position on May 20, 2008.

Facts reveal that Respondent is a home service company who sells life insurance primarily to lower-middle America. Respondent's President, is a Black man The Claimant's direct line Supervisor Staff Manager is also a Black female who was with the company from 2005 to March 2008 as a Staff Manager.

The Claimant executed her Arbitration Agreement with Respondent on June 6, 2005. Claimant filed a Demand for Arbitration on April 26, 2010.

ISSUES

(i) Whether or not the Claimant can establish a prima facie case of race discrimination by showing that she was performing her job satisfactorily at the time of any adverse action based on § 1981?

(ii) Whether or not the Claimant was subject to disparate treatment based on race as set forth in her Demand for Arbitration resulting in an actionable adverse employment action?

PERTINENT PROVISIONS

42 USCA § 1981

§ 1981 provides:

> All Persons within the jurisdiction of the United States shall have the same right in every State and Territory to make and enforce contracts, to sue, be parties, give evidence, and to the full and equal benefit of all laws and proceedings for the security of persons and property as is enjoyed by White citizens, and shall be subject to like punishment, pains, penalties, taxes, licenses, and exactions of every kind, and to no other.

§ 1981 was recodified in 1871, following the ratification of the 14th Amendment:

> No State shall make or enforce any law which shall abridge the privileges or immunities of citizens of the United States; nor shall any State deprive any person of life, liberty, or property without due process of law; nor deny to any person within its jurisdiction the equal protection of the laws.

POSITIONS OF THE PARTIES

It is the Claimant's position that the Respondent discriminated against her by both race and sex, as she is a Black female, a separate, protected class. That is, the Claimant argues that as a Black female, the only statistical pool of persons applicable to her are other Black females who were offered the position of Staff Manager, not just the category of Black males. Stated differently, the Claimant asserts that the Respondent cannot escape liability by showing that the Respondent did not discriminate against Blacks generally or that it does not discriminate against women. In essence, the Claimant asserts that to view otherwise would be to leave Black women without a viable Title VII remedy. Thus, the Claimant further argues that the fact that a Black man was awarded a promotion does not put him within the Claimant's protected class for purposes of her prima facie case.

Specifically, the Claimant points out that she was discriminated in three ways. First is by the discriminatory comment made by Manager that he could never put a Black female in a supervisory position. Second, the Claimant challenges the overall work record of both selectees for the positions of Staff Manager, as compared to Claimant. Third is the collective pattern of the then Regional Vice President's promotional practices.

The Claimant asserts that the omission to present Manager's testimony deserves a negative inference from the Arbitrator based upon the assumption he would have given damaging testimony against the Company. It is important to note, the Claimant emphasizes, that Manager was the only person who could have refuted the comment or explained its context or given any other explanation. Moreover, the Claimant contends that Manager was available and fully capable of testifying as he had a recent lunch with Regional Vice President, now District Manager, a few days earlier.

As to the discriminatory practices of the then Regional Vice President, the Claimant notes that the Vice President admits that Employee C, another Black female, was also overlooked. That is, the Claimant contends that it is the Respondent's pattern to put the onus on the Black female to request consideration for a supervisory Staff Manager position, in contrast to the Respondent's general practice of seeking out others, including Black males with inquiries of their professional interest in supervisory positions.

Therefore, the Claimant contends that it places an extra burden on Black women to seek out a supervisory position. Thus, the Claimant maintains that this amounts to an unfair, discriminatory practice regularly employed by the Respondent.

Although then Regional Vice President testified that all sales agents must have an exclusive relationship with only the Respondent, and that he checks these appointments every six (6) to twelve (12) months, the Claimant counters that evidence reveals that forty-three (43) agents had multiple licenses with other companies. Notwithstanding the fact that this is the current status with other agents, the Claimant asserts that the Respondent fired her for violating this same prohibition. Therefore, the Claimant asserts that it must conclude that such a practice is discriminatory and is dispositive of disparate treatment by the Respondent toward his sales agents.

In spite of the nine (9) documents as outlined in the Field Employee Handbook, detailing the steps of letters and paper work which document an agent on the decrease, the Claimant further asserts that

Claimant only received one of the nine documents. That is, the Claimant asserts that the Respondent offered no explanation as to the reason that the other eight documents for this planned intervention were not included in Claimant's file.

In addition, the Claimant claims that the Respondent attempted to unfairly discredit the testimony of a Former Sales Agent, called "Former Sales Agent," because he was the person who told Claimant of the derogatory comment made by Manager. However, the Claimant counters that Former Sales Agent did not lose his license, as the Vice President testified.

Most importantly, the Claimant emphasizes that Employee A, a Middle Eastern man, who had less qualifications and less than an acceptable track record than

Claimant, was promoted instead of her.Based on all the foregoing, the Claimant requests that the Arbitrator award Claimant fifteen (15) million dollars to deter the Respondent from discriminatory practices in the future and requests $ 7,572.29 in attorney's fees.

On the other hand, the Respondent counters that 42 USCA § 1981 is exclusively restricted in scope to race only. That is, the Respondent claims that it is not gender-based. In addition, the Respondent asserts that the Claimant is also precluded from utilizing the tenets of Title VII, as it was excluded due to the partial grant of the Motion to Dismiss as being time-barred.

Most importantly, the Respondent asserts that the Claimant has failed to establish a prima facie case with respect to either selection of the Staff Manager positions because Claimant was in a three fiscal quarter decrease via her book of premiums. Thus, the Respondent reasons that the Claimant was not eligible to be promoted when she requested to be in 2008.

In regards to the appropriate pool of sales agents, the Respondent retorts that then Regional Vice President inquired as to whether three Black male employees: Employee D, Employee E, and Employee F, were interested in a supervisory position. However, the Respondent asserts that none were interested. Prior to these Staff Manager openings, the Respondent asserts that Staff Manager, a Black female, was the incumbent manager. In spite of the Respondent's request for Staff Manager to continue her employment, she left to develop her own company.

* * * *

FINDINGS AND DISCUSSION

After a careful review of the record in its entirety, and after having had an opportunity to weigh and evaluate the testimony of the witnesses, this Arbitrator finds that this employment claim of race discrimination shall be denied for the following reasons.

First, both Title VII and 42 USCA Section § 1981 are based upon the same formula which must be evaluated for every discrimination claim (citation omitted). This four-prong test is delineated by *McDonnell Douglas Corporation vs. Green, 411 U.S. 792, 802, 36 L. Ed. 2nd 668, 93 Supreme Court 1817 (1973)*. The four elements which comprise a prima facie case are as follows:

(i) [the Claimant] belongs to a racial minority;

(ii) [the Claimant] applied and qualified for a job the Employer [the Respondent] was trying to fill;

(iii) though qualified, [the Claimant] was rejected;

(iv)thereafter the Employer [the Respondent] continued to seek applicants with [the Claimant's] qualifications

The burden is on the Claimant to prove all four prongs. However, once the Claimant establishes a prima facie case, the Respondent then has the burden of articulating a legitimate, nondiscriminatory reason for the employment decision.

Second, although the basis of this discriminatory claim is race and gender, however, Section § 1981 does not cover gender discrimination.

* * * *

As mentioned earlier, due to the earlier ruling of a prehearing motion which barred the use of Title VII for failure to abide by the time limitation, the analysis and coverage of Title VII is precluded from this employment claim for discrimination.

* * * *

Sixth, the McDonnell Douglas vs. Green, supra paradigm requires that the Claimant prove that: (i) she is a member of a racial minority; and (ii) that the Claimant was "qualified for a job" the Respondent "was trying to fill" to establish a prima facie case for the first two prongs.

Applying prong two (2) alone to that analysis, the record reflects that the Claimant was on a three quarter fiscal decrease in sales, thus was not qualified in 2008 for either promotion for the Silver Spring, Maryland District or the Northern Virginia District for the aforementioned reasons.

Seventh, although the Claimant is correct, this Arbitrator can make a negative inference of the omission of Manager to testify. He was well enough to be present at the forum, but was not called to rebut the alleged discriminatory statement that he would not hire a Black female to a supervisory position. This statement was allegedly made to "Former Sales Agent," Former Sales Agent, and subsequently told to Claimant. In light of Former Sales Agent's prior inconsistent statements made at the arbitration regarding the circumstances of his prior employment with Respondent, this Arbitrator finds that his testimony is tainted and must be discredited.

However, the record also reflects that the Respondent had forty-two (42) other sales agents who also violated this same prohibition. Notwithstanding this showing of unequal treatment of similarly-situated sales agents, the analysis of disparate treatment cannot be utilized in this claim under 42 USCA § 1981.

APPLICATION AND DISCUSSION QUESTIONS

1. Note that in employment arbitration cases, the claimant will typically allege a number of violations under various state and federal statutes, as well as under common law. Aside from the §1981 claim, what other legal claims were raised by the claimant that were not viable or withdrawn?

2. What are the elements of the *prima facie case* in a §1981 claim? Which element did the claimant fail to meet?

3. Unlike labor arbitrators, employment arbitrators must be aware of the statute of limitations under various employment laws. Which time frames did the claimant fail to meet?

2015 AAA EMPLOYMENT LEXIS 119
(2015, F. WEATHERSPOON)[*]

Employment Arbitration Tribunal
AWARD OF ARBITRATOR

Summary of Facts

The facts indicate that Claimant (hereinafter the Claimant) was an employee with the Respondent (hereinafter Respondent) at its Restaurant located in City, State. On August 20, 2013 Respondent terminated her employment. On September 18, 2013, the Claimant filed a civil action in the Court of County, State, alleging that Respondent violated the West Virginia Wage Payment and Collection Act (WVWPCA) that requires an employer who terminates an employee, to pay the final wages owed to the employee within four business days of the date of termination. Claimant alleges that she did not receive a check for her final wages until August 27, 2013, which caused her to suffer economic loss, annoyance and inconvenience. On February 19, 2014, the Court of County, State granted the defendant's motion to enforce an agreement between the parties to resolve any claims of dispute through the Dispute Resolution Program. On April 2, 2014, the Claimant filed a Demand for Arbitration with the American Arbitration Association. The arbitration was held on April 6, 2015.

Summary of the Issues Presented

During the hearing, the Claimant testified that after she was terminated on August 20, 2013; she called Respondent on at least two different days (August 22 and 23) and again on Monday, August 26 (i.e., the fourth business day) to inquire about a check for her final wages. She claims that Respondent did not make her final check available until August 27, 2013 thus violating the WVWPCA.

The WVWPCA, Section 21-5-4 (b) and (e) state in pertinent parts:

Whenever a person, firm or corporation [employer] discharges an employee, the [employer] shall pay the employee's wages in full no later than the next regular payday or four business days, whichever comes first. [b]... If [the employer] fails to pay wages as required under this section, [the employer], in addition to the amount which was unpaid when due, is liable to the employee for three times that unpaid amount as liquidated damages.

Section 21-5-12 (b) of the WVWPCA states that if the Claimant prevails and it is found that a violation of the statute occurred, then the employee is also entitled to reasonable attorney's fees and costs. Claimant's Aunt, testified that she was present with Claimant when Claimant called Respondent on August 22, 23 and 26, 2013, to inquire about her check. The witnesses further testified that each time when Claimant got off the phone with Respondent; Claimant was upset because her final check still was not available. Claimant testified that she is a single Mother who was raising a toddler (at the time she was terminated) and another young child; therefore, she needed her last check ASAP to support her children's financial needs and her rent that would soon be due.

General Manager at Respondent's Restaurant location, was Acting General Manager at the time Claimant was terminated. He testified that it was his decision to discharge Claimant from employment. General Manager inferred that it was common practice when terminating an employee, to immediately contact Respondent's Corporate HR Office to request that payroll cut a check ASAP and expeditiously send it to the facility where the employee worked, so that it would be available the next day for the employee to pick it up. General Manager testified that this process was adhered to in Claimant's case. Respondent provided a copy of an email showing that General Manager requested expeditious handling of Claimant's check. General Manager contends that Store delivered the check the following day, i.e., August 21st, 2013. Respondent produced a copy of a Store tracking document in an effort to substantiate General Manager' testimony. Respondent also produced copies of checks dated August 21, 2013 that were made out to Claimant. In addition, Respondent produced copies of Store delivery invoices showing that packages were delivered to the Restaurant location on August 21. General Manager claims that he called Claimant on her cell phone to notify her that she could come and pick up her check on August 21st, but he received her voice mail. He testified that he left a message on Claimant's cell phone, but Claimant denies receiving the message. The Claimant's attorney attempted to obtain cell phone records from the service provider, but since Claimant changed her service to a new provider, a backup of calls was not transferred; therefore, no records are available. Notwithstanding, General

Manager testified that Respondent also does not have a log directory record of calls outgoing and ingoing from the Restaurant.

Analysis of Issues Presented

The issue in this case is whether Respondent violated the WVWPCA? Both parties stipulated the basic facts; i.e., that Claimant was terminated on August 20, 2013; that the actual termination is not an issue in this case; that the issue revolves around whether Respondent notified Claimant that her last wages due were available within four business days of the date she was terminated; in light thereof, the check should have been available and Claimant notified not later than August 26, 2013 (that Saturday and Sunday should not be counted). Moreover, both parties agree that no damages are due to Claimant unless she can meet her burden of proof to show that the WVWPCA was violated. It is undisputed that the Claimant picked up the checks (there were two of them) on August 27, 2013 and cashed them at her bank. The parties also agree that there were two checks provided; one in the amount of $ 258.84 and another in the amount of $ 53.87; for a total of $ 312.71. If the statute was violated, Respondent would be liable for liquidated damages. Liquidated damages are calculated by multiplying the amount of wages due by three. Clamant would be due $ 938.13, less the amount already paid. The Clamant could also request interest, costs and reasonable attorney fees.

Claimant's Aunt, testified during the hearing and corroborated Claimant's testimony that she attempted to contact Respondent on three different occasions on three different days prior to the end of the four business days, but allegedly each time Respondent told Claimant that her check was not yet available. Claimant's Aunt admitted that she could not hear Respondent's responses on the other end of the cell phone. Although I find the witnesses' testimony credible and have no reason to doubt the veracity of their testimony; less weight is nevertheless accorded to their testimony because they are Claimant's relatives. The burden of proof is on the Claimant to provide some objective evidence to support her claim that she attempted to contact Respondent to inquire about her check and that Respondent did not inform her it was available prior to August 27, 2013.

Along the same lines, Respondent did not have any records to substantiate that they called Claimant. At the very least, Respondent could have asked one of its employees to witness the making of the call and to make a written note of the time and date of the call. Associate Manager was the Associate Manager at the Restaurant at the time the Claimant was terminated. Associate Manager was dealing with an illness and was at a different location around the time this matter was being adjudicated;

therefore, the parties agreed to take a deposition from him and then enter it into the record. Associate Manager recalled the incident which led up to Claimant's termination. However, he does not recall her ever calling the store to inquire about her check prior to the day she came to the restaurant to pick up her checks (i.e., August 27, 2013). In light thereof, Associate Manager did not corroborate Claimant's testimony. Respondent's Director of HR, testified at the hearing and corroborated Respondent's contention that General Manager requested expeditious handling of the final checks when he contacted the corporate office on August 20, 2013. Respondent's Director instructed payroll to cut the check immediately and he alleges that Store delivered the checks the following day, i.e., August 21st.

The Arbitrator must first decide whether the checks constituting Claimant's final wages were delivered to Respondent's place of business at Restaurant within four business days of the termination. The preponderance of the evidence shows that the checks were delivered on August 21, 2013. In addition to the persuasive testimony of General Manager and Respondent's Director; plus the deposition of Associate Manager; witness testimony on behalf of Respondent is more convincing than Claimant's and her Aunt's testimony to the contrary. In further corroboration of Respondent's position, the evidence combined of the email requesting expeditious handling of the last wages, the Store tracking document and the date of the checks; supports Respondent's contention that the checks were delivered in a timely manner.

Notwithstanding, the Arbitrator must also decide whether Respondent made a bona fide attempt to contact Claimant prior to or on August 26th (i.e., the fourth business day) to inform her that the check was available for pick up. Claimant proffers that since she introduced into evidence a copy of a bank record verifying that she cashed the check on August 27th; and that in light of her economic circumstances, she had a dire need to cash the checks as soon as she received them; that the Arbitrator should find her testimony more credible. Nevertheless, just because she cashed the checks on August 27th, does not mean that Respondent did not make the checks available for pick up prior to that day. Claimant admitted during the hearing that she was aware of the WVWPCA at the time she was terminated and knew about the fourth business day requirement. Considering that she acknowledged she was aware of the statutory requirement, it would have been reasonable for her to understand that, if she claimed a violation of the statute, she would have to come forward with persuasive evidence to support her claim.

When assessing Respondent's position that General Manager called Claimant and left a message on her cell phone that she could come to get her check prior to the fourth business day; the record is devoid of evidence to substantiate Respondent's claim. It could also be argued that Respondent could have made another attempt by calling the cell phone number again to ensure that Claimant received the voice mail message. However, the statute does not mandate that more than one attempt be made. Moreover, the Arbitrator must take into consideration that the burden of proof and persuasion remains with the Claimant. Although the Arbitrator finds the Claimant's argument that because she had two young children to support and her rent would soon be due; that she would have came to pick up the checks immediately if Respondent had contacted her to be reasonable; the record is still lacking of evidence that Respondent did not contact her sooner. This is a close case and both parties provided credible arguments. However, in evaluating the totality of the circumstances, this Arbitrator does not find that the Claimant met her burden of substantiating her claim by the preponderance of the evidence.

Conclusion

The evidence supports Respondent's position that it did not violate the WVWPCA. The totality of the evidence shows that Respondent made a good faith attempt to notify Claimant that her final wages were available for pick up prior to the expiration of the fourth business day, as required by the statute. Claimant could not meet her burden of proof to show that the statute was violated. Since she failed to meet her burden of proof, she is not entitled to any damages. Respondent requested that Claimant pay its attorney's fees and costs in the event her claim was not successfully adjudicated. The Claimant provided credible evidence to support her argument; it just fail short of meeting the burden of proof to support her claim. It does not appear that her claim was purely frivolous or spurious. Therefore, I deny the request for the Claimant to pay Respondent's attorney's fees and costs.

This Award is in full settlement of all claims and counterclaims submitted to this Arbitration. All claims not expressly granted herein are hereby, denied.

APPLICATION AND DISCUSSION QUESTIONS

1. What objective evidence could the claimant have presented that she attempted to contact respondent?

2. Was management's testimony more credible than the claimant's witness?

3. Did it appear that the claimant's claim was frivolous or spurious?

4. Why is the burden of proof placed on the employee and not on the company? Who is in control of issuing the check?

5. Is this the type of claim that should be presented in arbitration? Why was the civil claim referred to arbitration?

RESOURCES

RULES AND POLICIES

AMERICAN ARBITRATION ASSOCIATION®

Employment Arbitration Rules and Mediation Procedures

Rules Amended and Effective November 1, 2009

Fee Schedule Amended and Effective July 1, 2015

Available online at adr.org/employment

AMERICAN ARBITRATION ASSOCIATION®

Labor Arbitration Rules (Including Expedited Labor Arbitration Rules)

Rules Amended and Effective July 1, 2013

Fee Schedule Amended and Effective March 15, 2015

Available online at adr.org/labor

NATIONAL ACADEMY OF ARBITRATORS

Professional Responsibility Standards in Employment Arbitration

Available online at http://naarb.org/Guidelines_for_standard.asp

ORGANIZATIONS

AMERICAN ARBITRATION ASSOCIATION®

https://www.adr.org

FEDERAL MEDIATION AND CONCILIATION SERVICES

https://www. fmcs.gov.

JAMS® (formerly known as Judicial Arbitration and Mediation Services)

https://www.jamsadr.com

NATIONAL LABOR RELATIONS BOARD

https://www.nlrb.gov

NATIONAL MEDIATION BOARD

https://www.nmb.gov

INDEX